Fundamental Problems in Computing

Professor Daniel J. Rosenkrantz

S. S. Ravi · Sandeep K. Shukla

Editors

Fundamental Problems in Computing

Essays in Honor
of Professor Daniel J. Rosenkrantz

 Springer

S. S. Ravi
University at Albany—SUNY
Department of Computer Science
1400 Washington Avenue
Albany, NY 12222, USA
E-mail: ravi@cs.albany.edu

Sandeep K. Shukla
Virginia Tech
Bradley Dept. Electrical and
Computer Engineering
302 Whittemore (0111)
Blacksburg, VA 24061, USA
E-mail: shukla@vt.edu

ISBN 978-90-481-8183-4   e-ISBN 978-1-4020-9688-4

Printed on acid-free paper

9 8 7 6 5 4 3 2 1

springer.com

Foreword

Dan Rosenkrantz and I were colleagues for about 40 years, first at the General Electric Research and Development Center and then at the University at Albany. Thus I witnessed his career first hand and had the privilege of working with him on a number of topics.

Dan was very productive throughout his entire career and even into retirement. He worked in a variety of areas from the very theoretical to the very practical. This diversity is evident from the selection of papers in this book.

Dan is friendly and easy to work with. He is able to ask penetrating questions and get to the heart of a problem. He is also famous for his ability to find counter-examples. These exceptional qualities make him attractive as a collaborator and fun to work with. Consequently, he was successful in collaborating with a variety of researchers and producing papers with them.

Dan has excellent communication skills. This is evident in the clarity of his writing. These skills also made him effective as a teacher. Because of his teaching skills and his prowess as a researcher, students often sought him out as an advisor.

In summary, this book is a tribute to a great person, a great mentor, and a great career.

RICHARD E. STEARNS
Winner of ACM Turing Award (1993)
Distinguished Professor Emeritus
Department of Computer Science
University at Albany—SUNY
Albany, NY, USA

Preface and Introduction

S. S. RAVI

Department of Computer Science, University at Albany—SUNY, Albany, NY 12222, USA.
Email: ravi@cs.albany.edu

SANDEEP K. SHUKLA

Department of Electrical and Computer Engineering, Virginia Tech, Blacksburg, VA 24061,
USA. Email: shukla@vt.edu

Overview

The purpose of this volume is to honor Professor Daniel Jay Rosenkrantz ("Dan" to his friends) for his extensive research contributions which have enriched the field of Computer Science. The volume includes reprinted forms of ten of Dan's publications in archival journals and eight contributed chapters by various researchers.

A Biographical Sketch

Dan was born on March 5, 1943 in Brooklyn, New York. He attended Evander Childs High School in Bronx, New York, before proceeding to Columbia University for his undergraduate and graduate degrees in Electrical Engineering. He received his Bachelor's degree in 1963. He was a National Science Foundation Cooperative Graduate Fellow at Columbia University and received his Master's degree in 1964. His Ph.D. thesis, completed in 1967, was supervised by Professor Stephen H. Unger. Dan spent the last year of his graduate studies at Bell Telephone Laboratories in Murray Hill, New Jersey.

After receiving his Ph.D., Dan joined the General Electric Corporate Research and Development Center (GECRD) in Schenectady, New York. During his ten years at GECRD, Dan worked with Philip M. Lewis II and Richard E. Stearns on a number of fundamental research problems in many areas including formal languages, compilers, algorithms and database systems. Their research led to numerous seminal papers, four of which are reprinted in Part I of this book. Another outcome of their collaboration is an early and highly regarded textbook on compiler design [13], which made the topic accessible to undergraduate students in Computer Science. The following quote from the contributed chapter[1] by Phil Lewis, nicely summarizes the years spent by Dan at GECRD:

> "Those were magic years for Computer Science at G.E., and
> Dan made important contributions to that magic."

In 1977, Dan moved to the Computer Science Department at the University at Albany–State University of New York (UAlbany) as a Full Professor. Dan was a member of the Computer Science faculty at UAlbany for 28 years before retiring in June 2005. From 1983 to 1985, when he was on leave from UAlbany, Dan worked as a Principal Computer Scientist for Phoenix Data Systems, a company which developed design automation tools for very large scale integrated (VLSI) systems. During his tenure at UAlbany, Dan supervised or co-supervised seven Ph.D. students and a large number of Master's students. He also served as the Chair of the Computer Science Department during the period 1993 to 1999.

Dan's first paper was published in *IEEE Transactions on Electronic Computers* in 1966. For more than 40 years since his first publication, Dan has published extensively in prestigious conferences and journals. As of September 2008, Dan's publication list includes more than 140 papers with 38 collaborators. These publications cover many different areas of Computer Science including formal languages, compilers, algorithms, database systems, VLSI design and testing, fault-tolerant computing, hierarchical specifications, software engineering, high performance computing, operations research, discrete dynamical systems and data mining. A beautifully concise statement which captures the nature of Dan's research contributions is the following partial quote[2] provided by Jeffrey Ullman (Computer Science Department, Stanford University):

> "His work has been a model for how one uses theoretical skills to
> make an impact on real problems, ..."

Like his research record, Dan's record of service to the Computer Science community is also extensive. He was the Area Editor for Formal Languages and Models of Computation for the *Journal of the Association for Computing Machinery* (JACM) from 1981 to 1986 and then the Editor-in-Chief of the

---

[1] This chapter appears in Part II of this book.
[2] The full version of this quote appears on the back cover of this book.

same journal from 1986 to 1990. During his tenure as the Editor-in-Chief, three new areas (Logic in Computer Science, Computational Geometry and Deductive Systems and Equational Reasoning) were added to the journal [24]. Dan has served on the program committees of many well known conferences including IEEE Symposium on Foundations of Computer Science (FOCS) and its previous incarnation (IEEE Symposium on Switching and Automata Theory), ACM International Symposium on Principles of Database Systems (PODS), International Conference on the Management of Data (SIGMOD), IEEE Symposium on Reliable Distributed Systems (SRDS) and ACM Symposium on Programming Language Principles (POPL). He was the Chairman of the Program Committee for FOCS 1975 and also served as the Secretary of ACM SIGACT (Special Interest Group on Automata and Computability Theory) from 1977 to 1979. He was the General Chairman for PODS in 1984, 1990 and 1991 and served as a member of the PODS Executive Committee from 1990 to 1995. In addition, Dan has served on evaluation panels for the National Science Foundation (NSF) and the National Aeronautics and Space Administration (NASA).

Dan has received many awards in recognition of his research contributions. He was elected a Fellow of the Association for Computing Machinery (ACM) in 1995. His fellowship citation reads as follows:

> "For pioneering contributions to formal languages, compiler design, algorithm analysis, databases, parallel and fault-tolerant computing and for exemplary ACM service including Editorship of JACM."

In 2001, Dan received the "Contributions Award" from the ACM Special Interest Group on Management of Data (SIGMOD). In 1991, he received the "Excellence in Research Award" from the University at Albany–State University of New York. Dan has been listed in *Who's Who in America* since 1990. His academic honors include Sigma Xi, Eta Kappa Nu and Tau Beta Pi.

Summary of Part I

The collection of papers which are reprinted in Part I of this book cover four decades (1967 to 2008) of Dan's research career. Many of the papers in this collection represent seminal contributions to Computer Science.

Chapter 1 ("Matrix Equations and Normal Forms for Context-Free Grammars") is the reprinted form of Dan's second journal paper, which originally appeared in JACM in 1967. This paper shows how the Greibach Normal Form [11] of a context-free grammar, where the right side of each production begins with a terminal symbol,[3] can be constructed efficiently by exploiting the

---

[3] The grammar may also have productions of the form $A \rightarrow \lambda$, where λ represents the null string.

correspondence between the productions of the grammar and a set of linear equations. The approach used in the paper obviates the need for generating regular expressions from a directed graph representation of the linear equations. Moreover, the paper also shows how the grammar can be modified so that each production starts and ends with a terminal symbol. A detailed discussion of the algorithm appears in the classic text on formal languages by Harrison [12, Sect. 4.9].

Chapter 2 ("Attributed Translations") is reprinted from the *Journal of Computer and System Sciences* (1974). This paper formalized the notion of attributed translation which plays a central role in the design of compilers for high-level languages. The classic text on compiler design by Aho and Ullman [1, p. 295] mentions that this paper developed one of the "classes of translation schemes for which attributed and synthesized translations can be implemented efficiently".

Chapter 3 ("An Analysis of Several Heuristics for the Traveling Salesman Problem") is an early paper on the analysis of approximation algorithms. This paper, which originally appeared in *SIAM Journal on Computing* (1977) is considered a classic and has been cited in virtually every subsequent paper on the topic. The paper established a tight performance guarantee of $\Theta(\log n)$ for the well known "near-neighbor" heuristic for the problem, where n represents the number of cities. This paper also introduced the minimum spanning tree based heuristic which provides a performance guarantee of $2(1 - 1/n)$.

Chapter 4 ("System Level Concurrency Control for Distributed Database Systems") and Chap. 5 ("Consistency and Serializability in Concurrent Database Systems") represent seminal contributions to the area of transaction processing in concurrent databases. The ideas presented in these papers are discussed in standard texts on database concurrency control [8, 22]. The first of these papers, which is reprinted from *ACM Transactions on Database Systems* (1978), presents several designs for concurrency control schemes and formally proves that the schemes are free from phenomena such as deadlocks. The second paper, which is reprinted from *SIAM Journal on Computing* (1984), shows formally that serializability is both necessary and sufficient for consistency in concurrent databases. The book by Bernstein et al. [8, p. 23] calls the conference version of this paper [25] an "influential early paper" on the topic of concurrency control.

Chapter 6 ("An Efficient Method for Representing and Transmitting Message Patterns on Multiprocessor Interconnection Networks"), reprinted from the *Journal of Parallel and Distributed Computing* (1991), discusses research done jointly by Dan and his first Ph.D. student (Philip Bernhard). This paper describes a representation (called a **mask**) for messages in multiprocessor interconnection networks and shows how a number of properties of the messages can be determined efficiently from the corresponding mask. (An example of such a property is whether the messages represented by a given mask will cause congestion.) In addition, it is shown that under this representation, the problem of partitioning a given set of messages into a minimum number of conflict-free rounds can be solved efficiently.

The paper reprinted as Chap. 7 ("Representability of Design Objects by Ancestor-Controlled Hierarchical Specifications") originally appeared in *SIAM Journal on Computing* (1992). This was coauthored with Dan's second Ph.D. student (Lin Yu). This paper developed a model called **versioned dag** (VDAG) for succinctly representing hierarchically specified design data. The paper provides a complete characterization of the expressive power of the VADG model and presents complexity results for a number of related problems.

Chapter 8 ("The Complexity of Processing Hierarchical Specifications"), reprinted from *SIAM Journal on Computing* (1993), represents another important contribution to the topic of hierarchically specified objects. In that paper, it is shown that any hierarchically specified acyclic circuit can be simulated deterministically in space that is linear in the size of the representation, even when the description is not explicitly acyclic. This result settled an open problem due to Lengauer [21]. Further, it is shown that the problem of simulating a hierarchically specified acyclic monotone circuit is PSPACE-complete and that the simulation of any hierarchically specified acyclic circuit (even if it is not monotone) can be carried out in deterministic time $2^{O(\sqrt{n})}$, where n represents the size of the description. In addition, it is shown that the simulation problem for hierarchically specified cyclic circuits is EXPSPACE-complete.

Chapter 9 ("Approximation Algorithms for Degree-Constrained Minimum-Cost Network-Design Problems") is reprinted from *Algorithmica* (2001). This paper is one of the first to consider the idea of approximating several objectives simultaneously. The definition of multiobjective approximation introduced in the conference version of this paper [23] is widely used today. The paper considered several variants of the problem of constructing spanning trees that minimize two objectives, namely the total cost and the maximum node degree. Since the publication of this paper, the problem and its variants have been studied by many researchers (see for example [2] and the references cited therein).

Chapter 10 ("Efficient Algorithms for Segmentation of Item-Set Time Series"), reprinted from *Data Mining and Knowledge Discovery* (2008), represents Dan's joint work with another Ph.D. student (Parvathi Chundi). This paper considers the problem of mining a special form of time series data, called **item-set** time series. In such data sets, the information stored for each time instant is a group of items rather than a single item. For example, in a software repository, the data stored for each time instant may be the names of files that were changed at that time or the names of people who modified those files.

One way to extract useful patterns from such data sets is to first divide them into appropriate segments. The paper defines the notion of an optimal segmentation under different objectives and presents polynomial time algorithms that construct such segmentations. The paper also includes extensive experimental results obtained by applying the algorithms to several data sets.

Summary of Part II

Part II of this book contains eight chapters contributed by various researchers. Like Dan's research record, these chapters also cover a wide variety of areas.

Chapter 11 ("Structure Trees and Subproblem Independence") by Richard E. Stearns and Harry B. Hunt III shows that many constraint satisfaction problems (such as different versions of the Boolean Satisfiability problem, their counting versions, several graph theoretic problems, etc.) can be captured using a very general framework called the **sum-of-products** form. This framework enables one to formalize the notion of subproblem independence, which has important implications on the time needed to solve the corresponding problem. The chapter shows that when instances of the problem have bounded treewidth, one can readily obtain an efficient algorithm from the general framework. The topic of developing efficient algorithms for treewidth-bounded problem instances has been of interest to Dan since the 1990's, and he has published many papers on that topic (e.g. [6, 7, 19]).

The next two chapters are on transaction processing in concurrent databases. As mentioned earlier, this is a topic to which Dan has made several seminal contributions. Chapter 12 ("An Optimistic Concurrency Control Protocol for Replicated Databases") by Yuri Breitbart, Henry Korth and Abraham Silberschatz discusses a concurrency control protocol that guarantees serializability and freedom from deadlock for multi-site transactions. An important characteristic of the protocol is that it does not rely on any special properties of the database systems running at the individual sites. Further, the new protocol reduces the communication overhead needed to achieve serializability and deadlock freedom. Breitbart et al. compare their approach with the approach presented in one of Dan's papers on the topic [10].

Chapter 13 ("SNAPSHOT Isolation: Why do Some People Call it SERIAL-IZABLE?") by Philip M. Lewis is based on his popular lecture entitled "Why Does Oracle Make Fun of Theoreticians?". He points out that several commercial database systems use a relaxed consistency requirement called **snapshot isolation** (instead of serializability) for running concurrent transactions. It is known that snapshot isolation can result in nonserializable schedules. However, users of such systems do not complain about getting incorrect results from their transactions. The chapter offers a possible explanation for this phenomenon: those transactions are based on certain design patterns for which snapshopt isolation is sufficient to produce correct results. The chapter also presents an example of such a design pattern.

Chapter 14 ("A Richer Understanding of the Complexity of Election Systems") by Piotr Faliszewski, Edith Hemaspaandra, Lane Hemaspaandra and Jörg Rothe presents a detailed survey of recent results on the complexity of various election systems. They point out that in addition to political elections, the topic of voting arises naturally in a number of other contexts such as spam detection, web search engines, etc. They consider the effect of control, manipulation and bribery on the complexity of the underlying election problems. The chapter provides the necessary background on various election systems and an outline of the techniques used to establish the complexity results. The chapter also includes an extensive list of references. Dan has studied the complexity of problems arising in many different areas since the mid 1970's and has published extensively on the topic (e.g. [9, 14–18]).

The next two chapters deal with different forms of approximation algorithms for NP-hard problems, a topic in which Dan has had an active interest since the 1970's. Chapter 15 ("Fully Dynamic Bin Packing") by Zoran Ivković and Errol L. Lloyd considers the **fully dynamic** version of the online bin packing problem. In that version, requests to insert and delete new items arrive one at a time, and the online algorithm is required to maintain a packing with a small number of bins. To process a request, the online algorithm is allowed to do a limited amount of repacking. The performance of such an algorithm is measured by its **competitive ratio**, which is the worst-case ratio of the number of bins used by the algorithm to the minimum number of bins used by an optimal offline algorithm. The authors consider several variants of the problem and establish lower and upper bounds on achievable competitive ratios.

Chapter 16 ("Online Job Admission") by Sven O. Krumke, Rob van Stee and Stephen Westphal addresses an online scheduling problem. In this problem, each job has a release time and execution time which are revealed to the online algorithm only when the job arrives. A time horizon T is specified and the jobs must be scheduled up to time T in a nonpreemptive fashion on a given number of processors. As each job arrives, the online algorithm must make a decision whether to accept or reject the job without any knowledge of the future jobs. The goal is to accept a subset of jobs such that the total execution time of the accepted jobs is close to the maximum possible value obtainable using an optimal offline algorithm. The authors first present a lower bound on the achievable competitive ratio. Then they present deterministic and randomized algorithms which achieve competitive ratios that are close to the lower bound.

Chapter 17 ("A Survey of Graph Algorithms Under Extended Streaming Models of Computation") by Thomas C. O'Connell summarizes many known results on graph algorithms when the input to the algorithm is in the form of a data stream; thus, an algorithm can only make one pass over the entire input. In addition, there is a restriction on how much of the stream data can be stored by the algorithm. Using ideas from communication complexity [20], many natural graph problems have been shown to be inherently difficult under this streaming model. Therefore, researchers have proposed extensions of the streaming model under which one can solve some of the graph problems. The chapter provides descriptions of the various extensions and outlines known algorithms for several graph problems (e.g. finding connected components, computing shortest paths) under those models. Thomas O'Connell was a Ph.D. student in the Computer Science Department at UAlbany when Dan served as the Chair of the department.

Chapter 18 ("Interactions Among Human Behavior, Social Networks and Societal Infrastructures: A Case Study in Computational Epidemiology") was contributed by a group of researchers (Christopher Barrett, Keith Bisset, Jiangzhuo Chen, Stephen Eubank, Bryan Lewis, V. S. Anil Kumar, Madhav Marathe and Henning Mortveit) at the Network Dynamics and Simulation Science Laboratory (NDSSL), which is a part of the Virginia Bioinformatics Institute and Virginia Tech. This chapter gives an overview of the ongoing research on large scale simulations and computational epidemiology at NDSSL. The issues addressed by this research are extremely important in practice. To address those issues, ideas and techniques from a number of different fields (e.g. Computer Science, Mathematics, Biology, Sociology) are needed. The focus of the chapter is on some questions that are of interest to Computer Science researchers. Dan has been involved in joint research with several members of the NDSSL group for many years, and this collaboration has led to a number of publications (e.g. [3–7]).

Acknowledgments

We thank all the authors who contributed chapters for the second part of this book. We also thank ACM, SIAM and Elsevier for granting permission to reprint Dan's journal papers for the first part of this book. We thank Springer for publishing this book. In particular, we are grateful to Mark DeJongh and Cindy Zitter of Springer for their help and patience.

We owe a special thanks to Veronica Lee, who created latex source files for many of the papers that appear in Part I of this book. Without her help, it would have taken us even longer to finish this book.

One of the editors (Ravi) thanks Nandaki Systems and Glomantra e-Services (P) Limited (both located in Bangalore, India) for allowing him to use their networking facilities to work on this book while he was visiting India.

Last but not the least, we express our sincere thanks to Dan, who has been an exceptional colleague and mentor. We have benefitted significantly from his extensive knowledge, tremendous enthusiasm for research, exceptional problem solving skills and high ethical standards. It has been our pleasure and privilege to work with him. We hope to continue to work with him for many years to come.

References

[1] A. V. Aho and J. D. Ullman. *Principles of Compiler Design*. Addison–Wesley, Reading, 1977.

[2] N. Bansal, R. Khandekar, and V. Nagarajan. Additive guarantees for degree bounded directed network design. In *Proc. 40th annual ACM Symp. Theory of Computing*, pages 769–778, May 2008.

[3] C. L. Barrett, H. B. Hunt III, M. V. Marathe, S. S. Ravi, D. J. Rosenkrantz, and R. E. Stearns. Analysis problems for sequential dynamical systems and communicating state machines. In *MFCS*, pages 159–172, 2001.

[4] C. L. Barrett, H. B. Hunt III, M. V. Marathe, S. S. Ravi, D. J. Rosenkrantz, and R. E. Stearns. Predecessor and permutation existence problems for sequential dynamical systems. In *DMCS*, pages 69–80, 2003.

[5] C. L. Barrett, H. B. Hunt III, M. V. Marathe, S. S. Ravi, D. J. Rosenkrantz, and R. E. Stearns. Complexity of reachability problems for finite discrete dynamical systems. *J. Comput. Syst. Sci.*, 72(8):1317–1345, 2006.

[6] C. L. Barrett, H. B. Hunt III, M. V. Marathe, S. S. Ravi, D. J. Rosenkrantz, R. E. Stearns, and M. Thakur. Computational aspects of analyzing social network dynamics. In *IJCAI*, pages 2268–2273, Jan. 2007.

[7] C. L. Barrett, H. B. Hunt III, M. V. Marathe, S. S. Ravi, D. J. Rosenkrantz, R. E. Stearns, and M. Thakur. Predecessor existence problems for finite discrete dynamical systems. *Theor. Comput. Sci.*, 386(1-2):3–37, 2007.

[8] P. Bernstein, V. Hadzilacos, and N. Goodman. *Concurrency Control and Recovery in Database Systems*. Addison–Wesley, Reading, 1987.

[9] P. A. Bloniarz, H. B. Hunt III, and D. J. Rosenkrantz. Algebraic structures with hard equivalence and minimization problems. *J. ACM*, 31(4):879–904, 1984.

[10] P. Chundi, D. Rosenkrantz, and S. S. Ravi. Deferred updates and data placement in distributed databases. In *Proc. International Conference on Data Engineering*, pages 469–476, New Orleans, LA, Feb.–Mar. 1996.

[11] S. Greibach. A new normal-flow theorem for context-free phrase structure grammars. *J. ACM*, 12(1):42–52, Jan. 1965.

[12] M. A. Harrison. *Introduction to Formal Language Theory*. Addison–Wesley, Reading, 1978.

[13] P. M. Lewis II, D. J. Rosenkrantz, and R. E. Stearns. *Compiler Design Theory*. Addison–Wesley–Longman, Boston, 1976.

[14] H. B. Hunt III and D. J. Rosenkrantz. On equivalence and containment problems for formal languages. *J. ACM*, 24(3):387–396, 1977.

[15] H. B. Hunt III and D. J. Rosenkrantz. The complexity of testing predicate locks. In *SIGMOD Conference*, pages 127–133, May 1979.

[16] H. B. Hunt III and D. J. Rosenkrantz. The complexity of monadic recursion schemes: Executability problems, nesting depth, and applications. *Theor. Comput. Sci.*, 27:3–38, 1983.

[17] H. B. Hunt III and D. J. Rosenkrantz. The complexity of monadic recursion schemes: Exponential time bounds. *J. Comput. Syst. Sci.*, 28(3):395–419, 1984.

[18] H. B. Hunt III, D. J. Rosenkrantz, and P. A. Bloniarz. On the computational complexity of algebra on lattices. *SIAM J. Comput.*, 16(1):129–148, 1987.

[19] H. B. Hunt III, M. V. Marathe, V. Radhakrishnan, S. S. Ravi, D. J. Rosenkrantz, and R. E. Stearns. NC-approximation schemes for NP- and PSPACE-Hard problems for geometric graphs. *J. Algorithms*, 26(2):238–274, 1998.

[20] E. Kushilevitz and N. Nisan. *Communication Complexity*. Cambridge University Press, New York, 1996.

[21] T. Lengauer. Exploiting hierarchy in VLSI design. In F. Makedon et al., editor, *Proc. Aegean Workshop on Computing*. Lecture Notes in Computer Science, volume 227, pages 180–193. Springer, Berlin, 1986.

[22] C. Papadimitriou. *The Theory of Database Concurrency Control*. Computer Science Press, Rockville, 1986.

[23] R. Ravi, M. V. Marathe, S. S. Ravi, D. J. Rosenkrantz, and H. B. Hunt III. Many birds with one stone: multi-objective approximation algorithms. In *Proc. 25th Annual ACM symposium on Theory of Computing*, pages 438–447, May 1993.

[24] D. J. Rosenkrantz. JACM 1986–1990. *J. ACM*, 50(1):18, 2003.

[25] R. E. Stearns, P. M. Lewis II, and D. J. Rosenkrantz. Concurrency controls for database systems. In *Proc. 17th Annual Symp. on Foundations of Comptr. Sci.*, pages 19–32, Houston, Texas, Oct. 1976.

Table of Contents

Front Matter

Part I: Selected Reprints from Professor Rosenkrantz's Seminal Contributions

Part II: Contributed Articles

End Matter

Part I

Selected Reprints from Professor Rosenkrantz's Seminal Contributions

Chapter 1

MATRIX EQUATIONS AND NORMAL FORMS
FOR CONTEXT-FREE GRAMMARS*

DANIEL J. ROSENKRANTZ

Department of Electrical Engineering, Columbia University, New York, NY, USA

Reprinted from: *J. ACM*, Vol. 14, No. 3, Jul. 1967, pp. 501–507. © ACM

Abstract   The relationship between the set of productions of a context-free grammar and
the corresponding set of defining equations is first pointed out. The closure
operation on a matrix of strings is defined and this concept is used to formalize
the solution to a set of linear equations. A procedure is then given for rewriting
a context-free grammar in Greibach normal form, where the replacement string
of each production begins with a terminal symbol. An additional procedure is
given for rewriting the grammar so that each replacement string both begins
and ends with a terminal symbol. Neither procedure requires the evaluation of
regular expressions over the total vocabulary of the grammar, as is required by
Greibach's procedure.

Received May 1966.

1.   Preliminaries

A context-free grammar is a 4-tuple (V_T, V_N, P, S) where V_T is a finite set
of terminal symbols, V_N is a finite set of nonterminal symbols disjoint from V_T,
P is a finite set of productions, and S, the distinguished symbol, is a member
of V_N. The productions are of the form $A \rightarrow \psi$, where $A \in V_N$ is called the
generatrix of the production and ψ, the replacement string, is a finite string of
symbols from $V = V_T \cup V_N$. For convenience, we assume that ψ is nonnull
and cannot be a single nonterminal symbol, i.e., we cannot have a production

---

* This work was written while the author was a National Science Foundation Graduate Fellow.

S.S. Ravi, S.K. Shukla (eds.), *Fundamental Problems in Computing*,
© Springer Science + Business Media B.V. 2009

of the form $A \rightarrow B$ where $B \in V_N$. The language generated by the grammar is the set of finite strings of terminal symbols which can result from successive applications of the productions, beginning with the string consisting of the distinguished symbol. In applying a production to a string an occurrence in the string of the generatrix is replaced by the replacement string of the production.

Now a grammar is called right linear if all its rules are right linear (of the form $A \rightarrow aB$ with $a \in V_T$) or terminating (of the form $A \rightarrow a$) and is called left linear if every rule is left linear (of the form $A \rightarrow Ba$) or terminating. Every left or right linear grammar generates a finite state language, i.e., one corresponding to a regular expression, and every finite state language is generated by a left linear and by a right linear grammar [4, 5].

2.   Systems of Equations

A set of productions from a context-free grammar can be put in the form of a set of defining equations [4–6]. For instance, consider the following set of productions (where $V_N = \{x_1, x_2\}$).

EXAMPLE 1.

$$
\begin{array}{ll}
x_1 \rightarrow x_1 a x_2 & x_2 \rightarrow x_2 d \\
x_1 \rightarrow x_2 x_2 & x_2 \rightarrow x_2 x_1 a \\
x_1 \rightarrow b & x_2 \rightarrow a x_1 \\
& x_2 \rightarrow c
\end{array}
$$

These productions correspond to the following two equations:

$$
x_1 = x_1 a x_2 + x_2 x_2 + b,
$$
$$
x_2 = x_2 d + x_2 x_1 a + a x_1 + c.
$$

Each x_i can be considered as corresponding to a set of strings[1] over V_T which satisfy the equations with "+" standing for set union. Given a grammar with n nonterminal symbols, we can let $\mathbf{x}$ be an n-dimensional column vector, each of whose components is one of the nonterminals, the first component being the distinguished symbol. Defining equations can then be written in the form $\mathbf{x} = \mathbf{f}(\mathbf{x})$, where each component of $\mathbf{f}$ is a sum of terms, each of which corresponds to a production of the grammar.

---

[1] Each x_i can also be considered a formal power series [4, 5], where the "+" stands for addition of formal power series. The major effect of adopting this viewpoint is that each string of terminal symbols has an associated coefficient equal to the number of different ways that string can be generated from x_i by the grammar. For instance, under this interpretation of "+," $ab + ab = 2ab$.

3. Regular Expressions and the Closure of a Matrix

The equations for a finite state language whose productions are all right linear or terminating can be written in the form

$$\mathbf{x} = A\mathbf{x} + \mathbf{b},$$

where $\mathbf{b}$ is an n vector and A is an $n \times 1$ matrix. The components of A and $\mathbf{b}$ are finite sums of strings of terminal symbols. We call an element of a sum a term. A component can be φ, which denotes the empty set of strings. But no component contains the null length string, denoted by λ, as a term in the sum.

EXAMPLE 2.
$$\begin{bmatrix} x_1 \\ x_2 \end{bmatrix} = \begin{bmatrix} a & a+b \\ \varphi & ab \end{bmatrix} \begin{bmatrix} x_1 \\ x_2 \end{bmatrix} + \begin{bmatrix} a \\ ba \ +bb \end{bmatrix}$$
is equivalent to the equations

$$x_1 = ax_1 + ax_2 + bx_2 + a,$$
$$x_2 = abx_2 + ba + bb.$$

For the single linear equation $y = ay + b$ where, as before, a and b are finite sums of terminal strings not containing λ, the solution [1, 3, 2, 8] is $y = a^*b$, where ""* denotes the closure operation of regular expressions with $a^* = \lambda + a + a^2 + \cdots$. Also, the solution to $y = ya + b$ is $y = ba^*$.

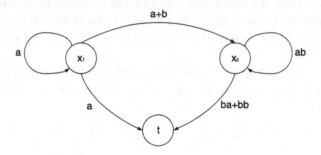

Figure 1.1. Flow graph for Example 2

Now consider the set of linear equations $\mathbf{x} = A\mathbf{x} + \mathbf{b}$. These equations can correspond to a directed graph with a node for each component of $\mathbf{x}$ plus an additional terminal node (labeled t). If $A_{i,j}$ (the element in the ith row and jth column of A) is not equal to φ then there is a branch from x_i to x_j whose label is $A_{i,j}$. If $b \neq \varphi$ then there is a branch from x_1 to t whose label is b_i. The graph for tile above example is shown in Fig. 1.1.

Now x_i can be identified with the set of labels corresponding to all the paths (of all lengths) from node x_i to node t. Such a set of paths would satisfy the equations; for each path which goes from x_i to t does so either directly in one step (corresponding therefore to a term in b_i) or else goes from x_i to some node x_j in one step (corresponding to a term in $A_{i,j}$) and then from x_j to t (corresponding to a member of x_j). A matrix A^* can now be defined whose (i,j)-th component, $A^*_{i,j}$, is the set of sequences of labels corresponding to all paths[2] from node x_i to node x_j. Then since each path from x_i to t must go from x_i to some node x_j (which is the next to last node in the path) and then from node x_j to t in one final step, the path consists of a term from $A^*_{i,j}$ concatenated with a term from b_j. Thus, the solution to the equation

$$\mathbf{x} = A\mathbf{x} + \mathbf{b} \quad \text{is} \quad \mathbf{x} = A^*\mathbf{b}.$$

Let an identity matrix I be defined as a square $n \times n$ matrix with the diagonal elements equal to λ and the off-diagonal elements equal to φ. Then since for any set of strings p, $\lambda p = p\lambda = p$, $IB = B$ for any matrix B with n rows, and $CI = C$ for any matrix C with n columns.

Now $A^* = I + A + A^2 + \cdots$. This is because $A^m_{i,j}$ is the set of paths from node x_i to node x_j traversing exactly m branches, as can be shown by induction. First $A^0_j = I_{i,j}$ is the set of paths from node x_i to node x_j of length 0. Next, assuming that $A^m_{i,j}$ is the set of paths from x_i to x_j of length m, note that

$$A^{m+1}_{i,j} = \sum_{k=1}^{n} A^m_{i,k} A_{k,j}.$$

Each term in the sum denotes a path beginning at x_i, going to x_k after m steps, and then having the last step go from x_k to x_j. Furthermore, each path of $m+1$ branches appears in the summation since after m branches, a path must be at node x_k for some k.

A^* can be obtained from A either by signal flow graph reduction techniques [9, 2] or algebraically by successive elimination of variables [1, 3]. In the example,

$$A^* = \begin{bmatrix} a^* & a^*(a+b)(ab)^* \\ \varphi & (ab)^* \end{bmatrix}$$

and

$$\begin{bmatrix} x_1 \\ x_2 \end{bmatrix} = A^*\mathbf{b} = \begin{bmatrix} a^*a + a^*(a+b)(ab)^*(ba+bb) \\ (ab)^*(ba+bb) \end{bmatrix}.$$

4.   Normal Form with Terminal Production Heads

A context-free grammar can be rewritten so that the head (first symbol) of the replacement string of each production in the rewritten grammar is a termi-

---

[2] If the formal power series approach is being taken, each sequence of labels in $A^*_{i,j}$ has an integer associated with it which equals the number of different paths from x_i to x_j with that sequence of labels.

nal symbol, as has been shown by Greibach [7]. However, Greibach's procedure requires the obtaining of regular expressions from a flow graph. In this section a procedure is presented which obtains the same normal form in a systematic manner in which the entire grammar is rewritten at one time and no regular expression needs to be evaluated.

First, in order to separate the productions which begin with nonterminal symbols from those beginning with terminal symbols, the defining equations are written in the form

$$\mathbf{x}' = \mathbf{x}'G + \mathbf{f}',$$

where ' stands for transposition, $\mathbf{f}'$ is an n vector, and G is an $n \times n$ matrix. The ith component of $\mathbf{f}'$ is the sum of the productions for x_i whose heads (initial symbols) are terminal symbols, while G_{ij} is the sum of the decapitated (with the head deleted) productions for x_j whose head is x_i. For Example 1 the equations are

$$[x_1 \quad x_2] = [x_1 \quad x_2] \begin{bmatrix} ax_2 & \varphi \\ x_2 & x_1a + d \end{bmatrix} + [b \quad ax_1 + c].$$

Now just as the solution to $\mathbf{x} = A\mathbf{x} + \mathbf{b}$ is $A^*\mathbf{b}$, the solution to $\mathbf{x}' = \mathbf{x}'A + \mathbf{b}'$ is $\mathbf{b}'A^*$. Therefore the solution to $\mathbf{x}' = \mathbf{x}'G + \mathbf{f}'$ is $\mathbf{x}' = \mathbf{f}'G^*$, where G^* is a matrix of regular expressions in terms of $V_T \cup V_N$. Noting that $G^* = I + GG^*$, we obtain $\mathbf{x}' = \mathbf{f}' + \mathbf{f}'GG^*$. Defining a new matrix $H = GG^*$, the equations for $\mathbf{x}'$ can be written $\mathbf{x}' = \mathbf{f}' + \mathbf{f}'H$. Now we introduce a new nonterminal symbol, $H_{i,j}$, for each component of H and can use $\mathbf{x}' = \mathbf{f}'H + \mathbf{f}'$ as the new defining equations for $\mathbf{x}'$.

It is possible for some components of H to be equal to φ, in which case they can be dropped from the grammar. A graph can be constructed from G with n nodes and an arrow from node i to node j if $G_{i,j}$ is not equal to φ. If there is no path of any length from node i to node j in this graph, then $H_{i,j} = \varphi$ since $H_{i,j}$ denotes the set of paths from i to j in the graph. In the example $H_{12} = \varphi$ and can be omitted from the grammar.

We thus introduce a new nonterminal symbol, $H_{i,j}$, for each nonnull component of H and use $\mathbf{x}' = \mathbf{f}'H + \mathbf{f}'$ as the new defining equations for $\mathbf{x}$. In the example, the defining equations for $\mathbf{x}$ in the new grammar are

$$[x_1 \quad x_2] = [b \quad ax_1 + c] \begin{bmatrix} H_{11} & \varphi \\ H_{21} & H_{22} \end{bmatrix} + [b \quad ax_1 + c].$$

Since each term in $\mathbf{f}$ begins with a terminal symbol, each term in the new equations begins with a terminal symbol.

Now H satisfies the equation $H = G + GH$, which can be used as the set of defining equations for the components of H. However, we want each

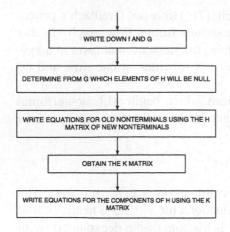

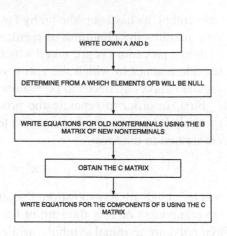

Figure 1.2. Procedure for rewriting a grammar so that each production begins with a terminal symbol

Figure 1.3. Procedure for rewriting a grammar which is already in Greibach normal form, so that each production begins and ends with a terminal symbol

production to begin with a terminal symbol. Therefore if the leftmost symbol of any term in G is a terminal symbol, leave it alone. If it is a nonterminal, say x_i, replace that symbol by the right-hand side of the new equation which defines x_i (each term of which begins with a terminal symbol). This procedure gives a new matrix, K, which is equivalent to G. In the example,

$$K = \begin{bmatrix} ax_2 & \varphi \\ ax_1 H_{22} + cH_{22} + ax_1 + c & bH_{11}a + ax_1 H_{21}a + cH_{21}a + ba + d \end{bmatrix}.$$

Now use $H = K + KH$ as the defining equations for H. Each term in these equations begins with a terminal symbol since each term in K begins with a terminal symbol.

Thus the equations for the new grammar are

$$\mathbf{x}' = \mathbf{f}'H + \mathbf{f}',$$
$$H = KH + K.$$

The procedure used to obtain these equations is summarized in Fig. 1.2.

Putting all the nonterminals in the new grammar for our example into one column vector gives the following final set of defining equations:

$$x_1 = bH_{11} + ax_1 H_{21} + cH_{21} + b,$$
$$x_2 = ax_1 H_{22} + cH_{22} + ax_1 + c,$$
$$H_{11} = ax_2 H_{11} + ax_2,$$
$$H_{21} = ax_1 H_{22} H_{11} + cH_{22} H_{11} + ax_1 H_{11} + cH_{11} + bH_{11}aH_{21}$$

$$+ ax_1 H_{21} a H_{21} + c H_{21} a H_{21} + ba H_{21} + d H_{21} + ax_1 H_{22}$$
$$+ c H_{22} + ax_1 + c,$$
$$H_{22} = b H_{11} a H_{22} + ax_1 H_{21} a H_{22} + c H_{21} a H_{22} + ba H_{22} + d H_{22}$$
$$+ b H_{11} a + ax_1 H_{21} a + c H_{21} a + ba + d.$$

5. Normal Form with Terminal Heads and Tails

In this section a procedure is obtained for rewriting the productions of a context-free grammar into a form where the head (first symbol) and tail (last symbol) of the replacement string for each production are both terminal symbols. Since the procedure is similar to that of the previous section an example is not given.

First by using the technique of the previous section obtain a grammar in the form where each production begins with a terminal symbol. Then use the procedure outlined in Fig. 1.3 to obtain productions whose tails are also terminal symbols. This latter procedure begins by writing the equations for the grammar in the form $\mathbf{x} = A\mathbf{x} + \mathbf{b}$, where $\mathbf{x}$ is the column vector corresponding to the nonterminals, b_i is the sum of productions for x_i which end in a terminal, and $A_{i,j}$ is the sum of productions for x_i which end in x_j (but with x_j deleted). Each term in A and b begins with a terminal.

Now the solution to the set of equations $\mathbf{x} = A\mathbf{x} + \mathbf{b}$ is $\mathbf{x} = A^*\mathbf{b} = \mathbf{b} + A\mathbf{b} + AB\mathbf{b}$, where $B = AA^*$ and can be defined by $B = A + AA + ABA$. A new nonterminal, $B_{i,j}$, is introduced for each component of B which is not equal to φ.

The new productions for $\mathbf{x}$ are obtained from the new defining equations

$$\mathbf{x} = \mathbf{b} + A\mathbf{b} + AB\mathbf{b},$$

each of whose terms begins and ends with a terminal.

A new matrix, C, is obtained from A as follows. If any term in A ends in a nonterminal, say x_i, then that appearance of x_i is replaced by the defining equation for x_i (each term of which ends in a terminal). Thus C is equivalent to A but each term in C both begins and ends in a terminal symbol.

The defining equations for B are now taken to be

$$B = C + AC + ABC.$$

The new grammar is now in the proper normal form.

Acknowledgment

The author is indebted to Professor Stephen H. Unger of Columbia University for suggesting that context-free grammars can be put in a form where all productions both begin and end with a terminal symbol, and for offering assistance and encouragement during the writing of this paper.

References

[1] D. N. Arden. Delayed logic and finite state machines. In *Theory of Computing Machine Design*, pages 1–35. Univ. of Michigan Press, Ann Arbor, 1960.

[2] J. A. Brzozowski. A survey of regular expressions and their applications. *IRE Trans.*, EC-11:324–335, 1962.

[3] J. A. Brzozowski and E. J. McCluskey Jr. Signal flow graph techniques for sequential circuit state diagrams. *IEEE Trans.*, EC-12:67–76, 1963.

[4] N. Chomsky, Formal properties of grammars. In R. D. Luce, R. R. Bush, E. Galanter, editors, *Handbook of Mathematical Psychology*, volume 11, pages 323–418. Wiley, New York, 1963.

[5] N. Chomsky and M. P. Schutzenberger. The algebraic theory of context-free languages. In P. Braffort and D. Hirshberg, editors, *Computer Programming and Formal Systems*, pages 118–161. North-Holland, Amsterdam, 1963.

[6] S. Ginsberg and H. G. Rice. Two families of languages related to ALGOL. *J. ACM*, 9(3):350–371, 1962.

[7] S. Greibach. A new normal-flow theorem for context-free phrase structure grammars. *J. ACM*, 12(1):42–52, 1965.

[8] S. C. Kleene. Representation of events in nerve nets and finite automata. In C. E. Shannon and H. McCarthy, editors, *Automata Studies*, pages 3–41. Princeton Univ. Press, Princeton, 1956.

[9] R. McNaughton and H. Yamada. Regular expressions and state graphs for automata. *IRE Trans.*, EC-9(1):39–47, 1960.

Chapter 2

ATTRIBUTED TRANSLATIONS*

P. M. Lewis, D. J. Rosenkrantz and R. E. Stearns

General Electric Company, Research and Development Center, Schenectady, NY 12345, USA

Reprinted from: *J. Computer and System Sciences*, Vol. 9, No. 3, Dec. 1974, pp. 279–307. © Elsevier

Abstract   Attributed translation grammars are introduced as a means of specifying a translation from strings of input symbols to strings of output symbols. Each of these symbols can have a finite set of attributes, each of which can take on a value from a possibly infinite set. Attributed translation grammars can be applied in depth to practical compiling problems.

Certain augmented pushdown machines are defined and characterizations are given of the attributed translations they can perform both deterministically and nondeterministically. Classes of attributed translation grammars are defined whose translation can be performed deterministically while parsing top down or bottom up.

Received August 30, 1973.

1.   Introduction

The purpose of this paper is to develop the concept of an "attributed translation," particularly attributed translations which can be described in a syntax-directed manner. The theory is developed with a particular application in mind, namely the specification of input-output relations of language processing devices such as the lexical and syntax boxes of a compiler. This application is reflected in our choice of mathematical terminology and in our illustrative examples.

---

* A preliminary version of this paper was presented at the 1973 Fifth Annual ACM Symposium on the Theory of Computing.

S.S. Ravi, S.K. Shukla (eds.), *Fundamental Problems in Computing*,
© Springer Science + Business Media B.V. 2009

The concept underlying the mathematics of this paper is the concept of an *attributed symbol*. A set of attributed symbols is specified by giving a finite set of basic symbols, a finite set of attributes for each basic symbol, and a set (possibly infinite) of values for each attribute. A particular attributed symbol consists of a basic symbol together with an associated attribute value for each attribute. Our customary notation is to display the attribute values as subscripts of the basic symbol. Our customary interpretation is that the values are "semantic" information associated with a particular occurrence of a basic symbol. Suppose, for example, that one basic symbol is the symbol CONSTANT specified to have one attribute and suppose it is specified that the attribute can take any integer as its value. Then the attributed symbol consisting of the basic symbol CONSTANT with associated attribute value 37 would be written $CONSTANT_{37}$. In a particular application, the subscript might be interpreted as semantic information giving the numerical value of a constant. (In other applications, an attribute might be interpreted as a pointer to a symbol table entry.)

By an "attributed translation," we mean a mapping of certain strings of attributed "input symbols" (i.e. an input language) into strings of attributed "action symbols." The terminology "action symbol" is in deference to the interpretation that an action symbol represents the performance of an arbitrary semantic action. In the simple applications illustrating this paper, the semantic actions are simply to emit a corresponding output. Thus for purposes of understanding this paper, it is satisfactory to think of the action symbols as "output symbols."

The attributed translations studied in this paper are translations that can be described by a grammar we call an "attributed translation grammar," which is a generalization of context-free grammar. The generalization is achieved in two steps. First a context-free grammar is generalized to a "translation grammar" describing translations without attributes. Then the attributes are added.

After considering attributed translation grammars as a means of specifying translations, we concentrate on performing these translations with augmented pushdown machines. Characterizations are given of the attributed translations that can be performed by both nondeterministic and deterministic augmented pushdown machines. Certain classes of attributed translation grammars are defined whose specified translation can always be performed by a deterministic augmented pushdown machine while parsing top down or bottom up.

Attributed translations are based on the ideas of attributed grammars [10] and syntax directed translations [7, 12]. The computation of attributes is also considered in [1]. Other relevant concepts are property grammars and table machines [14], attributed grammars with relations [3], and affix grammars [2, 11].

2.   Translation Grammars

We begin by introducing a new mechanism, called a translation grammar. The translation grammar concept is introduced as a way of specifying translations of input strings (without attributes) into action or output symbol strings (without attributes).

A *translation grammar* is a context free grammar in which the set of terminal symbols is partitioned into a set of *input symbols* and a set of *action symbols*. The strings in the language generated by a translation grammar are called *activity sequences*. The *input grammar* of a translation grammar is the grammar obtained by deleting all action symbols from the productions of the given grammar.

Given an activity sequence of input and action symbols, we use the term *input part* to refer to the sequence of input symbols obtained from the activity sequence by deleting all action symbols and we use the term *action part* to refer to the sequence of action symbols obtained from the activity sequence by deleting all input symbols. For each activity sequence, the action part is called a *translation* of the input part.

Given a translation grammar, each activity sequence in the language defined by that grammar pairs an input part with an action part. The set of all pairs that can be obtained in this way is called the *syntax directed translation* defined by that translation grammar.

The set of translations defined by translation grammars is exactly the same set as defined by the simple syntax directed transductions of [12], because the translation grammar provides an alternate notation for indicating "simple transduction elements." However, the activity sequence is a new mathematical object amenable to theoretical study. In practice, an activity sequence can be interpreted as a scenario specifying the operation of a language processor. An occurrence of an input symbol in an activity sequence can be interpreted (roughly) as the reading of that symbol by the processor. The occurrence of an action symbol in an activity sequence can be interpreted as the emitting of that symbol by the processor. Alternatively, the action symbols can be interpreted as the names of action (or semantic) routines that are to be called while processing the input sequence. The activity sequence can thus be interpreted as specifying both the sequence of action routine calls (or emitting of symbols) corresponding to the input sequence, and the timing of these action routine calls with respect to reading the input symbols.

The primary use of translation grammars in this paper is as a vehicle for describing translations.

3.   Attributed Translations

We now start the study of translations where the input and action symbols have associated attributes. As an aid to understanding the objectives of the theory, we begin with an English description of a particular language processor.

The input set of the processor is the set

$$\{(,),+,*,C\}$$

where C represents a constant. Furthermore, each occurrence of input C presented to the processor is accompanied by information giving the value of that constant. The processor accepts input sequences which constitute valid arithmetic expressions and emits the numerical value of the input expression.

To model the input of this processor as a string of attributed input symbols, we simply treat the value of the constant as an attribute. Under our convention that attributes are shown as subscripts, one of the permissible attributed input strings is

$$(C_2 + C_5) * (C_{11} + C_3)$$

To model the output activity of the processor, we invent the symbol ANSWER to represent the action of emitting the answer. We let ANSWER have an attribute which is to be the numerical answer emitted. The action sequence corresponding to the above input sequence would therefore be

$$ANSWER_{98}$$

In the next section, we present a method of describing certain attributed translations in a grammatical way. It will then be possible to replace the above English description of a processor with a precise grammatical specification of its input-output relation. In later sections, we show how suitable grammatical specifications can be used to obtain processors for performing the specified attributed translation.

4.   Attributed Translation Grammars

We now generalize translation grammars to accommodate attributes. Each symbol in the translation grammar (input, nonterminal or action symbol) is allowed to have attributes. Rules are then given by which values for the attributes of all the symbols on a derivation tree can be computed.

An *attributed translation grammar* is a translation grammar for which the following additional specifications are made.

1. Each input, nonterminal, and action symbol has an associated finite set of attributes, and each attribute has a (possibly infinite) set of permissible values.

2. Each nonterminal and action symbol attribute is classified as being either *inherited* or *synthesized*.

3. Rules for inherited attributes are specified as follows.

   (a) For each occurrence of an inherited attribute on the right-hand side of a given production, there is an associated rule which says how to compute a value for that attribute as a function of certain other attributes of symbols occurring in the left- or right-hand sides of the given production.

   (b) An initial value is specified for each inherited attribute of the starting symbol.

4. Rules for synthesized attributes are specified as follows.

   (a) For each occurrence of a synthesized nonterminal attribute on the left-hand side of a given production, there is an associated rule which says how to compute a value for that attribute as a function of certain other attributes of symbols occurring in the left- or right-hand sides of the given production.

   (b) For each synthesized action symbol attribute, there is an associated rule which says how to compute a value for that attribute as a function of certain other attributes of the action symbol.

Attributed translation grammars are to be used to define attributed derivation trees and then attributed activity sequences and attributed translations. The basic idea is as follows.

1. An unattributed derivation tree is constructed from the underlying translation grammar.

2. For each occurrence of an input symbol in the derivation tree, arbitrary permissible values are assigned to its attributes.

3. The attribute rules are then employed wherever possible in an attempt to supply attribute values for all the attributes of all the occurrences of non-terminal and action symbols in the derivation tree.

Before discussing the ramifications of Step 3, we first discuss and interpret the attributed translation grammar definition.

Part 1 of the definition simply says that the input, nonterminal, and action symbols are to be attributed symbols.

In part 2, a distinction is made between inherited and synthesized attributes to indicate whether their values are to be computed by rules specified by part 3 or by rules specified by part 4. The terms "inherited" and "synthesized" were introduced in [10], as was the term "attribute." A more detailed comparison with [10] is given at the end of this section.

Part 3 states what rules are needed to compute values for inherited attributes in a derivation tree. Each symbol in a derivation tree is either associated with the right-hand side of a production (i.e. the production which attaches the symbol to its parent in the tree) or is designated as the root of the tree (in which case the symbol is an occurrence of the starting symbol). These two cases account for the two sections A and B of part 3.

Section A says that each inherited attribute associated with a right-hand occurrence has a rule for computing its value based on some of its parent's attribute values, some of its sibling's attribute values, and even some of its own attribute values. The term "inherited" is suggestive of the idea that the rule is based on information obtained from the parent. The evaluation of the attribute rule can of course only be performed if the attribute values on which the rule depends have previously been computed.

Section B of part 3 says that initial values must be supplied for inherited attributes of the root of the derivation tree.

Part 4 states what rules are needed to compute values for synthesized attributes in a derivation tree. The case of a nonterminal attribute and an action symbol are treated separately.

Section A of part 4 deals with the nonterminal case. Because each nonterminal node in a derivation tree is associated with a left-hand side of a production, namely the production applied to that node, Section A ensures that there is a rule for each non- terminal synthesized attribute. The rule computes a value using some of the attribute values of the nonterminal's immediate descendants and possibly some of the non- terminal's own attribute values. The term "synthesized" is suggestive of the idea that a value is synthesized from the attributes of the descendants.

Section B of part 4 deals with the action symbol case. Here the rule is associated with the symbol itself (because the action symbol is not a left-hand side) and the rule is based solely on other attributes of the symbol (because the action symbol has no descendants). Synthesized action symbol attributes are almost completely neglected in the rest of the paper since an equivalent formulation with only inherited action symbol attributes can always be found for purposes of specifying a translation. Nevertheless, we believe it natural to include such attributes in modeling compilers.

Now we return to the problem of adding nonterminal and action symbol attributes to a derivation tree for which input symbol attribute values have been supplied. As a first step, values can be assigned to the inherited attributes of the root in accordance with the initial values required by Section 3B. Then perhaps rules can be found which depend only on the input attributes or the inherited attributes of the root, and the resulting values can be added to the tree.

Hopefully, as attribute values are added to the tree, the arguments of additional rules will be available, and still more values can be added until finally every attribute of each symbol on the derivation tree has an assigned value.

We say that an attributed translation grammar is *well defined* if and only if, for any derivation tree obtained from the underlying translation grammar, the process described above can be used to compute a value for each attribute of each symbol occurring in the derivation tree. This concept of "well defined" was introduced in [10], and the test given in [10] can be used with straightforward extensions to test an attributed translation grammar for the "well defined" condition. For application purposes, we are only interested in well defined attributed translation grammars, and our examples are all from this class.

Given an attributed translation grammar and given a derivation tree obtained from the grammar, the sequence of attributed input and action symbols obtained from the derivation tree is an *attributed activity sequence*. The attributed action part of this activity sequence is called a translation of the attributed input part. The set of attributed input part and action part pairs obtainable from the given grammar is called the *attributed translation* specified by the grammar. If an attributed translation grammar has an unambiguous input grammar, then each attributed input sequence has only one derivation tree and only one attributed translation.

Comparing the attributed translation grammars presented here with those of Knuth in [10], the principal difference is that we permit and require a certain class of terminal symbols (namely the input symbols) to have attributes whose values are not given by rules. There are also two minor differences. Knuth restricts terminals to have inherited attributes whereas we also permit synthesized attributes for our action terminals. Knuth also restricts the starting symbol to synthesized attributes only whereas we permit initialized inherited attributes. These two differences are minor in the sense that given any attributed translation grammar, the translation can be specified by an equivalent attributed translation grammar with all action symbol attributes inherited and all starting symbol attributes synthesized.

5. Examples

EXAMPLE 1. As a first example, we give an attributed translation grammar specifying the translation of expressions over constants mentioned previously.

The nonterminals $\langle E \rangle$, $\langle T \rangle$, and $\langle P \rangle$, each have an integer valued synthesized attribute. The input symbol C has one integer valued attribute and the action symbol ANSWER has an inherited integer valued attribute. The starting symbol is $\langle S \rangle$.

    1. $\langle S \rangle \rightarrow \langle E \rangle_a$ ANSWER$_b$

          $b \leftarrow a$

2. $\langle E \rangle_d \rightarrow \langle E \rangle_e + \langle T \rangle_f$

$$d \leftarrow e + f$$

3. $\langle E \rangle_g \rightarrow \langle T \rangle_h$

$$g \leftarrow h$$

4. $\langle T \rangle_i \rightarrow \langle T \rangle_j * \langle P \rangle_k$

$$i \leftarrow j * k$$

5. $\langle T \rangle_m \rightarrow \langle P \rangle_n$

$$m \leftarrow n$$

6. $\langle P \rangle_p \rightarrow (\langle E \rangle_q)$

$$p \leftarrow q$$

7. $\langle P \rangle_r \rightarrow \langle C \rangle_s$

$$r \leftarrow s$$

The notation used to describe the rules for computing attributes is that each attribute of a symbol in a production is given a name and the rules are written below the productions in terms of these names. For instance the rule

$$d \leftarrow e + f$$

below production 2 specifies that attribute d is computed by evaluating the sum $e + f$.

In any derivation tree obtained from this grammar, the value of the attribute of each nonterminal $\langle E \rangle$, $\langle T \rangle$ and $\langle P \rangle$ equals the numerical value of the subexpression generated by that nonterminal. The value of the attribute of ANSWER is the numerical value of the entire expression.

The input sequence

$$(C_2 + C_5) * (C_{11} + C_3)$$

has the attributed derivation tree shown in Fig. 2.1. The activity sequence corresponding to the tree is

$$(C_2 + C_5) * (C_{11} + C_3) \text{ANSWER}_{98}$$

and the action sequence is

$$\text{ANSWER}_{98}.$$

To see that the attribute values in Fig. 2.1 are in fact obtainable by successive applications of attribute rules, observe that the values can be added to the unattributed tree simply by computing the values in a bottom up order. In

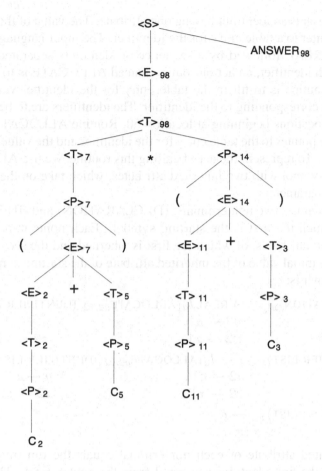

Figure 2.1.

other words, each nonterminal attribute can be computed as soon as the attribute values have been determined for the symbols below it, so its value can be computed by starting from the terminal attributes and working up the tree. The value of action ANSWER can be computed as the final step.

EXAMPLE 2. To show how an attributed translation grammar might be used in a compiler design, we consider the processing of declarations in a hypothetical programming language. The translation is one that the syntax box of a compiler might be required to perform. The input set consists of the three symbols:

1. REAL

2. *I*

3. ,

where I represents an identifier having one attribute. The value of this attribute is to be a pointer to a table entry for the identifier. The input language consists of the word REAL followed by a sequence of identifiers separated by commas. For each identifier, an action routine named ALLOCATE is to be called. This action routine is to fill in the table entry for the identifier with the run time location corresponding to the identifier. The identifiers are to be allocated consecutive locations beginning at location 50. Routine ALLOCATE has two parameters: a pointer to the table entry for the identifier and the value of the run time location. To represent the act of calling this routine, we use ALLOCATE as an action symbol with two inherited attributes, which take on the values of the routine's parameters.

The grammar has two nonterminals, $\langle$DECLARATION$\rangle$ and $\langle$IDENTIFIER LIST$\rangle$, of which the first is the starting symbol. Each nonterminal has two pointer-valued attributes, of which the first is inherited and the second is synthesized. The initial value of the inherited attribute of the starting symbol is 50.

The grammar is:

1. $\langle$DECLARATION$\rangle_{x1,z2} \rightarrow$ REALI_{a1}ALLOCATE$_{a2,x2}\langle$IDENTIFIER LIST$\rangle_{y,z1}$

$$a2 \leftarrow a1 \qquad\qquad\qquad y \leftarrow x1 + 1$$
$$x2 \leftarrow x1 \qquad\qquad\qquad z2 \leftarrow z1$$

2. $\langle$IDENTIFIER LIST$\rangle_{x1,z2} \rightarrow I_{a1}$ALLOCATE$_{a2,x2}\langle$IDENTIFIER LIST$\rangle_{y,z1}$

$$a2 \leftarrow a1 \qquad\qquad\qquad y \leftarrow x1 + 1$$
$$x2 \leftarrow x1 \qquad\qquad\qquad z2 \leftarrow z1$$

3. $\langle$IDENTIFIER LIST$\rangle_{x,z} \rightarrow \epsilon$

$$z \leftarrow x$$

The inherited attribute of each nonterminal equals the run time location available for the first identifier generated from the nonterminal. The synthesized attribute equals the next available runtime location after space has been allocated to all the identifiers generated from the nonterminal. In this example, the synthesized attributes do not affect the attributes of the action symbols, but they might if this grammar were part of some larger grammar.

The input sequence

$$\text{REAL } I_3, I_9, I_2$$

has the derivation tree shown in Fig. 2.2. The activity sequence is

$$\text{REAL } I_3 \text{ ALLOCATE}_{3,50}, I_9 \text{ ALLOCATE}_{9,51}, I_2 \text{ ALLOCATE}_{2,52}$$

The attribute values shown in Fig. 2.2 were obtained by first computing the inherited values and then the synthesized attributes. The inherited attributes were evaluated starting with the initial value of the top node and evaluating each attribute after those above and to the left were evaluated. The first synthesized attribute evaluated was the one lowest on the tree and then the other synthesized attributes were evaluated working up the tree. The order of evaluation

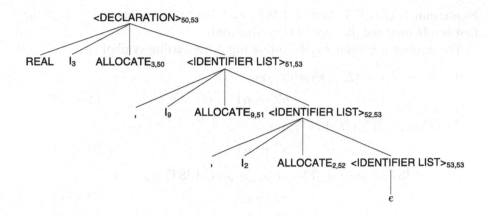

Figure 2.2.

illustrates a technique of sending information down the tree using inherited attributes and then sending it back up using synthesized attributes. Observe how the downward information is turned back up with the application of production 3.

EXAMPLE 3. As another example, we consider the translation of assignment statements in a hypothetical programming language. The input set is

$$\{(,), +, *, I, =\}$$

where I represents an identifier having one attribute whose value is to be a pointer to a table entry for the identifier.

The set of action symbols is

$$\{\text{ADD, MULTIPLY, ASSIGN}\}$$

where ADD and MULTIPLY each have three inherited attributes and ASSIGN has two inherited attributes. The attributes of ADD and MULTIPLY are to be pointers to the table entries for the left operand, right operand, and result of the operator. The attributes of ASSIGN are to be pointers to the table entries for an identifier being assigned to and the expression which is being assigned to the identifier.

The nonterminal set is

$$\{\langle S \rangle, \langle E \rangle, \langle T \rangle, \langle P \rangle, \langle E\text{-LIST} \rangle, \langle T\text{-LIST} \rangle\}.$$

Nonterminal $\langle S \rangle$ has no attributes. Nonterminals $\langle E \rangle$, $\langle T \rangle$, and $\langle P \rangle$ each have one attribute, which is synthesized. This attribute is to be a pointer to the table entry for the result of the subexpression generated by the nonterminal.

Nonterminals $\langle E\text{-LIST}\rangle$ and $\langle T\text{-LIST}\rangle$ each have two attributes, of which the first is inherited and the second is synthesized.

The attributed grammar is the following, with starting symbol $\langle S\rangle$.

1. $\langle S\rangle \rightarrow I_{a1} = \langle E\rangle_{b1}\text{ASSIGN}_{a2,b2}$

$$a2 \leftarrow a1 \qquad\qquad\qquad\qquad b2 \leftarrow b1$$

2. $\langle E\rangle_{b2} \rightarrow \langle T\rangle_{a1}\langle E\text{-LIST}\rangle_{a2,b1}$

$$a2 \leftarrow a1 \qquad\qquad\qquad\qquad b2 \leftarrow b1$$

3. $\langle E\text{-LIST}\rangle_{a1,d2} \rightarrow +\langle T\rangle_{b1}\text{ADD}_{a2,b2,c1}\langle E\text{-LIST}\rangle_{c2,d1}$

$$a2 \leftarrow a1 \qquad\qquad\qquad\qquad c2 \leftarrow c1$$
$$b2 \leftarrow b1 \qquad\qquad\qquad\qquad d2 \leftarrow d1$$
$$c1 \leftarrow \text{GETNEW}$$

4. $\langle E\text{-LIST}\rangle_{a1,a2} \rightarrow \epsilon$

$$a2 \leftarrow a1$$

5. $\langle T\rangle_{b2} \rightarrow \langle P\rangle_{a1}\langle T\text{-LIST}\rangle_{a2,b1}$

$$a2 \leftarrow a1 \qquad\qquad\qquad\qquad b2 \leftarrow b1$$

6. $\langle T\text{-LIST}\rangle_{a1,d2} \rightarrow *\langle P\rangle_{b1}\text{MULTIPLY}_{a2,b2,c1}\langle T\text{-LIST}\rangle_{c2,d1}$

$$a2 \leftarrow a1 \qquad\qquad\qquad\qquad c2 \leftarrow c1$$
$$b2 \leftarrow b1 \qquad\qquad\qquad\qquad d2 \leftarrow d1$$
$$c1 \leftarrow \text{GETNEW}$$

7. $\langle T\text{-LIST}\rangle_{a1,a2} \rightarrow \epsilon$

$$a2 \leftarrow a1$$

8. $\langle P\rangle_{a2} \rightarrow I_{a1}$

$$a2 \leftarrow a1$$

9. $\langle P\rangle_{a2} \rightarrow (\langle E\rangle_{a1})$

$$a2 \leftarrow a1$$

GETNEW is assumed to be a parameterless function procedure which supplies a pointer to some unused table entry that can be used to keep track of a partial result. Because different calls on GETNEW return different answers, GETNEW is not strictly speaking a function. Thus in using GETNEW, we are taking a small liberty with our formal definition. As an alternative to using GETNEW, extra attributes could be used to keep track of available table entries. However, the use of GETNEW is simpler and would be the likely choice in an actual design application.

Nonterminal $\langle E\text{-LIST}\rangle$ can be thought of as generating a list consisting of $+\langle T\rangle$ ADD repeated zero or more times. The inherited attribute of $\langle E\text{-LIST}\rangle$ corresponds to the left operand of the first $+$ (if any) on the list. The synthesized attribute of $\langle E\text{-LIST}\rangle$ corresponds to the result of the subexpression obtained by appending the string generated from $\langle E\text{-LIST}\rangle$ to the string representing the left operand. Nonterminal $\langle T\text{-LIST}\rangle$ is similar to $\langle E\text{-LIST}\rangle$.

For illustrative purposes, assume that GETNEW supplies consecutive locations beginning with location 200. Then the input sequence

$$I_7 = I_5 + I_2 * I_3$$

has the derivation tree shown in Fig. 2.3. The activity sequence is

$$I_7 = I_5 + I_2 * I_3 \text{MULTIPLY}_{2,3,200} \text{ADD}_{5,200,201} \text{ASSIGN}_{7,201}$$

and the action sequence is

$$\text{MULTIPLY}_{2,3,200} \text{ADD}_{5,200,201} \text{ASSIGN}_{7,201}$$

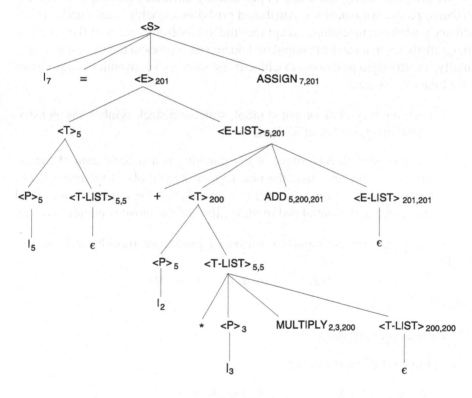

Figure 2.3.

The order of attribute evaluation in Fig. 2.3 is more complex than in the previous two examples. The most systematic order is to evaluate the inherited attributes of a given symbol before evaluating attributes of its descendants, to evaluate the synthesized attributes of a symbol after evaluating attributes for the descendants, and to evaluate all attributes of a left sibling before a right sibling. The $\langle E\text{-LIST}\rangle$ and $\langle T\text{-LIST}\rangle$ portions of the tree again illustrate the technique of sending down inherited information and then passing back up synthesized information. Productions 4 and 7 are the productions which turn this information around.

6. Attributed Pushdown Machines

We are interested in devices that "perform" the attributed translation specified by an attributed translation grammar. By a device performing an attributed translation we mean the device reads the input symbols including their attributes, verifies that the input sequence is in the language specified by the input grammar and outputs the attributed action symbols specified by the activity sequence corresponding to the input sequence.

We are particularly interested in performing attributed translations with *attributed pushdown machines*. Attributed pushdown machines are similar to ordinary pushdown machines, except that the symbols and states of the machine have attributes that can be manipulated during the moves of the machine. Informally, an attributed pushdown machine is the same as a conventional pushdown machine except that:

1. Each input symbol, output symbol, state, and stack symbol has an associated fixed number of attributes.

2. Associated with each move of the machine is a specification of the attributes of the new state, the new top stack symbols (if the move is not a pop) and the outputs (if any) as a function of the attributes of the old state, top stack symbol and input symbol (if the move is not an ϵ-move).

Formally, a (nondeterministic) attributed pushdown transducer is an 11-tuple

$$(Q, I, Y, \Gamma, \delta, q, Z, A, C, u, v)$$

where:

Q is a finite state of *states*.

I is a finite set of *input symbols*.

Y is a finite set of *output symbols*, disjoint from I.

Γ is a finite set of *stack symbols*.

q in Q is the *initial state*.

Z in Γ is the *initial stack symbol*.

A is the set of possible *attribute values*.

C is a function from $Q \cup I \cup Y \cup \Gamma$ to the nonnegative integers, specifying how many attributes each of these symbols have. We let $\bar{C}$ denote the extension of C to $(Q \cup I \cup Y \cup \Gamma)^*$ defined by $\bar{C}(\epsilon) = 0$ and $\bar{C}(\alpha\beta) = C(\alpha) + \bar{C}(\beta)$ for α a single symbol.

u in $A^{C(q)}$ is the attribute set of the starting state.

v in $A^{C(Z)}$ is the attribute set of the starting stack symbol.

δ is a mapping of $Q \times (I \cup \{\epsilon\}) \times \Gamma$ into a finite set of 4-tuples such that if $\delta(r, a, \beta)$ contains (p, γ, ξ, f) then p is in Q, γ is in Γ^*, ξ is in Y^*, and f is a computable function from $A^{C(r)+\bar{C}(a)+\bar{C}(\beta)}$ into $A^{C(p)+\bar{C}(\gamma)+C(\xi)}$. Furthermore each pair of 4-tuplets in $\delta(r, a, \beta)$ differs in at least one of the first three components.

We say that an attributed pushdown transducer is deterministic if

1. For each r in Q and β in Γ, whenever $\delta(r, \epsilon, \beta)$ is nonempty, then $\delta(r, a, \beta)$ is empty for all a in I;

2. δ never maps its argument into more than one element.

A configuration of an attributed pushdown translator is a 4-tuple (r, x, γ, y) where r is an attributed state, x is a string of attributed input symbols, γ is a string of attributed stack symbols, and y is a string of attributed output symbols. If a configuration is of the form $(r_g, a_h x, \beta_i \gamma, y)$ where r is a state with attributes g, a is in $I \cup \{\epsilon\}$ and has attributes h, β is a stack symbol with attributes i, and $\delta(r, a, \beta)$ contains (p, η, ξ, f) then we write $(r_g, a_h x, \beta_i \gamma, y) \vdash (\bar{p}, x, \bar{\eta}\gamma, y\bar{\xi})$ where $\bar{p}$, $\bar{\eta}$, and $\bar{\xi}$ are p, η, and ξ respectively with attributes computed by applying the function f to the attributes obtained by composing g, h, and i.

Let $\overset{*}{\vdash}$ denote the transitive reflexive closure of $\vdash$. Then if

$$(q_u, x, Z_v, \epsilon) \overset{*}{\vdash} (p, \epsilon, \epsilon, y)$$

we say that y is a translation of x performed by the machine. The *translation performed* by the machine is the set of all such pairs (x, y).

We say that a machine has an *endmarker* $\sharp$ for $\sharp$ in I if $C(\sharp) = 0$ and all input sequences for which the machine performs a translation are of the form $z\sharp$ where z is in $(I - \sharp)^*$. Note that the machine reads the endmarker in producing a translation. If a machine has endmarker $\sharp$, then we say that the translation *performed using an endmarker* by the machine is the set of pairs (z, y) such that $(z\sharp, y)$ is in the translation performed by the machine.

Note that the set of translations performed by nondeterministic attributed pushdown machines is identical to the set of translations performed using an endmarker by nondeterministic attributed pushdown machines.

7.   Performing Translations Nondeterministically

We define a subclass of attributed translation grammars and relate it to attributed pushdown machines.

An attributed translation grammar is called *L-attributed* if and only if the following three conditions hold.

1. For each attribute evaluation rule associated with an inherited attribute of some given symbol in the right-hand side of some given production, each argument of that rule is either an inherited attribute of the left-hand side or an arbitrary attribute of some right-hand side symbol appearing to the left of the given symbol.

2. For each attribute evaluation rule associated with a synthesized attribute of the left-hand side of some given production, each argument of that rule is either an inherited attribute of the given left-hand side or an arbitrary attribute of some right-hand side symbol.

3. For each attribute evaluation rule associated with a synthesized attribute of an action symbol, each argument of that rule is an inherited attribute of the given action symbol.

Comparing the above three conditions with the definition of attributed translation grammars, we see that 1, 2, and 3 above are restrictions on Sections 3A, 4A, and 4B, respectively. The only evaluation rules not constrained by the above three conditions are the initialization rules of Section 3B.

The L in the name "L-attributed" refers to the restriction (in condition 1 of the definition) that a rule for the inherited attribute of a given symbol in a production can use attributes of symbols to the left of the given symbol, but not attributes of symbols to the right. The intent of condition 1 is that the inherited attributes of a given node in the derivation tree should depend (either directly or indirectly) only on those input symbol attributes occurring to left of the given node, and be independent of the input symbol attributes below or to the right of the given node. A consequence of this intent is that the synthesized attributes of the given node should only depend on the input symbol attributes to the left or below the given node, and be independent of input symbol attributes to the right of the given node.

The purpose of conditions 2 and 3 is to ensure that the grammar is well defined. Together, the three conditions ensure that given a production such as

$A \rightarrow BC$, the attributes of A, B, and C can be evaluated in the following order:

1. Inherited attributes of A,

2. Inherited attributes of B,

3. Synthesized attributes of B,

4. Inherited attributes of C,

5. Synthesized attributes of C,

6. Synthesized attributes of A.

THEOREM 1. *Any translation specified by an L-attributed translation grammar can be performed by a nondeterministic attributed pushdown machine.*

Proof. We construct a one state machine which operates in a top down fashion. Let the translation grammar have input set I, action set Y, and nonterminal set N. If there are m productions, order them from 1 to m and let the ith production in the translation grammar have n_i symbols.

The machine is

$$(\{q\}, I, Y, \{Z\} \cup \{(i,j) | 1 \leq i \leq m \text{ and } 0 \leq j \leq n_i\}, \delta, q, Z, A, C, u, v)$$

where q and Z are arbitrary new names, A is the set of values that the attributes of the grammar can take us on, u is arbitrary, and C, v, and δ will be specified below.

For each symbol α in $I \cup Y$, $C(\alpha)$ equals the number of attributes α has in the grammar. For Z, $C(Z)$ equals 0, and so v is trivially a null vector. For q, $C(q)$ equals the maximum number of attributes of any symbol in the grammar. For each stack symbol of the form (i,j), $C((i,j))$ is equal to the sum of the number of attributes of the first $j-1$ symbols on the right-hand side of production i plus the number of inherited attributes of the left-hand nonterminal.

The machine parses top down, with stack symbol (i,j) representing a prediction of the rest of production i after the first j symbols. The machine operates so that when the top stack symbol is (i,j), the attributes of the stack symbol equal the inherited attributes of the left-hand nonterminal of production i, and the attributes of the first $j-1$ symbols on the right-hand side. Also, when $j > 0$ an appropriate number of attributes of the state will equal the attributes of the jth symbol on the right-hand side. Thus when (i,j) is on top of the stack the inherited attributes of the left-hand side of production i and all the attributes of the first j symbols of the right-hand side are available as attributes of the state and top stack symbol.

Stack symbol Z is used only to initialize the stack and disappears forever with the first machine operation. The first operation is to predict the production i applied to the starting symbol and replace the Z with the corresponding $(i, 0)$. Symbol $(i, 0)$ has an attribute for each inherited attribute of the starting symbol (left-hand side of production i) and these are initialized with the values specified as part of the grammar. Stated symbolically,

$$\delta(q, \epsilon, Z) = \{(q, (i, 0), \epsilon, f_i) \text{ for all productions } i \text{ with the starting symbol as left-hand side}\}$$

where f_i assigns the initial starting symbol inherited attribute values to the attributes of $(i, 0)$ and assigns arbitrary values to attributes of q.

When the top stack symbol of the machine has the form (i, j) where $j = n_i$, the machine predicts that an example of production i is over. The machine operation is to assign the attribute values of the left-hand side to a subset of the state attributes and to pop the stack to the symbol below. The inherited attributes of the left-hand side are immediately known since their values are given by corresponding attributes of (i, j). The synthesized attributes must now be computed, but this is easily done because of condition 2 of the L-attributed definition which says they can be computed from attribute values of the top stack symbol and the attributes of q.

$$\delta(q, \epsilon, (i, n_i)) \text{ is the one element set } \{(q, \epsilon, \epsilon, f)\}$$

where f is a function computing the left-hand side attributes of production i and assigning them to attributes of q (and assigning arbitrary values to any remaining state q attributes).

For a stack symbol of the form (i, j) where $j < n_i$ we consider three cases, depending on whether the $(j + 1)$st symbol on the right-hand side production i is in I, Y, or N. All three cases have the property that (i, j) is to be replaced with $(i, j + 1)$ and that the attribute values for this replacement symbol are already computed and are available as attributes of (i, j) and q. The actions taken in each case must also provide that the attributes for the j'th symbol are assigned to q, but the mechanism is different in each case. Letting α be the $(j + 1)$st symbol of production i, the three cases are as follows.

Case 1. α is an input symbol. In this case, the machine has an operation if and only if predicted input symbol α matches the current input. The obligation to make the attributes of state q equal the attributes of α is met simply by assigning the attributes of the machine input to q. Symbolically,

$$\delta(q, \alpha, (i, j)) \text{ is the one element set } \{(q, (i, j + 1), \epsilon, f)\}$$

where f fills in the values of $(i, j + 1)$ and q as described above.

Case 2. α is an action symbol. Conditions 1 and 3 of the L-attributed definition ensure that the attributes of α can be computed from the information at hand and be assigned as attributes of the state. Condition 1 says that the inherited attributes of α can be computed from the attribute values of top stack symbol (i, j) and the attributes of q. Condition 3 says that the synthesized attributes of α can then be computed from the inherited attributes. One other action associated with α is to put out α with its attribute values. Symbolically,

$$\delta(q, \epsilon, (i, j)) \text{ is the one element set } \{(q, (i, j + 1), \alpha, f)\}$$

where f fills in the values of stack symbol $(i, j + 1)$, state q, and output α as described above.

Case 3. α is a nonterminal symbol. Condition 1 of the L-attributed definition ensures that the inherited attributes can be computed from the attributes of the state and top stack symbol. The machine predicts a production k that generates the predicted occurrence of α, and places a symbol $(k, 0)$ on top of the stack (above the $(i, j + 1)$) assigning to its attributes the inherited attributes of α. Later, when the symbol $(i, j + 1)$ is exposed (due to popping a (k, n_k)), the attributes of α will appear as attributes of the state thus fulfilling the obligation to have $(i, j + 1)$ appear with the attributes of α as state attributes. Symbolically,

$$\delta(q, \epsilon, (i, j)) \text{ equals } \{(q, (k, 0)(i, j + 1), \epsilon, f_k) \text{ for all productions } k \text{ with}$$
$$\text{left-hand nonterminal } \alpha\}$$

where f_k computes the attributes of $(k, 0)$ and $(i, j + 1)$ and arbitrary values for q as described above.

This completes the construction. We have given arguments at each step to show that appropriate attribute values are always available and computed. The machine is otherwise a standard top down translator so we omit further arguments that it performs the desired attributed translation. $\square$

EXAMPLE 4. Consider the following L-attributed translation grammar with input set $\{a, b\}$, action set $\{d\}$, nonterminal set $\{S, B\}$, and starting symbol S. Symbols a and b each have one attribute; S and d each have one inherited attribute; and B has two attributes, of which the first is inherited and the second synthesized. The starting value of the attribute of S is 4. The productions are

1. $S_r \rightarrow a_s B_{t,u} d_v$

$$t \leftarrow r + s \qquad\qquad v \leftarrow 3 * u$$

2. $B_{r,s} \rightarrow b_t$

$$s \leftarrow r * t$$

The machine constructed by the procedure described above would have the following sequence of configurations for input sequence $a_2 b_5$. Wherever the machine can specify an arbitrary value for an attribute, the value 0 has been specified. The output sequence is d_{90}.

$$(q_{0,0}, a_2 b_5, Z, \epsilon) \vdash (q_{0,0}, a_2 b_5, (1,0)_4, \epsilon)$$
$$\vdash (q_{2,0}, b_5, (1,1)_4, \epsilon) \vdash (q_{0,0}, b_5, (2,0)_6 (1,2)_{4,2}, \epsilon)$$
$$\vdash (q_{5,0}, \epsilon, (2,1)_6 (1,2)_{4,2}, \epsilon) \vdash (q_{6,30}, \epsilon, (1,2)_{4,2}, \epsilon)$$
$$\vdash (q_{90,0}, \epsilon, (1,3)_{4,2,6,30}, d_{90}) \vdash (q_{4,0}, \epsilon, \epsilon, d_{90})$$

THEOREM 2. *Any translation performed by a nondeterministic attributed pushdown machine can be specified by an L-attributed translation grammar.*

Proof. We modify a standard technique for picking a grammar off a machine [6]. Let the machine be $(Q, I, Y, \Gamma, \delta, q, Z, A, C, u, v)$. The grammar has input set I, action set Y, and nonterminal set $(Q \times \Gamma \times Q) \cup \{S\}$ where S is a new symbol and is also the starting nonterminal. The productions are of two forms

1. $S \rightarrow (q, Z, p)$ for each p in Q,

2. $(r, A, p) \rightarrow a\xi(q_1, B_1, q_2)(q_2, B_2, q_3) \cdots (q_m, B_m, q_{m+1})$ for each r, $q_1, q_2, \ldots, q_{m+1}$ in Q where $p = q_{m+1}$, each a in $I \cup \{\epsilon\}$, and $A, B_1, B_2, \ldots, B_m$ in Γ, such that $\delta(r, a, A)$ contains $(q_1, B_1 B_2 \cdots B_m, \xi, f)$. (If $m = 0$ then $q_1 = p$, $\delta(r, a, A)$ contains (p, ϵ, ξ, f) and the production is $(r, A, p) \rightarrow a\xi$).

Each input and action symbol in the grammar has the same number of attributes as the corresponding symbol in the machine, and all action symbol attributes are inherited. Nonterminal S has no attributes. A nonterminal of the form (r, A, p) has $C(r) + C(A)$ inherited attributes and $C(p)$ synthesized attributes.

For a form 1 production, the rules for the inherited attributes of (q, Z, p) are that they equal u and v.

For a form 2 production, the function f from the machine specifies the attributes of q_1, ξ and $B_1 B_1 \cdots B_m$ in terms of the attributes of r, a, and A. The rules associated with the production for computing the inherited attributes of ξ are obtained from f, with the inherited attributes of the left-hand non-terminal used instead of the attributes of the symbols r and A in the machine. If $m = 0$ the rules for computing the synthesized attributes of the left-hand nonterminal are similarly obtained from f. If $m > 0$, the rules for the synthesized attributes of the left-hand nonterminal specify that they equal the synthesized attributes of (q_m, B_m, q_{m+1}). The rules for computing the inherited attributes of symbol

(q_i, B_i, q_{i+1}) use the rules from f to compute the attributes corresponding to B_i. For $i = 1$, the rules for the inherited attributes corresponding to q_i are obtained from f. For $i > 1$, the inherited attribute rules specify that these attributes equal the synthesized attributes of the symbol (q_{i-1}, B_{i-1}, q_i).   □

Note that the grammar is L-attributed.

THEOREM 3. *There exists a translation specified by an attributed translation grammar that cannot be performed by any nondeterministic attributed pushdown machine.*

Proof. The proof uses the following grammar, which is not L-attributed. The input set is $\{a, b, c\}$, action set is $\{1, 2, 3\}$, and starting nonterminal is S.

$$S \rightarrow 1_y Ac_x$$
$$y \leftarrow x$$
$$A \rightarrow a2A$$
$$A \rightarrow b3A$$
$$A \rightarrow \epsilon$$

Suppose this translation can be performed by a nondeterministic machine and that for some input string, the machine can produce the translation by emitting the 1 before reading the c, i.e.,

$$(q, stc_j, Z, \epsilon) \overset{*}{\vdash} (p, tc_j, \gamma, 1_j\xi) \overset{*}{\vdash} (r, \epsilon, \epsilon, 1_j\xi\eta)$$

But then for some other attribute k

$$(q, stc_k, Z, \epsilon) \overset{*}{\vdash} (p, tc_k, \gamma, 1_j\xi) \overset{*}{\vdash} (r, \epsilon, \epsilon, 1_j\xi\eta)$$

which is an incorrect translation.

If, on the other hand, 1 is never emitted before reading the c, then no output is produced until all inputs are read (1 being the first output symbol and c the last input symbol). Picking a grammar off this machine by the proof of Theorem 2, the underlying translation grammar would generate the set

$$L = \{wc1h(w) | w \text{ in } \{a, b\}^*\}$$

where h is the string homomorphism mapping a into 2 and b into 3. There is a string homomorphism which maps L into $\{ww | w \text{ in } \{a, b\}^*\}$, which is known to be not context free. Since context free languages are closed under homomorphisms, L is not a context free language. We conclude that no such grammar can be picked off a machine and hence no such machine can exist.   □

8. Performing Translations Deterministically

In this section we study the attributed translations that can be performed using an endmarker by deterministic attributed pushdown machines. First we note that any translation that can be performed by a deterministic machine can also be performed using an endmarker by a deterministic machine. However, there are translations that can be performed using an endmarker by a deterministic machine, but that cannot be performed by a deterministic machine, simply because more languages can be accepted when the endmarker is used [5]. First we consider the case when the input grammar is $LL(k)$ [12, 13], i.e., can be parsed top down without backtrack.

THEOREM 4. *Any translation specified by an L-attributed translation grammar with an $LL(k)$ input grammar can be performed using an endmarker by a deterministic attributed pushdown machine.*

Proof. First construction 1 of [13] can be applied to the grammar so that the input grammar is strong $LL(k)$. For this input grammar, the next k input symbols always determine which production should be applied to a nonterminal [13]. Now a construction similar to that for Theorem 1 can be used to obtain the attributed pushdown machine, assuming that the machine is capable of looking ahead at the next k input symbols when selecting a move. The construction is modified so that the next k input symbols are used to determine which production to apply to a nonterminal. The resulting machine is deterministic and performs the attributed translation.

Since attributed pushdown machines as defined in this paper are not capable of lookahead, the standard lookahead machine must be simulated by the type of machine defined in this paper. This can be done in a straightforward manner using the machine state to remember k inputs and the attributes of the state to remember the attributes of k inputs. The simulating machine needs an endmarker and so the translation is performed using an endmarker by the resultant deterministic machine. □

Note that Examples 2, 3, and 4 are all L-attributed and all have an $LL(1)$ input grammar.

L-attributed translations with an $LL(k)$ input grammar can also be performed using the method of recursive descent [4]. In this method there is a procedure for recognizing each nonterminal in the grammar. To perform an attributed translation, the procedure has a parameter for each attribute of the corresponding nonterminal. In terms of ALGOL 60, the parameters corresponding to inherited attributes can be called by value, and the parameters corresponding to synthesized values must be called by name. In the call of one of the procedures, an actual parameter corresponding to an inherited attribute is the value of the attribute, and an actual parameter corresponding to a synthesized attribute is a variable to which the value of the synthesized attribute should be assigned during the execution of the called procedure.

As an example, the following ALGOL-like program is a recursive descent processor based on the grammar of Example 4, assuming the attribute values are integers.

```
begin
procedure S(r); value r; integer r;
    comment This procedure translates an example of nonterminal S.
    All examples of S begin with input symbol a;
    if input symbol = a
    then begin integer s, t, u, v;
        s := attribute of input symbol;
        advance to next input symbol;
        t := r + s;
        B(t, u);
        v := 3 * u;
        output ("d", v)
        end
    else reject;
procedure B(r, s); value r; integer r, s;
    comment This procedure translates an example of nonterminal B.
    All examples of B begin with input symbol b;
    if input symbol = b
    then begin integer t;
        t := attribute of input symbol;
        advance to next input symbol;
        s := r * t;
        end
    else reject;
    comment execution starts here;
    S(4);
    if input symbol = end marker then accept else reject
    end
```

Bochman [1] independently shows that, in his model, if the attribute rules satisfy conditions similar to those in our definition of *L*-attributed grammars, the attributes can be evaluated in a top down scan of a derivation tree by calling recursive procedures.

We now study attributed translations that can be performed while parsing bottom up. First we need the following definition.

An attributed grammar is called *Polish* if and only if all action symbols occur only at the extreme right end of the right-hand sides of productions.

Any unattributed translation specified by a Polish translation grammar with an $LR(k)$ input grammar can be performed using an endmarker by a deterministic pushdown machine [12]. However this result does not hold when the grammar is L-attributed.

THEOREM 5. *There exists a translation specified by an L-attributed Polish translation grammar with an $LR(0)$ input grammar that cannot be performed by any deterministic attributed pushdown machine.*

Proof. Consider the following L-attributed grammar with input set $\{a, b, c, d\}$, action set $\{0, 1, 2\}$ and nonterminal set $\{S\}$. Nonterminal S has one inherited attribute for which the initial value is 1. Action symbol 2 has an inherited attribute.

$$S_x \rightarrow aS_yc0$$
$$y \leftarrow 2 * x$$
$$S_x \rightarrow aS_yd1$$
$$y \leftarrow 2 * x + 1$$
$$S_x \rightarrow b2_y$$
$$y \leftarrow x$$

Suppose this translation can be performed by a deterministic machine. The attribute of action symbol 2 cannot be determined by the machine until after the entire input sequence has been read, and so the machine cannot produce any output until after it reads the entire input sequence. The machine must therefore be able to read a sequence in $\{c, d\}^*$ and then output the same sequence with c replaced by zero and d by 1. However when the machine reaches the end of the input string, the first part of its output string is determined by the upper portion of its stack contents, and this upper portion can only reflect the end of the sequence in $\{c, d\}^*$. Therefore such a deterministic machine does not exist. □

An L-attributed grammar is called *S-attributed* if and only if all attributes of nonterminals are synthesized.

Many compilers that parse bottom up use a design method that only permits the call of a "semantic action" when a production is recognized. If furthermore, the information available to the semantic action is associated with the right-hand side of the recognized production, and the information returned by the semantic action is associated with the left-hand side, the design method corresponds to S-attributed Polish translation grammars.

THEOREM 6. *Any translation specified by an S-attributed Polish translation grammar with an $LR(k)$ input grammar can be performed using an endmarker by a deterministic attributed pushdown machine.*

Proof. The machine is based on the standard $LR(k)$ machine [6, 8] for recognizing the unattributed version of the input grammar in a bottom up fashion. Each stack symbol has a set of attributes equal to the attributes of the grammatical symbol it represents. When a production is recognized, the attributes of the action symbols and left-hand nonterminal are computed, and the outputs are emitted. □

However, S-attributed translation grammars cannot specify all translations that deterministic attributed pushdown machines can perform using an endmarker.

THEOREM 7. *There exists a translation specified by an L-attributed translation grammar with an $LL(1)$ input grammar that cannot be specified by any S-attributed translation grammar.*

Proof. Consider the following translation grammar with input set $\{a, b, c\}$, action set $\{1, 2, 3\}$, and starting nonterminal S. Nonterminal A and action symbol 2 each have one inherited attribute; and input a has one attribute. No other symbols have attributes.

$$S \rightarrow a_x A_y$$
$$y \leftarrow x$$
$$A_x \rightarrow b1 A_y c3$$
$$y \leftarrow x$$
$$A_x \rightarrow d2_y$$
$$y \leftarrow x$$

Observe that the grammar is L-attributed and has an $LL(1)$ input grammar. The activity sequences generated by this grammar have input part $a_x b^n dc^n$ and action part $1^n 2_x 3^n$ where $n \geq 0$ and the attribute of 2 equals the attribute of a.

Suppose this translation can be specified by an S-attributed translation grammar. Then it can be shown (see for instance the proof of the "$uvwxy$" theorem in [5]) that associated with the grammar there is an integer p such that all activity sequences of length greater than p can be written in the form $uvwxy$ where v and x are not both ϵ, and there is a nonterminal A such that the starting symbol of the grammar generates uAy and $A \overset{*}{\Rightarrow} vAx \overset{*}{\Rightarrow} vwx$. An implication of this is that all sequences of the form $uv^m wx^m y$ are generated by the grammar. Since an activity sequence containing $n + 2$ input symbols must contain exactly $n + 1$ action symbols, vx must contain an equal number of input symbols and action symbols.

Now consider an activity sequence generated from the hypothetical S-attributed grammar and having length greater than p. We wish to show that the single occurrence of a from the input part must be part of u and the single occurrence of 2 from the action part must be part of w.

The one occurrence of a cannot be in v or x because these sequences are repeated. The a could not occur in y because then y would contain all the input symbols and vx would contain only action symbols. Finally, the a cannot occur in w, because then all the input symbols in vx would be in x, and $uvvwxxy$ would have an input part that is not of the form $a_x b^n dc^n$. We conclude that a is in u.

The one occurrence of 2 cannot be in v or x because these sequences are repeated. The 2 cannot occur in u, because then vx would contain action symbol 3, but not action symbol 2. Similarly, 2 in y would imply that vx contains action symbol 1, but not action symbol 3. We conclude that 2 is in w.

From the "$uvwxy$" theorem, we now conclude that there is a derivation of an activity sequence where $A \overset{*}{\Rightarrow} w$ and w contains 2, but not a. Since the grammar is assumed to be S-attributed, the nonterminals have only synthesized attributes. Therefore the attributes of any action symbols generated from a nonterminal can only be computed in terms of the attributes of the input symbols actually generated from that nonterminal. Since a is not generated from nonterminal A, there is no way of specifying that the attribute of 2 equals the attribute of a.

We now give a characterization of the translations that can be performed by deterministic attributed pushdown machines, i.e., we define a class of attributed translation grammars which specify exactly the set of attributed translations that can be performed by deterministic attributed pushdown machines. The characterization is in terms of an extension of strict deterministic grammars [5] in which we take the attributes and action symbols into account.

An attributed translation grammar (with terminals and nonterminals V) is called *SD-attributed* if and only if it is L-attributed and there exists a partition π on V such that

1. All input symbols are in the same block of π.

2. For each action symbol y, $\{y\}$ is a block of π.

3. All the nonterminals in the same block of π have the same number of inherited attributes.

4. The inherited attributes of each nonterminal can be ordered so that for any nonterminals A and A' in the same block of π, if $A \rightarrow \alpha\beta$ and $A' \rightarrow \alpha\beta'$ are productions (α, β, β', in V^*) then either

(a) both β and $\beta' \neq \epsilon$, in which case the first symbol of β and β' are in the same block of π, and the rules for computing corresponding inherited attributes of these symbols (in terms of the attributes of α and corresponding inherited attributes of A and A') are the same, or

(b) $\beta = \beta' = \epsilon$ and $A = A'$. □

THEOREM 8. *Any translation performed by a deterministic attributed pushdown machine can be specified by an SD-attributed translation grammar.*

Proof. The grammar obtained from the machine by the construction used in the proof of Theorem 2 is SD-attributed. To construct the partition whose existence is required by the definition, place nonterminals of the form (r, A, p) in the same block if and only if they have the same first two components. Then place nonterminal S in a one element block, place the input symbols together as a block, and put each action symbol in a separate one element block. The attribute ordering required by condition 4 is then easily supplied. □

THEOREM 9. *Any translation specified by an SD-attributed translation grammar can be performed by a deterministic attributed pushdown machine.*

Proof. We extend the construction in [5]. Let the grammar have partition π and vocabulary V consisting of input set I, action set Y, and nonterminal set N.
  The machine is

$$(Q, I, Y, \Gamma, \delta, Z, A, C, u, v)$$

where $Q = \{q_j \mid 0 \leq j < $ maximum number of symbols in a block of $\pi\}$. $\Gamma = \{(V_i, \alpha) \mid A \rightarrow \alpha\beta$ for some A in block V_i and α, β in $V^*\} \cup \{(V_i, \alpha, V_j) \mid A \rightarrow \alpha B\beta$ for some A in block V_i, nonterminal B in block V_j and α, β in $V^*\}$. $Z = (V_0, \epsilon)$ where V_0 is the block containing the starting nonterminal.
  A is the set of values that the attributes of the grammar can take on.
  $C(a)$ for a in $I \cup Y$ equals the number of attributes a has in the grammar. $C((V_i, \alpha))$ equals the sum of the number of attributes of α in the grammar and the number of inherited attributes of a symbol in V_i. $C((V_i, \alpha, V_j))$ equals the sum of the number of attributes of α, the number of inherited attributes of a symbol in V_i, and the number of inherited attributes of a symbol in V_j. $C(q)$ for q in Q equals the maximum number of synthesized attributes of any nonterminal.

u is arbitrary.

v equals the inherited attributes of the starting nonterminal.

δ consists of the following five types of moves.

For any V_i, V_k blocks of nonterminals, α in V^*, a in I, y in Y, and q in Q.

(i) $\delta(q_0, a, (V_i, \alpha)) = \{(q_0, (V_i, \alpha a), \epsilon, f)\}$ if $A \to \alpha a \beta$ for some A in V_i and β in V^*.

(ii) $\delta(q_0, \epsilon, (V_i, \alpha)) = \{(q_0, (V_i, \alpha y), y, f)\}$ if $A \to \alpha y \beta$ for some A in V_i and β in V^*.

(iii) $\delta(q_0, \epsilon, (V_i, \alpha)) = \{(q_0, (V_k, \epsilon)(V_i, \alpha, V_k), \epsilon, f)\}$ if $A \to \alpha B \beta$ for some A in V_i, nonterminal B in V_k and β in V^*.

(iv) $\delta(q_0, \epsilon, (V_i, \alpha)) = \{(q_j, \epsilon, \epsilon, f)\}$ if $A \to \alpha$ is a production and A is the jth nonterminal in its block.

(v) $\delta(q_j, a, (V_i, \alpha, V_k)) = \{(q_0, (V_i, \alpha B), \epsilon, f)\}$ if B is the jth nonterminal in block V_k.

In case (iv), function f computes the synthesized attributes of A (from the attributes of (V_i, α)) and assigns them to q_j. In all other cases, f assigns arbitrary values to the attributes of the new state.

In case (i), f assigns to $(V_i, \alpha a)$ the attributes of (V_i, α) plus the attributes of a. In case (ii), f computes the attributes of y. It assigns these attributes to the output and (together with the attributes of (V_i, α)) to $(V_i, \alpha y)$. In case (iii), f computes the inherited attributes of B. Because the grammar is SD-attributed, all such B have the same rule for computing their attributes. Function f assigns these attributes to (V_k, ϵ) and (together with the attributes of (V_i, α)) to (V_i, α, V_k). In case (v), f assigns the attributes of q_j and (V_i, α, V_k) to $(V_i, \alpha B)$. $\square$

9. Performing Arbitrary Translations

In this section we show that if the attribute rules specify all the attribute values in a derivation tree, the attributes can be computed on a random access device in an amount of time proportional to the number of edges in the derivation tree. When the grammar is well defined, the attribute rules specify all the attribute values in all derivation trees.

THEOREM 10. *Given a derivation tree for which the attribute rules specify all the attribute values, and assuming that one unit of time is charged for the evaluation of an attribute rule, then the attributes can be computed in time linear with the number of edges in the derivation tree.*

Proof. Construct a directed graph containing a node for each attribute of each node of the derivation tree. The graph contains an edge from node a to node b if the rule for computing attribute b uses the value of attribute a. Since the rules for computing attributes can only depend on other attributes in the same production, the number of edges and nodes in the graph is bounded by some constant (based on the attributed grammar) times the number of edges in the derivation tree.

Since the attributed grammar specifies all the attributes of the tree (given the values of the input symbol attributes and starting symbol inherited attributes) the constructed graph has no cycles. Therefore a topological sort can be performed on the graph, using an algorithm whose time is linear with the size of the graph [9]. The attributes associated with the nodes of the graph can then be evaluated in the order produced by the topological sort. Each attribute will be evaluated after the attributes on which the rule for computing it depends. $\square$

10. Summary

A grammatical method of specifying attributed translations has been presented. The traditional top down and bottom up pushdown translators have been generalized to perform these translations. As with unattributed pushdown machines, the generalizations also operate in linear time (excluding the time required to evaluate the attribute evaluation functions).

Generalizations of $LL(k)$ and $LR(k)$ grammars are L-attributed $LL(k)$ and S-attributed $LR(k)$ grammars respectively. Neither of these grammars is sufficient to characterize deterministic attributed pushdown translations since $LL(k)$ grammars do not have sufficient syntactic power and S-attributed grammars do not have sufficient semantic power (Theorem 7). However, a characterization of deterministic attributed pushdown translations can be obtained by merging a top down attribute concept (L-attributed grammars) with a bottom up grammatical concept (SD grammars of [5]).

Taken together, the results show that grammatical specification and translation techniques can be generalized in a natural way to handle attributed translations without significant increases in processing cost. Thus attributed translation grammars can be a suitable basis for a theory of formal semantics of translation.

Acknowledgment

The authors wish to thank Professor Michael M. Hammer of the Massachusetts Institute of Technology for many useful comments concerning the presentation of this paper.

References

[1] G. V. Bochman. Semantics evaluated from left to right. Technical report, Departement d'Informatique, Univ. de Montreal, 1973.

[2] D. Crowe. Generating parsers for affix grammars. *Comm. Assoc. Computing Mach.*, 15:728–734, 1972.

[3] K. Culik. Attributed grammars and languages. Technical report, Departement d'Informatique, Univ. de Montreal, 1969.

[4] D. Gries. *Compiler Construction for Digital Computers*. Wiley, New York, 1971.

[5] M. A. Harrison and I. M. Havel. Strict deterministic grammars. *J. Comput. System Sci.*, 7:237–277, 1973.

[6] J. E. Hopcroft and J. D. Ullman. *Formal Languages and Their Relation to Automata*. Addison–Wesley, Reading, 1969.

[7] E. T. Irons. A syntax directed compiler for ALGOL 60. *Comm. Assoc. Comput. Mach.*, 4:51–55, 1961.

[8] D. E. Knuth. On the translation of languages from left to right. *Information and Control*, 8:607–639, 1965.

[9] D. E. Knuth. *The Art of Computer Programming: Fundamental Algorithms*, volume 1. Addison–Wesley, Reading, 1968.

[10] D. E. Knuth. Semantics of context free languages. *Math. Systems Theory*, 2:127–145, 1968.

[11] C. H. A. Koster. Affix grammars. In *ALGOL 68 Implementation*. North-Holland, Amsterdam, 1971.

[12] P. M. Lewis and R. E. Stearns. Syntax directed transduction. *J. Assoc. Comput. Mach.*, 15:465–488, 1968.

[13] D. J. Rosenkrantz and R. E. Stearns. Properties of deterministic top-down grammars. *Information and Control*, 17:226–256, 1970.

[14] R. E. Stearns and P. M. Lewis. Property grammars and table machines. *Information and Control*, 14:524–549, 1969.

Chapter 3

AN ANALYSIS OF SEVERAL HEURISTICS
FOR THE TRAVELING SALESMAN PROBLEM*

DANIEL J. ROSENKRANTZ, RICHARD E. STEARNS
AND PHILIP M. LEWIS II

General Electric Research and Development Center, Schenectady, NY 12345, USA

Reprinted from: *SIAM J. Computing*, Vol. 6, No. 3, Sept. 1977, pp. 563–581.
© SIAM

Abstract   Several polynomial time algorithms finding "good," but not necessarily optimal, tours for the traveling salesman problem are considered. We measure the closeness of a tour by the ratio of the obtained tour length to the minimal tour length. For the nearest neighbor method, we show the ratio is bounded above by a logarithmic function of the number of nodes. We also provide a logarithmic lower bound on the worst case. A class of approximation methods we call insertion methods are studied, and these are also shown to have a logarithmic upper bound. For two specific insertion methods, which we call nearest insertion and cheapest insertion, the ratio is shown to have a constant upper bound of 2, and examples are provided that come arbitrarily close to this upper bound. It is also shown that for any $n \geq 8$, there are traveling salesman problems with n nodes having tours which cannot be improved by making $n/4$ edge changes, but for which the ratio is $2(1 - 1/n)$.

Keywords: traveling salesman problem, approximation algorithm, k-optimal, minimal spanning tree, triangle inequality

Received by the editors July 19, 1976, and in revised form December 13, 1976.

---

* An extended abstract of this paper is in the Proceedings of the IEEE Fifteenth Annual Symposium on Switching and Automata Theory, 1974, under the title *Approximate algorithms for the traveling salesperson problem*.

S.S. Ravi, S.K. Shukla (eds.), *Fundamental Problems in Computing*,
© Springer Science + Business Media B.V. 2009

1.   Introduction

The traveling salesman problem has long been of great interest. The problem has been formulated in several different ways. We use the following formulation:

A traveling salesman graph G is a complete weighted undirected graph specified by a pair (N, d) where N is a set of nodes, d is a *distance function* mapping pairs of nodes (or edges) into real numbers, and d satisfies

(a) $d(i, j) = d(j, i)$ for all i and j in N,

(b) $d(i, j) \geq 0$ for all i and j in N,

(c) $d(i, j) + d(j, k) \geq d(i, k)$ for all i, j, k in N.

Condition (c) is referred to as the *triangle inequality*. The number $d(i, j)$ is called the *length* or *weight* of (i, j).

A *tour* for a traveling salesman graph G is a circuit on the graph containing each node exactly once (i.e. a Hamiltonian circuit). The *length* of a tour is the sum of the lengths of the edges composing the circuit. An *optimal tour* or *solution* for G is a tour of minimal length. The *traveling salesman problem* is to take a traveling salesman graph and find an optimal tour.

The traveling salesman problem is sometimes formulated (Bellmore and Nemhauser [1]) as the problem of finding a minimal length circuit containing each node at least once for an undirected graph in which the distances are not constrained by the triangle inequality. However, a problem stated in this manner can always be reduced (Hardgrave and Nemhauser [6]) to the problem considered here by the technique of changing each $d(i, j)$ to the length of the shortest path between i and j. This conversion can be done in time proportional to the cube of the number of nodes (Floyd [4]). Each tour in the new problem corresponds to a circuit of the same length in the original problem, and the two problems have solutions of the same length. Therefore, our results, which are stated in terms of the new problem, also apply to the original problem.

Another formulation requires that a shortest tour be found for distances not constrained by the triangle inequality. A problem stated this way can always be reduced to the type of problem considered here by adding a suitably large constant k to each distance. The altered problem has the same optimal tour as the original, but the lengths of the optimal tours will differ by the amount $n \cdot k$ where n is the number of nodes. Our results do not apply to this formulation, since our results pertain to the tour lengths.

The best known methods of solving the traveling salesman problem take an amount of time exponential in the number of nodes. Furthermore, the problem is easily seen to be *NP*-hard. Karp [8] shows that determining whether an undirected graph has a Hamiltonian circuit is *NP*-complete. This problem can be reduced to a traveling salesman problem by forming the complete weighted graph whose edges are of length one if there is a corresponding edge in the original graph, and of length two otherwise. For an n node graph, the minimal tour of the new graph has length n if and only if the original graph has a Hamiltonian circuit.

In view of the computational difficulties in obtaining optimal tours, a number of algorithms have been published which run faster but do not necessarily produce an optimal tour. A number of these approximation algorithms have been experimentally observed to perform well, but there has not been a theoretical characterization of how the obtained tours compare with the optimal.

In this paper, we analyze some of these methods to bound the ratio of the obtained tour length to the optimal tour length. In some cases, these bounds grow as a function of the number of nodes and in other cases a constant bound is found for all traveling salesman problems. In contrast, if the distance function is unconstrained by the triangle inequality then for any constant $k \geq 1$, the problem of finding a tour with a ratio bounded by k is *NP*-complete (Sahni and Gonzalez [16]).

Another approximation method was recently announced and analyzed in Christofides [2]. This method produces a better worst case approximation than the methods analyzed here, but requires more running time.

In the material which follows, we exclude the trivial case where the distance function is identically zero. This assumption together with the triangle inequality implies that every tour has a length greater than zero. We also adopt the convention that OPTIMAL represents the length of the optimal tour. Under the assumption of nontriviality,

$$\text{OPTIMAL} > 0. \tag{1.1}$$

2.   Nearest Neighbor Algorithm

The first approximation algorithm we study is the nearest neighbor method (Bellmore and Nemhauser [1]), also called the next best method in Gavett [5]. In this algorithm, a path is constructed as follows:

1. Start with an arbitrary node.

2. Find the node not yet on the path which is closest to the node last added and add to the path the edge connecting these two nodes.

3. When all nodes have been added to the path, add an edge connecting the starting node and the last node added.

We assume that when there are ties in step 2, they can be broken arbitrarily.

We note that the nearest neighbor algorithm can be programmed to operate in time proportional to n^2 where n is the number of nodes. This time is linear in the input length if the input is a list of all distances.

Let NEARNEIBER be the length of the tour obtained by the nearest neighbor algorithm. Let lg denote the logarithm to the base 2, and $\lceil x \rceil$ denote the smallest integer greater than or equal to x.

THEOREM 1. *For a traveling salesman graph with n nodes*

$$\frac{\text{NEARNEIBER}}{\text{OPTIMAL}} \leq \frac{1}{2}\lceil \lg(n) \rceil + \frac{1}{2}.$$

The proof of Theorem 1 is given after the proof of the following lemma.

LEMMA 1. *Suppose that for a n node graph (N, d) there is a mapping assigning each node p a number l_p such that the following two conditions hold:*

(a) $d(p,q) \geq \min(l_p, l_q)$ *for all nodes p and q.*

(b) $l_p \leq \frac{1}{2}$ OPTIMAL *for all nodes p.*

Then $\sum l_p \leq \frac{1}{2}(\lceil \lg(n) \rceil + 1)$ OPTIMAL.

Proof. We can assume without loss of generality that node set N is $\{i \mid 1 \leq i \leq n\}$ and that $l_i \geq l_j$ whenever $i \leq j$. The key to the proof is the following inequality:

$$\text{OPTIMAL} \geq 2 \sum_{i=k+1}^{\min(2k,n)} l_i \tag{2.1}$$

for all k satisfying $1 \leq k \leq n$.

To prove (2.1), we let H be the complete subgraph defined on the set of nodes

$$\{i \mid 1 \leq i \leq \min(2k, n)\}.$$

We let T be the tour in H which visits the nodes of H in the same order as these nodes are visited in an optimal tour of the original graph. Let LENGTH be the length of T. By the triangle inequality, each edge (b, c) of T must have a length which is less than or equal to the length of the path from b to c used in the optimal tour. Since the edges of T sum to LENGTH and the corresponding paths in the original graph sum to OPTIMAL we conclude that

$$\text{OPTIMAL} \geq \text{LENGTH}. \tag{2.2}$$

By condition (a) of the Lemma, for each (i, j) in T, $d(i, j) \geq \min(l_i, l_j)$. Therefore,

$$\text{LENGTH} \geq \sum_{(i,j) \in T} \min(l_i, l_j) = \sum_{i \in H} \alpha_i l_i \qquad (2.3)$$

where α_i is the number of edges (i, j) in T for which $i > j$ (and hence $l_i = \min(l_i, l_j)$).

We want to obtain a lower bound on the right hand side of (2.3). Observe that each α_i is at most 2 (because i is the endpoint of only two edges in tour T) and that the α_i sum to the number of edges in T. Because k is at least half of the number of edges in T, we certainly get a lower bound on the right hand side of (2.3) if we assume that the k largest l_i have $\alpha_1 = 0$ and the remaining $\min(2k, n) - k$ of the l_i have $\alpha_i = 2$. By assumption, the k largest are $\{l_i | 1 \leq i \leq k\}$ so the estimated lower bound is

$$\sum_{i \in H} \alpha_i l_i \geq 2 \sum_{i=k+1}^{\min(2k,n)} l_i \qquad (2.4)$$

and (2.2), (2.3), and (2.4) together establish (2.1).

We now sum inequalities (2.1) for all values of k equal to a power of two less than s, namely:

$$\sum_{j=0}^{\lceil \lg(n) \rceil - 1} \text{OPTIMAL} \geq \sum_{j=0}^{\lceil \lg(n) \rceil - 1} 2 \cdot \sum_{i=2^j+1}^{\min(2^{j+1},n)} l_i,$$

which reduces to

$$\lceil \lg(n) \rceil \cdot \text{OPTIMAL} \geq 2 \cdot \sum_{i=2}^{n} l_i. \qquad (2.5)$$

Now condition (b) of the lemma implies

$$\text{OPTIMAL} \geq 2 \cdot l_1 \qquad (2.6)$$

and (2.5) and (2.6) combine to give the conclusion of the lemma. $\square$

Proof of Theorem 1. For each node p, let l_p be the length of the edge leaving node p and going to the node selected as the nearest neighbor to p. We want to show that the l_p satisfy the conditions of Lemma 1.

If node p was selected by the algorithm before node q, then q was a candidate for the closest unselected node to node p. This means that edge (p, q) is no shorter than the edge selected and hence

$$d(p, q) \geq l_p. \qquad (2.7)$$

Conversely, if q was selected before p, then

$$d(p, q) \geq l_q. \tag{2.8}$$

Since one of the nodes was selected before the other, either (2.7) or (2.8) must hold and condition (a) of Lemma 1 must be satisfied.

To prove condition (b) it suffices to prove that for any edge (p, q)

$$d(p, q) \leq \frac{1}{2} \cdot \text{OPTIMAL}. \tag{2.9}$$

The optimal tour can be considered to consist of two disjoint parts, each of which is a path between nodes p and q. From the triangle inequality, the length of any path between p and q cannot be less than $d(p, q)$, establishing (2.9).

Because the l_p are the lengths of the pairs comprising tour T,

$$\sum l_p = \text{NEARNEIBER}. \tag{2.10}$$

The conclusion of Lemma 1 together with (2.10) and (1.1) imply the inequality of Theorem 1. □

THEOREM 2. *For each $m > 3$, there exists a traveling salesman graph with $n = 2^m - 1$ nodes such that*

$$\frac{\text{NEARNEIBER}}{\text{OPTIMAL}} > \frac{1}{3} \lg(n + 1) + \frac{4}{9}.$$

Proof. For all $i \geq 1$, we define an incomplete weighted graph F_i with three distinguished nodes. The distinguished nodes are called the *start node*, the *middle node*, and the *right node*. These graphs are defined recursively using Fig. 3.1 where the start node appears to the left, the middle node in the middle, and the right node on the right. Each F_i has a path P_i which goes from the start node to the middle node visiting each node of F_i on the way. The P_i are also defined recursively in Fig. 3.1.

Graph F_1 consists of precisely three nodes with each pair of nodes having an edge of weight 1. Path P_1 consists of two edges, the edge from the start node to the right node and the edge from the right node to the middle node.

To construct graph F_{i+1}, one takes two copies of F_i (which we call the *left copy* and *right copy*) and one additional node (which becomes the middle node of F_{i+1}). This additional node is called D in Fig. 3.1. The additional node D is connected to the right node of the left copy (node C) and the start node of the right copy (node E) by edges of length 1. The additional node D is also connected to the middle node of the right copy (node F) by an edge of length l_i (defined below). Finally, the middle node of the left copy (node B) is

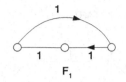

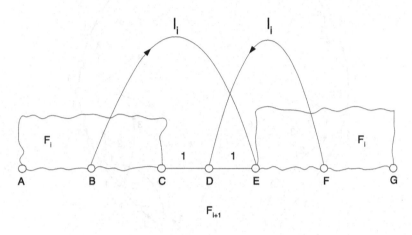

Figure 3.1.

connected to the start node of the right copy (node E) by an edge of length l_i. The start node of F_{i+1} is the start node of the left copy (node A) and the right node is the right node of the right copy (node G). The path P_{i+1} consists of the two copies of path P_i plus the two edges (B, E) and (F, D) of length l_i. The length l_i is given by the formula

$$l_i = \frac{1}{6}(4 \cdot 2^i - (-1)^i + 3). \tag{2.11}$$

Let L_i be the length of path P_i. Length L_i is described by the difference equation

$$L_{i+1} = 2 \cdot L_i + 2 \cdot l_i$$

since P_{i+1} consists of two copies of P_i and two edges of length l_i. Given that $L_1 = 2$, the solution of this difference equation is

$$L_i = \frac{1}{9}(6 \cdot i \cdot 2^i + 8 \cdot 2^i + (-1)^i - 9). \tag{2.12}$$

For each F_i, we define a graph G_i obtained by connecting the start and right nodes of F_i by an edge of length 1, and connecting the middle node to the start node with an edge of length $l_i - 1$. The start node of F_i is then also

52

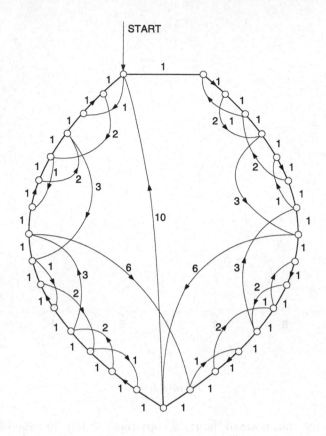

Figure 3.2.

referred to as the start node of G_i. Figure 3.2 is a picture of G_4. We define $\bar{G}_i$ to be the complete graph on the nodes of G_i where $d(a,b)$ is the length of the minimal path from a to b in G_i. Therefore, the distances in $\bar{G}_i$ satisfy the triangle inequality.

Graph $\bar{G}_i$ has two important properties:

(a) the edges of G_i have the same lengths in $\bar{G}_i$ as they have in G_i;

(b) if the nearest neighbor method is started with the start node of G_i, the method can (with suitable resolution of ties) produce path P_i followed by the edge of length $l_i - 1$ returning from the middle node (which is the last node of path P_i) to the start node.

We return to prove properties (a) and (b) after completing the main thread of the proof.

Each $\bar{G}_i$ has an optimal tour whose length is equal to the number of nodes n in $\bar{G}_i$ (namely $2^{i+1} - 1$). This tour is found, starting with the start node, by

visiting the nodes in left to right order and then returning from the right node
back to the start node. Each of the edges in this tour has weight one.

The example satisfying the theorem is $\bar{G}_{m-1}$. Its ratio is exactly

$$\frac{\text{NEARNEIBER}}{\text{OPTIMAL}} = (L_i + l_i - 1)/n \quad \text{where } i = \lg(n+1) - 1.$$

This ratio is greater than the ratio indicated in the theorem.

All that remains is to prove properties (a) and (b). Referring back to Fig. 3.1,
we first show that for each F_{i+1}

$$\overline{AB} = \overline{BC} = \overline{EF} = \overline{FG} = l_i - 1, \tag{2.13}$$
$$\overline{AC} = \overline{EG} = l_{i+1} - 2, \tag{2.14}$$
$$\overline{BE} = \overline{DF} = l_i, \tag{2.15}$$
$$\overline{AD} = \overline{DG} = l_{i+1} - 1, \tag{2.16}$$
$$\overline{AG} = l_{i+2} - 2. \tag{2.17}$$

The notation $\overline{XY}$ indicates the length of the shortest path between X and Y
in F_{i+1}. The equations are routinely verified for $i = 1$. We continue by
induction. Assume that (2.12)–(2.16) are true for $i \leq I - 1$ (i.e. for F_I).
Figure 3.3 shows the relevant nodes in F_{I+1} before the two copies of F_I are
connected. Associated with each pair of nodes from the same copy of F_I, an
edge is shown whose weight is the length of the shortest path in F_I connecting
these nodes. These shortest path lengths in F_I are specified by the induction
hypothesis. For instance, edge (A, B) in Fig. 3.3 connects the start and middle
nodes of F_I and from (2.15), the shortest path length in F_I connecting these
nodes is $l_I - 1$. Figure 3.4 shows Fig. 3.3 with the addition of the four edges
created in the construction of F_{I+1} from the two copies of F_I. Because each
of the edge weights in Fig. 3.3 represents a shortest path in F_I, by applying
formula (2.11) for l_I to all possible paths in F_{I+1}, we can conclude that each of
the edge weights in Fig. 3.4 is the length of the shortest path in F_{I+1} *connecting
the end nodes of the edges. This establishes equations (2.12)–(2.14) for F_{I+1}.*

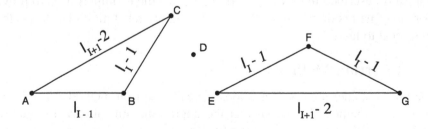

Figure 3.3.

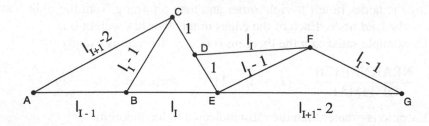

Figure 3.4.

Equations (2.15) and (2.16) are established by a similar consideration of all paths in Fig. 3.4. The path of length $l_{I+2} - 2$ from A to G is *ABEG*.

We note also that (2.12)–(2.15) also hold when F_{I+1} is converted to G_{I+1}. This is proven by connecting A and G in Fig. 3.4 by an edge of weight one and A and D by an edge of length $l_{I+1} - 1$ and again checking the paths. Note also that the shortest path from A to D is the edge (A, D).

Now we return to property (a). Equation (2.14) shows that, as each F_{i+1} is constructed, the newly added edges constitute the shortest paths between their endpoints. All distances among points in an F_i are maintained when that F_i is embedded in F_{i+1}, because the distances among the three exit points at F_i are maintained. (Compare (2.12) with (2.15) and (2.13) with (2.16).)

We have already noted that the final edge added in constructing a G_i is also a shortest path and the fact that the length one edges are also shortest paths requires no argument. Thus property (a) is established.

Property (b) is established by observing that the middle node of an F_i is reached only after all of the nodes of F_i have been visited, and the node at the end of the edge of length l_i is at least as close as any node reached by a path through the start or right nodes. These nodes are already distance l_{i-1} away from the middle node and are at least distance 1 from a node not yet selected. □

One way to improve a nearest neighbor result is to repeat the method for each possible starting node and then take the minimum solution among these. This idea is described in Gavett [5]. However, for the examples used to prove Theorem 2, the result of this method (with suitable resolution of ties) is also proportional to $\lg(n)$.

3.   Insertion Methods

We now consider a class of methods we call insertion methods. The basic idea of these methods is to construct the approximation tour by a sequence of steps in which tours are constructed for progressively larger subsets of the nodes.

DEFINITION. Given a traveling salesman graph (N, d), a tour T on a subset S of N will be called a *subtour* of (N, d). We write $a \in T$ to mean $a \in S$. We treat a one node subset as a tour without edges.

DEFINITION. Given a traveling salesman graph (N, d), a subtour T, and a node k in N which is not in T, we define TOUR(T, k) to be a subtour obtained as follows:

if T passes through more than one point, then

(a) find an edge (x, y) in T which minimizes

$$d(x, k) + d(k, y) - d(x, y), \tag{3.1}$$

(b) delete edge (x, y) and add edges (x, k) and (k, y) to obtain TOUR(T, k);

if T passes through a single node i, then make TOUR(T, k) the two node tour consisting of edges (i, k) and (k, i).

In either case, we say that TOUR(T, k) is obtained by *inserting* k into T.

Formula (3.1) represents the difference in length between tour T and the tour obtained by replacing (x, y) by (x, k) and (k, y). Thus, when T has two or more nodes, TOUR(T, k) is the shortest tour that can be obtained from T and k by the alteration described in step (b). When T has only one node, TOUR(T, k) is the only tour that can be made from k and the point in T.

DEFINITION. An approximation method is called an *insertion method* if it takes a traveling salesman graph (N, d) with n nodes and constructs a sequence of subtours $T_1, \ldots, T_n$ so that

1. T1 consists of a single node a_0,

2. for each $i < n$, there is a node a_i not in T_i such that

$$T_{i+1} = \text{TOUR}(T_i, a_i), \tag{3.2}$$

3. T_n is the approximation.

In later sections, we consider specific selection criteria for choosing the nodes a_i. Here we are concerned with results which hold regardless of the selection method.

DEFINITION. Given a subtour T and a node k not in T, we define COST(T, k) to be the length of TOUR(T, k) minus the length of T.

An important consequence of the triangle inequality is the following:

LEMMA 2. *If (N, d) is a traveling salesman graph, T is a subtour, k a node not in T, and j a node in T, then*

$$\text{COST}(T, k) \leq 2 \cdot d(k, j). \tag{3.3}$$

Proof. In the case that T has only one node, the result is obvious. When T consists of more than one node, j is an endpoint of some edge (i, j) in T. Because k is inserted to minimize (3.1),

$$\text{COST}(T, k) \leq d(i, k) + d(k, j) - d(i, j) \tag{3.4}$$

where the right-hand side is (3.1) with (i, j) substituted for (x, y). The triangle inequality says

$$d(i, k) - d(i, j) \leq d(j, k). \tag{3.5}$$

Inequalities (3.4) and (3.5) together with $d(j, k) = d(k, j)$ give (3.3). □

We let INSERT represent the length of a path constructed by an insertion algorithm.

THEOREM 3. *For a traveling salesman graph with n nodes,*

$$\frac{\text{INSERT}}{\text{OPTIMAL}} \leq \lceil \lg(n) \rceil + 1. \tag{3.6}$$

Proof. Let (N, d) be the graph and let T_i for $1 \leq i \leq n$ and a_i for $0 \leq i < n$ be the subtours and nodes referred to in the definition of an insertion method. An obvious consequence of the definition of cost is

$$\text{INSERT} = \sum_{i=1}^{n-1} \text{COST}(T_i, a_i) \tag{3.7}$$

For each node a_i in $N - \{a_0\}$, define

$$l_{a_i} = \frac{1}{2} \cdot \text{COST}(T_i, a_i) \tag{3.8}$$

and define

$$l_{a_0} = 0. \tag{3.9}$$

We want to show that the l_p for p in N satisfy the hypothesis of Lemma 1. To verify condition (a), consider two nodes a_i and a_j with $i > j$. By our naming conventions, $i > j$ means that a_j belongs to T_i and a_i was inserted in T_i. By Lemma 2,

$$\text{COST}(T_i, a_i) \leq 2 \cdot d(a_i, a_j). \tag{3.10}$$

With (3.8) this implies

$$l_{a_i} \leq d(a_i, a_j),\qquad(3.11)$$

which implies condition (a).

Condition (b) is trivial for l_{a_0}. For other l_{a_i}, (3.8) requires us to prove

$$\mathrm{COST}(T_i, a_i) \leq \mathrm{OPTIMAL}.\qquad(3.12)$$

In the case of a_1, this cost is just $2d(a_0, a_1)$ and by the triangle inequality, OPTIMAL is at least as large as the distance between two points and back. For $i > 1$, a_i is inserted between two distinct points x and y with cost

$$d(x, a_i) + d(a_i, y) - d(x, y),\qquad(3.13)$$

which is the length of the added edges minus the length of the deleted edge. There is a subpath of the optimal tour between x and a_i which does not contain y and a disjoint subpath between a_i and y not containing x. By the triangle inequality, these subpaths are no shorter than $d(x, a_i)$ and $d(a_i, y)$ respectively and hence (3.13) must be no greater than OPTIMAL and condition (b) is established.

Lemma 1 together with (3.8), (3.9), (3.7), and (1.1) imply the theorem. $\square$

We do not know if the logarithmic growth permitted by Theorem 3 can actually be achieved. In fact, we know of no examples such that INSERT/OPTIMAL > 4 so there could even be a constant upper bound. In the next section we present some insertion methods for which we can establish a constant upper bound.

4. Nearest Insertion and Cheapest Insertion

We now consider two insertion methods which produce a tour no longer than twice the optimal regardless of the number of nodes in the problem. We call these two methods the nearest insertion method and the cheapest insertion method.

Given a subtour T and a node p, we define the distance $d(T, p)$ between T and p as

$$\min\{d(x, p) \text{ for } x \text{ in } T\}.\qquad(4.1)$$

We say that a tour is constructed by *nearest insertion* if each $a_i, 1 \leq i < n$, in the definition of an insertion method satisfies

$$d(T_i, a_i) = \min\{d(T_i, x) \text{ for } x \text{ in } N - T_i\}.\qquad(4.2)$$

We say a tour is constructed by *cheapest insertion* if the a_i satisfy

$$\mathrm{COST}(T_i, a_i) = \min\{\mathrm{COST}(T_i, x) \text{ for } x \text{ in } N - T_i\}.\qquad(4.3)$$

The nearest insertion method is easily programmed to run in a time proportional to n^2. The only programming trick is to compute the value of $d(T_{i+1}, x)$ as the minimum of the two numbers $d(T_i, x)$ and $d(a_i, x)$. Thus the nearest insertion method runs in time proportional to the nearest neighbor method.

The cheapest insertion method is described in Nicholson [12]. The fastest algorithm we have devised for the cheapest insertion method runs proportional to $n^2 \cdot \log(n)$. Each time a node a_i is inserted in T_i, the new subtour T_{i+1} contains two new edges not in T_i. For each new edge (x, a_i) in T_{i+1}, the algorithm involves performing a sort of the $n - (i + 1)$ values of

$$d(x, k) + d(k, a_i) - d(x, a_i)$$

obtained for all k in $N - T_{i+1}$.

THEOREM 4. *If a tour of length* INSERT *is obtained by nearest insertion or cheapest insertion, then*

$$\frac{\text{INSERT}}{\text{OPTIMAL}} < 2. \tag{4.4}$$

We prove this theorem after proving the following lemma:

LEMMA 3. *Suppose that, for a traveling salesman graph* (N, d) *with n nodes, a tour of length* INSERT *is constructed by the insertion method of Sect. 3. Suppose further that for i satisfying* $1 \leq i < n$, *the tour* T_i *and node* a_i *selected by the insertion method satisfy*

$$\text{COST}(T_i, a_i) \leq 2 \cdot d(p, q) \tag{4.5}$$

for all nodes p and q such that p is in T_i *and q is not in* T_i. *Then*

$$\text{INSERT} \leq 2 \cdot \text{TREE}, \tag{4.6}$$

where TREE *is the length of a minimal spanning tree for* (N, d).

Proof. Let M be a minimal spanning tree. The idea of the proof is to establish a correspondence between steps in the insertion procedure and edges of M. For the step of inserting node a_i into T_i, the corresponding edge of M will have one endpoint in T_i and the other endpoint in $N - T_i$. Thus (4.5) can be used to show that the cost of each step is no more than twice the corresponding edge.

First, since M is a tree, there is a unique path in M connecting each pair of nodes. For each node a_i with $i > 0$, we say that node a_j is *compatible* with node a_i if $j < i$ and all the intermediate nodes in the unique path in M connecting a_i and a_j have indices greater than i. Thus a_j compatible with a_i

implies that a_j is the first node in T_i encountered in the path from a_i to a_j. For each a_i with $i > 0$, the *critical node* is the node with the largest index that is compatible with a_i. The *critical path* for a_i is the unique path in M between a_i and its critical node. The *critical edge* for a_i is the edge in the critical path, one of whose endpoints is the critical node. Observe that the critical edge for a_i has one endpoint (the critical node) in T_i, and the other endpoint in $N - T_i$.

We now show that no two nodes can have the same critical edge. Assume to the contrary that a_i and a_j (with $j > i$) have the same critical edge. Let the endpoints of this critical edge be a_k and a_l with $l > k$. For any critical edge, the node with the lower index is the critical node and the node with the higher index is on the critical path, so node a_k is the critical node for both a_i and a_j. Thus, the critical paths for a_i and a_j both pass through a_l before reaching a_k. Therefore, there is a path P in M connecting a_j and a_i, such that every edge in P belongs to either the critical path for a_j or the critical path for a_i (or both). Therefore every intermediate node on P has an index greater than i. Since the path P from a_j reaches a node of lower index (a_i), some node a_m along path P is compatible with a_j. Now $m \geq i$ because a_m is on path P and $i > k$ because a_k is a compatible node for a_i. This implies $m > k$ and so a_m is a compatible node for a_j with a higher index than a_k. This contradicts the assumption that a_k is critical for a_j. Therefore no two nodes can have the same critical edge. Thus given a minimal spanning tree we can associate a unique edge in that tree with each node inserted by the insertion method.

Let e_i be the critical edge for node a_i. Since one endpoint of e_i is in T_i and the other endpoint is not, by (4.5).

$$\mathrm{COST}(T_i, a_i) \leq 2 \cdot d(e_i). \tag{4.7}$$

Summing (4.7) gives

$$\sum_{i=1}^{n-1} \mathrm{COST}(T_i, a_i) \leq 2 \cdot \sum_{i=1}^{n-1} d(e_i). \tag{4.8}$$

The left-hand side of (4.8) is INSERT by (3.8). Since M consists of $n - 1$ edges, and each e_i is distinct, the right-hand side of (4.8) is $2 \cdot$ TREE. Thus (4.8) implies (4.6). □

Proof of Theorem 4. We first show that, for both insertion methods, (4.5) holds. For the nearest insertion, there is for each i by (4.2) a node y_i in T_i such that

$$d(y_i, a_i) \leq d(p, q) \tag{4.9}$$

for all p in T_i and q in $N - T_i$. Lemma 2 says that

$$\mathrm{COST}(T_i, a_i) \leq 2 \cdot d(y_i, a_i) \tag{4.10}$$

and (4.9) and (4.10) imply (4.5). For the cheapest insertion, the cost of inserting a_i is by (4.3) even less than the cost of inserting an a_i chosen to satisfy (4.2). Therefore (4.5) must also hold in this case and Lemma 3 applies to both cases.

The optimal tour can be made into a tree by deleting its longest edge and this longest edge has a length at least OPTIMAL$/n$ where n is the number of nodes in the problem. Since the minimal spanning tree is no longer than this tree,

$$\text{TREE} \leq \left(1 - \frac{1}{n}\right) \cdot \text{OPTIMAL}. \tag{4.11}$$

Equations (4.11), (4.6), and (1.1) imply (4.4). $\qquad\qquad\square$

COROLLARY. *For a traveling salesman graph on n nodes, (4.4) in Theorem 4 may be replaced by*

$$\frac{\text{INSERT}}{\text{OPTIMAL}} \leq 2 \cdot \left(1 - \frac{1}{n}\right). \tag{4.12}$$

For the nearest insertion method, a simpler correspondence than that in the proof of Lemma 3 can be established between the cost of the insertion steps and the edges of a minimal spanning tree. Since each a_i is selected in accordance with (4.2), there is an edge (x, a_i) such that x is in T_i and

$$d(x, a_i) = \min\{d(p, q) \text{ for } p \text{ in } T_i \text{ and } q \text{ in } N - T_i\}. \tag{4.13}$$

Let e_i be this edge (x, a_i) and observe from Lemma 2 that

$$\text{COST}(T_i, a_i) \leq 2 \cdot e_i.$$

Moreover, the set of edges $\{e_i \mid 1 \leq i < n\}$ constitute a minimal spanning tree since the method of selecting edges satisfying (4.13) is a method of constructing a minimal spanning tree (Kruskal [9], Prim [13]).

We now show that there exist traveling salesman graphs for which the bound (4.12) is actually achieved. The examples can be interpreted as cities placed uniformly on a circular road. The case for 8 nodes is shown in Fig. 3.5. The optimal path is simply to go around the circle. The insertion methods may construct a path such as that in the figure, a path which goes almost all the way around and then doubles back on itself. Thus, each edge of the circle (except one) is traveled twice instead of the one time actually required, and the ratio of the path obtained to OPTIMAL is roughly two.

THEOREM 5. *For $n \geq 6$, there exists a traveling salesman graph on n nodes such that*

$$\frac{\text{INSERT}}{\text{OPTIMAL}} = 2 \cdot \left(1 - \frac{1}{n}\right) \tag{4.14}$$

for either the nearest insertion or cheapest insertion methods.

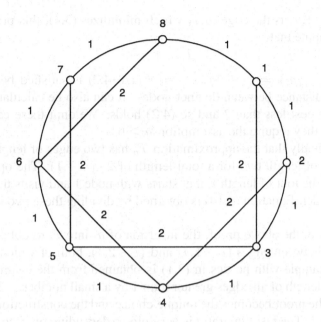

Figure 3.5.

Proof. We define graph (N_n, d_n) as follows:

$$N_n = \{i \mid 1 \leq i \leq n\},$$
$d_n(i, j) =$ smallest nonnegative integer m
such that $i - j \equiv m \pmod{n}$ or $j - i \equiv m \pmod{n}$.

We define T_1 to be the tour on set $\{1\}$, we define

$$T_2 = \{(1, 2), (2, 1)\}$$

and for $3 \leq i \leq n$ we define

$$T_i = \{(1, 2), (i - 1, i)\} \cup \{(j, j + 2) \mid 1 \leq j \leq i - 2\}.$$

Figure 3.5 shows T_8 for the case $n = 8$.
     We define

$$a_i = i + 1 \quad \text{for } 0 \leq i < n.$$

Obviously the T_i defined above are tours. We will show that the T_i together with the a_i satisfy (3.2), (4.2), and (4.3).
     T_{i+1} is obtained from T_i by deleting edge $(i - 1, i)$ and adding edges $(i - 1, i + 1)$ and $(i, i + 1)$.
     We compute that

$$\text{COST}(T_i, a_i) = 2$$

and that $(i - 1, i)$ is the edge in T_i which minimizes (3.1); this proves (3.2). We also compute that

$$d(T_i, a_i) = 1$$

because $d(a_{i-1}, a_i) = (i + 1) - i = 1$ and (4.2) is satisfied because 1 is the shortest distance between distinct nodes. It can also be calculated that no insertion can cost less than 2 and so (4.2) holds. We omit these calculations but note that they require the assumption $n \geq 6$.

We note finally that the approximation T_n has two edges of length one and $n - 2$ edges of length two for a total length of $2 \cdot (n - 1)$. The optimal tour is obviously the tour of length n that starts with node 1 and visits the nodes in numerical order. Equation (4.14) is obtained by dividing these two lengths. $\square$

For $i > 3$ in the above proof, the insertion of a_i into T_i to obtain T_{i+1} involves a tie between edges $(i - 1, i)$ and $(i - 2, i)$, both of which minimize (3.1). An example with no ties in (3.1) is obtained from the example by decreasing the length of all edges greater than 1 by a small number ε. The choice $(i - 1, i)$ of the proof becomes the unique choice and the construction proceeds as in the proof. The resulting ratio is very close (depending on ε) to (4.14).

Theorem 5 shows that, in the worst case, nearest insertion can create paths which double back on themselves and are roughly twice as long as necessary. We examined a number of problems with nodes placed randomly on a plane, and observed that the nearest insertion method often produced paths in which portions doubled back on themselves.

5. Farthest Insert

There is another insertion method which has some intuitive and empirical appeal, a method we call farthest insertion.

We say that a tour is constructed by *farthest insertion* if each $a_i, 1 \leq i < n$, in the definition of an insertion method satisfies

$$d(T_i, a_i) = \max\{d(T_i, x) \text{ for } x \text{ in } N - T_i\}. \tag{5.1}$$

Contrasting (5.1) with (4.2), we observe that farthest insertion has a max where nearest insertion has a min. The intuitive appeal is that the method establishes the general outline of the approximate tour at the outset and then fills in the details. The early establishment of a general outline is appealing because we expect better performance when the number of nodes is small. Inserting nearby points late in the approximation is appealing because the short edges used late in the procedure are less likely to be accidentally deleted by some still later insertion.

The empirical appeal is that, in a series of experiments, we found that farthest insertion usually produced a better tour than nearest insertion, cheapest insertion, and the nearest neighbor. For example, when tried on problems obtained by placing 50 nodes randomly on a unit square, nearest insertion was from 7 to 22% worse than farthest insertion, nearest neighbor was from 0 to 38% worse, and cheapest insertion ranged from 7% better to 12% worse. The usual ranking was thus farthest insertion first, cheapest insertion second, nearest insertion third, and nearest neighbor last.

The largest example we tried was 2000 points placed uniformly at random in the unit square. The score was farthest insertion 36.8, nearest insertion 41.4, and nearest neighbor 39.9. A path of length 37.2 was obtained by randomly selecting the order in which points were chosen for insertion. The farthest insertion path was no more than 1.25 times the optimal since the minimal spanning tree had length 29.5.

The advantage of picking random or arbitrary points for insertion is that virtually no computation time is needed to select an arbitrary point. On the 2000 city problem, the nearest neighbor tour was constructed in 751 seconds, the arbitrary insertion in 820 seconds, and the nearest and farthest insertions in 1628 seconds each.

Theorems 2 and 4 tell us that, in the worst case, the nearest neighbor paths become progressively worse than the nearest insertion paths as the number of nodes increase. We found no evidence of such a trend in our experiments. For example, in the 2000 node example described above, nearest neighbor actually did better than nearest insertion.

Altogether, our experiments suggest that the performance of the methods is not strongly tied to their worst case behavior.

6.   Some Other Approximation Methods

There are a variety of other approximation methods for which the cost of each step in the construction of the tour corresponds to a unique edge in a minimal spanning tree and for which the reasoning of Lemma 3 and Theorem 4 can be used to demonstrate a worst case ratio bound of 2. In this section, we discuss two such methods.

The first method, which we call *nearest addition*, is similar to nearest insertion. The nearest addition method takes a traveling salesman graph (N, d) with n nodes and constructs a sequence of subtours $T_1, T_2, \ldots, T_n$ so that

1. T_1 consists of a single node a_0;

2. for each $i < n$ there are nodes a_i in $N - T_i$ and b_i in T_i such that

    $$d(b_i, a_i) = \min\{d(y, x) \text{ for } y \text{ in } T_i \text{ and } x \text{ in } N - T_i\}. \qquad (6.1)$$

    and T_{i+1} is constructed from T_i by deleting some edge (c, b_i) from T_i and adding the two edges (c, a_i) and (b_i, a_i);

3. T_n is the approximation.

At each step of the procedure, the closest node is selected and added to the subtour next to the node to which it is the closest.

The increase in length between T_i and T_{i+1} is

$$d(c, a_i) + d(b_i, a_i) - d(c, b_i). \tag{6.2}$$

From the triangle inequality

$$d(c, a_i) \leq d(c, b_i) - d(b_i, a_i) \tag{6.3}$$

so that (6.2) is bounded by $2 \cdot d(b_i, a_i)$. The set of edges (b_i, a_i) selected in accordance with (6.1) is identical to the set of edges that would be selected for the nearest insertion method in accordance with (4.2), and constitutes a minimal spanning tree. Therefore results similar to Lemma 3 and Theorem 4 apply, and the ratio of the obtained tour length to the optimal tour length is bounded by 2.

Another approximation method is one we call *nearest merger*. First, given two disjoint subtours (i.e., subtours having no nodes in common) T_1 and T_2, their merger $\text{MERGE}(T_1, T_2)$ is defined as follows:

(a) If T_1 consists of a single node k, then

$$\text{MERGE}(T_1, T_2) = \text{TOUR}(T_2, k)$$

else if T_2 consists of a single node k_1, then

$$\text{MERGE}(T_1, T_2) = \text{TOUR}(T_1, k).$$

(b) If T_1 and T_2 each contain at least two nodes, let a, b, c, d be nodes such that (a, b) is an edge in T_1, (c, d) is an edge in T_2 and

$$d(a, c) + d(b, d) - d(a, b) - d(c, d) \tag{6.4}$$

is minimized. Then $\text{MERGE}(T_1, T_2)$ is the tour obtained from T_1 and T_2 by deleting (a, b) and (c, d) and adding (a, c) and (b, d).

The *nearest merger* method takes a problem (N, d) with n nodes and constructs a sequence $S_1, \ldots, S_n$ such that each S_i is a set of $n - i + 1$ disjoint subtours covering all the nodes in N. The sequence is constructed as follows:

1. S_1 consists of n subtours, each containing a single node.

2. For each $i < n$, find an edge (a_i, c_i) such that

$$d(a_i, c_i) = \min\{d(x, y) \text{ for } x \text{ and } y \text{ in different subtours in } S_i\}. \tag{6.5}$$

Then S_{i+1} is obtained from S_i by merging the subtours containing a_i and c_i.

At each step in the procedure, the two closest subtours are merged.

Observe that in a merger corresponding to (6.4), from the triangle inequality

$$d(b, d) \leq d(b, a) + d(a, c) + d(c, d)$$

so that (6.4) is bounded by $2 \cdot d(a, c)$. Also observe that the set of edges (a_i, c_i) chosen in accordance with (6.5) form a minimal spanning tree (Kruskal [9]). From these facts, results similar to Lemma 3 and Theorem 4 can be proved for nearest merger, and so the ratio of the obtained tour length to the optimal tour length is bounded by 2.

We also observe that Theorem 5 is also true for both nearest addition and nearest merger. For the examples in the proof of Theorem 5 both of these methods produce the same approximate tour as nearest insertion and cheapest insertion.

One possible way to improve nearest insertion, cheapest insertion, and nearest addition is to repeat each of these methods for each possible starting node and then take the minimum solution among these. However, for the examples in the proof of Theorem 5, these methods produce tours of the same length for all starting nodes. Therefore the approach of trying all starting nodes does not improve the worst case ratio.

The methods of this section and Sect. 4 are all proven to have constant bounds because of comparisons with the minimal spanning tree. There are also known bounded methods which actually construct a tour by first constructing the minimal spanning tree. One widely known but unpublished method is to construct the minimal spanning tree, double its edges to obtain an Eulerian circuit containing each point at least once, and then make the circuit into a tour by removing extra occurrences of each node. This method also has an upper bound of 2.

The method of Christofides [2] also starts with the minimal spanning tree, but this is converted into an Eulerian circuit by solving the matching problem among the nodes of odd order. This method has an upper bound of $\frac{3}{2}$, an improvement on the bounds for the methods studied here. However, the running time of this method is n^3, which is slower than the n^2 methods studied here.

7. k-Optimality

One approach to obtaining approximate solutions is to first find some tour and then perturb it somewhat to see if a better tour results. If a better tour does result, the original tour is discarded and perturbations on the new tour are tried. Methods of this kind are described in Croes [3], Lin [10], Reiter and Sherman [14], Roberts and Flores [15] and Nicholson [12]. The local optimum obtained by these perturbation methods can be further adjusted to obtain a global optimum (Croes [3]). Lin and Kernighan [11] generalize these techniques in a powerful way.

Define a *k-change* of a tour as the deletion of k edges and their replacement by k other edges so that another tour is obtained.

Define a tour as *k-optimal* (Lin [10]) if no k-change produces a better tour.

Lin [10] describes a method whereby several random initial tours are obtained, each is improved until a 3-optimal tour is obtained and the best of these 3-optimal tours is used.

In this section, we investigate how far a k-optimal tour can be from the optimal tour.

THEOREM 6. *For each $n \geq 8$ there exists a traveling salesman graph having a tour which is k-optimal for all $k \leq n/4$, and for which the length of that tour, LOCALOPT, satisfies*

$$\frac{\text{LOCALOPT}}{\text{OPTIMAL}} = 2 \cdot \left(1 - \frac{1}{n}\right). \tag{7.1}$$

Proof. The example is the graph (N_n, d_n) and tour T_n constructed in the proof of Theorem 5. In particular, the tour shown in Fig. 3.5 will be shown to be 2-optimal.

For each n, define the set of edges

$$E_n = \{(1, n)\} \cup \{(i, i + 1) \text{ for } 1 \leq i < n\}$$

E_n is the set of edges which have length one. Because of the way function d_n is defined, each pair of points (a, b) from N_n is connected by some path in E_n of length equal to $d_n(a, b)$. For each tour T, there is a circuit $\alpha(T)$ obtained by replacing each edge of T by a path of equal length from E_n. Circuit $\alpha(T)$ has the same length as T and visits each node at least once. Circuit $\alpha(T_n)$ visits node 1 and n once and every other node twice.

For each edge e in E_n and each tour T, we let COUNT(e, T) be the number of times edge e occurs in circuit $\alpha(T)$. For tour T_n we have

$$\text{COUNT}((i, i + 1), T_n) = 2 \quad \text{for } 1 \leq i < n, \tag{7.2}$$

$$\text{COUNT}((1, n), T_n) = 0. \tag{7.3}$$

Because the edges of E_n are of unit length, the length $L(T)$ of tour T is given by

$$L(T) = \sum_{e \text{ in } E_n} \text{COUNT}(e, T). \tag{7.4}$$

We say that a tour T is *even* if COUNT(e, T) is even for all e in E_n. We say that a tour T is *odd* if COUNT(e, T) is odd for all e in E_n. We next show that any tour must be either odd or even.

By construction, each node a is the endpoint of exactly two edges of E_n, namely $(a, a + 1)$ and $(a, a - 1)$ (mod n). Since each occurrence of a in $\alpha(T)$ is associated with two edges of $\alpha(T)$

$$\text{COUNT}((a, a + 1), T) + \text{COUNT}((a, a - 1), T) = 2 \cdot j_a \qquad (7.5)$$

where j_a is the number of times node a occurs in circuit $\alpha(T)$. Therefore, $\text{COUNT}((a, a + 1), T)$ and $\text{COUNT}((a, a - 1), T)$ sum to an even number and are either both even or both odd. Since the edges in E_n form a connected graph, if T were neither odd nor even, some node would have one incident edge with an odd count and its other incident edge with an even count. This contradicts (7.5), so T is either odd or even.

For any tour T, there can be only one edge e in E_n such that $\text{COUNT}(e, T)$ $= 0$ since otherwise the tour could not be connected. Therefore, T_n with its one edge of count 0 and other edges of count 2 (see (7.1) and (7.2)) is the shortest even tour. Consequently, any tour improving on T_n must be odd.

Now suppose that tour T_n is changed by a k-change to an odd tour. Since the largest edges of T_n, are of length 2, the decrease resulting from deleting k edges is at most $2k$. Since at most $2k$ of the counts in $\alpha(T)$ are reduced, and since E_n has n edges, $n - 2k$ edges of E_n do not get their counts decreased. When edges are added to complete the k-change, the counts for the edges not decreased must in fact be increased in order to change from an even number to an odd number. Therefore, the increases are at least $n - 2k$. If the k-change is to improve the tour length, the decreases must be greater than the increases or

$$2k > n - 2k.$$

This inequality is only true when $k > n/4$ so T is indeed k-optimal for $k \leq n/4$.

We already know from the proof of Theorem 5 that T_n and the optimal tour have ratio $2 \cdot (1 - 1/n)$ so the theorem is proved. $\qquad \square$

COROLLARY. *For any k and n such that $4 \cdot k \leq n$, the nearest insertion and cheapest insertion methods can result in a k-optimal tour such that*

$$\frac{\text{INSERT}}{\text{OPTIMAL}} = 2 \cdot \left(1 - \frac{1}{n}\right).$$

Proof. We have just shown that the example used to establish Theorem 5 is also k-optimal if $4 \cdot k \leq n$. $\qquad \square$

References

[1] M. Bellmore and G. L. Nemhauser. The traveling salesman problem: A survey. *Operations Res.*, 16:538–558, 1968.

[2] N. Christofides. Worst-case analysis of a new heuristic for the traveling salesman problem. In *Symp. on New Directions and Recent Results in Algorithms and Complexity*. Carnegie-Mellon Univ., Pittsburgh, 1976.

[3] G. A. Croes. A method for solving traveling salesman problems. *Operations Res.*, 6:791–812, 1958.

[4] R. Floyd. Algorithm 97, Shortest path. *Comm. ACM*, 5:345, 1962.

[5] J. Gavett. Three heuristic rules for sequencing jobs to a single production facility. *Management Sci.*, 11:166–176, 1965.

[6] W. W. Hardgrave and G. L. Nemhauser. On the relation between the traveling salesman and the longest path problem. *Operations Res.*, 10:647–657, 1962.

[7] L. L. Karg and G. L. Thompson. A heuristic approach to solving traveling salesman problems. *Management Sci.*, 10:225–248, 1964.

[8] R. M. Karp. Reducibility among combinatorial problems. In R. E. Miller and J. W. Thatcher, editors, *Complexity of Computer Computations*, pages 85–103. Plenum, New York, 1972.

[9] J. B. Kruskal. On the shortest spanning subtree of a graph and the traveling salesman problem. *Proc. Amer. Math. Soc.*, 2:48–50, 1956.

[10] S. Lin. Computer solution of the traveling salesman problem. *Bell System Tech. J.*, 44:2245–2269, 1965.

[11] S. Lin and B. W. Kernighan. An effective heuristic algorithm for the traveling salesman problem. *Operations Res.*, 21:498–516, 1973.

[12] T. A. J. Nicholson. A sequential method for discrete optimization problems and its application to the assignment, traveling salesman, and three machine scheduling problems. *J. Inst. Math. Appl.*, 3:362–375, 1967.

[13] R. C. Prim. Shortest connection networks and some generalizations. *Bell System Tech. J.*, 36:1389–1401, 1957.

[14] S. Reiter and G. Sherman. Discrete optimizing. *J. Soc. Indust. Appl. Math.*, 13:864–889, 1965.

[15] S. M. Roberts and B. Flores. An engineering approach to the traveling salesman problem. *Management Sci.*, 13:269–288, 1966.

[16] S. Sahni and T. Gonzales. P-complete problems and approximate solutions. In *IEEE Fifteenth Ann. Symp. on Switching and Automata Theory*, pages 28–32, 1974.

Chapter 4

SYSTEM LEVEL CONCURRENCY CONTROL
FOR DISTRIBUTED DATABASE SYSTEMS*

DANIEL J. ROSENKRANTZ

Computer Science Department, State University of New York at Albany, Albany, NY 12222, USA

RICHARD E. STEARNS AND
PHILIP M. LEWIS II

General Electric Company, Research and Development Center, Schenectady, NY 12345, USA

Reprinted from: *ACM Trans. Database Systems*, Vol. 3, No. 2, June 1978, pp. 178–198. © ACM

Abstract   A distributed database system is one in which the database is spread among several sites and application programs "move" from site to site to access and update the data they need. The concurrency control is that portion of the system that responds to the read and write requests of the application programs. Its job is to maintain the global consistency of the distributed database while ensuring that the termination of the application programs is not prevented by phenomena such as deadlock. We assume each individual site has its own local concurrency control which responds to requests at that site and can only communicate with concurrency controls at other sites when an application program moves from site to site, terminates, or aborts.

This paper presents designs for several distributed concurrency controls and demonstrates that they work correctly. It also investigates some of the implications of global consistency of a distributed database and discusses phenomena that can prevent termination of application programs.

Keywords: distributed, database, consistency, lock, concurrency, transaction, integrity, readers and writers, deadlock, deadly embrace, rollback, restart

* A preliminary version of this paper appeared in the Proceedings of the Second Berkeley Workshop on Distributed Data Management and Computer Networks, Berkeley, California, May 1977.

S.S. Ravi, S.K. Shukla (eds.), *Fundamental Problems in Computing*,
© Springer Science + Business Media B.V. 2009

Received August 1977; revised January 1978.

1.   Introduction

It is frequently desirable to structure a database system so that different parts of the database are stored at different sites, perhaps widely separated geographically, interconnected into a network. Individual application programs, which we call processes, may need to access and update data at different sites. We envision a process as starting at one site and moving from site to site as necessary to do its job. (In practice moving from one site to another is likely to be implemented by calling a routine at the second site.) Systems of this type are called *distributed* database systems in contrast to *centralized* systems in which the whole database is stored on one computer.

An important consideration in the design of distributed systems is the concurrency control. The concurrency control is that portion of the system that is concerned with deciding what actions should be taken in response to requests by the individual processes to read and write into the database. We are interested in those database systems in which concurrency control is performed at the system level and is invisible to individual users. Individual processes do not contain statements to lock and unlock database entities they access and in fact each process is written as if it were the only process running on the system.

The concurrency control is concerned with avoidingdeadlocks or similar occurrences and with maintaining the consistency of the database. Assuming that each process when run by itself will eventually terminate without destroying the consistency of the database, the job of the concurrency control is to ensure that during the concurrent operation of any set of processes:

1. Each process sees a consistent picture of the database.

2. Each process eventually terminates.

3. The final database after all the processes terminate is consistent.

The second condition refers to the elimination of deadlocks and other occurrences which may prevent process termination. (We assume the existence of some type of system scheduler which operates in such a manner that each process allowed to run by the concurrency control will eventually be given enough of the system resources so that it could terminate in the absence of deadlocks or similar occurrences caused by the concurrency control.)

The concurrency control has the same task whether the database is centralized or distributed. One design to be considered for a distributed system is to have all conflicting read or write requests referred back to some master site for resolution. If communication costs are low, this design choice may be attractive. However, such a design is merely a centralized control whose database happens to be distributed. Our interest is in concurrency control designs in which both the database and its control are distributed. Each site has its own local concurrency control which must make decisions about database conflicts that occur at that site. For a distributed control of this type, the local control at a given site may not have all the information that a centralized control would have. Therefore, a local control may need to take a more severe action (such as aborting a process) than a centralized control might take. Thus, in designing a particular system, our decentralized designs must be evaluated against centralized designs taking into account the trade-off between communication costs and conflict resolution abilities.

In our designs, we use three types of communication among local concurrency controls at different sites:

1. When a process moves from site to site, it is accompanied by a small amount of information to be used by concurrency controls at each site it visits.

2. When a process terminates or aborts at some site, the concurrency control at that site sends a message to all the sites that process has visited.

3. When a database conflict occurs at some site, the concurrency control at that site sometimes sends a message to all sites visited by one of the processes involved in that conflict.

We make no assumptions about the time required for a message to reach a site or the order in which messages reach various sites.

Despite these communication constraints the concurrency control must maintain the global consistency of the entire distributed database and must ensure that each process terminates. In particular, any read/write conflicts that occur between two processes at one site must be resolved by the local concurrency control at that site without communicating with any other sites to determine the outcomes of any previous conflicts that may have occurred between those processes.

In this paper we present the design of several distributed concurrency controls and demonstrate that they work correctly. We discuss some of the implications of maintaining global database consistency in distributed systems and investigate phenomena that can prevent process termination. We define and study the properties of a class of concurrency controls we call superstrict. This class includes the specific controls that we consider.

In [26] we present a mathematical approach to concurrency control in both the centralized and distributed case, including some results used in this paper.

Some of the issues involved in database concurrency control are discussed in [12, 13]. Issues involved in distributed database systems are discussed in [1,

6, 10, 15, 27]. Our model of database consistency, described in Sect. 2, is identical to that in [11], in which database consistency and its implication for the locking sequence of concurrent processes is discussed. Consistency and appropriate data manipulation language primitives to facilitate concurrency control are discussed in [18].

The problems involved in scheduling readers and writers of a single entity are discussed in [8, 17, 19]. In [5] a centralized concurrency control based on processes locking groups of entities before writing is discussed, and a system of this type, is mentioned in which a fixed order among processes is used. Various means of giving preference to the eldest process in a system of this type are considered in [3].

A centralized concurrency control based on preassigned linear ordering of the resources appears in [25]. Distributed systems using a preassigned linear ordering of the sites are described in [6], and a general discussion of distributed systems using orderings of the resources appears in [15]. In [6, 27], distributed systems are mentioned that are based on a centralized design, with one site acting as a central control that responds to all requests. The use of timestamps in the synchronization of distributed systems is discussed in [22], and the use of timestamps for synchronization and consistency of duplicate databases is discussed in [20].

The centralized dynamic WAIT system of Sect. 14 is similar to many systems that have been implemented, including IMS, System R [2], and MADMAN [14]. Various issues in deadlock detection are discussed in [7]. Deadlock detection by database concurrency controls is discussed in [3, 16, 21, 23, 24].

Issues concerning when the changes made by a process can be made permanent are discussed in [4, 9].

2. Consistency

We use the word *entity* to describe the smallest unit of the database accessible to the concurrency control. In a particular database system the entities might be files, pages, records, items, etc. Each entity can be assigned a *value*. Examples of values are character strings, integers, vectors of integers, etc. We assume that a *database* consists of a finite set of entities, each assigned a value. A particular assignment of values may be considered to be either *consistent* or *inconsistent*.

In practice, assignments are considered consistent if they satisfy certain consistency requirements. Examples of possible consistency requirements are:

1. In a banking system—the sum of the values assigned to the loans for a particular account must be less than the line of credit of that account.

2. In an airline reservation system—the number of assigned seats must not be greater than the capacity of the aircraft.

3. In a distributed system for a group of warehouses, consisting of a head-quarters site containing summary information and a number of local sites, each containing information about a local warehouse—the value of the entity in the headquarters site giving the total number of widgets must be the sum of the values of the entities in the local sites giving the number of widgets in the local warehouse.

4. In some distributed systems—the value of an entity at one site must be equal to the value of another entity at a different site.

Note that the consistency requirements can be defined globally over the entire distributed database.

We assume that each process has been designed in such a manner that if run by itself and given an input database which is consistent, it will eventually terminate and produce a consistent database as output. We assume the concurrency control does not know what the consistency requirements are, but nevertheless must operate in such a manner that during the concurrent operation of the processes, each process sees a consistent input database, and eventually terminates producing a consistent output database.

In our model the processes change the values of entities but do not change the number of entities; e.g. they do not store or delete entities. This model is equivalent to a model where processes allocate and deallocate entities, but where the total number of entities is constrained to be less than some fixed bound.

3.   Process Termination and Abortion

In our model a process is initiated at one site and then moves from site to site (perhaps returning to sites previously visited). The decision to move from site to site is controlled by the process itself. At any instant, the process is *active* at one site and *inactive* at all other sites it has visited. The process receives inputs from the database by reading entities and produces output by writing entities. The read and write activity is described in more detail in Sect. 5. The activity of a process can be stopped in two ways, either by *termination* or *abortion*.

Aborting a process consists of first stopping the running of the process at its active site, and then undoing all changes to the database made by the process. We use the term *rollback* to refer to the undoing of all the changes made by a process at a given site, i.e. rollback is the restoration of each entity (changed by the process) at the given site to the value it had before the process changed it. An aborted process must be rolled back at all sites it has visited. We assume that this rollback is caused by a "rollback" message sent from the active site to all visited sites.

Terminating a process consists of first stopping the running of the process at its active site and then making its changes to the database available to subsequent processes. Each site the process has visited must be informed that the values written by the process are now "official" and are to be "made permanent" and supplied to other processes. We assume that this notification is made by a "terminate" message sent from the active site to all sites visited.

Once a site has received a terminate or rollback message, made the required database operations, and continued the appropriate propagation of the message, the site can destroy all bookkeeping information it was saving about the process.

To understand the intuition behind our model of a process, consider a system in which programs are executed at single sites but can call other programs as subroutines at other sites. To fit our model, the execution of a program together with the execution of all associated subroutine calls are treated as the execution of a single process. At any time during this execution, the active site is the site of the subroutine being executed and the inactive sites are those where programs are waiting for subroutines to return or where subroutines have finished their execution. When a program at one site calls a program at another site, both programs together are responsible for maintaining global consistency. Either program, if run by itself, might violate a consistency requirement, since that program is only part of the overall process. Similarly, if either the program or any of its subroutines requests abortion, the entire program, including all of its subroutines, must be rolled back in order to guarantee global consistency. Also, none of the results of the program or subroutines can be made permanent until the program terminates, since at any time before termination the process may be aborted and hence rolled back at each site.

Systems in which rollback messages can be sent without first stopping a process are considered in [26]. For such systems, there is a potential danger that a process will be rolled back at one site and "made permanent" at another site, thereby violating global consistency requirements. In some of these systems the termination of a process is considered a "termination request," to which the concurrency control can respond in several ways besides compliance.

4.   Linearizing Concurrency Controls

We say that a concurrency control is *linearizing* if the effect of running a set of concurrent processes to termination is the same as if the processes had been run sequentially in some order. In other words it must be possible to order the processes $P_1, P_2, \ldots, P_n$, such that P_1 "sees" the initial database, P_2 "sees" the database that would have been produced if P_1 had run to completion, etc. This sequential running of the processes is called a *linearization* of the processes.

Since we are assuming that each process transforms a consistent input database into a consistent output database, each process in a linearization "sees" a consistent database, and the final database resulting from a linearization of the processes is consistent. Thus a linearizing concurrency control preserves the consistency of a database in the sense of conditions 1 and 3 of Sect. 1.

This observation appears in [11] and demonstrates that linearization is a sufficient condition for a concurrency control to preserve consistency. In [26] it is shown that if each process is constrained to read an entity before it writes that entity, then to preserve consistency, it is necessary that there be a linearization of all processes that write at least once.

5.   Conflicts

The concurrency control must select a response to the individual read and write requests of the processes. More precisely, we assume that the first request (whether a read or write request) on an entity and the first write request (if the previous requests were read requests) on the entity by any given process invoke the concurrency control, which must select a response. We assume that any subsequent read request on the same entity by the process is automatically granted and results in the process seeing the same version of the entity as the last request. Any subsequent write request by the process on the entity is automatically granted and overwrites the version of the entity produced by the preceding write request.

We now show by an example that if the concurrency control is too promiscuous in granting requests, an inconsistent database may be produced.

Suppose that there are two processes, S and T, and two entities, A and B. Assume that there is a single consistency requirement, namely that $A = 0$ or $B = 0$. Suppose that the two processes are:

$$S: \quad \text{if } A = 0 \quad \text{then } B = B + 1,$$
$$T: \quad \text{if } B = 0 \quad \text{then } A = A + 1.$$

Observe that each of these processes, when presented with a consistent database, terminates and produces a consistent database. Suppose that in the initial database, A and B are both 0. Running S to completion followed by running T to completion will produce a database with $A = 0$ and $B = 1$. Running T to completion, and then S, produces a database with $A = 1$ and $B = 0$. However, if S and T are run in an interleaved fashion, and all requests are granted, the following scenario of granted requests may occur:

S reads $A = 0$;

T reads $B = 0$;

S reads $B = 0$;

S writes $B = 1$;

T reads $A = 0$;

T writes $A = 1$.

The final database produced has $A = 1$ and $B = 1$, and is therefore inconsistent.

Observe that the above scenario is not linearizable. The write by S of entity B changed the version of that entity previously seen by T. Therefore any sequential running of the processes that is to produce the same effect as the above scenario must have T before S. However, the write by T on entity A changed the value seen by S and therefore requires that in the sequential running, S must come before T. Since S and T cannot be run before each other, there is no equivalent linearization.

We say that two requests by different processes on a given entity are *in conflict* if one of the requests is a write request and the site containing the entity has not received a termination message or rollback message for either process. A process which makes a request in conflict with a previously made request is said to *cause* the conflict. Note that the conflict occurs whether or not the previously made request has been granted. Also note that a conflict no longer exists when a termination or rollback message for one of the processes involved is received.

A conflict is caused either by a read request of an entity for which there is a previous write request or by a write request of an entity for which there is a previous read or write request. However, a conflict is not caused by a read request of an entity for which there are previous read requests.

6. Strict Concurrency Controls

We say that a concurrency control is *strict* if it is designed so that a request is never granted at a time when the request is in conflict with a granted request of another process. One obvious property of strict concurrency controls is that if several processes manage to write a given entity, each process has its write request granted after all the processes that have already written that entity have terminated. When a read request on the entity is granted, there is no ambiguity as to which version of the entity to use in granting the request; the version supplied is the one produced by the most recently terminated writer.

We define the *current database* at any instant of time as the database that would result if all unterminated processes were to be aborted. For a strict concurrency control, the version of an entity in the current database is that produced by the most recently terminated process that wrote on the entity.

We assume it is meaningful to talk of the order in which processes terminate (i.e. initiate termination). In the event of several processes terminating simultaneously at different sites, any resolution of the ties can be considered to be the termination order. (Note that we are talking about the existence of a conceptual order of termination. There is no requirement that a control actually compute this order.)

We now show that the effect of running a set of processes to completion under a strict concurrency control is the same as the linearization based on ordering the processes by their time of termination. We begin with a lemma.

LEMMA 1. *For a strict concurrency control, if a given process has a read request on an entity granted, then the entity value supplied to the process is in the current database from the time the request is granted until the process terminates or aborts.*

Proof. Because the concurrency control is strict, at the time the read request was granted, no unterminated process had a granted write request on the entity. Once the read request was granted, any request by another process to write the entity would cause a conflict, and so would not be granted while the given process is unterminated or unaborted. Therefore, until the given process terminates or aborts, no other process can write the entity version read by the given process. □

THEOREM 1. *For a strict concurrency control, the current database is obtainable by a linearization of the terminated processes, ordered by their time of termination.*

Proof. The proof is by induction on the number of processes that have terminated. The statement of the theorem is true if zero processes have terminated, since in that case the current database is the initial database.

Now assume that the theorem is true if n processes have terminated, and suppose the $(n+1)$-st process, which we call P, terminates. At the instant just before P terminates, the current database is (from the induction hypothesis) obtainable by a linearization of the then terminated processes in their termination order. From Lemma 1, each entity version supplied to a granted read request of P is in the current database just before P terminates. The current database just after P terminates is therefore obtainable by running P alone with the previous current database as input. □

Theorem 1 is closely related to a result in [11] that "legal" transaction schedules maintain consistency.

Consider a scenario of processes initiating and running under the operation of a concurrency control. We say that a process *runs forever* in a scenario if each request issued by the process is granted (perhaps after waiting some finite amount of time), but the process neither terminates nor aborts. We now show that for a strict concurrency control, no process runs forever.

THEOREM 2. *For a strict concurrency control, no process can run forever.*

Proof. Suppose there is a scenario in which a process runs forever. Since the set of entities composing the database is finite, the subset of these entities accessed by the process during the scenario must also be finite. Thus there must be a time, say T, at which each entity in the set accessed by the process has had the initial request by the process on the entity granted. From Lemma 1, the process sees the current database at time T. From Theorem 1, this current database is obtainable by a linearization of terminated processes and is consistent by the results cited in Sect. 4. Since we are assuming that a process will terminate if run by itself and given a consistent input database, the process must eventually terminate. □

The assumption in our model that there are only a finite number of entities is essential to the proof of Theorem 2. If the number of entities were infinite, a process might run forever (even if there is only one site). For example, suppose there is an infinite set of entities, each numbered by a positive integer and each having a value of zero or one. Suppose that the consistency requirement is that only a finite number of entities have a nonzero value. Consider a process, say P, that reads the entities in numerical order until encountering an entity whose value is zero, changes the value of this entity to one, and terminates. If P is run alone and given a consistent input database, it will terminate and produce a consistent output database. However, suppose P is run under a concurrency control, and before P issues a read request on any given entity, some new process initiates, writes a one on that entity, and terminates. In this scenario there are no conflicts at all, each request is granted, and the current database is always consistent. However, since P never encounters an entity value of zero, it runs forever.

We note that there exist concurrency controls that are not strict and that are linearizable, but for which the termination order is not equivalent to the linearization. (See [26].)

Finally, we give a sufficient condition, to be used later, for a concurrency control to be strict.

THEOREM 3. *Suppose a concurrency control has the property that a request is not granted unless a termination message or rollback message has been received for each of the processes it caused a conflict with. Then the concurrency control is strict.*

Proof. Suppose a given request is issued at time T_1, and granted at time T_2. Then by time T_2, a termination or rollback message has been received for each process the given request caused a conflict with. If between T_1 and T_2 any other process issues a request causing a conflict with the given request, that request will not be granted during this time interval. Therefore at time T_2, when the given request is granted, it is not in conflict with any granted request. Hence the concurrency control is strict. $\square$

Note that the definition of strict requires that a request not be granted when it is in conflict with a granted request, whereas the condition of the theorem requires that the request not be granted when it is in conflict with any request it caused a conflict with, whether or not the request has been granted.

7. Responses to Conflicts

When a request is made in conflict with another request, the concurrency controls considered in this paper take one of the following two actions.

1. WAIT. The requesting process is made to wait until the process (or processes) with which it is in conflict terminates or is aborted (and the requests are therefore no longer in conflict).

2. RESTART. Either the requesting process or some of the processes it is in conflict with can be restarted. Restarting a process means first aborting it and then beginning the process again at its original initial site.

There is a potential timing problem which we assume is accounted for in the implementation of restart. The problem is that, when the restarted process reaches a site visited during the aborted run, the arrival of the restarted process could precede the "rollback" message from the earlier run. If this can occur, it is important that the site not mistake the new version as a return of the old version. It is also important that the site rollback the old version and not the new one.

In the systems considered in this paper, restarting is invoked by the concurrency control using one of the following primitives:

DIE. The process making the request is restarted. Since that process is active at the site at which it made the request, abortion can be immediately initiated.

WOUND. When the concurrency control at some site selects wound, the process the requestor is in conflict with is said to be *wounded*. A message is sent to all the sites the wounded process has visited saying that it is wounded. If that message gets to the site at which the process is active (or if the process returns to a site that has received the message) and the process has not yet initiated termination, the concurrency control at that site initiates an abort of that process. If the process has already initiated termination, the wound message is ignored. In this case, as discussed in Sect. 3, the process will eventually be terminated at all sites. Meanwhile at the site of the original conflict, the process in conflict with the wounded process waits for the wounded process. The wounded process will eventually either be restarted or terminated, at which time (in either event) the conflicting process can proceed.

A concurrency design using WOUND must take into account that a "wound" message, a "rollback" message, and the arrival of a restarted version could occur in any order at a particular site. In particular the new version must not be rolled back because of a wound message intended for the old version.

Also note that if a "terminate" or "rollback" message for a particular process has begun to propagate to sites a process has visited, it is no longer necessary to notify any sites that the process has been wounded. Therefore a site can destroy its bookkeeping information about a process after receiving a "terminate" or "rollback" message for the process.

Finally we note that the possibility of several wound messages for the same process does not cause a problem.

The above primitives result in a strict concurrency control if used in the following way: Whenever a process causes a conflict, the process either dies or is made to wound or wait for each of the processes it caused a conflict with.

8. Waiting Forever

The response of the concurrency control to conflicts must be designed to ensure that every process terminates. Consequently, the use of WAIT as a possible response must be restricted. For example, consider again processes S and T from Sect. 5. Suppose the concurrency control always resolves conflicts by selecting WAIT. Then the following scenario might occur.

S reads $A = 0$;

T reads $B = 0$;

S reads $B = 0$;

S attempts to write B and is made to wait for T;

T reads A;

T attempts to write A and is made to wait for S.

This is an example of a *deadlock*, where S and T are waiting for each other, and so will never terminate. Although this deadlock is easy to detect on a

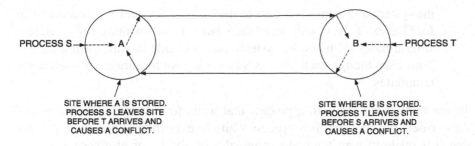

SITE WHERE A IS STORED.
PROCESS S LEAVES SITE
BEFORE T ARRIVES AND
CAUSES A CONFLICT.

SITE WHERE B IS STORED.
PROCESS T LEAVES SITE
BEFORE S ARRIVES AND
CAUSES A CONFLICT.

Figure 4.1. Conflicts at different sites

centralized system, it may be more difficult to detect on a distributed system because when a conflict occurs at one site the concurrency control at that site cannot communicate with the concurrency controls at other sites. Figure 4.1 shows an example of what may happen. Entities A and B are assumed to be at different sites. Process S starts at the site with A, has a request for A granted, and then moves to the site with B. Meanwhile, process T starts at the site with B, has a request for B granted, and then moves to the site with A, where it issues a request on A that causes a conflict. Simultaneously, process T issues a request on B that causes a conflict. The concurrency control at each site must respond to the conflict at its site without communicating with the other site. Therefore, the concurrency controls must be designed so that they do not both select wait.

Deadlock is only one possible reason why a process might wait forever. More generally, suppose a concurrency control permits a scenario where a process issues a request and is made to wait forever without having its request granted. (Note that WAIT and WOUND both cause a process to wait.) Then the scenario must contain one of the four following cases:

1. Deadlock. A deadlock occurs when there is a finite set of processes waiting for each other.

2. Infinite Chain of Distinct Waiting Processes. An infinite chain of waits occurs if there is a scenario where one process waits forever for a second process, which waits forever for a third, etc., and all these processes are distinct. (At any instant of time, only a finite number of processes in the chain have actually started, but the number increases without limit as new processes enter the system and cause older processes to wait.)

3. Waiting for a Process That Runs Forever.

4. Waiting for an Infinite Number of New Processes Each of Which Terminates or Aborts. For example, suppose process S wishes to access a particular entity and is made to wait for process T. Later process U enters

the system and requests access to the same entity, and S is made to wait for U also. T eventually terminates but S is still waiting for U. Before U terminates V enters the system and S is made to wait for it also, etc. Thus even though each process S is waiting for terminates, S itself never terminates.

To see that a scenario with a process that waits forever must contain one of these cases, observe that if a process waits forever then either some process that it is made to wait for never terminates or aborts, or else case 4 occurs. If case 4 does not occur then the process being waited for either runs forever (case 3) or waits forever. If no process in the scenario runs forever then case 1 or case 2 occurs.

We now present conditions on a concurrency control that preclude cases 2, 3, and 4.

We say that a concurrency control is *superstrict* if

(1) a request is not granted unless a termination message or rollback message has been received for each of the processes it caused a conflict with, and

(2) a process is only made to wait for processes that it causes a conflict with.

From Theorem 3, every superstrict concurrency control is also strict.

LEMMA 2. *A scenario produced by a superstrict concurrency control cannot contain a process waiting for an infinite number of new processes (case 4) and cannot contain an infinite chain of distinct waiting processes (case 2).*

Proof. A process cannot wait for an infinite number of new processes because for a superstrict concurrency control, a process can only be made to wait for processes that have previously issued requests.

Now suppose there is an infinite chain of distinct processes, in which each process in the chain waits for the next. Let P_i be the ith process in the chain, so that P_i waits for P_{i+1} for $1 \leq i$.

We say that P_i *involves* a given entity if P_i waits for P_{i+1}, because of a request on that entity. Because there is a conflict, either P_i or P_{i+1} has issued a write request on the given entity. We call the request by P_i that caused it to wait forever its *critical request*.

Let C be the set of entities involved in the chain. Since the total number of entities is finite, C is also finite. Therefore, there is some time, T, when for each entity in C, a process on the chain has been made to wait because of a critical request involving that entity. Any request issued after time T on an entity in C will not be granted since the request will cause a conflict with a previously issued write request by a process that waits forever.

Since only a finite number of processes can be initiated during a finite time interval, there is an integer J such that for every P_k with $k > J$, P_k is a process that is initiated after time T. Since at any given time only a finite number of requests can have been issued, there must be a time when for some $i > J$, the critical request of P_i has been issued, but the critical request by P_{i+1} has not yet been issued. Let e be the entity (in C) involved in the critical request by P_i. Since the concurrency control is superstrict, in order for P_i to wait for P_{i+1}, process P_{i+1} must issue a request on e prior to the request by P_i. However, since process P_{i+1} is initiated after time T, a request by P_{i+1} on e results in P_{i+1} waiting forever. Therefore the request by P_{i+1} on e is the critical request of P_{i+1}, contradicting the assumption that P_i issues its critical request before P_{i+1}. □

THEOREM 4. *If a superstrict concurrency control is not subject to deadlock, then no scenario can contain a process that waits forever.*

Proof. From Theorem 3, Theorem 2, and Lemma 2. □

The implication of this theorem for distributed systems is that if the concurrency control at each site of a distributed system is designed to be superstrict, the only phenomenon that can cause processes to wait forever is deadlock.

9. Fixed Order Concurrency Controls

The concurrency control designs given in this paper make use of a fixed ordering of the processes. When each process is first initiated, it is given a unique number (which may be a function of the time of day the process initially started, the number of its initial site, and its priority). This number is carried with the process when it moves from site to site and is retained if the process is restarted. The numbers associated with the processes specify a particular total order of the processes.

If a process should have a conflict with some other process, the concurrency control selects its response based on a comparison of the numbers of the two processes (e.g. if the number of the process causing the conflict is larger than that of the other process, one particular response is selected; if it is smaller, another response is selected).

This method of selecting responses guarantees that if two processes have conflicts at different sites (for example the situation shown in Figure 4.1), the conflict will be resolved at both sites on the basis of the same pair of numbers associated with the processes.

We say that a method of assigning numbers to processes is a *valid numbering method* if each process is assigned a unique positive integer. A property of valid numbering methods is that once a process has been assigned a number, only a finite set of other processes can be assigned a lower number. In the concurrency control designs we present, a low number is a desirable asset for a process. When comparing the numbers of two processes that have been assigned numbers by a valid numbering method, we say that the process with the lower number is *older* and the process with the higher number is *younger*.

As a specific example of a valid numbering method, assume first that each site has a unique site number, with all site numbers containing the same number of bits. Also assume that each site has a clock, although the clocks at different sites need not be synchronized, or even run at the same rate. Then the number of a process is the initiation time (as determined at its initial site) concatenated with the site number of the initial site.

One variation in the above method is to let high priority processes "lie" about their age by subtracting a constant from their actual initiation time. Another variation, for systems without clocks, is that the jth process that initiates at the site with site number i is assigned as its number the result of concatenating j and i.

The fixed order produced by a valid numbering method may differ from the order of process termination and may not correspond to a valid linearization. For example, consider the following scenario involving processes S and T. Note that the scenario takes place at only one site, and does not involve any conflict.

S initiates;

T initiates;

T reads entity A;

T writes entity A;

T terminates;

S reads entity A;

S terminates.

The termination order has T before S. Since S read A after T had written it and terminated, S must be after T in any linearization that is equivalent to the above scenario. However, note that S started before T and may very well be before T in the ordering implied by the numbers associated with the processes and used by the concurrency control to resolve conflicts. Thus the linearization implied by the associated numbers may be different from any of the linearizations equivalent to the concurrent running of the processes.

10. Restarting Forever

Just as an injudicious selection of WAIT by a concurrency control can result in processes waiting forever and hence never terminating, an injudicious selection of restart can result in processes being repeatedly restarted forever and hence never terminating. For instance, suppose that in the situation described in Fig. 4.1 the concurrency control at each site decides to restart the process issuing the request that causes the conflict. Then S and T will both be restarted. After S and T are rolled back and reinitiated, the same situation may repeat itself. Therefore S and T may perpetually cause each other to be restarted and so never terminate.

As another example, suppose processes U and V have a conflict and U is restarted. The new incarnation of U has a conflict with V and this time V is restarted. The new incarnation of V conflicts with U and U is restarted. This cycle of restarts may repeat indefinitely with the result that the processes never terminate. Specific examples of concurrency control designs subject to this type of cyclic restart are given in [26].

In this paper we consider concurrency controls that use a valid numbering method to prevent a process from being repeatedly restarted forever. We say that for a given concurrency control, restart is *based on a valid numbering method* if whenever a process is wounded or dies, it is in conflict with a lower numbered process.

THEOREM 5. *If a superstrict concurrency control is not subject to deadlock and has restart based on a valid numbering method then every process terminates.*

Proof. Suppose there is a scenario in which one of the processes never terminates. There are three possible reasons for a process not to terminate:

1. The process has each of its requests granted, but runs forever.

2. The process waits forever.

3. The process is repeatedly restarted forever.

From Theorem 2, no process can fail to terminate because of reason 1. From Theorem 4, no process can fail to terminate because of reason 2.

Now consider reason 3. Assume there is a set of processes that are repeatedly restarted forever, and let P be the member of this set with the lowest number. Because no process can be unterminated for reason 1 or reason 2, there is some time when all processes having a lower number than P have terminated. Process P cannot be restarted after this time, since P can only be restarted because of a conflict with a lower numbered process and there are no lower numbered processes for P to conflict with. Therefore P cannot be

Assume process Q issues a request causing a conflict with a request previously made by another process P. Let N_Q and N_P be the unique numbers assigned to Q and P respectively by a valid numbering method. The conflict is resolved using the following rule:

If requester is older then requester waits, else requester dies, i.e.

if $N_Q < N_P$ **then** WAIT **else** DIE

Notes:

1. WAIT means Q waits for P to terminate or abort. DIE is described in the text (Sect. 7).

2. If this request puts Q in conflict with more than one process, apply the above rule to each process Q is in conflict with. If any application indicates DIE, then Q is restarted; otherwise Q waits for all the processes.

Figure 4.2. WAIT-DIE system

repeatedly restarted forever, contradicting the assumption that there is a set of processes that are restarted forever. □

11. The WAIT-DIE System

Figure 4.2 gives the specifications of a distributed concurrency control that we call the WAIT-DIE system because the requesting process either waits or dies.

THEOREM 6. *The WAIT-DIE system is a strict concurrency control for which every process terminates.*

Proof. The WAIT-DIE system is designed to be superstrict, and have restart based on a valid numbering method. There cannot be a deadlock because for any finite set of processes, the youngest one cannot be made to wait for any of the others. Therefore, from Theorem 5, all processes terminate. □

12. The Wound-Wait System

Figure 4.3 gives the design of a distributed concurrency control that we call the WOUND-WAIT system because the requesting process in any conflict either waits or wounds the other process (or processes).

Assume process Q issues a request causing a conflict with a request previously made by another process P. Let N_Q and N_P be the unique numbers assigned to Q and P respectively by a valid numbering method. The conflict is resolved using the following rule:

If requester is older then requester wounds, else requester waits, i.e.

if $N_Q < N_P$ **then** WOUND **else** WAIT

Notes:

1. WAIT means Q waits for P to terminate or abort. WOUND is described in the text (Sect. 7).

2. If this request puts Q in conflict with more than one process, apply the above rule to each process Q is in conflict with.

Figure 4.3. WOUND-WAIT system

THEOREM 7. *The WOUND-WAIT system is a strict concurrency control for which every process terminates.*

Proof. The WOUND-WAIT system is designed to be superstrict and have restart based on a valid numbering method. There cannot be a deadlock because for any finite set of processes, the oldest cannot wait for any other process unless it has first sent out a wound message for that process. The wounded process cannot be part of a deadlock because the wound message must eventually reach any site where that process is waiting and cause it to be aborted. Therefore, from Theorem 5, every process terminates. □

Alternate Definition of Wound. The WOUND-WAIT system of Fig. 4.3 will still operate correctly using a somewhat different interpretation of WOUND: If a wound message reaches the site at which the process is active and the process has not initiated termination then that process is restarted only if it is waiting. Otherwise it is allowed to proceed (even to other sites) until it either initiates termination or becomes involved in a conflict that would normally cause it to wait (in which case it is restarted).

The same argument used to demonstrate the correct operation of the original WOUND-WAIT system can be used for the new one. The advantage of the new one is that fewer restarts occur.

13.   Comparison of WAIT-DIE and WOUND-WAIT Systems

Both the WAIT-DIE and the WOUND-WAIT systems work correctly in the sense that they maintain the global consistency of the database and guarantee that all processes terminate. Nevertheless, there are significant differences in how they operate in certain situations.

Waiting Processes. In the WAIT-DIE system an older process is made to wait for younger ones and as it gets still older it tends to wait for more and more younger processes. Although the older process will eventually terminate, it tends to slow down as it gets older.

By contrast, in the WOUND-WAIT system, an older process never waits for a younger one except when the older process has wounded the younger and is waiting for the wound to take its effect. The oldest process therefore runs roughshod through the system wounding any younger process in its path. Thus, the older process get increased priority.

Restarted Processes. Suppose that processes A and B have a conflict and A is restarted. The new incarnation of A may issue the same sequence of requests as before and thus reach the site of the previous conflict. At this site, a new conflict will result if B is still unterminated.

In the WAIT-DIE system A was the requestor that caused the original conflict (recall that only the requestor can die). In the new conflict A is still the requestor and dies again. Thus there can be a long sequence of DIEs and while both B and A will eventually terminate, the repeated attempts to run A will consume system resources.

By contrast, in the WOUND-WAIT system A was not the requestor in the original conflict and A was younger than B. In the new conflict A is still younger than B, but this time A is the requestor and hence waits. Process A presumably consumes far less system resources if it is waiting than if it is continually being restarted.

Interfacing with External Devices. In many applications, processes first access a database and then interact with some external device such as a printer, a drill press, or a nuclear reactor. It might be very awkward if the concurrency control caused such a process to restart after its external interactions had started. (How do you deal with the initial output of the printer which is now to be disregarded or how do you undrill a hole?)

The WAIT-DIE system has the property that a process can only be restarted when it makes a request to read or write a database entity for the first time. Thus, if the process is designed so that it completes all of these requests before initiating any interactions with external devices, then it is guaranteed not to be restarted by the concurrency control during or after these interactions.

Assume process Q issues a request causing a conflict with a request previously made by another process P. Let N_Q and N_P be the unique numbers assigned to Q and P respectively by a valid numbering method. The conflict is resolved using the following rule:

If requester can wait, then requester waits, else younger restarts, i.e.

if Q CAN-WAIT-FOR P **then** WAIT

else if $N_Q < N_P$ **then** WOUND **else** DIE

Notes:

1. WAIT means Q waits for P to terminate or abort. DIE and WOUND are described in the text (Sect. 7).

2. Process Q CAN-WAIT-FOR P if there is no chain of processes from P to Q, in which each process is waiting for the next.

3. If a request puts Q in conflict with more than one process, apply the above rule to each process Q is in conflict with. However, if any application indicates DIE then Q is restarted, but no other process is wounded.

Figure 4.4. Centralized dynamic WAIT system

By contrast, in the WOUND-WAIT system a process can be restarted at any time after it has had a request on a particular entity granted, when another process requests access to that same entity. Thus there is no guarantee that a process that has accessed an entity in the database will not be restarted after it initiates an interaction with an external device. However, if the alternate definition of WOUND is used, once a process completes all its database requests, it is guaranteed not to be restarted by the concurrency control.

14. Centralized Concurrency Control

The WAIT-DIE and WOUND-WAIT systems may select "unnecessary" process restarts because the concurrency control at a given site does not know what is happening at other sites and so selects a primitive causing restart whenever selecting WAIT could potentially cause a deadlock.

In contrast if there is only one site or a centralized concurrency control that selects the response for all sites, the concurrency control knows exactly which processes are waiting for which and so need only restart a process when selecting WAIT would actually create a deadlock. The design of a centralized system, which we call the centralized dynamic WAIT system, is shown in Fig. 4.4. This concurrency control uses a valid numbering method to determine which of two processes to restart, but makes the decision between WAIT and restart on the basis of the current situation of waiting processes. Thus process S *IS-WAITING-FOR* process T if the concurrency control selected WAIT when S previously caused a conflict with T. The concurrency control uses the relation *CAN-WAIT-FOR*, which is the complement of the transitive closure of the *IS-WAITING-FOR* relation.

THEOREM 8. *The centralized dynamic WAIT system is a strict concurrency control for which every process terminates.*

Proof. The concurrency control is designed to be superstrict and have restart based on a valid numbering method. There cannot be a deadlock, because WAIT is only selected when the CAN-WAIT-FOR relation permits. Therefore Theorem 5 applies and every process terminates. □

15. Hybrid Concurrency Controls

To reduce the number of process restarts caused by conflicts, the distributed systems described earlier can be modified to include certain features of the centralized dynamic WAIT system. Figures 4.5 and 4.6 describe two such hybrid systems, which we call the hybrid WAIT-DIE system and the hybrid WOUND-WAIT system. Both of these systems distinguish between *local* processes that have not left their initial site and *global* processes that have. If all processes were local, these systems would reduce to the centralized dynamic WAIT system. If all processes were treated as global, they would reduce to the WAIT-DIE or WOUND-WAIT system. However, they have the advantage over the WAIT-DIE and WOUND-WAIT systems that if there are many local processes, fewer restarts are to be expected.

The systems of Figs. 4.5 and 4.6 differ in whether for two global processes, the older is allowed to wait for the younger or the younger is allowed to wait for the older. This difference is reflected in the definition of the CAN-WAIT-FOR relation (Note 2) and the action taken when a local process becomes global (Rule B).

THEOREM 9. *The hybrid WAIT-DIE system is a strict concurrency control for which every process terminates.*

Proof. The concurrency control is designed to be superstrict and have restart based on a valid numbering method.

A. Assume process Q issues a request causing a conflict with a request previously made by another process P. Let N_Q and N_P be the unique numbers assigned to Q and P respectively by a valid numbering method. The conflict is resolved using the following rule:

If requester can wait then requester waits, else younger restarts, i.e.

if Q CAN-WAIT-FOR P **then** WAIT

else if $N_Q < N_P$ **then** WOUND **else** DIE

B. Suppose a local process Q wishes to become global, i.e. leave its initial site for the first time. Then WOUND each global process P that is younger than Q and for which there is a chain of processes from P to Q, in which each process is waiting (at that site) for the next.

Notes:

1. WAIT means Q waits for P to terminate or abort. DIE and WOUND are described in the text (Sect. 7).

2. Process Q CAN-WAIT-FOR P at a given site if there is no chain of processes from P to Q in which each process AWAITS the next at the given site. Process S AWAITS process T at the site if either S is waiting for T at the site, or S and T are both global processes that have visited the site and S is older than T.

3. If a request puts Q in conflict with more than one process, apply rule A to each process Q is in conflict with. However, if any application indicates DIE then Q is restarted, but no other process is wounded.

4. A process is local if it has not yet left its initial site and global if it has.

Figure 4.5. Hybrid WAIT-DIE system

Assume the system is subject to deadlock, so that there is a finite cycle of processes waiting for each other. Since WAIT is only selected when the CAN-WAIT-FOR relation permits, the cycle cannot consist of processes waiting for each other at a single site. Therefore the cycle must involve more than one site and at least two global processes. Consider the youngest global process, say P, involved in the deadlock. P must have been global prior to the request that made it wait forever, since it does not have an opportunity to become global once it is made to wait forever.

A. Assume process Q issues a request causing a conflict with a request previously made by another process P. Let N_Q and N_P be the unique numbers assigned to Q and P respectively by a valid numbering method. The conflict is resolved using the following rule:

If requester can wait then requester waits, else younger restarts, i.e.

if Q CAN-WAIT-FOR P **then** WAIT

else if $N_Q < N_P$ **then** WOUND **else** DIE

B. Suppose a local process Q wishes to become global, i.e. leave its initial site for the first time. Then select DIE if there is a global process P that is older than Q and for which there is a chain of processes from P to Q, in which each process is waiting (at that site) for the next.

Notes:

1. WAIT means Q waits for P to terminate or abort. DIE and WOUND are described in the text (Sect. 7).

2. Process Q CAN-WAIT-FOR P at a given site if there is no chain of processes from P to Q in which each process AWAITS the next at the given site. Process S AWAITS process T at the site if either S is waiting for T at the site or S and T are both global processes that have visited the site and S is younger than T.

3. If a request puts Q in conflict with more than one process, apply rule A to each process Q is in conflict with. However, if any application indicates DIE then Q is restarted, but no other process is wounded.

4. A process is local if it has not yet left its initial site and global if it has.

Figure 4.6.   Hybrid WOUND-WAIT system

The deadlock must include a chain of processes from P to some other global process Q, with each process waiting for the next at the same site. Let this chain be $R_0, R_1, \ldots, R_n$ where $n \geq 1$, $R_0 = P$, and $R_n = Q$. For each $i < n$, process R_i is waiting for R_{i+1} because of some request issued by R_i at the site. Let R_j be the process in the chain that issued the last such request.

Let T be the time of the request by R_j. At time T, the other requests in the chain have already been issued and resulted in the selection of WAIT. Therefore at time T from Note 2 in Fig. 4.5, R_i AWAITS R_{i+1} for all $i \neq j$. Now suppose that process Q was already a global process at time T. Then since Q

is older than P, from Note 2 in Fig. 4.5, at T it is the case that Q AWAITS P. Therefore at time T there is a chain from R_{j+1} to R_j such that each process in the chain AWAITS the next at the same site. Therefore at time T, it is false that R_j CAN-WAIT-FOR R_{j+1}, and the concurrency control would respond to the request by R_j with either WOUND or DIE, but not with WAIT.

This contradicts the assumption that Q was already a global process at time T. The fact that the request by R_j resulted in the selection of WAIT therefore implies that Q did not become global until after the chain from P to Q was already established. But since P is younger than Q, Rule B of the hybrid WAIT-DIE system would result in process P being restarted when Q wishes to become global. This contradicts the assumption that there is a deadlock.

Therefore, from Theorem 5, every process terminates. $\qquad\square$

THEOREM 10. *The hybrid WOUND-WAIT system is a strict concurrency control for which every process terminates.*

Proof. Similar to the proof of Theorem 9, except that under the assumption of a deadlock, consider the oldest global process involved. $\qquad\square$

Consider again the three points of comparison between systems discussed in Sect. 13.

Waiting Processes. The hybrid WOUND-WAIT system differs from the WOUND-WAIT system in that the oldest process may be made to wait. However, when it was young, it was less likely to have been restarted.

Restarted Processes. The hybrid WOUND-WAIT system differs from the WOUND-WAIT system in that if a process is restarted and the new incarnation of the process issues the same sequence of requests as before, the original conflict that caused it to be restarted can cause it to be restarted again. For instance, suppose there are three processes, $\{A, B, C\}$, with $N_B < N_A < N_C$. Suppose that A and C are global, and B is local. Suppose further that a request by B caused it to wait for C. Now if A issues a request causing a conflict with B, WAIT cannot be selected (since B AWAITS C, and C AWAITS A). Since A is younger than B, A is restarted. If the new incarnation of A returns and the situation remains unchanged, A will be restarted again.

Interfacing with External Devices. If the alternate definition of WOUND is used, then a process that completes its database requests and begins interacting with external devices is guaranteed not to be restarted by either the hybrid WAIT-DIE system or the hybrid WOUND-WAIT system.

In summary, the hybrid systems have the advantage of treating local processes like a centralized control, while working correctly for global processes.

References

[1] F. Achim. Data base networks–an overview. *Management Informatics*, 3(1):13–29, 1974.

[2] M. M. Astrahan et al. System R: Relational approach to database management. *ACM Trans. Database Syst.*, 1(2):97–137, 1976.

[3] R. Bayer. On the integrity of data bases and resource locking. In H. Hasselmeier and W. G. Spruth, editors, *Data Base Systems*. Lecture Notes in Computer Science, volume 39. Springer, Berlin, 1976.

[4] L. A. Bjork. Recovery scenario for a DB/DC system. In *Proceedings of the ACM National Conference*, pages 142–146, 1973.

[5] D. D. Chamberlin, R. F. Boyce, and I. L. Traiger. A deadlock-free scheme for resource locking in a database environment. In *Information Processing 74*, pages 340–343. North-Holland, Amsterdam, 1974.

[6] W. W. Chu and G. Ohlmacher. Avoiding deadlock in distributed data bases. In *Proceedings of the ACM National Conference*, pages 156–160, 1974.

[7] E. G. Coffman, Jr., M. J. Eliphick, and A. Shoshani. System deadlocks. *Computing Surveys*, 3(2):67–78, 1971.

[8] P. J. Courtois, F. Heymans, and D. L. Parnas. Concurrent control with "readers" and "writers". *Comm. ACM*, 14(10):667–669, 1971.

[9] C. T. Davies. Recovery semantics for a DB/DC system. In *Proceedings of the ACM National Conference*, pages 136–141, 1973.

[10] M. E. Deppe and J. P. Fry. Distributed data bases–a summary of research. *Computer Networks*, 1(3):130–138, 1976.

[11] K. P. Eswaran, J. N. Gray, R. A. Lorie, and I. L. Traiger. On the notions of consistency and predicate locks in a database system. *Comm. ACM*, 19(11):624–633, 1976.

[12] G. C. Everest. Concurrent update control and data base integrity. In J. W. Klimbie and K. L. Koffeman, editors, *Data Base Management*, pages 241–270. North-Holland, Amsterdam, 3rd edition, 1974.

[13] B. M. Fossum. Database integrity as provided for by a particular data base management system. In J. W. Klimbie and K. L. Koffeman, editors, *Data Base Management*, pages 271–288. North-Holland, Amsterdam, 3rd edition, 1974.

[14] General Electric Research and Development Center. *MADMAN user manual*. Schenectady, NY, 1976.

[15] J., Gray. Locking in a decentralized computer system. Technical Report Res. Rep. RJ 1346, IBM Res. Lab., San Jose, Calif., 1974.

[16] J. N. Gray, R. A. Lorie, and G. R. Putzolu. Granularity of locks in a shared data base. In *Proc. Int. Conf. on Very Large Data Bases*, pages 428–451, Framingham, 1975. (Available from ACM, New York).

[17] I. Greif. Formal problem specifications for readers and writers scheduling. In *Proc. MRI Symp. on Comptr. Software Eng.*, 1976. Polytechnic Inst. of New York.

[18] D. A. Hawley, J. S. Knowles, and E. E. Tozer. Database consistency and the CODASYL DBTG proposals. *Computer J.*, 18(3):206–212, 1975.

[19] C. A. R. Hoare. Monitors: An operating system structuring concept. *Comm. ACM*, 17(10):549–557, 1974.

[20] P. R. Johnson and R. H. Thomas. The maintenance of duplicate databases. Technical Report Doc. 31507, Network Information Center (NIC), 1975.

[21] P. F. King and A. J. Collmeyer. Database sharing–an efficient mechanism for supporting concurrent processes. In *Proc. AFIPS 1973 NCC*, volume 42, pages 271–275. AFIPS Press, Montvale, 1973.

[22] L. Lamport, Time clocks and the ordering of events in a distributed system. Technical Report, Massachusetts Computer Associates, Wakefield, Mass., March 1976.

[23] P. P. Macri. Deadlock detection and resolution in a CODASYL based data management system. In *ACM-SIGMOD Int. Conf. on Management of Data*, pages 45–49, 1976.

[24] G. Schlageter. Access synchronization and deadlock-analysis in database systems: An implementation-oriented approach. *Inform. Syst.*, 1:97–102, 1975.

[25] L. C. Sekino. Multiple concurrent updates. In *Proc. Int. Conf. on Very Large Data Bases*, pages 505–507, Framingham, 1975. (Available from ACM, New York).

[26] R. E. Stearns, P. M. Lewis II, and D. J. Rosenkrantz. Concurrency controls for database systems. In *Proc. 17th Annual Symp. on Foundations of Comptr. Sci.*, pages 19–32. Houston, 1976. (Available from IEEE, Long Beach, Calif.).

[27] M. Stonebraker and E. Neuhold. A distributed data base version of INGRES. In *Proc. Second Berkeley Workshop on Distributed Data Management and Computer Networks*, pages 19–36, 1977.

Chapter 5

CONSISTENCY AND SERIALIZABILITY IN CONCURRENT DATABASE SYSTEMS

D. J. ROSENKRANTZ* AND R. E. STEARNS†

Department of Computer Science, State University of New York at Albany, Albany, NY 12222, USA

P. M. LEWIS II

General Electric Corporation, Research and Development Center, Schenectady, NY 12301, USA

Reprinted from: *SIAM J. Computing*, Vol. 13, No. 3, Aug. 1984, pp. 508–530. © SIAM

Abstract
The main results of this paper show that serialization is both necessary and sufficient for consistency in concurrent database systems. This is true for both the final database and the views of the database seen by individual transactions. The model of a transaction includes both read and write operations which may be performed in any order (except an entity must be read before being written).

The main results are presented in terms of an information flow model describing the source of each value read and the use of each value written. Since the model does not involve any concept of the "time" a value was read or written, it models any concurrency system producing information flow among transactions.

There is a section discussing the effect of changing the model to include write operations without preceding reads, and a section discussing the restriction to straight-line programs.

Keywords: database, concurrency control, consistency, serialization, transaction

* The research of this author was supported in part by the National Science Foundation under grant MCS 78-03157.
† The research of this author was supported in part by the National Science Foundation under grant MCS 79-03770.

S.S. Ravi, S.K. Shukla (eds.), *Fundamental Problems in Computing*,
© Springer Science + Business Media B.V. 2009

Received by the editors September 26, 1980, and in final revised form August 29, 1983.

1. Introduction

There has been a lot of activity in the area of database concurrency controls. The goal of concurrency control is to allow transactions accessing a common database to run as concurrently as possible without destroying database consistency or preventing a transaction from eventually running to completion. It has generally been appreciated that consistency can be insured by designing a serializable control, where serializability means that the effect of running transactions concurrently is the same as if the transactions have been run in some serial order. Many practitioners have in fact made serializability a design requirement.

This paper investigates the relationship between serializability and consistency. We first develop a general concurrency control model based on information flow between transactions. We then show that serializability is both necessary and sufficient for consistency. (There is a small loophole for read-only transactions.) We consider both the consistency of the final database produced by the transactions and the consistency of the view seen by each transaction.

Our concurrency model is developed to reflect assumptions we believe appropriate for concurrency controls in mainstream commercial database systems. These assumptions and our reason for making them are as follows:

ASSUMPTION A1. The control can distinguish between a read access and a write access. *Reason*. Data manipulation languages have this feature.

ASSUMPTION A2. The control does not know the consistency criterion. *Reason*. In practice, consistency conditions are too complex to expect a user to write them down (or even fully comprehend them).

ASSUMPTION A3. The control does not make inferences from the particular values read or written. *Reason*. Because of Assumption A2, this information is, for practical purposes, useless. (In theory, inferences could be made from testing values for equality.)

ASSUMPTION A4. The control may respond to a read request with a value other than the last value written. *Reason*. Concurrency control designs have been proposed which have this feature [1, 2, 13–15].

ASSUMPTION A5. A value written in the database during the run of the transaction must be considered functionally dependent on all values read, rather than functionally dependent only on those read by the transaction before writing the value. *Reason*. Data manipulation languages usually permit branching and rewriting values. The control must assume a value written might have been rewritten if values read subsequently had been different.

ASSUMPTION A6. Before a transaction can write an entity, it must read the entity. *Reason*. The "necessity" results are false without this assumption. (See Sect. 11.)

ASSUMPTION A7. There are no "lost updates." More precisely, the history of changes to a given entity is a sequence of changes, each change overwriting the change made by the preceding transaction in the sequence. *Reason*. Lost updates are usually considered undesirable. Also, the "necessity" results are false without this assumption. For instance, consider a concurrency control that presents each transaction with the original contents of the database, and, when a transaction terminates, throws out the values it wrote. This concurrency control preserves consistency (since the final database is identical to the initial database), but is not serializable.

We believe Assumptions A1 to A5 to be both reasonable and desirable. Assumption A6 is also reasonable in that most state-of-the-art database systems interface with the operating system and concurrency control by first reading a page from the disk and then perhaps writing the page. Once Assumption A6 is made, we believe Assumption A7 to be both reasonable and desirable. It implies that all but one version of each entity is overwritten. The single version that is not overwritten can be thought of as being retained in a final database produced by the transactions. Therefore every version of the entity is actually "used" in the sense that it is either overwritten or else is the unique "surviving" version of the entity.

When we say that serialization is necessary, we mean that in all nonserializable situations, there could be (from the viewpoint of the concurrency control) an inconsistency. Our results do not exclude the possibility that for specific consistency criteria or for specific transactions, consistency may be preserved in nonserializable situations, and indeed such cases have been considered in the literature [6–9, 11].

This paper addresses two consistency questions:

(1) Under what conditions is the final database consistent?

(2) Under what conditions does an individual transaction see a consistent view of the database?

The second question is very important for several reasons:

(a) The view of the individual user is the view seen by transactions. A report produced by a transaction which sees an inconsistent view might be regarded by a user as evidence that the database is being mismanaged.

(b) A transaction may not be properly designed to accommodate "impossible" data, and may behave unpredictably when given an inconsistent view.

(c) In a system which is always running transactions, there may never be a well-defined "final database," and consistency for individual transactions may be the only meaningful concept.

Previous papers on serialization have concentrated on question 1. Question 2 requires more complex proof techniques because inconsistency must be demonstrated using only that portion of the database that a transaction sees.

Most papers on serializability use the concept of a "schedule of accesses" (or history or log). This concept is not adequate here because of Assumption A4. Instead we use the concept of a "version graph" showing information flow. The version graph might appear inadequate because it does not show the order in which an individual transaction makes its requests. However, the order of requests is irrelevant because of Assumption A5. We examine this issue more closely in Sect. 12.

The early work of [5] is based on "schedules." A *schedule* is *defined* to be consistent if it is serializable, and a database *state* is *defined* to be consistent if it satisfies a set of consistency constraints. The authors note that if the initial database state is consistent and if each transaction transforms a consistent state into a consistent state, then serializable schedules maintain consistency. From a schedule, they construct a "dependency" relation that is similar to the "augmented version graph" of this paper, and show that the schedule is serializable if and only if the dependency relation is acyclic.

Kung and Papadimitriou [10] show that for systems with only one type of access, which is a combined read-write access, a "schedule" maintains full database consistency if and only if it is serializable. They do not address the consistency of the view seen by individual transactions. The model in [10] differs from ours in Assumptions A1 and A5. In each case, we are making the more general assumption.

Casanova [3] and Casanova and Bernstein [4] study consistency in a model where all reads occur in a single combined access and then all writes occur in a single access. This does not permit all the possibilities of information flow permissible under our model. However, unlike our model, theirs allows the write to include entities which were not read.

The results in this paper improve an earlier version announced in [15, Thm. 1] without proof.

2.   Concurrency Control

In this section, we describe in nonmathematical terms our concept of a concurrency control. In later sections, we formalize those aspects of the control that pertain to consistency.

We think of a *transaction* as a computer program that reads information from and writes information into a database. The interface to the database is through system procedures READ and WRITE. A call on READ is referred to as a "read request" and a call on WRITE is referred to as a "write request."

If transactions were run on a system one at a time, read requests could be responded to by reading the value from the database, and write requests by replacing the old database value with the new. The problem comes with systems which attempt to run a number of transactions concurrently. The part of the system which determines the response to the read and write requests is called a *concurrency control*.

The concurrency control can grant read requests by supplying an input, and can grant write requests by saving the output somewhere. These values are not necessarily read or written directly into the database, as the control may sometimes have a temporary need to remember several different values for a single entity.

If a read request by a given transaction on a given entity is not the first request by that transaction on that entity, and if the concurrency control grants the read request, then the value supplied to the transaction is assumed to be the value associated with the preceding request on the entity by the transaction. If the preceding request was a write request, the value written is supplied to the new read request. If the preceding request was a read request, the value supplied to that request is assumed to be also supplied to the new read request. Thus the only time a concurrency control must make a choice as to what value of an entity to supply when granting a read request is when the read request is the first request of the transaction on the entity. The value that the concurrency control is allowed to supply is either the value of the entity in an initial database, or the final value written by some other transaction that wrote the entity.

Database consistency deals with data values, and is independent of other aspects of the concurrency control. Thus we base our mathematical treatment of consistency on a model of data flow, rather than a model of concurrency control. As with any mathematical model, the appropriateness for the intended application is an issue to be addressed. Towards this end, we will relate our formal definitions to the above notion of a concurrency control and to Assumptions A1 to A6 of the introduction.

3.   Databases

We now present our formal concepts of databases and database consistency.

DEFINITION 3.1. A *database* is specified by a pair (E, V) where E is a set of entities and V is a set of *values*. A mapping from E into V is called a *database state*.

In practice, a database entity could be an item, record, page, or file, depending on at what level a given system applies a concurrency control discipline. If s is a database state and e is an entity, then $s(e)$ is interpreted as the value stored in entity e.

DEFINITION 3.2. A *consistency criterion* for a database (E, V) is a set C of database states. A database state s in C is said to be *consistent*.

This definition of consistency allows for an arbitrary classification of database states being "consistent" or "inconsistent." There is no need to compute C, and in fact our interest is in controls which work for arbitrary criteria (Assumption A2).

It is our opinion that this definition is too weak to capture all aspects of preserving consistency. However, it serves the purposes of this paper very well, since this weak definition already gives the strongest possible result, namely that serialization is necessary.

4.   Transactions

A given run of a transaction reads certain entity values and writes certain entity values. To study consistency, the run can be represented mathematically by the entities and entity values read and written. We call this mathematical object a "transaction effect." Unlike most other authors, we do not put the order of reads and writes into our model. The reason is Assumption A5, which implies the order is not relevant.

DEFINITION 4.1. Given a database (E, V), a *transaction effect* is specified by a four-tuple (READSET, WRITESET, r, w) where

(a) READSET is a nonempty subset of E,

(b) WRITESET is a subset of READSET,

(c) r is a function r: READSET $\rightarrow V$ called the *input function*, and

(d) w is a function w: WRITESET $\rightarrow V$ called the *output function*.

READSET represents the set of entities read by the run of the transaction and function r gives the values read. We rule out the trivial case where no entities are read, since we are only concerned with transactions that interact with the database. WRITESET represents the set of entities written by the run of the transaction and function w gives the values written. We require that WRITESET be a subset of READSET to conform to Assumption A6.

A given transaction can produce a variety of effects, depending on the values supplied in response to its read requests. Even the READSETs and WRITESETs can vary because the transaction can branch on values read.

DEFINITION 4.2. Given a database state s and a transaction effect $\sigma =$ (READSET, WRITESET, r, w) for database (E, V), we say that σ is *matched to s* if and only if $r(e) = s(e)$ for all e in READSET. We say that transaction effect σ *transforms* database state s to database state t if and only if σ is matched to s and

(a) $t(e) = w(e)$ for e in WRITESET,

(b) $t(e) = s(e)$ otherwise.

The idea behind this definition is that when a transaction that can produce effect σ is run with a database state s matched to σ, the transaction changes the values in database state s to obtain database state t. If this same transaction were run with a database state u not matched to σ, then a different unspecified transaction effect would occur, one matched to u.

DEFINITION 4.3. Given a database (E, V) and a consistency criterion C, a transaction effect σ is said to be *valid* if and only if, for all database states s such that s is C and σ is matched to s, transaction effect σ transforms s to a database state in C.

Intuitively, a debugged transaction can only produce valid transaction effects. If a debugged transaction terminates when run by itself with a consistent initial database state, the final database state when it terminates is also consistent. No matter what the consistent initial database state matched to the transaction effect is, the transaction effect transforms this consistent state into another consistent database state.

Note that a given transaction effect may not be matched to any consistent database state. From Definition 4.3, such a transaction effect is valid. It could be the effect of debugged program presented with an inconsistent database (i.e. garbage in, garbage out).

The running of a sequence of transactions produces a sequence of transaction effects in the obvious way:

DEFINITION 4.4. Let $\sigma_1, \sigma_2, \ldots, \sigma_n$ be a sequence of transaction effects and let s_0 be a database state. The sequence is called a *serial run* on s_0 if and only if there exist database states $s_1, s_2, \ldots, s_n$ such that for $1 \leq i \leq n$, σ_i is matched to s_{i-1} and transforms s_{i-1} to s_i. Database state s_n is called the *result* of the serial run.

Note that if the s_i exist, they are unique. Thus, if the result exists, it is unique. The well known fact that serial runs preserve consistency is expressed in our notation follows.

THEOREM 4.5. *If $\sigma_1, \ldots, \sigma_n$ is a serial run of valid transaction effects on consistent state s_0 and $s_1, \ldots, s_n$ are database states as given in Definition 4.4, then all the s_i are consistent.*

Proof. By induction on i using Definition 4.4. □

5. Version Graphs

The outcome of concurrency decisions is a flow of information among transactions. We model this flow on two levels. One level is the "version graph" to be defined in this section. The other (more detailed) level is the "datatrace" defined in Sect. 7.

The version graph represents those facts about concurrency decisions available to the concurrency control. These are the facts the concurrency control can use to assure that consistency is maintained or that a given transaction sees a consistent view of the database. In particular, these facts do not include knowledge of specific entity values (Assumption A3) or what the consistency criterion is (Assumption A2).

The "version graph" is a mathematical concept that models how versions of entities flow between transactions. The version graph has a node for each transaction, plus an extra node for the initial database state. The edges reflect the source of entity values read or overwritten by the transactions.

DEFINITION 5.1. Given a set of entities E, a *version graph* G for E is a directed graph with a finite number of nodes such that:

(a) there is exactly one node I having no entering edges;

(b) each edge is labelled R_e or W_e where e is in E;

(c) for each node x and each e in E, node x has at most one entering edge labelled R_e and at most one entering edge labelled W_e;

(d) if there is an edge from node x to node y labelled W_e, then there is also an edge from x to y labelled R_e;

(e) if there is an edge labelled R_e or W_e leaving node x, then either x is the node I or x has an entering edge labelled W_e;

(f) for each e in E, the edges labelled W_e form a chain (i.e. a cycle free path, possibly of zero length) beginning at I.

The node I with no entering edges represents the initial database state. Any other node represents a transaction, and will be called a *transaction node*. A transaction node with an entering edge labelled W_e for some e is called a *writing transaction node*, and is considered to have overwritten entity e. A transaction node that is not a writer is called a *read-only transaction node*. A node that is either I or a writing transaction node is said to be a *producer node*, and is considered to produce the value of some entity. Producer node I is considered to produce an initial value for each entity. A writing transaction node q with an entering edge labelled W_e is considered to produce a value for entity e. The entity value produced by q is considered to overwrite the value produced by the node exited by the edge (from Definition 5.1(e) this node produces a value for entity e).

As an example, Fig. 5.1 shows a version graph with $E = \{\alpha, \beta, \gamma\}$. For convenience, the transaction nodes have been labelled with transaction names. From the graph it is evident that transaction a reads and writes entity set $\{\alpha\}$, transaction b reads $\{\alpha, \gamma\}$ and writes $\{\gamma\}$, and transaction c reads $\{\alpha, \gamma\}$ and writes the null set. Entity β is not accessed. The edge labelled R_α from a to c means that c reads the version of entity α that transaction a wrote.

The edges of a version graph can be considered to represent "information flow relations." For each e in E there is a relation R_e such that xR_eq holds

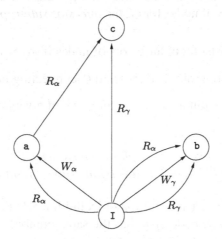

Figure 5.1. Version graph

if the version graph contains an edge labelled R_e from node x to node q, and signifies that the value of e produced by x was read by q. Relation xW_eq holds if the version graph contains an edge labelled W_e from node x to node q, and signifies that the value of e created by x was changed by q.

Each condition of Definition 5.1 has an interpretation in terms of the application we are modelling. Definition 5.1(a) reflects the inclusion of the initial database state in the version graph, and the assumption that each transaction actually accesses the database. Definition 5.1(b) merely says that an entity is associated with each read or write. Definition 5.1(c) reflects the assumption that the concurrency control need only supply an appropriate entity value when a transaction makes its initial request, since it supplies each subsequent request with the value from the preceding request. Definition 5.1(d) reflects Assumption A6. Definition 5.1(e) merely says that the source of each entity value is actually a producer of a value for that entity. Definition 5.1(f) reflects Assumption A7. The single version of an entity at the end of a chain is the version that is retained in a final database state produced by the transactions in the graph.

6.   Version Graph Analysis

In the preceding section, version graphs were used to model the information flow between transactions. We will subsequently characterize consistency in terms of version graph analysis. The key concepts behind this analysis are "individual version graphs," "writers version graphs" and "augmented version graphs." These concepts, together with certain lemmas used in later sections, are developed below.

DEFINITION 6.1. Given a directed graph G, node x is called an *ancestor* of node y if and only if there is a directed path (perhaps of zero length) from x to y. Given a subset S of nodes for G, the *ancestor subgraph* for S is the graph with

(a) node set A consisting of ancestors of nodes from S, and

(b) edge set consisting of all edges from G connecting nodes in A.

An important fact about an ancestor subgraph of a version graph is that it is a version graph:

LEMMA 6.2. *If G is a version graph for entity set E, and H is a nonempty ancestor subgraph of G, then H is a version graph for entity set E.*

Proof. We check H for each condition of Definition 5.1. For Definition 5.1(a), first note that since each node of H has the same number of entering edges as the corresponding node of G, H has at most one node with no entering edges. Next, note that from Definition 5.1(e) and (f), node I is an ancestor of every node of G. Since H is nonempty, node I is included in H, and so H satisfies Definition 5.1(a).

Definition 5.1(b) and (c) are obvious because the edges in the ancestor subgraph H are a subset of the edges in version graph G.

Definition 5.1(d) and (e) hold because the required edges are inherited from G.

For Definition 5.1(f), observe that the chain for e in H must have a node x which is at maximal distance from I on the chain. Because H is an ancestor subgraph, the nodes between x and I are also in H, so the W_e edges in H also form a chain. $\square$

A node of an ancestor subgraph participates in the same chains as in the original graph:

LEMMA 6.3. *Let x be a node common to version graphs G and A where A is an ancestor subgraph of G. Then node x is the kth node on the chain for entity e in version graph G if and only if x is the kth node on the chain for e in version graph A.*

Proof. The portion of the chain from I to x is the same in both graphs. $\square$

Certain ancestor subgraphs, defined below, play a key role in database consistency.

DEFINITION 6.4. Let G be a version graph. For each node x of G, the ancestor subgraph of G for $\{x\}$ is called the *individual version graph* (ivg) for x in G, and is denoted as ivg(G, x).

Let WRITERS be the set of nodes of G having an entering edge labelled W_e for some e. Define the *writers version graph* for G to be the ancestor subgraph for WRITERS.

For version graph G and entity e, define chainend (G, e) as the last node in G on the chain (see Definition 5.1(f)) for e. Define ivg(G, e) as ivg$(G,$ chainend $(G, e))$.

As an example, consider the version graph, G, of Fig. 5.1. The individual version graph for transaction c, i.e. ivg(G, c), is shown in Fig. 5.2(a). The writers version graph is shown in Fig. 5.2(b). Also note that chainend $(G, \alpha) = a$, chainend $(G, \beta) = I$, and chainend $(G, \gamma) = b$.

LEMMA 6.5. *For every version graph G and node x of G;*

(a) *Every node of ivg(G, x) except possibly x is a producer node;*

(b) *Every node of the writers version graph is a producer node.*

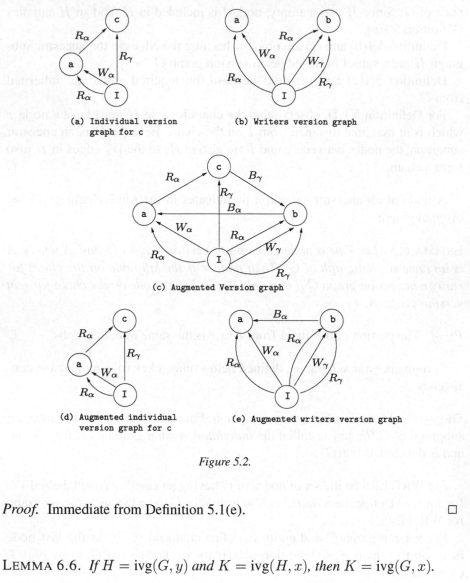

(a) Individual version
graph for c

(b) Writers version graph

(c) Augmented Version graph

(d) Augmented individual
version graph for c

(e) Augmented writers version graph

Figure 5.2.

Proof. Immediate from Definition 5.1(e). □

LEMMA 6.6. *If* $H = \mathrm{ivg}(G, y)$ *and* $K = \mathrm{ivg}(H, x)$, *then* $K = \mathrm{ivg}(G, x)$.

Proof. Node x has the same set of ancestors in G and H. □

We now consider extra edges that can be added to a version graph in order to indicate when one transaction reads an entity version that was overwritten by a second transaction.

DEFINITION 6.7. Given a version graph G and given a database entity e, define the relation B_e among nodes of G by pB_eq if and only if $p \neq q$ and for some node x in G, $x R_e p$ and $x W_e q$. Define the *augmented graph* for G, denoted as $\mathrm{aug}(G)$, to be G with directed labelled edges added for the relations B_e for all entities e.

The relationship $p B_e q$ can be interpreted to mean that transaction p read the value of e that was changed by transaction q. More briefly, p read the value of entity e that existed *before* q overwrote that value. Note that since node I has no entering R_e or W_e edges, node I has no entering or exiting B_e edges.

Figures 5.2(c), 5.2(d) and 5.2(e) show the augmented graphs for Figs. 5.1, 5.2(a) and 5.2(b) respectively.

7.   Datatraces

In studying consistency considerations, we are concerned not only with information flow, but also with the actual entity values that are read and written. This is because it is the actual values that determine if the data seen or the database state produced are actually consistent. In the following definition, we combine a version graph with the effects of its transactions to form a "datatrace." The datatrace represents both the flow and values of database information involved in the running of a finite set of transactions.

DEFINITION 7.1. Given a database (E, V), a *datatrace* is a triple (G, σ, s) where:

 (a) G is a version graph for E;

 (b) σ is a function that maps each transaction node p of G into a transaction effect $(\mathrm{READSET}_p, \mathrm{WRITESET}_p, r_p, w_p)$;

 (c) s is a database state (the *initial* state);

 (d) for each transaction node p in G, $\mathrm{READSET}_p$ equals the set of entities e such that an edge labelled R_e enters node p, and $\mathrm{WRITESET}_p$ equals the set of entities e such that an edge labelled W_e enters node p;

 (e) if $q R_e p$ in G then e is in $\mathrm{WRITESET}_q$ and $w_q(e) = r_p(e)$, where the notation is extended by defining $\mathrm{WRITESET}_I = E$ and $w_I(e) = s(e)$.

Datatraces lead naturally to a concept of a final database state.

DEFINITION 7.2. Given a database (E, V) and a datatrace (G, σ, s), define the final database state t for the trace to be the function such that $t(e)$ is given by the output function of chainend (G, e) (so that $t(e)$ equals $w_{\mathrm{chainend}(G,e)}(e)$).

We now show that if a version graph is associated with a trace, then each nonempty ancestor subgraph is the version graph of an appropriately defined subtrace of the given trace.

LEMMA 7.3. *If (E, V) is a database, (G, σ, s) a datatrace and G' a nonempty ancestor subgraph of G, and if σ' is σ restricted to the nodes of G', then (G', σ', s) is a datatrace.*

Proof. From Lemma 6.2, G' is a version graph, so condition (a) of Definition 7.1 is satisfied. The other conditions of Definition 7.1 carry over directly from G, σ and s. $\qquad\square$

Consider the flow of information when a set of transactions are run in order $p_1, \ldots, p_n$ with each transaction terminating before the next one begins. Describing this flow with a version graph, an edge $p_j R_e p_i$ is included whenever transaction p_i reads the value written by p_j. Because of the sequential order of execution, $p_j R_e p_i$ in the flow graph implies $j < i$ and further implies that e is not in WRITESET of any p_k for $j < k < i$. It is this characteristic that we build into the following definition:

DEFINITION 7.4. A *serialization* of datatrace (G, σ, s) is an ordering $p_0, \ldots, p_n$ of the nodes of G such that

(a) $p_0 = I$ and

(b) $p_j R_e p_i$ implies

$$j = \max\{k \mid k < i \text{ and } e \text{ is in WRITESET}_{p_k}\}.$$

A datatrace is *serializable* if it has a serialization.

The "serialization" of a datatrace is thus an ordering which shows that the trace could have resulted from a sequential running of the transactions. A "serializable trace" is a datatrace which has such an explanation.

As defined, serializability is essentially a property of the version graph rather than the whole datatrace. The next result addresses the entire datatrace and relates serializations of datatraces with serial runs.

THEOREM 7.5. *If $p_0, \ldots, p_n$ is a serialization of datatrace (G, σ, s) then*

(a) $\sigma(p_1), \ldots, \sigma(p_n)$ *is a serial run on s, and*

(b) *the result of the serial run is identical to the final state of the datatrace.*

Proof. (a) The database states required by Definition 4.4 are defined as follows. For $1 \leq i \leq n$, let $s_i(e) = w_{p_l}(e)$ where $l = \max\{k \mid k \leq i \text{ and } e \text{ is in}$

WRITESET$_{p_k}$}, and let $s_0 = s$. We will show that σ_{p_i} is matched to s_{i-1} and transforms s_{i-1} to s_i.

To prove that σ_{p_i} is matched to s_{i-1}, we must show that $r_{p_i}(e) = s_{i-1}(e)$ for all e in READSET$_i$. From Definition 7.1, $r_{p_i}(e) = w_{p_j}(e)$ where $p_j R_e p_i$ in G. By Definition 7.4(b), $j = \max\{k \mid k < i$ and e is in WRITESET$_{p_k}\}$. Obviously $j = \max\{k \mid k \le i-1$ and e is in WRITESET$_{p_k}\}$, and so $s_{i-1}(e) = w_{p_j}(e)$ by construction of s_{i-1}.

To prove that σ_{p_i} transforms s_{i-1} into s_i, consider e in WRITESET$_{p_i}$. From the construction of s_i, $s_i(e) = w_{p_i}(e)$ because the maximum possible value of k satisfying $k \le i$ is $k = i$. For e not in WRITESET$_{p_i}$, $\{k \mid k \le i$ and e is in WRITESET$_{p_k}\} = \{k \mid k \le i - 1$ and e is in WRITESET$_{p_k}\}$, so $s_i(e)$ and $s_{i-j}(e)$ both equal $w_{p_l}(e)$ for the same value of l.

(b) The result of the serial run is the constructed s_n. Let t be the final state of the datatrace. For the entity e, the ordering of nodes of the writers chain for e conforms to the serialization order because of Definition 7.4(b). Let chainend $(G, e) = p_j$. Then $j = \max\{k \mid k \le i$ and e is in WRITESET$_{p_k}\}$ and $s_n(e) = w_{p_j}(e)$ by construction of s_n. Thus $t(e) = s_n(e)$. □

We now characterize the serializable traces. First, given an acyclic graph, a *topological sort* of the graph is an ordering of the nodes $p_0, \ldots, p_n$ such that (p_i, p_j) an edge implies $i < j$. Note that an acyclic graph may have more than one topological sort. We now show that if the augmented version graph of a trace is acyclic, then any topological sort of the augmented version graph is a serialization of the trace.

LEMMA 7.6. *Let (E, V) be a database and let (G, σ, s) be a datatrace. Suppose the nodes of* aug(G) *can be ordered $p_0, \ldots, p_n$ so that (p_i, p_j) an edge of* aug(G) *implies $i < j$. Then this order is a serialization of the trace.*

Proof. To see that $p_0 = I$, observe that every transaction node of G has an entering edge, and so cannot be the first node in the linear sequence. Thus, Definition 7.4(a) is satisfied.

Now assume that $p_i R_e p_j$ but that the equation in Definition 7.4(b) fails because of a k such that $i < k < j$ and e is in WRITESET$_{p_k}$. Nodes p_k and p_i are both on the chain for e (Definition 5.1(e)). Each step in the chain must by hypothesis have a larger subscript so there must be a k' such that $p_i W_e p_{k'}$ and $k' \le k$. (Node $p_{k'}$ is the next node on the chain after p_i and cannot come after p_k.) But $p_i R_e p_j$ and $p_i W_e p_{k'}$ implies $p_j B_e p_{k'}$ contrary to $k' \le k < j$ and the hypothesis. Thus k cannot exist and j must satisfy the condition of Definition 7.4. Order $p_0, \ldots, p_n$ is therefore a serialization. □

We next prove a converse to Lemma 7.6. It says that running transactions serially imposes an order on the nodes of the augmented version graph, an order which agrees with the direction of the edges of the graph.

LEMMA 7.7. *Let (G, σ, s) be a datatrace serialized by ordering $p_0, \ldots, p_n$ of the nodes of G. Then (p_i, p_j) an edge of $\text{aug}(G)$ implies $i < j$.*

Proof. If $p_i R_e p_j$, the equation of Definition 7.4 requires $i < j$. If $p_i W_e p_j$, then also $p_i R_e p_j$ (Definition 5.1(d)) and again $i < j$.

If $p_i B_e p_j$, this means there is a p_k such that $p_k W_e p_j$ and $p_k R_e p_i$. We have already shown this implies $k < j$ and $k < i$. If $j < i$, then

$$k \neq \max\{l \mid l < i \text{ and } e \text{ is in WRITESET}_{p_l}\}$$

because of the possibility $l = j$. This violates Definition 7.4(b) and $j < i$ has led to a contradiction. Therefore $j > i$ and the lemma is proved. $\square$

THEOREM 7.8. *A datatrace (G, σ, s) is serializable if and only if $\text{aug}(G)$ is acyclic.*

Proof. This follows from Lemmas 7.6 and 7.7. $\square$

Theorem 7.8 is the expression in our model of the well-known result from [5] that a schedule is serializable if and only if the constructed dependency relation is acyclic.

8. Main Results

We now present two "if and only if" theorems to support our claims that serializability is equivalent to preserving consistency. The first addresses the issue of preserving consistency of the final database. By assumption, the concurrency control knows G and does not know V, C, σ, or s. The theorem says that consistency of the final database is guaranteed to be preserved if augmented G_w is acyclic, and consistency can be violated if it is not.

THEOREM 8.1. *For all entity sets E and all version graphs G on E, the augmented writers version graph is acyclic if and only if, for all sets of values V, all consistency criteria C on (E, V) and all datatraces (G, σ, s) such that s is in C and each $\sigma(p)$ is valid, the final database state is in C.*

THEOREM 8.2. *For all entity sets E and all version graphs G on E and all transaction nodes i of G, the augmented ivg of i is acyclic if and only if, for all sets of values V, all consistency criteria C on (E, V), and all datatraces*

(G, σ, s) *such that s is in C and each $\sigma(p)$ is valid, $\sigma(i)$ is matched to some database state in C.*

These theorems are consequences of Theorems 9.1 and 10.1, proven in the next two sections.

Since serializability has been equated with acyclic version graphs by the results of the preceding section, Theorems 8.1 and 8.2 say that serializability is equivalent to preserving consistency.

9. Assuring Consistency

We are now prepared to give sufficient conditions for a concurrency control to maintain consistency. Specifically, we combine the "only if" parts of Theorems 8.1 and 8.2 into a single theorem. For readability, the conjunction of the two "only if" parts is expressed in a logically equivalent form with the universal quantifiers moved to the front.

THEOREM 9.1. *Let (E, V) be a database, C a consistency criterion for the database, and (G, σ, s) a datatrace such that s is in C and transaction effect $\sigma(p)$ is valid for each transaction node p of G. If the augmented ivg for a given transaction node p is acyclic, then $\sigma(p)$ is matched to some database state in C. If the augmented writers version graph for G is acyclic, then the final database state for the trace is in C.*

Proof. Let G' be $\mathrm{ivg}(G, p)$ for a given transaction node p, and let σ' be the restriction of σ to the nodes of G'. Then from Lemma 7.3, (G', σ', s) is a datatrace. If $\mathrm{aug}(G')$ is acyclic, (G', σ', s) is serializable by Theorem 7.8 and $\sigma(p)$ is matched to a database state in a serial run (Theorem 7.5(a)). Since the transaction effects are valid, Theorem 4.5 says the state in the serial run is consistent.

Now let G' be the writers version graph and σ' again be the restriction of σ. Again (G', σ', s) is a trace and an acyclic $\mathrm{aug}(G')$ implies that (G', σ', s) is serializable. Since G' contains all the writers from G, the final database state of (G', σ', s) is identical to the final database state for (G, σ, s) (from Lemma 6.3 and Definition 7.2). Since (G', σ', s) is serializable, Theorem 7.5 says that the final state of the datatrace is identical to the result of a serial run. Theorem 4.5 implies that the result of a serial run is consistent. □

COROLLARY 9.2. *Given a database consistency criterion and datatrace as in the statement of Theorem 9.1, the $\sigma(p)$ are matched to consistent database states and the final database state is consistent if the augmented graph for version graph G is acyclic.*

Proof. The augmented individual version graphs and the augmented writers version graph are all subgraphs of augmented G and inherit the acyclic property from G.   □

Thus serializability of a trace is sufficient to ensure that the final database state is consistent and each transaction has seen a consistent database. The implication for concurrency control is the following:

COROLLARY 9.3. *A concurrency control starting with a consistent database state and running valid transactions will maintain database consistency if the overall effect of the granted requests is the same as if the transactions were run serially.*

Proof. Lemma 7.6 tells us that the serial run does produce an acyclic augmented version graph and the theorem applies.   □

We note that these results can be applied to concurrency control design without any special knowledge about the consistency criterion. By keeping a record of which transactions supply information read by other transactions and preventing cycles in the augmented version graph, the concurrency control is assured that, starting with a consistent database state, a set of valid transactions will receive and produce a consistent database state.

As an example, consider Fig. 5.1. First we check if the transactions produce a consistent final database state. The augmented writers version graph is shown in Fig. 5.2(e). The graph is acyclic and the one node order satisfying Lemma 6.5 is I, b, a. Thus if the initial database state is consistent and transactions a and b are valid, the final database state is the one obtainable by running first transaction b to completion and then transaction a. This same order says that transactions b and a are also matched to consistent databases. The general principle is:

COROLLARY 9.4. *Under the conditions of Theorem 9.1, if the augmented writers version graph is acyclic, then each writing transaction is matched to a consistent database state and the final database state is consistent.*

Proof. The augmented individual version graph for each writing transaction is a subgraph of the augmented writers version graph and must also be acyclic. The conclusion is then immediate from the theorem.   □

There remains transaction c which only read and did not write during its execution. The augmented individual version graph for c is shown in Fig. 5.2(d) and is acyclic. The one order satisfying Lemma 6.5 is I, a, c and transaction c is matched to the result of applying transaction a to the initial database.

Now look at the augmented version graph itself. It is shown in Fig. 5.2(c) and does have a cycle, so the graph is not part of a serializable trace. The conditions of Corollaries 9.2 and 9.3 are violated, yet each transaction was given a consistent database state and the final database state was consistent.

The loophole is that read-only transactions need not be checked in determining the consistency of the final database state, and certain "relativity effects" can occur. From the relative viewpoint of transaction c, the database appeared to be the result of applying transaction a to the initial database state. From the relative viewpoint of the final database state, transaction a was run after transaction b.

10. The Converse Result

We are now prepared to address the "if" parts of Theorems 8.1 and 8.2. We actually prove a stronger result. The theorems of Sect. 8 require that, given entities and a cyclic augmented version graph G, there exist some value set, consistency criterion, initial database state and datatrace for G whereby there is an inconsistency. We show here that, in fact, the values, criterion and initial database can be constructed before G is given. This implies that, even if the consistency criterion is announced in advance and the designer is permitted to tailor the control to the criterion, serializability is still necessary for certain criteria.

We also strengthen the theorems by showing that one construction works for both Theorems 8.1 and 8.2. We thus get the following strengthened converse to Theorem 9.1:

THEOREM 10.1. *Given a set of entities E, there exist*

(a) *a set of values V,*

(b) *a consistency criterion C for database (E, V) and*

(c) *an (initial) database state s in C such that for every version graph G, there exists a function σ mapping the transaction nodes of G into valid transaction effects such that (G, σ, s) is a datatrace for (E, V) and*

(d) *if the augmented writers version graph for G is cyclic, then the final database state for the datatrace is not in C, and*

(e) *if the augmented ivg for a given transaction node p of G is cyclic, then transaction effect $\sigma(p)$ is not matched to any element in C.*

Proof. Assume a set of entities E is given. We will construct V, C and s.

Construction of values V. Let V be the set of pairs (G, n) where G is a version graph, n is a node of G, and $G = \text{ivg}(G, n)$.

We now define a function TE that maps a value v from V into a transaction effect.

Construction of TE. Let $v = (G, n)$. Define

$$TE(v) = (\text{READSET}, \text{WRITESET}, r, w)$$

as follows:

$$\text{READSET} = \{e \text{ in } E \mid xR_en \text{ for some node } x \text{ in } G\},$$
$$\text{WRITESET} = \{e \text{ in } E \mid xW_en \text{ for some node } x \text{ in } G\},$$
$$r(e) = (\text{ivg}(G, x), x) \text{ where } xR_en,$$
$$w(e) = v.$$

For convenience, we write $TE(G, n)$ as an abbreviation for $TE((G, n))$.

Construction of initial database state s_0. Let s_0 be the constant mapping of E into the pair (G_0, I) where G_0 is the version graph consisting of a single node I and no edges.

Construction of consistency criterion C. s is in C if and only if $s = s_0$ or there is a sequence of values

$$(G_1, n_1), \ldots, (G_k, n_k)$$

such that $TE(G_1, n_1), \ldots, TE(G_k, n_k)$ is a serial run on s_0 resulting in s.

LEMMA 10.2. *For all v in V, transaction effect $TE(v)$ is valid.*

Proof. If $TE(v)$ is matched to state s which is in C because of sequence of values $v_1, \ldots, v_k$, then the result of transforming s by $TE(v)$ is in C because this state is the result of serial run $TE(v_1), \ldots, TE\ TE(v_k), TE(v)$. □

Continuing the proof of Theorem 10.1, we now assume some version graph G is given and construct σ.

Construction of datatrace from version graph G. The datatrace is (G, σ, s_0) where $\sigma(p)$ for transaction node p is $TE(\text{ivg}(G, p), p)$.

It is easily verified that the constructed (G, σ, s_0) satisfies Definition 7.1, the definition of a datatrace.

If the final database state or a state matched to an individual transaction is consistent, then it must be producible as the result of a serial run. This run conceivably could contain effects not part of (G, σ, s_0) and conceivably could contain part of this trace more than once or not at all. The object of the subsequent lemmas is to show that, in all runs, the effects of producer nodes from the constructed datatrace must appear exactly once. Furthermore, their order in the run must agree with edges in the augmented version graph. Therefore the existence of a run will imply no cycles in the graph.

The next lemma says that transaction effects preserve the ivg's of nodes in the values read. Thus the information read is not destroyed by a write operation, and in effect the transactions only append information to an entity.

LEMMA 10.3. *Let database state s_l be matched to transaction effect $t =$ TE(G, n) and let s_2 be the result of transforming s_1 by t. For some entity e, let $s_1(e) = (G_1, n_1)$ and $s_2(e) = (G_2, n_2)$. Let p be any node of G. Then p is a node of G_2 and $\mathrm{ivg}(G_1, p) = \mathrm{ivg}(G_2, p)$.*

Proof. Case 1. *e is not in* WRITESET *of t.* By Definition 4.2 of "transforms," $s_2(e) = s_1(e)$, and the result is immediate.

Case 2. *e is in* WRITESET *of t.* By Definition 4.2 of "transforms" and construction of TE, $s_2(e) = (G, n)$, so $G_2 = G$ and $n_2 = n$. From the construction of function TE, the value of e read is $(\mathrm{ivg}(G, x), x)$ where $x R_e n$ in G. By Definition 4.2 of "matched to," the value of e read equals $s_1(e)$. Hence

$$s_1(e) = (G_1, n_1) = (\mathrm{ivg}(G, x), x).$$

Thus $n_1 = x$ and $G_1 = \mathrm{ivg}(G, x)$. Since $G = G_2$,

$$G_1 = \mathrm{ivg}(G_2, n_1).$$

Since G_1 is a subgraph of G_2, p is a node of G_2 and it remains to be shown that $\mathrm{ivg}(G_1, p) = \mathrm{ivg}(G_2, p)$. Substituting for G_1, this is equivalent to

$$\mathrm{ivg}(\mathrm{ivg}(G_2, n_1), p) = \mathrm{ivg}(G_2, p),$$

which says we must show that p has the same set of ancestors in both $\mathrm{ivg}(G_2, n_1)$ and G_2. Obviously ancestors of p in subgraph $\mathrm{ivg}(G_2, n_1)$ are in G_2, so we must show ancestors of p in G_2 are in $\mathrm{ivg}(G_2, n_1)$.

By hypothesis, p is in G_1 which is $\mathrm{ivg}(G_2, n_1)$, so p is an ancestor of n_1 in G_2. This implies all ancestors of p in G_2 are also ancestors of n_1 and so belong to $\mathrm{ivg}(G_2, n_1)$. $\square$

The next lemma says that a noninitial value read during a serial run must correspond to an earlier transaction in the run.

LEMMA 10.4. *Suppose a consistent database state results from s_0 by a serial run of transaction effects*

$$\mathrm{TE}(G_1, n_1), \ldots, \mathrm{TE}(G_k, n_k).$$

Suppose for some (G_j, n_j) in the run, there is a transaction node x of G_j and an entity e such that $x R_e n_j$ in G_j. Then there exists an $i < j$ such that $(G_i, n_i) = (\mathrm{ivg}(G_j, x), x)$.

Proof. Let $s_1, \ldots, s_k$ be the sequence of states specified in Definition 4.4. Since s_{j-1} is matched to $\text{TE}(G_j, n_j)$, the definition of TE implies that $s_{j-1}(e) = (\text{ivg}(G_j, x), x)$. Since $s_{j-1}(e)$ does not equal $s_0(e)$, one of the transactions must have written $s_{j_1}(e)$. The only transaction effect that writes this value is $\text{TE}(\text{ivg}(G_j, x), x)$. $\qquad\square$

Next, the preceding lemma is generalized to show that every transaction node in a graph written during a serial run must correspond to an earlier transaction in the serial run.

LEMMA 10.5. *Suppose a consistent database state results from s_0 by a serial run of transaction effects*

$$\text{TE}(G_1, n_1), \ldots, \text{TE}(G_k, n_k).$$

Suppose for some (G_j, n_j) in the run, x is a transaction node of G_j. Then there exists an $i \leq j$ such that $(G_i, n_i) = (\text{ivg}(G_j, x), x)$.

Proof. Because x is in $\text{ivg}(G_j, n_j)$, there is a path from x to n_j in G_j. Let the nodes on this path be $x_1 = x, \ldots, x_m = n_j$ such that for all l satisfying $1 \leq l < m$ there is an entity e such that $x_l R_e x_{l+1}$. The lemma is true if $x = n_j$. Assume the lemma is true for x related to n_j by a path of length m or less, and consider x related to n_j by a path of length $m + 1$. Then there is a y such that $x R_e y$ in G_j and a path of length m from y to n_j. From the induction hypothesis, there exists $q \leq j$ such that $(G_q, n_q) = (\text{ivg}(Gj, y), y)$. Since $x R_e y$ in G_j, we also have $x R_e y$ in G_q. Thus from Lemma 10.4 there exists $i < q$ such that $(G_i, n_i) = (\text{ivg}(G_q, x), x)$. From Lemma 6.6, $\text{ivg}(G_q, x) = \text{ivg}(G_j, x)$. Thus $(G_i, n_i) = (\text{ivg}(G_j, x), x)$. $\qquad\square$

COROLLARY 10.6. *If s is a consistent state, $s(e) = (G, n)$ for some entity e, and x is a transaction node of G, then every serial run of transaction effects that results in s includes $\text{TE}(\text{ivg}(G, x), x)$.*

Proof. In a serial run that results in s, the last transaction effect whose WRITESET contains e must be $\text{TE}(G, n)$. Apply Lemma 10.5 with $(G_j, n_j) = (G, n)$. $\qquad\square$

Corollary 10.6 has established that for each node of the final value of entity e, a transaction effect occurs in the serial run. Next we show that members of the writers chain for an entity e actually occur in their chain order.

LEMMA 10.7. *Let s be a consistent database state resulting from s_0 by a serial run of transaction effects, let e be an entity, and let $\text{TE}(G_1, n_1), \ldots,$*

$TE(G_k, n_k)$ *be the subsequence of the transaction effects which have* e *in* WRITESET. *Let* $s(e) = (G, n)$.

Then $n_1, \ldots, n_k$ is the sequence of transaction nodes on the writers chain for e in G, and for $1 \leq i \leq k$

$$G_i = \mathrm{ivg}(G, n_i).$$

Proof. For $1 \leq j \leq k$, let P_j be the following predicate:

for $1 \leq i \leq j$, n_i is the ith transaction node on the chain for e in G_j and $G_i = \mathrm{ivg}(G_j, n_i)$.

We want to prove P_j by induction on j.

Consider $j = 1$. The only permitted value of i is $i = 1$. Because (G_1, n_1) is in the constructed set of values V, n_1 is in G_1 and $G_1 = \mathrm{ivg}(G_1, n_1)$. Thus to prove P_1, we need only show that n_1 is the first transaction node on the writers chain for e in G_1. We know n_1 is on the writers chain because e is in the WRITESET for $TE(G_1, n_1)$. Let x be the node such that $x W_e n_1$ (and hence also $x R_e n_1$) in G_j. Since $x R_e n_j$, the value of entity e read is $(\mathrm{ivg}(G_1, x), x)$ by construction of TE. This value equals the value of e in the database state transformed by the transaction effect. Since the transaction effect is the first to write entity e, the value read is the value from the initial database state s_0, namely (G_0, I). Thus $x = I$ and so n_1 is the first transaction node on the chain for e in G_1.

Now assume that P_j is true for some $j < k$, and consider P_{j+1}.

Case 1. $i < j + 1$. Transaction effect $TE(G_{j+1}, n_{j+1})$ reads the value (G_j, n_j) that was written by the preceding writer of entity e, and writes the value (G_{j+1}, n_{j+1}). Since P_j is assumed to be true, n_i is the ith transaction node on the chain for e in G_j and $G_i = \mathrm{ivg}(G_j, n_i)$. From Lemma 10.3, n_i is a node of G_{j+1} and $\mathrm{ivg}(G_j, n_i) = \mathrm{ivg}(G_{j+1}, n_i)$.

From Lemma 6.3, the ith transaction node (namely n_i) on the chain for e in G_j is also the ith transaction node in $\mathrm{ivg}(G_j, n_i)$. Thus n_i is the ith transaction node in the identical graph $\mathrm{ivg}(G_{j+1}, n_i)$ and (from Lemma 6.3 again) is the ith transaction node in G_{j+1}.

Case 2. $i = j + 1$. Because (G_{j+1}, n_{j+1}) is in the constructed set of values V, n_{j+1} is in G_{j+1} and $G_{j+1} = \mathrm{ivg}(G_{j+1}, n_{j+1})$. We now show that n_{j+1} is the $(j+1)$st transaction node on the writers chain for e in G_{j+1}. We know n_{j+1} is on the writers chain because e is in the WRITESET for $TE(G_{j+1}, n_{j+1})$. Let x be the node such that $x W_e n_{j+1}$ (and hence also $x R_e n_{j+1}$) in G_{j+1}. Since $x R_e n_{j+1}$, the value of entity e read is $(\mathrm{ivg}(G_{j+1}, x), x)$ by construction of TE. This value equals the value of e in the database state transformed by the transaction effect, namely the value (G_j, n_j). Therefore $x = n_j$ and $n_j W_e n_{j+1}$ (definition of x). From case 1, letting $i = j$, node n_j is the jth transaction node on the chain in G_{j+1}. Since $n_j W_e n_{j+1}$ is in G_{j+1}, node n_{j+1} is the $(j+1)$st transaction node on the chain in G_{j+1}.

The proof of P_j is now completed. To prove the lemma, observe that since the last value written on e is (G_k, n_k), $s(e) = (G_k, n_k)$, and hence $G_k = G$ and $n_k = n$. With these substitutions, P_k implies $G_i = \text{ivg}(G, n_i)$.

Finally, Corollary 10.6 implies that for every transaction node x on the writers chain for e in G, the serial run of transaction effects includes $\text{TE}(\text{ivg}(G, x), x)$. Since every such x has e in WRITESET, the transaction effect appears in the subsequence, and x is one of the n_i. Thus $n_i \cdots n_k$ is the entire writers chain. $\square$

COROLLARY 10.8. *Let* $\sigma = \text{TE}(G, n)$ *be a transaction effect in a serial run on* s_0. *Then if* WRITESET (σ) *is nonnull,* $\text{TE}(G, n)$ *occurs only once in the serial run.*

Proof. Let e be an entity in WRITESET of σ. Let s be the result of the run. From Lemma 10.7, the subsequence of transaction effects from the serial run which have e in WRITESET are distinguished by their position on the chain for e in $s(e)$. $\square$

We now complete the proof of Theorem 10.1.

Proof of Theorem 10.1(d). Assume the final database s for the constructed datatrace (G, σ, s_o) is consistent and results from the serial run $\text{TE}(G_1, n_1)$, $\ldots, \text{TE}(G_k, n_k)$ applied to s_o. Let G_w be the writers version graph for G and let x be any transaction node of G_w. Node x writes some entity e (Lemma 6.5(b)) and is a member of the writers chain for e in G_w. Value $s(e)$ is the output of σ (chainend (G, e)) which is constructed to be $(\text{ivg}(G, \text{chainend } (G, e))$, chainend $(G, e))$. Let $H = \text{ivg}(G, \text{chainend } (G, e))$. Thus $s(e) = (H, \text{chainend } (G, e))$. Since x is on the chain for e in G, x is a transaction node of H. From Corollary 10.6, the serial run of transaction effects includes $\text{TE}(\text{ivg}(H, x), x)$. From Lemma 6.6, $\text{ivg}(H, x) = \text{ivg}(G, x)$. Thus the serial run includes $\text{TE}(\text{ivg}(G, x), x)$, which is the constructed $\sigma(x)$. Since this transaction effect has a nonnull WRITESET, Corollary 10.8 applies and $\sigma(x)$ only occurs once in the serial run.

We now know that each transaction node x of G_w corresponds to a unique transaction effect $\sigma(x)$ in the serial run. Define the *serial order* of the transaction nodes of G_w to be the order in which the corresponding transaction effects occur in the serial run. The serial order extends to all nodes of G_w by putting node I first. We want to show that the edges in $\text{aug}(G_w)$ always go from an earlier node in the serial order to a later node. This will imply that $\text{aug}(G_w)$ is acyclic.

Suppose xR_ey in G. Node y must be a transaction node. Assume x is also a transaction node. The corresponding transaction effects in the run are $\sigma(x)$ and $\sigma(y)$. Event $\sigma(y)$ by construction reads (ivg(ivg$(G, y), x), x$) from entity e because xR_ey in ivg(G, y). By Lemma 6.6, this value read is (ivg$(G, x), x$). This value can only have been written by $\sigma(x)$, so the one occurrence of $\sigma(x)$ in the run must precede the occurrence of $\sigma(y)$. In the case where $x = I$, node x is defined to precede y in the serial order.

Suppose xW_ey. Then also xR_ey (Definition 5.1(d)), and again x precedes y in the serial order.

Suppose xB_ey. Then there is a z such that zR_ex and zW_ey. The value of e produced by z is the value read and overwritten by $\sigma(y)$. This value cannot be the value of entity e after $\sigma(y)$ occurs in the serial run. Since this value is the value read by $\sigma(x)$, $\sigma(x)$ must precede $\sigma(y)$ in the serial run. □

Proof of Theorem 10.1(e). Assume that transaction effect $\sigma(p)$ is matched to a consistent database state, say s. Then s results from a serial run TE(G_1, n_1), $\ldots$, TE(G_k, n_k) applied to s_0. Without loss of generality, it can be assumed that each transaction effect in the serial run has a nonnull WRITESET, since a transaction with a null WRITESET can be deleted, yielding a shorter serial run that also results in state s.

Since s is matched to $\sigma(p)$ we can append $\sigma(p)$ to the above serial run, and obtain a longer serial run,

$$\text{TE}(G_1, n_1), \ldots, \text{TE}(G_k, n_k), \text{TE}(\text{ivg}(G, p), p).$$

The remainder of the proof refers to this longer serial run.

From Lemma 10.5, since TE(ivg$(G, p), p$) is a member of the run, then for all transaction nodes x in ivg(G, p), the serial run includes TE(ivg(ivg(G, p), $x), x$). From Lemma 6.6 ivg(ivg$(G, p), x$) = ivg(G, x), so the serial run includes TE(ivg$(G, x), x$) which is the constructed $\sigma(x)$.

From Lemma 6.5(a), every node in ivg(G, p), except possibly p, is a producer node and, from Corollary 10.8, occurs only once in the serial run. If p is not a producer node, then $\sigma(p)$ has a null WRITESET, and so $\sigma(p)$ occurs only once in the serial run (since the original serial run resulting in s was assumed to have no read-only transactions).

We now know that each transaction node x of ivg(G, p) corresponds to a unique transaction effect $\sigma(x)$ in the serial run. As in the proof of Theorem 10.1(d), we can define the *serial order* of these nodes, and extend the order to all nodes of ivg(G, p) by putting node I first. In a manner similar to that in the proof of Theorem 10.1(d), it can be shown that the edges of aug(ivg(G, p)) always go from an earlier node in the serial order to a later node. This implies that aug(ivg(G, p)) is acyclic. □

Discussion of proof techniques. The version graphs in the proof can be thought of as "generalized Herbrand values." Each entity value incorporates the total historic record of the flow of information used to create the value. The usual Herbrand technique [12] involving strings as values does not work here because the strings can only be defined if the values are developed in a sequential manner (each string includes as substrings the relevant previously computed values). However, our model does not have sequential evaluations and, when a version graph (not augmented) is cyclic, there is no sequence of operations which represents the flow.

Theorem 10.1 shows the necessity of serializability for both the consistency of the final state (part (d)) and the consistency of the view seen by individual transactions (part (e)). The complexity of the proof is due to part (e). If Theorem 10.1 were stated without part (e), a much simpler proof would suffice. Instead of writing version graphs, the transactions would need to write only enough information so that the edges of the version graph could be deduced from the final database state. The consistency criterion would be that the augmented deduced graph be acyclic. For example, a transaction could append to entities written a set of pairs each of which is the name of an entity read and the name of the producer node that created the value read.

11.   The Read-Before-Write Assumption

As discussed in Sect. 4, Definition 4.1(b) embodies Assumption A6 that a transaction reads an entity before it writes. Here we want to consider the possibility that a transaction could instruct the concurrency control to write an entity without having read the entity. Will Theorem 10.1 generalize to such situations? We show here by example that the answer is "no."

Consider three transactions P, Q, and R which are run concurrently and access the database with the following schedule of events:

P Writes α (and terminates)

Q Reads α

R Reads α

Q Writes β

Q Writes α (and terminates)

R Reads β

R Writes γ (and terminates).

The "generalized augmented version graph" showing the information flow is shown in Fig. 5.3. It is no longer appropriate to show W_e edges because writes

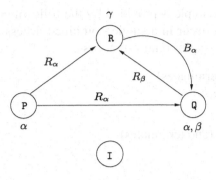

Figure 5.3.

may not replace a specified value. Instead the entities written are indicated beside each transaction node. The augmented edge from R to Q was added because the value of α read by R was read and then overwritten by Q.

As indicated by the cycle in the graph, the schedule of events is not serializable. Entity β was written by Q and then read by R so Q must be scheduled before R. On the other hand, the value of α written by P was read by R before being overwritten by Q so R must be scheduled before Q.

If Theorem 10.1 were generalized, an interpretation would exist such that R was not matched to any consistent database state and the final database state was not consistent. However, this cannot be true since R sees the database state obtained by running the sequence

$$P, Q, P$$

and the final database is that obtained by running the sequence

$$P, Q, P, R.$$

REMARK. In going from a schedule to a "generalized version graph," information about the final database state can be lost as the chainend concept depends on the read-before-write assumption, and the information flow may not show which value was written last. Thus the graph may be inadequate for further study of the write-without-read case.

REMARK. It should be remembered that the counterexample is for the consistency concept given in Definition 3.2. It is possible that some intuitive but stronger criteria can be found which do imply serialization. Producing the example result of P, Q, P, R is intuitively unsatisfactory when transaction P has in fact been initiated only once by a system user.

REMARK. Another example is provided by the following schedule, where all reads of a transaction occur in a single combined access, and all writes of a transaction occur in a single combined access:

S Writes α (and terminates)

R Reads α

P Writes α and β (and terminates)

Q Reads β and γ

Q Writes δ (and terminates)

R Writes γ (and terminates).

The final database state is consistent because it can be obtained by running the sequence P, Q, S, R, P. Any serial schedule producing the final database state must repeat a transaction.

12.   Time Assumptions

By looking at datatraces in terms of information flow instead of schedules, certain timing information is lost. For example, the version graph makes no distinction between the following two schedules:

P READS α	P READS α
P READS β	P WRITES α
P WRITES α	P READS β

The second schedule gives the illusion that the value written into entity α is unrelated to the value read from β, since α was written before the value of β was known. However, it must be remembered that the schedule is not a program, and the transaction might have produced a different schedule had the data read from the database been different.

To be more specific, suppose P read the value 1 from α, wrote the value 2 into α, then read the value 2 from β. Is it a coincidence that the transaction leaves α and β with the same value? It would be if the program for the transaction were the following:

$I \leftarrow$ ENTITY (α)

ENTITY $(\alpha) \leftarrow I + 1$

$J \leftarrow$ ENTITY (β).

If, however, the program were

$I \leftarrow \text{ENTITY} (\alpha)$

$\text{ENTITY} (\alpha) \leftarrow I + 1$

$J \leftarrow \text{ENTITY} (\beta)$

If $J \neq I + 1$ THEN $\text{ENTITY} (\beta) \leftarrow I + 1$,

then the transaction would always produce a database state with ENTITY $(\alpha) = \text{ENTITY}(\beta)$. The two programs often produce different results, but they have the same effect when presented with a database state with value 1 for α and 2 for β.

The point is that the values read and the values written could have any relationship, regardless of the order in which the reads and writes are performed in the particular running of the transaction. Thus it is reasonable to work with a model (the datatrace in our case) where the ordering is not considered.

Some authors have worked with models in which transactions are taken to be straight-line programs accessing a fixed sequence of entities. In this case, the order of access operations influences consistency.

For example, consider the following sequences of actions by two consistency preserving straight-line programs P and Q:

P reads α Q reads β
P writes α Q writes β
P reads β Q reads α

These programs can be run concurrently as follows so that the information flow is that shown in Fig. 5.4(a):

P reads α
Q reads β
P writes α
Q writes β
P reads β
Q reads α

The version graph and its augmented graph are cyclic. The run is not serializable: P must precede Q because P reads the value of α written by Q, and Q must precede P because of β.

However, it programs P and Q are modified to end after the final write and to omit subsequent reads, the programs produce the same effect on the database as the original. The modified programs therefore also preserve consistency when run alone. Concurrent running of the modified programs produces:

P reads α
Q reads β
P writes α
Q writes β

128

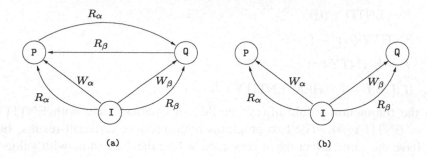

Figure 5.4.

which gives the information flow shown in the version graph of Fig. 5.4(b) (which is Fig. 5.4(a) with the two read operations deleted). Augmented 5.4(b) is acyclic (hence serializable) and produces a consistent final database state. But the two sequences of operations produce the same database state, and the final database state is the same for both 5.4(a) and 5.4(b). The final database state in 5.4(a) is consistent in spite of not being serializable. Thus the "if" part of Theorem 8.1 fails for straight-line programs.

Understanding consistency for the straight-line case involves the concept of a "trailing read." We refer to READ operations after the last WRITE operation performed by a process as *trailing* READs. These reads are the ones that do not affect the values written and can be deleted from the straight-line transactions without affecting their validity.

The following can be proven for the straight-line case:

Modify the version graph by deleting edges corresponding to trailing READs. If the transactions are valid, if the original database is consistent, and if the augmented version graph is acyclic, then the final database state is consistent. If the augmented version graph is cyclic, there exist a consistency criterion, a set of valid straight-line transactions, and an initial consistent database state such that the given history transforms the initial state into an inconsistent state.

Thus the straight-line case provides a loophole for trailing reads.

The problem of describing the consistency of data read is more complex. Consider the following three straight-line programs P, Q, and R:

P reads α Q reads β R reads α
P reads γ Q writes β R reads β
P writes α Q reads γ
P reads β Q writes γ
P reads δ
P writes δ

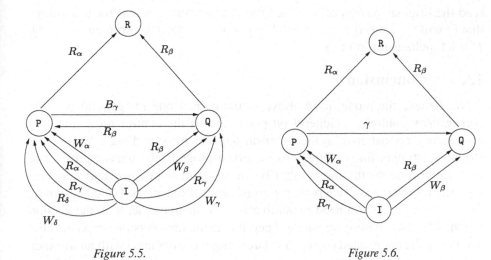

Figure 5.5.   Figure 5.6.

These programs can be run concurrently as follows, so that the information flow is that shown in the augmented version graph of Fig. 5.5:

$$P \text{ reads } \alpha$$
$$P \text{ reads } \gamma$$
$$P \text{ wries } \alpha$$
$$Q \text{ reads } \beta$$
$$Q \text{ writes } \beta$$
$$P \text{ reads } \beta$$
$$R \text{ reads } \alpha$$
$$R \text{ reads } \beta$$
$$Q \text{ reads } \gamma$$
$$Q \text{ writes } \gamma$$
$$P \text{ reads } \delta$$
$$P \text{ writes } \delta$$

In spite of the cycle in the ivg of transaction R, R does see consistent data as demonstrated by running the transactions in order P, Q, R. This serial schedule produces a different version graph from Fig. 5.5, but R gets the same information in both cases. This example shows that the "if" part of Theorem 8.2 fails for straight-line programs.

The information from Fig. 5.5 relevant to the consistency of data read by transaction R is shown in Fig. 5.6. A number of edges have been deleted because they did not impact on the data seen by R. For example, the edge from Q to P labelled R_β was deleted because the value read does not affect any entity value read by R. A new kind of edge labelled γ between P and Q was added because transaction R read a value of α reflecting the fact that P

read the original version of γ. Since the straight-line program for Q requires that Q write γ, from R's viewpoint P must precede Q. The serialization P, Q, R is a topological sort of Fig. 5.6.

13.   Conclusion

We believe the model used above is the correct one for general purpose concurrency controls. "General purpose" means the control must maintain consistency no matter what the criterion happens to be and regardless of the structure (straight-line or otherwise) used to program the transactions. The only imposition on the user is that he or she start with consistent data and only run transactions which preserve consistency if run alone. For consistency, the concurrency control need remember no information other than the version graph. The control must operate to keep the augmented version graph acyclic, for *any* cyclic augmented (writers) version graph is associated with an instance of inconsistency.

There is also danger in allowing a temporary cyclic flow of information, even when the control plans to break the cycle later with a rollback. The danger is that *any* cyclic augmented individual version graph is associated with an inconsistency and the individual transaction may be processing garbage.

There is a loophole for read-only transactions, although it is probably not worth exploiting in practice. Also, such exploitation may be considered unsatisfactory if one takes a stronger view of consistency than our admittedly weak mathematical definition. The definition is good for inferring things that should not be allowed (e.g. cyclic information flow), but additional criteria may be appropriate in deciding what should be allowed.

The general conclusion is that general purpose concurrency controls should be designed so that the augmented version graph is acyclic. Except for the minor read-only loophole, this is the only way to maintain consistency.

References

[1] R. Bayer, E. Elhardt, H. Heller, and A. Reiser. Distributed concurrency control in database systems. In *Proc. Sixth International Conference on Very Large Data Bases*, pages 275–284, Montreal, Oct. 1980.

[2] R. Bayer, H. Heller, and A. Reiser. Parallelism and recovery in database systems. *ACM Trans. Database Systems*, 5:139–156, 1980.

[3] M. A. Casanova. *The Concurrency Control Problem for Database Systems*. Lecture Notes in Computer Science, volume 116. Springer, Berlin, 1981.

[4] M. A. Casanova and P. A. Bernstein. General purpose schedules for database systems. *Acta Inform.*, 14:195–220, 1980.

[5] K. P. Eswaran, J. N. Gray, R. A. Lorie, and I. L. Traiger. The notions of consistency and predicate locks in a database system. *Comm. ACM*, 19(11):624–633, 1976.

[6] G. Gardarin. Contributions to the theory of concurrency in databases. In J. Winkowski, editor, *Mathematical Foundations of Computer Science*. Lecture Notes in Computer Science, volume 64, pages 201–212. Springer, Berlin, 1978.

[7] G. Gardarin and P. Lebeux. Scheduling algorithms for avoiding inconsistency in large databases. In *Proc. Third International Conference on Very Large Data Bases*, pages 501–506, Tokyo, 1977.

[8] G. Gardarin and M. Melkanoff. Proving consistency of database transactions. In *Proc. Fifth International Conference on Very Large Data Bases*, pages 291–298, Rio de Janeiro, Oct. 1979.

[9] J. N. Gray, R. A. Lorie, G. R. Putzolu, and I. L. Traiger. Granularity of locks and degrees of consistency in a shared data base. In G. M. Nijssen, editor, *Modelling in Data Base Management Systems*, pages 365–394. North-Holland, Amsterdam, 1976.

[10] H. T. Kung and C. H. Papadimitriou. An optimality theory of concurrency control for databases. In *Proc. SIGMOD International Conference on Management of Data*, pages 116–126, Boston, MA, May 1979.

[11] L. Lamport. Towards a theory of correctness for multi-user data base systems. Technical Report CA-7610-0712, Mass. Comput. Assoc. Inc., Oct. 1976.

[12] Z. Manna. *Mathematical Theory of Computation*. McGraw–Hill, New York, 1974.

[13] D. P. Reed. Naming and synchronization in a decentralized computer system. Technical Report MIT/LCS/TR-205, Dept. of Electrical Engineering and Computer Science, Massachusetts Inst. of Technology, Cambridge, MA, Sept. 1978. (Ph.D. thesis).

132

[14] R. E. Stearns and D. J. Rosenkrantz. Distributed database concurrency controls using before values. In *Proc. SIGMOD International Conference on Management of Data*, pages 74–83, Ann Arbor, MI, Apr. 1981.

[15] R. E. Stearns, P. M. Lewis II, and D. J. Rosenkrantz. Concurrency controls for database systems. In *Proc. 17th Annual Symp. on Foundations of Comptr. Sci.*, pages 19–32, Houston, TX, 1976.

Chapter 6

AN EFFICIENT METHOD FOR REPRESENTING AND TRANSMITTING MESSAGE PATTERNS ON MULTIPROCESSOR INTERCONNECTION NETWORKS[*]

P. J. BERNHARD[†]

Department of Computer Science, Clemson University, Clemson, SC 29634, USA

D. J. ROSENKRANTZ[‡]

Department of Computer Science, State University of New York at Albany, Albany, NY 12222, USA

Reprinted from: *J. Parallel and Distributed Computing*, Vol. 11, No. 1, Jan. 1991, pp. 72–85. © Elsevier

Abstract We describe a formalism for representing address sets, and for representing message patterns for multiprocessor interconnection networks. In this formalism a descriptor called a *mask* is used to represent a set of equal length bit vectors. Such a set can be interpreted as a set of processor addresses, or as a set of messages. We focus on the implications that this formalism has for routing message patterns on bundled omega networks. Specifically, we show that when a message pattern is represented in this formalism, a number of properties of the message pattern can be determined in polynomial time. This includes such things as determining whether the message pattern contains congestion. In addition, we show that the formalism defines a subclass of message patterns for which the *minimum round partitioning problem*, which in general is NP-hard, is solvable in linear time. We show this result to be true for both broadcast and

---

[*] An abbreviated version of this paper appears in *Proc. of the 1988 Symposium on the Frontiers of Massively Parallel Computation*, George Mason Univ., Fairfax, Virginia.
[†] Research supported in part by NSF Grant DCR 86-03184.
[‡] Research supported in part by NSF Grants DCR 86-03184 and CCR88-03278.

S.S. Ravi, S.K. Shukla (eds.), *Fundamental Problems in Computing*,
© Springer Science + Business Media B.V. 2009

134

non-broadcast bundled omega networks. This generalizes a known result for bit-permute-complement permutations to a more general class of message patterns, and to a larger class of networks.

Received July 28, 1989; revised February 8, 1990; accepted April 15, 1990.

1. Introduction

Consider an SIMD multiprocessor that consists of a large number $N = 2^m$ of processing elements each having an m bit binary address, an interconnection network through which the processing elements communicate, and a host computer that broadcasts instructions to the processing elements. In addition, suppose that in such a multiprocessor some message is to be sent from one processing element to another. In such a case the message can be represented by an (s, d)-*pair*, where s is the binary address of the source processor and d is the binary address of the destination processor. More generally, a *message pattern*, which is a set of messages, can be represented by a set of (s, d)-pairs, where each (s, d)-pair corresponds to one message. For example, in Fig. 6.1 we show a message pattern consisting of four (s, d)-pairs.

0000, 0101
0010, 0111
0101, 1100
0111, 1110

Figure 6.1. A message pattern consisting of four (s, d)-pairs

In this paper we discuss a formalism for representing and transmitting message patterns in multiprocessors such as the one described above. In this formalism a message pattern is represented by a descriptor called an (s, d)-*mask*. For example, if x_0 and x_1 are Boolean variables, then the (s, d)-mask $(0x_0x_1x_0, x_01x_1\overline{x}_0)$ can be used to represent the message pattern in Fig. 6.1. Similarly, the message pattern in Fig. 6.2 can be represented by the (s, d)-mask $(0x_011, 11x_0x_1)$. The basic idea is that each assignment to the variables in the (s, d)-mask specifies one (s, d)-pair in the corresponding message pattern.

The (s, d)-mask formalism is a generalization of a method commonly used to describe *bit-permute-complement permutations* [15]. The main difference, is that the class of bit-permute-complement permutations is more restricted than the class of message patterns defined by the (s, d)-mask formalism. More specifically, bit-permute-complement permutations are restricted in that every processor must send exactly one message and every processor must receive

0011, 1100
0011, 1101
0111, 1110
0111, 1111

Figure 6.2. The message pattern corresponding to the (s, d)-mask $(0x_011, 11x_0x_1)$

exactly one message. In contrast, the (s, d)-mask formalism, in addition to bit-permute-complement permutations, defines a number of non-permutation type message patterns. This includes message patterns that involve broadcasts, multiple destination requests, and message patterns that involve proper subsets of the processing elements. For example, consider the (s, d)-mask $(0x_011, 11x_0x_1)$ and its corresponding message pattern shown in Fig. 6.2. In this message pattern the processors with addresses 0011 and 0111 are each broadcasting a message to two different processors. Similarly, the message pattern corresponding to the (s, d)-mask $(00x_0x_1, 11x_10)$ contains multiple messages with the same destination.

Using (s, d)-masks to describe message patterns has a number of advantages. First, since a set of (s, d)-pairs can be exponentially large compared with a corresponding (s, d)-mask, simply storing the message pattern as an (s, d)-mask requires far less space than storing it as a *list* of (s, d)-pairs. Second, the host computer can direct the processing elements to implement a variety of communication patterns simply by broadcasting a single (s, d)-mask. Third, if message patterns are represented by (s, d)-masks then, as we shall show in Sect. 6, a variety of efficient preprocessing algorithms can be used by the host computer or by a preprocessor when preparing message patterns for routing. These algorithms determine such things as whether a given message pattern, specified as an (s, d)-mask, contains communication conflicts. Finally, one consequence of the conciseness of the formalism, is that it defines a subclass of the class of *all* possible message patterns. More formally, if $F = \{S \mid S$ is a message pattern that can be represented by a single (s, d)-mask$\}$ and $A = \{S \mid S$ is a message pattern$\}$ then it follows that $F \subset A$. This can be seen by noting that if an (s, d)-mask M contains r variables then the corresponding message pattern contains 2^r (s, d)-pairs. Hence, any message pattern containing a number of (s, d)-pairs that is not a power of 2 cannot be represented by a single (s, d)-mask. It can also be proven by a counting argument showing that the number of message patterns is larger than the number of (s, d)-masks [3].

The reason this fact is useful is because problems that are intractable for arbitrary message patterns can be considered on this restricted subclass. It is hoped that when restricted to this subclass, these problems will be efficiently solvable. This approach appears promising in light of the fact that many routing algorithms have already been developed for the class of bit-permute-complement permutations. These algorithms make use of a number of different routing strategies and apply to a number of different networks, including delta networks [19, 22], meshes [15], cubes [17], Benes [14, 16], omega [11, 24], and shuffle-exchange networks [10]. Conceivably, algorithms such as these, and other results that apply to bit-permute-complement permutations, may be generalizable to apply to all message patterns that can be represented by (s, d)-masks.

In this paper we exploit the above ideas in developing an efficient message routing algorithm. Specifically, we consider a message routing technique that we call *minimum round partitioning*. In this strategy a set of conflicting messages is partitioned into a minimum number of conflict-free subsets. The set of messages is then transmitted by successively transmitting the messages in each subset. For arbitrary message patterns it is known that minimum round partitioning is NP-hard [2]. In light of this fact it is highly unlikely that a polynomial time algorithm for the problem exists (unless $P = NP$). Consequently, two approaches to the problem are appropriate. The first is to develop polynomial time heuristics that have near optimal performance. Research along these lines has been reported in [5, 7, 23]. The second is to identify subclasses of message patterns such that the problem becomes solvable in polynomial time when restricted to those subclasses.

In this paper we take the second approach and show that the minimum round partitioning problem is solvable in linear time when restricted to the subclass of message patterns that are representable by a single (s, d)-mask. We show that this result applies to the class of *bundled omega networks* (these networks are sometimes referred to as *dilated* omega networks and have been studied in [12, 21]). This generalizes a result in [19] that applies only to bit-permute-complement permutations. Finally, we consider problems that deal with determining if a message pattern contains communication conflicts when that message pattern is represented by one or more (s, d)-masks.

The rest of this paper is organized as follows. In Sect. 2 we describe the omega network, its generalized version the bundled omega network, and a number of their properties. In Sect. 3 we define the (s, d)-mask formalism in detail. In Sect. 4 we define a "normal form" for masks and (s, d)-masks. In Sect. 5 we describe how the formalism generalizes the class of bit-permute complement permutations. In Sect. 6 we consider a number of problems that deal with determining if a given message pattern contains conflicts or congestion when the message pattern is represented by a set of (s, d)-masks. Finally, in Sect. 7 we consider the minimum round partitioning strategy. We show that when restricted to the subclass of message patterns that can be represented by a single (s, d)-mask, the problem becomes solvable in linear time for the class of bundled omega networks.

2.   The Omega Network

Following Lawrie [13], an N-input, N-output omega network (also called an $N \times N$ omega network), where $N = 2^m$, consists of m identical stages. Each stage consists of a *perfect shuffle* wire interconnection [20] followed by $N/2$ switching elements. In Fig. 6.3(a) we show an 8×8 omega network, and in Figs. 6.3(b)–(g) we show the possible states for each of the switches. Figure 6.3(b) shows the "straight through" state where the input signals are sent directly to the corresponding outputs, Fig. 6.3(c) shows the "interchange" state where the input signals are first interchanged before being sent to the outputs, and Figs. 6.3(d)–(g) show "incomplete" states. For example, in Fig. 6.3(d) a signal is passed from the upper input to the upper output while nothing is on the lower input or lower output. It should be noted that the network described here differs from the one in [13] since switches are not allowed to "broadcast" messages. However, in Sect. 7.2 we shall consider the network when broadcasts are allowed. In Fig. 6.3(a) we have labeled the interconnection links for each stage, from the top down, with a $\log_2 N$ bit binary address. We have numbered each of the stages, and we have shown two paths through the network, one from input 000 to output 011 and the other from input 100 to output 000.

A particular path through the network can be represented by a source-destination pair, abbreviated as an (s, d)-pair, where the source $s = s_0 s_1 \cdots s_{m-1}$ is the binary address of the input at the first stage, the destination $d = d_0 d_1 \cdots d_{m-1}$ is the binary address of the output at the last stage, and $m = \log_2 N$. Careful examination of the network shows that the *path code* $s_0 s_1 \cdots s_{m-1} d_0 d_1 \cdots d_{m-1}$ completely specifies a unique path through the network. Specifically, if we define an m bit window W_i as the bit pattern beginning at bit position i of the path code, we see that at stage i in the network, where $0 \leq i \leq m$, the path that goes from input $s_0 s_1 \cdots s_{m-1}$ to output $d_0 d_1 \cdots d_{m-1}$ makes use of the link with address $W_i = s_i s_{i+1} \cdots s_{m-1} d_0 d_1 \cdots d_{i-1}$. For example, Fig. 6.3(a) shows a path from 000 to 011. For this path $W_2 = 001$ and at stage 2 the path makes use of the link with address 001.

The fact that a path code specifies a unique path through the network enables communication conflicts in the network to be detected easily. Two messages that are being transmitted through the network at the same time will conflict if and only if they require use of a common link in the network. Hence, in light of the window property mentioned above, two (s, d)-pairs are said to **conflict** if and only if there exists an i such that the two (s, d)-pairs have the same bit pattern on window W_i. For example, Fig. 6.3(a) shows the paths $(000, 011)$

138

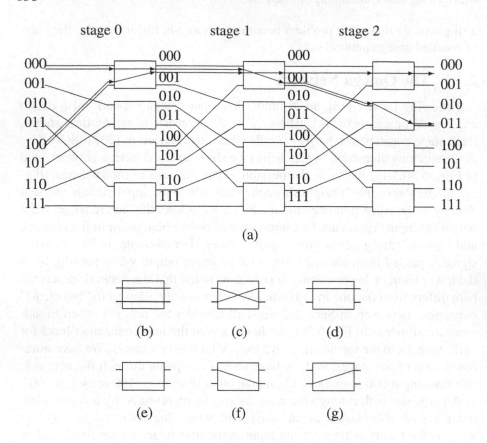

stage 0   stage 1   stage 2

(a)

(b)   (c)   (d)

(e)   (f)   (g)

Figure 6.3. An Omega Network and possible switch states

and $(100, 000)$. Both (s, d)-pairs have $W_1 = 000$, and at stage 1 both pass through the link with address 000.

The definition of the omega network can be generalized by the addition of another parameter b called the **bundle size** of the network. Specifically, we define a $(b)N \times (b)N$ omega network, where $N = 2^m$, to have bundle size b if each switch in the network has two bundles of inputs and two bundles of outputs, each of size b. For example, in Fig. 6.4 we show a $(3)4 \times (3)4$ omega network. The advantage of such a network is that message patterns containing conflicts on a standard omega network may be conflict-free on a bundled omega network with $b > 1$. In such a network, each bundle can carry b or fewer signals into a switch. Hence, a total of at most $2b$ signals can be input to a switch at any given time. Similarly, each output bundle can carry b or fewer signals out of a switch. For each input bundle, the incoming signals can be sent to the upper or lower output bundle. However, all the signals on a given input bundle don't necessarily have to go to the same output bundle.

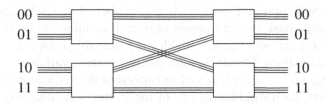

Figure 6.4. A $(3)4 \times (3)4$ Omega Network

Some can go to the upper output bundle, while others can go to the lower. Similarly, two signals on different input bundles can go to the same output bundle. The only constraint is that at most b signals can use a particular output bundle at any given time. If more than b require use of the same output bundle, then we say that **congestion** occurs.

The definition of the standard omega network is a special case of the generalized definition, where $b = 1$. Similarly "conflict" is a special case of "congestion". Recall that two (s, d)-pairs are said to conflict at stage i in the network if and only if they have the same bit pattern on window W_i. However, when $b > 1$ the fact that two (s, d)-pairs have the same bit pattern on window W_i doesn't necessarily imply that *congestion* occurs. In order for congestion to occur at stage i, at least $b + 1$ (s, d)-pairs must have the same bit pattern on window W_i. For example, consider the paths $(0000, 1000)$ and $(1100, 1001)$ on a $(2)16 \times (2)16$ omega network. Both (s, d)-pairs have the same bit pattern 0010 on W_2 and consequently the bundle at stage 2 with address 0010 would be full if the two paths were in use at the same time. If we now consider the path $(0100, 1010)$ we see that at stage 2 this also requires use of bundle 0010. Hence, if all three paths were required to be in use at the same time, congestion would occur. An example of a bundled omega network with $b = 16$ is in the proposed G.E. Cross Omega machine [9].

Finally, define a **message pattern** to be a set of (s, d)-pairs. Each (s, d)-pair in the set represents the fact that a message is to be sent from input s to output d of the network. Define a **permutation** to be a message pattern where each input of the network is the source of exactly one message, and each output is the destination of exactly one message. Define a **partial permutation** to be a message pattern where each input of the network is the source of *at most* one message, and each output is the destination of *at most* one message.

3. Definition of a Mask Formalism

Define a mask formalism as follows. **Symbols** include constants and literals. **Constants** are 0 and 1, **literals** include variables "x_0", "x_1", "x_2", ... and their complements. A literal l is said to be **derived** from the variable x_i if $l = x_i$ or $l = \overline{x}_i$. A **mask** is any finite sequence of symbols such as $x_0 1 0 x_1 1$

or $x_0x_1\overline{x}_2$. The length of a mask M is the number of symbol occurrences in the mask. Each mask has an implicit universal quantifier to its left for each variable that it contains, where variables are quantified over the set $\{0,1\}$. A mask M containing literals that are derived from r variables, denoted by $V(M) = \{x_0, x_1, \ldots, x_{r-1}\}$, is said to **represent** the set, denoted by $S(M)$, of 2^r addresses, each specified by one of the 2^r functions mapping each variable to the set $\{0,1\}$. Each address in the set $S(M)$ is said to be **covered** by the corresponding mask M. For example, the mask $M = x_01x_10$ represents the set of addresses $S(M) = \{0100, 0110, 1100, 1110\}$. In the case where a mask contains no variables, such as the mask 101, then the mask represents the set that contains only itself $\{101\}$.

Let M be a mask and f a function from the set $V(M)$ to the set $\{0, 1, x_0, \overline{x}_0, x_1, \overline{x}_1, \ldots\}$. Then define the **natural extension** of the function f to masks, to be a function $\hat{f}$ such that if $c \in \{0,1\}$ then $\hat{f}(c) = c, \hat{f}(x_i) = f(x_i), \hat{f}(\overline{x}_i) = \overline{f(x_i)}$, and if $M = a_0a_1 \cdots a_{m-1}$ then $\hat{f}(M) = \hat{f}(a_0)\hat{f}(a_1) \cdots \hat{f}(a_{m-1})$. It follows that a particular address A is in the set $S(M)$ if and only if there exists a function f from the set $V(M)$ to the set $\{0,1\}$ such that $\hat{f}(M) = A$. Finally, two masks M_1 and M_2 are said to be **disjoint** if $S(M_1) \cap S(M_2) = \emptyset$.

An (s, d)-**mask** consists of a left hand side (LHS) and a right hand side (RHS), where each is a mask of the same length. Examples of (s, d)-masks are $(001, 010), (1x_0, 01)$ and $(x_010x_1x_2, x_110x_2x_0)$. As with a mask, an (s, d)-mask has an implicit universal quantifier to its left for each variable that it contains. Hence, an (s, d)-mask is said to represent the corresponding set of (s, d)-pairs. For example, the (s, d)-mask $M = (x_010, \overline{x}_01x_1)$ represents the set $S(M) = \{(010, 110), (010, 111), (110, 010), (110, 011)\}$.

In addition, we shall make use of the following notation. The **cardinality** of a set S will be denoted by $|S|$. If S_1 represents the set of all addresses of length m, where $m \geq 1$, and $S_2 \subseteq S_1$, then $\overline{S}_2$ is $S_1 - S_2$. Finally, if $I_1 = \{i_0, i_1, \ldots, i_{k-1}\}$ is a subset of $I = \{0, 1, \ldots, m - 1\}$, where $i_0 \leq i_1 \leq, \ldots, \leq i_{k-1}$ and $M = a_0a_1 \cdots a_{m-1}$ is a mask, then the **projection** of M onto I_1, denoted by $M(I_1)$, is the mask $a_{i_0}a_{i_1} \cdots a_{i_{k-1}}$. For example, if $m = 7, I_1 = \{0, 3, 4, 6\}$ and $M = x_0\overline{x}_0110\overline{x}_0x_1$ then $M(I_1) = x_010x_1$. Note that all of the notation for masks can be applied to (s, d)-masks in the obvious way.

One observation is that any (s, d)-mask can, in many circumstances, be treated just like a mask, simply by concatenating the left hand side to the right hand side. For example, the (s, d)-mask $(x_01x_1, x_0x_1x_1)$ can be thought of as the mask $x_01x_1x_0x_1x_1$. The reason for doing this, is that many of the results for masks can be extended directly to (s, d)-masks simply by taking this into consideration.

4. Mask Normal Form

The definition of the mask formalism has the flexibility that a number of different masks can represent the same set of addresses. For example, all three of the masks $x_0x_1\overline{x}_0$, $\overline{x}_0x_1x_0$, and $x_1x_0\overline{x}_1$ represent the set $\{001, 011, 100, 110\}$. Given this, define two masks to be **equivalent** if they represent the same set of addresses. Similarly, we can define two (s, d)-masks to be equivalent if they represent the same set of (s, d)-pairs.

In light of the fact that a number of different masks can represent the same set of addresses, define a mask $M = a_0a_1\cdots a_{m-1}$ to be **normalized** if the following properties hold for M.

1. If x_i appears in M then for all $0 \le j < i, x_j$ also appears in M.

2. If there exists a u and i such that $a_u = \overline{x}_i$ then there exists a v, where $0 \le v < u$, such that $a_v = x_i$.

3. If $i < j, r = \min\{u \mid a_u = x_i\}$ and $s = \min\{v \mid a_v = x_j\}$ then $r < s$.

In other words, while performing a left to right scan of a mask no variables are "skipped," the first occurrence of x_i appears before any occurrence of $\overline{x}_i$, and if $i < j$ then the first occurrence of x_i appears before the first occurrence of x_j. A normalized mask will also be referred to as being in **normal form**. For example, the mask $x_0x_1\overline{x}_0x_2x_3$ is in normal form but the equivalent mask $\overline{x}_2x_0x_2x_5x_3$ is not. Similarly, the (s, d)-mask $(0x_01x_1, 00\overline{x}_0x_2)$ is in normal form but the equivalent (s, d)-mask $(0\overline{x}_11x_0, 00x_1x_2)$ is not. It can easily be shown that for every mask or (s, d)-mask, there exists a unique equivalent normalized mask or (s, d)-mask, respectively. In addition, suppose $M_1 = a_0a_1\cdots a_{m-1}$ and $M_2 = b_0b_1\cdots b_{m-1}$ are two normalized masks and let $p = \max\{q \mid x_q$ is a variable that occurs in $M_1\}$. Then a normalization of M_2 *with respect to M_1* is a replacement of each occurrence of the variable x_i and its complement $\overline{x}_i$ in M_2, by the literals x_{i+p+1} and $\overline{x}_{i+p+1}$, respectively.

LEMMA 1. *Given normalized masks M_1 and M_2, M_2 can be normalized with respect to M_1 in $O(m)$ time.*

Proof. Follows directly from the above discussion.[1] □

The main purpose of renormalizing one mask with respect to another is to ensure that they contain disjoint sets of variables. This fact shall be used by algorithms that are presented in following sections. Finally, the concept of equivalence can be extended to *sets* of masks and *sets* of (s, d)-masks. For

---

[1] We assume in this paper that accessing a symbol, such as a constant or a literal, requires unit time.

example, it can easily be verified that the message pattern represented by the set $S_1 = \{(0011, 110x_0), (x_0111, \overline{x}_0\overline{x}_0\overline{x}_0\overline{x}_0), (0111, 1110)\}$ is equivalent to the one represented by the set $S_2 = \{(0x_011, 11x_0x_1), (1111, 0000)\}$. Hence, the sets S_1 and S_2 are equivalent.

5. Classes of Message Patterns Representable by (s, d)-Masks

In this section we describe some of the different types of message patterns that can be represented by a single (s, d)-mask. Among other things, this will serve to emphasize how the (s, d)-mask formalism generalizes the class of bit-permute-complement permutations. In the following, let M be a normalized (s, d)-mask, and let V_1 and V_2 be the sets of variables that appear or whose complements appear in the LHS and RHS, respectively, of M.

OBSERVATION. If $V_1 = V_2$ then the corresponding message pattern is a partial permutation. Examples of such (s, d)-masks are $(00x_0x_1, 01x_1\overline{x}_0)$ and $(0x_00x_1, x_01\overline{x}_0\overline{x}_1)$.

OBSERVATION. If $V_2 \subset V_1$ then multiple (s, d)-pairs have the same destination address in the corresponding message pattern. Furthermore, if $k = |V_1| - |V_2|$ then 2^k (s, d)-pairs share each of the $2^{|V_2|}$ destination addresses. Examples of such (s, d)-masks are $(1x_0x_1x_2, x_1\overline{x}_000)$ and $(x_00x_1x_2, x_011\overline{x}_1)$.

OBSERVATION. If $V_1 \subset V_2$ then multiple (s, d)-pairs have the same source address in the corresponding message pattern. Furthermore, if $k = |V_2| - |V_1|$ then 2^k (s, d)-pairs share each of the $2^{|V_1|}$ source addresses. Examples of such (s, d)-masks are $(0x_0x_1x_2, x_1\overline{x}_0x_2x_3)$ and $(x_00x_1x_2, x_0\overline{x}_1x_2x_3)$.

OBSERVATION. If $V_1 \not\subset V_2$, $V_2 \not\subset V_1$ and $k = |V_1 \cap V_2|$ then each of the $2^{|V_1|}$ sources broadcasts to $2^{|V_2|-k}$ destinations, and each of the $2^{|V_2|}$ destinations is shared by $2^{|V_1|-k}$ sources. Examples of such (s, d)-masks are $(x_0x_1x_2, x_1\overline{x}_0x_3)$ and $(x_00x_1x_2, x_0x_1\overline{x}_1x_3)$.

DEFINITION. Let π be a permutation and suppose that for all k, where $0 \leq k \leq m - 1$, $y_k = x_k$ or $y_k = \overline{x}_k$. Then a **bit-permute-complement permutation,** abbreviated BPC, is a message pattern that can be described by an (s, d)-mask of the following form

$$(x_0x_1 \cdots x_{m-1}, y_{\pi(0)}y_{\pi(1)} \cdots y_{\pi(m-1)}). \tag{5.1}$$

Simply stated, the left hand side has a distinct uncomplemented variable in each bit position and the right hand side consists of a permutation of those variables with the possibility that some of them are complemented. Examples of such message patterns include the identity permutation $(x_0 x_1 \cdots x_{m-1},$ $x_0 x_1 \cdots x_{m-1})$, the bit reversal permutation $(x_0 x_1 \cdots x_{m-1}, x_{m-1} \cdots x_1 x_0)$, the perfect shuffle permutation $(x_0 x_1 \cdots x_{m-1}, x_1 \cdots x_{m-1} x_0)$ and the exchange permutation $(x_0 x_1 \cdots x_{m-1}, x_0 x_1 \cdots \overline{x}_{m-1})$.

OBSERVATION. If $V_1 = V_2$ and the LHS contains no constants or repeated instances of variables, and if the same is true of the RHS, then the corresponding message pattern is a bit-permute-complement (BPC) permutation.

If the LHS contains no constants then each position must contain a literal derived from some variable. Furthermore, if the LHS contains no repeated instances of variables then each position must contain a variable unique within the LHS. Since M is normalized, it follows that the LHS is of the form $x_0 x_1 \cdots x_{m-1}$. Similarly, since the same restrictions apply to the RHS and since $V_1 = V_2$, it follows that each position in the RHS must contain a literal derived from a variable that occurs exactly once in the RHS and exactly once in the LHS. Hence, the message pattern is a bit-permute-complement permutation.

THEOREM 2. *A permutation is representable by a single* (s, d)-*mask if and only if it is a bit-permute-complement permutation.*

Proof. (if) If a message pattern is a bit-permute-complement permutation, then by definition it can be represented by a single (s, d)-mask as in (5.1).

(only if) Suppose that a given permutation can be represented by the (s, d)-mask M. Assume without loss of generality that M is normalized, and consider the LHS of the (s, d)-mask. Since the message pattern represented by M forms a permutation, it follows that the that the LHS cannot contain any constants. For example, if the LHS of the (s, d)-mask had a 1 on position 5, then no processor whose address had a 0 on position 5 would send a message. Similarly, no two literals in the LHS can be derived from the same variable. Since the (s, d)-mask is normalized, it follows that the LHS is of the form $x_0 x_1, \ldots, x_{m-1}$. Now consider the RHS of the (s, d)-mask. As with the LHS, no position in the RHS can contain a constant. Furthermore, each variable occurring in the RHS must occur in the LHS, otherwise the message pattern would contain broadcasts. Similarly, each variable in the LHS must appear in the RHS. It follows that each variable from the LHS occurs exactly once in some literal in the RHS, in complemented or uncomplemented form. It follows that the (s, d)-mask has form given by (1) where π is a permutation, and for all k, where $0 \leq k \leq m - 1$, $y_k = x_k$ or $y_k = \overline{x}_k$. Hence, the message pattern forms a bit-permute-complement permutation. $\square$

COROLLARY 3. *Not all permutations can be represented by a single* (s, d)-*mask.*

Proof. From Theorem 2 it follows that if a given permutation can be represented by a single (s, d)-mask, then that permutation must be a bit-permute-complement permutation. In addition, since the RHS of any BPC permutation consists of a permutation of m variables, with the possibility that some of these variables are complemented, it follows that the total number of BPC permutations is $m!2^m$. In contrast, the total number of permutations on an $N = 2^m$ input omega network is $(2^m)!$. It can easily be verified that $m!2^m < (2^m)!$, for all $m \geq 2$. Hence, the theorem follows. □

THEOREM 4. *Given a normalized* (s, d)-*mask, determining if the corresponding message pattern is a partial permutation, bit-permute-complement permutation, contains multiple messages with the same destination, or broadcasts, can be done in* $O(m)$ *time.*

Proof. Using two bit vectors, construct the sets of variables in the LHS and the RHS of the (s, d)-mask. Next, compare the bit vectors to determine which of the properties from the above observations is true. Since the (s, d)-mask is normalized, it follows that at most $2m$ variables appear in the (s, d)-mask. Hence, the bit vectors need only be of length $2m$. It follows that both of the above steps can be performed in $O(m)$ time, and hence the lemma follows. □

6. (s, d)-Masks and Detecting Congestion

Suppose that a message pattern is to be routed on a bundled omega network such as the one described in Sect. 2. Since congestion is not permitted on such a network, the following two-step message routing procedure could be used. In the first step, the message pattern to be routed is tested for congestion. If the message pattern is found to be congestion-free then in the second step the messages are transmitted directly through the network. On the other hand, if the message pattern is not congestion-free then in the second step some routing strategy is used that transmits the messages to their destinations in a congestion-free manner.

The second step in this process, the problem of routing message patterns that contain conflicts or congestion, will be considered in Sect. 7. In this section, we focus on the first step in this process. Specifically, we consider algorithms for determining if a message pattern contains conflicts or congestion when that message pattern is represented by a set of one or more (s, d)-masks. We begin by describing a structure called a *conflict-cube* [19] that can be used to determine a number of properties of a message pattern. We then show how conflict-cubes can be used in a number of algorithms for detecting conflicts

(0000,1000)	(0001,1000)
(0000,1001)	(0001,1001)
(0000,1010)	(0001,1010)
(0000,1011)	(0001,1011)
(0010,1000)	(0011,1000)
(0010,1001)	(0011,1001)
(0010,1010)	(0011,1010)
(0010,1011)	(0011,1011)

Figure 6.5. Partition induced by $S_{M,1}$ on the message pattern corresponding to $(00x_0x_1, 10x_2x_3)$

and/or congestion. Such algorithms could be used in a host computer that is preparing message patterns for routing. Note that, in the following, we will sometimes informally speak of "conflicts in an (s, d)-mask" when in fact what we are referring to are conflicts in the corresponding message pattern.

DEFINITION. Let M be an (s, d)-mask and V_j the set of variables that occur or whose complements occur in window W_j, where $0 \leq j \leq m$. The **conflict-cube** $S_{M,j}$ of M corresponding to window W_j is the set $S_{M,j} = V(M) - V_j$. For example, if $M = (x_0 11 x_1, x_2 \bar{x}_1 x_3 x_0)$ then the conflict-cubes are $S_{M,0} = \{x_2, x_3\}$, $S_{M,1} = \{x_0, x_3\}$, $S_{M,2} = \{x_0, x_3\}$, $S_{M,3} = \{x_0\}$ and $S_{M,4} = \emptyset$.

The above definition is a generalization of one given in [19]. The main difference is that the above definition applies to any (s, d)-mask, and not just those corresponding to bit-permute-complement permutations. In addition, the above specifies conflict-cubes for W_0 and W_m. The reason conflict-cubes are important is because they can be used to determine a number of properties of the message pattern corresponding to an (s, d)-mask. Specifically, if $k = |S_{M,j}|$, for some j, then the (s, d)-pairs can be grouped into $2^{|V(M)|-k}$ sets, each containing 2^k (s, d)-pairs, where the (s, d)-pairs in each set use the same link in the network at stage j. The link used at stage j by the (s, d)-pairs in each of these sets is specified by an assignment to the variables in V_j.

For example, consider the (s, d)-mask $(00x_0x_1, 10x_2x_3)$. Note that if $j = 1$, then it follows that $k = |S_{M,j}| = 2$, and since $|V(M)| = 4$ it follows that the set of (s, d)-pairs can be grouped into 4 sets each containing 4 (s, d)-pairs, as shown in Fig. 6.5. Note that within each of these sets the (s, d)-pairs conflict (have the same bit pattern) on W_1, where the link through which the messages pass at stage 1 is specified by an assignment to the variables in $V_1 = \{x_0, x_1\}$.

In Sects. 6.1 and 6.2 we show how conflict-cubes can be used to determine a number of properties of (s, d)-masks and their corresponding message patterns. In addition, in Sect. 7 we show how conflict-cubes can be exploited in the solution to the minimum round partitioning problem, for any message pattern that can be represented by a single (s, d)-mask.

6.1 Detecting Conflicts in an (s, d)-Mask

In this section we are concerned with determining if a message pattern, represented by a given set of one or more (s, d)-masks, contains conflicts. Note that in this section we are concerned only with standard omega networks with bundle size $b = 1$. In Sect. 6.2 we will consider similar problems where $b \geq 1$. We begin by considering message patterns that are represented by a single (s, d)-mask. As stated above, detecting if a single (s, d)-mask contains conflicts is the same as detecting if it has a nonempty conflict-cube. Hence, we have the following.

THEOREM 5. *Given a normalized* (s, d)-*mask* M *of length* $2m$, *determining if the message pattern* $S(M)$ *is conflict-free can be done in* $O(m)$ *time.*

Proof. An algorithm that tests for conflicts need only construct and then examine each of the conflict-cubes for the (s, d)-mask. If a nonempty conflict-cube is detected then conflicts exist. Let $r = \max\{i \mid x_i$ is a variable that occurs in the (s, d)-mask $M\}$. Then each conflict-cube $S_{M,i}$ can be represented by an r bit vector. By making one "scan" of the (s, d)-mask we can determine the size of each of the conflict-cubes. If during this process a nonempty conflict-cube is detected then it must be the case that conflicts exist.

An algorithm that performs such a scan is shown in Fig. 6.6. Since the omega network described in Sect. 2 does not allow broadcasts it follows that an (s, d)-mask containing broadcasts will be interpreted by the algorithm to contain conflicts. The algorithm operates by scanning the windows beginning with W_0 and ending with W_m. For each window, the algorithm will determine if the corresponding conflict-cube is nonempty. If a nonempty conflict-cube is detected then the loop beginning on line 24 terminates and the algorithm returns on line 41. The algorithm keeps track of conflict-cubes by maintaining a count of the number of times that a variable or its complement occurs in the window currently under examination. For each variable x_i, vcount[i] contains this value. If at any time it is determined that some variable x_j occurs in the (s, d)-mask but does not appear in the current window, in which case vcount$[j] = 0$, then a nonempty conflict-cube is detected. Since the algorithm begins with window W_0, lines 16–21 scan the right half of the (s, d)-mask to determine if W_0 has a corresponding non-empty conflict-cube.

```
(0)   procedure detect;
(1)   input: M[0, 2m − 1]-array of 2m symbols representing
(2)                         a normalized (s, d)-mask
(3)   begin
(4)       cube-size := 0;
(5)       (*initialize the count array *)
(6)       for i := 0 to 2m − 1 do
(7)           begin
(8)               vcount[i] := 0;
(9)           end;
(10)      for i := 0 to m − 1 do
(11)          begin
(12)              if (M[i] is a literal derived from x_j, for some j) then
(13)                  vcount[j] := vcount[j] + 1;
(14)          end;
(15)      (* check if W_0 has a non-empty conflict-cube *)
(16)      for i := m to 2m − 1 do
(17)          begin
(18)              if (M[i] is a literal derived from x_j, for some j,) and
(19)                  (vcount[j] = 0) then
(20)                      cube-size := cube-size + 1;
(21)          end;
(22)      (* check each of the m windows for conflicts *)
(23)      i := 0;
(24)      while (i ≤ m − 1) and (cube-size = 0) do
(25)          begin
(26)              if (M[i] is derived from x_j, for some j) then
(27)                  begin
(28)                      vcount[j] := vcount[j] − 1;
(29)                      if (vcount[j] = 0) then
(30)                          cube-size := cube-size + 1;
(31)                  end;
(32)              if (M[i + m] is derived from x_j, for some j) then
(33)                  begin
(34)                      vcount[j] := vcount[j] + 1;
(35)                      if (vcount[j] = 1) then
(36)                          cube-size := cube-size − 1;
(37)                  end;
(38)              i := i + 1;
(39)          end;
(40)      if (cube-size > 0) then
(41)          return ("conflict on window ", i);
(42) end;
```

Figure 6.6. Algorithm for detecting conflicts in an (s, d)-mask

The ith iteration of the main loop on lines 24–39 corresponds to the examination of W_i, where $0 \le i \le m$. First, line 24 terminates the loop if W_i has a corresponding non-empty conflict-cube. If not, then the algorithm "slides" the window to W_{i+1}. As the window slides to W_{i+1} line 26 determines if the symbol falling off the left side of the window is a literal. If so, then the variable x_j from which the literal is derived appears one fewer time in W_{i+1} than in W_i.

Hence, vcount[j] is decremented on line 28. On the other hand, if the symbol entering the window on the right side is a literal derived from some variable x_j then that variable appears one more time in W_{i+1} than in W_i. This is detected on line 32. Hence, vcount[j] is incremented on line 34. Of course, if the symbol leaving the window and the symbol entering the window are derived from the same variable x_j then that variable occurs an equal number of times in W_i and W_{i+1}. Hence, vcount[j] is decremented on line 28 and then incremented on line 34, in which case vcount[j] stays the same. The variable *cube-size* contains an integer representing a count of the number of variables that are missing from the window currently being examined. After examining the entire current window, if the variable *cube-size* contains an integer that is greater than 0, then the conflict-cube corresponding to that window is nonempty. Hence, a conflict exists. The algorithm then terminates the loop on line 24 and returns on line 41. It can be verified that the algorithm in Fig. 6.6 operates in $O(m)$ time, where $2m$ is the length of the (s, d)-mask. □

Recall from Sect. 1 that there exist message patterns that cannot be represented by a single (s, d)-mask. In light of this fact, one dimension along which the above problem can be generalized is in n, the number of (s, d)-masks. Hence, we consider the problem of determining if a set of (s, d)-pairs, represented by a set S of $n \geq 1$ disjoint (s, d)-masks, is conflict-free. First, we describe a polynomial time algorithm that will solve the problem when $n = 2$. We then generalize it to show that the problem can be solved in polynomial time for any $n \geq 1$. In doing so we make use of the following lemma.

LEMMA 6. *Given normalized masks M_1 and M_2, determining if $S(M_1)$ and $S(M_2)$ have nonempty intersection can be done in $O(m)$ time.*

Proof. We reduce the problem to the 2-satisfiability problem [8] in linear time. Since the 2-satisfiability problem is solvable in linear time [6] it follows that detecting if two masks have nonempty intersection can also be solved in linear time.

Let $M_1 = a_0 a_1 \cdots a_{m-1}$ and $M_2 = b_0 b_1 \cdots b_{m-1}$. First normalize M_2 with respect to M_1. By Lemma 1, this step can be performed in $O(m)$ time. Second, a set C of clauses is constructed as follows. Consider each bit position i, where $0 \leq i \leq m - 1$.

Case 1: $a_i = c_1$ and $b_i = c_2$, where $c_1, c_2 \in \{0, 1\}$. Clearly, for $S(M_1)$ and $S(M_2)$ to have nonempty intersection it must be the case that $c_1 = c_2$. Hence, we need only verify that this is true.

Case 2: $a_i = l$ and $b_i = c$, where l is a literal and $c \in \{0, 1\}$. Since $b_i = c$, every address covered by M_2 will have a c on bit position i. If $c = 1$ then a clause consisting of the literal 1 is added to C and otherwise a clause consisting of the literal $\bar{l}$ is added to C. Similarly if $a_i = c$ and $b_i = l$.

Case 3: $a_i = l_1$ and $b_i = l_2$, where l_1 and l_2 are both literals. If there exists an address $e = e_0 e_1 \cdots e_{m-1}$, where $e \in S(M_1) \cap S(M_2)$, then by definition there exist functions f_1 and f_2 such that $\hat{f}_1(M_1) = \hat{f}_2(M_2) = e$, in which case $\hat{f}_1(a_i) = \hat{f}_2(b_i) = e_i$. In other words, $\hat{f}(l_1) = \hat{f}(l_2)$. This implies that $(l_1 \wedge l_2) \vee (\bar{l}_1 \wedge \bar{l}_2)$ is satisfiable, which is equivalent to $(l_1 \vee \bar{l}_2) \wedge (\bar{l}_1 \vee l_2)$. Hence, clauses $(l_1 \vee \bar{l}_2)$ and $(\bar{l}_1 \vee l_2)$ are added to C.

Clearly, this reduction can be performed in $O(m)$ time. Furthermore, it can be verified that the resulting set C of clauses is satisfiable if and only if $S(M_1)$ and $S(M_2)$ have nonempty intersection. Since the 2-satisfiability problem can be solved in linear time [6], it follows that determining if $S(M_1)$ and $S(M_2)$ have nonempty intersection can also be solved in linear time. □

LEMMA 7. *Given a set S of two disjoint normalized* (s, d)*-masks, where each* (s, d)*-mask is of length* $2m$*, determining if the message pattern represented by S is conflict-free can be done in* $O(m^2)$ *time.*

Proof. Let S consist of two *disjoint* normalized (s, d)-masks $M_1 = a_0 a_1 \cdots a_{2m-1}$ and $M_2 = b_0 b_1 \cdots b_{2m-1}$. Clearly, if $S(M_1) \cup S(M_2)$ is conflict-free then both M_1 and M_2 must individually be conflict-free. From Theorem 5 we know M_1 and M_2 can each individually be checked for conflicts in $O(m)$ time. In addition, in order for the union of the two (s, d)-masks to be conflict-free, no (s, d)-pair covered by M_1 can conflict with any other (s, d)-pair covered by M_2. This can be determined as follows.

First, M_2 is normalized with respect to M_1. By Lemma 1, this step can be performed in $O(m)$ time. Next, if some (s, d)-pair covered by M_1 does conflict with some (s, d)-pair covered by M_2 then there exists an i, where $0 \le i \le m$, such that the two (s, d)-pairs have the same bit pattern on W_i. This determination can be made by constructing the sub-masks of M_1 and M_2 on W_i and then testing the two sub-masks to see if they have nonempty intersection. To construct the sub-masks, both M_1 and M_2 are projected onto $I = \{i, i+1, \ldots, i+m-1\}$ giving the masks $M_1(I)$ and $M_2(I)$. This step can be performed in $O(m)$ time. These sub-masks will have nonempty intersection if and only if M_1 and M_2 contain (s, d)-pairs that have the same bit pattern on W_i. By Lemma 6 determining if $M_1(I)$ and $M_2(I)$ have nonempty intersection can be done in $O(m)$ time. Hence, determining if two (s, d)-masks contain (s, d)-pairs conflicting on W_i can be done in $O(m)$ time. Since there are a total of $m + 1$ windows, it follows that checking all of the windows can be done in $O(m^2)$ time. □

We now further generalize the above problem to show the following.

THEOREM 8. *Given a set S of disjoint normalized* (s, d)*-masks, where* $|S| = n$ *and each* (s, d)*-mask is of length* $2m$*, determining if S is conflict-free can be done in* $O(m^2n^2)$ *time.*

Proof. Clearly, each (s, d)-mask must individually be conflict-free. As stated in Theorem 5, this can be determined in $O(m)$ time for each (s, d)-mask. Since there are n (s, d)-masks, a total time of $O(mn)$ is required for this initial test. Next, we must determine if (s, d)-pairs covered by different (s, d)-masks conflict. As in the case where $n = 2$, this can be done by examining each of the $m + 1$ windows. The main difference is that each pair of (s, d)-masks must be examined to see if they conflict on some window. By Lemma 7 this can be determined for each pair of (s, d)-masks in $O(m^2)$ time. Since there are $(\frac{n(n-1)}{2})$ pairs of (s, d)-masks it follows that the total time used is $O(m^2n^2)$. □

6.2   Detecting Congestion in an (s, d)-Mask

In Sect. 6.1 we focused on problems concerned with determining if a set of one or more (s, d)-masks contained conflicts. However, these problems were considered only for standard omega networks, where the bundle size of the network is $b = 1$. In this section we consider many of these same problems for bundled omega networks where $b \geq 1$. For example, consider the problem of determining if the message pattern corresponding to a given (s, d)-mask M is congestion-free for an omega network with bundle size $b \geq 1$. Using a proof similar to that for Theorem 5 we can show the following.

THEOREM 9. *Given a normalized* (s, d)*-mask M of length* $2m$ *and an integer b, determining if $S(M)$ is congestion-free for an omega network with bundle size b can be done in $O(m)$ time.*[2]

Proof. From Theorem 5 it follows that if $b = 1$ then the problem can be solved in $O(m)$ time. More generally, if $b \geq 1$ then the problem can be solved in $O(m)$ time, since determining if an (s, d)-mask is congestion-free for an omega network with bundle size b is the same as determining if the (s, d)-mask has a conflict-cube of size k, where $2^k > b$. In light of this, letting $c = $ cube-size, the algorithm in Fig. 6.6 would only have to be modified by changing line 40 to "if $(2^c > b)$ then" and line 24 to "while $(i \leq m - 1)$ and $(2^c \leq b)$ do." □

---

[2] In this paper we assume that performing a comparison to an integer such as b can be done in unit time.

We now consider an additional generalization of the conflict detection problem. Specifically, we consider the problem of determining if a set of n normalized (s, d)-masks is congestion-free for an omega network with bundle size $b \geq 1$. We show that the problem can be solved in polynomial time if n is fixed. In doing so, we shall make use of the following fact from [3].

FACT 1. *Given two normalized masks M_1 and M_2, each of length m, determining if $S(M_1) \cap S(M_2) = \emptyset$ can be done in $O(m)$ time. In addition, if $S(M_1) \cap S(M_2) \neq \emptyset$, then a normalized mask M_3 such that $S(M_3) = S(M_1) \cap S(M_2)$ can be constructed in $O(m)$ time.*

Note that given a set of n normalized (s, d)-masks, a normalized (s, d)-mask representing the intersection of all of the (s, d)-masks can be computed in $O(mn)$ time, simply by repeatedly applying Fact 1. Using this, we can prove the following.

THEOREM 10. *Given a set of n disjoint normalized (s, d)-masks, where n is fixed and each (s, d)-mask is of length $2m$, determining if the set is congestion-free for an omega network with bundle size $b \geq 1$ can be done in $O(m^2)$ time.*

Proof. As in Theorem 9, each of the $m+1$ windows must be examined for the (s, d)-masks. The main difference is that we must now perform two steps for each window W_j:

1. First we must determine if some subset of the n (s, d)-masks cover a set of (s, d)-pairs that have the same bit pattern on W_j. As in Lemma 7 we must check each window to determine if a set of (s, d)-pairs covered by the (s, d)-masks conflict on that window. This will be done by computing a number of sub-mask intersections using Fact 1.

2. Second, if such a set of (s, d)-pairs exist then we must determine if they create congestion. In other words, if there are more than b (s, d)-pairs having the same bit pattern on W_i. As in Theorem 9 this can be deduced from the size of the appropriate conflict-cubes. We now describe the two steps in further detail.

First, "relabel" the variables in the (s, d)-masks so that each contains a distinct set of variables. If the (s, d)-masks are $M_0, M_1, M_2, \ldots$ then this can be accomplished by renormalizing M_1 with respect to M_0, M_2 with respect to M_1, etc. Since the (s, d)-masks are normalized, it follows from Lemma 1 that this can be performed in $O(mn)$ time. Now consider a subset containing i of the (s, d)-masks, and for each j, where $0 \leq j \leq m$, do the following. First, project the i (s, d)-masks onto window W_j. This step can be performed in $O(mi)$ time. Next, construct a mask representing the intersection of these sub-masks. This can be done by performing $i - 1$ intersections. The resulting sub-mask will be nonempty if and only if there exists a set of (s, d)-pairs covered by the i (s, d)-masks, at least one per (s, d)-mask, having the same bit pattern on W_j. By Fact 1, this step can be performed in $O(mi)$ time. If the resulting mask is empty then we just proceed on to the next window. On the other hand, if the mask is nonempty, then we have detected a set of i (s, d)-masks, $M_{r_0}, M_{r_1}, \ldots, M_{r_{i-1}}$ that covers a set of (s, d)-pairs conflicting on W_j. In such a case, we must count the number of (s, d)-pairs in the set to determine if congestion occurs. Letting $c = |S_{M,j}|$, where M is an (s, d)-mask, it follows that the number of (s, d)-pairs having the same bit pattern on W_j for an (s, d)-mask M is equal to 2^c. It follows that the total number of (s, d)-pairs having the same bit pattern on window W_j is given by

$$p = 2^{c_0} + 2^{c_1} + \cdots + 2^{c_{i-1}} \tag{6.1}$$

where $c_k = |S_{M_{r_k}, j}|$, and $0 \leq k \leq i - 1$. If $p > b$ then since p (s, d)-pairs make use of the same bundle at stage j it follows that congestion occurs. On the other hand, if $p \leq b$ then we just continue on to the next window. Since the conflict-cubes can be computed from the i masks in $O(mi)$ time, it follows that this step can be performed in $O(mi)$ time. Since there are a total of $m + 1$ windows, it follows that we can determine if a subset of i of the (s, d)-masks contains congestion in $O(m^2 i)$ time. In addition, since the total number n of (s, d)-masks is fixed, it follows that there is a constant number of such subsets (2^n), which can each be enumerated in $O(m)$ time. It follows that the total time used is $O(m^2)$. $\qquad\square$

7.   Minimum Round Partitioning for (s, d)-Masks

Once it has been determined that a message pattern creates conflicts or congestion, some routing strategy must be used that transmits the messages through the network in a congestion-free manner. For this purpose, we consider a message routing technique that we call *minimum round partitioning*. In this strategy a set of messages containing congestion is partitioned into a minimum number of *congestion-free* subsets, which we call *rounds*. The set of messages is then transmitted by successively transmitting the messages in each subset.

Minimum round partitioning has been studied by a number of researchers. For example, it is shown in [1] that any message pattern forming a permutation will require at most $O(\sqrt{N})$ rounds. The authors also present a method for calculating a lower bound on the number of rounds required by any given message pattern. In [2] it was shown that the problem is NP-hard for the class of bundled omega networks. Heuristics for the problem are presented in [5, 7, 23]. In [19] and [22] an algorithm is developed for constructing a "partitioning function" for any message pattern that forms a bit-permute-complement permutation. Finally, the relation between the problem and "bottlenecks" in butterfly networks is discussed in [18].

In this section we consider the computational complexity of the minimum round partitioning problem when restricted to the subclass of message patterns that are representable by a single (s, d)-mask. As we shall show, the problem becomes solvable in linear time when restricted to this subclass. This generalizes and extends a result in [19], originally established for bit-permute-complement permutations. We begin by considering the problem for bundled omega networks as described in Sect. 2. The omega network described there had the property that messages could not be "broadcast" to multiple destinations at the same time, or rather, within the same round. This was reflected by the switch states in Figs. 6.3(b)–(g). Hence, two (s, d)-pairs with the same source address were considered to be in conflict. With regards to bundled omega networks where $b \geq 1$, this means that two (s, d)-pairs with the same source address are treated as two different messages. Consequently, the two messages require two different wires when they are transmitted over the same bundle. In Sect. 7.2 we shall reconsider minimum round partitioning for a modified version of the network where broadcasts are allowed to occur.

7.1   Minimum Round Partitioning for Non-Broadcast Omega Networks

In this section we consider the minimum round partitioning problem for those message patterns that can be represented by a single (s, d)-mask. We consider the problem for the omega network as described in Sect. 2. We begin by mentioning a result from [19].

FACT 2. *Given an (s, d)-mask M representing a bit-permute-complement permutation, as in (1), a function $f : S(M) \rightarrow \{0, 1, \ldots, k - 1\}$ can be constructed that defines a partitioning of the message pattern $S(M)$ into a minimum number of rounds.*

It should be noted that the function constructed by the algorithm from [19] is in the form of a polynomial, whose variables are the same as those in the (s, d)-mask M. For example, for the (s, d)-mask $(x_0 x_1 x_2 x_3 x_4, x_4 x_3 x_2 x_1 x_0)$ the function constructed by the algorithm would be $f(x_0, x_1, x_2, x_3, x_4) = x_0 + 2x_1$. We shall provide other examples below, but first we will generalize this result to apply to any (s, d)-mask, bit-permute-complement or otherwise.

LEMMA 11. *Given a normalized (s, d)-mask M, which is of length $2m$, a function $f : S(M) \rightarrow \{0, 1, \ldots, k - 1\}$ that defines a partitioning of the message pattern $S(M)$ into a minimum number of rounds can be computed in $O(m)$ time.*

```
(0)    procedure partition;
(1)    input: M-array of 2m elements representing a normalized (s, d)-mask
(2)    let s = max{i | a literal derived from xᵢ is in the LHS of M}
(3)        t = max{i | a literal derived from xᵢ is in the RHS of M}
(4)    begin
(5)        for i := 0 to 2m − 1 do
(6)            begin
(7)                SOURCE[i] := 0; WT[i] := 0; CUBE[i] := 0; DEST[i] := 0;
(8)            end;
(9)        for i := 0 to m − 1 do
(10)           begin
(11)               if (M[i] is a literal derived from xⱼ, for some j) then
(12)                   SOURCE[j] := SOURCE[j] + 1;
(13)           end;
(14)       if (t ≤ s) then
(15)           big := −1
(16)       else begin
(17)               b := s + 1;
(18)               big := t − s − 1;
(19)               for i := 0 to big do
(20)                   CUBE[b] := 1; WT[b] := i; b := b + 1;
(21)           end;
(22)       for i := 0 to m − 1 do
(23)           begin
(24)               if (M[i + m] is a literal derived from xₚ) then
(25)                   begin
(26)                       if (SOURCE[p] = 0 and DEST[p] = 0) then
(27)                           push(WT[p], Q);
(28)                       DEST[p] := 1;
(29)                   end;
(30)               if (M[i] is a literal derived from x_q) then
(31)                   begin
(32)                       SOURCE[q] := SOURCE[q] − 1;
(33)                       if (SOURCE[q] = 0 and DEST[q]=0) then
(34)                           begin
(35)                               CUBE[q] := 1;
(36)                               if (not empty(Q)) then
(37)                                   WT[q] := pop(Q)
(38)                               else begin
(39)                                       big := big + 1; WT[q] := big;
(40)                                   end;
(41)                           end;
(42)                   end;
(43)           end;
(44)   end;
```
(45) Define: $f_M(x_0, x_1, \ldots, x_{2m-1}) = \sum_{i=0}^{2m-1} \text{CUBE}[i]x_i 2^{\text{WT}[i]} \bmod 2^{\text{big}+1}$

Figure 6.7. Algorithm for computing a partitioning function for a message pattern that is represented by a single (s, d)-mask

Proof. In Fig. 6.7 is an algorithm that will construct such a function. As mentioned above, given the omega network as defined in Sect. 2, a message pattern containing broadcasts will be interpreted to contain conflicts. Hence, the resulting function will define a partition of the message pattern where each broadcast is partitioned into multiple non-broadcast (s, d)-pairs. The algorithm in Fig. 6.7 operates as follows.

Since each (s, d)-pair in the message pattern is specified by an assignment of 0's and 1's to the variables in $V(M)$ it follows that if $k = |S_{M,i}|$ then 2^k (s, d)-pairs have the same bit pattern on window W_i. The algorithm in Fig. 6.7 operates by scanning the (s, d)-mask from left to right. As it scans, it examines each window W_i to determine which variables are, and are not in $S_{M,i}$. This is kept track of by the $2m$ bit arrays SOURCE and DEST.

A particular window W_i currently under examination consists of two parts. One part is that portion of W_i that overlaps with the LHS of the (s, d)-mask, and the other is that portion that overlaps with the RHS. The SOURCE and DEST arrays represent the sets of variables contained in these two portions of W_i, respectively. Hence, lines 9–13 initialize SOURCE$[i] := c$, if c literals appear in W_0 that are derived from x_i. In addition, since window W_0 does not overlap with the right hand side, it follows that for all $0 \le j \le 2m - 1$, DEST$[j]$ is initialized to 0. This takes place on line 7.

For each window W_i and variable $x_p \in S_{M,i}$, an associated "weight" WT$[p]$ is assigned, such that no two variables in $S_{M,i}$ are assigned the same weight. This property guarantees that each of the (s, d)-pairs having the same bit pattern on window W_i are assigned a different value, or round, by the function f. Which weights have, and have not been assigned is kept track of by the variable "big" and the stack "Q." If a variable x_q is in $S_{M,i}$, for any i, where $0 \le i \le m-1$, then CUBE$[q]$ is assigned a 1. Since CUBE$[q]$ is non-zero, this fact will allow WT$[q]$ to be included in the partitioning function (see line 45). If $V(W_0) \subset V(M)$, in which case $t > s$, then those variables in $V(M) - V_0$ must initially be assigned weights. This is done on lines 14–21.

Let $k = \max\{|S_{M,i}|$ such that $0 \le i \le m - 1\}$. Then since there exists a set of 2^k messages having the same bit pattern on some window, it follows that any function that defines a partitioning of the BPC permutation into 2^k rounds is optimum. It can be verified that the function f constructed by the algorithm in Fig. 6.7 is such a function. The proof of correctness for the algorithm is similar to the one given in [19]. Hence, we refer the interested reader there. In addition, it can be verified that the algorithm in Fig. 6.7 operates in $O(m)$ time. $\qquad\square$

It should be noted that given an arbitrary normalized (s, d)-mask, literals derived from any of the variables $x_0, x_1, \ldots, x_{2m-1}$ may appear in the (s, d)-mask. Hence, the arrays DEST, WT and CUBE must be of length $2m$. In addition, the array SOURCE is also of length $2m$. However, since the (s, d)-mask is normalized, the LHS will contain literals derived only from the variables $x_0, x_1, \ldots, x_{m-1}$. Hence, SOURCE actually need only be of length m.

One implication of the above result is that if M is an (s, d)-mask and $k = \max\{|S_{M,i}|$ such that $0 \le i \le m\}$ then 2^k rounds are both necessary and sufficient for the message pattern. The fact that it is necessary follows since 2^k messages conflict on some window, and hence, require use of the same link in the network. The fact that it is sufficient follows from the proof of correctness for the algorithm in Fig. 6.7 and the fact that the resulting function defines a partitioning of the message pattern into 2^k rounds. As an example, one can verify that for the (s, d)-mask $(1x_00x_0x_1x_200, x_3x_4000x_0\overline{x}_1x_2)$ the algorithm in Fig. 6.7 will construct the function $f = 2x_0 + x_1 + 2x_2 + x_3 + 2x_4$.

We now generalize the above result so that it applies to *bundled* omega networks where $b \ge 1$. Before stating and proving the result, we first note that a *round* for an omega network with bundle size $b \ge 1$ is a message pattern S such that for all j, where $0 \le j \le m$, at most b (s, d)-pairs in S have the same bit pattern on W_j. One consequence of this fact is that a *round* for a bundled omega network with $b \ge 1$ is not necessarily a partial permutation.

LEMMA 12. *Given an (s, d)-mask M of length $2m$ and a bundle size $b \ge 1$, a function $f : S(M) \to \{0, 1, \dots, k-1\}$ that defines a partitioning of the message pattern $S(M)$ into a minimum number of congestion-free rounds for an omega network with bundle size b can be computed in $O(m)$ time.*

Proof. Suppose the function f' defines a partition of the message pattern S into a minimum number of rounds $r_0, r_1, \dots, r_{q-1}$ as described in Lemma 11. Construct rounds $r_0', r_1', \dots, r_{n-1}'$, where $n = \lceil q/b \rceil$ by placing all messages from r_i into r_j', where $j = i \bmod n$. Note that the resulting message sets r_i', where $0 \le i \le n-1$, are all congestion-free for an omega network with bundle size b. In proof, consider the messages in the set $r_i' = r_i \cup r_{i+n} \cup r_{i+2n} \cup \cdots$ as they are routed on an omega network with bundle size b. Specifically, consider the number of messages that make use of any particular bundle. Since each message set r_j is a conflict-free round, it follows that each message set r_j that was placed into r_i' contains at most one message that makes use of any particular bundle. Since $n = \lceil q/b \rceil$ it follows that at most b rounds are placed into r_i', and hence, that at most b messages make use of any particular bundle. Hence, r_i' is congestion-free for an omega network with bundle size b.

It also follows that $n = \lceil q/b \rceil$ is the minimum number of congestion-free rounds into which the message pattern can be partitioned, for the following reasons. As discussed above following Lemma 11, if $k = \max\{|S_{M,i}|$ such that $0 \le i \le m\}$ and $q = 2^k$, then the message pattern contains q messages having the same bit pattern on some window. Consequently, these q messages require use of the same bundle in the network. Hence, $\lceil q/b \rceil$ is a lower bound on the number of congestion-free rounds into which S can be partitioned, for an omega network with bundle size $b \ge 1$. It follows that if $n = \lceil q/b \rceil$, then defining $f = f' \bmod n$, gives a function f that minimizes the total number of rounds on the bundled network. Since f' can be constructed from the (s,d)-mask in $O(m)$ time, it follows that f can also be constructed from the (s,d)-mask in $O(m)$ time. □

Note that the algorithm suggested by Lemmas 11 and 12 constructs the function f from an (s,d)-mask rather than the corresponding set of (s,d)-pairs. This fact suggests the following related problem. Suppose a set of (s,d)-pairs is given, *instead of an* (s,d)-*mask*. In the following, we show that Lemma 12 can be used to partition the set into a minimum number of congestion-free rounds in polynomial time when the set can be represented by a single (s,d)-mask. As we shall show, the key to the algorithm lies in the following.

FACT 3. *Let S be a set of (s,d)-pairs that can be represented by a single (s,d)-mask, where $|S| = n$ and each (s,d)-pair is of length $2m$. Then the normalized (s,d)-mask M such that $S = S(M)$ can be computed in $O(mn)$ time* [4].

Using Fact 3 we can now prove the main result of this section.

THEOREM 13. *Let S be a set of (s,d)-pairs that can be represented by a single (s,d)-mask of length $2m$. In addition, let b be an integer $b \geq 1$. Then S can be partitioned into a minimum number of congestion-free rounds for an omega network with bundle size b in $O(mn)$ time.*

Proof. By Fact 3, the set S can be converted into an (s,d)-mask in $O(mn)$ time. Using the algorithm in Fig. 6.7, a function f that defines a partition of the set S into a minimum number of rounds can be constructed from the (s,d)-mask in $O(m)$ time. This function can then be used to partition the set S in $O(mn)$ time. It follows that the total time used is $O(mn)$. □

7.2 Minimum Round Partitioning for Broadcast Omega Networks

As it was used in Sect. 7.1 and described in Sect. 2, the bundled omega network did not allow broadcasts to occur within the same round. For a standard omega network, where $b = 1$, this meant that if a message were to be broadcast to multiple destinations then that message would have to be partitioned into multiple (s,d)-pairs. For a bundled omega network where $b \geq 1$, this meant that two (s,d)-pairs with the same source required the use of 2 different wires when the corresponding messages made use of the same bundle. However, if the switches in the network were modified to allow broadcasts, as shown in Fig. 6.8, then the algorithm in Fig. 6.7 could be modified so that

158

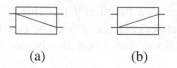

(a)   (b)

Figure 6.8.   Broadcast switch states

broadcasts would not be interpreted as conflicts or congestion. For a standard omega network, where $b = 1$, the function f would then be defined so that it did not "split up" broadcasts. For a bundled omega network where $b \geq 1$, messages with the same source address would use the same wire when the corresponding messages make use of the same bundle. In other words, two messages with the same source address are treated as a single message with 2 destinations. The message is "duplicated" into multiple messages at the switch where the broadcast takes place, as shown in Fig. 6.8. In order to do this, the algorithm in Fig. 6.7 would have to modified as follows.

Let M be an (s, d)-mask and V the set of all variables such that for each $x_i \in V$ there exists a literal in the LHS of M that is derived from x_i. In addition, let V_j be the set of variables that occur or whose complements occur in window W_j, where $0 \leq j \leq m$. Then the conflict-cube $S_{M,j}$ of the (s, d)-mask M corresponding to window W_j would then be redefined to be the set $V - V_j$. Note how this differs from the definition given in Sect. 6, since the set V contains a variable only if that variable occurs *at least once* in the LHS of the (s, d)-mask. This takes account of the fact that those variables occurring *only* in the RHS are responsible for the broadcasts. Given this, it can be verified that the algorithm in Fig. 6.7 can be modified so that it will construct a function that defines a partitioning of the message pattern corresponding to the (s, d)-mask M, into a minimum number of rounds where broadcasts are tolerated.

In the same way that broadcasts were not allowed in the omega network as defined in Sect. 2, multiple messages to the same destination were also not allowed. However, such message patterns might have a legitimate interpretation. For example, if a number of messages are sent to a particular processor and if each message consists of an operand, then the job of the destination processor might be to perform some operation on all of the operands. In such a case, if a switch were given the ability to perform the operation, and if two messages input to a switch were destined for the same processor, then that switch could perform the operation itself. The result of the operation could then be transmitted on the appropriate output (this would of course depend on the algebraic properties of the operation itself, i.e. associativity, etc.). Hence, in the same way that the algorithm in Fig. 6.7 could be modified to tolerate broadcasts, it could instead be modified to tolerate message patterns containing multiple messages with the same destination. To do this, let V be the set of all variables such that if $x_i \in V$ then there exists a literal in the RHS of M that is derived from x_i. The conflict-cube $S_{M,j}$ would then be defined as above.

8. Conclusion

The results in this paper show that the (s, d)-mask formalism is a useful method for describing message patterns. We have shown that the formalism defines a practical, non-trivial generalization of the class of bit-permute-complement permutations. In addition, we have shown that the minimum round partitioning problem, which in general is NP-hard, can be solved in linear time when restricted to those message patterns that can be represented by a single (s, d)-mask. This extends and generalizes a known result in [19]. Finally, we have shown that when message patterns are represented by (s, d)-masks, conflicts and congestion, under many circumstances, can be detected in polynomial time. Such algorithms operate directly upon (s, d)-masks rather than the much larger corresponding message patterns. If message patterns or sets of processor addresses were specified by masks in a multiprocessor, then algorithms that perform computations on masks and/or (s, d)-masks could be helpful or even required.

References

[1] D. P. Agrawal. Graph theoretical analysis and design of multistate interconnection networks. *IEEE Trans. Computers*, C-32(7):637–648, 1983.

[2] P. J. Bernhard and D. J. Rosenkrantz. The complexity of routing through an omega network. In *Proc. Twenty-Fifth Annual Allerton Conf. on Communication, Control and Computing*, 1987. Also Appears as a Technical Report: Comput. Sci. Dept., SUNY Albany, Albany, N.Y., TR 87-12, 1987.

[3] P. J. Bernhard and D. J. Rosenkrantz. Algebraic structure of mask-representable address sets and message patterns. Technical Report, Comput. Sci. Dept., Clemson University, Clemson, SC, 1990.

[4] P. J. Bernhard, H. B. Hunt III, and D. J.Rosenkrantz. Compaction of message patterns into space-efficient representations for multiprocessor interconnection networks. In *Proc. of 1989 Int. Conf. on Parallel Processing*, volume I, pages 111–115. Pennsylvania State Univ., University Park, 1989.

[5] J. S. Deogun and Z. Fang. A heuristic algorithm for conflict resolution problem in multistage interconnection networks. In *Proc. of 1988 Int. Conf. on Parallel Processing*, pages 475–478. Pennsylvania State Univ., University Park, 1988.

[6] S. Even, A. Itai, and A. Shamir. On the complexity of timetable and multicommodity flow problems. *SIAM J. Comput.*, 5:691–703, 1976.

[7] Z. Fang. Mathematical theory of multistage interconnection networks analysis. PhD Thesis, Dept. of Computer Science, University of Lincoln, Nebraska, 1984.

[8] M. R. Garey and D. S. Johnson. *Computers and Intractability: A Guide to the Theory of NP-Completeness*. Freeman, New York, 1979.

[9] R. M. Hardy. Personal communication, 1986.

[10] S. T. Huang and S. K. Tripathy. Self-routing technique in perfect-shuffle networks using control tags. *IEEE Trans. Computers*, 37(2):251–256, 1988.

[11] J. Keohane and R. E. Stearns. Routing linear permutations through the omega network in two passes. In *Proc. of the 1988 Symposium on the Frontiers of Massively Parallel Computation*, George Mason Univ., Fairfax, 1988. Also available as a technical report: Comput. Sci. Dept. SUNY Albany, Albany, N.Y., 1988.

[12] R. R. Koch. Increasing the size of a network by a constant factor can increase performance by more than a constant factor. In *Proc. of the 29th Annual Symposium on Foundations of Computer Science*, pages 221–230, White Plains, 1988.

[13] D. H. Lawrie. Access and alignment of data in an array processor. *IEEE Trans. Computers*, C-21(12):1145–1155, 1975.

[14] D. Nassimi. A fault-tolerant routing algorithm for BPC permutations in parallel computers. In *Proc. of 1989 Int. Conf. on Parallel Processing*, volume 1, pages 278–287. Pennsylvania State Univ., University Park, 1989.

[15] D. Nassimi and S. Sahni. An optimal routing algorithm for mesh-connected parallel computers. *J. ACM*, 27(1):6–29, 1980.

[16] D. Nassimi and S. Sahni. A self-routing Benes network and parallel permutation algorithms. *IEEE Trans. Computers*, C-30(5):332–340, 1981.

[17] D. Nassimi and S. Sahni. Optimal BPC permutations on a cube connected SIMD computer. *IEEE Trans. Computers*, C-31(4):338–341, 1982.

[18] R. E. Newman-Wolfe. Communication issues in parallel computation. PhD Thesis, TR200, Dept. of Computer Science, The University of Rochester, Rochester, NY, 1986.

[19] C. S. Raghavendra and A. Varma. Fault-tolerant multiprocessors with redundant-path interconnection networks. *IEEE Trans. Computers*, C-35(4):307–316, 1986.

[20] H. S. Stone. Parallel processing with the perfect shuffle. *IEEE Trans. Computers*, C-20(2):153–161, 1971.

[21] T. H. Szymanski and V. C. Hamacher. On the permutation capability of multistage interconnection networks. *IEEE Trans. Computers*, C-36(7):810–822, 1987.

[22] A. M. Varma. Design and analysis of reliable interconnection networks. PhD Thesis, Dept. of Elect. Eng. Systems, University of Southern Cal., Los Angeles, CA 90089-0781, 1986.

[23] C. L. Wu and T. Y. Feng. On a class of multistage interconnection networks. *IEEE Trans. Computers*, C-29(8):694–702, 1980.

[24] P. C. Yew and D. H. Lawrie. An easily controlled network for frequently used permutations. *IEEE Trans. Computers*, C-30(4):296–301, 1981.

Chapter 7

REPRESENTABILITY OF DESIGN OBJECTS BY ANCESTOR-CONTROLLED HIERARCHICAL SPECIFICATIONS*

LIN YU AND DANIEL J. ROSENKRANTZ

Department of Computer Science, State University of New York at Albany, Albany, NY 12222, USA

Reprinted from: *SIAM J. Computing*, Vol. 21, No. 5, Oct. 1992, pp. 824–855. © SIAM

Abstract   A simple model, called a VDAG, is proposed for succinctly representing hierarchically specified design data in CAD database systems where there are to be alternate expansions of hierarchical modules. The model uses an ancestor-based expansion scheme to control which instances of submodules are to be placed within each instance of a given module. The approach is aimed at reducing storage space in engineering design database systems and providing a means for designers to specify alternate expansions of a module.

  The expressive power of the VDAG model is investigated, and the set of design forests that are VDAG-generable is characterized. It is shown that there are designs whose representation via VDAGs is exponentially more succinct than is possible when expansion is uncontrolled. The problem of determining whether a given design forest is VDAG-generable is shown to be NP-complete, even when the height of the forest is bounded. However, it is shown that determining whether a given forest is VDAG-generable and producing such a VDAG if it exists, can be partitioned into a number of simpler subproblems, each of which may not be too computationally difficult in practice. Furthermore, for forests in a special natural class that has broad applicability, a polynomial time algorithm is provided that determines whether a given forest is VDAG-generable, and produces such a VDAG if it exists. However, the paper shows that it is NP-hard

* This research was supported in part by the National Science Foundation under grants DCR86-03184 and CCR88-03278. A preliminary extended abstract of this paper appeared in Proceedings of the Ninth Annual ACM SIGACT-SIGMOD-SIGART Symposium on Principles of Database Systems, April 1990, Nashville, Tennessee.

S.S. Ravi, S.K. Shukla (eds.), *Fundamental Problems in Computing*,
© Springer Science + Business Media B.V. 2009

164

to produce a minimum-sized such VDAG for forests in this special class, even
when the height of the forest is bounded.

Keywords: hierarchical modules, databases, design objects, versions, module alternatives,
conditional expansion, configuration control

AMS (MOS) subject classifications: 68P15, 68Q25, 68R05

Received by the editors July 10, 1989; accepted for publication (in revised form) August 26,
1991.

1. Introduction

We investigate a model of hierarchically represented design objects, which
accommodates design versions and alternatives by permitting the inclusion of
a submodule within a larger module to be conditional on the identity of the
ancestors of the larger module. This concept of ancestor-controlled expansion
of hierarchical modules is formalized by a simple model called a VDAG. The
expressibility of the VDAG model is explored, and the design objects that are
directly representable via the VDAG model are characterized. Several computational problems dealing with the representability of objects via this model
are considered. The computational complexity of these problems is studied,
and several appropriate algorithms are developed.

In many design applications, designs are both specified and represented *hierarchically*, where each design object can contain instances of lower level
objects within it. This use of hierarchy expedites the design process, and permits very large design objects to be represented relatively succinctly. The issue
of storing designs is complicated by the need for *version control* [2, 3, 8, 10,
13, 15, 19] and *design alternatives* [1, 11, 17]. Version control has to deal
with multiple versions of a given design object, with the possibility that these
versions differ only slightly. Design alternatives involve multiple designs, with
the possibility that a given higher level object contains somewhere within it
more than one alternative design for instances of a given lower level object.
For a recent survey of version control issues, see [9].

In existing version control systems for software engineering and document
generation systems, the differences between two versions are usually described
on a line basis [13, 15]. The differences between two given files can be computed by algorithms such as those in [6, 7] and the utility program *diff* in Unix
system [16]. With this approach, version differences that are kept track of are
line differences. Sometimes, the differences being kept track of are database
units, such as *record differences* [14]. In [3], a technique is proposed for storing different versions of a text file, based on a model in which each version can

be envisioned as an AVL tree, each of whose vertices represents a line of text. The set of trees may share common subtrees, and a data structure is proposed that keeps only one copy of certain common subtrees. From an abstract perspective, the method used in [3] is a particular technique for storing a forest of trees compactly, by storing only one copy of common subtrees. This raises the general issue of how to produce a compact representation of a given forest. For this problem, the kind of ancestor-based control of tree expansion considered here can lead to more compact representations.

In this paper, we consider hierarchically specified design objects, and focus on *module differences* in that the basic granularity of differences that are kept track of are instances of submodules within a higher level module. Using module differences to support design alternatives has emerged as an issue in CAD systems. Several schemes have been incorporated in [17]. For instance, one scheme allows a module to have alternate *bodies* that share a common *interface*, and a *configuration* of a module can be created by specifying which alternative body to use for submodules within that module. A configuration can have a different expansion specification for each instance of the same module type within it. Another mechanism provided in [17] is conditional expansions, which can be based on the values of generic parameters. Conditional expansion involves a test to determine whether given submodule instances should be placed within a given module body. The generic parameters, which are typically involved in such tests, are passed in a top-down manner to a given module, and so represent control passed to the module from its ancestors in the hierarchy. A model is proposed in [1] whereby a module can have alternate implementations (corresponding to bodies in VHDL), which share a common interface. A body can have *instantiations* of submodules, and can be *parameterized* by a specification of which body to use for specified occurrences of submodules. However, the model in [1] does not provide any explicit mechanism to control expansion. Furthermore, in the model of [1] certain kinds of alternatives are not supported conveniently, in the sense that they require the creation of separate implementations, even though they may differ only slightly. For example, suppose we want module A to contain certain submodules when it is used as a submodule of B and to contain some other submodules when it is used as a submodule of C. In this case, the model in [1] would require two distinct implementations for module A.

In this paper, a *hierarchically specified* set of *modules* is a collection of modules, each of which can have a body. A module body contains *instances* of lower level modules, where some of these instances might only be conditionally included in the body. A given *hierarchically specified design module* can be envisioned as a *design tree*. For example, suppose that within the body of design module Z there are three *submodules*, where two are instances of

X and the other is an instance of Y; within the body of each module X there are submodules U and V; within the body of each module Y there are two submodules that are instances of W; and the body of each W contains two submodules that are instances of T. Figure 7.1 shows module Z at different levels of abstraction, and the tree representation of module Z is shown in Fig. 7.2. Note that module Z includes the vertex Z and all of its descendants in the tree. In the tree, for each arc $a = (u, v)$, there is a function $st(a)$ (where "st" standards for *stamp*) that provides information about the occurrence of v as a submodule within u.

In the tree of Fig. 7.2, there are two copies of X, U, V, and W, respectively, and four copies of T. If the tree were to be stored directly, there would be a copy of the design data for each *instance* of a module within Z; e.g., there would be four copies of T. However, in CAD systems, a more succinct representation is usually used for hierarchically specified designs; namely, a *directed acyclic multigraph* (*dag*). The dag representation for module Z is shown in Fig. 7.3. Thus, a hierarchically specified set of modules can be represented as a multigraph, where each vertex represents a module. If the body of module Z contains an instance of module X, we say "X is a direct submodule of Z." Corresponding to this instance of X within the body of Z, the dag contains an arc from the vertex representing Z to the vertex representing X. If there is a directed path from Z to X, we say "X is a submodule of Z."

In this dag representation, only one copy of the design data for each module is kept, regardless of the number of the instances of the module involved in the design. The dag representation uses an appropriate stamp to keep track of information about instances of submodules within other modules, such as the two instances of T within W. Since the dag representation reduces duplication of design module descriptions, it is more space efficient to store hierarchically specified design data this way. Also, designers typically use a hierarchical approach to design their modules, so the dag would typically capture the design in the form specified by the designer.

An issue in the formulation of the dag model is that sometimes designers want to have alternative designs for a given module, and sometimes want to use different designs for different instances of a given submodule within a higher level module. We consider the following problem: how to succinctly represent hierarchically specified design module data that supports design alternatives and version control. To illustrate this problem, consider the example shown in Fig. 7.4, where the three multigraphs represent three different versions of a design module H.

The conventional dag representation, as depicted in Fig. 7.3, involves no control over expansion. In the forest represented by such a dag, all the subtrees corresponding to a given vertex of the dag are identical; therefore, expansion

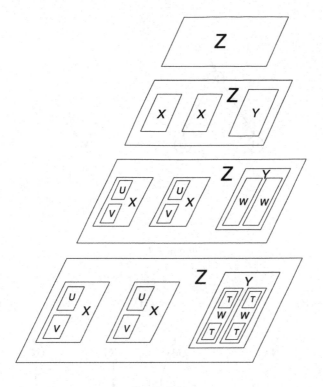

Figure 7.1.

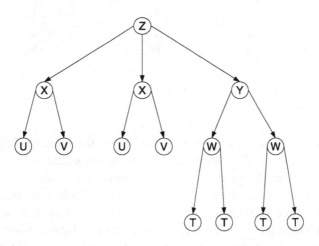

Figure 7.2.

control is needed to represent versions and alternatives. The emphasis of this work is on the foundation of mechanisms for controlling expansions. We focus on using the identity of ancestors to control expansion.

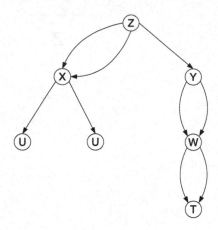

Figure 7.3.

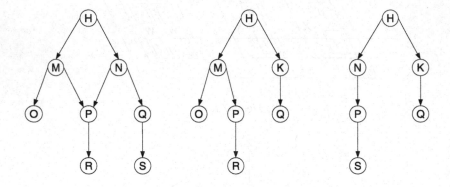

Figure 7.4.

Since we do not want to keep multiple copies of the same module for differ-ent versions, we can use the following scheme, as illustrated in Fig. 7.5, to store *versioned* hierarchically specified design module data. Under this scheme, we create one source vertex for each design version of module H (note that these newly added source vertices are "dummies" that do not contain actual design data), and we place labels on each arc to indicate to which version or versions the arc belongs. Since the amount of storage for the labels would generally be relatively small compared with the amount of storage saved from eliminating duplicated copies of submodules, this representation is more succinct than a method that keeps all of the design data for each version in separate files. If the number of versions is large and the differences between versions are rela-tively small, the storage savings can be quite significant.

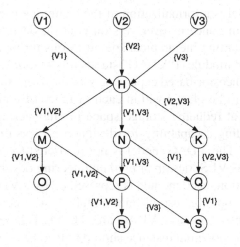

Figure 7.5.

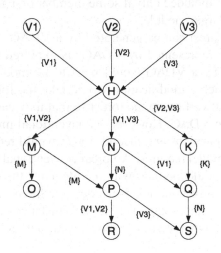

Figure 7.6.

Of course, since we are concerned with succinctness of the design representation, we would like to represent the labels succinctly. For example, in Fig. 7.5, we might use $\{M\}$ as the label for the arc from M to O, instead of $\{V1, V2\}$, since every instance of M in the forest of Fig. 7.4 contains an instance of O. Thus it is appealing to consider a more general scheme in which the elements of a label for an arc from u to v are either u or some ancestors of u in the dag. The example in Fig. 7.6 illustrates how the generalized scheme can be used to represent the three designs of Fig. 7.4.

The VDAG model is a formalization of the technique used in Figs. 7.5 and 7.6, which blends in concerns over version control, design alternatives, and hierarchy by representing hierarchical specifications through alternate expansions of hierarchical modules ("VDAG" stands for *versioned dag*). The VDAG model features an ancestor-based expansion scheme to control which instances of submodules are to be placed within each instance of a given module. The approach is aimed at reducing storage space in engineering design database systems and providing a capability for designers to specify alternate expansions of a module. The VDAG model is not restricted to any specific design applications, such as VLSI design or civil engineering design.

In this formalization, each module is represented by a VDAG vertex having a unique tag. Each possible use of one module as a direct instance within a larger module is represented as a VDAG arc. The arc is labeled with a specification as to when the potential instance should indeed be a real instance within the larger module. This specification is ancestor-based. It can say that the instance should always be included within the larger module, or it can say that the instance should be included only if some member of a given list of modules is an ancestor of the larger module.

Not every design forest can be generated by a VDAG. The issue of which design forests can be represented by VDAGs is explored here. A forest that cannot be generated by a VDAG would have to be modified in order to be VDAG-generable. Such a modification would take the form of changing the identity of some of the vertices in the forest so that they can be represented by distinct vertices in the VDAG. However, a conventional model of hierarchical designs, where all expansions are unconditional, would require more duplication than the VDAG model requires. Atypical conventional CAD system might have a file for each module, perhaps with the file name the same as the module name. If a variant of a given module is needed, the file is copied, modified appropriately, and the variant module is renamed. Instances of the given module (within larger modules) that are to use the new variant are modified to use the new module name.

In [18] we introduced the VDAG model, provided some algorithms to process VDAGs, and investigated some combinatorial problems involved in processing a given VDAG.

The remaining sections are organized as follows. In Sect. 2, we present some basic definitions and concepts. In Sect. 3, we investigate the expressive power of the VDAG model. The complexity of determining whether a design forest can be generated by a VDAG is examined in Sect. 4. An important natural class of design forests is identified in Sect. 5, and a polynomial time algorithm is provided to build a VDAG, when one exists, for a given design forest in that class. In Sect. 6, we address the search space issue in construction of arc labels. In Sect. 7, non-VDAG-generable forests are dealt with. The relative conciseness of the VDAG model in comparison with the conventional dag model is examined in Sect. 8. Simplification problems are considered in Sect. 9.

2. Basic Definitions and Concepts

DEFINITION. In a dag $G(V, A)$, where V is a set of vertices and A a set of arcs, a vertex u is an ancestor of a vertex v if u is v or there is a directed path from u to v in G.

DEFINITION. A *design tree* is a triple (T, t, st) where T is a tree, t is a function that assigns each vertex v of T a value $t(v)$ called the *tag* of v, and st is a function that assigns each arc a of T a value $st(a)$ called the *stamp* of a.

In a design tree, each vertex v represents a *module*. The tag $t(v)$ on a vertex v contains the design data for the module represented by that vertex. We assume that a portion of a tag serves as a module identifier. The information in the tag may also include an interface description describing how the module is connectable when used as a direct submodule within a larger module. For example, the tag might contain a formal parameter list, comparable to a list of input and output ports of a VLSI module.

An arc a from vertex u to vertex v represents an instance of module v as a submodule occurring within module u. For arc a, the stamp $st(a)$ is the information specifying how the instance of v occurs inside u. For example, the stamp may specify the location and/or orientation of the instance within u. The stamp might also contain an actual parameter list; for instance, in the VLSI application $st(a)$ might specify which signal of u is connected to each port of the instance.

Note that a design tree is an unordered tree. If it is desired that the ordering of children of a vertex should have some significance, this ordering information can be incorporated in the stamps on the arcs going to the children. In that case, the arcs existing from the same vertex will have distinct stamps.

DEFINITION. A *design forest* is a set of design trees such that each tag of a root vertex contains an identifier occurring nowhere else in the forest.

The tag on the root of each tree serves to uniquely identify the tree as a design module, or perhaps as a particular version or alternative of a design module.

In the future we often use "tree" and "forest" to mean design tree and design forest, respectively.

DEFINITION. A VDAG is a four tuple (G, t, st, l), where G is a directed, acyclic multigraph with vertex set V and arc set A; t is a function mapping each vertex v to a unique value denoted by $t(v)$, (t for *tag*); st is a function mapping each arc a to a value denoted by $st(a)$, (st for *stamp*); and l is a function mapping each arc a to a nonempty subset of ancestors of the vertex exited by a, and is denoted by $l(a)$ (l for *label*).

Since each VDAG vertex has a tag containing a unique identifier, we assume that a label $l(a)$ for an arc a is represented as a list of tag identifiers. (For convenience in presenting results and examples, we will often equate a tag with its tag identifier, but in practice we anticipate that a vertex would contain an entire tag, and a label would contain just tag identifiers.) The interpretation of element w in $l(a)$, where arc a goes from u to v, is that whenever an instance of module w has an instance of u as a submodule, or a submodule of a submodule, etc., then each instance of u within the instance of w should contain an instance of v within the instance of u. This concept is formalized below in the definition of a "generating path."

Each vertex of the VDAG might have the format shown in Fig. 7.7, where vertex v has k exiting arcs pointing to (not necessarily distinct) submodules $v_1, \ldots, v_k$. The *connection data* contains stamps, labels, and pointers to submodules. The *design data* contains the tag of v. Fig. 7.7 is only intended to be suggestive of how the design information might be stored, and many variations are possible. For instance, there might be a separate file for each VDAG vertex.

EXAMPLE. Given a forest of two trees representing two versions of a design as shown in Fig. 7.8(a), a possible VDAG representation is shown in Fig. 7.8(b). (In this example, the arcs all have stamp δ.)

From the examples given above, we observe that if there is a path in the forest that starts at a root vertex with tag A and ends at a vertex with tag B, then module A contains an instance of B as a submodule. Each such path in the forest corresponds to a VDAG path that starts at the vertex with tag A and ends at the vertex with tag B, and has appropriate labels and stamps on its arcs. Similarly, for each properly labeled path in the VDAG, there should be a corresponding path in the design forest. However, care is needed in formalizing

Design data for vertex v		
tag(v)		
Connection data	Connection data	Connection data
for arc a_1:	for arc a_2:	for arc a_k:
stamp(a_1),	stamp(a_2),	$\ldots$ stamp(a_k),
label(a_1),	label(a_2),	label(a_k),
pointer to(v_1)	pointer to(v_2)	pointer to(v_k)

Figure 7.7.

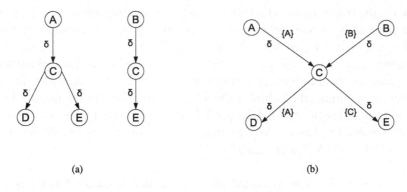

Figure 7.8.

the concept of properly labeled paths. For instance, in Fig. 7.8(a), A contains D but B does not, even though there may seem to be a path from B to D in Fig. 7.8(b). To capture the concept of a properly labeled VDAG path, which corresponds to the containment relationship, we formulate the following definition. The idea behind this definition is that a given path can be extended by a given arc exiting the path's endpoint only if the path contains at least one vertex that is an element of the given arc's label.

DEFINITION. In a given VDAG (G, t, st, l), a valid path is either a single vertex v_0, or is a sequence of arcs $a_1, a_2, \ldots, a_k$ in A, $k \geq 1$, such that there exist vertices $v_0, v_1, \ldots, v_k$ for which for all i, $1 \leq i \leq k$, arc a_i connects v_{i-1} to v_i, and the intersection of $l(a_i)$ and $\{v_0, v_1, \ldots, v_{i-1}\}$ is nonempty. A *generating path* is a valid path whose initial vertex is a source of G.

Note that, by the definition of a generating path, for each source vertex v in V, there is a generating path from v to v, and if a sequence of arcs $a_1, a_2, \ldots, a_k$ is a generating path, then so are each of its prefixes of the form $a_1, a_2, \ldots, a_j$, where $1 \leq j < k$. The significance of a generating path from v_0 to v_k is that an instance of module v_0 contains an instance of v_k as a submodule because of that generating path. In particular, v_0 contains an instance of v_1, which in turn contains an instance of v_2, etc. The generating path corresponds to this sequence of nested module instances.

DEFINITION. Given a VDAG β, the *exploded forest generated by* β is a forest F with a distinct vertex for each distinct generating path in β. The tag on the vertex corresponding to such a path is the same as the tag of the last vertex in the path. For each source vertex v_0 in β, forest F contains a root vertex corresponding to the generating path consisting of the single vertex v_0. For each generating path consisting of a single arc a from a source vertex v_0 to a vertex v_1, the tree vertex corresponding to the generating path v_0 is the parent of the tree vertex corresponding to the generating path a. For each generating path $a_1, \ldots, a_k$, having at least two arcs, the tree vertex corresponding to the generating path $a_1, \ldots, a_{k-1}$ is the parent of the tree vertex corresponding to $a_1, \ldots, a_k$. There are no other vertices and arcs in F. The stamp on the tree arc between a parent and a child is the same as the stamp of the last arc in the generating path for the child. Given a VDAG β, we will denote the exploded forest generated by β as F_β. We say that a design forest F is *VDAG-generable* if there exists a VDA β such that $F = F_\beta$.

Given a VDAG β, the exploded forest generated from the VDAG is a set of design trees, with a tree root for each source vertex in β. The relationship between a given VDAG and this set of design trees constitutes the meaning of the VDAG; the purpose of the VDAG is to represent the set of design trees that it generates.

Recalling Fig. 7.8, the exploded forest generated by the VDAG in Fig. 7.8(b) is the forest shown in Fig. 7.8(a). Figure 7.9 is the exploded forest generated by the VDAG in Fig. 7.6.

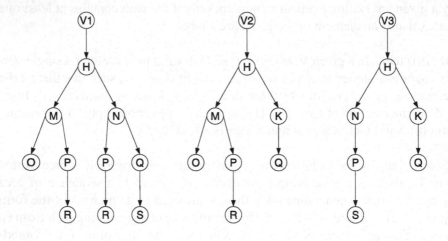

Figure 7.9.

We now show that the problem of finding a VDAG that generates a given forest is no harder than the problem of finding a VDAG that generates a given tree. Consider an algorithm SUPERTREE, which given a forest F containing k trees with source tags $s_1, s_2, \ldots, s_k$, as shown in Fig. 7.10(a), returns a forest consisting of a single tree, as follows. (1) Add a "super source" with a tag S not in F; (2) make $s_1, s_2, \ldots, s_k$ each a child of S where the stamps on the arcs from S to its children are assigned arbitrary unique values $\delta_1, \delta_2, \ldots, \delta_k$, as shown in Fig. 7.10(b).

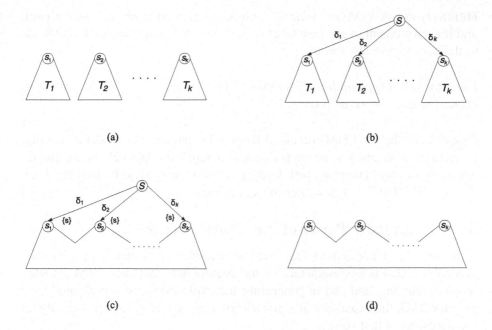

Figure 7.10.

PROPOSITION 2.1. *A forest F is* VDAG-*generable if and only if* SUPER-TREE(F) *is* VDAG-*generable.*

Proof. (if) Suppose that a VDAG α, as shown in Fig. 7.10(c), generates SUPERTREE(F). A VDAG β generating F can be constructed from α as follows. First vertex S and its exiting arcs are deleted. Then each occurrence of S as a label element in a remaining arc, say from vertex u to vertex v, is replaced by those members of the set $\{s_1, s_2, \ldots, s_k\}$ that are ancestors of u. (VDAG α and β are illustrated in Figs. 7.10(c) and (d), respectively.) It is easy to see that β generates F.

(only if) Suppose a VDAG β, as shown in Fig. 7.10(d), generates F. Then SUPERTREE(F) is generated by the VDAG a shown in Fig. 7.10(c), which is obtained from β by adding a new vertex of tag S and for each i, $1 \le i \le k$, one arc from S to s_i with stamp δ_i and label $\{S\}$. $\square$

From the proof of Proposition 2.1, we observe that the problem of finding a VDAG that generates a given forest is not significantly harder for forests containing multiple trees than for forests containing a single tree.

A VDAG arc, vertex, or label element that is uninvolved in any generating path is useless in producing the exploded forest represented by the VDAG. The set of VDAGs without such useless components can be formalized as follows.

DEFINITION. A VDAG is *valid* if each arc occurs on some generating path, and if each element of each arc label occurs on some generating path that leads to the vertex exited by the arc.

LEMMA 2.2. *Given an invalid* VDAG α, *here exists a valid* VDAG *that generates the same forest as* α *does.*

Proof. Let β be the VDAG obtained from α by deleting vertices and arcs that do not occur on any generating paths, and deleting arc label elements that do not occur on any generating path leading to the vertex exited by the arc. Then β is a valid VDAG that generates the same forest as α.   □

3.   Expressive Power of the VDAG Model

In Sect. 1, we pointed out that there are certain forests that are not VDAG-generable. This is a consequence of the requirement that each VDAG vertex has a unique tag, and that in generating the exploded forest represented by a given VDAG, the expansion of a given vertex in the forest can depend only on the ancestors of that vertex.

For example, there are no VDAGs that generate the design forests in Fig. 7.11(a) and Fig. 7.11(b), since each tree contains two instances of B that are indistinguishable by the tags of their ancestors, but which are expanded differently. It is also the case that the VDAG model cannot be used for forests that represent recursively defined design modules. An example of such a forest is shown in Fig. 7.11(c).

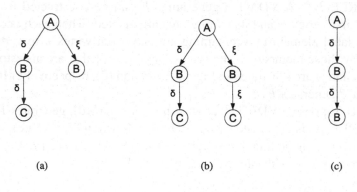

(a)   (b)   (c)

Figure 7.11.

If a given design forest cannot be generated by a VDAG, the forest can be modified by using new tag values for certain vertices. For instance, in each of the examples of Fig. 7.11, one of the B vertices could have its tag changed to B', and the modified design forest would be VDAG-generable. The VDAG would have separate vertices with tags B and B', with replication of data in the tag.

We now investigate the conditions under which a design forest F can be generated by a VDAG.

DEFINITION. Given a vertex u in a forest F, pathtag(u) is the set of all tags of vertices on the path from a forest root to u (including the tag of u itself). For each tag in F, anctag(t) is the union of pathtag(u) over all vertices having tag t.

Consider a forest F and a given tag t. Consider the set of paths starting at a root and ending at a vertex with tag t. As shown in Fig. 7.12, let these paths be $p_1, p_2, \ldots$, and p_k, having endpoints $u_1, u_2, \ldots, u_k$, respectively. Suppose there is a u_i, $1 \le i \le k$, having m exiting arcs with stamp δ that enter vertices with tag t', $m \ge 0$, and there is a u_j, $i \le j \le k$, $j \ne i$, having n exiting arcs with stamp δ that enter vertices with tag t', where $n > m$. Then in each VDAG that generates F, if any, there must be at least n arcs with stamp δ going from t to t'. Furthermore, of this set of arcs, there must be $n - m$ arcs having labels that are each disjoint from pathtag(u_i) but not disjoint from pathtag(u_j). In other words, there must be $n - m$ arcs whose label l satisfies the conditions that $l \cap \text{pathtag}(u_i) \ne \emptyset$ and $l \cap \text{pathtag}(u_j) \ne \emptyset$. An obvious necessary condition for this is that pathtag(u_j) − pathtag(u_i) is nonnull. However, the requirements on the VDAG are more subtle.

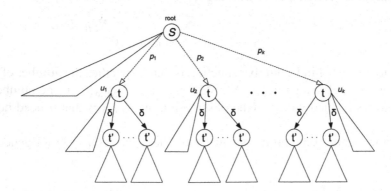

Figure 7.12.

DEFINITION. For a given forest F, tag t, tag t', and stamp δ, if F contains at least one arc with stamp δ going from a vertex with tag to a vertex with tag t', we say that (t, t', δ) is a *relevant triple* for F. We call a forest or VDAG arc that exits a vertex with tag t, enters a vertex with tag t', and has stamp δ, a (t, t', δ)-arc.

It will turn out that whether or not a given forest is VDAG-generable involves a certain combinatorial property for each relevant triple. First consider the following definitions pertaining to relevant triples.

DEFINITION. Given a vertex u with tag t, a tag t', and a stamp δ in a forest F, let $\mathrm{num}(u, t', \delta)$ be the number of (t, t', δ)-arcs exiting from u. Given a relevant triple (t, t', δ) for F, let $\mathrm{maxnum}(t, t', \delta)$ be the maximum number of (t, t', δ)-arcs exiting from a vertex with tag t, i.e.,

$$\mathrm{maxnum}(t, t', \delta) = \max\{\mathrm{num}(u, t', \delta) \mid u \text{ has tag } t\},$$

and let $\mathrm{totnum}(t, t', \delta)$ be the total number of (t, t', δ)-arcs, i.e.,

$$\mathrm{totnum}(t, t', \delta) = \sum_{\text{vertices } u \text{ with tag } t} \mathrm{num}(u, t', \delta).$$

To capture the labeling requirements imposed by F, we define the concept of a "number function" for a relevant triple, as follows.

DEFINITION. Given a design forest F and a relevant triple (t, t', δ), a *number function* $N_{t,t',\delta}$ for F and (t, t', δ) is a mapping from the nonempty subsets of $\mathrm{anctag}(t)$ to the nonnegative integers, i.e.,

$$N_{t,t',\delta} : (2^{\mathrm{anctag}(t)} - \emptyset) \to \mathbf{N},$$

such that for all vertex u in F with tag t,

$$\mathrm{num}(u, t', \delta) = \sum_{\gamma \text{ such that } \gamma \cap \mathrm{pathtag}(u) \neq \emptyset} N_{t,t',\delta}(\gamma).$$

The intuition behind a number function is that it specifies the number of arcs having each label in a particular VDAG for F; i.e., $N_{t,t',\delta}(\gamma)$ is the number of (t, t', δ)-arcs labeled with γ. One observation on $N_{t,t',\delta}$ is that it need not be unique.

We now define some properties that will characterize the VDAG-generable forests.

DEFINITION. A design forest F is *tag-acyclic* if merging vertices of F with the same tag does not create cycles.

DEFINITION. A relevant triple for a design forest is *labelable* if a number function exists for it. A design forest is *labelable* if all of its relevant triples are labelable.

DEFINITION. A design forest is *well structured* if it is tag-acyclic and labelable.

It will be shown that a given forest is VDAG-generable if and only if it is well structured.

LEMMA 3.1. *Every well-structured design forest is* VDAG-*generable*.

Proof. Consider a well-structured design forest F. Consider any directed multigraph with a vertex for each tag occurring in F, and a set of arcs satisfying the constraint that there is an arc from the vertex with tag t to the vertex with tag t' only if F contains an arc from a vertex with tag t to a vertex with tag t'. Since F is tag-acyclic, any such multigraph is acyclic.

Now consider the following directed acyclic multigraph a of the above form. Multigraph α has a vertex for each tag occurring in F. For each relevant triple (t, t', δ), let $N_{t,t',\delta}$ be a number function; since F is labelable, such a number function exists. Based on this number function, multigraph α is given a set of labeled (t, t', δ)-arcs. For each set γ such that $N_{t,t',\delta}(\gamma)$ is nonzero, the number of (t, t', δ)-arcs with label γ in a is $N_{t,t',\delta}(\gamma)$. Note that the elements of each such label γ are ancestors of the vertex for t in α; therefore, the labeled directed acyclic multigraph α is a VDAG. The constraints on $N_{t,t',\delta}$ guarantee that the exploded forest generated by α is the original design forest. $\square$

LEMMA 3.2. *If a design forest is* VDAG-*generable, it is well structured*.

Proof. Consider a design forest F. Suppose F is generated by VDAG α. By Lemma 2.2, we may assume that α is valid.

Since α does not contain cycles and each arc of F corresponds to an arc of whose endpoints have the same tags as the arc in F, F must be tag-acyclic.

The remaining task is to show that F is labelable. We claim that for each relevant triple (t, t', δ) for F, a number function $N_{t,t',\delta}$ exists. For a given tag t, let v_t be the vertex of α whose tag is t. Because α is valid, every label element x occurring in the label of an arc exiting the VDAG vertex v_t has the property that α has a generating path p going from a source vertex to vertex v_t, such that x occurs on p. Since forest F is the exploded forest generated from α, F contains a vertex u corresponding to path p. This vertex u has tag t, and has x as a member of $\mathrm{pathtag}(u)$. Consequently, x is a member of $\mathrm{anctag}(t)$. Since this is true for each label element of each arc exiting v_t, the label of each arc exiting v_t is a nonempty subset of $\mathrm{anctag}(t)$. Now, on the basis of α, define a function $N_{t,t',\delta}$ from $(2^{\mathrm{anctag}(t)} - \emptyset)$ to **N** as follows. For each nonempty subset γ of $\mathrm{anctag}(t)$, define $N_{t,t',\delta}(\gamma)$ to be the number of (t, t', δ)-arcs in α with label γ.

We now show that the specified function $N_{t,t',\delta}$ is indeed a number function for F. Consider a vertex u of F having tag t. Since F is the exploded forest generated from α, VDAG α has a generating path p corresponding to u, such that this generating path ends at the vertex v_t, whose tag is t. Furthermore, each (t, t', δ)-arc exiting vertex u in F corresponds to an extension of path p to a longer generating path by the use of a VDAG arc having stamp δ that exits v_t and enters the vertex $v_{t'}$, having tag t', such that the arc's label γ has a nonnull intersection with the vertices in path p. Since γ is a subset of $\mathrm{anctag}(t)$, this arc contributes to the value of $N_{t,t',\delta}(\gamma)$. Thus $\mathrm{num}(u, t', \delta)$ equals the number of (t, t', δ)-arcs in α having a label whose intersection with the vertices on path p is nonempty. Furthermore, each such arc has a label that is a subset of $\mathrm{anctag}(t)$. Consequently,

$$\sum_{\substack{\gamma \text{ such that} \\ \gamma \cap \mathrm{pathtag}(u) \neq \emptyset}} N_{t,t',\delta}(\gamma) = \mathrm{num}(u, t', \delta).$$

Therefore, for each relevant triple (t, t', δ), the specified function $N_{t,t',\delta}$ is indeed a number function for F. Hence F is labelable. □

A consequence of Lemmas 3.1 and 3.2 is the following.

THEOREM 3.3. *A design forest is* VDAG-*generable if and only if it is well structured.*

4. VDAG Construction

We now consider the problem of determining if a given design forest F is well structured. First consider tag-acyclicity. To test tag-acyclicity, a given forest can be collapsed into a graph having single vertex for each tag in the forest (thereby merging all forest vertices having the same tag), and having a single arc for all the forest arcs whose endpoints have the same tag. This conversion is described in algorithm COLLAPSE, shown in Fig. 7.13.

ALGORITHM COLLAPSE

Input: forest $F = (T, t, st)$
Output: a graph

    1 for each distinct tag t in F, create a vertex with tag t and call the vertex t;

    2 for each pair of tags (t, t') such that in F, a vertex with tag t is a parent of a vertex with tag t', create an edge from t to t' in the graph.

Figure 7.13.

PROPOSITION 4.1. *A forest F is tag-acyclic if and only if* COLLAPSE(F) *is acyclic.*

Proof. The proof is obvious. □

An observation on the tag-acyclicity of a forest F is that it can be tested in linear time. The graph COLLAPSE(F) can be constructed in linear time, and a topological sorting on COLLAPSE(F) can be done in time linear in its size [12].

If a given forest F is tag-acyclic, we can perform a labelable test on F to determine whether it is well structured. Detecting the labelable condition, however, can be a difficult computational task, as indicated by the following result. The problem of determining if a forest is VDAG-generable is *NP*-complete; furthermore, the problem is *NP*-complete even for forests of bounded height.

DEFINITION. The *height* of a forest F is the number of arcs on a longest path from a source vertex to a leaf vertex. The *depth* of a vertex u in a forest is the number of arcs on the path from a source vertex to u.

We observe that Proposition 2.1 implies that (1) if the VDAG-generability problem for forests of height h is *NP*-hard, the VDAG-generability problem for trees of height $h + 1$ is also *NP*-hard; and (2) if the VDAG-generability problem for trees of height h is computationally easy, the VDAG-generability problem for forests of height $h - 1$ is also easy.

The following result concerns the size of a VDAG with respect to the size of a forest it represents.

THEOREM 4.2. *For a VDAG-generable forest F and a number function $N_{t,t',\delta}$ for F, it is the case that*

$$\sum_{\gamma \in (2^{\text{anctag}(t)} - \emptyset)} N_{t,t',\delta}(\gamma) \leq \text{totnum}(t, t', \delta).$$

Proof. Consider a number function $N_{t,t',\delta}$ for relevant triple (t, t', δ). For each vertex u with tag t and at least one exiting (t, t', δ)-arc, it is the case that

$$\text{num}(u, t', \delta) = \sum_{\gamma \text{ such that } \gamma \cap \text{pathtag}(u) \neq \emptyset} N_{t,t',\delta}(\gamma).$$

Because of the above equality, it is possible to associate each of the forest arcs that contribute to $\text{num}(u, t', \delta)$ with a set γ having a nonnull intersection with $\text{pathtag}(u)$, such that exactly $N_{t,t',\delta}(\gamma)$ of these arcs are associated with each set γ. Since the association can be done for each vertex u having tag t, each arc that contributes to $\text{totnum}(t, t', \delta)$ is associated with exactly one set γ.

Now consider a set γ such that $N_{t,t',\delta}(\gamma)$ has a nonzero value, say k. Because γ is a nonnull subset of $\text{anctag}(t)$, F contains a vertex u with tag t such that $\gamma \cap \text{pathtag}(u)$ is nonnull. Consequently, there are k arcs exiting u that have been associated with γ. Since this is true for each γ, and the total number of arcs available for association is only $\mathrm{totnum}(t, t', \delta)$, it is the case that

$$\sum_{\gamma \in (2^{\mathrm{anctag}(t)} - \emptyset)} N_{t,t',\delta}(\gamma) \le \mathrm{totnum}(t, t', \delta).$$

$\square$

THEOREM 4.3. *For each $h \ge 4$, given a design tree F of height h that is tag-acyclic, the problem of determining if F is VDAG-generable is NP-complete.*

Proof. Theorem 3.3 implies that F has a VDAG representation if and only if a labeling can be found. By Theorem 4.2, for each relevant triple (t, t', δ), the number of sets γ such that $N_{t,t',\delta}(\gamma)$ is nonzero cannot exceed the number of vertices in F. Thus a nondeterministic Turing machine can guess a labeling and verify in time polynomial in the size of F that the labeling satisfies the constraints of the labelable condition. Consequently, the set of well-structured forests is in *NP*.

The *NP*-hardness is by a reduction from the Graph 3-Coloring Problem (for undirected graphs) [4].

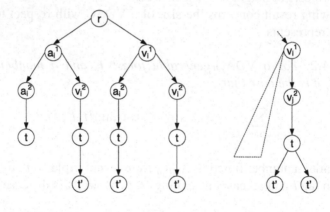

Figure 7.14.   *Figure 7.15.*

Consider graph $G(V, E)$, where $V = \{v_1, v_2, \ldots, v_n\}$, which is to be 3-colored. We construct a design tree F as follows. The root of F, denoted *root*, has tag r. For each v_i in V, F contains four distinct tags, v_i^1, v_i^2, a_i^1, and a_i^2. Also, for each v_i in V, *root* has two subtrees, headed by v_i^1 and a_i^1 respectively, as shown in Fig. 7.14. For each edge (v_i, v_j) in V, $i < j$, the vertex with tag v_i^1 previously placed in F has a subtree, headed by v_j^2, as shown in Fig. 7.15. F also contains three distinct tags, b^1, b^2, and Q, where *root* has two subtrees, headed by Q and b^1, respectively, as shown in Fig. 7.16. All arcs in F have stamp δ.

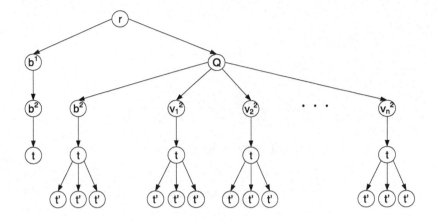

Figure 7.16.

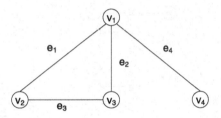

Figure 7.17.

For instance, given the Graph 3-Coloring instance shown in Fig. 7.17, the constructed forest F is shown in Fig. 7.18. A VDAG generating F is shown in Fig. 7.19.

Note that the size of F is linear in the size of the given graph, that F has height 4, and that F is tag-acyclic. Also, as illustrated in Fig. 7.19, we observe that all arcs, except for (t, t', δ)-arcs, can be labeled by $\{r\}$; so there is clearly a number function for each relevant triple, with the possible exception of the triple (t, t', δ).

Suppose F can be generated by a VDAG. Consider VDAG arcs from t to t'. Since the forest paths r, b^1, b^2, t and r, a_i^1, a_i^2, t, for $1 \le i \le n$, end in vertices with no children, the VDAG cannot contain any (t, t', δ)-arc whose label contains r, t, b^1, b^2, a_i^1, or a_i^2.

For each i, $1 \le i \le n$, the paths r, a_i^1, v_i^2, t and r, v_i^1, a_i^2, t require that v_i^1 and v_i^2 each must appear in exactly one (t, t', δ)-arc label, since each of the occurrences of t on the two paths has only one child whose tag is t'. Because the occurrence of t in path r, v_i^1, v_i^2, t has exactly one child of tag t', tags v_i^1 and v_i^2 must appear in the same (t, t', δ)-arc label.

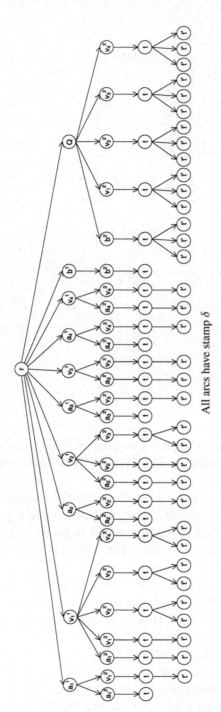

All arcs have stamp δ

Figure 7.18.

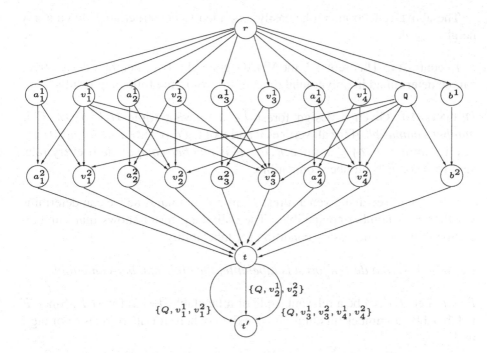

Figure 7.19.   All arcs whose label is not shown have label $\{r\}$. All arcs have stamp δ

Consider the path r, Q, b^2, t. Since this t has 3 children whose tag is t', the VDAG must contain exactly three (t, t', δ)-arcs whose labels contain Q. For each i, $1 \leq i \leq n$, because of the path r, Q, v_i^2, t, where this occurrence of t has 3 children whose tag is t', the (t, t', δ)-arc in whose label v_i^1 and v_i^2 occur must be one of the three (t, t', δ)-arcs whose label contains Q. All possible label elements have now been accounted for. The VDAG must have exactly three (t, t', δ)-arcs. The label of each of these three arcs must contain Q, plus some subset of tags corresponding to the members of V, with each v_i^1, v_i^2 pair occurring on exactly one of these three arcs. The occurrence of tags corresponding to each member of V in the label of exactly one of these three VDAG arcs represents an assignment of one of three colors to each member of V.

Now consider each edge e in E. Suppose $e = (v_i, v_j)$, where $i < j$. F contains a path r, v_i^1, v_j^2, t, where this occurrence of t has two children whose tags are t'. This requires that $\{v_i^1, v_i^2\}$ and $\{v_j^1, v_j^2\}$ occur in the labels of two distinct (t, t', δ)-arcs of the VDAG, i.e., v_i and v_j must be assigned different colors in G. Thus if F is VDAG-generable, then graph G is 3-colorable.

If G is 3-colorable, we can construct a labeling for (t, t', δ) as follows. For each set of vertices $v_{c_1}, \ldots, v_{c_k}$ of G which have the same color, let there be a VDAG arc with label $\{Q, v_{c_1}^1, v_{c_1}^2, \ldots, v_{c_k}^1, v_{c_k}^2\}$. By the previous discussion, this is indeed a labeling for (t, t', δ). Hence F is VDAG-generable.

The above reduction can be easily extended to construct an F having any height $h \geq 4$. □

In contrast to Theorem 4.3, the VDAG-generability of height 3 design trees can be determined in polynomial time, as shown in the following results.

DEFINITION. Given a design forest F, a relevant triple (t, t', δ) of F is *number-compatible* if for all vertices u and v of tag t, $\text{pathtag}(u) \subseteq \text{pathtag}(v)$ implies $\text{num}(u, t', \delta) \leq \text{num}(v, t', \delta)$. F is *number-compatible* if every relevant triple of F is number-compatible.

It is easy to see that given a forest F, in polynomial time we can determine whether F is number-compatible. The following result shows that number-compatibility is a necessary condition for labelability.

LEMMA 4.4. *If a design forest is labelable, then it is number-compatible.*

Proof. Let (t, t', δ) be a relevant triple of a labelable design forest F. Since F is labelable, a number function $N_{t,t',\delta}$ exists, where for all vertices w of tag t in F,

$$\sum_{\gamma:\, \gamma \cap \text{pathtag}(w) \neq \emptyset} N_{t,t',\delta}(\gamma) = \text{num}(w, t', \delta).$$

Now consider two vertices of tag t in F, say u and v, such that $\text{pathtag}(u) \subseteq \text{pathtag}(v)$. Then for all $\gamma \in (2^{\text{anctag}(t)} - \emptyset)$, if $\gamma \cap \text{pathtag}(u) \neq \emptyset$ then $\gamma \cap \text{pathtag}(v) \neq \emptyset$. But this in turn implies that

$$\sum_{\gamma:\, \gamma \cap \text{pathtag}(u) \neq \emptyset} N_{t,t',\delta}(\gamma) \leq \sum_{\gamma:\, \gamma \cap \text{pathtag}(v) \neq \emptyset} N_{t,t',\delta}(\gamma).$$

Hence $\text{num}(u, t', \delta) \leq \text{num}(v, t', \delta)$, so (t, t', δ) is number-compatible. Since this is true for all relevant triples, F is number-compatible. □

Our next results show that a design tree of height at most 3 is VDAG-generable if and only if it is tag-acyclic and number-compatible.

LEMMA 4.5. *Let F be a tag-acyclic design tree of height at most 3. If F is number-compatible, then F is labelable.*

Proof. Let (t, t', δ) be a relevant triple of F, and let

$$\text{minnum}(t, t', \delta) = \min\{\text{num}(u, t', \delta) \mid u \text{ has tag } t\}.$$

If $\text{maxnum}(t, t', \delta) = \text{minnum}(t, t', \delta)$, then for all vertices u and v with tag t, $\text{num}(u, t', \delta) = \text{num}(v, t', \delta)$, and (t, t', δ) is labelable since we can specify a number function $N_{t,t',\delta}$ by assigning $N_{t,t',\delta}(\{t\}) = \operatorname{minnum}(t,t',\delta)$, and for all nonempty $\gamma \subseteq \operatorname{anctag}(t)$ where $\gamma \neq \{t\}$, $N_{t,t',\delta}(\gamma) = 0$.

So now suppose that $\operatorname{minnum}(t,t',\delta) < \operatorname{maxnum}(t,t',\delta)$, and we need to find a number function for (t,t',δ). Note that for any vertex u, with tag t, occurring at depth 0 or 1 in F, $\operatorname{num}(u,t',\delta) = \operatorname{minnum}(t,t',\delta)$. Also, since the height of F is at most 3, if there is a vertex u of depth 3 with tag t, this u has no children; so, in this case, $\operatorname{num}(u,t',\delta) = 0 = \operatorname{minnum}(t,t',\delta)$. Thus, every vertex u for which $\operatorname{num}(u,t',\delta) > \operatorname{minnum}(t,t',\delta)$ is of depth 2. Suppose q is the tag of a depth 1 vertex, having a (depth 2) child whose tag is t. Since F is number-compatible, all depth 2 vertices u having tag t and a parent whose tag is q have the same value for $\operatorname{num}(u,t',\delta)$. Let this value be designated as $\operatorname{enum}(q,t,t',\delta)$. For a tag q' that is not the tag of any depth 1 vertex having a child whose tag is t, let $\operatorname{enum}(q',t,t',\delta)$ be undefined.

We now construct $N_{t,t',\delta}$ as follows. We assign $N_{t,t',\delta}(\{t\}) = \operatorname{minnum}(t,t',\delta)$. For each q for which $\operatorname{enum}(q,t,t',\delta)$ is defined, we assign $N_{t,t',\delta}(\{q\}) = \operatorname{enum}(q,t,t',\delta) - \operatorname{minnum}(t,t',\delta)$. For all other nonempty subsets γ of $\operatorname{anctag}(t)$, we assign $N_{t,t',\delta}(\{\gamma\}) = 0$. By number-compatibility of F and our previous discussion, it is easily verified that $N_{t,t',\delta}$ is indeed a number function for (t,t',δ).

Since the above construction of a number function can be applied to all of the relevant triples of F, F must be labelable. $\qquad \Box$

THEOREM 4.6. *A design tree F of height at most 3 is* VDAG-*generable if and only if it is tag-acyclic and number-compatible.*

Proof. The proof is a direct result from Theorem 3.3 and Lemmas 4.4 and 4.5. $\Box$

THEOREM 4.7. *The* VDAG-*generability problem for trees of height at most 3 can be solved in polynomial time.*

Proof. Tag-acyclicity and number-compatibleness of design trees can each be tested in polynomial time. By Theorem 4.6, these tests are sufficient to determine whether a design tree of height 3 is VDAG-generable. $\qquad \Box$

5. Stamp Uniqueness Property and the Effect of Bounded Stamp Multiplicity

It is likely that in many design applications, for instance, applications in civil engineering design, mechanical design, or VLSI layout, the stamps on the arcs exiting from any given design tree vertex and entering vertices with the same tag would have to be distinct (e.g., it is not meaningful or useful in the design application for two instances of the same type of submodule to be placed in exactly the same position within a larger module). The class of design objects having this property is important, and covers the forests that would arise in many design systems. In this section we formalize this class of design forests, characterize the VDAGs that generate members of this class, and show that it is computationally easy to determine if a given forest in this class is VDAG-generable. This contrasts with the computational difficulty of determining if an arbitrary forest is VDAG-generable.

DEFINITION. Given a design forest F, let

$$\text{stpmult}(F) = \max_{u, t', \delta}\{\text{num}(u, t', \delta)\}$$

Given a VDAG α, let

stpmult(α) = max$\{m \mid \alpha$ contains vertices u and v such that there are m arcs from u to v having the same stamp.$\}$

Stpmult stands for *stamp multiplicity*.

We now show that determining whether a given forest is VDAG-generable is NP-complete, even for forests whose stamp multiplicity is 2.

THEOREM 5.1. *It is NP-complete to determine whether a given forest F, where* stpmult(F) $= 2$, *is* VDAG-*generable*.

Proof. The argument for membership in *NP* is the same as in the proof of Theorem 4.3. The *NP*-hardness proof is by a reduction from Not-All-Equal 3SAT, which is known to be NP-complete [4]. A Not-All-Equal 3SAT instance consists of a set of variables X and a set of clauses C, each of which contains three literals. The computational problem is whether there is a truth assignment to the variables such that each clause has at least one literal *true* and at least one literal *false*.

Consider a given Not-All-Equal 3SAT instance with $X = \{x_1, x_2, \ldots, x_n\}$ and $C = \{c_1, c_2, \ldots, c_m\}$, where for each j, $1 \leq j \leq m$, c_j contains literals l_j^1, l_j^2, and l_j^3, and the index of the variable corresponding to l_j^1 is less than the index of the variable corresponding to l_j^2, which in turn is less than the index of the variable corresponding to l_j^3. Construct the forest F consisting of the single tree whose form is shown in Fig. 7.20. For example, given the Not-All-Equal 3SAT instance shown in Fig. 7.21, the constructed forest F is shown in Fig. 7.22, and a VDAG generating F is shown in Fig. 7.23. Note that stpmult(F) $= 2$, F is tag-acyclic, and the size of F is linear in m and n. Also note that there is a number function for each relevant triple, with the possible exception of (A, B, δ).

Suppose the forest is VDAG-generable, and consider relevant triple (A, B, δ). Consider the occurrences of A in paths S, W, A; S, Y, A; $S,$

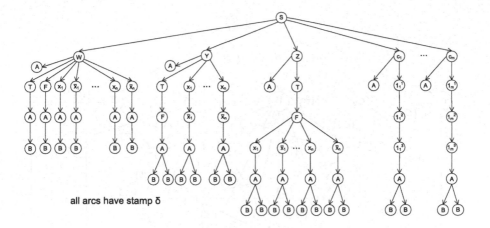

Figure 7.20.

$$X = \{x_1, x_2, x_3\}$$
$$C = \{(x_1, \bar{x}_2, x_3), (x_1, x_2, \bar{x}_3)\}$$

Figure 7.21.

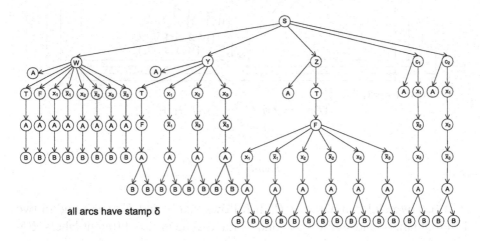

Figure 7.22.

Z, A and for each j, $1 \leq j \leq m$, S, c_j, A. Since each such A has no child with tag B, it follows that S, W, Y, Z, c_j, and A cannot appear in the label of any VDAG arcs from A to B. Consider paths S, W, T, A; S, W, F, A and for each i, $1 \leq i \leq n$, S, W, x_i, A and S, W, $\bar{x}_i$, A. Since each occurrence of A in each of these paths has exactly one child with tag B, it follows that T, F, x_i, $\bar{x}_i$ each appears in the label of exactly one VDAG arc from A to B. Consider paths S, Y, T, F, A and S, Y, x_i, $\bar{x}_i$, A, where each occurrence

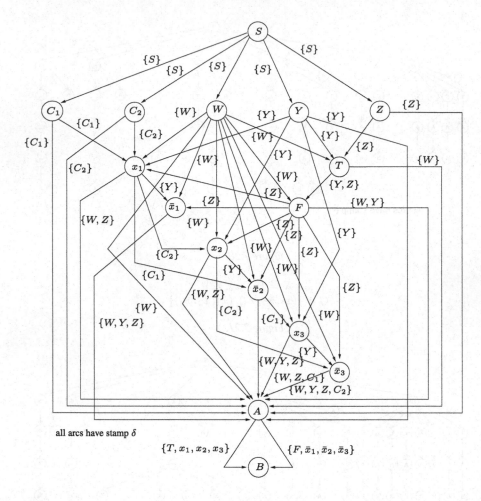

Figure 7.23.

of A has two children with tag B. It follows that T and F have to be in two different labels; and similarly, x_i and $\bar{x}_i$ have to be in two different labels. Because each occurrence of A on paths S, Z, T, F, x_i, A and S, Z, T, F, $\bar{x}_i$, A has two children with tag B, x_i and $\bar{x}_i$ must be in the labels containing T or F. It follows that there must be exactly two VDAG arcs with stamp δ from A to B. Now consider, for each j, $1 \le j \le m$, the occurrence of A in the path S, c_j, l_j^1, l_j^2, l_j^3, A. This A has two children with tag B, hence at least one of the three literals must appear in the label containing T and at least one of the three literals must appear in the label containing F. We may interpret the literals in the label containing T as being assigned *true* and the literals in the label containing F as being assigned *false* in the truth assignment for the Not-All-Equal 3SAT instance. Thus the appearance of literals in the two arcs from A to B in a VDAG generating F represent a not-all-equal satisfying truth assignment.

By the above discussion, the given Not-All-Equal 3SAT has a satisfying truth assignment if and only if there is a labeling on VDAG arcs from A to B, that is, if and only if F is VDAG-generable. □

DEFINITION. Let UnqStamp be the set of design forests such that no two arcs exiting from the same vertex and entering vertices with the same tag have the same stamp, i.e., forests whose stamp multiplicity is 1. Let $\mathrm{VD}_{\mathrm{UnqStamp}}$ be the set of VDAGs such that no two arcs with the same endpoints have the same stamp, i.e., VDAGs whose stamp multiplicity is 1.

Later we will show that there is a close correspondence between UnqStamp and $\mathrm{VD}_{\mathrm{UnqStamp}}$.

We now consider VDAG-generability problem for forests in UnqStamp. First, note that from Theorem 3.3, a given member of UnqStamp is VDAG-generable if and only if it is well structured. To be well structured, the design forest must be both tag-acyclic and labelable. Since even for arbitrary forests, tag-acyclicity is testable in linear time, the main computational issue is labelability. The forests in Figs. 7.11(a) and (b) are examples of forests in UnqStamp that are tag-acyclic, but not labelable, and therefore not VDAG-generable. In both these examples, a number function for relevant triple (B, C, δ) does not exist because the forest contains vertices u and v with tag B such that $\mathrm{num}(u, C, \delta) = 1$, $\mathrm{num}(v, C, \delta) = 0$, and $\mathrm{pathtag}(u)$ is contained in $\mathrm{pathtag}(v)$. This phenomenon can serve as the basis for a polynomial time test for labelability, as follows.

LEMMA 5.2. *The problem of determining whether a member of* UnqStamp *is* VDAG-*generable can be solved in polynomial time.*

Proof. Consider a given forest F in UnqStamp. Using the algorithm COL-LAPSE from Proposition 4.1, F can be tested for tag-acyclicity in linear time. If F is not tag-acyclic, then it is not VDAG-generable. Thus, assume F is tag-acyclic, and consider its labelability.

Note that since F is in UnqStamp, for any vertex u, tag t', and stamp δ, $\mathrm{num}(u, t', \delta)$ is at most 1. Given a relevant triple (t, t', δ), let the set of all paths from a root to a vertex u with tag t, where $\mathrm{num}(u, t', \delta) = 0$ be $P_0(t, t', \delta)$, and the set of all paths from a root to a vertex u with tag t, where $\mathrm{num}(u, t', \delta) = 1$ be $P_1(t, t', \delta)$. Let $\Gamma_0(t, t', \delta)$ be the set of all tags occurring in the paths in $P_0(t, t', \delta)$. Similarly, let $\Gamma_1(t, t', \delta)$ be the set of all tags occurring in the paths in $P_1(t, t', \delta)$. For each p in $P_1(t, t', \delta)$, we check if the set of tags of vertices on path p is contained in $\Gamma_0(t, t', \delta)$. If one such p exists, $N_{t,t',\delta}$ cannot exist, and F is not labelable. Otherwise, let $N_{t,t',\delta}(\Gamma_1(t, t', \delta) - \Gamma_0(t, t', \delta)) = 1$, and for all $\gamma \neq \Gamma_1(t, t', \delta) - \Gamma_0(t, t', \delta)$, let $N_{t,t',\delta}(\gamma) = 0$. It is easy to see that $N_{t,t',\delta}$ satisfies the requirements for a number function. If for each relevant triple (t, t', δ), $N_{t,t',\delta}$ is found, F is labelable. Otherwise, F is not labelable. Note that the above test can be done in polynomial time. □

If a forest F in UnqStamp is well structured, then Algorithm VDAGCONS, shown in Fig. 7.24, constructs a VDAG that generates F.

ALGORITHM VDAGCONS

Input: a forest F in UnqStamp

Output: a VADG α generating F, if F is well structured

1. if F is not ta-acyclic, **exit**;

2. apply algorithm used in the proof of Lemma 5.2 to F;

   if F is not well structured, **exit**;

3. let α have a vertex for each tag occurring in F;

   for relevant triple (t, t', δ) **do**

      let α have an arc a with stamp δ going from the vertex with tag t to the vertex with tag t', and label arc a with $(\Gamma_1(t, t', \delta) - \Gamma_0(t, t', \delta))$ as described in the proof of Lemma 5.2.

Figure 7.24.

THEOREM 5.3. *Given a member of* UnqStamp, *say F, we can in polynomial time,* (1) *determine whether F is* VDAG-*generable; and* (2) *if F is indeed* VDAG-*generable, construct a VDAG that generates F.*

Proof. Algorithm VDAGCONS terminates in polynomial time. If it terminates by *exit*, the given forest is not VDAG-generable, as implied by the proof of Lemma 5.2; otherwise, it is VDAG-generable. If Algorithm VDAGCONS constructs a VDAG, then from the proof of Lemma 5.2, this VDAG generates F. □

We next note that the algorithm in the proof of Lemma 5.2 is applicable not only to forests in UnqStamp, but to any relevant triples for which the value of maxnum is 1, even if other relevant triples have a larger value of maxnum.

DEFINITION. A relevant triple (t, t', δ) for a design forest F has the *unique stamp property* if $\text{maxnum}(t, t', \delta) = 1$.

THEOREM 5.4. *If a relevant triple (t, t', δ) for a forest F has the unique stamp property, then we can in polynomial time* (1) *determine if (t, t', δ) is labelable; and* (2) *if it is, construct a number function for (t, t', δ).*

Proof. Apply the algorithm from the proof of Lemma 5.2. □

We now show that the set of forests generated by members of $\text{VD}_{\text{UnqStamp}}$ is identical to the set of VDAG-generable members of UnqStamp.

THEOREM 5.5. *The set of forests generated by members of* $\text{VD}_{\text{UnqStamp}}$ *is precisely the set of forests in* UnqStamp *which are* VDAG-*generable.*

Proof. Consider a forest F which is a well-structured member of UnqStamp. Then, $\alpha = \text{VDAGCONS}(F)$ is a VDAG generating F. Since for each relevant triple (t, t', δ), the constructed VDAG α has exactly one (t, t', δ)-arc, α is a member of $\text{VD}_{\text{UnqStamp}}$.

Now consider a member α of $\text{VD}_{\text{UnqStamp}}$. No two arcs of α with the same endpoints have the same stamp; therefore, if a vertex of forest F_α has more than one child with the same tag, the stamps on the arcs from the vertex to these children must have distinct stamps. Hence F_α is a member of UnqStamp. □

6. Construction of Number Functions

Theorems 4.3 and 5.1 imply that finding a labeling for a forest is *NP*-hard. If $P \neq NP$, this task cannot be done in polynomial time. However, finding a labeling can be divided into a set of independent subtasks, namely finding a number function for each relevant triple (t, t', δ). In searching for a number function for a given relevant triple, an obvious approach is to enumerate potential number functions in a canonical order, and check whether the labelable condition is satisfied. The search space can be reduced because if a given forest is labelable, its number functions are "sparse," in a sense formalized by the following result. The next result shows that if there is a number function, then there is one in which $N_{t,t',\delta}(\gamma)$ is nonzero for only a small number of sets γ.

THEOREM 6.1. *If a relevant triple* (t, t', δ) *for a forest F is labelable, then it has a number function* $N_{t,t',\delta}$ *for which*

$$\sum_{\gamma \in (2^{\text{anctag}(t)} - \emptyset)} (|\gamma| \cdot N_{t,t',\delta}(\gamma)) \leq \text{totnum}(t, t', \delta).$$

Proof. Let α be a valid VDAG generating F. For each relevant triple (t, t', δ), consider the (t, t', δ)-arcs in α. From the proof of Theorem 4.2, each (t, t', δ)-arc in F can be associated with one of these arcs in α; and each of these arcs in α is associated with at least one of these arcs in F. This association can be strengthened by associating each F arc with a single element of the label of its associated α arc. In particular, since an F arc exiting a vertex u is associated with an α arc having label γ such that $\gamma \cap \text{pathtag}(u)$ is nonnull, let the F

arc be associated with some arbitrary member of $\gamma \cap \text{pathtag}(u)$. Note that because α is valid, each arc label in α will have at least one F arc associated with at least one of the elements of the label.

Now, modify the arc labels in α by deleting every label element that has no F arc associated with it. Let β be the resulting VDAG. Then β is a valid VDAG that generates F. Let $N_{t,t',\delta}$ be the number function for (t, t', δ) that is embodied in β. Each arc of F that contributes to $\text{totnum}(t, t', \delta)$ is associated with some label element in β, and each label element is associated with at least one such arc. A label γ in β is, therefore, associated with at least $|\gamma|$ arcs of F. Since there are only $\text{totnum}(t, t', \delta)$ arcs available for this association, it is the case that

$$\sum_{\gamma \in (2^{\text{anctag}(t)} - \emptyset)} (|\gamma| \cdot N_{t,t',\delta}(\gamma)) \leq \text{totnum}(t, t', \delta). \qquad \square$$

COROLLARY 6.2. *If a given design forest F is* VDAG-*generable, then there exists a* VDAG α *generating F whose size is linearly bounded by the size of F.*

Proof. First, note that the number of vertices in a valid VDAG generating F cannot exceed the number of distinct tags on vertices in F. Theorem 6.1 implies that the total number of occurrences of label elements in α need not exceed the number of vertices in F. Since arc labels are nonempty, the total number of arcs cannot exceed the total number of label elements, and thus cannot exceed the total number of vertices in F. $\qquad \square$

Another observation that can sometimes reduce the search space for a number function is that the members of $\text{anctag}(t)$ for tag t can be partitioned on the basis of occurrences in paths, and only one representative from each block of the partition need be considered. This concept can be formalized as follows.

DEFINITION. Given a forest F and a tag t, two tags p, q in $\text{anctag}(t)$ are *equivalent* with respect to t if for every vertex u such that $t(u) = t$, either p and q are both in $\text{pathtag}(u)$ or neither is. Let $\text{neqtag}(t)$ be a set that contains exactly one member from each tag equivalence class with respect to t.

For each relevant triple (t, t', δ), the search space for a number function $N_{t,t',\delta}$ can be reduced to nonnull subsets of $\text{neqtag}(t)$, instead of $\text{anctag}(t)$, as shown by the following result.

DEFINITION. For each γ that is a subset of $\text{anctag}(t)$, let $\text{neq}(\gamma)$ be the subset of $\text{neqtag}(t)$ defined as follows: a member w of $\text{neqtag}(t)$ is in $\text{neq}(\gamma)$ if and only if γ contains at least one member of the equivalence class represented by w.

LEMMA 6.3. *If a relevant triple* (t, t', δ) *for a forest* F *is labelable, then it has a number function for which each argument having a nonzero value is a nonnull subset of* neqtag(t).

Proof. Suppose that there is a number function $N_{t,t',\delta}$ for (t, t', δ). On the basis of this number function, define a function $M_{t,t',\delta}$ from $(2^{\text{anctag}(t)} - \emptyset)$ to $\mathbf{N}$ as follows. For each nonnull subset ξ of neqtag(t), let

$$M_{t,t',\delta}(\xi) = \sum_{\gamma:\text{neq}(\gamma)=\xi} N_{t,t',\delta}(\gamma).$$

For each set ξ that contains a member of $(\text{anctag}(t) - \text{neqtag}(t))$, let $M_{t,t',\delta}(\xi) = 0$.

Note that from the definition of the equivalence relation used to construct neqtag(t), for each vertex u with tag t in F, and each subset γ of anctag(t), $\gamma \cap \text{pathtag}(u)$ is nonnull if and only if $\text{neq}(\gamma) \cap \text{pathtag}(u)$ is nonnull; therefore, since $N_{t,t',\delta}$ is a number function for (t, t', δ), so is $M_{t,t',\delta}$. Furthermore, $M_{t,t',\delta}$ only has a nonzero value for subsets of neqtag(t). $\square$

The search space for a number function can be reduced even further, as follows.

DEFINITION. Given a forest F and a relevant triple (t, t', δ), let $\Gamma_0(t, t', \delta)$ be the set of tags that occur in pathtag(u) for some vertex u of the forest having tag t and for which num(u, t', δ) equals zero. Let candtag(t, t', δ) be $(\text{neqtag}(t) - \Gamma_0(t, t', \delta))$.

Note that a member of $\Gamma_0(t, t', \delta)$ cannot be a member of any set γ for which a number function for (t, t', δ) has a nonzero value. Thus we can confine the search for a number function for (t, t', δ) to nonnull subsets of candtag(t, t', δ). This can be formalized as follows.

THEOREM 6.4. *If a relevant triple* (t, t', δ) *for a forest* F *is labelable, then it has a number function for which each argument having nonzero value is a nonnull subset of* candtag(t, t', δ).

The search space can be reduced still further by observing that two vertices in a forest having the same tag t and whose ancestors include the same subset of candtag(t, t', δ) are equivalent with respect to finding a labeling. If forest F contains two vertices u and v with tag t such that pathtag$(u) \cap$ candtag$(t, t', \delta) = \text{pathtag}(v) \cap \text{candtag}(t, t', \delta)$, then for (t, t', δ) to be labelable it must be the case that num$(u, t', \delta) = \text{num}(v, t', \delta)$. Suppose that this condition is not violated for relevant triple (t, t', δ). Let $\psi(t, t', \delta)$ be the collection of subsets of candtag(t, t', δ) such that γ is in $\psi(t, t', \delta)$ if and only if

F contains a vertex u with tag t such that $\gamma = \text{pathtag}(u) \cap \text{candtag}(t, t', \delta)$. Also, let $\text{numc}(\gamma, t, t', \delta)$ be the value of $\text{num}(u, t', \delta)$ for some vertex u with tag t for which $\gamma = \text{pathtag}(u) \cap \text{candtag}(t, t', \delta)$. Let

$$\text{totnum}(t, t', \delta) = \sum_{\gamma \in \psi_{t,t',\delta}} \text{numc}(\gamma, t, t', \delta).$$

Then, from the reasoning used in the proof of Theorem 6.1, we have the following result.

THEOREM 6.5. *If a relevant triple (t, t', δ) for a forest F is labelable, then it has a number function $N_{t,t',\delta}$ that only has nonzero values for subsets of* $\text{candtag}(t, t', \delta)$, *and for which*

$$\sum_{\gamma \in (2^{\text{candtag}(t,t',\delta)} - \emptyset)} (|\gamma| \cdot N_{t,t',\delta}(\gamma)) \leq \text{totnumc}(t, t', \delta).$$

7.   Handling Non-VDAG-Generable Forests

We pointed out earlier that a given forest that is not well structured can be made well structured by modifying the tags of its vertices. This concept can be formalized as follows.

DEFINITION. A *homomorphism* h from design forest F *onto* design forest G is a mapping from the tags occurring in F onto the tags occurring in G, such that applying mapping h to F produces G. A VDAG α *embodies* design forest G if there exists a homomorphism from F_α onto G.

Note that a homomorphism can map several tags of F onto the same tag of G. From a different perspective, G is the same as F, except that each tag of G has been split into one or more tags in F and for each vertex of G the corresponding vertex in F has as its tag some member of the split tag set.

An observation is that if a given forest F is modified to have a distinct tag on each of its vertices, then there is a homomorphism from the modified forest F^* to F. Furthermore, F^* is well structured, and each valid VDAG generating F^* is simply F^* with appropriate labels on its arcs. One such labeling scheme is for each arc exiting a vertex with tag t to be assigned label $\{t\}$. We thus see that every forest is embodied by some VDAG. Furthermore, it is embodied by a VDAG whose expansion is unconditional, where VDAGs with unconditional expansion, corresponding to the conventional dag representation of hierarchically specified design objects, can be formalized as follows.

DEFINITION. An UncVDAG is a VDAG where the label of each arc contains only the tag of the vertex exited by the arc.

"UncVDAG" stands for *Uncontrolled-expansion VDAG*. The UncVDAGs are a subclass of VDAGs, corresponding to conventional dags with uncontrolled expansion. The only difference between a UncVDAG and a conventional dag is that an UncVDAG has the extra overhead of storing a one-element label for each arc.

From the preceding discussion, we have the following observation.

PROPOSITION 7.1. *Every design forest is embodied by some* UncVDAG.

A natural computational problem is minimizing the amount of splitting needed to obtain a VDAG embodying a given forest. This problem can be posed as a decision problem, as follows.

MINIMUM TAG SPLIT (MTS).

Instance: A design forest F with m distinct tags $t_1, t_2, \ldots, t_m$, positive integers sp_i, $1 \leq i \leq m$.

Question: Is there a VDAG generating design forest F^*, where F^* is obtained from F via replacing tag t_i by at most sp_i modified versions of t_i, $1 \leq i \leq m$?

The following result shows that this problem is *NP*-complete.

THEOREM 7.2. MTS *is NP-complete*.

Proof. The membership of MTS in *NP* is obvious. The *NP*-hardness proof is by a simple reduction from the problem: "Given a forest F, determine whether there is a VDAG generating F," which has been shown to be *NP*-complete by Theorem 4.3. For a given forest F with m distinct tags, we construct an MTS instance by assigning $sp_i = 1$ for all i, $1 \leq i \leq m$. It is straightforward to verify that there is a positive answer for the constructed MTS instance if and only if there exists a VDAG generating F. $\qquad\square$

8. Relative Conciseness of VDAG Model

As mentioned in Sect. 1, one of the purposes of the VDAG model is to succinctly represent design versions and alternatives. It is well known that conventional dags can be exponentially more succinct than trees. For instance, consider a UncVDAG β_n with n vertices, numbered $v_1, v_2, \ldots, v_n$ such that v_i has two arcs going to v_{i+1}, for $1 \leq i < n$. Then F_{β_n} is a tree with $2^n - 1$ vertices; so F_{β_n} is exponentially larger than β_n.

We now show that VDAGs, utilizing controlled expansion, can be exponentially more succinct than UncVDAGs, where expansion is uncontrolled.

Given a positive integer n, let VDAG α_n be that shown in Fig. 7.25. All stamps in α_n are δ. The label on the arc from B_n to C_i is $\{A_i\}$, $1 \leq i \leq n$,

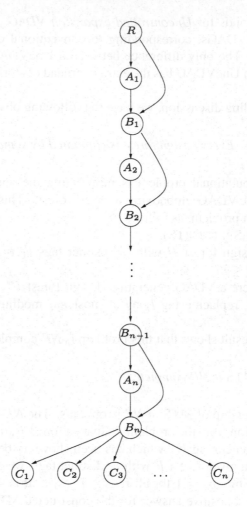

Figure 7.25. All arcs have stamp δ

and all the remaining arcs are labeled by $\{R\}$. It is easily verified that there are $3n + 1$ vertices, $4n$ arcs and $4n$ label elements in α_n.

Now consider F_{α_n}. It is easily seen that there are 2^n generating paths in α_n from R to B_n, where for each i, $1 \le i \le n$, each such path either goes through or bypasses A_i. In particular, each of these 2^n generating paths to B_n goes through a distinct subset of the A_i vertices. The instance of B_n in F_{α_n} corresponding to a generating path in α_n, say path p, has an instance of C_i as a child if and only if p goes through A_i. Hence F_{α_n} contains 2^n distinct subtrees rooted by instances of B_n. The leaves of each of these subtrees correspond to a distinct member of the power set of $\{C_1, C_2, \ldots, C_n\}$. More generally, for each i, $1 \le i \le n$, there are 2^i distinct subtrees rooted by instances of B_i

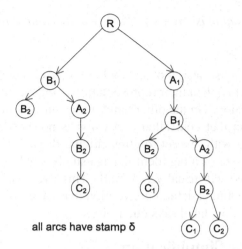

Figure 7.26.

and 2^{i-1} distinct subtrees rooted by instances of A_i. For example, Fig. 7.26 shows F_{α_2}.

Let D be a UncVDAG embodying F_{α_n}. Since for each i, $1 \leq i \leq n$, each of the 2^i vertices with tag B_i in F_{α_n} is the root of a distinct subtree, D must split tag B_i into 2^i tags, i.e., D must have a separate vertex for each of these 2^i vertices of F_{α_n}. Similarly, D must have a separate vertex for each of the 2^{i-1} vertices with tag A_i in F_{α_n}. Thus D must have at least

$$\sum_{i=0}^{n-1} 2^i + \sum_{i=1}^{n} 2^i + n + 1 = 3 \cdot 2^n + n - 2$$

vertices. Since there must be

$$\sum_{i=0}^{n-1} i \cdot \binom{n}{i} = n \cdot 2^{n-1}$$

arcs exiting from instances of B_n and entering instances of C, and each instance of A and each instance of B must have exactly 1 entering arc, D must have

$$\sum_{i=0}^{n} i \cdot \binom{n}{i} + \sum_{i=0}^{n-1} 2^i + \sum_{i=1}^{n} 2^i = (n+6) \cdot 2^{n-1} - 3$$

arcs.

We have just shown the following result.

THEOREM 8.1. *For each positive integer n, there exists a VDAG α_n with $3n + 1$ vertices, $4n$ arcs, and $4n$ label elements, such that every UncVDAG* *embodying F_{α_n} has at least $(n + 6) \cdot 2^{n-1} - 3$ arcs and at least $3 \cdot 2^n + n - 2$ vertices.*

Therefore, there exist design objects whose VDAG representation is exponentially more succinct than their representation using a conventional dag with uncontrolled expansion. On the other hand, if design versions and alternatives are not involved, so that controlled expansion is not needed, the only extra overhead of VDAG with respect to conventional dags is a one-element label per arc. Since the size of a tag identifier is usually smaller than the size of a stamp, this overhead will usually be small. This overhead could be reduced even further by adopting a default convention that an arc is to be included unconditionally, unless the label says otherwise.

9. Automatic Simplification

In this section we consider the problem of, given a well-structured forest F, finding a VDAG that generates F and has as small a size as possible.

DEFINITION. Two VDAGs are *equivalent* if the forests they produce are identical. VDAG α is *smaller* than VDAG β if α has fewer arcs than β, or if α and β have the same number of arcs and α has a smaller total label size than β. A VDAG α is *minimum-sized* if there is no equivalent VDAG β such that is smaller than α.

Since the size of a VDAG is finite, for each VDAG there exists some equivalent minimum-sized VDAG.

THEOREM 9.1. *For each $h \geq 5$, given a well-structured design tree F in* UnqStamp *with height h, it is NP-hard to find a minimum-sized VDAG generating F.*

Proof. We show *NP*-hardness by a reduction from the Vertex Cover Problem [4]. The Vertex Cover decision problem consists of determining for a given undirected graph G and integer k, whether there is a set of at most k vertices such that each edge is incident on at least one vertex in the set. Given a Vertex Cover instance involving graph G with the set of vertices $V = \{v_1, v_2, \ldots, v_n\}$ and the set of edges $E = \{e_1, e_2, \ldots, e_m\}$, we construct a forest F as follows. F consists of one tree where the root has tag S. For each i, $1 \leq i \leq m$, root S has a child with tag e_i. Suppose the two endpoints of e_i are v_{i_1} and v_{i_2}, where $i_1 < i_2$. Then e_i has two children: one with tag A and the other with tag v_{i_1}. This vertex with tag v_{i_1} has a child with tag v_{i_2}, which in turn has a child with tag A, which has a child with tag B. Stamp δ is assigned to all arcs in F. F is

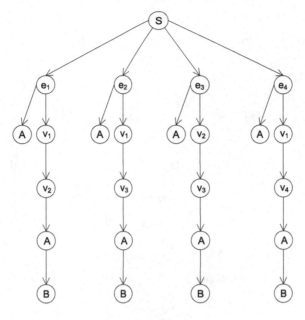

all arcs have stamp δ

Figure 7.27.

in UnqStamp since no two children of a vertex have the same tag. Note that the height of F is 5.

For example, given the Vertex Cover instance shown in Fig. 7.17, the constructed forest is shown in Fig. 7.27, and a VDAG generating that forest is shown in Fig. 7.28.

To see that the constructed F is well structured in general, first note that F is tag-acyclic. Next, consider labelability. For relevant triples of the form (S, e_i, δ), the label can be $\{S\}$. For relevant triples whose first component is e_i, the label can be $\{e_i\}$. For relevant triples of the form (v_i, v_j, δ), $i < j$, the label can be $\{e_k\}$, where e_k is the edge of G which is incident on both v_i and v_j. For relevant triples of the form (v_j, A, δ), the label can be the set of e's that have v_i and v_j as endpoints for some $i < j$. For relevant triple (A, B, δ), the label can be V. Thus F is well structured, and hence VDAG-generable.

Theorem 5.5 asserts that there is a VDAG in $\text{VD}_{\text{UnqStamp}}$ that generates F. Hence in each minimum-sized VDAG generating F, only one (A, B, δ)-arc is needed. Let α be a minimum-sized VDAG in $\text{VD}_{\text{UnqStamp}}$ and let the label on the (A, B, δ)-arc in α be l. For each i, $1 \le i \le m$, because of the path S, e_i, A in F, where this occurrence of A has no children, S, A, and e_i do not occur in l. Hence only v_i's can appear in l, $1 \le i \le n$. Note that a minimum-sized VDAG generating the forest in Fig. 7.27 may have $l = \{v_1, v_3\}$, and $\{v_1, v_3\}$

202

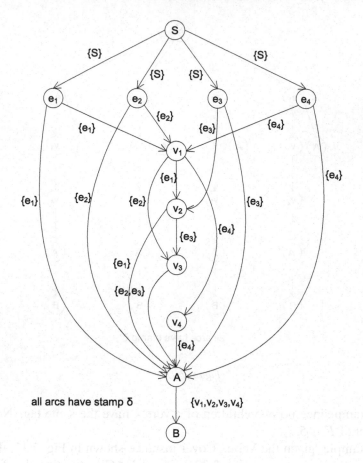

Figure 7.28.

is a minimum cover for the given vertex cover instance in Fig. 7.17. In general, for each e_i, the generating path in α from S to e_i to v_{i_1} to v_{i_2} to A must involve at least one member of l. Therefore, l contains at least one of $\{v_1, v_{i_2}\}$.

Hence, set l covers all elements of E and is indeed a vertex cover; therefore, there exists a k-element label for arc (A, B) if and only if graph G has a vertex cover of size k.

The above reduction can be easily extended to construct an F having any height $h \geq 5$. □

From Theorem 9.1, we obtain the following results.

COROLLARY 9.2. *For each $h \geq 4$, given a well-structured design forest in* UnqStamp *of height h, it is NP-hard to find a minimum-sized* VDAG *generating that forest.*

Proof. The proof is similar to that in Theorem 9.1, with the root and its associated arcs removed from the constructed tree. □

   In contrast to Theorem 9.1, minimum-sized VDAGs can be efficiently found
for VDAG-generable trees of height 4 or less.

THEOREM 9.3. *For each* VDAG-*generable tree F in* UnqStamp *of height 4 or
less, a minimum-sized* VDAG *generating F can be found in polynomial time.*

Proof. Let (t, t', δ) be a relevant triple. Then by Theorem 5.5, a minimum-
sized VDAG generating F has exactly one (t, t', δ)-arc. A minimum size label
for this arc must be found.
   If $\Gamma_0(t, t', \delta)$ is null, then $\{t\}$ can serve as a minimum size label for this arc.
Thus assume that $\Gamma_0(t, t', \delta)$ is nonnull. Then both t and the tag of the root
vertex are in $\Gamma_0(t, t', \delta)$, and so neither can be elements of the label.
   Let *relvert* be the set of vertices u of F such that the tag of u is t and
$\text{num}(u, t', \delta) = 1$. Note that each member of *relvert* has depth 2 or 3 in F.
   For vertex u of *relvert*, let

$$\text{ptag}(u) = \text{pathtag}(u) - \Gamma_0(t, t', \delta).$$

Note that $|\text{ptag}(u)|$ must be either 1 or 2. Let onecand be the set of members
u of *relvert* such that $|\text{ptag}(u)| = 1$. Let

$$\text{mustintag} = \bigcup_{u \text{ in onecand}} \text{ptag}(u).$$

Note each member w of mustintag is a tag that is the only ancestor of some
member u of *relvert*, such that $\{w\} = \text{pathtag}(u) - \Gamma_0(t, t', \delta)$, so w must be
an element of the label being constructed. For a vertex u of *relvert*, let

$$\text{ctag}(u) = \text{ptag}(u) - \text{mustintag}.$$

Note that if $|\text{ctag}(u)| = 1$, then one of the ancestors of u is a member of
mustintag, and the presence of this tag in the label will account for vertex u. If
$|\text{ctag}(u)| = 0$, then u is a member of onetag, so an ancestor of u is a member
of mustintag.
   Let twocand be the set of members u of relvert such that $|\text{ctag}(u)| = 2$. The
members of twocand present a design choice in constructing the label. Each
member u of twocand must be accounted for by having at least one member
of $\text{ctag}(u)$ included in the label, but it is not necessary for both members of
$\text{ctag}(u)$ to be included. This gives rise to a Vertex Cover Problem as follows.
   We construct a Vertex Cover instance $G(V, E)$ as follows. Let

$$V = \bigcup_{u \text{ in twocand}} \text{ctag}(u).$$

For each u in twocand, E contains an undirected edge between the two members of ctag(u). A minimum size label consists of the union of mustintag and a minimum size vertex cover of graph G.

Now, we show that graph G is bipartite. First note that for each u in twocand, the two vertices of F that contribute to ctag(u) occur at depth 1 or 2, respectively. Let A be a member of V. Suppose that there is a vertex at depth 1 with tag A that is an ancestor of a member of twocand. Then, there are tags S and B such that S, A, B, t, t' are the tags along a path in F. Suppose that there is also a vertex at depth 2 with tag A that is an ancestor of a member of twocand. Then there is a tag C such that S, C, A, t, t' are the tags along a path in F. Let α be a VDAG generating F; since F is VDAG-generable, such a VDAG exists. Because of the two forest paths described above, VDAG α must have an arc from S to C labeled $\{S\}$, an arc from C to A whose label contains S or C, an arc from A to B whose label contains S or A, an arc from B to t whose label contains S, A or B, and an arc from t to t' whose label contains A or B. But then α contains a generating path with tags S, C, A, B, t, t'. This generating path would correspond to a depth 5 vertex in F, contradicting the assumption that F has height 4. Thus either all the vertices with tag A that are ancestors of members of twocand have depth 1, or they all have depth 2. Consequently, the constructed graph G is bipartite, with each edge of G connecting a depth 1 tag and a depth 2 tag.

Given a bipartite graph, a minimum size vertex cover can be found in polynomial time [4, 5]. Therefore, a minimum size label for (t, t', δ) can be found in polynomial time. □

An immediate consequence is the following.

COROLLARY 9.4. *For* VDAG-*generable design forests in* UnqStamp *of height at most* 3, *a minimum-sized* VDAG *generating a given forest can be found in polynomial time.*

We now consider the issue of whether the value of maxnum(t, t', δ) for a relevant triple in a forest can be used to limit the number of VDAG (t, t', δ)-arcs. The next result shows that the number of such arcs in the VDAG may have to be arbitrarily larger than maxnum(t, t', δ), that is, in general, the stamp multiplicity of a VDAG cannot be bounded by the stamp multiplicity of the forest it generates.

THEOREM 9.5. *For each integer* $k \geq 2$, *there exists a* VDAG-*generable forest* F, *such that* stpmult$(F) = 2$ *and for each* VDAG α *generating* F, stpmult$(\alpha) = k$.

Proof. For a given k, consider the complete undirected graph of k vertices, and consider the forest F_k produced from this graph by the construction used in the proof of Theorem 4.3, except with the subtree rooted by Q removed. It is easily seen that $\text{stpmult}(F_k) = 2$ and that F_k is VDAG-generable. Suppose that VDAG α generates F_k. By an argument similar to that used in the proof of Theorem 4.3, it can be seen that the number of (t, t', δ)-arcs in α must be k. Thus $\text{stpmult}(\alpha) = k$. □

10. Conclusion

The VDAG model proposed in this work can be used to concisely represent hierarchically specified design data in a flexible way that supports design alternatives in engineering design database systems. In fact, there are designs whose representation via VDAGs is exponentially more succinct than is possible with the conventional model of uncontrolled expansion. However, only those design forests which are well structured can be generated via the VDAG paradigm of ancestor based expansion. Problems such as determining whether a forest can be generated by a VDAG are *NP*-complete, even for forests whose heights are bounded. However, for an important class of design forests that include objects from many design applications, namely UnqStamp, the problem of determining whether a given forest is generable from a VDAG can be solved in polynomial time. If the answer is "yes," an appropriate VDAG can be generated in polynomial time, although finding a minimum-sized VDAG for a forest in UnqStamp is *NP*-hard, even if the height of that forest is bounded.

References

[1] D. S. Batory and W. Kim. Modeling concepts for VLSI CAD objects. *ACM Trans. Database Systems*, 10:322–346, 1985.

[2] K. R. Dittrich and R. A. Lorie. Version support for engineering database systems. *IEEE Trans. Software Engrg.*, 14:429–437, 1988.

[3] C. W. Fraser and E. W. Myers. An editor for revision control. *ACM Trans. Programming Languages and Systems*, 9:277–295, 1987.

[4] M. R. Garey and D. S. Johnson. *Computers and Intractability: A Guide to the Theory of NP-Completeness*. Freeman, San Francisco, 1979.

[5] F. Harary. *Graph Theory*. Addison–Wesley, Reading, 1969.

[6] P. Heckel. A technique for isolating differences between files. *Comm. ACM*, 21:264–268, 1978.

[7] J. W. Hunt and M. D. McIlroy. An algorithm for differential file comparison. Comput. Sci. Tech. Report 41, AT&T Bell Laboratories, Murray Hill, NJ, 1976.

[8] R. H. Katz. A database approach for managing VLSI design data. In *ACM IEEE 19th Design Automation Conf.*, Las Vegas, NV, pages 274–282, June 1982.

[9] R. H. Katz. Toward a unified framework for version modeling in engineering databases. *ACM Comput. Surveys*, 22:375–408, 1990.

[10] R. H. Katz and T. J. Lehman. Database support for versions and alternatives of large design files. *IEEE Trans. Software Engrg.*, SE-10:191–200, 1984.

[11] R. H. Katz, R. Bhateja, E. E. Chang, D. Gedge, and V. Trijanto. Design version management. *IEEE Design & Test*, 4:12–22, 1987.

[12] D. E. Knuth. *The Art of Computer Programming, Fundamental Algorithms*, volume 1. Addison–Wesley, Reading, 2nd edition, 1973.

[13] M. J. Rochkind. The source code control system. *IEEE Trans. Software Engrg.*, SE-1:364–370, 1975.

[14] D. G. Severance and G. M. Lohman. Differential files: their application to the maintenance of large databases. *ACM Trans. Database Systems*, 1:256–267, 1976.

[15] W. F. Tichy. RCS–a system for version control. *Software–Practice and Experience*, 15:637–684, 1985.

[16] Unix User's Reference Manual, 1986. Department of Electrical Engineering and Computer Science, University of California, Berkeley, CA.

[17] VHDL Language Reference Manual, Draft Standard 1076/B, 1987. IEEE.

[18] L. Yu and D. J. Rosenkrantz. Ancestor controlled submodule inclusion in design databases. In *Proc. 2nd Intl. Conf. on Data and Knowledge Sys-

208

tems for Manufacturing and Engineering, pages 28–37, IEEE, Gaithersburg, 1989. (Full version to appear in IEEE Trans. on Knowledge and Data Engineering).

[19] L. Yu and D. J. Rosenkrantz. Minimizing time-space cost for database version control. *Acta Inform.*, 27:627–663, 1990.

Chapter 8

THE COMPLEXITY OF PROCESSING HIERARCHICAL SPECIFICATIONS

DANIEL J. ROSENKRANTZ* AND HARRY B. HUNT III†

Department of Computer Science, State University of New York at Albany, Albany, NY 12222, USA

Reprinted from: *SIAM J. Computing*, Vol. 22, No. 3, June 1993, pp. 627–649.
© SIAM

Abstract   Hierarchical object descriptions consisting of a set of module descriptions are considered, where each module is either a primitive module or has a body that is an interconnection of submodules. The description represents a flattened object, whose size can be exponential in the size of the description. The complexity of processing and/or analyzing such hierarchically specified objects is considered. The simulation of hierarchically specified circuits is emphasized, but the results are applicable to other kinds of hierarchically specified objects.

It is shown that hierarchically specified acyclic circuits can be simulated deterministically in space linear in the size of the description, even when the description is not explicitly acyclic. $\Theta(n^2)$-size-bounded reductions are given from the languages in $\mathrm{DSPACE}(n)$ to the problem of simulating hierarchically specified acyclic monotone circuits. This implies that this simulation problem is PSPACE-complete and that any algorithm for it that operates faster than $2^{O(\sqrt{n})}$ deterministic time could be used to recognize all $\mathrm{DSPACE}(n)$ languages in less than $2^{O(n)}$ deterministic time. It is then shown that the simulation problem for hierarchically specified acyclic circuits (not necessarily monotone) can indeed be solved in $2^{O(\sqrt{n})}$ deterministic time. Moreover, every hierarchically specified acyclic circuit is shown to have an equivalent flat circuit of size $2^{O(\sqrt{n})}$. For binary circuits the size of the equivalent flat circuit is $O(n^{3/2}2^{1.53\sqrt{n}})$. It

* This research was supported by the National Science Foundation grants DCR 86-03184 and CCR 88-03278.
† This research was supported by the National Science Foundation grants DCR 86-03184 and CCR 89-03319.

S.S. Ravi, S.K. Shukla (eds.), *Fundamental Problems in Computing*,
© Springer Science + Business Media B.V. 2009

is also shown that the problem of simulating hierarchically specified circuits is EXPSPACE-complete for cyclic circuits.

Keywords: hierarchical specification, CAD systems, acyclic circuits, combinational circuits, cyclic circuits, sequential circuits, simulation, computational complexity

AMS (MOS) subject classifications: 68Q25, 94C10, 68M15

Received by the editors November 13, 1989; accepted for publication (in revised form) February 18, 1992.

1.   Introduction

Hierarchical object design permits the overall design of an object to be partitioned into the design of a collection of modules, each of whose design is a more manageable task than producing a complete design in one step. It also facilitates the development of computer-aided design (CAD) systems since low-level objects can be incorporated into libraries and thus can be made available as submodules to designers of larger-scale objects. In particular, hardware description languages usually permit circuits to be hierarchically specified (see, e.g., [5, 15, 18, 19]). Hierarchical description languages are also useful for describing the configuration of distributed software systems [17].

An important feature of hierarchical specifications is that they permit more concise descriptions of circuits than do flat nonhierarchical descriptions. A consequence of this is that the complexity of analyzing or otherwise processing a given hierarchically presented object can be different from that when the object is presented as a flat combination of primitives. For example, in VLSI mask specifications, analyzing a flat list of rectangles for overlap can be done in polynomial time, whereas this problem is NP-complete for hierarchically specified sets of rectangles [3]. On the other hand, when restrictions are imposed on the hierarchical mask specifications, they can be processed more efficiently [3, 20, 21, 23]. Certain graph-analysis problems for hierarchically specified undirected graphs can be solved efficiently in polynomial time [10, 11, 13]. The effect of hierarchical specifications on VLSI design problems is investigated in [9], and their effect on more general combinatorial problems is investigated in [12]. In [9] and [12] it is shown that the problem of simulating a hierarchically specified Boolean circuit, where the specification is explicitly acyclic at every level of the hierarchy, is a PSPACE-complete problem, where [9] covers the upper bound and [12] covers the lower bound. In [9] it is also shown that an explicitly acyclic Boolean circuit can be simulated within space that is linear in the size of the hierarchical description and a nonexplicitly acyclic circuit in quadratic space. The question of whether a nonexplicitly acyclic circuit can be simulated in linear space is left open, and it is conjectured that such an efficient deterministic space simulation is unlikely.

Here we study the complexity of processing and/or analyzing hierarchically specified objects, emphasizing the simulation of hierarchically specified circuits. A hierarchically specified object is presented as a set of modules, each of which is classified as either a primitive module or a composite module. Each composite module has a body, whose description consists of an interconnection of instances of lower-level modules. Each module has a corresponding flattened body, which is an interconnection of primitive modules that can be obtained by repeatedly replacing each instance of a composite module with its body. We are concerned with analyzing a hierarchically specified object for some given property, where the property is a property of the flattened object. An issue is, for which properties can the analysis be performed in a more efficient way than constructing the flattened object and then analyzing it? We focus on the problem of circuit simulation, which reflects the semantics of what circuits actually do.

In Sect. 2 we present definitions and terminology for hierarchically specified objects.

In Sect. 3 we show that hierarchically specified acyclic circuits can be simulated in deterministic space linear in the size of the description, even when the description is not explicitly acyclic at every level. This answers the open problem from [9] that was mentioned above.

In Sect. 4 we generalize and strengthen the PSPACE-hard lower bound in [12] for explicitly acyclic logic-circuit simulation to explicitly acyclic monotone logic-circuit simulation. We accomplish this in a very general algebraic setting by means of $\Theta(n^2)$-size bounded reductions from the languages in DSPACE(n). As a consequence, if there are languages in DSPACE(n) whose recognitions requires $2^{\Omega(n)}$ deterministic time, then this simulation problem requires $2^{\Omega(\sqrt{n})}$ deterministic time. In contrast, the reduction in [12] is a $\Theta(n^4)$-size bounded reduction from the languages in DSPACE(n); so even if there is such a language requiring $2^{\Omega(n)}$ time, the reduction only implies that the acyclic circuit simulation problem requires $2^{\Omega(n^{1/4})}$ deterministic time.

In Sect. 5 we show that hierarchically specified acyclic circuits can indeed by simulated in deterministic $2^{O(\sqrt{n})}$ time. This contrasts with the traditional approach of first flattening the hierarchically specified circuit and then simulating this flattened circuit [14, 2]. In the worst case the size of the flattened circuit is $2^{\Omega(n)}$ and thus the overall time required is $2^{\Omega(n)}$. However, we show that every hierarchically specified acyclic circuit has an equivalent flat circuit of size $2^{O(\sqrt{n})}$. Furthermore, this equivalent circuit can be constructed and thus simulated in time $2^{O(\sqrt{n})}$. Results on the size of acyclic circuit descriptions also appear in [8], where the focus is on the effect of requiring that a description be explicitly acyclic at every level of the hierarchy. In [8] it is shown that there are acyclic circuits that have a hierarchical description of size n such that any description that is explicitly acyclic at every level of the hierarchy must be of size $2^{\Omega(n)}$, and it is also shown that for every acyclic circuit that has a hierarchical description of size n there is an equivalent circuit that has a $O(n^3)$-size hierarchical description that is explicitly acyclic at every level of the hierarchy.

Sections 4 and 5 present lower and upper complexity bounds that match, given the current state of knowledge about computational complexity. A $\Theta(n^p)$-size-bounded reduction from the languages in DSPACE(n) to the simulation problem for acyclic circuits and an $2^{O(n^q)}$ algorithm for this simulation problem can be combined, implying that all languages in DSPACE(n) are recognizable in time $2^{O(n^{pq})}$. Thus an improvement either to the size bound of $O(n^2)$ in the reduction from Sect. 4 or to the time bound of $2^{O(\sqrt{n})}$ for the simulation algorithm from Sect. 5 would imply that all languages in DSPACE(n) are recognizable in less than $2^{\Theta(n)}$ deterministic time. This would be a surprising breakthrough in complexity theory.

In Sect. 6 we consider cyclic hierarchically specified logic circuits. Under fairly loose assumptions, the simulation problem for such logic circuits is shown to be EXPSPACE-complete by means of $\Theta(n)$-size-bounded reductions from the languages accepted by 2^n-space-bounded Turing machines. This suggests that to solve this type of problem, one might as well construct and then simulate the flattened circuit.

We assume that the reader is familiar with complexity classes and reductions; otherwise, see, e.g., [1, 6].

2. Definitions and Terminology of Hierarchical Specifications

We define the class of hierarchically specified objects as follows. An object is described as a set of *modules*, where each module is either a *primitive module* or a *composite module*. Each module (whether primitive or composite) has an *interface*, and each composite module has a *body*. A module interface specifies the *module name* and a set of *module ports*. Each module port has a *port name* and is specified to be either an *input port* or an *output port*. For a given module, the module port names are unique. A module body consists of an interconnection of *module instances*. A given module instance can be an instance of either a primitive module or a composite module. A given module body may contain more than one instance of the same module.

As an example, Fig. 8.1(a) shows an interface for a module named P with input ports $\{U, V, W\}$ and output ports $\{X, Y\}$. In the graphical representation used in our diagrams, input ports are denoted by incoming arrows and output ports are denoted by exiting arrows. Figure 8.1(b) shows a body for module P.

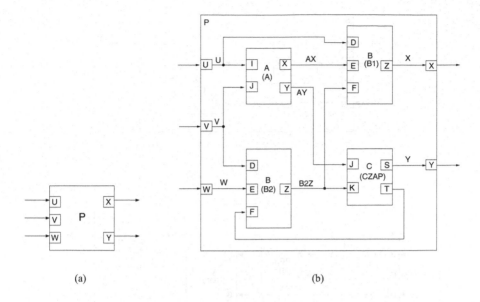

Figure 8.1. (a) Interface for module P; (b) body for module P

The module body contains two instances of module B, an instance of module A, and an instance of module C. Each module instance in a body has an *instance name*. In Fig. 8.1(b) the instance names are $B1$, $B2$, A, and *CZAP*. For a given module body the instance names are unique.

A module body contains two kinds of ports: *instance ports* and *body ports*. An *instance port* is a port of an instance within the body. Examples of instance ports in Fig. 8.1(b) are port J of instance *CZAP* and port Z of instance $B2$. A *body port* is a port of the module whose composition is described by the body. In Fig. 8.1(b), P has five body ports: U, V, W, X, and Y.

The interconnections within a module body are specified by *signals*. Each signal is given a *signal name* and is *connected* to a set of ports within the body. For example, in Fig. 8.1(b) signal $B2Z$ is connected to instance ports Z of $B2$, F of $B1$, and K of *CZAP*. Signal U is connected to body port U of P and instance ports I of A and D of $B1$. Note that Fig. 8.1(b) uses the convention of giving a signal connected to exactly one body port the same name as that body port. For a given module body the signal names are unique.

We assume that a set of modules satisfies certain restrictions. First, define the *DIRECTLY-WITHIN* relation on modules as follows: module α is *DIRECTLY-WITHIN* module β if the body of β contains an instance of α. We assume that the set of modules satisfies the *nesting restriction* that the *DIRECTLY-WITHIN* relation is acyclic. The nesting restriction ensures that the description of a set of modules is a meaningful hierarchical description of a finite object.

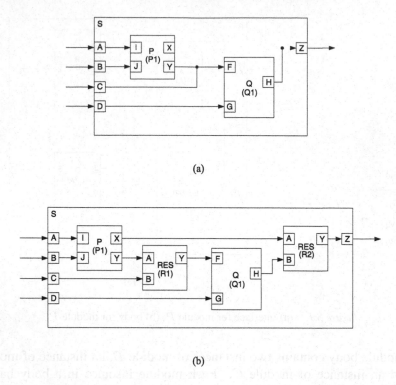

(a)

(b)

Figure 8.2. (a) Body with violations of wiring restriction; (b) body with extra instances to satisfy wiring restriction

In a module body define a *driver port* to be either a body input port or an instance output port. Define a *drivable port* to be either a body output port or an instance input port. We assume that each module body satisfies the *wiring restriction* that no signal in the body is connected to two driver ports.

The wiring restriction prevents direct connections between drivers. However, real circuit technologies often permit drivers to be connected together, with a technology-dependent rule resolving the situation when connected drivers supply conflicting values. To model a circuit design that uses this capability, we would require the placement of a module instance having inputs connected to these drivers and having a single output. The semantics of this additional module would represent the conflict resolution function. For example, Fig. 8.2(a) shows a module body containing two violations of the wiring restriction. Figure 8.2(b) shows a corresponding body that satisfies the wiring restriction, with instances of module *RES* inserted to resolve conflicts.

For a given module in a hierarchically specified object, the *flattened body* for that module is the interconnection of instances of primitive modules, obtained by repeatedly replacing instances of composite modules in the body by their bodies.

A *module description* consists of a module interface, together with either an indication that the module is primitive or a body for the module. A *hierarchical object description* consists of a set of module descriptions, one of which is designated as the *root module*, such that the set includes every module that occurs as a module instance within any of the module bodies. The root module is said to be *hierarchically specified*. The *hierarchically specified object* corresponding to a hierarchical object description is the flattened body of the root module. A *flat object description* is a hierarchical object description involving a single composite module. Thus the body of this module is an interconnection of instances of primitive modules.

The *size* of a module interface is 1 plus the number of module ports. The *size* of a module body is the sum of the size of the interface of the module, the number of signals in the body, and the sizes of the interface for each module instance within the body. Note that this is the same as the sum of 1, the number of signals within the body, the number of module instances within the body, and the number of ports (both instance ports and body ports) within the body. The *size* of a module description is the sum of the sizes of its interface and body. The *size* of a hierarchical object description is the sum of the sizes of the module descriptions occurring in the overall object description. This definition of size measures the number of symbols occurring in a typical representation of the object description. The number of bits in the representation would be larger since each symbol might be represented by a number of bits equal to the logarithm of the number of distinct symbols. We regard the number of symbol occurrences in the description to be the more practical measure of its size.

We now consider acyclic hierarchically described objects. An *instance dataflow graph* for a given composite module is a directed graph describing the dataflow within the body of the module. The graph has a vertex for each module instance within the body and a vertex for each body port. There are edges corresponding to connections from driver ports to drivable ports within the body. Specifically, there is a directed edge for each of the following four cases:

(a) Edge from instance A to instance B if an output port of A is connected to an input port of B.

(b) Edge from body input port X to instance B if X to connected an input port of B.

(c) Edge from instance A to body output port Y if an output port of A is connected to Y.

(d) Edge from body input port X to body output port Y if X is connected to Y.

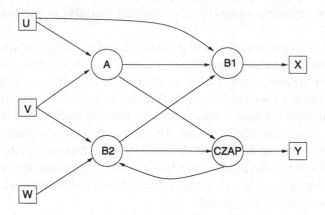

Figure 8.3. Instance dataflow graph

As an example, Fig. 8.3 shows the instance dataflow graph for module P described in Fig. 8.1.

A composite module is said to be *locally acyclic* if its instance dataflow graph is acyclic. A composite module is said to be *weakly acyclic* if the instance dataflow graph for its flattened body is locally acyclic. A composite module M is said to be *strongly acyclic* if module M is locally acyclic and every composite module Q such that Q *DIRECTLY-WITHIN* M is strongly acyclic [9].

Strong acyclicity is a special case of weak acyclicity. Let the relation *SOME-WHERE-WITHIN* be the transitive closure of *DIRECTLY-WITHIN*. Then an equivalent definition of M being strongly acyclic is that M is locally acyclic and every composite module Q such that Q *SOMEWHERE-WITHIN* M is locally acyclic. Strong acyclicity requires not only that the flattened circuit be acyclic but also that at every level of the hierarchy each module body be described as an acyclic combination of the instances occurring directly within it. Given a hierarchical description, it is clear that strong acyclicity can be determined in polynomial time. In addition, weak acyclicity can be determined in polynomial time, using a bottom-up dataflow analysis [13].

3. Linear Space Simulation of Weakly Acyclic Circuits

In this section we show that weakly acyclic hierarchically specified logic circuits can be simulated deterministically using only linear space. First, we define the simulation problem as follows: the *simulation problem* for a weakly acyclic module consists of computing the values of the output ports of the module, given a value for each input port of the module and a hierarchical circuit description for which it is the root module.

We make several assumptions to ensure that the simulation problem and the complexity analysis of simulation algorithms are well defined. First, we assume that the domain of signal values is finite. (Equivalently, the amount of space required to represent a signal value is fixed.) Second, we assume that each primitive module is a memoryless combinatorial element whose input values determine its output values. Third, we assume that the input-output behavior of each primitive module is polynomial-time computable, i.e., given input values, the output values can be computed in polynomial time. Finally, we assume that if the flattened body of the module being simulated contains a primitive module instance port that is unconnected to a driver, there is a rule for what value to use for that input port.

Reference [9] contains a sketch of how a strongly acyclic hierarchically specified circuit whose primitive modules are logic gates can be simulated deterministically in space that is linear in the size of the hierarchical circuit description. It is also pointed out that a weakly acyclic circuit can be simulated nondeterministically in linear space and deterministically in quadratic space. The problem of finding a deterministic linear space algorithm for this case is left as an open question, and Lengauer says that it is questionable whether such a method exists. The next result shows that weakly acyclic circuits can indeed be simulated deterministically in linear space.

THEOREM 3.1. *A weakly acyclic hierarchically specified object can be simulated in space linear in the size of the hierarchical circuit description.*

Proof. First, consider the case when the hierarchically specified object is strongly acyclic, as described in [9]. In this case, since each module is locally acyclic, its instance dataflow graph is acyclic. Each instance dataflow graph can be topologically sorted, and the instances within it can be simulated in this order. Consider a given module to be simulated, with given values for its input ports. If the given module is primitive, its simulation consists of computing the values of the output ports using the values of the input ports. If the given module is composite, then each of the instances in the body is simulated, in topological sort order. In any stage of simulating a given module body, the algorithm maintains a record of the input-port values of the body and of the output-port values of instances simulated thus far. Consequently, when a given instance in the body is to be simulated, all drivers of the input-ports of the given instance have known values. When the last instance in the body of the given composite module has been simulated, the value of the drivers of the output ports of the given module are known and the simulation of the given module is complete.

Figure 8.4 shows an example in which A, B, and C are composite modules; left-to-right order in the figure corresponds to a topological sort of the instances

218

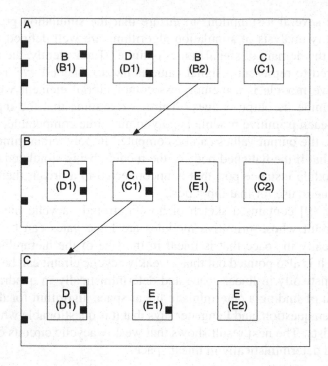

Figure 8.4. Snapshot of simulation of a strongly acyclic circuit

within each body. Figure 8.4 shows a snapshot of the simulation of module A, where recorded values are indicated by darkening the appropriate driving ports. In the snapshot the simulation of instances $B1$ and $D1$ within A have been completed and the simulation of instance $B2$ within A is in progress. In this subsimulation, the simulation of $D1$ within module B has been completed and the simulation of $C1$ within B is in progress. In this subsimulation, the simulations of $D1$ and $E1$ have been completed and the simulation of $E2$ is about to begin.

Now consider a weakly acyclic hierarchically specified circuit. Consider the subsimulation problem of simulating a given composite module in the hierarchy, where a subset (not necessarily proper) of the input ports of the module have specified values. The subsimulation computes the values of all those output ports whose values are determined by the specified input-port values. More precisely, a given output-port value is computed if a value has been specified for every input port for which the instance dataflow graph for the flattened body of the module has a path to the given output port.

In the subsimulation of a given body we use two lists of module instances occurring in the body. We call these two lists *FULL* and *PARTIAL*. List *FULL* contains module instances for which all the instance input-port values are known and the module instance can be simulated to obtain all its instance output-port values. List *PARTIAL* contains module instances for which some (possibly none), but not all, of the instance input-port values are known and for which the module can be simulated to obtain those instance output-port values that do not depend on unknown input-port values.

Initially in the subsimulation some of the body input-port values are known. Each of these known driver values specifies the values of all drivable ports to which it is connected. Also, each unconnected instance input port is assigned a special driver value, say, UNCONNECTED, during the simulation. List *FULL* is initialized with those module instances for which all instance input-port values are known, based on the above information. List *PARTIAL* is initialized with all remaining module instances.

The subsimulation proceeds until lists *FULL* and *PARTIAL* are both empty. If both lists are nonempty, a module instance is deleted from FULL and is simulated. If *FULL* is empty and *PARTIAL* is nonempty, a module instance is deleted from *PARTIAL* and is simulated. When both lists are empty, the subsimulation returns all the output-port values for which the driving values have been computed during the subsimulation. As the subsimulation proceeds a record of known driver values is maintained, i.e., a record of the given body input-port values and the instance output-port values that have been obtained thus far.

Now consider what happens in a simulation upon completion of the subsimulation of a given module instance within the body being simulated. For each instance output-port value computed by the subsimulation such that this output-port value was not known prior to the subsimulation, this value is recorded. Furthermore, each module instance having an input port driven by this driver is checked. If the module instance does not yet have all its output values computed, then it is a candidate for subsimulation. If all its input-port values are now known, it is placed on list *FULL* (and removed from list *PARTIAL* if it is currently on that list); otherwise, it is placed on list *PARTIAL* if it is not already on that list.

An example is shown in Fig. 8.5, in which A, B, and C are composite modules. In this example, for both B and C the lower output port is determined solely by the lower input port and the upper output port is determined by both input ports. Figure 8.5 shows a snapshot of the simulation in which recorded values are indicated by darkening the appropriate driving ports. Within module A instance $B1$ was simulated with only its lower input port known, producing the value of its lower output port. The instance $B2$ was simulated with its lower input port known, producing the value of its lower output port. Then instance $C1$ was simulated with its lower input port known, producing the value of its lower output port. Then instance $B1$ was simulated again, this time with both input ports known, and the value of its upper output port was

220

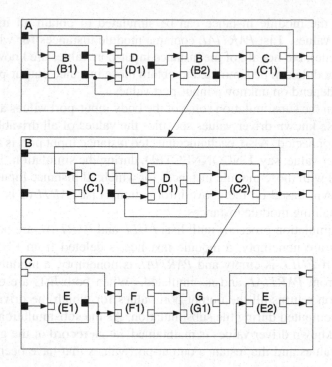

Figure 8.5. Snapshot of simulation of a weakly acyclic circuit

obtained. Then instance D was simulated. The simulation of instance $B2$ with
both input ports known is in progress. In this subsimulation of B, $C1$ has
already been simulated with its lower input port known, producing the value of
its lower output port. The simulation of $C2$ with its lower input port known is
in progress. In this subsimulation of C the simulation of instance $E1$ has been
completed and the simulation of $E2$ is about to begin.

The data recorded at any point in the overall algorithm is a set of values for drivers within the bodies of modules occurring in a directed path of
the *DIRECTLY-WITHIN* relation. Since the *DIRECTLY-WITHIN* relation is
acyclic, each module occurs at most once in such a directed path. Thus the
number of values to be remembered at any time does not exceed the size of the
hierarchical description.   □

Although the algorithm of Theorem 3.1 requires only linear space, it may
entail fruitless subsimulations. The subsimulation of a module instance from
list *PARTIAL* is fruitful only if it produces an instance output-port value that
was not previously known. Fruitless subsimulations can be avoided by using
auxiliary information. For each module an interface dataflow graph can be
computed in a bottom-up manner [13], where this graph indicates which input

ports determine which output ports. Then a module is placed on list *PARTIAL* only if its known input-port values determine a not yet known output port. Since the size of an interface dataflow graph can be the product of the number of input ports and number of output ports, the use of this technique may require quadratic space.

4. Acyclic Circuits: Lower Bounds

In this section we investigate the inherent computational complexity of several analysis problems for hierarchically described acyclic circuits and focus on the simulation problem.

Reference [12] presents a sketch of a proof that the simulation problem is PSPACE-hard for strongly acyclic hierarchically specified logic circuits. The reduction used is from the quantified Boolean formula logical validity problem [22] and is itself $\Theta(n^2)$-size-bounded. The reduction in [22] used to prove that the quantified Boolean formula logical validity problem is PSPACE-hard is a $\Theta(n^2)$-size-bounded reduction from the membership problem for linear-bounded automata. Thus the reduction in [12] provides a $\Theta(n^4)$-size-bounded reduction from the membership problem for linear-bounded automata. If it is assumed that there are languages in DSPACE(n) whose recognition requires $2^{\Omega(n)}$ time, the reduction in [12] only provides evidence that the simulation problem for strongly acyclic hierarchically specified logic circuits requires time $2^{\Omega(n^{1/4})}$. Also, it can readily be seen that the logical validity problem for quantified monotone Boolean formulas is decidable deterministically in polynomial time and thus cannot be used to prove the PSPACE-hardness of the simulation problem for hierarchically specified monotone logic circuits. (This contradicts an apparent claim in [12].)

Here we present a polynomial-time $\Theta(n^2)$-size-bounded reduction from the membership problem for deterministic linear-bounded automata to the simulation problem for explicitly acyclic hierarchically specified monotone circuits. If it is assumed that there are languages in DSPACE(n) whose recognition requires $2^{\Omega(n)}$ time, our reduction provides evidence that the simulation problem for strongly acyclic hierarchically specified logic circuits requires $2^{\Omega(\sqrt{n})}$ time. In Sect. 5 below we present a matching upper bound. Our reduction and lower bound apply not only to the simulation of monotone circuits but also to the simulation or evaluation of all classes of strongly acyclic hierarchically specified functions, for which the allowed primitive function modules can emulate monotone Boolean logic. Thus our reduction and lower bound apply to strongly acyclic hierarchically specified functions on many different algebraic structures with a 0 and 1. These include all of the following algebraic structures (provided that they have at least two elements): lattices, rings with a multiplicative identity, idempotent semirings with a multiplicative identity, finite semirings with a multiplicative identity that are not rings, etc. For examples of these structures see [4, 7, 16], and [24]. In particular, our reduction and lower bound apply to the various lattice-theoretical structures used to simulate faults, errors, transients, unknown states, variable strength signals, etc., in digital logic both at the gate and transistor levels [7].

Before presenting our reduction, we need the following definition.

DEFINITION 4.1. We say that a set of primitive modules has *monotone logic expressibility* if there exist two values ϕ and τ, in the domain of values operated on by the primitive modules, and two modules *OR* and *AND*, either available as primitive modules or constructible as composite modules by an interconnection of primitive modules, with the following properties. Modules *OR* and *AND* each have two inputs and one output. If both outputs of *OR* equal ϕ, the output value is ϕ; if one input value is ϕ and the other is τ, the output is τ; and if both inputs are τ, the output is τ. If both inputs of *AND* are ϕ, the output is ϕ; if one input is ϕ and the other is τ, the output is ϕ; and if both inputs are τ, the output is τ.

THEOREM 4.2. *Let* Π *be a set of primitive modules with monotone logic expressibility. Then each language in DSPACE* (n) *is polynomial time and* $\Theta(n^2)$*-size-bounded reducible to the following problem* Γ*: Given a strongly acyclic hierarchical object description whose primitive modules are in the set of primitive modules* Π*, an assignment of values to the input ports of the root module, and a specified value for one of the output ports of the root module, determine whether the specified object, given the specified input values, produces the specified output value.*

Proof. Consider a deterministic linear-bounded automaton M. The description of M can be modified, if necessary, so that once it accepts an input string, it cycles in an accepting state. Also, M can be modified, if necessary, so that its head never moves off the end of its tape. There is a constant $c > 0$ such that for any input sequence x to M, where x includes endmarkers and $n = |x|$, if M accepts x, it does so within 2^{cn} moves. Thus M accepts x if and only if after 2^{cn} moves M is in an accepting state.

As shown below, M and x can be encoded into a strongly acyclic hierarchical monotone object description and an input value assignment such that the hierarchically specified object produces output τ for the given input assignment if and only if M accepts x. With M fixed, this encoding represents a polynomial-time algorithm whose input is x and whose output, consisting of a hierarchical object description together with an input value assignment, is of size $\Theta(|x|^2)$. Thus the algorithm is the required reduction from $L(M)$

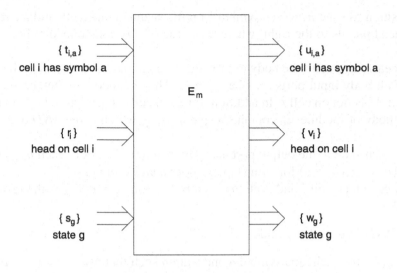

Figure 8.6. Ports of module E_m

to the simulation problem for strongly acyclic hierarchical monotone object descriptions.

For each m, where $0 \le m \le cn$, there is a composite module E_m. The ports of these modules are summarized in Fig. 8.6. For each tape cell i of M, where $1 \le i \le n$, and each tape symbol a of M, each module E_m has an input port $t_{i,a}$ and an output port $u_{i,a}$. In addition, for each tape cell i, $1 \le i \le n$, each module E_m has an input port r_i and an output port v_i. Finally, for each state g of M each module E_m has an input port s_g and an output port w_g. The purpose of the input ports is to encode a configuration of M. The value of input port $t_{i,a}$ indicates whether, in the configuration, cell i has tape symbol a written on it. A value of τ indicates that this is so, and a value of ϕ indicates that it is not so. Input port r_i indicates whether the tape head is scanning cell i. Input port s_g indicates whether the state is state g. The output ports encode a configuration in a similar manner. Note that since M is fixed, the number of ports is proportional to n, the length of x.

For each m, where $0 \le m \le cn$, module E_m will be designed so that if the inputs encodes a length n configuration of M, then the outputs of E_m will encode the configuration that results after 2^m moves by M.

Consider E_0, whose purpose is to simulate one move of automaton M. The body of E_0 is constructed by using instances of modules *OR* and *AND*. For simplicity, we describe E_0 as though *OR* and *AND* can have multiple inputs, with the understanding that the circuit is actually constructed by using two-input module instances.

Suppose that automaton M has transition function δ, where $\delta(g, a) = (h, b, p)$ means that when M is in state g and scanning tape symbol a, it makes a transition to state h, writes symbol b on the scanned tape cell, and moves its tape head p cells to the right, where the value of p is constrained to be -1, 0, or $+1$.

For each tape cell i the body of module E_0 contains a signal q_i, which is the OR of all body input ports r_j, where $j \neq i$. Thus q_i encodes whether the tape head of M is not on cell i. In addition, for each cell i, tape symbol a, and state g, the body of module E_0 contains a signal $y_{i,a,g}$, which is the AND of $t_{i,a}$, r_i and s_g.

For each state h, the output port w_h is the result of the OR of each $y_{i,a,g}$ such that $\delta(g, a) = (h, b, p)$ for some tape symbol b and some p.

For each tape cell i and each tape symbol b, output port $u_{i,b}$ is the result of the OR of

(i) AND of q_i and $t_{i,b}$, and

(ii) $y_{i,a,g}$ for each tape symbol a and state g such that $\delta(g, a) = (h, b, p)$ for some state h and some p.

For each tape cell i, output port v_i is the result of the OR of

(i) $y_{i,a,g}$ for each tape symbol a and state g such that $\delta(g, a) = (h, b, 0)$ for some state h and tape symbol b,

(ii) $y_{i-1,a,g}$ for each tape symbol a and state g such that $\delta(g, a) = (h, b, +1)$ for some state h and tape symbol b, provided cell i is not the leftmost tape cell, and

(iii) $y_{i+1,a,g}$ for each tape symbol a and state g such that $\delta(g, a) = (h, b, -1)$ for some state h and tape symbol b, provided cell i is not the rightmost tape cell.

E_0 has been designed so that if its inputs encode a configuration of M, then its outputs encode the configuration that results from one move of M. Note that the size of E_0, measured in terms of the number of instances of two input AND and OR modules, is quadratic in n.[1]

Next, consider the body of each E_m, where $1 \leq m \leq cn$. The body of each such E_m is constructed by using two instances of module E_{m-1}, connected as shown in Fig. 8.7. The body input ports of E_m drive the input ports of the first instances of E_{m-1}, whose output ports drive the input ports of the second instance of E_{m-1}, whose output ports drive the body output ports of E_m. Since the outputs of each instance of E_{m-1} encode the configuration of M produced after 2^{m-1} moves from the configuration encoded by its inputs, the outputs of

---

[1] Although it is possible to design E_0 so that its size is linear in n, this entails providing extra ports to hold complementary values and would not strengthen the result.

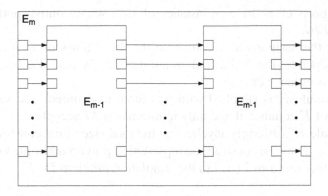

Figure 8.7. Body of E_m for $m > 0$

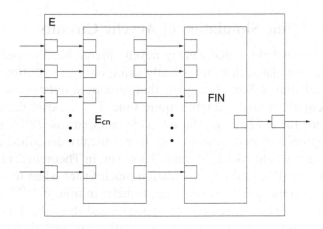

Figure 8.8. Body of root module E

E_m encode the configuration produced after 2^m moves from the configuration encoded by the inputs of E_m.

Note that the size of the description of the body of each such E_m is linear in n and that the number of such descriptions is cn.

Let *FIN* be a module with one output port and a number of input ports equal to the number of output ports of E_0. The body of *FIN* consists of instances of *OR* modules that compute the result of the *OR* of those input-port variables that represent an accepting state of M. Thus when the input ports of *FIN* encode a configuration of M, the output of *FIN* encodes whether the configuration is an accepting configuration.

Let E be a module with one output port and a number of input ports equal to the number of input ports of E_0. The body of E is shown in Fig. 8.8. The body input ports of E drive an instance of E_{cn}, whose output ports drive an instance of *FIN*.

Consider the assignment of values to the input ports of E such that this assignment encodes the initial configuration of M given x. (Each value in this assignment is either τ or ϕ.)

When module E is supplied with this input assignment, the value of the output port of E equals τ if and only if automaton M accepts x.

The module E is strongly acyclic, and the total size of the constructed modules is $\Theta(n^2)$. Thus the construction represents a polynomial-time $\Theta(n^2)$-size-bounded reduction from $L(M)$ to the simulation problem for E. □

An immediate consequence of Theorem 4.2 is that problem Γ is PSPACE-hard. Moreover, if some language in $\text{DSPACE}(n)$ requires time $2^{\Omega(n)}$, then problem Γ requires time $2^{\Omega(\sqrt{n})}$.

5. $2^{O(\sqrt{n})}$ time Simulation of Acyclic Circuits

In this section we show that weakly acyclic hierarchically specified logic circuits can be simulated deterministically using only $2^{O(\sqrt{n})}$ time. The linear space simulation of Sect. 3 suggests that perhaps simulation of an acyclic hierarchical circuit of size n might require time $2^{\Theta(n)}$. Also, the size of the flattened circuit for a size n acyclic hierarchical circuit is $2^{\Theta(n)}$, so that the traditional approach of first flattening the hierarchically described circuit and then simulating it would take $2^{O(n)}$ time. However, in Theorem 5.11 below we show that it is possible to do the simulation much faster when the domain of values involved in the simulation is finite, namely, in time $2^{O(\sqrt{n})}$. Moreover, we carefully analyze the constant in the exponent and show that it is of reasonable size. To do this we need the following notation and technical lemmas.

DEFINITION 5.1. The *submodule size* of a module M equals 1 if M is primitive and equals the number of occurrences of submodules appearing directly in the body of M otherwise. The *submodule size* of a hierarchical description D is the sum of the submodule sizes of the modules appearing in D.

DEFINITION 5.2. The *module expansion tree M-Tree(D)* of a hierarchically specified module D is defined as follows: *M-Tree(D)* is a labeled unordered tree such that

(i) each node of *M-Tree(D)* is labeled by the name of a module Z such that Z *SOMEWHERE-WITHIN* D,

(ii) the root of *M-Tree(D)* is labeled by the name of the root module D,

(iii) each node of *M-Tree(D)* labeled by the name of a primitive module has no children,

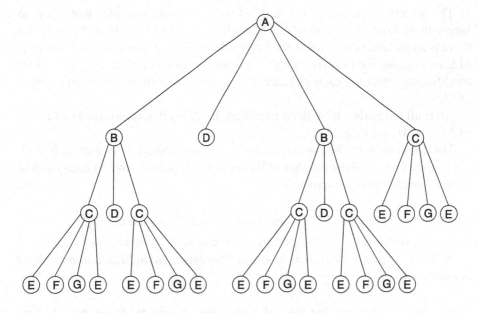

Figure 8.9.   Module expansion tree *M-Tree(A)*

(iv) each node of *M-Tree(D)* labeled by the name of a composite module, say, module Z, has a child for each module instance in the body of Z. Each child is labeled with the module name of the instance.

As an example, Fig. 8.9 shows *M-Tree(A)* for the module A that appears in Fig. 8.5. (Note that module D is primitive.)

LEMMA 5.3. *Let $n \geq 1$ be an integer. The maximum number of leaves in the expansion tree of a hierarchically specified module whose hierarchical description is constrained to have submodule size at most n occurs when only one kind of submodule occurs at each level in the expansion tree of the hierarchically specified module.*

Proof. The following algorithm, given a hierarchically specified module M, produces a hierarchically specified module N whose hierarchical description has submodule size no greater than that of M, such that

  (i) the number of leaves in *M-Tree(M)* is less than or equal to the number of leaves in *M-Tree(N)*, and

 (ii) only one kind of submodule occurs at each level in the expansion tree of hierarchically specified module N.

The algorithm processes the body of the composite modules that occur as labels in *M-Tree(M)* as follows. For each body let Q be a module such that there is an instance of Q within the body and *M-Tree(Q)* has a maximal number of leaves among the kinds of modules having instances in the body. The body is modified by replacing each instance of a module other than Q with an instance of Q.

After all the bodies have been modified, modules that no longer label nodes in *M-Tree(M)* are deleted.

The correctness of the lemma follows since the submodule size of each module is unchanged and the number of leaves in the expansion tree of each module is either unchanged or increased. □

LEMMA 5.4. *Let m, k, $i_1, \ldots,$ and i_k be integers ≥ 1 such that $\sum_{j=1}^{k} i_j = m$. Then the product $\prod_{j=1}^{k} i_j$ is less than or equal to 3^r if $m = 3 \cdot r$, $3^{r-1} \cdot 2^2$ if $m = 3 \cdot r + 1$, and $3^r \cdot 2$ if $m = 3 \cdot r + 2$. Moreover, the indicated upper bound is obtainable.*

Proof. It is easily seen that the indicated upper bound is obtainable. To verify that the claimed upper bound is an upper bound, we need only verify the following: Let $m, k, i_1, \ldots,$ and i_k be integers ≥ 1. Let m be fixed.

(1) The product $i_1 \cdots i_k$, subject to the constraint $i_1 + \cdots + i_k = m$, is maximized when $i_1, \ldots, i_k \in \{2, 3\}$.

(2) Given that $i_1, \ldots, i_k \in \{2, 3\}$, the product $i_1 \cdots i_k$, subject to the constraint $i_1 + \cdots + i_k = m$, is maximized when at most two of the integers $i_1, \ldots, i_k$ equal 2.

To see the correctness of (1), we observe the following:

(1a) Suppose some $i_l \geq 5$. Then the product $i_1 \cdots i_k < (\prod_{j=1, j \neq l}^{k} i_j) \cdot 2 \cdot (i_l - 2)$ (since $i_l < 2 \cdot (i_l - 2)$) and $\sum_{j=1, j \neq l}^{k} i_j + 2 + (i_l - 2) = m$.

(1b) Suppose some $i_l = 4$. This occurrence of 4 can be replaced by two occurrences of 2; the sum and product of the integers will be unchanged.

To see the correctness of (2), we observe that $6 = 2 + 2 + 2 = 3 + 3$ *but* $2^3 < 3^2$. □

DEFINITION 5.5. A set of primitive modules Π is *complete* over a domain D of values if D is the domain over which the primitives operate and if every function of the form $D^k \to D$ for finite k can be computed by a finite interconnection of modules in Π.

LEMMA 5.6. *For any set Π of primitive modules that is complete over a finite domain with d values, there is a constant c such that any acyclic circuit with z ports has an equivalent circuit of size at most czd^z.*

Proof. Of the z ports, let x be the number of input ports and let y be the number of output ports. The circuit computes a function from d^x to d^y. Let each of the d^x input value assignments be called a *minterm*.

Since Π is complete, a circuit of a fixed size can perform each of the binary operations in Z_d. Thus for each minterm a circuit that computes a signal whose value is 1 if the input assignment corresponds to that minterm, and whose value is 0 otherwise, can be constructed. The size of the circuit for each minterm is at most $c_1 x$, where constant c_1 depends on Π. Each of the y outputs can be computed by a circuit that combines the values of the d^x minterms, and the size of this circuit is at most $c_2 d^x$, where constant c_2 depends on Π. If c is $\max(c_1, c_2)$, the size of the overall circuit is at most czd^z. $\qquad\square$

DEFINITION 5.7. Consider a hierarchical circuit description D of size n. Let M be a hierarchically described module occurring in D such that the number of ports of M is at least $\sqrt{n}$. The *module semiexpansion tree* of M, denoted by *S-Tree(M)*, is a labeled unordered tree such that

(i) each node of *S-Tree(M)* is labeled by the name of a module that occurs in the description D and that has at least $\sqrt{n}$ ports,

(ii) the root of *S-Tree(M)* is labeled by the name of module M,

(iii) each node of *S-Tree(M)* labeled by the name of a primitive module has no children,

(iv) each node of *S-Tree(M)* labeled by the name of a composite module, say, module Z, has a child for each instance in the body of Z of a module with at least $\sqrt{n}$ ports. Each child is labeled with the module name of the instance.

Note that *S-Tree(M)* corresponds to the expansion tree of M that would be produced if D were modified by deletion of all occurrences of modules and module instances having less than $\sqrt{n}$ ports.

LEMMA 5.8. *Consider a hierarchical description D of size n, and a module M occurring in D such that M has at least $\sqrt{n}$ ports. Then*

(1) *S-Tree(M) has depth at most $\sqrt{n}$, and*

(2) *S-Tree(M) contains at most $3^{\lceil \sqrt{n}/3 \rceil}$ leaves.*

Proof. (1) Since each node along a path from the root to a leaf of *S-Tree*(M) corresponds to a distinct module whose description is of size at least $\sqrt{n}$, the number of such modules cannot exceed $\sqrt{n}$.

(2) Note that the proof of Lemma 5.3 applies to *S-Trees*. Thus for a given value of n the number of leaves is maximized when each module body contains instances of only one module type. Thus assume that at each level of *S-Tree*(M) all the nodes at that level are labeled by the same module. Let $M_0, M_1, \ldots, M_k$ be the module labeling the root, children of the root, etc. For $1 \le i \le k$ let i_j be the number of instances of module M_j within the body of module M_{j-1}. Since the total size of the description is n and each module instance has size at least $\sqrt{n}$, there can be at most $\sqrt{n}$ module instances contributing to *S-Tree*(M). Thus it must be the case that $\sum_{j=1}^{k} i_j \le \sqrt{n}$. Therefore, from Lemma 5.4, $\prod_{j=1}^{k} i_j$ does not exceed $3^{\lceil \sqrt{n}/3 \rceil}$. But this product is the number of leaves of *S-Tree*(M). □

THEOREM 5.9. *For any set Π of primitive modules that is complete over a finite domain with d values there is a constant c such that any acyclic circuit specified by a hierarchical description of a size n has an equivalent circuit whose flat description is of size at most* $cn^{3/2}2^{((1/3)\log_2 3 + \log_2 d)\sqrt{n}}$.

Proof. Suppose a module M has at most $\sqrt{n}$ ports. Then from Lemma 5.6 it has an equivalent circuit of size at most $c_1\sqrt{n}d^{\sqrt{n}}$, where c_1 depends on Π.

Suppose M has more than ports. From Lemma 5.8, *S-Tree*(M) contains at most $3^{\lceil \sqrt{n}/3 \rceil}$ leaves. Each of these leaves has a module body containing at most n module instances, and each of these module instances has at most $\sqrt{n}$ ports. Therefore, if M were expanded by continually replacing module instances with more than $\sqrt{n}$ ports by their bodies and not expanding any module instance with at most $\sqrt{n}$ ports, the resulting circuit would contain at most $n3^{\lceil \sqrt{n}/3 \rceil}$ instances of modules, each with at most $\sqrt{n}$ ports. From Lemma 5.6 each of these module instances can be replaced by a flat circuit containing at most $c_1\sqrt{n}d^{\sqrt{n}}$ instances of primitive modules. If we let $c = 3c_1$, the overall circuit contains at most $cn^{3/2}2^{((1/3)\log_2 3 + \log_2 d)\sqrt{n}}$ instances of primitive modules. □

Note that since $\log_2 3$ is less than 1.59, the bound from the preceding theorem is $cn^{3/2}2^{(0.53 + \log_2 d)\sqrt{n}}$. When the domain of the circuit is binary, so that $d = 2$, the bound is $cn^{3/2}2^{1.53\sqrt{n}}$.

THEOREM 5.10. *For any set Π of primitive modules that is complete over a finite domain with d values, there is a constant c such that for any acyclic circuit specified by a hierarchical description of size n an equivalent flat description can be constructed in time* $cn^{5/2}2^{((1/3)\log_2 3 + \log_2 d)\sqrt{n}}$.

Proof. Let c_1 be the constant in the statement of Theorem 5.9. Let M be the module whose description is to be constructed. Then working from the bottom up in accordance with the *DIRECTLY-WITHIN* relation, an "official" flat circuit is constructed for each of the modules that are involved in the hierarchical description of M and have fewer than $\sqrt{n}$ ports. Finally, the flat circuit for M is constructed. For each module N considered with fewer than $\sqrt{n}$ ports, the official flat circuit is constructed as described in Lemma 5.6. To use this construction we need a table that gives the output values for each assignment of input values. This table is constructed by first producing a "working body" for N and then simulating the working body for each input assignment. The working body is constructed as described by Theorem 5.9, continually substituting the body for each instance of a module, but when an instance of a module with less than $\sqrt{n}$ ports is encountered, its already constructed official body is directly substituted for the instance. The result is that the working body for N is of size at most $c_1 n^{3/2} 2^{((1/3) \log_2 3 + \log_2 d)\sqrt{n}}$. The table for N requires $d^{\sqrt{n}}$ rows, and each row can be filled in by simulating the working body for N, given the input assignment corresponding to that row. Thus the time to fill in the table is proportional to $n^{3/2} 2^{((1/3) \log_2 3 + \log_2 d)\sqrt{n}}$.

After at most n official bodies are constructed, the fiat circuit for M can be constructed as described in Theorem 5.9. $\square$

THEOREM 5.11. *For any set Π of primitive modules that is complete over a finite domain with d values, there is a constant c such that any acyclic circuit specified by a hierarchical description of size n can be simulated in time at most $cn^{5/2} c^{((1/3) \log_2 3 + \log_2 d)\sqrt{n}}$.*

Proof. A flat circuit equivalent to the module to be simulated can be constructed as described in Theorem 5.10 and then can be directly simulated. $\square$

In performing a simulation it is not really necessary to construct the circuits for modules with fewer than $\sqrt{n}$ ports. Rather, each such module can be represented by a table that provides the output values for each input assignment. Each such table can be initially empty. Each time the module is simulated with an input assignment that has not been submitted thus far, the output values in the appropriate row can be filled in. When the module is to be simulated with an input assignment that has already been simulated, the output values in the appropriate row can be used (without having to repeat this simulation). Thus a given overall simulation might take less time than the construction that is the basis of Theorem 5.11 would take.

Note that given a hierarchically described circuit, the size of the flattened circuit can be computed in linear time by using a bottom-up method. A choice can than be made between using the algorithm of Theorem 5.11 and simulating the flattened circuit, depending on a comparison of the size of the flattened circuit and the bound of Theorem 5.11. This hybrid algorithm never uses more time or more space than the traditional method of constructing the flattened circuit and then simulating it. Since the flattened circuit can be of size $2^{\Omega(n)}$, the hybrid algorithm often uses less time and much less space. If space is of the utmost importance, the algorithm of Theorem 3.1 can be used.

6. Analysis Problems for Circuits with Cycles

In this section we consider hierarchical module descriptions in which dataflow cycles are permitted. Simulation for circuits with dataflow cycles involves computing the values of the output ports of a module, given its hierarchical description, a specification of the sequence of values for each input port, a specification of the initial state of the module, and a specification of which values should be reported.

As for acyclic modules, we assume that the domain of signal values is finite. We also assume that for each input port of a primitive module there is a rule for what value to use should the port be unconnected to a driver.

Because of the presence of cycles, timing issues arise. We assume that for any given set of primitive modules, all delays are multiples of some basic unit of time. We also assume that each primitive module can have a state (where combinational modules are a special case that have only a single state). For each primitive module we assume that there is a rule computable in polynomial time and linear space that when given a state and input-port values, determines a next state and output-port values, perhaps with a specified delay.

Consider a set of primitive modules that satisfy the conditions described above. The *input information* for a *simulation problem* consists of a hierarchical module description, the specification of a sequence of values for each input port of the root module, the specification of initial values for states of some of the primitive modules and some signals in the flattened body of the module, the specification of a condition of when to stop the simulation, and the specification of conditions for when the output values should be reported. We make the following assumptions about the language in which these specifications are expressed. We assume that time can be written in binary. We assume that the language for expressing the sequence of values for an input port can enumerate values at given times or during given time intervals, can specify repetition of a sequence of values, and can specify default values for times not explicitly described. We assume that the language for expressing initial values for states or signals in the flattened body can specify a value for certain explicitly listed signals and primitive module instances in the flattened body and can specify default values for those not explicitly listed. We assume that for explicitly listing a signal or module its *hierarchical name* is given, where the hierarchical name begins with the name of the root module and consists of an identifying sequence of names separated by periods. The size of a hierarchical name is the number of names in the sequence. For instance, hierarchical name $A.B.C.D.$ refers to D within instance C within instance B of module A. The size of this hierarchical name is 4. We assume that the stop condition can be either a specified time or a specified value for one of the output ports. We assume that the report condition can be a list of times or time intervals or can be a Boolean combination of output-port values.

The *output information* for a simulation problem is the values of the output ports of the root module at those times satisfying the specified report conditions, up to the time the stop condition is satisfied.

PROPOSITION 6.1. *For a given set of primitive modules, the simulation problem for flat circuit descriptions can be solved in linear space.*

Proof. The simulation can keep track of the value of each signal in the flat body plus, if appropriate, states of the primitive modules. □

THEOREM 6.2. *A hierarchically specified circuit can be simulated in exponential space.*

Proof. The size of the flattened body of the module is at most exponential in the size of the hierarchical description. Thus the flattened body can be constructed in exponential space and then simulated. □

We now show that the simulation problem requires exponential space.

We say that a set of primitive modules has *flip-flop expressibility* if there exist two values ϕ and τ in the domain of values operated on by the primitive modules and if there exist four modules {*AND, OR, NOT, FLIP-FLOP*} either available as primitive modules or constructible as composite modules by an interconnection of primitive modules such that these modules behave like the standard logic modules with these names. The *FLIP-FLOP* module can behave like any of the standard flip-flop types. (The *FLIP-FLOP* module can be a composite module constructed out of the gate-type modules.)

For a set of primitive modules with flip-flop expressibility, a linear-bounded automaton with a given input string can be described as a flat module whose size is proportional to the length of the input string. Consequently, the simulation problem for fiat modules constructed from primitive modules that have flip-flop expressibility is PSPACE-hard. Because of Proposition 6.1, the problem is PSPACE-complete. Hierarchical descriptions permit an exponential increase in conciseness but involve a corresponding exponential increase in the space required for the simulation problem, as described in the following result.

THEOREM 6.3. *For a set* Π *of primitive modules with flip-flop expressibility, there exists a constant* $d > 0$ *such that the simulation problem for hierarchical module descriptions requires space at least* 2^{dn} *on any Turing machine.*

Proof. Let M be an arbitrary 2^{cn}-space-bounded Turing machine for some constant $c > 0$. Assume that M serves as a language recognizer. Also assume that M has an explicit accept state and an explicit reject state. Without loss of generality it can be assumed that for every input string, M eventually enters either its explicit accept or explicit reject state without having touched more than its 2^{cn} leftmost tape cells, and it then moves to the right indefinitely in its accept or reject state.

Consider an input string x of length n, where x is assumed to include end markers. In processing x machine M uses at most 2^{cn} tape cells and then keeps moving to the right in either the accept or reject state.

The overall circuit to be specified hierarchically will contain an implementation of Turing machine M and enough tape cells to determine whether M accepts x. In this implementation each tape cell will be implemented explicitly by an instance of a submodule, called module D_0, that can both record the contents of a tape cell and simulate the operation of M's finite state control when the tape head of M is on that cell. A transition of M will be implemented by changes of signal values involved in instances of D_0 corresponding to the tape cells affected by the transition, with other instances of D_0 remaining unchanged.

Given x, a hierarchical circuit description can be constructed as follows. The circuit description depends only on n, the length of x. For each m, where $0 \leq m \leq cn$, there is a composite module D_m. In the overall circuit that is specified hierarchically, each instance of D_m represents a segment of 2^m contiguous cells of M's tape. The flip-flops in this instance of D_m record the contents of the tape cells in this segment, whether or not the tape head is residing on this segment and, if so, the state of M and on which cell in the segment the head is residing. The ports of D_m are summarized in Fig. 8.10. For each state g of M input port xl_g encodes whether the tape head, in state g, is moving onto the represented tape segment from the left. Similarly, input port xr_g encodes whether the tape head, in state g, is moving onto the tape segment from the right. Output port yl_g encodes whether the tape head, in state g, is moving off the tape segment to the left. Similarly, output port yr_g encodes whether the tape head, in state g is moving off the tape segment to the right.

Consider D_0, whose purpose is to simulate one cell of M. The body of D_0 can be constructed by using instances of modules *FLIP-FLOP*, *OR*, *AND*, and *NOT*. The flip-flops are used to remember the contents of the tape cell, whether or not the tape head is on the cell, and, if so, the state. A straightforward implementation can have a flip-flop for each tape symbol and a flip-flop for

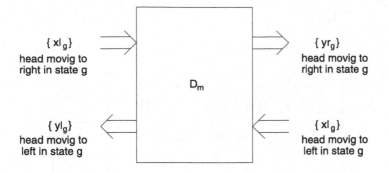

$$\{\,xl_g\,\}$$
head movig to
right in state g

$$\{\,yr_g\,\}$$
head movig to
right in state g

D_m

$$\{\,yl_g\,\}$$
head movig to
left in state g

$$\{\,xl_g\,\}$$
head movig to
left in state g

Figure 8.10. Ports of module D_m

each state. At each step of the computation by M, the head of M resides at some given tape cell, say, cell α. On the basis of the contents of cell α and the current state, M makes a transition that involves a next state, new contents of cell α, and the determination of whether the head of M remains stationary, moves one cell to the left, or moves one cell to the right. Corresponding to this step of M, the instance of D_0 representing cell α uses its recorded value of the state and cell contents to simulate the transition. The new contents of cell α are recorded in this instance of D_0. If the transition involves no head movement, then the next state and the fact that the head is residing on this cell is recorded in this instance of D_0. If the transition involves movement of the tape head, then the appropriate output port of this instance of D_0 is given a value indicating the movement of the tape head onto an adjacent cell and the new state of M. This value on the output port causes the instance of D_0 representing the adjacent tape cell to record the fact that the tape head is now residing on it. (Note that for all instances of D_0 other than the one that represents cell α, the values on the output ports remain unchanged.) The details of the construction of the body of D_0 are routine and are left to the reader.

Now consider the body of each D_m where $1 \leq m \leq cn$. The body of each D_m is constructed by using two instances of module D_{m-1} interconnected as shown in Fig. 8.11.

Note that the size of the description of each D_m is independent of n and that the number of such descriptions is cn.

Let *INIT* be a module whose body consists of a sequence of n instances of D_0 connected together. The purpose of *INIT* is to represent the first n tape cells of M, which are initially to contain string x. (All other cells of M are initially to contain the blank tape symbol.) Module *INIT* has the same set of ports as described in Fig. 8.10. Note that the size of the description of *INIT* is proportional to n.

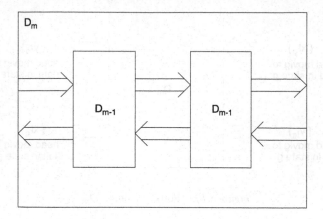

Figure 8.11. Body of D_m for $m > 0$

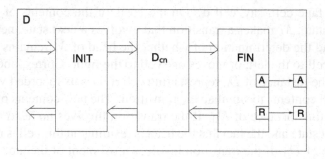

Figure 8.12. Body of root module D

Let *FIN* be a module with two output ports $\{A, R\}$ and a number of input ports equal to the number of right output ports of D_{cn}. The body of *FIN* computes whether its input ports indicate that the tape head is moving to the right in the explicit accept or reject state. Output port A is given a special value when *FIN* detects the tape head moving to the right in the accept state, and output port R is given a special value when *FIN* detects the tape head moving to the right in the reject state.

Let D be a module with two output ports and no input ports. The body of D is shown in Fig. 8.12. In Fig. 8.12 the left input ports of *INIT* and the right input ports of D_{cn}, are shown as unconnected. This assumes that the unconnected input ports of D_0 are interpreted as representing the absence of tape head movement. If this is not the case for the primitive modules used in the body of D_0, the body of D could be given additional module instances to generate the appropriate input-port values.

Consider the following instance of the simulation problem. The hierarchical module description consists of the description of D, *INIT*, *FIN*, $D_0, \ldots, D_{cn}$, with D designated as the root module. The specification of the initial values of flip-flops in the flattened circuit is that the n instances of D_0 within *INIT* are initialized with the n symbols of x and that all the instances of D_0 within D_{cn} are initialized with the blank symbol. Also, the leftmost instance of D_0 within *INIT* is specified to be initialized with the tape head present and the starting state of M. All other occurrences of D_0 are initialized with the tape head absent. The condition for both reporting the output and stopping the simulation is that either output of D has the special value that indicates acceptance or rejection by M.

For this simulation problem the simulation always halts, only one set of output-port values is reported, and the reported values indicate whether M accepts or rejects x.

Note that the size of the hierarchical object description is proportional to n. The size of the initialization specification is proportional to n since the size of the hierarchical name of each instance of D_0 within *INIT* is constant. (If the language for specifying initialization conditions were more restricted, the construction could be modified so that all flip-flops would be specified to be in the same neutral state and D would be given an input that could be used to load specified values into the first n cells and then initiate the operation of M.) Thus the construction represents a linear size (and polynomial time) reduction from the acceptance problem for M to the simulation problem for D. Since the size of the input information for the simulation problem is proportional to n, there is a constant $d > 0$ such that the simulation problem requires space at least 2^{dn}. □

Combining Theorems 6.2 and 6.3 gives the following result.

COROLLARY 6.4. *The simulation problem is EXPSPACE-complete for hierarchically specified objects when the set of primitive modules has flip-flop expressibility.*

Acknowledgments

We wish to acknowledge one of the referees for pointing out a flaw in our original proof of Theorem 3.1.

References

[1] A. V. Aho, J. E. Hopcroft, and J. D. Ullman. *The Design and Analysis of Computer Algorithms*. Addison–Wesley, Reading, 1974.

[2] J. Benkoski and A. J. Strojwas. A new approach to hierarchical and statistical timing simulations. *IEEE Trans. Computer-Aided Design*, CAD-6:1039–1052, 1987.

[3] J. L. Bentley and T. Ottman. The complexity of manipulating hierarchically defined sets of rectangles. In J. Gruska and M. Chytil, editors, *Proc. Mathematical Foundations of Computer Science*. Lecture Notes in Computer Science, volume 118, pages 1–15. Springer, Berlin, 1981.

[4] P. A. Bloniarz, H. B. Hunt III, and D. J. Rosenkrantz. Algebraic structures with hard equivalence and minimization problems. *J. Assoc. Comput. Mach.*, 31:879–904, 1984.

[5] J. D. Crawford. EDIF: A mechanism for the exchange of design information. *IEEE Design and Test*, 2:63–69, 1985.

[6] M. R. Garey and D. S. Johnson. *Computers and Intractability*. Freeman, San Francisco, 1979.

[7] J. P. Hayes. Digital simulation with multiple logic values. *IEEE Trans. Computer-Aided Design*, CAD-5:274–283, 1986.

[8] R. Kolla and B. Serf. The virtual feedback problem in hierarchical representations of combinatorial circuits. *Acta Informatica*, 28:463–476, 1991.

[9] T. Lengauer. Exploiting hierarchy in VLSI design. In F. Makedon et al., editor, *Proc. Aegean Workshop on Computing*. Lecture Notes in Computer Science, volume 227, pages 180–193. Springer, Berlin, 1986.

[10] T. Lengauer. Hierarchical planarity testing algorithms. In L. Kott, editor, *Proc. 13th International Colloquium on Automata, Languages and Programming*. Lecture Notes in Computer Science, volume 226, pages 215–225. Springer, Berlin, 1986.

[11] T. Lengauer. Efficient algorithms for finding minimum spanning forests of hierarchically defined graphs. *J. Algorithms*, 8:260–284, 1987.

[12] T. Lengauer and K. W. Wagner. The correlation between the complexities of the nonhierarchical and hierarchical versions of graph problems. In E. J. Brandenburg et al., editors, *Proc. 4th Annual Symposium on Theoretical Aspects of Computer Science*. Lecture Notes in Computer Science, volume 247, pages 100–113. Springer, Berlin, 1987.

[13] T. Lengauer and E. Wanke. Efficient solution of connectivity problems in hierarchically defined graphs. *SIAM J. Comput.*, 17:1063–1089, 1988.

[14] Y. Levendel and P. R. Menon. Fault simulation. In D. K. Pradhan, editor, *Fault-Tolerant Computing: Theory and Techniques*, volume 1, pages 184–264. Prentice Hall, Englewood Cliffs, 1986.

[15] R. Lipsett, E. Marschner, and M. Shahdad. VHDL–the language. *IEEE Design and Test*, 3:28–41, 1986.

[16] S. Maclane and G. Birkhoff. *Algebra*. MacMillan, New York, 1967.

[17] J. Magee, J. Kramer, and M. Sloman. Constructing distributed systems in conic. *IEEE Trans. Software Engrg.*, 15:663–675, 1989.

[18] C. Mead and L. Conway. *Introduction to VLSI Systems*. Addison–Wesley, Reading, 1980.

[19] C. Niessen. Hierarchical design methodologies and tools for VLSI chips. *Proc. IEEE*, 41:65–75, 1983.

[20] J. K. Ousterhout, G. T. Hamachi, R. N. Mayo, W. S. Scott, and G. S. Taylor. The magic VLSI layout system. *IEEE Design and Test*, 2:19–30, 1985.

[21] L. K. Scheffer and R. Soetarman. Hierarchical analysis of IC artwork with user defined abstraction rules. In *Proc. ACM/IEEE 22nd Design Automation Conference*, pages 293–298, 1985.

[22] L. J. Stockmeyer and A. R. Meyer. Word problems requiring exponential time. In *Proc. 5th Annual ACM Symposium on Theory of Computing*, pages 1–9, 1973.

[23] T. J. Wagner. Hierarchical layout verification. *IEEE Design and Test*, 2:31–37, 1985.

[24] U. Zimmerman. *Linear and Combinatorial Optimization in Ordered Algebraic Structures*. North-Holland, Amsterdam, 1981.

Chapter 9

APPROXIMATION ALGORITHMS FOR DEGREE-CONSTRAINED MINIMUM-COST NETWORK-DESIGN PROBLEMS*

R. RAVI

Graduate School of Industrial Administration, Carnegie Mellon University, Pittsburgh, PA 15213-3890, USA. Email: `ravi@cmu.edu`

MADHAV V. MARATHE

Los Alamos National Laboratory, P.O. Box 1663, MS B265, Los Alamos, NM 87545, USA.
Email: `marathe@lanl.gov`

S. S. RAVI, DANIEL J. ROSENKRANTZ AND HARRY B. HUNT III

Department of Computer Science, University at Albany—SUNY, Albany, NY 12222, USA.
Emails: `ravi@cs.albany.edu`, `djr@cs.albany.edu`,
`hunt@cs.albany.edu`

Reprinted from: *Algorithmica*, Vol. 31, No. 1, May 2001, pp. 58–78.
© Springer

Abstract   We study network-design problems with two different design objectives: the total cost of the edges and nodes in the network and the maximum degree of any node in the network. A prototypical example is the degree-constrained node-weighted Steiner tree problem: We are given an undirected graph $G(V, E)$, with a non-negative integral function d that specifies an upper bound $d(v)$ on the degree of each vertex $v \in V$ in the Steiner tree to be constructed, nonnegative costs on the nodes, and a subset of k nodes called *terminals*. The goal is to

* A preliminary version of this paper appeared as [26]. R. Ravi's research was supported by a NSF CAREER grant 96-25297. The work by Madhav Marathe was supported by the Department of Energy under Contract W-7405-ENG-36. The last three authors were supported by NSF Grants CCR 89-03319, CCR 90-06396, CCR 94-06611 and CCR 97-34936.

S.S. Ravi, S.K. Shukla (eds.), *Fundamental Problems in Computing*,
© Springer Science + Business Media B.V. 2009

construct a Steiner tree T containing all the terminals such that the degree of any node v in T is at most the specified upper bound $d(v)$ and the total cost of the nodes in T is minimum. Our main result is a bicriteria approximation algorithm whose output is approximate in terms of both the degree and cost criteria—the degree of any node $v \in V$ in the output Steiner tree is $O(d(v) \log k)$ and the cost of the tree is $O(\log k)$ times that of a minimum-cost Steiner tree that obeys the degree bound $d(v)$ for each node v. Our result extends to the more general problem of constructing one-connected networks such as generalized Steiner forests. We also consider the special case in which the edge costs obey the triangle inequality and present simple approximation algorithms with better performance guarantees.

Keywords: approximation algorithms, network design, bicriteria problems

Received December 21, 1998; revised September 24, 1999. Communicated by G. N. Frederickson. Online publication May 22, 2001.

1.   Introduction and Motivation

Several problems in the design of communication networks can be modeled as finding a network obeying certain connectivity specifications. For instance, the network may be required to connect all the nodes in the graph (a spanning tree problem), a specified subset of the nodes in the graph (a Steiner tree problem) or to only interconnect a set of pairs of nodes (a generalized Steiner forest problem). The goal in such network-design problems can usually be expressed as minimizing some measure of cost associated with the network. Several examples of such cost measures have been considered in the literature. For example, if we associate costs with edges and nodes that can be used to build the network, then we may seek a network such that the cost of construction is minimized. This is the *minimum-cost network design* problem and has been well studied. A notion of cost that reflects the vulnerability of the network to single point failures and the amount of load at a given point in the network is the maximum degree of any node in the network. Minimizing this cost gives rise to the *minimum-degree network design* problem, which has also been well studied. Another common cost measure is the maximum cost of any edge in the network. This goal falls under the category of *bottleneck problems* that have also received considerable attention.

Finding a network of sufficient generality and of minimum cost with respect to any one of these measures is often NP-hard [14]. Hence much of the work mentioned above focuses on approximation algorithms for these problems. However, in applications that arise in real-world situations, it is often the case that the network design problem involves the minimization of more than one of these cost measures simultaneously [9, 16].

In this paper, we concentrate on two objectives: (i) the degree of the network and (ii) the total cost of the network. Typically, our goal will be to find networks of minimum cost subject to degree constraints. For example, consider the following problem: Given an undirected graph $G = (V, E)$ with nonnegative costs on its edges and an integer $b \geq 2$, find a spanning tree in which the maximum degree of any node is at most b and the total cost is a minimum. Such *degree-constrained minimum-cost network* problems arise in diverse areas such as VLSI design, vehicle routing and communication networks. For example, Deo and Hakimi [8] considered this problem in the context of backplane wiring among pins, where no more than a fixed number of wires can be wrapped around any pin on the wiring panel. In communication literature, this problem is commonly known as the *teleprocessing design problem* or as the *multidrop terminal layout problem* [2]. Here, we investigate the complexity and approximability of a number of such degree-constrained minimum-cost network-design problems. The main focus of our work is to develop a general technique for constructing near-optimal solutions to such problems.

The remainder of the paper is organized as follows. Section 2 contains basic definitions and formal statements of the problems considered in this paper. It also discusses a framework for evaluating approximation algorithms. Section 3 summarizes the results in the paper. Section 4 discusses related work. In Sect. 5 we present our algorithm for degree-bounded node-weighted networks. In that section we also discuss an extension of the algorithm to networks represented using proper functions. In Sect. 6, we outline the algorithms with improved performance and running times for constructing networks when restricted to input graphs obeying the triangle inequality. Section 7 contains negative results on the approximabilities of some problems. Finally, Sect. 8 discusses some implications and directions for future research.

2. Basic Definitions and Problem Formulations

Following the framework developed in [21], a generic bicriteria network design problem, denoted by $(\mathbf{A}, \mathbf{B}, \mathcal{S})$, is defined by identifying two minimization objectives, denoted by $\mathbf{A}$ and $\mathbf{B}$, from a set of possible objectives, and specifying a membership requirement in a class of subgraphs, denoted by $\mathcal{S}$. The problem specifies a budget value on the first objective $(\mathbf{A})$ under one cost function, and the goal is to find a network having minimum possible value for the second objective $(\mathbf{B})$ under another cost function, such that this network is within the budget on the first objective. The solution network must belong to the subgraph-class $\mathcal{S}$.

The two objectives we consider in this paper are: (i) degree of the network and (ii) the cost of the network. We consider two extensions of these objectives. The first extension deals with the budgeted objective, namely degree, and the second deals with the minimization objective, namely the total cost. The two versions of degree constraints that we consider are: (i) non-uniform degree (denoted by N-DEGREE) and (ii) uniform degree (denoted by U-DEGREE). In the *non-uniform degree* version, a possibly different degree bound $d(v)(\geq 2)$ is specified for each vertex v. The *uniform degree* version is a special case where $\forall v \in V, d(v) = b$ for some integer b; i.e., all the vertices have the same degree constraint. Thus, for the problems considered in this paper $\mathbf{A} \in \{\text{U-DEGREE}, \text{N-DEGREE}\}$. For the minimization objective, we focus on the total cost of the network. We assume we are given nonnegative costs on the edges and/or nodes of the input undirected graph. The *total cost* is given by the sum of the costs of all the edges (denoted by E-TOTAL-COST) or all the nodes (denoted by N-TOTAL-COST) in the network. Thus, $\mathbf{B} \in \{\text{N-TOTAL-COST}, \text{E-TOTAL-COST}\}$. Finally, the class of subgraphs $\mathcal{S}$ studied here includes SPANNING TREES, STEINER TREES, GENERALIZED STEINER TREES and networks specified using proper 0–1 functions introduced in [15].

Using the above notation, the problem of finding a minimum-cost spanning tree in which each node has degree at most b is denoted by (U-DEGREE, E-TOTAL COST, SPANNING TREE). Similarly, given a node weighted graph $G(V, E)$, an integer function d specifying the upper bound on the degree of each node and a set of terminals $\mathcal{T}$, the (N-DEGREE, N-TOTAL-COST, STEINER TREE) problem is to find a minimum-cost tree T spanning the nodes in $\mathcal{T}$ such that the nodes in T obey the degree constraints. Problems in which the desired network is a generalized Steiner forest or a graph specified by a proper 0–1 function can be formulated along similar lines.

Some of the problems considered in this paper also involve the maximum cost of any edge in the network, i.e., the bottleneck cost, as a minimization objective. We use E-BOTTLENECK-COST to denote this objective. For the rest of the paper, we use the term "$d(v)$-bounded network" to mean a network in which the degree of node v is at most $d(v)$ for all v.

Most of the degree-constrained network-design problems considered in this paper are NP-hard. In fact, for several problems (e.g. (U-DEGREE, E-TOTAL COST, SPANNING TREE)) we show (Theorem 7.1) that it is NP-hard to find a solution that is within any factor of the optimal objective value, if the solution is required to satisfy the budget constraint; alternatively, if the solution must achieve exactly the minimum value of the total cost objective, then it is NP-hard to find one which satisfies the budget within any given factor. Motivated by these hardness results for unicriterion approximations, we focus on finding bicriteria approximations, that is, efficient algorithms that guarantee a solution which is approximate in terms of both the budget and the objective function.

An (α, β) approximation algorithm for a generic bicriteria problem $(\mathbf{A}, \mathbf{B}, \mathcal{S})$ is a polynomial-time algorithm that produces a solution in which the objective value for **A** is at most α times the budget and the cost of the solution with respect to **B** is at most β times the value of an optimal solution with respect to **B** that respects the budget constraint with respect to **A**. Our algorithms provide bicriteria approximations in the sense described above for a wide variety of one-connected network-design problems.

3. Summary of Results

3.1 Hardness Results

Our lower bound results on finding near-optimal solutions include the following. Additional hardness results are discussed in Sect. 7.

1. For general graphs, unless P = NP, for any $\rho > 1$, there is no polynomial time $(1, \rho)$ approximation algorithm for the (U-DEGREE, E-TOTAL COST, SPANNING TREE) problem.

2. For general graphs, unless P = NP, for any $\rho > 1$, there is no polynomial time $(\rho, 1)$ approximation algorithm for the problem (U-DEGREE, E-TOTAL-COST, STEINER TREE).

3. For general graphs, unless P = NP, for any $\varepsilon > 0$ and $\rho > 1$, there is no polynomial time $(2 - \varepsilon, \rho)$-approximation algorithm for the (N-DEGREE, E-TOTAL-COST, STEINER TREE) problem.

4. For general graphs, unless P = NP, for any $\varepsilon > 0$ and $\rho > 1$, there is no polynomial time $(\rho, \tau - \varepsilon)$-approximation algorithm for the (N-DEGREE, E-TOTAL-COST, STEINERTREE) problem. Here τ is the lower bound on the performance guarantee of any algorithm for finding minimum Steiner trees (see Chapter 10 of [10] for the best bounds). This result is an immediate corollary of hardness results for the minimum Steiner tree problem.

These hardness results motivate the need for bicriteria rather than unicriterion approximation algorithms for these problems.

3.2 Approximation Algorithms

A problem with costs on nodes as well as edges can be transformed (for the purposes of designing approximation algorithms) into one with only node costs as follows: subdivide each edge by introducing a new node with cost equal to the cost of the edge.[1] Therefore, in stating our approximation results, we focus on the node-weighted case. To keep the description of our main result simple, we present below the result for the case of degree-constrained node-weighted

---

[1] This transformation is not applicable to minimum cost spanning trees, for which the node weighted case is trivial.

Steiner trees. The extension of this theorem to more general classes of one-connected networks representable as cut-covers of proper functions is deferred to Sect. 5.7.

THEOREM 3.1. *There is a polynomial-time algorithm that, given an undirected graph G on n nodes with nonnegative costs on its nodes, a subset of k nodes called terminals, and a degree bound $d(v) \geq 2$ for every node v, constructs a Steiner tree spanning all the terminals, with degree $O(d(v) \log k)$ at a node v and of cost $O(\log k)$ times that of the minimum-cost Steiner tree of G that spans all the terminals and obeys all the degree bounds.*

A proof of this theorem is provided in Sect. 5. The positive result presented in this theorem should be contrasted with the hardness results mentioned earlier stating that there is no $(2 - \varepsilon, \rho)$ or $(\rho, \tau - \varepsilon)$ (for any $\rho > 1$ and some $\epsilon > 0$) approximation algorithm for the (N-DEGREE, E-TOTAL-COST, STEINERTREE) problem unless P = NP. Combining the above observations we get that finding an approximation algorithm with performance guarantee $(2 - \varepsilon, \tau - \varepsilon)$ is NP-hard. Note that the performance guarantee on the node-cost in the above theorem cannot be asymptotically improved (even if the other performance ratio is arbitrarily weakened) since one of the problems included in the framework of Theorem 3.1 is the node-weighted Steiner tree problem considered by Klein and Ravi in [18]. By a reduction from the set cover problem and the known non-approximability results for the latter problem, they note that the best possible performance ratio achievable for this problem (even without the degree restrictions imposed in Theorem 3.1) is logarithmic unless P = NP [20, 3, 27]. As an immediate corollary of Theorem 3.1, we obtain an $(O(\log n), O(\log n))$ approximation algorithm for the (U-DEGREE, E-TOTAL COST, SPANNING TREE) problem introduced earlier.

In Sect. 6, we address the special case in which the edge costs obey triangle inequality and present *simple* approximation algorithms with better performance guarantees. Further, for the problem of constructing spanning networks in this special case, we show that our algorithms also simultaneously approximate yet another objective, namely the maximum cost of any edge in the network.

4. Related Work

Much work has been done on approximating each of the two cost measures that we simultaneously minimize (see [4, 5] and the references therein). We also refer the reader to the comprehensive book edited by Hochbaum [10] for recent results and techniques for solving these problems.

There has also been extensive work on bicriteria network design problems. The (U-DEGREE, E-TOTAL COST, SPANNING TREE) problem, originally posed and studied in [8], has been recently considered in Boldon, Deo and Kumar [4]. They present heuristics and their parallel implementations but do not provide worst case performance guarantees. Papadimitriou and Vazirani [23] studied the Euclidean version of this problem for the case when $d = 3, 4$. Monma and Suri [22] showed that for any set of points in the plane, a minimum spanning tree with $d = 5$ can be constructed efficiently. Khuller, Raghavachari and Young [17] gave approximation algorithms with performance guarantees of $3/2$ and $5/4$ for $d = 3$ and $d = 4$ respectively for points in the plane. They also presented an approximation algorithm with a performance guarantee of $5/3$ for point sets in higher dimensions when $d = 3$. Iwainsky et al. [16] formulated a version of the minimum-cost Steiner problem with an additional cost based on node-degrees. Duin and Volgenant [9] formulated the degree-bounded Steiner tree problem motivated by practical considerations. In other related work, Fischer [12] considered the problem of finding a MST of minimum possible maximum degree in a weighted undirected graph. He showed that the techniques of Fürer and Raghavachari [13] can be applied to find a MST of approximately minimum degree.

In [26], we presented early versions of the results in this paper giving specific algorithms for the edge-cost versions, and using a simpler version of the techniques in this paper to give results for the uniform degree node-weighted versions. Building on our work there, in [21], we studied other bicriteria network design problems. There we also presented a polynomial-time algorithm for the (U-DEGREE, E-TOTAL COST, SPANNING TREE) problem when inputs are restricted to treewidth-bounded graphs. In [24], Ravi has applied some of the ideas here to solve a bicriteria problem that forms the basis for finding an approximately minimum broadcast-time scheme in an arbitrary graph.

5.   Degree-Constrained Node-Weighted Steiner Trees

In this section, we present our algorithm in detail for the degree-constrained node-weighted Steiner tree problem. In Sect. 5.7, we briefly indicate how the algorithm can be extended to accommodate more general connectivity specifications.

Recall that, as input to the problem, we are given an undirected graph $G(V, E)$, with nonnegative costs on the nodes and a set of *terminals* to be connected together into a Steiner tree. In addition, for each vertex v, a budget $d(v)$ on its degree in the Steiner tree is specified. The goal is to find a Steiner tree of minimum node cost that obeys the degree constraint at every node. There are no edge costs in this version since the problem with node and edge costs can be transformed into one involving just node costs (see Sect. 3.2). We shall assume for the sake of simplicity that such a Steiner tree always exists on the input graph and address the problem of computing one that approximately obeys the degree budgets as well as minimizes the total node cost. In the description of the algorithm and its analysis, we use $c_G(v)$ to denote the cost of a node $v \in V$. We omit the subscript G when there is no ambiguity.

5.1   High Level Description

The algorithm maintains a set S of nodes and a set F of edges. Initially S contains all the terminals and F is empty. During the course of the algorithm, the connected components of the graph (S, F) are node-disjoint trees whose union contains all the terminals. Define a connected component of (S, F) to be *active* if it contains at least one terminal but not all of the terminals. The algorithm works in $O(\log k)$ iterations. In each iteration, we run a greedy algorithm to choose a subgraph (a collection of many smaller subgraphs called *spiders*) of small degree and small node-cost such that the addition of this subgraph to the current solution reduces the number of connected components of (S, F) by a constant factor.

We first define a few additional terms used in describing our algorithm. We use OPT to denote the minimum cost of any Steiner tree that obeys the degree restrictions in the input.

DEFINITION 5.1 [18]. A *spider* is a tree with at most one node of degree greater than two. A *center* of a spider is a node from which there are node-disjoint paths (called *legs*) to the leaves of the spider. Note that if a spider has at least three leaves, its center is unique. The leaves of the spider are also called the *feet* of the spider. A *nontrivial spider* is one with at least two feet.

5.2   The Algorithm and Its Performance Guarantee

The rest of Sect. 5 is devoted to describing the algorithm and its performance for approximately solving the (N-DEGREE, E-TOTAL-COST, STEINER TREE). ALGORITHM-DEGREE-STEINER gives the details of the entire algorithm.

5.3   A Procedure to Find Minimum Ratio Spiders

The heart of ALGORITHM-DEGREE-STEINER is Step 8—a procedure that chooses a nontrivial spider of minimum "ratio-cost". We describe this procedure informally. Consider a generic step of ALGORITHM-DEGREE-STEINER (Step 4). Observe that we maintain a current graph G' and the current partial solution (S, F). Let the connected components of (S, F) be denoted by $\{C_1, \ldots, C_q\}$. The spider we use to merge these components must have a real node of G' as the center and some of these components as its feet. During the course of an iteration, we may delete a node v from G' if the degree of v due

---

ALGORITHM-DEGREE-STEINER:

Input: An undirected graph $G(V, E)$ with nonnegative costs on its nodes, a set $\mathcal{T} \subseteq V$ of terminals (where $|\mathcal{T}| = k$), and a function d assigning nonnegative values (each value is at least two) to the nodes of G. Let $b = \min_v \{d(v)\}$.
Output: A Steiner tree T spanning the terminals $\mathcal{T}$ such that the degree of any node v in T is at most is $O(d(v) \log k)$ and the cost of T is at most $O(\log k)$ times that of a minimum-cost degree-constrained Steiner tree spanning the terminals $\mathcal{T}$.

1   Initialization: $S = \mathcal{T}$ and $F = \phi$.

2   **Repeat** while there are active components in (S, F)

3   Let $\mathcal{C}$ be the set of active components of (S, F). Let $\mathcal{C} = \{C_1, \ldots, C_q\}$ where $q = |\mathcal{C}|$. Set $G'(V', E') := G(V, E)$.

4   **While** $|\mathcal{C}| \geq 11q/12$ **and** $q > 6$ **do**

5   Construct an auxiliary graph H as follows: Starting with $G(V, E)$ delete the nodes in $V - V'$ to get a graph G' on V'. For every component surviving (as active) in $\mathcal{C}$, contract all nodes within this component occurring in G' to a single supernode.

6   **For** every node $v \in V'$, consider v as the center of a spider.

7   If v is in a supernode of H, then uncontract v from this supernode and attach a zero-cost edge between them; if no nodes from V' remain in the supernode after uncontracting v, then add a new dummy supernode to H representing the active component containing v and a zero-cost edge to it from v.

8   **For** $j = 2$ to $d(v) + 1$ **do** Find a minimum-cost spider centered at v in H with j supernodes as its feet using PROCEDURE-FIND-SPIDER.

9   Among all the spiders produced in Step 6, choose one of minimum ratio-cost, defined as the ratio of the cost of all the real nodes in the spider to the number of feet in it.

10   Let v be the center node and $C_1, \ldots, C_r$ be the components in $\mathcal{C}$ chosen as the feet of the spider in Step 9. Let $P_1, \ldots, P_r$ be the legs of the spider connecting v to $C_1, \ldots, C_r$ respectively. Add $\bigcup_{a=1}^{r} P_a$ to the current solution (S, F) so as to merge $C_1, C_2, \ldots, C_r$ into one active component. Update $\mathcal{C}$.

11   For every node $v \in V'$, if the degree of this node using edges added so far in this iteration (Steps 5 through 11) is between $2d(v)$ and $3d(v)$, then update $V' = V' - \{v\}$.

12   **If** $q \leq 6$ **then**

13   **Repeat** while there are active components

14   Run Steps 5 to 10.

15   Set $V' = \phi$.

16   **else** Goto Step 2. ($|\mathcal{C}|$ is now less than $\frac{11q}{12}$.)

17   Output (S, F) as the solution.

---

to the addition of edges in the generic step is between $2d(v)$ and $3d(v)$; i.e., a constant factor of the degree bound for v. We must then choose in the current graph G' a spider of minimum ratio-cost, namely the ratio of the cost of all the nodes of $G' - S$ in the spider and the number of feet of the spider.

Although the concept of a spider is similar to the one used in [18], the degree constraint makes the problem of finding a "good spider" harder. As a result, the procedure in [18] for finding spiders cannot be used in place of PROCEDURE-FIND-SPIDER described below.

We find a spider of minimum ratio-cost by using several calls to a minimum-cost flow algorithm on the auxiliary graph H. We describe how to find a minimum ratio spider centered at a specific node $v \in G'$, the current graph. By trying all nodes, we can choose the overall minimum ratio spider. To find a minimum ratio spider centered at v, it suffices to find a spider centered at v containing exactly j feet such that it has minimum total node cost. By trying all values of j in the set $\{2, 3, \ldots, d(v) + 1\}$, we can find the value of j minimizing the ratio cost of the resulting spider for v. PROCEDURE-FIND-SPIDER given below describes a method to find a minimum node-cost spider centered at v with exactly j feet.

PROCEDURE-FIND-SPIDER:

Input: An undirected graph H containing real nodes and supernodes, a real node v as the center and a number j specifying the number of feet in the spider to be constructed.
Output: A minimum-cost spider centered at v with j feet that are supernodes.

1   Bi-direct all the undirected edges in H giving each resulting arc the cost of the node at its tail. (Supernodes have zero cost.)

2   Reassign the cost of all the arcs leaving the center node v to be $\frac{c(v)}{j}$.

3   Attach a new sink node t_v with new arcs of zero-cost coming to it from all the supernodes.

4   In this digraph, impose a capacity bound of one unit on all nodes except v and t_v and find a minimum-cost flow of value j from v to t_v.

REMARKS.

1. The solution to the above flow problem (when feasible) can be found in polynomial time and is integral (see [2] or Chap. 4 of [6]).

2. Such a flow gives a minimum-cost set of node-disjoint paths originating at v and ending at a set of j supernodes.

3. The cost of real nodes in H other than v that occur in flow paths are accounted for in the cost of the arcs leaving them. Node v has exactly j

arcs leaving it in the flow solution, each of cost $\frac{c(v)}{j}$ for a total of $c(v)$. Thus, the total cost of the flow solution is equal to the cost of all the real nodes in the spider that are not in any component of (S, F).

4. The set of edges in the solution to the flow problem contains no cycles. Consequently, the set of undirected edges from the original graph that correspond to these flow paths (i.e., ignoring the arcs into t_v) contain no cycles.

We now prove the claimed performance guarantee of the algorithm. For ease of exposition the proof is broken down into a sequence of lemmas and theorems.

PROPOSITION 5.2. *The number of iterations of Step 2 in the algorithm is* $O(\log k)$ *where k is the number of terminals.*

The above proposition follows by observing that in each iteration of Step 4, we reduce the number of active components by a constant factor. We start with k components and the last iteration runs to completion when this number drops to 6 or below.

PROPOSITION 5.3. *For each node v, the increase in the degree of v in (S, F) due to edges added in one iteration of Step 2 is at most* $3d(v)$.

Proof. Consider a node v and fix an iteration i (Step 4). If degree of v exceeds $2d(v)$ using edges in this iteration, then it is deleted from further consideration in Step 11 and no more edges are added in this iteration that are adjacent to it. Furthermore, in Step 8 the increase in degree of v is either (i) at most $d(v) + 1$ if it is the center of the chosen spider or (ii) at most 2 which is in turn at most $d(v)$ if it is a non-center node of the chosen spider (since for all v, $d(v) \geq 2$). Thus, if the degree of v is no less than $2d(v)$ to begin with, it never exceeds $3d(v)$ after executing Step 8. In the last iteration, we merge at most 6 components using an acyclic set of edges. Thus, the degree of v increases by at most $6 \leq 3d(v)$, since for all v, $d(v) \geq 2$. $\square$

Combining Propositions 5.2 and 5.3 immediately leads to the performance guarantee on the degree of a node in the final solution. We now bound the total cost of the subgraph added in one iteration. Lemma 5.4 along with Proposition 5.2 yield the required performance guarantee on the total cost of the final solution, completing the entire proof.

LEMMA 5.4. *The cost of the set of nodes added to the solution in each iteration of Step 2 is at most* $O(\text{OPT})$.

First we complete the proof with regard to the cost added in the last iteration. Recall that at the beginning of the last iteration, the number of active components is at most 6. For this iteration, our algorithm reduces to that of Klein and Ravi [18] for node-weighted Steiner trees. Hence using their result with the number of "terminals" to be connected being at most 6, the cost of the nodes added is at most $O(\text{OPT} \log 6) = O(\text{OPT})$.

The proof of the lemma for the remaining iterations is more involved and is described in Sects. 5.4 through 5.6. The proof proceeds by deriving a decomposition of an optimal solution and using it as a witness to the performance of the algorithm in each iteration. In particular, we use the decomposition to prove an averaging lemma and use this in conjunction with a potential function argument due to Leighton and Rao [19] to prove Lemma 5.4. We begin by proving a bound on the total degree of all the nodes that are deleted from G' in any iteration.

5.4   Bounding the Total Degree of Deleted Nodes

Fix an iteration i. Let the active components in the beginning of this iteration i be $C_1, C_2, \ldots, C_q$. At the beginning of this iteration, we initialize the graph $G' := G$. During the course of this iteration, we may delete nodes from G' in Step 11.

LEMMA 5.5. *In each iteration of Step 2 of the algorithm, the sum of the degrees of all the nodes deleted from G' due to edges added in this iteration is at most q.*

The proof relies on the following observations.

1. The subgraph added in a given iteration is acyclic.

2. The iteration terminates when at most $\frac{q}{12}$ of the active components are merged using edges added in a given iteration.

Using these observations we can show that a large fraction of the degree of the deleted nodes contributes to merging the q active components. This implies an upper bound on the sum of the degrees.

Proof. Let m be the number of components that were merged in this iteration. Note that $m \leq \frac{q}{12}$. We can assume without loss of generality that the m components are merged into a single component. (It is easy to see that in other cases we obtain better bounds.)

Let $\mathcal{R}$ denote the acyclic subgraph added to merge the m components. By the working of the algorithm, the leaves of $\mathcal{R}$ are precisely the m components that were merged. By our assumption, $d(v) \geq 2$ for all v. Thus, all vertices of degree 2 in $\mathcal{R}$ do not contribute to the degree sum of deleted nodes. Hence we modify $\mathcal{R}$ to obtain $\mathcal{R}'$ as follows: We contract all simple paths in which each internal node has degree 2 into a single edge. Now each internal node in $\mathcal{R}'$ has a degree of at least 3. Let $\mathcal{N} = \{w_1, w_2, \ldots, w_P\}$ denote the internal nodes of $\mathcal{R}'$. Note that some of these nodes might not have been deleted. Let $\mathcal{D}(w_i)$, $1 \leq i \leq P$ denote the degree of w_i in $\mathcal{R}'$. We now prove a stronger statement and show that

$$D = \sum_{i=1}^{P} \mathcal{D}(w_i) \leq q. \tag{5.1}$$

Note that $1 \leq i \leq P$, $\mathcal{D}(w_i) \geq 3$. Thus $D \geq 3P$. But since $\mathcal{R}'$ is a tree we know that the number of edges $|E(\mathcal{R}')|$ is given by $|E(\mathcal{R}')| = P + m - 1$. Thus

$$2|E(\mathcal{R}')| = 2(P + m - 1) = D + m \geq 3P + m \tag{5.2}$$

implying that $P \leq m - 2$. This gives an upper bound on the total number of internal nodes in $\mathcal{R}'$.

$$D + m = 2|E(\mathcal{R}')| = 2(P + m - 1) \leq 2(m - 2 + m - 1) \leq 3m - 5. \tag{5.3}$$

Combining this with the upper bound on m we get

$$D \leq 2m - 5 \leq 2\frac{q}{12} - 5 \leq \frac{q}{6}$$

proving (5.1). □

5.5 Spider Decompositions and an Averaging Lemma

We employ the notion of spider decompositions introduced by Klein and Ravi [18] in showing that the each node chosen in Step 9 has small ratio-cost with respect to the optimal solution.

Let G be a graph, and let M be a subset of its nodes. A *spider decomposition* of M in G is a set of node-disjoint nontrivial spiders in G such that the union of the feet and the centers of the spiders in the decomposition contains M.

THEOREM 5.6 [18]. *Let G be a connected graph, and let M be a subset of its nodes such that $|M| \geq 2$. Then G contains a spider decomposition of M.*

Let v be a node chosen in Step 9 of the algorithm. Let C denote the cost of the subgraph added subsequently in Step 10. Let this subgraph merge r trees. We prove the following claim.

CLAIM 5.7.

$$r \geq \frac{5}{12} \frac{Cq}{\text{OPT}}. \tag{5.4}$$

Proof. Let T^* be a minimum-cost degree-bounded Steiner tree of cost OPT. Let $C_1, \ldots, C_p$ be the active components when a spider centered at node v was chosen by the algorithm. Let $T^*(v)$ be the graph obtained from T^* by contracting each C_j to a supernode of zero cost. $T^*(v)$ is connected and contains all supernodes. We then remove edges from $T^*(v)$ so as to make it acyclic; thus $T^*(v)$ is a tree.

Delete all edges incident on nodes in $V - V'$ (the deleted nodes) in $T^*(v)$. Consider a node u. By construction of $T^*(v)$, u's degree in $T^*(v)$ (denoted by $d_T(u)$) is at most $d(u)$. Furthermore, u is deleted in our algorithm only if its degree, denoted by $d^i(u)$, exceeds $2d(u)$ due to the edges added in a given iteration of Step 2. Thus we have

$$\forall u \in V - V', \quad d^i(u) \geq 2d(u) \quad \text{and} \quad d_T(u) \leq d(u).$$

Combining these observations with Lemma 5.5, we get

$$\sum_{u \in V - V'} d_T(u) \leq \frac{1}{2} \sum_{u \in V - V'} d^i(u) \leq q/2.$$

Thus, the total number of edges deleted from $T^*(v)$ is also at most $\frac{q}{2}$. Since there were p active components (and hence supernodes) when v was chosen, the tree $T^*(v)$ has p supernodes in it. Since we deleted at most $\frac{q}{2}$ edges from this tree, at least $p - \frac{q}{2}$ of the supernodes are in subtrees with at least two or more supernodes. Since $p \geq \frac{11q}{12}$, at least $\frac{5q}{12}$ supernodes are in such trees. We summarize this in the following proposition.

PROPOSITION 5.8. *Let M denote the subset of supernodes that are in subtrees with two or more supernodes. Then $|M| \geq \frac{5q}{12}$.*

We apply Theorem 5.6 to each subtree of $T^*(v)$ with at least two supernodes to obtain a spider decomposition of M. We now compare the ratio cost of spider chosen by the algorithm with that of each spider in the decomposition. To do this however, we must ensure that the following two conditions hold.

(i) the center of each spider in the decomposition must be a real node (not a supernode) and

(ii) the number of legs of each spider must be at most $d(v) + 1$.

We achieve this as follows. We further partition a spider centered at a supernode into many nontrivial spiders each centered at a real node v contained in this supernode such that the union of their feet contains the feet of the original spiders and the number of legs of the spider centered at v is at most $d(v) + 1$. To do this, first consider all the real nodes in the central supernode with at least one leg of the spider incident on them. Each such real node can be made the center of a nontrivial spider (satisfying (i)) with all the legs incident on it as the legs of the spider, along with a zero cost leg to the supernode that it belongs to. Since the degree of any real node in T^* is at most $d(v)$, the number of legs of any such spider is at most $d(v) + 1$ satisfying (ii).

Let the centers of the resulting spider decomposition satisfying (i) and (ii) be the set of real nodes $v_1, \ldots, v_t$. Let $\ell_1, \ldots, \ell_t$ denote the number of nodes of M (feet) in each of these spiders respectively. Since every spider in the decomposition is nontrivial and is derived as above, each ℓ_j is at least two and at most $d(v) + 1$. Moreover, a spider with center v_j induces a subset of the current active components, namely the ℓ_j components whose supernodes belong to this spider. Let the cost of the spider centered at v_j (i.e., cost of v_j plus the sum of the node-costs of the paths from v_j to the ℓ_j components—if v_j is already in a supernode, we may assume its cost to be zero since it has already been paid for in the formation of the supernode) be Cost_j. Then the ratio cost of the spider centered at v_j in the auxiliary graph H constructed in this loop is at most $\frac{\text{Cost}_j}{\ell_j}$.

Since the algorithm chooses a spider of minimum ratio-cost in H, for each spider in the decomposition we have $\frac{\text{Cost}_j}{\ell_j} \geq \frac{C}{r}$. Summing over all the spiders in the decomposition yields

$$\sum_{j=1}^{t} \text{Cost}_j \geq \frac{C}{r} \sum_{j=1}^{t} \ell_j. \tag{5.5}$$

Combining Proposition 5.8 with the observation that the union of the feet of the spiders contains M, we get

$$\sum_{j=1}^{t} \ell_j \geq |M| \geq \frac{5q}{12}. \tag{5.6}$$

Also note that

$$\sum_{j=1}^{t} \text{Cost}_j \leq \text{COST}(T^*(v)) \leq \text{OPT} \tag{5.7}$$

since (i) the cost of the nodes in the tree $T^*(v)$ is at most OPT and (ii) each real node in $T^*(v)$ appears in at most one spider. Combining (5.5), (5.6) and (5.7) yields Claim 5.7. $\qquad\square$

5.6 A Potential Function Argument

Now we are ready to complete the proof of Lemma 5.4. Fix an iteration i and let the set of nodes chosen in Step 9 of the algorithm in this iteration be $v_1, \ldots, v_f$ in the order in which they were chosen.

Let ϕ_j denote the number of active components in the solution after choosing vertex v_j in this iteration. Thus, for instance, $\phi_0 = q$, the number of active components at the beginning of this iteration in (S, F), $\phi_{f-1} > \frac{11q}{12}$ and $\phi_f \leq \frac{11q}{12}$. Let the number of trees merged using vertex v_j be r_j. Then we have

$$\phi_j = \phi_{j-1} - (r_j - 1). \tag{5.8}$$

Let C_j denote the cost of the subgraph added by the algorithm in the step when vertex v_j was chosen. Then by Claim 5.7, we have

$$r_j \geq \frac{5}{12} \frac{C_j q}{\mathrm{OPT}} \geq \frac{5}{12} \frac{C_j \phi_{j-1}}{\mathrm{OPT}}. \tag{5.9}$$

We now use an analysis technique due to Leighton and Rao [19] to complete the proof as in [18]. Substituting (5.9) into (5.8) and simplifying using $r_j \geq 2$ gives

$$\phi_j \leq \phi_{j-1}\left(1 - \frac{5}{24} \frac{C_j}{\mathrm{OPT}}\right). \tag{5.10}$$

Simplifying (5.10), we obtain

$$\phi_{f-1} \leq \phi_0 \prod_{j=1}^{f-1}\left(1 - \frac{5}{24} \frac{C_r}{\mathrm{OPT}}\right).$$

Taking natural logarithms on both sides and simplifying using the approximation $\ln(1 + x) \leq x$, we obtain

$$\frac{24}{5}\mathrm{OPT}\ln\left(\frac{\phi_0}{\phi_{f-1}}\right) \geq \sum_{j=1}^{f-1} C_j.$$

Note that $\phi_0 = q$ and $\phi_{f-1} > \frac{11q}{12}$ and so we have

$$\sum_{j=1}^{f-1} C_j < 5\,\mathrm{OPT}\ln\frac{12}{11} = O(\mathrm{OPT}). \tag{5.11}$$

Note that the cost of the nodes added in this iteration is exactly the sum $\sum_{j=1}^{f} C_j$.

To complete the proof, we bound the cost of the subgraph associated with v_f, the last node chosen in this iteration. Using Claim 5.7 and noting that $r_f \leq q$ we have

$$C_f \leq \frac{12}{5}\mathrm{OPT}.$$

Using the above equation and (5.11), we have that the cost of the set of nodes added in this iteration is

$$\sum_{j=1}^{f} C_j = O(\text{OPT}).$$

This completes the proof of Lemma 5.4.

The performance of our approximation algorithm was summarized in Theorem 3.1.

5.7 Extension to Proper Function Cut Covers

The extension of Theorem 3.1 to construct cut-covers defined by proper 0–1 functions is fairly straightforward, and the algorithm for this case follows the same outline as the one above. The reader is referred to [15, 10] for the definition of proper 0–1 functions. The algorithm begins with the set S being the set of terminals defined by the proper function. The definition of active components in the algorithm is now based on the f-values given to cuts by the input proper function. In other words, a component is deemed active if the cut around it is. Note that when all components are inactive, the set of edges added by the algorithm until then constitutes a feasible cut-cover.

The only additional issue is that in the proof of the upper bound on the cost of the subgraph added in each iteration, the optimal solution is a forest instead of a single tree. However, as in [18], we can use the fact that each tree in the forest must contain at least two active components to infer that this forest contains at least as many edges as half the number of active components. This observation is sufficient to prove a modified version of Claim 5.7 with slightly worse constants. The details are straightforward and omitted to avoid repetition. Thus we have the following theorem.

THEOREM 5.9. *There is a polynomial-time algorithm that, given an undirected graph G with nonnegative costs on its nodes, a proper function f defined on the node subsets of G, and a function d assigning a nonnegative value $d(v) \geq 2$ to each node v of G, constructs a cut-cover for the family of cuts defined by f in which the maximum degree of any node v is at most $O(d(v) \log k)$ and the cost of the cover is at most $O(\log k)$ times that of the "minimum-cost degree-constrained cut cover" for f. Here k represents the number of terminals defined by f. A degree-constrained cut cover is a subgraph which covers (i.e., contains at least one edge in) all the cuts defined by f and has degree at most $d(v)$ at node v, for all v.*

6. Algorithms Under Triangle Inequality

One way to circumvent the difficulty of approximating the problems studied is to consider more structured cost functions on the edges. In this direction, we turn to the case where the underlying graph is assumed to be complete with costs only on the edges and these costs obey the triangle inequality. Define the *bottleneck cost* of a network to be the maximum cost of any edge in it. In this case, we present approximation algorithms that strictly conform to the degree restriction in the input problem and approximate the bottleneck cost of the output network as well. Most of the results in this section are straightforward and we discuss it here for the sake of completeness.

6.1   Results for Spanning Trees

PROPOSITION 6.1.

1. *There is a polynomial time approximation algorithm for* (N-DEGREE, E-TOTAL COST, SPANNING TREE) *problem restricted to edge-weighted graphs that satisfy triangle inequality. Its performance guarantee is* $(1, (2 - \frac{(d_{\min}(v)-2)}{(n-1)}))$. *Moreover, the bottleneck cost of the tree produced by* ALGORITHM-TI-SPANNING-TREE *is at most twice that of the minimum-bottleneck spanning tree. Here* $d_{\min}(v)$ *denotes the smallest degree constraint.*

2. *There is a polynomial-time algorithm that, given a undirected graph with edge costs satisfying the triangle inequality, outputs a TSP tour of total cost at most two times the cost of a MST and of bottleneck cost at most three times that of a minimum bottleneck-cost spanning tree.*

Proof. First we sketch the proof of Part 1. The algorithm starts by constructing an MST. It then partitions the edges of the MST into claws and sorts the edges in every claw in the order of non-decreasing cost. Each claw is short-cut locally by replacing edges from the internal node to its children (except the very first child) with edges between consecutive children. Let T denote the resulting tree.

To prove the first part of the proposition, for any set E' of edges, let $c(E')$ denote the sum of the costs of all the edges in E'. We have the following relations.

$$c(\text{MST}) = \sum_{v\,:\,v \text{ is not a leaf of the MST}} c(\text{claw}(v)).$$

For an internal node v, let $t(v)$ denote the number of children of v in the rooted MST. For the solution T, we have

$$c(T) = \sum_{v\,:\,v \text{ is not a leaf of the MST}} \left[c(\text{claw}(v)) - \sum_{i=2}^{t(v)-d(v)+2} c(v, v_i) + \sum_{i=2}^{t(v)-d(v)+2} c(v_{i-1}, v_i) \right].$$

By triangle inequality on the costs c, we have

$$c(v_{i-1}, v_i) \leq c(v_{i-1}, v) + c(v, v_i) \leq 2c(v, v_i)$$

The last inequality follows from the way we ordered the edges in each claw in non-decreasing order of costs. Putting the above three equations together, we get the following bound on the cost of the output tree T.

$$\frac{c(T)}{c(\text{MST})} \leq \left(2 - \frac{(d_{\min}(v) - 2)}{(n - 1)}\right).$$

Since the cost of any $d(v)$-bounded spanning tree is at least as much as that of the MST, this gives the bound on the cost of the tree output by the algorithm.

We now complete proof by proving the bound of two on the bottleneck cost. It is well known that an MST is also an optimum bottleneck spanning tree. Since each short-cut used in forming the output tree T is made up of at most two edges, the bottleneck cost of T is at most twice that of the MST. Since the bottleneck cost of any b-bounded spanning tree is at least as much as that of the bottleneck spanning tree, the resulting tree has bottleneck cost at most twice the optimum.

Part 2 of the proposition follows from standard constructions based on a recursive short-cutting procedure using edges from the cube of the Minimum Spanning Tree. This is also hinted at in [7] (see problem 37.2-3 on p. 975). □

6.2 Extension to Higher Connectivities

Now we are ready to prove our result for networks with higher connectivities. The result is proved by using short-cuts that induce higher-connected graphs.

THEOREM 6.2. *There is a polynomial-time algorithm that, given an undirected graph with edge costs satisfying the triangle inequality, and an integer $k \geq 2$ (the vertex-connectivity requirement), outputs a k-connected spanning subgraph of G in which the degree of every node is exactly k, the total cost of all the edges in the subgraph is at most $\frac{k+4}{2}$ times that of a minimum-cost k-connected subgraph, and the bottleneck cost of the subgraph is at most $3 \cdot \lceil \frac{k}{2} \rceil$ times that of a minimum bottleneck-cost spanning tree.*

Proof. Let c^* and β^* denote the cost of an MST and the optimum bottleneck cost of a spanning tree of the input graph. By Proposition 6.1, we can obtain a TSP tour T of cost $c(T)$ and bottleneck cost $\beta(T)$ such that $c(T) \leq 2c^*$ and $\beta(T) \leq 3\beta^*$. Let the vertices in this tour be numbered $v_1, v_2, \ldots, v_n$. Now, we add extra edges to this cycle as follows: For every node, add edges joining it to vertices to its left in the cycle that are within $\lceil \frac{k}{2} \rceil$ edges from it and all vertices to its right in the cycle that are within $\lfloor \frac{k}{2} \rfloor$ edges from it. It is not hard to see that this graph is k-vertex-connected (by showing $\lceil \frac{k}{2} \rceil$ disjoint paths between any pair of nodes going clockwise in the cycle and another $\lfloor \frac{k}{2} \rfloor$ disjoint paths going counter-clockwise). The degree of every node in this graph is exactly k. Since each shortcut employed replaces a path of at most $\lceil \frac{k}{2} \rceil$ edges, the bottleneck cost goes up by this factor. This proves that the bottleneck cost of this subgraph is within $3 \cdot \lceil \frac{k}{2} \rceil$ of optimal.

The total cost of the graph obtained this way can be computed by bounding how many newly added edges contain a given edge in the TSP tour within their span of $\frac{k}{2}$ or less. We can compute this for an edge uv by counting all the added edges that originate at u or to the left of it and end at v or to its right. The number of such edges originating at u is $\lceil \frac{k}{2} \rceil$, and the number originating at the node before u crossing over uv is $\lceil \frac{k}{2} \rceil - 1$ and so on, giving a total of at most $\frac{k(k+2)}{8} + 1$. Thus the total cost of this graph is at most $\frac{k(k+2)}{8} + 1$ times that of the TSP tour T that we started with. This in turn is at most $(\frac{k(k+2)}{4} + 1)c^*$. However, we can apply an approximate min-max relation between a MST and a packing of cuts in the graph that is derived in [1, 15] in proving a better performance guarantee of $\frac{k+2}{2} + 1$ for the total cost.

In particular, if OPT_k denotes the cost of a minimum k-connected subgraph, we show that $\mathrm{OPT}_k \geq \frac{kc^*}{2}$. This would prove that the cost of the k-connected subgraph output by our algorithm is at most $(\frac{k+2}{2} + 1)\mathrm{OPT}_k$ as claimed in Theorem 6.2.

It remains to prove that $\mathrm{OPT}_k \geq \frac{kc^*}{2}$. We do this in the remainder of this section. Before that we need some definitions. Given a graph G, recall that an edge cut in the graph can be written as $\Gamma(W)$, where W is a node subset of the graph, and $\Gamma(W)$ denotes the set of edges with exactly one endpoint in W. A fractional packing of cuts is a family of cuts $\Gamma(W_1), \Gamma(W_2), \ldots, \Gamma(W_k)$, together with a rational *weight* for each cut. A (fractional) w-*packing* of cuts is a weighted collection of cuts that have the following property: for each edge (u, v) of cost $w(u, v)$, the sum of the weights of all the cuts in this collection containing the edge is at most $w(u, v)$. The *value of the packing* is the sum of the weights of all the cuts in the packing. A *maximum packing* is one of maximum value. The following theorem is a consequence of the results in [1, 15]. $\square$

THEOREM 6.3. *Given an undirected graph with edge-weights, a minimum-weight spanning tree has weight at most twice the value of a maximum packing of cuts.*

The algorithms in [1, 15] find a greedy packing of cuts and simultaneously build a minimum spanning tree of weight at most twice the value of this packing.

Note that any k-connected spanning subgraph must have at least k edges crossing any cut since this subgraph has k disjoint connections between every pair of vertices. Thus we have the following lemma.

LEMMA 6.4. *The weight of any k-connected subgraph is at least k times as much as the value of a maximum packing of cuts.*

Applying the above lemma to the optimum k-connected subgraph of cost OPT_k and combining with Theorem 6.3 above we conclude that $\text{OPT}_k \geq \frac{kc^*}{2}$.

7. Hardness Results

In this section, we prove hardness results that motivate the need for bicriteria approximations rather than approximating only one objective while strictly obeying the budget on the other. We first prove the results for spanning trees and then strengthen the results for Steiner trees.

7.1 Hardness Results for Spanning Tree Problems

THEOREM 7.1.

1. *Unless* P $=$ NP, *for any* $\rho > 1$, *there is no polynomial time* $(1, \rho)$ *approximation algorithm for the problem* (U-DEGREE, E-TOTAL COST, SPANNING TREE).

2. *Unless* P $=$ NP, *for any* $\rho > 1$, *there is no polynomial time* $(1, \rho)$ *approximation algorithm for the problem* (U-DEGREE, E-BOTTLENECK-COST, SPANNING TREE).

3. *Unless* P $=$ NP, *for any* $1 \leq \rho < 2$, *there is no polynomial time* $(1, \rho)$ *approximation algorithm for the problem* (U-DEGREE, E-BOTTLENECK-COST, SPANNING TREE), *even when edge weights satisfy triangle inequality.*

Proof. The NP-hardness of (U-DEGREE, E-TOTAL COST, SPANNING TREE) and (U-DEGREE, E-BOTTLENECK-COST, SPANNING TREE), follows via a straightforward reduction from the HAMILTONIAN PATH problem in which we add a the right number of distinct leaves to each node of the original graph.

To prove the third part, we use the cost assignment as in the first part of the proof that obeys the triangle inequality. Under this assignment, the maximum cost of any b-bounded spanning tree of the resulting graph is at most one if the original graph is Hamiltonian and is at least two otherwise. Hence an approximation algorithm with performance ratio less than two in this case would be able to recognize Hamiltonian graphs. This completes the proof of Theorem 7.1. □

7.2 Hardness Results for Steiner Tree Problems

Since a spanning tree is a special case of a Steiner tree, it follows from Part 1 of Theorem 7.1 that unless P = NP, there is no polynomial time $(1, \rho)$ or $(\rho, 1)$ approximation algorithm for the (U-DEGREE, E-TOTAL-COST, STEINER TREE) problem for any $\rho > 1$. Furthermore, since the problem of computing a Steiner tree of minimum total edge weight (even without any degree constraints on nodes) is NP-hard, it follows that unless P = NP, there is no polynomial time $(\rho, 1)$ approximation algorithm for the (U-DEGREE, E-TOTAL-COST, STEINER TREE) problem for any $\rho > 1$.

These hardness results require either the budget to be satisfied exactly or the cost of the network to be optimal. We now present a result which points out the difficulty of solving the Steiner version of the non-uniform degree bounded problem within constant factors. This result is obtained by a reduction from the SET COVER problem. Recently, Arora and Sudan [3], and independently Raz and Safra [27] have shown the following non-approximability result for MIN SET COVER.

THEOREM 7.2. *Unless* P = NP, *the* MIN SET COVER *problem, with a universe of size k, cannot be approximated to better than a $\ln k$ factor.*

THEOREM 7.3. *Unless* P = NP, *for any $\varepsilon > 0$, there is no polynomial time $(2 - \varepsilon)$-approximation algorithm for the non-uniform degree-bounded Steiner tree problem.*

Proof. Suppose there is a polynomial time $(2 - \varepsilon)$-approximation algorithm A for the problem. We will show that A can be used to obtain a polynomial time 2-approximation for the MIN SET COVER. In view of Theorem 7.2, the required result would follow.

Given an instance of MIN SET COVER, we construct the natural bipartite graph with one partition for set nodes (denoted by $Q_1, Q_2, \ldots, Q_m$) and the other for element nodes (denoted by $q_1, q_2, \ldots, q_n$), and edges representing element inclusion in the sets. To this bipartite graph, we add an "enforcer" node (denoted by x) which is adjacent to each of the set nodes. Let G denote the resulting bipartite graph. The set R of terminals for the Steiner tree instance is given by $R = \{x, q_1, q_2, \ldots, q_n\}$.

In this way, we create a sequence of m instances of the problem (N-DEGREE, E-TOTAL-COST, STEINER TREE). In all these instances, the degree bound for each element node is chosen as 1 and the degree bound for each set node is chosen as $n + 1$. For the jth instance of the (N-DEGREE, E-TOTAL-COST,

STEINER TREE) problem, the degree bound on the enforcer node is chosen as j ($1 \leq j \leq m$).

Suppose there is an optimal solution $Q' = \{Q_{i_1}, Q_{i_2}, \ldots, Q_{i_k}\}$ consisting of k sets to the MIN SET COVER instance. Then the Steiner tree T in G consisting of x, the edges (x, Q_{i_j}), $1 \leq j \leq k$, and one edge from each element node to some set node in Q' satisfies all the degree constraints. The cost of T is equal to k.

Suppose we run the approximation algorithm A successively on instances $1, 2, \ldots, m$ of the (N-DEGREE, E-TOTAL-COST, STEINER TREE) problem. Note that A may fail to produce a Steiner tree on some of these instances since there may be no Steiner tree satisfying the degree constraints, even after allowing for degree violations by a factor of $2 - \varepsilon$. We stop as soon as A produces a solution. We now argue that from this solution, we can obtain a 2-approximate solution to the MIN SET COVER instance. To see this, note that when we run A on instance k, A must produce a Steiner tree T', since as argued above, there is a feasible solution to instance k. Since the degree requirement for each element node is 1 and the violation factor is less than 2, the degree of each element node in T' is 1. Similarly, the degree of the enforcer node x in T' is less than $2k$. The set nodes adjacent to x must cover all the element nodes since the degree of each element node is 1. We thus have a solution of size at most $2k$ for MIN SET COVER and this completes the proof. $\square$

COROLLARY 7.4. *Unless* P = NP, *for any* $\varepsilon > 0$ *and* $\rho > 1$, *there is no polynomial time* $(2 - \varepsilon, \rho)$-*approximation algorithm for the* (N-DEGREE, E-TOTAL-COST, STEINER TREE) *problem*.

8.   Concluding Remarks

We have introduced bicriteria approximation algorithms for degree-constrained minimum-cost one-connected network problems, that allow general degree specifications and node costs. Our results for bicriteria problems can be used to improve previous results on approximating certain minimum degree network problems. In particular, Theorem 5.9 implies a polynomial-time approximation algorithm for a class of minimum-degree forest problems considered by Ravi, Raghavachari and Klein [25]. They address the problem of finding one-connected networks that are cut-covers of proper functions such that the maximum degree of any node in the network is minimum. This is a single criterion problem without the node weight objective. They provide a quasi-polynomial ($n^{O(\log_{1+\epsilon} n)}$-time) approximation algorithm for these problems on an n-node graph that provides a solution of degree at most $(1+\epsilon)$ times the minimum with an additive error of $O(\log_{1+\epsilon} n)$, for any $\epsilon > 0$. A prototypical example of the one-connected network problem considered in [25] is the minimum-degree generalized Steiner forest problem: given an undirected graph with site-pairs of nodes, find a generalized Steiner forest for the site-pairs in which the maximum degree is minimum. The techniques in [25] can be adapted to provide polynomial-time approximation algorithms with performance ratio $\Omega(n^\delta)$ for any constant $\delta > 0$ (by setting $\epsilon = n^{\frac{1}{\delta}}$). By a direct application of Theorem 5.9, an improved (logarithmic) approximation ratio can be achieved in polynomial time for this problem.

Subsequent Work

In subsequent work, we have used a similar framework to devise approximation algorithms for other bicriteria problems (see [21, 24]). An obvious open problem resulting from this work is to improve the performance ratios in all our results; although different techniques than those given seem to be required. In this context, it would be interesting to investigate whether the primal-dual method [1, 15] can be applied to provide such better guarantees and also provide a general framework for bicriteria network-design problems. Another interesting question is to investigate the extension of our work to higher-connected degree-constrained networks without the triangle inequality.

In other follow-up to our work, the special case of the (U-DEGREE, E-TOTAL COST, SPANNING TREE) problem in the Euclidean plane was addressed in [17], and improvements to the short-cutting scheme of Proposition 6.1 using network flow techniques are presented in [11].

Acknowledgments

We thank the referee for several valuable suggestions. We gratefully acknowledge helpful conversations with M. X. Goemans, P. N. Klein, G. Konjevod, S. Krumke, B. Raghavachari, V. S. Ramakrishnan, S. Subramanian and R. Sundaram.

References

[1] A. Agrawal, P. Klein, and R. Ravi. When trees collide: An approximation algorithm for the generalized Steiner problem on networks. *SIAM J. Computing*, 24:440–456, 1995.

[2] R. Ahuja, T. Magnanti, and J. Orlin. *Network Flows: Theory and Algorithms*. Prentice Hall, Englewood Cliffs, 1993.

[3] S. Arora and M. Sudan. Improved low-degree testing and its applications. In *Proc. 29th Annual ACM Symposium on Theory of Computing (STOC'97)*, pages 485–496, 1997.

[4] B. Boldon, N. Deo, and N. Kumar. Minimum weight degree constrained spanning tree problem: Heuristics and implementation on a SIMD parallel machine. *Parallel Computing*, 22(3):369–382, 1996.

[5] P. M. Camerini, G. Galbiati, and F. Maffioli. The complexity of weighted multi-constrained spanning tree problems. In *LOVSZEM: Colloquium on the Theory of Algorithms*. North-Holland, Amsterdam, 1985.

[6] W. Cook, W. Cunningham, W. Pulleybank, and A. Schrijver. *Combinatorial Optimization*. Wiley–Interscience Series on Discrete Mathematics and Optimization. Wiley, New York, 1998.

[7] T. H. Cormen, C. E. Leiserson, and R. L. Rivest. *Introduction to Algorithms*. McGraw–Hill, Cambridge, 1990.

[8] N. Deo and S. L. Hakimi. The shortest generalized Hamiltonian tree. In *Proc. 6th Annual Allerton Conference*, pages 879–888, 1968.

[9] C. W. Duin and A. Volgenant. Some generalizations of the Steiner problem in graphs. *Networks*, 17:353–364, 1987.

[10] D. Hochbaum (Editor). *Approximation Algorithms for NP-Hard Problems*. PWS, Boston, 1997.

[11] S. Fekete, S. Khuller, M. Klemmstein, B. Raghavachari, and N. Young. A network flow technique for finding low-weight bounded-degree spanning trees. *J. Algorithms*, 24(2):310–324, 1997.

[12] T. Fischer. Optimizing the degree of minimum weight spanning trees. Technical Report TR 93-1338, Department of Computer Science, Cornell University, Ithaca, New York, Apr. 1993.

[13] M. Fürer and B. Raghavachari. Approximating the minimum-degree Steiner tree to within one of optimal. *J. Algorithms*, 17(3):409–423, 1994.

[14] M. R. Garey and D. S. Johnson. *Computers and Intractability: A Guide to the Theory of NP-Completeness*. Freeman, San Francisco, 1979.

[15] M. Goemans and D. Williamson. A general approximation technique for constrained forest problems. *SIAM J. Computing*, 24:296–317, 1995.

[16] A. Iwainsky, E. Canuto, O. Taraszow, and A. Villa. Network decomposition for the optimization of connection structures. *Networks*, 16:205–235, 1986.

[17] S. Khuller, B. Raghavachari, and N. Young. Low-degree spanning trees of small weight. *SIAM J. Computing*, 25(2):355–368, 1996.

[18] P. Klein and R. Ravi. A nearly best-possible approximation for node-weighted Steiner trees. *J. Algorithms*, 19(1):104–115, 1995.

[19] F. T. Leighton and S. Rao. An approximate max-flow min-cut theorem for uniform multicommodity flow problems with application to approximation algorithms. *J. ACM*, 46(6):787–832, 1999.

[20] C. Lund and M. Yannakakis. On the hardness of approximating minimization problems. *J. ACM*, 41(5):960–981, 1994.

[21] M. V. Marathe, R. Ravi, R. Sundaram, S. S. Ravi, D. J. Rosenkrantz, and H. B. Hunt III. Bicriteria network design problems. *J. Algorithms*, 28(1):142–171, 1998.

[22] C. Monma and S. Suri. Transitions in geometric minimum spanning trees. *Discrete & Computational Geometry*, 8(3):265–293, 1992.

[23] C. Papadimitriou and U. Vazirani. On two geometric problems related to the traveling salesman problem. *J. Algorithms*, 4:231–246, 1984.

[24] R. Ravi. Rapid rumor ramification. In *Proc. 35th Annual IEEE Symp. Foundations of Computer Science (FOCS'94)*, pages 202–213, 1994.

[25] R. Ravi, B. Raghavachari, and P. N. Klein. Approximation through local optimality: Designing networks with small degree. In *Proc. 12th Annual Conference on Foundations of Software Technology and Theoretical Computer Science (FST & TCS)*. Lecture Notes in Computer Science, volume 652, pages 279–290. Springer, Berlin, 1992.

[26] R. Ravi, M. V. Marathe, S. S. Ravi, D. J. Rosenkrantz, and H. B. Hunt III. Many birds with one stone: Multi-objective approximation algorithms. In *Proc. 25th Annual ACM Symposium on Theory of Computing (STOC'93)*, pages 438–447, 1993.

[27] R. Raz and S. Safra. A sub-constant error-probability low-degree test and a sub-constant error-probability PCP characterization of NP. In *Proc. 29th Annual ACM Symposium on Theory of Computing (STOC'97)*, pages 475–484, 1997.

[28] D. J. Rosenkrantz, R. E. Stearns, and P. M. Lewis II. An analysis of several heuristics for the traveling salesman problem. *SIAM J. Computing*, 6(3):563–581, 1977.

Chapter 10

EFFICIENT ALGORITHMS FOR SEGMENTATION OF ITEM-SET TIME SERIES

PARVATHI CHUNDI

Computer Science Department, University of Nebraska at Omaha, Omaha, NE 68106, USA.
Email: `pchundi@mail.unomaha.edu`

DANIEL J. ROSENKRANTZ

Computer Science Department, SUNY at Albany, Albany, NY 12222, USA.
Email: `djr@cs.albany.edu`

Reprinted from: *Data Mining and Knowledge Discovery Journal*, Published online April 18, 2008. © Springer

Abstract   We propose a special type of time series, which we call an *item-set time series*, to facilitate the temporal analysis of software version histories, email logs, stock market data, etc. In an item-set time series, each observed data value is a set of discrete items. We formalize the concept of an item-set time series and present efficient algorithms for segmenting a given item-set time series. Segmentation of a time series partitions the time series into a sequence of *segments* where each segment is constructed by combining consecutive time points of the time series. Each segment is associated with an item set that is computed from the item sets of the time points in that segment, using a function which we call a *measure function*. We then define a concept called the *segment difference*, which measures the difference between the item set of a segment and the item sets of the time points in that segment. The segment difference values are required to construct an optimal segmentation of the time series. We describe novel and efficient algorithms to compute segment difference values for each of the measure functions described in the paper. We outline a dynamic programming based scheme to construct an optimal segmentation of the given item-set time series. We use the item-set time series segmentation techniques to analyze the temporal content of three different data sets—Enron email, stock market data, and a synthetic data set. The experimental results show that an optimal segmentation of item-set time series data captures much more temporal content than a segmentation constructed based on the number of time points in each segment, without examining

S.S. Ravi, S.K. Shukla (eds.), *Fundamental Problems in Computing*,
© Springer Science + Business Media B.V. 2009

the item set data at the time points, and can be used to analyze different types of temporal data.

Keywords: item-set time series, measure function, segment difference, segmentation algorithms, optimal segmentation

Received: 5 February 2008 / Accepted: 28 March 2008. Responsible editor: Eamonn Keogh.

1.   Introduction

Time series data is generated by many measurement and monitoring applications [5, 16, 18, 27], and accounts for a large fraction of the data available for analysis purposes. Time series data is collected and analyzed for an enhanced understanding of the phenomenon being observed. Numerous data mining methods have been applied to the time series data including segmentation, forecasting, periodicity detection, and rule discovery [9, 18, 20, 22, 27].

A time series is a sequence of observations of some phenomenon, where the observations are ordered in time. Usually, each observation (also known as a data point) is a numeric value or a vector of numeric values for a set of variables [16, 22]. In this paper, we discuss a new type of time series, which we call an **item-set** time series, where each data point is a set of discrete items. The notion of an item-set time series is motivated by applications where the values observed at each time point are sets of items. As an example, consider software repositories such as Mozilla and Apache. These repositories store many kinds of information collected during the evolution of a software project, such as the developers working on the project, the modules and files of the project, version histories as recorded by version management programs, and bug reports. Thus, a temporal representation of the activity recorded in a software repository may contain the ids of developers involved in the project at any point of time during the life cycle of the project, the ids of files that were being changed, or the most frequently reported bug topics. The temporal activity may be represented as a set of developer ids, file ids, etc. [29].

Another application that can be modeled using an item-set time series is the analysis of email data. The email data of an organization includes the email ids of senders and receivers (in the *To, CC and BCC* fields), the subject and body of the messages, and the time each message was sent. Analyzing email data has been shown to be extremely valuable for uncovering organizational structure in terms of hidden social networks and discussion threads [10, 26, 28]. An email data set may be represented as a set of email ids that sent/received large amounts of emails at any given time. These email ids may correspond to individuals who are central to some important activity at the time the emails were sent. By modeling email data as an item-set time series, one may be able to identify employees of organizational importance at each point in time, other employees these important individuals are in touch with, and the topics of emails sent/received among these employee groups.

The item-set time series notion also enables us to analyze stock market data from a novel perspective. Instead of analyzing the highs and lows of a stock price or traded volumes, one can use the notion of an item-set time series and its segmentation to study the set of stocks that were traded in high volumes or contributed to large gains during a time period.

Traditionally, time series data may contains hundreds or thousands of observations. One may wish to extract time segments where the observations are somewhat similar to each other or distinct from the rest of the time period. Time series segmentation algorithms are typically employed to compactly represent a time series in a way so that segments with similar observations are highlighted [1, 5, 18–22]. Given a time series T containing n observations (or time points), a p-segmentation (where typically $p \ll n$) of T consists of partitioning the time range of T into p segments. The data associated with each segment is constructed by merging the consecutive observations (or time points) in the segment into a single observation.

There are many ways to construct a segmentation of a time series. One can simply combine all observations appearing in the same day/week/month/year etc. into a single segment. Another way is to combine an equal number of consecutive observations to form each segment.[1] We refer to these segmentations as **oblivious** segmentations since they are constructed without examining the data at the time points. Although these methods are efficient and easy to implement, they may not result in a good segmentation for data mining and analysis purposes.

In this paper, we focus on the problem of constructing an **optimal segmentation** of a given item-set time series. We define the notion of an *optimal* segmentation of an item-set time series and describe methods to construct it. Intuitively, an optimal segmentation of a time series is one where the observation associated with each segment represents the time series in a best possible manner. A set of items, which we call the **segment item set**, is associated with each segment. The segment item set of a given segment is computed from the individual item sets in that segment using a function, which we call a **measure function**.[2] We describe two different measure functions, the **count** measure and the **density** measure. The difference between the item set of a given seg-

---

[1] In cases where n is not a multiple of p, one of the segments in such a segmentation may have fewer observations than the other segments.

[2] The term *measure function* first appeared in [2], but had a different meaning than here, returning a value for a given keyword in a given set of documents.

ment and the individual item sets in that segment is formalized via the concept of a **segment difference** value. We will also define the notion of the **non-homogeneity** of a segmentation as a function of the segment difference values of the segments in the segmentation. We define an optimal segmentation as a segmentation with minimal non-homogeneity, subject to specified constraints on the segmentation.

The optimal segmentation problem takes as input a time series T and an upper bound p on the desired number of segments. The output is a segmentation of T with at most p segments, having the minimum amount of non-homogeneity among such segmentations. An alternative formulation of the problem is to provide as input an upper bound on the non-homogeneity value. The output is a segmentation of T with a minimum number of segments that satisfies the given upper bound on non-homogeneity.

The construction of an optimal segmentation uses the segment differences of each of the $O(n^2)$ segments of the input time series T (where n is the number of time points in T). The computation of segment differences has received little attention in the literature. This issue is especially important for an item-set time series, where computing segment differences involves set operations over the item sets of time points and segments, which can be very time-consuming. In this paper, we describe efficient procedures, which we refer to as **SD-Count-Eff** and **SD-Density-Eff**, to compute segment item sets and segment differences for the measure functions discussed in the paper. The proposed procedures consider segments of increasing sizes starting at a given time point i ($1 \leq i \leq n$) and use the measure function definition to determine which new items should be added to the current segment item set and which items, if any, should be dropped from the current segment item set. This information is used to update intermediate count values used in the computation. Our experiments show that computations *SD-Count-Eff* and *SD-Density-Eff* result in significant time savings, compared to more straightforward algorithms.

This paper makes three main contributions. First, it formulates the notion of an item-set time series. The items in an item set are assumed to be atomic, with no (useful) internal structure. Hence, the concept of an item-set time series is very general, and likely to have wide applicability. Second, it presents novel and efficient methods to compute the segment difference values required to construct optimal segmentations of an item-set time series. Third, the paper presents the results of several experiments on different kinds of data sets. The experimental results highlight the general nature of the item-set time series notion and the variety of useful information captured by the segmentation of item-set time series data.

We applied the item-set time series segmentation techniques of this paper to three different data sets—Enron email data [11], $S\&P$ 500 stock market data, and a synthetic data set. The Enron email data has been analyzed in many contexts [10, 23, 26, 28]. We represent the Enron data as an item-set series of users with a special property. In this paper, we identified all users who sent an unusually high amount of email at a particular time. Frequent senders may be people of importance or may belong to a sub-entity of an organization with an unusually high amount of email activity. Constructing an optimal p-segmentation of such an item-set time series identifies p segments and a set of users for each segment that sent email frequently during that segment. This information can then be used to analyze the spots of high activity in an organization and how these spots change over time. We considered all emails exchanged in 2000 and 2001 and constructed an item-set time series from the data, with a time point for each of the 105 weeks during 2000–2001.

The $S\&P$ 500 stock market data was downloaded from http://kumo.swcp. com. The data contained, for each of the $S\&P$ 500 stocks and each trading day between Feb 21, 2007 and Feb 20, 2008, the ticker symbol, the opening price, the highest traded price, the lowest traded price, the closing price, and the volume traded for that day. Using this data, we calculated the top 5 stocks in terms of the volume traded on each day in the data set. This resulted in an item-set time series containing 252 time points.

We constructed several segmentations for the item-set time series constructed from the Enron corpus and the stock market data. Optimal and oblivious segmentations were compared using the non-homogeneity of a segmentation as a metric. As expected, the non-homogeneity of optimal segmentations was smaller compared to oblivious segmentations of the same size in all cases.

The experiments illustrated the interplay between the user defined threshold value used in deciding which items belong in the item set of a segment, and the constraint on the number of segments of a segmentation. For example, when the upper bound on the number of segments in a segmentation is set to a small value and the threshold is set to a higher value, the non-homogeneity of the optimal segmentations constructed was high. For most segmentation sizes, threshold values of around 0.5 for the density measure yielded segmentations with the lowest values of non-homogeneity.

A simple random data generator was used to generate item-set time series containing different numbers of time points and items. The randomly generated item-set time series were used to conduct scalability experiments. We generated item-set time series with 50, 100, 200, 400, 800, and 1600 time points. For each item-set time series and each measure function defined in the paper, we measured the time taken to compute the segment differences using the efficient method as well as a straightforward computation. The time taken by the efficient methods was much smaller than that taken by the straightforward computations. As the number of time points of an item-series time series increased, the difference between times taken by the straightforward computations and the efficient methods increased dramatically.

We also measured the time taken for the construction of an optimal segmentation of each of the above item-set time series by the dynamic programming scheme described in the paper. For an item-set time series containing 1,600 time points, the construction of an optimal segmentation took about 580 seconds. The computation of segment difference values for the same data set using the *SD-Count-Eff* procedure took about 490 seconds. Therefore, the total time to construct an optimal segmentation of the given item-set time series was approximately 1,070 seconds.

The rest of the paper is organized as follows. In Sect. 2, we describe the terminology and definitions. In Sect. 3, we describe novel algorithms for computing the segment differences for the two measure functions discussed in Sect. 2. In Sect. 4, we discuss optimal segmentations and dynamic programming schemes for constructing them. In Sect. 5, we describe the experiments. Section 6 describes related work, and Sect. 7 concludes the paper.

2.   Terminology and Definitions

Let $\mathcal{I}$ be a finite set of discrete items $d_1, d_2, \ldots, d_m$. An **item set** is a subset of $\mathcal{I}$. The **fractional difference** between two item sets x and y is $(|x - y| + |y - x|) / (|x \cup y|)$ if $x \cup y$ is nonempty, and is 0 otherwise.

An **item-set time series** T consists of a finite sequence of n samples $x_1, \ldots, x_n$ where each x_k is an item set, recorded at successive time points $t_1, \ldots, t_n$.

A **segment** $s(a, b)$ ($1 \leq a \leq b \leq n$) of a time series T consists of the consecutive time points $t_a, \ldots, t_b$. Suppose that a given segment s_1 ends immediately before another given segment s_2 begins, so that $s_1 = s(a, b)$ and $s_2 = s(b + 1, c)$, for some a, b, and c. In this case, the **concatenation** of s_1 and s_2, denoted as $s_1 s_2$, is defined, and is the segment $s(a, c)$.

A **measure function** (denoted by f) is used to assign a numeric value to each pair consisting of an item and a segment.

There are many possible types of measure functions that can be formulated. In this paper, we define two measure functions, both based on the occurrence frequency of an item in a segment.

- The *count measure* (f_c) takes an item d_q and a segment $s(a, b)$ as input, and returns the number of item sets in $s(a, b)$ that contain d_q.

- The *density measure* (f_d) takes an item d_q and a segment $s(a, b)$ as input, and returns the fraction of the item sets in $s(a, b)$ that contain d_q.

The numeric values assigned to items by a measure function f in a given segment $s(a, b)$ are used to identify items that are deemed to be significant for that segment, as follows. Let α be a user specified threshold. An item d_q is called **significant** in segment $s(a, b)$ if $f(d_q, s(a, b)) \geq \alpha$. The **segment item** set of segment $s(a, b)$, denoted by $I_\alpha(s(a, b), f)$, is the set of significant items in $s(a, b)$.

Let $s(a, b)$ be a segment and t_h be a time point such that $a \leq h \leq b$. Let δ_h denote the fractional difference between $I_\alpha(s(a, b), f)$ and x_h. The **segment difference** of segment $s(a, b)$, denoted by $\delta(s(a, b))$, is $\sum_{a \leq h \leq b} \delta_h$.

A segmentation Π of a time series T is a sequence $s(b_0, b_1)$, $s(b_1 + 1, b_2)$, $\ldots, s(b_{l-1} + 1, b_l)$ of segments such that the concatenation $s(b_0, b_1)$ $s(b_1 + 1, b_2) \cdots s(b_{l-1} + 1, b_l) = s(1, n)$. The **size** of Π, denoted by $|\Pi|$, is l, the number of segments in Π.

3. Computation of Segment Differences

Optimal segmentation construction algorithms require access to the segment difference values of all of the $O(n^2)$ segments of the input time series T, where n is the number of item sets in T. Efficient algorithms for computing segment differences have received little attention in the time series segmentation literature. This computation is especially important for item-set time series segmentation, since the computation requires set operations over $\mathcal{I}$, which is possibly a very large set.

For both the count and density measure functions, in a straightforward computation, the item set $I_\alpha(s(a, b), f)$ of a given segment $s(a, b)$ can be computed by processing all of the item sets in $s(a, b)$ and applying measure function f on each of the items. Let $m = |\mathcal{I}|$. This computation takes time $O(nm)$ per segment, and the item sets of all segments can be computed in $O(n^3 m)$ time. (A more efficient computation can compute all the item sets in time $O(n^2 m)$.)

Now consider computing the segment differences. The segment difference of a segment $s(i, j)$ is a summation of fractional differences between the item sets x_h of the time points t_h in the segment and the item set $I_\alpha(s(i, j), f)$. To compute $\delta(s(a, b))$, each fractional difference δ_h between an x_h ($a \leq h \leq b$) and $I_\alpha(s(a, b), f)$ can be computed in $O(m)$ time, and these fractional differences can be summed up. The segment difference of $s(a, b)$ can thus be computed in $O(nm)$ time, and all of the $O(n^2)$ segment differences can be computed in time $O(n^3 m)$ time.

The segment difference computation algorithms described in this paper combine the item set and difference computation of a segment into one step to achieve time savings. We first describe an efficient algorithm for computing the segment differences for the count measure.

3.1 Segment Difference Computation for the Count Measure

We assume that the items in $\mathcal{I}$ are represented by consecutive integers, which we refer to as *item ids*. We assume that each item set x_h in the input time series is represented as a sorted list of the item ids of those items that are in x_h. Let K denote the total size of all these lists together. Note that K is at most mn. In practice, item sets may be much smaller than $\mathcal{I}$, so that it will often be the case that $K \ll mn$.

Given the set of lists x_h, we can in time $O(K)$, transform this set of lists into a data structure *Item_Occurrences*, that has embedded within it both the list x_h for each of the n time points, and a list τ_q for each of the m items d_q in $\mathcal{I}$. List τ_q is a list of those time points in which item d_q appears, sorted in ascending order. A given entry in *Item_Occurrences* corresponds to a given time point t_h and item d_q. The entry contains four fields: the value of h, the value of q, a pointer to next entry for t_h (i.e a pointer to the next member of x_h), and a pointer to next entry for d_q (i.e a pointer to the next member of τ_q).

A segment difference $\delta(s(a,b))$ is computed by adding up the fractional difference of each of the time points t_h in the segment. The fractional difference δ_h is the size of the symmetric difference between x_h and $I_\alpha(s(a,b),f)$ normalized by the size of $x_h \cup I_\alpha(s(a,b),f)$.

Let P and Q be two sets of items. Then, the fractional difference between P and Q is $\frac{|P-Q|+|Q-P|}{|P \cup Q|}$ when $|P \cup Q| > 0$, and is 0 otherwise. Let $\omega(P,Q) = P \cap Q$. Then the fractional difference can be calculated as $\frac{|P|+|Q|-2|\omega(P,Q)|}{|P|+|Q|-|\omega(P,Q)|}$ when $|P|+|Q| > 0$.

To compute δ_h, we compute the sizes of $I_\alpha(s(a,b),f)$, and $\omega(x_h, I_\alpha(s(a,b),f))$.

An observation crucial to the algorithm is that, for the count measure function, if an item is in the item set of a segment s, then it is also in the item set of all segments s' that can be obtained by combining s with one or more adjacent time points. In particular, we utilize this observation as follows. Suppose that for a given item d_q and time point t_i, $f_c(s(i,n),d_q) \geq \alpha$. Let t_j be the first time point such that $f_c(s(i,j),d_q) = \alpha$. Then for each g, where $i \leq g < j$, d_q is not in $I_\alpha(s(i,g),f)$, and for each g, where $j \leq g \leq n$, d_q is in $I_\alpha(s(i,g),f)$. We call t_j the *critical point* for d_q and t_i.

The algorithm, which we refer to as **SD-Count-Eff**, is outlined in Fig. 10.1. To elucidate the algorithm, we define several abstract variables, as follows.

Definitions of Abstract Variables

$count_{i,j,q}$ is the number of x_h, $i \leq h \leq j$, such that $d_q \in x_h$, i.e. the number of occurrences of d_q in $s(i,j)$.

$\omega_{i,j,h} = |x_h \cap I_\alpha(s(i,j),f)|$ for $i \leq h \leq j$, and 0 otherwise.

$new\_to\_omega_{i,j,h}$ is the number of d_q such that $d_q \in x_i \cap x_h$ and $count_{i,j,q} = \alpha$ for $i < h \leq j$, is the number of d_q such that $d_q \in x_i$ and $count_{i,j,q} \geq \alpha$ for $i = h \leq j$, and is 0 otherwise.

Computation of Segment Difference Values for Count Measure

Input: Set of items x_h for each time point t_h

Output: Segment difference value for each segment $s(i,j)$,
$1 \leq i \leq j \leq n$, stored in variable $seg\_diff[i,j]$.

begin
       From the set of lists x_h, construct the data structure $Item\_Occurrences$;
       for each item d_q, $count[q] = 0$; /* Initialize vector $count$. */
       for $start = n$ down to 1
           for $future\_end = start$ to n
              $newly\_critical[future\_end]$ = NULL;
              $previously\_critical[future\_end]$ = NULL;
           $num\_items[start] = 0$;
           /* Initialize $num\_significant$. */
           /* As end varies, $num\_significant$ will store $|I_\alpha(s(start,end),f)|$. */
           $num\_significant = 0$;
           /* $num\_critical[start]$ will store $num\_critical_{start,start}$. */
           $num\_critical[start] = 0$;
           for each d_q in x_{start}
              increment $num\_items[start]$ by 1;
              increment $count[q]$ by 1;
              if $count[q] \geq \alpha$ **then**
                 $first\_occurrence[q]$ = pointer to entry in $Item\_Occurrences$ for t_{start} and d_q;
                 let new_crit be the time point of the αth entry in τ_q, beginning with
                             $first\_occurrence[q]$.
                 increment $num\_critical[new\_crit]$ by 1;
                 insert q in $newly\_critical[new\_crit]$;
              if $count[q] > \alpha$ **then**
                 let old_crit be the time point for $\alpha + 1^{th}$ entry in τ_q, beginning with
                              $first\_occurrence[q]$;
                 decrement $num\_critical[old\_crit]$ by 1;
                 insert q in $previously\_critical[old\_crit]$;

           for $end = start$ to n
              $num\_significant = num\_significant + num\_critical[end]$;
              $new\_to\_omega[end] = 0$;
              for each q in $newly\_critical[end]$
                 for each time point h of first α entries in τ_q, beginning with $first\_occurrence[q]$
                     increment $new\_to\_omega[h]$ by 1;
              for each q in $previously\_critical[end]$
                 for each time point h of the first $\alpha - 1$ entries in τ_q,
                       beginning after $first\_occurrence[q]$
                     decrement $new\_to\_omega[h]$ by 1;
              /* Initialize $omega[start,end]$, which will store the value of $\omega_{start,end,start}$. */
             $omega[start,end] = 0$;
             $seg\_diff[start,end] = 0$;
             for $h = start$ to end
                $omega[h,end] = omega[h,end] + new\_to\_omega[h]$;
                if $(num\_items[h] + num\_significant) > 0$
                then $delta = \frac{(num\_items[h] + num\_significant - 2*omega[h,end])}{num\_items[h] + num\_significant - omega[h,end]}$;
                else $delta = 0$;
                $seg\_diff[start,end] = seg\_diff[start,end] + delta$;
end

Figure 10.1. *SD-Count-Eff*: Segment Difference Computation for the Count Measure

$num\_critical_{i,j}$ is the number of items d_q for which t_j is the critical point for d_q and x_i.

$newly\_critical_{i,j} = \{q \mid q \in x_i \cap x_j \text{ and } count_{i,j,q} = \alpha\}$.

$previously\_critical_{i,j} = \{q \mid q \in x_i \cap x_j \text{ and } count_{i,j,q} = \alpha + 1\}$.

The algorithm contains a triply nested loop: the outermost loop ranges over a time-point valued variable $start$, the middle loop ranges over a time-point valued variable end, and the innermost loop ranges over a time-point valued variable h.

The values of program variables in the algorithm are related to the abstract variables defined above as follows.

Consider a given iteration of loop variable $start$. The algorithm contains two vectors, $count$ and $first\_occurrence$, each with an element for each item id. Vector element $count[q]$ equals $count_{start,n,q}$. The given loop iteration only accesses the elements of vector $first\_occurrence$ corresponding to those items d_q such that d_q is in x_{start} and $count_{start,n,q}$ is at least α. For each such item d_q, vector element $first\_occurrence[q]$ contains a pointer to the entry in $Item\_Occurrences$ for t_{start} and d_q, i.e. a pointer to the entry corresponding to the occurrence of d_q in x_{start}. The algorithm also contains the three vectors $num\_critical$, $newly\_critical$, and $previously\_critical$. Each of these three vectors has an entry for each time point from $start$ to n. Consider time point j, where $start \leq j \leq n$. Vector element $num\_critical[j]$ equals $num\_critical_{start,j}$. Vector element $newly\_critical[j]$ is a list of the members of $newly\_critical_{start,j}$. Vector element $previously\_critical[j]$ is a list of the members of $previously\_critical_{start,j}$.

Consider a given iteration of loop variable end within a given iteration of loop variable $start$. Program variable $num\_significant$ equals $|I_\alpha(s(start, end), f)|$. The algorithm contains vector new_to_omega, with an entry for each time point from $start$ to end. Consider time point j, where $start \leq j \leq end$. Vector element $new\_to\_omega[j]$ equals $new\_to\_omega_{start,end,j}$.

Consider a given iteration of loop variable h within a given iteration of loop variable end, within a given iteration of loop variable $start$. The algorithm contains a two-dimensional array, $omega$, where for $start \leq h \leq end$, $omega[h, end]$ equals $\omega_{start,end,h}$.

Each iteration of the outermost loop (with loop variable $start$) computes the segment differences of all segments starting at time point t_{start}, considering these time points in reverse chronological order (i.e., $start$ goes from n to 1). Each time point in segment $s(start, n)$ is considered as an end point t_{end}. Each iteration of the middle loop (with loop variable end) computes the segment difference for segment $s(start, end)$. During a given iteration of the $start$ loop, vector new_to_omega is computed, and used to update array $omega$, which in turn is used to compute the segment differences for the segments starting at t_{start}.

At the beginning of a given iteration of the $start$ loop, the previous iteration has left $omega[h, end]$, for $start < h \leq end \leq n$, equal to $\omega_{start+1,end,h}$. Such a value $omega[h, end]$ needs to be incremented for each item d_q such that $d_q \in x_h$, $d_q \in x_{start}$, and $count_{start,end,q} = \alpha$, i.e., for each item contributing to $new\_to\_omega_{start,end,h}$. Thus, for $start < h \le end \le n$,

$$\omega_{start,end,h} = \omega_{start+1,end,h} + new\_to\_omega_{start,end,h}.$$

Moreover, $\omega_{start,end,start} = new\_to\_omega_{start,end,start}$.

A given item d_q will only cause changes to array $omega$ if $d_q \in x_{start}$, and $count_{start,n,q} \ge \alpha$. For such an item d_q, let new_crit be the index of the time point t_{new_crit} such that $d_q \in x_{new\_crit}$, and $count_{start,new\_crit,q} = \alpha$, i.e. t_{new_crit} is the critical point for d_q and t_{start}. Suppose that $count_{start,n,q} = \alpha$. Then d_q contributes to $new\_to\_omega_{start,end,h}$ for all h and end, such that $d_q \in x_h$ and $start \le h \le new\_crit \le end$. Suppose now that $count_{start,n,q} > \alpha$. Let old_crit be the index of the time point t_{old_crit} such that $d_q \in x_{old\_crit}$, and $count_{start,old\_crit,q} = \alpha+1$, i.e. t_{old_crit} is the critical point for d_q and $t_{start+1}$. Then d_q contributes to $new\_to\_omega_{start,end,h}$ for all h and end, such that $d_q \in x_h$ and $start < h \le new\_crit \le end < old\_crit$, or $start = h$ and $end \ge new\_crit$.

For a given value of $start$, before executing the end loop, the algorithm scans the item set x_{start} to compute the number of items occurring in x_{start}, update vector $num\_critical$, and compute the vectors $newly\_critical$ and $previously\_critical$. Suppose that for a given item d_q in x_{start}, it is the case that $count_{start,n,q} \ge \alpha$. Let new_crit be the critical point for d_q and t_{start}. The algorithm records this fact by incrementing the vector element $num\_critical[new\_crit]$ by 1, and inserting q into the list-valued vector element $newly\_critical[new\_crit]$. Consider the more special case where $count_{start,end,q} > \alpha$. In this special case, $count_{start+1,end,q} \ge \alpha$. Let old_crit be the critical point for d_q and $t_{start+1}$. Then, a previous iteration of the $start$ loop would have considered d_q to be a contributor to the vector element $num\_critical[old\_crit]$. Because of the change in the critical point for d_q, the algorithm decrements the vector element $num\_critical[old\_crit]$ by 1, and inserts q into the list-valued vector element $previously\_critical[old\_crit]$.

Thus, vector $num\_critical$ is updated as follows. Consider a non-initial iteration of the $start$ loop. For the current value of loop variable $start$, the previous iteration of the outer loop has left vector element $num\_critical[j]$, for $start < j \le n$, equal to $num\_critical_{start+1,j}$. However, $num\_critical[j]$ must be updated to equal $num\_critical_{start,j}$. This update is carried out by incrementing $num\_critical[j]$ by 1 for each item d_q such that $d_q \in x_{start}$, $d_q \in x_j$, and $count_{start,j,q} = \alpha$; and decrementing $num\_critical[j]$ by 1 for each item d_q such that $d_q \in x_{start}$, $d_q \in x_j$, and $count_{start,j,q} = \alpha + 1$. Moreover, each of the former items is inserted into $newly\_critical[j]$, and each of the latter items is inserted into $previously\_critical[j]$.

Now consider a given iteration of the end loop, within a given iteration of the $start$ loop. From the preceding iteration of the end loop, each vector element $new\_to\_omega[h]$, for $start \le h < end$, stores the value of

$new\_to\_omega_{start,end-1,h}$, and should now be updated to store $new\_to\_omega_{start,end,h}$. The update of vector new_to_omega is done as follows. First consider each q in $newly\_critical_{start,end}$. For each of the α values of h between $start$ and end, such that d_q is in x_h, item d_q is a contributor to $new\_to\_omega_{start,end,h}$, but not a contributor to $new\_to\_omega_{start,end-1,h}$. Consequently, because of d_q, each of these α elements of the vector new_to_omega should be incremented by 1. Now consider each q in $previously\_critical_{start,end}$. For each of the $\alpha - 1$ values of h such that $start < h < end$ and d_q is in x_h, item d_q is a contributor to $new\_to\_omega_{start,end-1,h}$ and is a contributor to $\omega_{start,end,h}$, but is not a contributor to $new\_to\_omega_{start,end,h}$. Consequently, because of d_q, each of these $\alpha - 1$ elements of vector new_to_omega should be decremented by 1. Overall, the updating of vector new_to_omega is based on the following identity. For $start \leq h < end$,

$$
\begin{aligned}
new\_to\_omega_{start,end,h} = \ & new\_to\_omega_{start,end-1,h} \\
& + |x_h \cap newly\_critical_{start,end}| \\
& - (\text{if } h = start \text{ then } 0 \\
& \qquad \text{else } |x_h \cap previously\_critical_{start,end}|)
\end{aligned}
$$

For $start < h = end$,

$$
new\_to\_omega_{start,end,h} = |x_h \cap newly\_critical_{start,end}|.
$$

We now consider the complexity of the algorithm. There are $O(n)$ iterations of the $start$ loop, each containing $O(n)$ iterations of the end loop, each containing $O(n)$ iterations of the h loop, each of whose iterations takes $O(1)$ time. Thus, the total time taken by all the iterations of the h loop is $O(n^3)$. Each list x_{start} is scanned once. The processing of each item d_q in list x_{start} takes time $O(\alpha)$, and may result in the insertion of q on a list in vector $newly\_critical$, and on a list in vector $previously\_critical$. The subsequent processing of each such occurrence of d_q on these lists also takes time $O(\alpha)$. The total number of entries on all the x_{start} lists is K, with a total processing time of $O(\alpha K)$. The overall algorithm takes $O(n^3 + \alpha K)$ time in total when all of the n starting points are considered.

3.2 Segment Difference Computation for the Density Measure

Given an item d_q and a segment $s(i,j)$, density measure f_d returns the fraction of item sets in $s(i,j)$ that contain item d_q. Item d_q is included in the segment item set if this fraction is at least α. As more time points are added to a segment, d_q may or may not be in the corresponding segment item sets. Indeed, the value of f_d for d_q may alternate between below α and above α as the segment length increases. This behavior differs from that for the count measure, where once an item is in at least α time points in a segment, it will not fall below α as a segment is lengthened. Because of this behavior, the algorithm for the count measure cannot be used for the density measure.

We say that the *status* of a given item d_q in $s(i,j)$ is *significant* if and only if d_q is in $I_\alpha(s(i,j),f)$. For a given i and j, where $i < j \leq n$, we say that d_q *changes status* at j if d_q is significant in $s(i,j-1)$ and not significant in $s(i,j)$, or vice versa. We will show that for a given value of i, item d_q can change status at most $\lceil 3\alpha n \rceil$ times as j varies between $i+1$ and n. To see this, let $\theta = \lceil 1/\alpha \rceil$, and consider any sequence of θ consecutive time points t_j through $t_{j+\theta-1}$, starting after t_i. Suppose that d_q changes status at least three times in this sequence of time points. Suppose that the first three of these status changes occur at j', j'', and j'''. Note that $j \leq j' < j'' < j''' < j + \theta$. Suppose that d_q is not significant in $s(i,j-1)$, changes status to significant at j', changes to not significant at j'', and changes to significant at j'''. Because of the first status change, the number of occurrences of d_q between i and j' is at least $\alpha(j' - i + 1)$. Moreover, there is an occurrence of d_q at j''', so the density of occurrences of d_q in the at most $\theta - 1$ time points between $j' + 1$ and $j + \theta - 1$ is at least α. Consequently, the status of d_q cannot change a fourth time until after $j + \theta - 1$. Similar reasoning applies if d_q is significant in $s(i,j-1)$, changes status to not significant at j', changes to significant at j'', and changes to not significant at j'''. Then the density of d_q in $s(i,j-1)$ is at least α, and given the occurrence of d_q at j'', j''' must be $j + \theta - 1$. So, there cannot be a fourth status change until after $j + \theta - 1$. Thus, there are at most three status changes in t_j through $t_{j+\theta-1}$. Note that n or fewer time points can be partitioned into at most $\lceil \alpha n \rceil$ groups of consecutive time points, where the length of each group is at most θ. Thus, for any given value of *start*, as *end* ranges from *start* to n, the number of times item d_q changes status is at most $\lceil 3\alpha n \rceil$.

In Fig. 10.2, we outline an algorithm called **SD-Density-Eff** to compute the segment difference values for the density measure. Each iteration of the *start* loop computes the segment difference of all segments starting at time point t_{start}. These segments are considered in increasing order of their end point. To elucidate the algorithm, we define the following abstract variables.

$add_{i,j}$ is the set of items that are not significant for $s(i,j-1)$, but are significant for $s(i,j)$, where $1 \leq i < j \leq n$.

$drop_{i,j}$ is the set of items that are significant for $s(i,j-1)$, but are not significant for $s(i,j)$, where $1 \leq i < j \leq n$.

The algorithm is based on the following identities.

$$I_\alpha(s(i,j),f) = I_\alpha(s(i,j-1),f) \cup add_{i,j} - drop_{i,j}, \quad \text{for } 1 \leq i < j \leq n.$$

Computation of Segment Difference Values for the Density Measure

Input: Set of items x_h for each time point t_h

Output: Segment difference value for each segment $s(i, j)$, $1 \leq i \leq j \leq n$, stored in variable $seg\_diff\,[i, j]$.

begin
    From the set of lists x_h, construct the data structure $Item\_Occurrences$;
    for $start = n$ down to 1
        $num\_items[start] = 0$;
        for each d_q in x_{start}
            increment $num\_items[start]$ by 1;
        for each item d_q
            $count[q] = 0$;
            $is\_significant[q] = false$;
        $number\_significant = 0$;
        for $future\_end = start$ to n
            $drop_list[future_end] = $ NULL;
        for $end = start$ to n
            $omega[end] = 0$;
            $threshold = \lceil \alpha\,(end - start + 1) \rceil$;
            for each d_q in x_{end}
                increment $count[q]$ by 1;
                if $(count[q] \geq threshold)$ **then**
                    increment $omega[end]$ by 1;
                    $drop\_point = \lfloor \frac{count[q]}{\alpha} \rfloor + start$;
                    if (τ_q has a next occurrence after that in x_{end})
                    then $next_occurrence = $ time point index of this next occurrence;
                    else $next\_occurrence = n + 1$;
                    if ($drop\_point < next\_occurrence$) **then**
                        insert pointer to $Item\_Occurrences$ entry for d_q and t_{end} into $drop\_list[drop\_point]$;
                    if (**not** $is\_significant[q]$) **then**
                        $is\_significant[q] = true$;
                        increment $number\_significant$ by 1;
                        for each time point t_h in an entry in τ_q such that $start \leq h < end$
                            increment $omega[h]$ by 1;
             for each entry in $drop\_list[end]$
                let q be the item id in that entry;
                $is\_significant[q] = false$;
                decrement $number\_significant$ by 1;
                for each time point t_h on list τ_q such that $start \leq h < end$
                    decrement $omega[h]$ by 1;
             $seg\_diff\,[start, end] = 0$;
            for $h = start$ to end
                if ($num\_items[h] + num\_significant > 0$)
                then $delta = \frac{(num\_items[h] + num\_significant - 2 * omega[h])}{num\_items[h] + num\_significant - omega[h]}$;
                else $delta = 0$;
                $seg\_diff\,[start, end] = seg\_diff\,[start, end] + delta$;
end

Figure 10.2. *SD-Density-Eff*: Segment Difference Computation Algorithm for the Density Measure

$$\omega_{i,j,h} = \omega_{i,j-1,h} + |x_h \cap add_{i,j}|$$
$$- |x_h \cap drop_{i,j}|, \quad \text{for } 1 \leq i \leq h < j \leq n.$$
$$\omega_{i,j,j} = |x_j \cap I_\alpha(s(i, j), f)|, \quad \text{for } 1 \leq i \leq j \leq n.$$

The algorithm also uses the concept of a $drop\_point$, defined as follows. Suppose that d_q is in $x_j \cap I_\alpha(s(i, j), f)$. Then $\frac{count_{i,j,q}}{j - i + 1} \geq \alpha$. Suppose that time point t_j were to be followed by a sequence of time points that do not contain d_q. Item d_q would remain significant until a time point $t_{j'}$ was reached such that $\frac{count_{i,j,q}}{j'-i+1} < \alpha$. At this time point $t_{j'}$, item d_q would change status to not significant. The value j' is given by the formula $\lfloor \frac{count_{i,j,q}}{\alpha} \rfloor + i$. We define $drop\_point_{i,j,q}$ as j'. If $drop\_point_{i,j,q} \leq n$ and there is no occurrence of d_q at time points t_{j+1} through $t_{drop\_point_{i,j,q}}$, then d_q will indeed change status to not significant at $drop\_point_{i,j,q}$, and d_q is in $drop_{i,drop\_point_{i,j,q}}$.

We now consider the complexity of the algorithm. There are n iterations of the $start$ loop, each containing $O(n)$ iterations of the end loop, each containing $O(n)$ iterations of the h loop, each of whose iterations takes $O(1)$ time. Thus, the total time taken by all the iterations of the h loop is $O(n^3)$. In addition, for a given iteration of the $start$ loop, each list x_{end}, for $start \leq end \leq n$, is scanned once, thereby scanning at most K item occurrences. For the given value of $start$, as end ranges from $start$ to n, each item d_q changes status at most $\lceil 3\alpha n \rceil$ times. Let K_q be the total number of occurrences of item d_q. Each change of status of d_q entails processing each occurrence of d_q between $start$ and end, of which there are at most K_q such occurrences. For the given value of $start$, the total time required for this processing of d_q is $O(\alpha n K_q)$. Since K equals $\sum_{q=1}^{m} K_q$, the total time for the given value of $start$, over all d_q, is $O(\alpha n K)$. Summing over the n iterations of the $start$ loop gives $O(\alpha n^2 K)$ time. Thus, the total time for the algorithm is $O(n^3 + \alpha n^2 K)$.

4. Optimal Segmentations

A desirable property of a time series segmentation is that the item set of each of the segments closely reflects the item sets of the time points contained in that segment. The segment difference of a given segment is a measure of how internally homogeneous that segment is. There are a variety of ways to measure the non-homogeneity of a given segmentation of a time series, given the segment difference of each segment in the segmentation. We describe three such measures here. The **summation difference** measure, denoted by Δ_{sum}, is the sum of the segment differences of the segments in the segmentation. The **average difference** measure, denoted by Δ_{avg}, is the average segment difference (ratio of the summation difference to the size of the segmentation). The **max difference** measure, denoted by Δ_{max}, is the maximum segment difference. Segmentation of a time series reduces the number of samples to be examined, while hopefully preserving much of the information of the original time series. For a given measure function and difference measure, the **optimal segmentation problem** is to take as input an item-set time series, and an upper bound p on the size of the desired segmentation of the input time series, and construct a segmentation of at most p segments with minimum non-homogeneity. A dual formulation of the optimal segmentation problem is to take as input an item-set time series and an upper bound on the amount of non-homogeneity, and construct a minimum size segmentation whose non-homogeneity does not exceed the given limit.

Increasing the size of a segmentation does not necessarily guarantee that the amount of non-homogeneity will decrease. The following simple example illustrates a scenario where a smaller size segmentation is better than any bigger size alternative.

EXAMPLE 4.1. Let $\mathcal{I} = \{a, b\}$. Time series T contains three time points. The items sets in the time series are $\{a\}$, $\{b\}$, $\{a\}$. The measure function is the density measure f_d and $\alpha = 0.66$. Let Δ_{sum} be the measure of non-homogeneity of a segmentation.

We first consider the segmentation $\Pi_1 = s(1, 3)$ of T, of size one. $I_\alpha(s(1, 3), f_d) = \{a\}$. The non-homogeneity of Π_1 is $\delta(s(1, 3))$, which equals $\sum_{1 \leq j \leq 3} \delta_j$. $\delta_1 = 0$, $\delta_2 = 1$, and $\delta_3 = 0$. Therefore, $\Delta_{sum}(\Pi_1) = 1$.

Now consider a segmentation of size two. There are two possible size two segmentations of T. Let $\Pi_2 = s(1, 1), s(2, 3)$. (The other segmentation of size two is $s(1, 2)$, $s(3, 3)$, and is symmetric to Π_2.)

$$I_\alpha(s(1, 1), f_d) = \{a\} \quad \text{and} \quad I_\alpha(s(2, 3), f_d) = \{\}.$$
$$\delta(s(1, 1)) = 0, \qquad \delta(s(2, 3)) = \sum_{2 \leq j \leq 3} \delta_j = 2.$$
$$\Delta_{sum}(\Pi_2) = 2.$$

Therefore, in this case the non-homogeneity of every size 2 segmentation is greater than that of the size 1 segmentation.

The above observation is true even if we use Δ_{max} as the measure of non-homogeneity. However, if Δ_{avg} is used, then, for this example, both Π_1 and Π_2 have the same non-homogeneity, namely 1.

To solve the optimal segmentation problem, given an item-set time series of n item sets (or time points) and a size constraint p, an *optimal* segmentation, satisfying the given size constraint and with minimum non-homogeneity, is typically constructed using dynamic programming [16, 18]. The dynamic programming approach uses as input data the non-homogeneity measure for each of the $O(n^2)$ segments of the input time series, i.e. the $\delta(s(i, j))$ value for each segment $s(i, j)$ $(1 \leq i \leq j \leq n)$. Prior to carrying out the dynamic programming algorithm, these non-homogeneity values for all segments are computed, using the measure function specified by the user.

An upper bound p on the size of an optimal segmentation is input to the dynamic programming algorithm, which operates as follows. We assume that the item set time series to be segmented begins at index 1 and that $p \leq n$.

A two-dimensional table R is maintained by the dynamic programming algorithm. Entry $R[j, k]$ in the table records the minimum possible amount of non-homogeneity that can be incurred in combining time points 1 through j into k segments ($j \geq 1$, $k \leq j$, $k \leq p$). If k is 1, the value of $R[j, k]$ is set to $\delta(s(1, j))$. Otherwise, a recursive equation is used to compute the value of $R[j, k]$ from previously computed entries in the table. The specifics of the recursive equation depends on which non-homogeneity measure is being used. Entry $R[j, 1]$ (that is $k = 1$) is set to $\delta(s(1, j))$ in all cases. For the summation difference measure of non-homogeneity, each entry $R[j, k]$, when $k > 1$, is set to $min_{k-1 \leq z < j} (R[z, k - 1] + \delta(s(z + 1, j)))$. For the max difference measure of non-homogeneity, $R[j, k]$, when $k > 1$, is set to $min_{k-1 \leq z < j} max(R[z, k - 1], \delta(s(z + 1, j)))$. Finally, for the average difference measure of non-homogeneity, $R[j, k]$, when $k > 1$, is set to $min_{k-1 \leq z < j}$ $((k - 1) * R[z, k - 1] + \delta(s(z + 1, j)))/k$. It can be easily seen that the average difference measure value of an entry $R[j, k]$ is simply the summation difference measure of $R[j, k]$ divided by k. Equivalently, the average difference measure of an entry $R[j, k]$ multiplied by k gives the summation difference measure.

A dynamic programming algorithm based on the above recursive equations can be used to construct table R in $O(n^2 p)$ time. Since each computed value $R[n, k]$ in the last row of the R table is the minimum possible cost of segmenting the time series into k segments, and p is the given constraint on the number of segments, the optimum segmentation non-homogeneity value is given by the minimum value of $R[n, k]$, $1 \leq k \leq p$. The dynamic programming algorithm typically uses an additional two-dimensional table T, where $T[j, k]$ records the value of z that minimizes the $R[j, k]$ entry. Table T is used to construct an optimal segmentation that achieves the minimal cost.

5. Experiments

This section describes the outcomes of applying the segmentation algorithms to the *Enron Corpus*, *S&P 500* stock market data, and synthetic data.

5.1 Comparison of Optimal and Oblivious Segmentations

The *Enron Corpus* was made public during the legal investigation of the Enron Corporation. It contains about 200,000 email messages [11]. We considered the email messages exchanged in the years 2000 and 2001. The item-set time series constructed from the data, denoted by T_E, contained 105 time points, one time point for each week during this time period. Each time point is associated with an item set consisting of the email ids of *frequent senders*. We computed the set of frequent senders as follows. For each email id, we counted the number of emails sent using that email id in a given week. Let a_i be the average value of these counts for week t_i. An email id e is a frequent sender during week t_i if the number of emails sent by e during t_i is greater than a_i. Frequent senders can be used to discover egocentric social networks, as these employees may have organizational significance during the period of activity [7]. There are about 2150 email ids who were frequent senders in at least one of the 105 time points. About 66% of these users were frequent senders in at most two time points.

The stock market data set contained, for each *S&P* stock, and each trading day between Feb 21st, 2007 and Feb 20th, 2008, the date, the ticker symbol, the opening price, the highest traded price, the lowest traded price, the closing price, and the volume traded for that day. Using this data, we calculated the top 5 stocks in terms of the volume traded for each day in the data set. This resulted in an item-set time series, denoted by T_S, containing 252 time points. There are 72 unique ticker symbols that appear in at least one of the 252 time points. Unlike T_E, more than 50% of the stocks appeared in 3 or more item sets.

We processed T_E and T_S as follows. For each segment, we used the density measure to compute the segment item sets from the item sets of the time points in that segment. We first fixed the value of α at 0.5 and constructed optimal as well as oblivious segmentations of several different sizes. The optimal segmentations of different sizes were constructed using the dynamic programming scheme outlined in Sect. 4. The non-homogeneity of an optimal segmentation was computed using the summation difference measure. We constructed the oblivious segmentations as follows. Let n be the number of time points and p be the desired segmentation size. If n is a multiple of p, then each segment contains n/p time points. If n is not a multiple of p, then each of the first $p-1$ segments contains $\lfloor n/(p-1) \rfloor$ time points, and the pth segment contains $n \bmod (p-1)$ time points.

Figure 10.3 displays the experimental results for T_E. Figure 10.3(a) plots the non-homogeneity of a segmentation as a function of the segment size. As can be seen from the figure, the non-homogeneity of a segmentation drops as its size increased. For this experiment, the non-homogeneity of an oblivious segmentation was always higher than that of an optimal segmentation of the same size. Of course, since oblivious segmentations are constructed with no attention to their non-homogeneity, one would expect them to be suboptimal.

Figure 10.3(b) displays the number of frequent senders in a segmentation as a function of segmentation size. For each segmentation constructed, we counted the total number of distinct users that are frequent senders in at least one of its segments. The total number of distinct frequent senders of a segmentation is the cardinality of the union of all segment item sets in that segmentation. For optimal segmentations, the number of distinct frequent senders always increased with the size of a segmentation, but this was not the case for

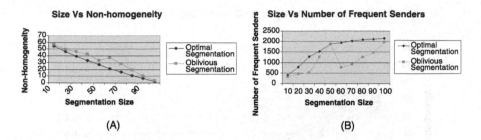

Figure 10.3. (a) Size Vs Non-homogeneity for Optimal and Oblivious Segmentations of T_E.
(b) Size Vs the Total Number of Frequent Senders for Optimal and Oblivious Segmentations
of T_E

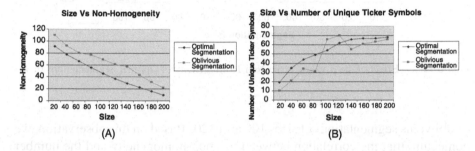

Figure 10.4. (a) Size Vs Non-homogeneity for Optimal and Oblivious Segmentations of T_S.
(b) Size Vs the Total Number of Frequent Senders for Optimal and Oblivious Segmentations
of T_S

oblivious segmentations. Moreover, the number of frequent senders for each
size was much greater for the optimal segmentation when compared to the
oblivious segmentation of the same size. The only exception occurred for size
50. The number of frequent senders of the oblivious segmentation containing
50 segments was 1,875, which was close to the number of frequent senders in
the same size optimal segmentation, 1,871.

Figure 10.4 displays similar plots for T_S. Figure 10.4(a) plots the non-
homogeneity as a function of segmentation size for both optimal and oblivious
segmentations. As can be seen from the figure, the non-homogeneity of an
optimal segmentation was always lower than that of the same size oblivious
segmentation. Figure 10.4(b) plots the segmentation size versus the number
of unique ticker symbols appearing in a segmentation. As the segmentation
size increases, the number of unique ticker symbols increases. The number
of unique ticker symbols of an optimal segmentation was higher than that of
a same size oblivious segmentation in most cases. However, for segmentation
sizes 100 and 120, the oblivious segmentations contained a greater number
of unique ticker symbols than the same size optimal segmentations. This is
because almost all of the 72 ticker symbols appeared in the segment item sets

286

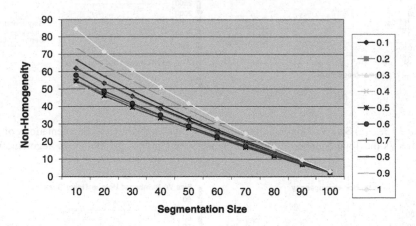

Figure 10.5.   Effect of the α value on the Non-Homogeneity of Optimal Segmentations of T_E

of oblivious segmentations of sizes 100 and 120. Based on this observation, we conjecture that the correlation between the non-homogeneity and the number of distinct items of an optimal segmentation may depend on how the items are distributed over the time points of the input item-set time series. We plan to study this further.

Next we analyzed the effect of the threshold α on the non-homogeneity a segmentation. Consider the time series T_E. If the specified value of α is small, for a user to be deemed a frequent sender in a given segment of T_E, the user needs to be a frequent sender in only a small fraction of time points in the segment. This may lead to high values of segment differences and non-homogeneity. We computed several segmentations of T_E and T_S for different values of α. The result is plotted in Figs. 10.5 and 10.6 for T_E. In both figures, the x-axis plots the segmentation size and y-axis plots the non-homogeneity. There is one curve for each value of α in the range 0.1 to 1, in steps of 0.1. For all values of α, the non-homogeneity of an optimal segmentation dropped consistently as segmentation size increased. For oblivious segmentations, the relationship between segmentation size and non-homogeneity was not as consistent. As can be seen from Fig. 10.6, for the oblivious segmentations, there were many instances where non-homogeneity increased as segmentation size increased, before eventually dropping as the segmentation size approaches n (the number of time points in the input time series).

From Fig. 10.5 it can also be seen that for all segmentation sizes studied, α values 0.4 and 0.5 produced the lowest values of non-homogeneity for the data set T_E (The difference between the plots for α equal to 0.4 and 0.5 is

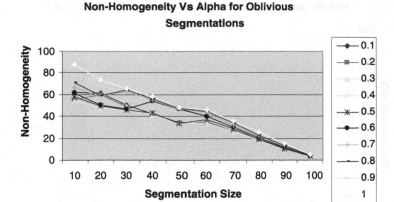

Figure 10.6. Effect of the α value on the Non-Homogeneity of Oblivious Segmentations of T_E

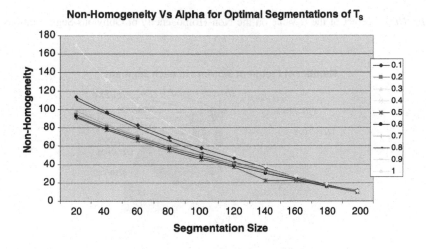

Figure 10.7. Effect of the α value on the Non-Homogeneity of Optimal Segmentations of T_S

minor.) For oblivious segmentations, the lowest non-homogeneity values were achieved for α values 0.3, 0.4, and 0.5.

Figures 10.7 and 10.8 report the experimental results from the same study on T_S. Again, the non-homogeneity of a segmentation did not fall consistently for oblivious segmentations of T_S. For every size tried, the non-homogeneity of optimal segmentations of T_S was smallest when α was 0.4. For oblivious segmentations of T_S, the non-homogeneity of a segmentation was minimum for α values of both 0.4 and 0.5.

Finally, we chose the size 25 optimal segmentation of T_E to study how well a segmentation captures the time varying information for each user. There are approximately 975 users that are frequent senders in at least one of the

288

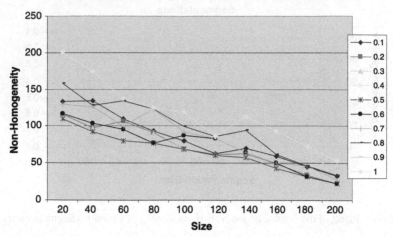

Figure 10.8. Effect of the α value on the Non-Homogeneity of Oblivious Segmentations of T_S

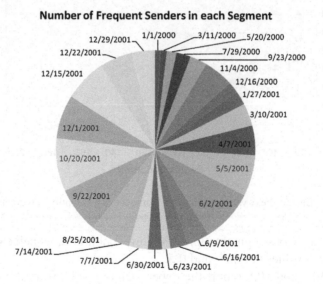

Figure 10.9. Number of Frequent Senders in Each Segment of the Size 25 Segmentation

25 segments. Figure 10.9 shows the distribution of these users over the entire segmentation. The figure shows a pie chart where the label of each pie slice is the starting date of that segment and the size of each pie slice denotes the percent of users in that segment. The length of most segments is approximately 4–6 weeks. Some segments are only one week long.

Segments	03/11/2000-05/19/2000	11/04/2000-12/15/2000	10/20/2001-11/30/2001
Emails Sent To	mark.courtney@enron.com, rebecca.cantrell@enron.com, steve.hooser@enron.com, jennifer-gillaspie@reliantenergy.com, eric.gillaspie@enron.com	amcmullen@canscot.com, mark.whitt@enron.com, ipc_oil@msn.com, mandy.bowles@email.moore.com, htebs@huber.com	kim.ward@enron.com, barry.tycholiz @enron.com, rank.vickers@enron.c om, t..hodge@enron.com, sara.shac kleton@enron.com
Frequent Subject Keywords	Agreement, CA, Gallup, Gas, Interconnect	Agreement, GTC, Huber, Revised, Crescendo	Gas, Invoice, Review, Dow, Contract

Figure 10.10. Information Captured for the Frequent Sender *Gerald Nemec*

To illustrate the frequent sender information captured in the segmentation, we focus on a particular user, called *gerald.nemec@enron.com*, who is one of the two most frequent senders in 23 of the 25 segments.[3] Figure 10.10 shows, for a few segments, which users Gerald Nemec frequently sent emails to and the top five most frequent keywords in the subjects of the emails sent during this time.

It can be seen from Fig. 10.10 that user Gerald Nemec was in touch with different people at different time intervals. The frequently occurring subject keywords during these time intervals are also different, indicating a shift in Gerald Nemec's interests/responsibilities.

5.2 Study of the Performance of Proposed Methods

We used a Red Hat Linux machine with a dual core Intel Xeon 3.73 GHz processor with a 3 GB of RAM to study the scalability of the algorithms described in this paper. We implemented, in Perl, the *SD-Count-Eff, SD-Density-Eff* procedures, and the straightforward computations described in Sect. 3 to compute the segment differences. The straightforward computation considers each segment $s(i, j)$ $(1 \le i \le j \le n)$ separately, computes the segment item set for a given measure function and an α value for the segment, and then computes the segment difference value. We refer to the straightforward computation of segment differences for the count (density) measure as **SD-Count-SF** (**SD-Density-SF**). To study the time taken to construct an optimal segmentation, we implemented the dynamic programming scheme using the summation difference measure. We used Perl's *time* function to measure the time taken by each of these computations in seconds.

We implemented a simple random data generator to generate many item-set time series. The random data generator takes three inputs: m, the number of distinct items in $\mathcal{I}$; n, the number of time points; and b, an upper bound on the cardinality of the item set at each time point. The random data generator outputs an item-set time series containing n item sets, where each item set contains

---

[3] The other such user was elizabeth.sager@enron.com.

n	SD-Count-Eff	SD-Count-SF
50	0	1
100	1	5
200	1	51
400	9	259
800	65	2916
1600	487	25319
3200	3667	—

(A)

n	SD-Density-Eff	SD-Density-SF
50	0	1
100	1	3
200	1	21
400	7	160
800	43	1301
1600	308	10561
3200	2519	—

(B)

n	Time for Optimal Segmentation Construction
50	0
100	1
200	2
400	10
800	73
1600	578
3200	4999

(C)

m	SD-Count-Eff	SD-Count-SF
100	1	21
200	1	22
400	1	25
800	1	27

(D)

Figure 10.11. (a) Time to Compute the Segment Differences for the Count Measure as n grows ($m = 100$). (b) Time to Compute the Segment Differences for the Density Measure as n grows ($m = 100$). (c) Time to Compute an Optimal Segmentation as n grows ($m = 100$ and $p = n$). (d) Time to Compute the Segment Differences for the Count Measure as m grows ($n = 200$)

at most b items. The data generator does not ensure that every one of the m items actually occurs in the generated time series. For each item-set time series generated from the random data generator, segment differences were computed using all four procedures: *SD-Count-Eff*, *SD-Count-SF*, *SD-Density-Eff*, and *SD-Density-SF*. Figure 10.11(a) shows the computation times for *SD-Count-Eff* and *SD-Count-SF*. The first column in the table in Fig. 10.11(a) shows the number of time points n in the input time series, the second column gives the time taken by *SD-Count-Eff* and the third column gives the time taken by *SD-Count-SF*. The α value for $n = 50$ was set to 10. For all other runs, α was set to 50. It can be observed from this figure that *SD-Count-Eff* takes much less time to compute segment differences than does *SD-Count-SF*. It can also be observed that the difference between the computation time of *SD-Count-Eff* and *SD-Count-SF* increases substantially as n increases. From Fig. 10.11(b), similar observations can be made for *SD-Density-Eff* and *SD-Density-SF*. The value of α was always set to 0.5 in the density function experiments. For $n = 3,200$, procedures *SD-Count-SF* and *SD-Density-SF* did not terminate after running for 5 days.

We measured the time taken to construct an optimal segmentation for different values of n. We set p, the constraint on the number of segments, to n in our experiments. Figure 10.11(c) shows the time taken by the dynamic programming algorithm to construct an optimal segmentation of size at most p, as n grows. It can be seen from this table that the effort to construct an optimal segmentation is somewhat evenly divided between the computation of segment differences and the construction of an optimal segmentation. When $n = 6,400$, the dynamic programming algorithm ran out of memory.

To study the effect of big item sets on the computation of segment differences, we conducted an experiment where the number of items in $\mathcal{I}$ were increased while keeping n constant at 200. We compared the time taken by *SD-Count-Eff* and *SD-Count-SF* in each case. The result is displayed in Fig. 10.11(d). The first column in the table in Fig. 10.11(d) shows the m value, the second column shows the time taken by *SD-Count-Eff* and the third column shows the time taken by *SD-Count-SF*. As can be observed from the table, both computations cope well with increasing m, and *SD-Count-Eff* outperforms *SD-Count-SF* in every case.

6. Related Work

Segmentation algorithms for time series data is an active and a classic area of research [1, 16, 18, 19, 21, 22]. Most of this work is focused on time series where each observed value in a given time series is a numeric value or a set of numeric values, whereas in this paper we assume that each observed value is a set of discrete items. A time series as a sequence of symbols is explored in [24], which proposes a symbolic representation of a time series for dimensionality reduction. A piecewise aggregate approximation is first computed, based on which the symbolic representation is generated.

Mining data streams is also an active research area (see [13] and the references contained therein), where segmentation of streams is an important problem [24]. Our paper is focused on processing time series data in a batch mode.

Segmenting sequence data such as DNA sequences or any sequence of characters has also received considerable attention [8, 12, 14, 15, 17, 25]. We can model such sequence data as an item-set time series where each item set is a singleton. We plan to study how this perspective compares with the prior literature.

In our earlier work [2–4, 6], we studied time decompositions based on time stamped documents, with a focus on keywords appearing in these documents. This earlier work utilized a more complex model than item sets. Each time point had an associated set of documents, and each document had an associated set of keyword occurrences, with possibly multiple occurrences of a given keyword in a given document. Each segment in a time decomposition was associated with a keyword set computed by applying one of three measure functions (count, ratio, and rank) to the keywords appearing in the document set of the interval. Segment difference (referred to as *information loss*) values were defined as a function of set difference cardinalities. An efficient algorithm to compute the information loss values for the count measure was described in [6].

The segment difference computation for the count measure, *SD-Count-Eff*, described here is different from our previous work in two significant ways. First, it assumes that each item (or keyword) appears in each time point just once, whereas our previous algorithm assumed that each keyword might appear multiple times in a time point. Second, and more important, the segment difference definition used in this paper is different from our previous work. The current definition normalizes the symmetric difference between a segment item set and an item set in that segment by using fractional differences, whereas our previous work did not use normalization. This normalization precludes the techniques used in [6]. The density measure studied in this paper was not meaningful for the model used in our earlier work on document-based time series, since the measure functions in this earlier work were applied to the set of documents in a given segment, with no regard to which particular time points in the segment contained a given document or keyword occurrence. Thus, the segment difference definitions and the *SD-Density-Eff* algorithm described in this paper have not appeared elsewhere.

Optimal segmentation problems are typically solved via dynamic programming [16, 18]. The dynamic programming schemes outlined in this paper to construct an optimal segmentation have appeared before [3, 16, 29].

Our earlier work in [29, 30] applied the concept of item-set time series segmentation to analyze the version control repositories of several large open source projects—Mozilla, Apache, and Eclipse.

7. Conclusions

In this paper, we propose a special type of time series, which we refer to as an *item-set* time series. Each observation in an item-set time series is a set of discrete items. We extend the segmentation framework to item-set time series by defining the notion of a measure function to compute the segment item sets from the item sets of the time points in the segment, and the notion of segment difference to compute the non-homogeneity of segmentations. We described three separate, yet related, dynamic programming schemes to compute the optimal segmentation of an item-set time series. Segment difference values for each segment of a given item-set time series must be available to the dynamic programming schemes to construct the optimal segmentations. An efficient algorithm is presented to compute the segment difference values for each of the two measure functions defined in the paper. We used item-set time series segmentation methods to analyze Enron email data and stock market data. Several optimal as well as oblivious segmentations of the time series were constructed and studied. As expected, the experiments showed that the non-homogeneity of optimal segmentations is less than that of oblivious segmentations of the same size. The value of the user-specified threshold α also affected the amount of non-homogeneity of a segmentation. We studied the information captured in a segmentation by focusing on one user that appeared in the optimal segmentation of size 25 of the time series constructed from the Enron email data. We identified when and which employees the user was in touch with, and the most frequently used email subject keywords during these periods. We studied the scalability of the proposed techniques using synthetic data. The efficient procedures *SD-Count-Eff* and *SD-Density-Eff* described in the paper outperformed the straightforward segment difference computation in all cases.

Acknowledgments

P. Chundi's work was supported in part by NSF Grant IIS-0534616 and by Grant Number P20 RR16469 from the National Center for Research Resources (NCRR), a component of the National Institutes of Health (NIH).

References

[1] R. Bellman. On the approximation of curves by line segments using dynamic programming. *Commun. ACM*, 4(6):284, 1961.

[2] P. Chundi and D. J. Rosenkrantz. Constructing time decompositions for analyzing time-stamped documents. In *Proceedings of the 4th SIAM International Conference on Data Mining*, pages 57–68, Orlando, FL, Apr. 2004.

[3] P. Chundi and D. J. Rosenkrantz. On lossy time decompositions of time-stamped documents. In *Proc. 13th ACM Conference on Information and Knowledge Management (CIKM)*, pages 437–445, Washington, DC, Nov. 2004.

[4] P. Chundi and D. J. Rosenkrantz. Information preserving time decompositions of time stamped documents. *Data Min. Knowl. Discov.*, 13(1):41–65, 2006.

[5] P. Chundi and D. J. Rosenkrantz. Segmentation of time series data. In J. Wang, editor, *Encyclopedia of Data Warehousing and Mining*. Information Science Reference, Hershey, 2nd edition, pages 1753–1758, 2008.

[6] P. Chundi, R. Zhang, and D. J. Rosenkrantz. Efficient algorithms for constructing time decompositions of time stamped documents. In K. V. Andersen, J. K. Debenham, and R. Wagner, editors, *Proc. 16th International Conference on Database and Expert Systems Applications (DEXA)*. Lecture Notes in Computer Science, volume 3588, pages 514–523. Springer, Berlin, 2005.

[7] K. K. S. Chung, L. Hossain, and J. Davis. Exploring sociocentric and egocentric approaches for social network analysis. In *Proc. 2nd International Conference on Knowledge Management in Asia Pacific*, 2005.

[8] P. Cohen and N. Adams. An algorithm for segmenting categorical time series into meaningful episodes. In *Proc. 4th International Symposium on Intelligent Data Analysis*. Lecture Notes in Computer Science, volume 2189, pages 198–207. Springer, Berlin, 2001.

[9] G. Das, K. Lin, H. Mannila, G. Renganathan, and P. Smyth. Rule discovery from time series. In *Proc. 4th International Conference on Knowledge Discovery and Data Mining (KDD)*, pages 16–22. AAAI Press, Menlo Park, 1998.

[10] J. Diesner and K. Carley. Exploration of communication networks from the Enron Email Corpus. In *Proc. 2005 Workshop on Link Analysis, Counterterrorism, and Security (held in conjunction with SDM 2005)*, 2005.

[11] Enron, 2005, Enron Email Corpus. http://www.cs.cmu.edu/~enron/.

[12] J. A. Flanagan, J. Mantyjarvi, and J. Himberg. Unsupervised clustering of symbol strings and context recognition. In *Proc. 2nd IEEE International Conference on Data Mining*, page 171, 2002.

[13] M. M. Gaber, A. Zaslavsky, and S. Krishnaswamy. Mining data streams: A review. *ACM SIGMOD Record*, 34(2):18–26, 2005.

[14] X. Ge, W. Pratt, and P. Smyth. Discovering Chinese words from unsegmented text. In *Proc. 22nd International Conference on Research and Development on Information Retrieval (SIGIR)*, pages 271–272, Berkeley, CA, 1999.

[15] A. Gionis and H. Mannila. Finding recurrent sources in sequences. In Proc. 7th International Conference on Research in Computational Molecular Biology (RECOMB), pages 123–130, 2003.

[16] A. Gionis and H. Mannila. Segmentation algorithms for time series and sequence data. In *Tutorial at 5th SIAM International Conference on Data Mining*, 2005.

[17] R. Gwadera, A. Gionis, and H. Mannila. Optimal segmentation using tree models. In *Proc. 6th International Conference on Data Mining (ICDM)*, pages 244–253, 2006.

[18] J. Himberg, J. Toivonen, K. Korpiaho, and H. Mannila. Time series segmentation for context recognition in mobile devices. In *Proc. 1st International Conference on Data Mining (ICDM)*, pages 203–210, 2001.

[19] A. Kehagias and V. Petridis. Time-series segmentation using predictive modular neural networks. *Neural Computation*, 9(8):1691–1709, 1997.

[20] E. J. Keogh and S. Kasetty. On the need for time series data mining benchmarks: A survey and empirical demonstration. *Data Min. Knowl. Discov.*, 7(4):349–371, 2003.

[21] E. J. Keogh and M. J. Pazzani. An enhanced representation of time series which allows fast and accurate classification, clustering and relevance feedback. In *Proc. 4th International Conference on Knowledge Discovery and Data Mining (KDD)*, pages 239–243. AAAI Press, Menlo Park, 1998.

[22] E. J. Keogh, S. Chu, D. Hart, and M. J. Pazzani. An online algorithm for segmenting time series. In *Proc. 1st IEEE International Conference on Data Mining (ICDM)*, pages 289–296, 2001.

[23] B. Klimt and Y. Yang. Introducing the Enron Corpus. In *First Conference on Email and Anti-Spam (CEAS)*, 2004.

[24] J. Lin, E. J. Keogh, S. Lonardi, and B. Chiu. A symbolic representation of time series, with implications for streaming algorithms. In *Proc. 8th ACM SIGMOD Workshop on Research Issues in Data Mining and Knowledge Discovery (DMKD)*, pages 2–11, 2003.

[25] H. Mannila, H. Toivonen, and A. I. Verkamo. Discovery of frequent episodes in event sequences. *Data Min. Knowl. Discov.*, 1(3):259–289, 1997.

[26] N. Pathak, S. Mane, and J. Srivastava. Who thinks who knows who? Socio-cognitive analysis of Email networks. In *Proc. 6th IEEE International Conference on Data Mining (ICDM)*, pages 466–477, 2006.

[27] E. Perlman and A. Java. Predictive mining of time series data in astronomy. *Proc. Astronomical Data Analysis Software and Systems XII, ASP Conference Series*, 295:431–434, 2003.

[28] J. Shetty and J. Adibi. Discovering important nodes through graph entropy – the case of Enron Email Database. In *Workshop on Link Discovery: Issues, Approaches and Applications (held in conjunction with ACM SIGKDD 2005)*, pages 74–81, 2005.

[29] H. Siy, P. Chundi, D. J. Rosenkrantz, and M. Subramaniam. Discovering dynamic developer relationships from software version histories by time series segmentation. In *Proc. 23rd IEEE International Conference on Software Maintenance (ICSM)*, pages 415–424, Paris, Oct. 2007.

[30] H. Siy, P. Chundi, D. J. Rosenkrantz, and M. Subramaniam. A segmentation-based approach for temporal analysis of software version repositories. *J. Software Maintenance and Evolution: Research and Practice*, 20(3):199–222, 2008.

Part II
Contributed Articles

Chapter 11

SUMS-OF-PRODUCTS AND SUBPROBLEM INDEPENDENCE

RICHARD E. STEARNS AND HARRY B. HUNT III

Department of Computer Science, University at Albany—SUNY, Albany, NY 12222, USA.
Email: res@cs.albany.edu, hunt@cs.albany.edu

Abstract   Sums-of-products provide a basis for describing certain computational problems, particularly problems related to constraint satisfaction including SAT,
MAX SAT, and #SAT. They also can be used to describe many problems arising
from graph theory. By modeling a problem as a sum-of-products problem, the
concept of "subproblem independence" takes on a clear meaning. Subproblem
independence has immediate computational implications since it can be used
to create programs with reduced levels of nesting and programs which exploit
memoization. The concept of subproblem independence also extends to quantified sums.

   Subproblem independence can be linked directly to structural concepts associated with tree decompositions for graphs and the closely related structure trees
for algebraic problems. Thus methods of finding tree decompositions apply directly to finding independent subproblems.

Keywords: sums-of-products, quantifiers, generic algorithms, constraint satisfaction problems, computational complexity, tree decompositions, treewidth, structure trees,
quantified sums

1.   Introduction

We are interested in the complexity of solving sum-of-products problems
where the sum is taken over all assignments to a set of finite domain variables
and the quantities summed are products of terms. As discussed later, many
problems of interest can be described by sums-of-products even though the
problems are not initially expressed that way. Symbolically, we want to find
$\sum_{\alpha \in \Gamma(V)} \prod_{p \in P} p[\alpha]$ where

S.S. Ravi, S.K. Shukla (eds.), *Fundamental Problems in Computing*,

1. V is a finite set of finite domain variables,

2. $\Gamma(V)$ is the set of assignments to variables in V,

3. P is a set of terms of the form $f(x_1, \ldots, x_k)$ for some k where f is a function symbol and $x_1, \ldots, x_k$ are variables in V,

4. $p[\alpha]$ is the value of term p obtained by replacing the variables in p by the values from assignment α.

The sum-of-products can thus be specified by a pair (V, P) where V is a set of finite domain variables and P is a set of terms involving variables from V.

Computational complexity is usually associated with a set of problem instances expressed as strings. The theory addresses the question "what is the worst case computation time (or space) as a function of instance size?". Here, we associate complexity with problem instances. We ask "what is the number of plus and times operations needed to compute a specified sum-of-products?" This question can be asked about any sum-of-products instance and the answer is independent of any set of problem instances from which the sum-of-products instance was taken. As discussed in Sect. 3, we assume that the sum and product operators are taken from a commutative semi-ring. This insures that the sum-of-products is well-defined and can be manipulated using standard algebraic techniques. We want to compute sum-of-product values "generically" using operator sequences that produce the correct value regardless of the particular plus and times operations involved and of the actual value of the terms. In other words, except for the semi-ring assumption, our solution methods are independent of the interpretation of the operators and terms.

Computational complexity is usually associated with algorithms which take problem instances as input and output the answer to some question about the input instance. Here we are concerned about algorithms designed to compute the sum-of-products value for a particular problem instance. Algorithms 1 and 2 are two examples of such algorithms. The algorithms are "generic" in that they work for any interpretation of the operations and terms. Because of their generic nature, the number of operations performed by the algorithms is a function of domain sizes. This enables us to make complexity comparisons in the usual way. For example, Algorithms 1 and 2 both compute the same sum-of-products, but Algorithm 2 is preferred because the number of operations performed grows only as the square of domain size whereas the number of operations performed by Algorithm 1 grows as the cube of domain size.

We want to apply our understanding of "the complexity of instances" to the following kind of computation problem: given a sum-of-products instance from a set of sum-of-products instances, find the value of that sum-of-products. Many problems of interest can be expressed naturally as sum-of-products problems including satisfiability, counting, and optimization problems. This is elaborated upon in Sect. 3 where several semi-rings and their applications are discussed.

Another feature of the sum-of-products problems and the generic algorithms that solve them is that the concepts of "subproblem" and "subproblem independence" have clear meanings. These concepts are understood on the basis of sub-calculations which are also described as sums-of-products. Subproblem independence can make particular instances of hard problems easier.

Many quantifiers are sum-like. For example, $\exists_x f(x)$ is the disjunction (a sum using $\vee$) of the $f(c)$ for c in the finite domain of x. The quantified formulas $\mathrm{MAX}_x f(x)$ is the maximum (a sum using the MAX operator) of all $f(c)$ for c in a non-empty finite domain. Because of this similarity, the sum-of-products model can be extended to the problem of evaluating quantified sums. First, several kinds of summation operators are allowed on the same set (MAX and MIN on numbers for example). Then the original plus operations are turned into quantifiers and the original times operator is then called plus. The concept of subproblem independence and the methods of exploiting it carry over exactly. *The one extra consideration is that the order of quantifiers becomes important when different kinds of quantifiers are used together and then conditions restricting the interchange of quantifiers must be respected.* Subproblem independence plays an important role in determining when two quantifiers may be interchanged. These matters are discussed in Sect. 4.

CNF Satisfiability (sometimes called SAT) plays a central role in the theory of NP-completeness because the operation of a non-deterministic Turing machine operating in polynomial time can be described efficiently by a CNF formula of polynomial size. Since every SAT instance can be viewed efficiently and naturally as an instance of a sum-of-products problem (see Sect. 2), one can say it is a sum-of-products problem that plays this central role. Again, subproblem independence shows up in an interesting way. Now, subproblem independence becomes associated with restricted nondeterministic space computations. This matter is the subject of Sect. 5. This is evidence that subproblem independence is more pervasive than one might first suppose.

2. Examples

In this section, we look at some sum-of-products examples and see how to display and exploit "subproblem independence" with a "structure tree". Throughout this paper, we use the following conventions:

1. All variables have finite domains.

2. The domain of variable x is D_x.

3. $\sum_x$ means sum over all values in domain D_x.

Now consider the following problem:

$$\text{Find } \sum_x \sum_y \sum_z [p(x,z) \cdot q(y,z)].$$

This problem is described in "(V, P) notation" as "find the sum-of-products with variable set $V = \{x, y, z\}$ and with term set $P = \{p(x,z), q(y,z)\}$."

The most straightforward way of computing the sum's value is with Algorithm 1. Although we haven't given a meaning to the sum and product operations, we can describe the algorithm's complexity by counting the number of operations performed. The operations are performed at line 5 which is inside the nested loops so the number of additions is clearly $|D_x| \cdot |D_y| \cdot |D_z|$ and so is the number of multiplications. Assuming all variables have the domain D, we can say that the number of operations is $\Theta(|D|^3)$.

Algorithm 1 Compute $\sum_x \sum_y \sum_z [p(x,z) \cdot q(y,z)]$

1: $sum \leftarrow 0$
2: **for** all x in D_x **do**
3:     **for** all y in D_y **do**
4:         **for** all z in D_z **do**
5:             $sum \leftarrow sum + p(x,z) \cdot q(y,z)$
6:         **end for**
7:     **end for**
8: **end for**
9: **output** sum

Observe that

$$\sum_x \sum_y \sum_z [p(x,z) \cdot q(y,z)] \quad \text{equals} \quad \sum_z [[\sum_x p(x,z)] \cdot [\sum_y q(y,z)]]$$

Using the right hand expression as a guide, we see that the sum-of-products can be solved using Algorithm 2. In this program, the depth of nesting is just two. The operations are performed at lines 5, 9, and 11 and the number of additions is now $|D_z| \cdot (|D_x| + |D_y| + 1)$ which is just $\Theta(|D|^2)$ and the number of multiplications is just $|D_z|$.

The improvement here in complexity can be attributed naturally to "subproblem independence". Specifically, once a value has been assigned to z, the problems $\sum_x p(x,z)$ and $\sum_y q(y,z)$ are "independent" in that they have no unassigned variables in common. They are "subproblems" in that their answers are computed as part of the overall computation.

The problem structure exploited by Algorithm 2 is shown by the "structure tree" shown in Fig. 11.1.

DEFINITION 2.1. A **structure tree** for a sum-of-products problem (V, P) is given by a tree T and two functions α and β such that

Algorithm 2 Compute $\sum_z([\sum_x p(x, z)] \cdot [\sum_y q(y, z)])$

1: $sum \leftarrow 0$
2: **for all** z in D_z **do**
3:     $sum_x \leftarrow 0$
4:     **for all** x in D_x **do**
5:         $sum_x \leftarrow sum_x + p(x, z)$
6:     **end for**
7:     $sum_y \leftarrow 0$
8:     **for all** y in D_y **do**
9:         $sum_y \leftarrow sum_y + q(y, z)$
10:     **end for**
11:     $sum \leftarrow sum + sum_x \cdot sum_y$
12: **end for**
13: **output** sum

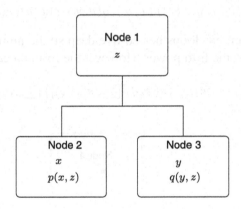

Figure 11.1. Structure Tree for $(\{x, y, z\}, \{p(x, z), q(y, z)\})$

1. the tree T has a root,

2. each variable v in V has been assigned to a node $\alpha(v)$ of T,

3. each term p in P has been assigned to a node $\beta(p)$ of T,

4. if variable $v \in V$ appears in term $p \in P$, then the node $\alpha(x)$ is between $\beta(p)$ and the root.

Note that, unlike our simple examples, several variables or several terms can be assigned to the same structure tree node. The relationship between structure trees and corresponding programs is this: *for any term, the variables on the path from the term's node to tree's root correspond to the variables in the loops enclosing that term.* The maximum number of variables on a path from root to leaf is called the **weighted depth** of the tree. The number of operations performed by the corresponding program is exponential (as a function of domain size) only in the weighted depth.

A sum-of-products problem can have many structure trees and the minimum weighted depth among the structure trees for the problem is called the **weighted depth** of the problem. A structure tree may suggest nesting the variables in a different order than that suggested by the original sum-of-products description. In the simple example just discussed, the program Algorithm 2 indicated by the structure tree of Fig. 11.2 has variable z in the outermost loop whereas the original description has variable x first.

Now consider a problem a little more complicated:

$$\textbf{Find } \sum_v \sum_w \sum_x \sum_y \sum_z [p(x, w) \cdot q(v, w) \cdot r(x, y) \cdot s(x, z)]$$

or in (V, P) notation

$$\textbf{Find } (\{v, w, x, y, z\}, \{p(x, w), q(v, w), r(x, y), s(x, z)\}).$$

The obvious program has loops nested five deep so the number of operations is the domain size to the fifth power. However the formula can be rewritten as

$$\sum_w [\sum_x \{p(x, w)[\sum_y r(x, y)][\sum_z s(x, z)]\}\{\sum_v q(v, w)\}]$$

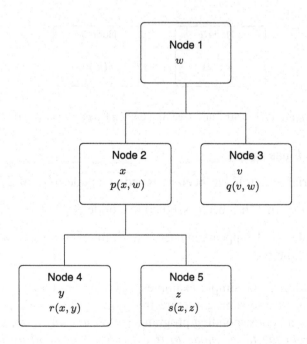

Figure 11.2. Structure Tree for $(\{v, w, x, y, z\}, \{p(x, w), q(v, w), r(x, y), s(x, z)\})$

Algorithm 3 Compute $\sum_w[\sum_x\{p(x,w) \cdot [\sum_y r(x,y)] \cdot [\sum_z s(x,z)]\} \cdot \{\sum_v q(v,w)\}]$

```
 1: sum ← 0
 2: for all w in D_w do
 3:     sum_x ← 0
 4:     for all x in D_x do
 5:         sum_y ← 0
 6:         for all y in D_y do
 7:             sum_y ← sum_y + r(x,y)
 8:         end for
 9:         sum_z ← 0
10:         for all z in D_z do
11:             sum_z ← sum_z + s(x,z)
12:         end for
13:         sum_x ← sum_x + p(x,w) · sum_y · sum_z
14:     end for
15:     sum_v ← 0
16:     for all v in D_v do
17:         sum_v ← sum_v + q(v,w)
18:     end for
19:     sum ← sum_x · sum_v
20: end for
21: output sum
```

The corresponding program is Algorithm 3 and the corresponding structure tree is shown in Fig. 11.2. Because the structure has weighted depth 3, the program is only nested to depth 3. The number of operations is thus only $\Theta(|D|^3)$.

An alternative view is that a structure tree defines a function for each node. In the case of Fig. 11.2, the five nodes 1 to 5 correspond to the following functions F_1 to F_5:

1. F_1 returns $\sum_w[F_2(w) \cdot F_3(w)]$.

2. $F_2(w)$ returns $\sum_x[p(x,w) \cdot F_4(x) \cdot F_5(x)]$.

3. $F_3(w)$ returns $\sum_v q(v,w)$.

4. $F_4(x)$ returns $\sum_y r(x,y)$.

5. $F_5(x)$ returns $\sum_z s(x,z)$.

If one calls the function corresponding to the root, namely F_1, the value returned is the value of the sum-of-products. The number of operations performed will be the same as in Algorithm 3 because the two methods execute the same sequence of operations.

This functional description exposes a kind of inefficiency not yet discussed. The function F_4 is called $|D_w|$ times for each x in D_x. Time can be saved (at the cost of some space) if $F_4(x)$ is computed once for each x in D_x and the result saved in some table where the value of $F_4(x)$ can subsequently be looked up rather than be recomputed.

Now think of the F_i as tables rather than functions. By constructing the tables in some bottom-up order such as F_5, F_4, F_3, F_2, F_1, the appropriate values from the lower tables will be available when needed to compute the values for the higher tables. Table F_2 has $|D_w|$ entries, each entry is computed using $|D_x|$ additions, and thus Table F_2 is computed with $|D_w| \cdot |D_x|$ additions, Tables F_3, F_4, and F_5 are also computed in "square time" and F_1 is computed in $|D_w|$ time. Table F_1 will have one entry and it will contain the answer to the problem.

Can this square time method be inferred from the structure tree? The answer is "yes" if we compute the set of "channel variables" for each node. Variable x is called a **channel variable** at node n if and only if the node associated with x is at or above n and some term containing x is at or below n. (By "above", we mean closer to the root.) The channel variable set at a node n is the set of variables involved in computing the function or table for node n. For the function, the channel variables v such that $\alpha(v)$ is above node n are the parameters of the function. The channel variables v such that $\alpha(v) = n$ are local variables used in the body of the function procedure to index loops. The table for n has one entry for each assignment to the variables v such that $\alpha(v)$ is above n.

For a given structure tree, the size of its largest channel variable set is called the **channelwidth** of the tree. For a given problem, the minimum channelwidth among all the trees for the problem is called the **channelwidth** of the problem.

In Fig. 11.3, the channel variable sets have been added to the structure tree from Fig. 11.3. Because the largest channel variable set has size two, we know that computing the sum-of-products using look-up tables takes only $\Theta(|D|^2)$ operations.

The cause of the improvement is evident at node 4. There are three branch variables at node 4, namely w, x, and y, but only the two channel variables x and y. This indicates that $r(x, y)$ is calculated independently of w even though it is inside the w loop. The term $r(x, y)$ is computed $|D_w|$ times for each possible assignment to x and y and the sub-calculation uses $|D_x| \cdot |D_y|$ operations. However with tables, that sub-calculation is only performed once thereby saving a factor of $|D_x|$.

The bottom-up table method is often called "non-serial dynamic programming" [3, 11]. The tables mapping channel variable assignments to semi-ring

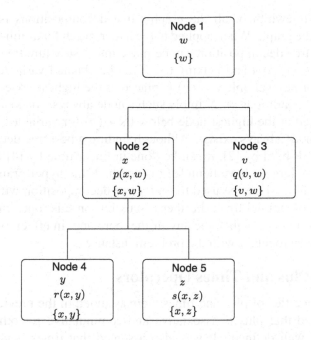

Figure 11.3. Structure Tree from Fig. 11.2 with Channel Variables

values will be called **node tables**. These tables can also be used to compute the sum-of-products top-down if one computes and records each node table entry at the time it is first needed. Then the method is called "memoization" [9].

To apply our methods to sets of sum-of-products instances, it becomes necessary to deal with the following structure tree problem: given a sum-of-products problem (V, P) from a set of sum-of-product problems, find a best structure tree for the problem. The complexity of this problem depends on the particular set of problems from which problem instances are taken.

In (V, P) notation, we can associate problem instance (V, P) with a hyper-graph (N, E) where N has one node for each variable in V and one hyper-edge for each term in P. The hyper-edge for term p is the set of nodes corresponding to the variables in p. Because the structure trees are defined without any consideration to the meaning of the variables or terms, structure trees for a given problem can be derived directly from its hyper-graph. This enables graph theory tools to be used for structure tree construction. The concept of tree decompositions for graphs is particularly relevant.

Tree decompositions for graphs were defined in [1] and the extension to hyper-graphs is straightforward. A tree decomposition for a graph is an unordered tree where, for each tree node n, there is an associated set of graph nodes $X(n)$ where the $X(n)$ must satisfy certain conditions. The size of the largest $X(n)$ minus one is called the **treewidth** of the decomposition.

The smallest treewidth of all the graph's tree decompositions is called the **treewidth** of the graph. When applied to the hyper-graph for a sum-of-products problem, any tree decomposition can be made into a structure tree by picking any node to be the root and making the $X(n)$ be channel variable sets. This means that, for any variable v, $\alpha(v)$ is placed at the highest node n such that $v \in X(n)$ (the conditions on X imply such a node always exists) and $\beta(p)$ for term p is placed at the highest node below the $\alpha(v)$ for variables v of p (and again such a node always exists). Although finding a best tree decomposition in general is NP-hard by [2], it can be done in linear time by [4] if the problems in the problem set have bounded treewidth. If the hyper-graph is planar, the methods of [7, 8] can be used to find a tree decomposition with treewidth $O(\sqrt{|V|})$ in polynomial time. Further discussion on this topic can be found in [13]. We don't cover this topic any further here and, in effect, we assume a structure is given together with the problem instances.

3.   The Plus and Times Operators

Certain properties of plus and times were assumed in the previous section. It was assumed that plus is associative and commutative for otherwise $\sum_x$ would not be well defined. It was also assumed that times is commutative and associative so that we could pick the products apart to form independent subproblems. We assumed that times distributes over plus so that the product of two independent problems would be the solution to a larger problem.

We now add assumptions that there is a **zero element** 0 satisfying $0 + a = a$ and $a \cdot 0 = 0$ for all a and a **unit element** 1 satisfying $1 \cdot a = a$ for all a. The zero element represents the sum of an empty set of terms and was used in our programs (e.g. lines 1, 3, and 7 in Algorithm 2) to initialize variables. The unit element represents the product of an empty set of terms and is needed to express subproblem independence in situations such as $\sum_x \sum_y p(y) = [\sum_x 1] \cdot [\sum_y p(y)]$. As described in the next section, constraints are modeled by zero/unit-valued terms

A set of elements and operators satisfying the above properties is called a "commutative semi-ring", "commutative" because times is commutative and "semi" because there is no minus operator.

DEFINITION 3.1. $\mathcal{R} = (S, +, \cdot, 0, 1)$ is called a **commutative semi-ring** if and only if

1. S is a set of **elements**,

2. $+$ (**plus**) is an associative and commutative binary operator on S,

3. $\cdot$ (**times**) is an associative and commutative binary operator on S such that times distributes over plus (i.e. $a \cdot (b + c) = a \cdot b + a \cdot c$),

4. $0 \in S$ (the **zero element**) satisfies $a + 0 = a$ and $a \cdot 0 = 0$ for all a,

5. $1 \in S$ (the **unit element**) satisfies $a \cdot 1 = a$ for all a.

The problem we want to solve is the following: **given a set of variables and a set of semi-ring valued terms, find the sum over all variable assignments of the products of the terms.**

Note that the variable domains are distinct from the semi-ring elements and the set of semi-ring elements can be infinite whereas variable domains are always finite. The complexity of performing the semi-ring operations is not an issue here because we measure the complexity of our algorithms by counting operations. Obviously, the cost of performing operations and evaluating terms must be considered when describing time complexity.

We now define and discuss some useful semi-rings:

Semi-ring $\mathcal{B}_\vee = (\{\text{TRUE}, \text{FALSE}\}, \vee, \wedge, \text{FALSE}, \text{TRUE})$:
This semi-ring is used to model **satisfiability** problems. Replacing plus and times by their $\mathcal{B}_\vee$ interpretations gives expressions such as $\vee_x \vee_y \vee_z [p(x, z) \wedge q(y, z)]$. This sum-of-products is TRUE if and only if the terms are simultaneously satisfiable. Equivalently, one can replace $\vee$ by $\exists$ as in $\exists_x \exists_y \exists_z [p(x, z) \wedge q(y, z)]$.

Semi-ring $\mathcal{B}_\wedge = (\{\text{TRUE}, \text{FALSE}\}, \wedge, \vee, \text{TRUE}, \text{FALSE})$:
This semi-ring is used to model **tautology** problems. Replacing plus and times by their $\mathcal{B}_\wedge$ interpretations gives expressions such as $\wedge_x \wedge_y \wedge_z [p(x, z) \vee q(y, z)]$. This sum-of-products is TRUE if and only if, for each assignment, some term is satisfied. Equivalently, one can replace $\wedge$ by $\forall$ as in $\forall_x \forall_y \forall_z [p(x, z) \vee q(y, z)]$.

Semi-ring $\mathcal{I} = (\text{NUMBERS}, +, \cdot, 0, 1)$ (ordinary arithmetic):
The set NUMBERS can be integers, rationals, non-negative integers, or (depending on the application) any subset of numbers closed under plus and times and containing zero. One application is for counting the number of satisfying assignments to a set of Boolean valued terms. Here we can take NUMBERS to be the set of non-negative integers. For this application, we consider TRUE terms to have value one and FALSE terms to have value zero. Then the product of these terms is one if all terms are satisfied and is zero otherwise. Thus the sum-of-products **counts the number of satisfying assignments**.

Semi-ring $\mathcal{I}_{\text{MAX}} = (\text{NUMBERS} \cup \{-\infty\}, \text{MAX}, +, -\infty, 0)$:
Here $+$ is ordinary addition and NUMBERS can be any set of numbers (such as the integers) closed under addition and containing zero. Operations MAX and plus satisfy the distributive law because $a + \text{MAX}(b, c) = \text{MAX}(a + b, a + c)$. Sums-of-products here have the form $\text{MAX}_x \text{MAX}_y \text{MAX}_z [p(x, z) + q(y, z)]$. The sum-of-products is the **maximum sum of terms**. A special case of this is **MAXSAT** which is solved using the non-negative integers as NUMBERS by making the Boolean-valued terms integer-zero/integer-one-valued with one representing TRUE and zero representing FALSE.

Semi-ring $\mathcal{I}_{\text{MIN}} = (\text{NUMBERS} \cup \{\infty\}, \text{MIN}, +, \infty, 0)$:
Here NUMBERS is the same as in $\mathcal{I}_{\text{MAX}}$. The sum-of-products is the **minimum sum of terms**.

Semi-ring ZOM $= (\{0, 1, 2\}, \oplus, \otimes, 0, 1)$ where $a \oplus b = \text{MIN}(a + b, 2)$ and $a \otimes b = \text{MIN}(a \cdot b, 2)$:
Elements 0, 1, and 2 are interpreted as "zero", "one", and "many". The distributive law holds because of the equation $\text{MIN}(a \cdot \text{MIN}(b + c, 2), 2) = \text{MIN}(\text{MIN}(a \cdot b, 2) + \text{MIN}(a \cdot c, 2), 2)$. This semi-ring can be used to test for **unique satisfiability** using terms which are 0/1-valued, 1 for TRUE and 0 for FALSE. The terms are uniquely satisfiable if and only if the sum-of-products is one. A sum of two means the terms have more than one solution and a sum of zero means the terms have no solution.

Observe that, given a set of Boolean-valued terms, testing for satisfiability, tautology, counting solutions, maximizing the number of satisfied terms, or testing uniqueness all involve sums-of-products with the same variables and the similar terms. The terms differ only in the interpretations of TRUE or FALSE. Thus, for a given set of terms and variables, the corresponding sums-of-products all have the same structure trees and our algorithms compute each sum-of-products value with the same sequence of operations.

We are also interested in "constrained sums-of-products":

DEFINITION 3.2. A **constrained sum-of-products problem** is a problem of the following form: Given a commutative semi-ring, a set of variables, a set of semi-ring valued terms, and a set of Boolean valued terms, find the sum-of-products of the semi-ring valued terms for all assignments which satisfy all the Boolean-valued terms.

A constrained problem can always be modeled as an unconstrained problem by making the Boolean terms be zero/unit-valued terms (unit for TRUE and zero for FALSE) and treating them like any other term. A product will have its original value if all Boolean terms are one and value zero if any Boolean term is zero. For example, to minimize the sum of terms subject to some constraints, use semi-ring $\mathcal{I}_{\text{MIN}}$, change the constraints so that TRUE becomes zero (the semi-ring unit) and FALSE becomes ∞ (the semi-ring zero), and put the constraints and numeric terms together. The constraints are thus modeled as terms with a large penalty (namely ∞) if they are unsatisfied and no effect on the sum if satisfied. If the constraints cannot be satisfied, then the sum will be ∞, and otherwise the sum will be the minimum value.

For some semi-rings, any sum-of-products is equal to one of its products. A variable assignment producing such a product can be thought of as "causing" the sum-of-products value and one may want to output such an assignment together with the sum-of-products value. Semi-ring $\mathcal{B}_\lor$ is one such semi-ring.

If the sum-of-products is TRUE, one of the products is TRUE and the assignment which produced it is called a "satisfying assignment". If the sum-of-products is FALSE, all products are FALSE and all assignments produce a FALSE term. In this case, the associated assignments are not of special interest.

Other examples are $\mathcal{I}_{\text{MAX}}$ and $\mathcal{I}_{\text{MIN}}$. In these cases, assignments which produces a maximum or minimum product are known as "optimal assignments".

In order for every sum to be equated with one of its terms, the semi-ring must satisfy $a + b = a$ or $a + b = b$ for all semi-ring elements a and b. Defining the relation $\leq$ by $a \leq b \iff a + b = b$, a total ordering is placed on the set of semi-ring elements and a sum-of-products becomes the maximum product under this ordering. An assignment producing this maximum is a maximizing assignment. Alternatively, one can define relation $\leq$ by $a \leq b \iff a + b = a$ and then the problem is viewed as a minimization problem.

In all cases, the algorithms can easily be modified to compute the corresponding optimal assignment. Whenever two quantities are added, remember the assignment whose quantity became the sum. Whenever two sums are multiplied, combine the two assignments associated with the sums (the two assignments will be based on disjoint variable sets.) The impact of performing this extra work is not significant.

4. Quantified Sums

Now we consider how the "subproblem independence" concept can be applied to problems involving quantified variables. As a starting point, observe that semi-ring summation operators behave as a kind of quantifier and therefore sum-of-product problems can be interpreted as a quantified-product problems. For example, the sum $\vee_x f(x)$ in $\mathcal{B}_{\vee}$ means exactly the same thing as $\exists_x f(x)$. Under this equivalence, sum-of-products problem $\vee_x \vee_y \vee_z (f(x,z) \wedge g(y,z))$ means the same thing as $\exists_x \exists_y \exists_z (f(x,z) \wedge g(y,z))$. Rather than talking about "quantified product problems", we prefer to call the connecting operator "plus" instead of "times" and talk about "quantified sum problems". We are thus using $+$ as we did in semi-rings $\mathcal{I}_{\text{MAX}}$ and $\mathcal{I}_{\text{MIN}}$.

We will to consider quantified sums involving more that one quantifier and it is instructive to consider how MAX and MIN can be used together. They clearly work together on non-empty sets of numbers, but there is a problem with empty domains. The maximum of an empty set is $-\infty$ in $\mathcal{I}_{\text{MAX}}$ and the minimum of an empty set is ∞ in $\mathcal{I}_{\text{MIN}}$. We can't put both $-\infty$ and ∞ into a set of numbers because the sum $-\infty + \infty$ has no meaning. Therefor we consider the MAX and MIN combination defined only for non-empty finite domains. Consequently, unlike the sum operators MAX and MIN, quantifiers MAX and MIN are not associated with identities.

The sum operations associated with quantified sums will be modeled by plus operators from commutative monoids:

DEFINITION 4.1. A **commutative monoid** is given by $\mathcal{M} = (S, +, 0)$ where

1. S is a set of elements,

2. $+$ (**plus**) is an associate and commutative binary operator on S,

3. $0 \in S$ (the **zero** element) satisfies $a + 0 = a$ for all $a \in S$.

Our notation for a quantified variable is q_x where q is the name of a quantifier and x is the name of a variable. The meaning of quantifier q for a monoid $\mathcal{M} = (S, +, 0)$ is specified by a functional which takes functions of the form $f : D_x \rightarrow S$ and produces a value $q_x f(x)$ in S. However, in order to obtain a suitable notion of "subproblem independence", we need to put restrictions on the quantifiers considered:

DEFINITION 4.2. A quantifier q defined on domains in a set $\mathcal{D}$ is called a **quantifier** for commutative monoid $\mathcal{M} = (S, +, 0)$ if and only if

1. for all $f : D_x \rightarrow S$ and $c \in S$, $q_x(f(x) + c) = (q_x f(x)) + c$,

2. for all $g : D_x \times D_y \rightarrow S$: $q_x q_y g(x, y) = q_y q_x g(x, y)$.

The first condition says that q obeys a kind of distributive law and the second says q obeys a commutative law. There is no condition asserting that different quantifiers can be interchanged. In general they can't be because $\text{MAX}_x \text{MIN}_y g(x, y)$ is not necessarily equal to $\text{MIN}_y \text{MAX}_x g(x, y)$. Thus we define a **quantified sum problem** (Q, P) as given by a list (rather than a set) of quantified variables Q and a set of terms P where each variable of each term in P is quantified by Q. If quantifier q_x comes before quantifier r_y in Q, we also say that variable x comes before variable y in Q.

The conditions of Definition 4.2 arc satisfied by "sum-based quantifiers" σ_x described by the following proposition:

PROPOSITION 4.3. *Let $\mathcal{R} = (S, +, \cdot, 0, 1)$ be a commutative semi-ring. For the monoid $\mathcal{M} = (S, \cdot, 1)$ and variable x with finite domain D, define σ_x by*

$$\sigma_x f(x) = \sum_{d \in D} f(d).$$

Then σ is a quantifier for finite domains on $\mathcal{M}$. Quantifiers so defined are called **sum-based** *quantifiers.*

Proof. Easily verified. $\qquad\qquad\qquad\qquad\qquad\qquad\qquad\qquad\qquad\qquad\qquad\qquad$ $\square$

Given a quantified expression where all the quantifiers are sum-based, the expression can be evaluated by the same methods as sum-of-product problems. For a quantified variable q_x applied to some subexpression $f(x)$, the value $q_x f(x)$ can be obtained by summing the various $f(x)$ using the sum-based operator used to define q. Even if a quantifier is not based on any method of summing, the value can still be computed by a loop. The values associated with each domain element can be stored as they are computed (rather than summed as they are computed) and the result of the quantification computed from the stored values after all the associated values have been computed.

Some quantifier examples:

DEFINITION 4.4. Quantifiers $\forall$, $\exists$, MAX, MIN, and $\Re$ are defined as follows:

1. For the Boolean monoids $\mathcal{B}_\wedge = (\{\text{TRUE}, \text{FALSE}\}, \wedge, \text{TRUE})$ and $\mathcal{B}_\vee = (\{\text{TRUE}, \text{FALSE}\}, \vee, \text{FALSE})$ and for any variable x with finite domain D, define $\exists_x f(x) = \bigvee_{d \in D} f(d)$ and $\forall_x f(x) = \bigwedge_{d \in D} f(d)$.

2. For any ordered commutative monoid $\mathcal{M} = (S, +, 0, \leq)$ and for any variable x over a finite non-empty domain D, define $\text{MAX}_x f(x) = \text{MAX}\{f(d) \mid d \in D\}$ and $\text{MIN}_x f(x) = \text{MIN}\{f(d) \mid d \in D\}$.

3. Let $\mathcal{F} = (S, +, \cdot, 0, 1)$ be a commutative field containing the integers. For the monoid $(S, +, 0)$ and any x having a finite non-empty domain D, define the **stochastic quantifier** $\Re_x f(x) = (\sum_{d \in D} f(d)/|D|)$.

The quantifiers $\exists$, $\forall$, MAX, and MIN are all sum-based. The stochastic quantifier, taken from [10], gives the average value for $f(x)$ when the value of x is selected uniformly at random. This is also defined as a summation but using a more complicated sum then those described in Proposition 4.3.

For sums-of-products, a structure tree with good channelwidth suggested a good order for performing the summation operations, namely sum over variables high in the tree (close to the root) before summing over variables further down in the tree. In a similar way, we want a structure tree for a quantified sum to be defined in such a way that it represents an equivalent quantified expression. However "equivalence" here must take into account equivalent orderings of quantifiers.

To illustrate the point, the quantified expression $q_x q_y f(x, y)$ is equivalent to the expression $q_y q_x f(x, y)$ by Property 2 of Definition 4.2. However $q_x r_y f(x, y)$ may or may not have the same value as $r_y q_x f(x, y)$ depending on the interpretations of f, q_x and r_y. We want structure trees to represent equivalent expressions for all interpretations and thus, for $q_x r_y f(x, y)$, we must exclude structure trees which reorder q_x and r_y.

Sometimes, we can infer that two quantifiers are interchangeable for all interpretations. For example,

$$q_x r_y(f(x) + g(y)) = q_x f(x) + r_y g(y) = r_y q_x(f(x) + g(y))$$

because of Property 1 of Definition 4.2. There is a way to tell if a structure tree represents an equivalent quantified formula for all interpretations. It is based on the concept of an "influence relation" defined as follows:

DEFINITION 4.5. Let $f = (Q, P)$ be a quantified formula and let q_x and r_y be quantifiers in Q. We write $x \prec y$ or x **influences** y if and only if $q \neq r$ and there exists a sequence of variables $z_1 \ldots z_k$ quantified with quantifiers in Q such that

1. $z_1 = x$ and $z_k = y$;

2. for each i, $1 \le i < k$, there is a term t_i in P such that both z_i and z_{i+1} are variables of t_i;

3. x occurs in Q before z_i for $1 < i \le k$;

4. there does not exist a j, $1 < j < k$, such that the quantifier for z_j is not r and z_j appears before z_i in Q for all i, $j < i \le k$.

The sequence $z_1, \ldots, z_k$ is called an **influence sequence** from x to y.

Simply stated, the last condition says that no suffix of an influence sequence is an influence sequence.

The influence relation has several important properties, proven in [14] and not reproved here:

1. The influence relation is a partial ordering (a sub-ordering of Q).

2. The influence relation is easily computed (by a variation on transitive closure).

3. If q_x appears immediately before r_y in Q and $x \not\prec y$, interchanging q_x and r_y gives a new quantifier list Q' such that (Q, P) and (Q', P) have the same value for all interpretations of the quantifiers and terms. Furthermore, (Q, P) and (Q', P) have the same influence relation.

4. If q_x appears immediately before r_y in Q and $x \prec y$, interchanging q_x and r_y gives a new quantifier list Q' such that (Q, P) and (Q', P) have different values for some interpretation of the quantifiers and terms.

To illustrate the above, consider the following three quantified expressions, each with the same sets of quantifiers and terms:

1. $\mu_v \nu_z \mu_w \nu_x \mu_y (p(x,w) + q(v,w) + r(x,y) + s(x,z))$

2. $\mu_v \mu_w \nu_z \nu_x \mu_y (p(x,w) + q(v,w) + r(x,y) + s(x,z))$

3. $\mu_w [\nu_x [p(x,w)[\mu_y r(x,y)][\nu_z s(x,z)]][\mu_v q(v,w)]]$

Expressions 1 and 2 are identical except that adjacent quantifiers ν_z and μ_w in the quantifier lists have been interchanged.

Looking at expression 1, we see that $z \prec w$ because of influence sequence z, x, w and therefore the quantifiers cannot be interchanged without changing the value of the expression for some interpretation of the quantifiers and terms. Looking at expression 2, we come to the same conclusion because now $w \prec z$ by sequence w, x, z.

Expression 3 is suggested by the structure tree in Fig. 11.3, but obviously expression 3 cannot be equivalent to both expression 1 and expression 2. The structure tree is in conflict with expression 1 because the tree puts w above z whereas the influence relation requires that ν_z proceed μ_w. Therefore the expressions will have different values for some interpretation of the quantifiers and terms. The structure tree is in agreement with expression 2 because the partial ordering described by the tree is in agreement with the influence relation. Expression 3 therefore has the same value as expression 2 for all interpretations of the quantifiers and terms.

As suggested by the above discussion, structure trees for quantified expressions are defined as follows:

DEFINITION 4.6. Let (Q, P) be a quantified sum and let V be the set of variables quantified by Q. A **structure tree** for (Q, P) is a structure tree (T, α, β) for (V, P) such that $\alpha(x)$ is at or above $\alpha(y)$ for all x and y such that $x \prec y$.

Structure trees for quantified sums have weighted depths and channelwidths in the same way as structure trees for sum-of-product problems and the smallest weighted depths and channelwidths for a problem are considered the **weighted depth** and **channelwidth** of the problem.

The structure tree in Fig. 11.3 is a structure tree for

$$(\mu_v \mu_w \nu_z \nu_x \mu_y, \{p(x,w), q(v,w), r(x,y), s(x,z)\})$$

which is expression 2 in (Q, P) notation and has weighted depth 3 and channelwidth 2. It implies equivalence of expressions 2 and 3. In expression 3, the quantifiers are nested only three deep which enables faster evaluation than brute-force depth five evaluation. As with sums of products, the structure tree nodes can be viewed as defining functions or tables in which case F_1 returns $q_w[F_2(w) + F_3(w)]$ and so forth, the computation cost being reduced further to $\Theta(|D|^2)$.

It can happen that, for certain quantifiers and monoids, the influence relation is too strict and certain quantifiers can be interchanged in spite of the influence relation. An example of this is a τ-quantifier defined as follows:

DEFINITION 4.7. For idempotent commutative monoid $\mathcal{M} = (S, +, 0)$ and finite domain D, define

$$\tau_x f(x) = \sum_{d \in D} f(d).$$

Two examples come to mind. For $\mathcal{M} = (\{\text{TRUE}, \text{FALSE}\}, \wedge, \text{TRUE})$, $\forall$ is a τ-quantifier. For $\mathcal{M} = \{\text{TRUE}, \text{FALSE}\}, \vee, \text{FALSE})$, $\exists$ is a τ-quantifier.

A τ-quantifier has the special property that $\tau_x(f(x) + g(x)) = \tau_x f(x) + \tau_x g(x)$ so $\tau_x f(x)$ and $\tau_x g(x)$ behave as independent subproblems even though they each have an instance of the same quantified variable. An influence relation that take into account the special properties of τ-quantifiers are developed in [14] and are not discussed further here.

5.   Connection to Memory-Bounded Nondeterminism

Now we discuss connections between subproblem independence and memory-bounded nondeterministic computation. When talking about memory bounds (often called space bounds), it is customary to assume that a problem is presented to a computing device on read-only memory and that only read-write memory will be counted as memory used. The value of this assumption is that it becomes meaningful to talk about solving problems using sub-linear memory bounds. For example, for certain problems of size n, it can happen that only $\sqrt{n}$ read-write memory locations are needed.

Sub-linear nondeterministic memory can be the basis for deterministic computing in less than 2^n time. If an input of size n can be solved non-deterministically using only m binary memory locations, the problem can be solved deterministically by considering all $n2^m$ configurations of the computing device (n possible locations on the input and 2^m possible memory configurations) and the graph connecting each configuration to each of its permissible successor configurations. Potentially, the analysis can be done in $O(n2^m)$ time if the graph can be efficiently constructed and traversed.

Here now we have a new basis for speeding up computation, namely the use of reduced memory. This basis seems to be more general than subproblem independence. However, we now present circumstances in which reduced memory and subproblem independence are interchangeable. The material in this section summarizes some of our work reported in [15].

Because nondeterminism is usually defined only for YES/NO problems and because nondeterministic acceptance is defined as at least one computation branch accepting, nondeterminism is best understood using the semi-ring $\mathcal{B}_\vee$. Accordingly, we will confine our discussion to this semi-ring.

As discussed in Sect. 3, we can use $\exists$ in place of sum operator $\vee$. Suppose we want to evaluate $\exists_z([\exists_x p(x,z)] \wedge [\exists_y q(y,z)])$. This can be done nondeterministically with the following "guess and verify program":

GUESS a value for z.

GUESS a value for x.

VERIFY $p(x,z)$.

RELEASE x.

GUESS a value for y.

VERIFY $q(y,z)$.

RELEASE y.

RELEASE z.

ACCEPT if all conditions were verified.

By "guess", we mean select a memory location to store the associated variable and non-deterministically assign a value to that variable. By "verify", we mean fail to accept if the associated condition is FALSE. By "release", we mean make the memory location of the released variable available for another variable.

Observe that the number of statements in the program is linear in the size of the problem and (there being no loops) each statement is executed at most once. Notice also that variables x and y can share space since x is released before y is initialized. With space sharing, only two variables need be stored in memory at any one time. The scopes of the variables are nested in the manner suggested by the structure tree in Fig. 11.1 and consequently the number of memory locations needed for variables is equal to the weighted depth of the tree in Fig. 11.1.

Now suppose we are given a guess and verify program where the variable scopes are not nested. For each VERIFY statement, some set of variables may be classified as "visible", namely those variables such that their GUESS statements come before the VERIFY and their RELEASE statements come after the VERIFY. The size of the largest set of visible variables is obviously equal to the number of locations needed to store variables.

This time, the number of locations needed can be described as the channel-width of a one-branch structure tree. The structure tree has one node for each VERIFY and the term to be verified is placed at that node by β. The node corresponding to the last VERIFY is designated as the root and the node for each of the other VERIFY statements is made the child of the VERIFY which follows it. Finally, for each variable x, $\alpha(x)$ is placed with the last VERIFY where x is visible. Alternatively, one can similarly construct a corresponding one-branch tree making the first VERIFY correspond to the root. In either case, the channel variables at a node are just the visible variables at the corresponding VERIFY statement so the size of the largest such set is the channelwidth of the tree which we also call the **line channelwidth** of the one-branch tree. For a given problem, the minimum channelwidth among the one-branch structure trees for the problem is called the **line channelwidth** of the problem.

Given the one-branch tree, satisfiability can be tested by computing the node table for the first VERIFY, then the second, and so forth. Recall from Sect. 2 that a node table assigns a semi-ring value (in this case TRUE or FALSE) for each assignment to the channel variables (in this case the visible variables). An entry is TRUE if the corresponding assignment is compatible with some assignment at the previous node and FALSE otherwise. Entries can be interpreted as indicating if a certain configuration can be reached nondeterministically, namely the configuration with the input at the current node and the variables assigned as described by the name of the table entry.

Now assume the functions used to construct conditions are from a finite set of Boolean-valued functions on Boolean-valued variables. Under this assumption, and assuming other obvious conditions are met, sequences of GUESS, VERIFY, and RELEASE statements become nondeterministic programs. By "obvious conditions", we mean things such as "variable values must be guessed before they are used".

A guess and verify program can be "compiled" in polynomial time into an input sequence for a certain Turing machine T which then "executes" the program. The key feature of compiled sequence is that the number of tape squares needed to execute the sequence is $O(m)$ where m is the maximal number of variables visible at any point in the original program. Because a Turing machine cannot access its tape memory randomly, some extra moves must be taken shifting the memory tapes in order to retrieve the desired sequence of values. By clever programming (discussed in [15]) the input sequence can be constructed so as to have length $O(n \log m)$ where n is the number of statements in the original program.

The states of T are used as storage for $k + 1$ binary variables where k is the maximum arity of the permitted binary-valued functions. The purpose of k variables is to store the parameters of the function appearing in a corresponding VERIFY statement. This enables the control of T to evaluate the function in one step. The purpose of the other variable is to store a flag which is set to FALSE if any verification fails. When all inputs are processed, T accepts if and only if the flag is TRUE. Thus a failed verification causes the corresponding branch of the nondeterministic computation to fail after the complete input sequence has been processed.

Machine $\mathcal{T}$ has two work tapes which can store one binary value on each tape square. Each input symbol of $\mathcal{T}$ instructs $\mathcal{T}$ to perform some elementary action. One such action is to take the value from one location and put it in another (such as from a tape square to a state variable). Another is to verify that the state values make a corresponding term TRUE (as discussed above). A third is to nondeterministically assign a location a binary value (this is the only nondeterministic action). A fourth is to shift a tape such as "move left on tape 1". The final input symbol tells $\mathcal{T}$ to stop and accept if the flag variable is TRUE. Further details such as how to get the right information to the right place may be found in [15] and are beyond the scope of this paper.

The time taken by the compiling process is of little consequence as long as it is accomplished in polynomial time. This is because it is the nondeterministic space which caused the corresponding deterministic machine to run in exponential time. For example, if restricted to problems of $\sqrt{n}$ line channelwidth, the compiled program uses $\sqrt{n}$ nondeterministic space. When made deterministic using node tables, the tables have $\sqrt{n}$ entries and the time complexity is $2^{\sqrt{n}}$ times the length of the input. This dominates any polynomial time used to perform the compilation.

The constructed $\mathcal{T}$ is an example of a "choice oblivious" Turing machine defined as follows:

DEFINITION 5.1. A nondeterministic Turing machine is called **choice oblivious** if and only if, for any given input string, motions of the tape heads are identical for all computation branches.

In particular, any deterministic Turing machine is choice oblivious, there being only one computation branch per input.

To summarize, we have seen that, for $\mathcal{B}_\vee$ sum-of-product problems, subproblem independence implies that a certain nondeterministic choice oblivious Turing machine can compute the answer using only the amount of space implied by the subproblem independence. The reverse is also true:

THEOREM 5.2. *Let $\mathcal{L}$ be a decision problem, $\mathcal{T}_\mathcal{L}$ be a choice oblivious nondeterministic multi-tape Turing machine, and m a function of integers to integers. Let R be a function mapping instances of $\mathcal{L}$ into input strings for $\mathcal{T}_\mathcal{L}$ such that $R(\ell)$ is processed using only $m(|\ell|)$ tape squares and $\ell \in \mathcal{L}$ is TRUE if and only if $R(\ell)$ causes $\mathcal{T}_\mathcal{L}$ to accept. Then a sum-of-products instance for $\mathcal{B}_\vee$ can be constructed from $R(\ell)$ such that the sum-of-products is TRUE if and only if ℓ is a TRUE instance of $\mathcal{L}$.*

This theorem is implied by the results in [15] but a proof is beyond the scope of this paper.

The construction of a sum-of-products instance for $R(\ell)$ can be performed in time $t(n)$ for some t which is almost linear. (Specifically $t(n)$ is $O(n^{1+\epsilon})$ for all $\epsilon > 0$.) This means the time needed to perform R dominates the time needed to change $R(\ell)$ into a sum-of-products problem and so, if R is performed in polynomial time, the reduction of $\mathcal{L}$ to a sum-of-products problem is polynomial.

In the absence of subproblem independence, a sum-of-products can be solved in $2^{O(n)}$ time if the operations are sufficiently easy to perform. There are many NP-hard problems which can be solved in time $2^{O(n^a)}$ for some $a < 1$. Can the smaller time complexity of these problems be attributed to subproblem independence even if there is no obvious sup-problem independence? Theorem 5.2 says we can transform the problem into a sum-of-products problem with subproblem independence if we can give a nondeterministic input oblivious method of solving the problem in sub-linear space. We conclude with two examples from [15] where the Theorem applies even though there is no obvious subproblem independence.

In [5], Gary and Johnson give special attention to six NP-complete problems from Karp's original list [6]. They call these the "six basic NP-complete problems" because they have been found so useful as source problems for proving NP-hardness. Four of these (3SAT, 3DM, VC, and HC) have the same time complexity in the sense that they have the same "power index" as defined in [12]. No solution methods have been found so far that solve these problems in time 2^{n^a} for any $a < 1$. The other two basic problems, namely CLIQUE and PARTITION, appear to be easier in that we know how to solve them in $2^{O(\sqrt{n})}$ time. As discussed below, these two problems can be solved in $\sqrt{n}$ nondeterministic space by an input oblivious Turing machine. Details about how this is done may be found in [15]. The implication is that the improvement in solution times for these problems can be ascribed to subproblem independence even though this interpretation is not immediately apparent.

The NP-complete problem known as CLIQUE, namely does graph G have a clique of size k, can be solved in time $2^{O(\sqrt{k})}$ for the simple reason that a graph with a clique of size k must have at least $O(k^2)$ nodes. This reason seems unrelated to subproblem independence. Yet in [15], we show how this problem can be solved nondeterministically and choice obliviously using $O(\sqrt{n})$ space. This means the problem can be reduced to a set of sum-of-products problems having line-channelwidth $O(\sqrt{n})$ and this sum-of-products problem can be evaluated in $2^{O(\sqrt{n})}$ time because of subproblem independence.

Another such NP-complete problem is PARTITION, namely can a set of integers be divided into two sets which have the same sum. This problem can be solved in time $2^{O(\sqrt{k})}$ because the hardest instances are composed of $O(\sqrt{n})$

numbers, each number having $O(\sqrt{n})$ bits. The solution method involves treating the short numbers differently from the long numbers, and will not be repeated here. Again this reason seems unrelated to subproblem independence. Yet in [15], we show how this problem can be solved nondeterministically and choice obliviously using $O(\sqrt{n})$ space. This means the problem can be reduced to a set of sum-of-products problems having line-channelwidth $O(\sqrt{n})$ and this sum-of-products problem can be evaluated in $2^{O(\sqrt{n})}$ time because of subproblem independence.

6.   Measures of Independence

We have discussed three methods of measuring subproblem independence, namely weighted depth, channelwidth, and line channelwidth. For a sum-of-products problem, we use the notation WD, CW, and LCW to refer to the minimum weighted depth, channelwidth, and line channelwidth for all the problem's structure trees. These quantities are closely related as follows:

PROPOSITION 6.1. *For sum-of-product problems of size n,*

$$CW \cdot \log n \geq WD \geq LCW \geq CW.$$

The reasons for these inequalities are fairly simple. Any line is a tree so $LCW \geq CW$. A structure tree of weighted depth WD can be made into a line of nodes having line channelwidth LCW by ordering the tree nodes by a depth first search. Thus $WD \geq LCW$. A structure tree of weighted depth $CW \cdot \log n$ can be constructed from a structure tree of channelwidth CW by rearranging the tree nodes (and changing α) to get a tree in which no branch is longer than $\log n$. After the transformation, the branch variables at each node are subsets of the union of the channel variables sets the path nodes had in the original tree. Details may be found in [13].

For quantified sums, the transformation from weighted depth to line channelwidth preserves the influence relation, but the method of rearranging nodes to get good weighted depth from good channelwidth fails to preserve influence. Thus we have

PROPOSITION 6.2. *For quantified sum problems of size n,*

$$WD \geq LCW \geq CW.$$

An example of a quantified sum with weighted depth n but channelwidth two is given in [14].

324

7.   Thank You Dan

The authors are thankful to Dan Rosenkrantz for many years of friendship (forty and thirty respectively), for productive research relationships, and for his strong support of the Computer Science Department at the University at Albany. He has enriched many lives. Best wishes Dan for a happy and productive retirement.

References

[1] A. Arnborg and A. Proskurowski. Linear time algorithms for np-hard problems on graphs embedded in k-trees. Technical Report TRITA-NA-8404, Department of Numerical Analysis and Computer Science, Royal Institute of Technology, Stockholm, Sweden, 1984.

[2] A. Arnborg, D. G. Corneil, and A. Proskurowski. Complexity of finding embeddings in a k-tree. *SIAM J. Alg. and Discr. Methods*, 8:277–284, 1987.

[3] U. Bertele and F. Brioschi. *Nonserial Dynamic Programming*. Academic, New York, 1972.

[4] H. L. Bodlaender. A linear-time algorithm for finding tree-compositions of small treewidth. *SIAM Journal on Computing*, 25:1305–1317, 1996.

[5] M. R. Garey and D. S. Johnson. *Computers and Intractability: A Guide to the Theory of NP-Completeness*. Freeman, San Francisco, 1979.

[6] R. M. Karp. Reducibility among combinatorial problems. In R. E. Miller and J. W. Thatcher, editors, *Complexity of Computer Computations*, pages 85–103. Plenum, New York, 1972.

[7] R. L. Lipton and R. E. Tarjan. Applications of a planar separator theorem. *SIAM J. Comput.*, 9:615–629, 1980.

[8] R. L. Lipton, D. J. Rose, and R. E. Tarjan. Generalized nested dissection. *SIAM J. Numer. Analysis*, 16:346–358, 1979.

[9] D. Michie. 'Memo' functions and machine learning. *Nature*, 218:19–22, 1968.

[10] C. H. Papadimitriou. Games against Nature. *J. Comput. System Sci.*, 31:288–301, 1985.

[11] A. Rosenthal. Dynamic programming is optimal for non-serial optimization problems. *SIAM J. Comput.*, 11:47–59, 1982.

[12] R. E. Stearns and H. B. Hunt III. Power indices and easier NP-complete problems. *Mathematical Systems Theory*, 23:209–225, 1990.

[13] R. E. Stearns and H. B. Hunt III. An algebraic model for combinatorial problems. *SIAM J. Comput.*, 25(2):448–476, 1996.

[14] R. E. Stearns and H. B. Hunt III. Exploiting structure in quantified formulas. *J. Algorithms*, 43:220–263, 2002.

[15] R. E. Stearns and H. B. Hunt III. Resource bounds and subproblem independence. *Theory Comput. Systems*, 38:731–761, 2005.

Chapter 12

AN OPTIMISTIC CONCURRENCY CONTROL PROTOCOL FOR REPLICATED DATABASES

YURI BREITBART

Department of Computer Science, Kent State University, Kent, OH 44240, USA.
Email: yuri@cs.kent.edu

HENRY F. KORTH

Department of Computer Science and Engineering, Lehigh University, Bethlehem, PA 18015,
USA. Email: hfk@lehigh.edu

AVI SILBERSCHATZ

Department of Computer Science, Yale University, New Haven, CT 06520, USA.
Email: avi@cs.yale.edu

Abstract   This paper presents an optimistic approach to transaction management for replicated databases. We propose a new transaction management protocol that guarantees global serializability and freedom from distributed deadlocks without relying on any properties of the DBMSs running at the local sites. In comparison
to prior protocols, this protocol reduces the communication required to coordinate transactions by a factor of r, where r is the average number of operations
per transaction. We also consider implementation issues in reducing message
overhead and discuss failure recovery.

Our approach is based on the concept of virtual sites introduced in Breitbart
and Korth (*Proc. SIGACT-SIGART-SIGMOD Symp. Principles of Database
Systems*, pages 173–184, Tucson, AZ, 1997; *J. Computer and System Sciences*,
59(1):29–69, 1999). The optimistic protocol of this paper allows a significantly
higher degree of concurrency than the protocol presented there.

Keywords: concurrency control, replication, distributed databases

S.S. Ravi, S.K. Shukla (eds.), *Fundamental Problems in Computing*,
© Springer Science + Business Media B.V. 2009

1.   Introduction

The management of replicated data in a distributed database is an old and well-studied problem. However, the classic solutions to the replicated data problem are applicable mainly to distributed systems with a relatively low transaction-processing rate. With distributed data warehouses and data marts at the high end, and distributed data in often-disconnected mobile computers at the low end [18], the problem of consistent access to replicated data with reasonably high transaction throughput represents a difficult challenge [9, 14, 15, 26, 28]. It was shown [14] that many proposed solutions do not scale up to meet the demands of systems that either require a high throughput rate, or a high degree of replication, or both. Furthermore, it does not appear that straightforward modifications of classic solutions will eliminate these deficiencies. Even 10 years after the publication of [14], the management of replicated data remains a vexing problem. The fundamental problem, as identified by [14], is that the standard transactional approach to the propagation of updates to replicas is unstable—deadlocks increase as the cube of the number of network sites and as the fourth power of transaction size. This is particularly problematic with relatively long data-mining queries and with mobile transactions. The former access many data items; while the latter effectively live for a long period of time. Thus, deadlock is no longer a rare event with a negligible effect on performance; instead, it is a barrier to the ability of systems to scale.

Several authors considered the problem of ensuring global serializability and atomicity without the use of an atomic commit protocol. They assumed that only transactions that execute at the *primary site* for a data item may initiate an update to that data item, and that propagation of updates to replicas occurs only after the update transaction has committed at the primary site [9, 14, 28, 5]. Such an approach was termed *lazy-master*.

To guarantee global serializability, the lazy-master approach must be augmented with one of the following:

- Restrictions on placement of primary copies of data among different sites [9].

- Restrictions on the order of replica updates propagation after the primary copy has been updated.

- A global concurrency-control mechanism that minimizes coordination among sites.

In this paper, we choose the *lazy-master* approach. We require that transaction executions be serializable and atomic, and that the transactions read only committed data. The atomicity protocol, however, should not cause blocking. We extend here the notion of lazy replica propagation and present an optimistic approach to transaction management for replicated databases. We propose a new protocol that guarantees global serializability and freedom from distributed deadlocks without relying on any properties of the DBMSs running at the local sites. In comparison to prior protocols, the new protocol reduces the communication required to coordinate transactions by a factor of r, where r is the average number of operations per transaction.

Our approach is based on the concept of virtual sites introduced in [5, 3], and expanded upon in [6]. The notion of a virtual site used in this paper is identical to the one used in [6]. Finally, we consider implementation issues in reducing message overhead and discuss failure recovery.

2.   Related Work

Initial work on replicated databases has concentrated on the issues of how to guarantee global serializability and atomicity in an environment where the sites as well as communication between them are subject to failures [4]. Global serializability can be achieved by using a distributed version of any protocol that guarantees serializability, such as two-phase locking or timestamp protocols [4], in combination with one of the replica update-propagation schemes (read-one, write-all or read any, write all available, etc.). To ensure atomicity despite failures, the two-phase commit protocol in combination with a replica-coherency scheme is used. The various published protocols vary in their degree of central control and the specific techniques used [10, 29, 12, 22]. These approaches guarantee the ACID (atomicity, consistency, isolation, and durability) properties of transactions [13]. The problem, however, is that such approaches are susceptible to deadlocks, transaction aborts, and site blocking. As the number of sites, data items, and the degree of replication grow, the frequency of these undesirable effects rises dramatically. We shall not elaborate on these approaches further and refer the reader to [15]. Rather, we wish to emphasize that to generate a practical algorithm for updating replicated data, some compromise is needed to achieve better performance. Either the notion of correctness must be relaxed or the set of allowed actions by transactions must be restricted, or both. For example, [23, 24] proposes dropping updates during periods of high load to increase performance while settling for approximate correctness. [11] takes specific application features into account to achieve better performance. [2] propose a notion of data "freshness" to increase performance of transactions that do not require the latest data copy.

Gray et al. [14] proposed a taxonomy of replication management strategies that is based on who may update what data and how updates are propagated to other replicas. Their taxonomy is based on the concepts of *regulation* and it propagation:

- *Regulation*: *Group* permission, in which any site holding a replica may initiate an update, versus *master* permission, in which only the primary site (that is, the site that contains a primary copy of the data item) for the data item may initiate an update to that data item.

- *Propagation*: *Eager* propagation by the update transaction itself, versus *lazy* propagation by a separate asynchronous transaction.

Agrawal et al. [1] considered a lazy propagation of transactions that guarantees both global serializability and transaction atomicity. They describe two algorithms for update propagation: pessimistic and optimistic. The former approach guarantees global serializability, provided that each local DBMS employs the strict two-phase locking protocol [4]. Transaction atomicity is achieved by using a standard version of the two-phase commit protocol. The latter approach, on the other hand, may improve transaction throughput but may sometimes generate non-serializable executions. The use of the two-phase commit protocol exposes both approaches to blocking, the probability of which grows with the number of sites.

Several papers have considered the issues of global serializability and atomicity without an atomic commit protocol. For example, [9, 28] propose an approach that is based on either group or master permission and lazy replica propagation. Global serializability is achieved by means of a distributed version of one of the standard concurrency control protocols, but when a transaction ends at some site, it commits locally and releases its locks without waiting for commitment at other sites. There are potential data inconsistencies resulting from certain replicated data items holding obsolete data. Thus, there must be a mechanism that ensures replica convergence [14].

In [9] database consistency is guaranteed by ensuring the acyclicity of a directed graph (which they call the *data placement graph*). Two sites are connected by an edge if one of the sites contains a primary copy of the data item and the other site contains a secondary copy of the same data item. If the data placement graph is acyclic, each local DBMS employs the rigorous two-phase locking protocol, and propagation messages are sent and received in commit order, then global serializability is guaranteed. However, the probability that the data placement graph is acyclic in a realistic application is low, since each site normally contains a large database and the number of sites is usually much smaller than the number of data items. In [8] authors proposed two protocols that impose an order on the replica propagation scheme. Both their protocols guarantee global serializability.

In [28] another approach to data replication is described that is based on lazy propagation and master permission. It appears that the system ensures eventual replica convergence but does not guarantee global serializability.

In [27], the authors propose a decentralized propagation algorithm that guarantees data convergence with a limited number of messages exchanged between sites. Their approach, however, does not guarantee global serializability.

3. System Model

Our system model is that of [5, 6]. The database consists of data distributed over k sites. Data may be replicated at any number of sites. For a given data item a, there is a unique site $p(a)$, called the primary site of a, which is responsible for the updates of a. The copy of a located at $p(a)$ is called the *primary copy*. Every other copy of a is called a secondary copy. Each local DBMS generates a local serializable schedule of transactions executing at the local site, and is responsible for managing local deadlocks. The site at which T_i is submitted is called the *origination site* of transaction T_i and is denoted by $o(T_i)$. Each transaction T_i can read data only at its origination site $o(T_i)$. A transaction is called *local* if it runs only at the site where it is submitted. Otherwise, it is *global*. A global transaction is represented by several local subtransactions—one for each site that holds replicas of one or more data items updated by the transaction. For simplicity of notation, we denote a global transaction and all its local subtransactions by the same name (e.g., T_i).

A local transaction, T_i, is a partial order, $<_i$, on a set of read and write operations (denoted by r_i and w_i, respectively) with either $commit_i$ (denoted by c_i) or $abort_i$ (denoted by a_i) (but not both) as a single maximal element of $<_i$. A *read-only* transaction is one that contains no write operations. An *update* transaction contains at least one write operation.

A *local schedule* S over a set of transactions T is a partial order $<_S$ of all operations of all transactions in T such that for any transaction T_i in T, $<_i$ is a subset of $<_S$. If $o_i <_S o_j$ in S, then we say that operation o_i is executed before operation o_j in S. Transaction T_i is *committed* (*aborted*) in schedule S if S contains c_i (a_i) operation. Transaction T_i is *active* in S if it is neither committed nor aborted in S. We say that schedule S is serial if for every two transactions T_i and T_j in S either all operations of T_i appear before any operation of T_j or vice versa.

A transaction T_i can update data item a only if $o(T_i) = p(a)$. This significantly restricts the set of data items that can be updated by a single transaction. However, this restriction is less serious in practice than it may appear since any application in which each data item has a specific "owner" adheres to this restriction. When the primary copy of data item a is updated, the new value of a must be propagated to all other replicas. This propagation can commence at any time. However, the new value of a at a's secondary site can be installed only after the transaction updating the primary copy of a has committed at site $p(a)$.

We note two consequences of our model.

- If two transactions T_i and T_j have a write operation on the same data item a, then $o(T_i) = o(T_j)$. Indeed, if transactions T_i and T_j originate at different sites s_l and s_k, then only one of these sites (say s_l) is the primary site for a. Thus, the transaction that originated at s_k cannot update a.

- Each read-only transaction is local. An update transaction is local if it does not update any replicated data item.

If two transactions perform write operations on the same replicated data item a, then updates at secondary sites can be easily coordinated by using the Thomas Write Rule [4]. This rule uses data and transaction timestamps to order events and transaction local commits. Write operations with a timestamp older than the timestamp of the data item can be ignored. Consequently, any replication coherency protocol need only consider coordination of *read/write* and *write/read* conflicts. A read/write (write/read) conflict occurs if a transaction reads (writes) a data item before another transaction writes (reads) it. We refer to read/write and write/read conflicts collectively as r-conflicts. We define r-conflict equivalent and r-conflict serializable schedules in a manner similar to the standard definition of conflict equivalent and conflict serializable schedules [4]. Two schedules are r-conflict equivalent if they are defined over the same set of transactions and have the same set of r-conflicts. A schedule is r-conflict serializable (or just r-serializable) if it is r-conflict equivalent to a serial schedule.

Following [7], we say that local schedule S over the set of transactions T is an *sp-schedule* if and only if there exists a mapping sp from T to the set of operations of transactions in T such that both of the following hold:

- If T_i is in T, then $sp(T_i)$ is an operation of T_i.

- If T_i and T_j is in T, and $sp(T_i)$ occurs before $sp(T_j)$ in S, then there exists a serial schedule equivalent to S in which T_i precedes T_j.

As shown in [7], not every local schedule is an sp-schedule. If a schedule is an sp-schedule, then $sp(T_i)$ is called the *serialization point operation (sp-operation)* of T_i.

A union of local schedules is called a global schedule. We say a global schedule is globally serializable if and only if there is a total order of all transactions such that if T_i precedes T_j in the total order, then T_i is serialized before T_j at all local sites at which these two transactions are executed together.

Each transaction T_i can be in one of the following four global transaction states at any point in time:

- **aborted**, if T_i has aborted at its origination site $o(T_i)$;

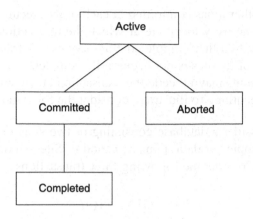

Figure 12.1. State Transition Diagram

- **active**, if T_i is active at its origination site $o(T_i)$;

- **committed**, if T_i has either committed or executed its sp-operation at its origination site $o(T_i)$, but is not yet in the **completed** state;

- **completed**, if at every site at which T_i executes, it has executed its sp-operation (if the local schedule is a sp-schedule) or has committed (if the local schedule is not sp-schedule) and is preceded in that site's *local* serialization order only by **completed** transactions.

Figure 12.1 depicts a state transition diagram for global transaction states.

Local transactions' states may differ from the global transaction state because of the delay between the time at which a global transaction state change occurs and the time remote sites are informed of the transaction. We show here that our protocol is robust in the face of arbitrary delays in the communication of global state transitions, though performance may suffer. Henceforth, by transaction state we mean a global transaction state unless we explicitly state differently.

Each transaction eventually enters either the **committed** or **aborted** state. If a transaction is in the **active** or **aborted** state, then the transaction did not execute any operations at sites other than its origination site. From the **active** state, the transaction may transfer either into the **aborted** or **committed** state, or remain in the **active** state. It cannot transfer directly into the **completed** state. When the transaction has entered into the **aborted** state, it remains there. If a global transaction is in the **committed** state, then it may have started propagation of its updates to sites other than its origination site. From the **committed** state, the transaction can be transferred only into the **completed** state.

We assume a local DBMS does not generate sp-schedule unless there is information to the contrary. To decide whether the transaction has completed, we first check whether it has committed at each of its execution sites and then we check whether at every local site at which the transaction was executing, it is preceded only by other completed transactions. A transaction that has committed at each of its sites is not necessarily completed since some of non-completed transactions may precede the transaction at some of the local sites at which it was executing. To illustrate, consider the following example.

EXAMPLE 1. Consider a database consisting of two sites s_1 and s_2. Site s_1 contains primary copies of data items a, b, and c. Site s_2 contains secondary copies of b and c. Consider the following three transactions:

$$T_1: \quad r_1(b); w_1(b)$$
$$T_2: \quad r_2(a), w_2(c)$$
$$T_3: \quad r_3(b); r_3(c)$$

Transactions T_1 and T_2 originate at s_1, while T_3 originates at s_2. Assume that the global execution is as follows (an operation superscript indicates the site at which the transaction operation is executed and a subscript indicates the transaction to which the operation belongs):

$$r_1^1(b), w_1^1(a), w_1^1(b), c_1^1, r_3^2(b), w_1^2(b), c_1^2, r_2^1(a), w_2^1(c), c_2^1,$$
$$w_2^2(c), c_2^2, r_3^2(c), c_3^2$$

Then, the following local schedules are generated at each site:

$$S_1: \quad r_1(b), w_1(a), w_1(b), c_1, r_2(a), w_2(c), c_2$$
$$S_2: \quad r_3(b), w_1(b), c_1, w_2(c), c_2, r_3(c), c_3$$

It is simple to see that the above schedule is not globally serializable. T_1 precedes T_2 at s_1, while at s_2, T_2 precedes T_3 which precedes T_1. At the point where T_1 has committed everywhere (just after c_1^2 in the global execution order), T_3 is still active. By our definition, T_1 is not in the **completed** state, although it has committed at each site. Furthermore, at the point where T_3 has committed, transaction T_1 is still not in the **completed** state, since it is preceded by T_2 and T_3 neither of which has completed. If a global concurrency control protocol chose no longer to worry whether T_1 has completed after it has committed everywhere, it would not be possible to detect the non-serializability of the execution. For this reason, our protocol keeps transactions under consideration until they enter the **completed** state. We shall see that, under our protocol, once a transaction reaches the **completed** state, it can no longer cause non-serializability of the global schedule.

If a transaction has committed at all sites, but has not yet completed it may eventually complete. For example, suppose that site s_1 contains primary copies of a and b, while site s_2 contains their secondary copies. We assume that the DBMS at s_2 does not guarantee the generation of sp-schedules. Further suppose that at sites s_1 and s_2 the following local schedules:

$$S_1: \quad w_1(a), c_1, r_2(a), w_2(b), c_2$$
$$S_2: \quad r_3(b), w_2(b), c_2, w_1(a), c_1, r_3(a), c_3$$

When T_2 commits at both sites, it is not yet completed, since it is preceded by an uncompleted transaction T_3 at site s_2. However, when T_3 commits at s_2, it becomes completed and, consequently, T_2 becomes completed also. Observe that T_1 is completed as soon as it has committed at s_2, since it is not preceded at either site by any non-completed transaction.

4. Virtual Sites and Replication Graph

In this section, we present the concept of a replication graph from [5], which we use to coordinate transaction execution. We begin by defining a notion of a virtual site. Following that, we define a replication graph whose nodes are virtual sites.

In our discussion, we use the term *access* of a data item a at site s by transaction T_i to mean that T_i has executed a read of a at s or has executed a write of any replica of a regardless of site.

4.1 Virtual Sites

To guarantee global serializability, global transactions must compete for local sites as a resource [9]. Since the number of global transactions is usually much higher than the number of local sites, contention is high, resulting in a high probability of waits and deadlocks. For this reason, we divide each physical site into a set of *virtual sites*. A set of virtual sites and transactions running on them must satisfy data model restrictions stated above. To achieve that, we construct virtual sites dynamically based on the following rules.

- **Locality rule.** All data items site that a transaction T_i has accessed so far at a given physical site s_j belong to the virtual site of T_i at s_j. Transaction T_i executes at exactly one virtual site at each physical site at which it executes.

- **Union rule.** If two transactions T_i and T_j conflict (directly or indirectly) on a primary data item or r-conflict (directly or indirectly) on a secondary data item at physical site s_k, then their virtual sites at s_k are the same and include all data accessed up to that point by either T_i or T_j at s_k.

- **Split rule.** If transaction T_i is in the completed or aborted state, then all data items accessed only by T_i are removed from the virtual sites where T_i was active. In addition, if transactions T_m and T_n have a conflicting operation with T_i at site $s_l = o(T_i)$ or a r-conflicting operation with T_i at site $s_l \neq o(T_i)$, then the virtual sites of T_n and T_m at site s_l are separated into two sites by having each of these sites contain data items of T_n and T_m, respectively, subject to the union rule.

If two transactions execute write operations on the same data item at the same physical site, then their ww conflict can be handled by the Thomas Write Rule [4] at any site that contains a primary or secondary copy of the data item (as we shall see in the protocol definitions). If a ww conflict is on the primary data item, however, it needs to be recorded in the virtual site of the transaction-origination site to guarantee global serializability in the presence of local transactions that conduct write operation on non-replicated data items. There is, however, no need to merge virtual sites due to a ww conflict on a secondary data item, since transactions that have such a conflict have originated at the same site and the DBMS at that site has already recorded this conflict. This makes it possible to keep virtual sites smaller and to reduce the amount of contention during replica propagation.

The locality and union rules are requirements for correctness. The split rule is aimed at necessary performance improvements that make the protocol practical. The power of the protocol arises from keeping virtual sites as small as possible. Thus, when transaction T_i enters the **aborted** or **completed** state, it is desirable to use this information to split, shrink, or eliminate virtual sites.

We always can select a set of virtual sites for a set of given transactions. If the selected set of virtual sites satisfies the locality, union, and split rules, we call such a set an *acceptable* set of virtual sites for a given set of transactions. For a given set of transactions there is at least one set of *acceptable* virtual sites. Specifically, the set of physical sites at which the transactions are executing is an acceptable set of virtual sites.

4.2 Replication Graph

Let T be a set of transactions, S be a schedule over the set T, and VS be a set of acceptable virtual sites for T. We define a replication graph $RG = \langle V, E \rangle$ as follows [5]. RG is a nondirected bipartite graph whose set of nodes are virtual sites from VS and transactions from T. Edge $\langle vs_i, T_j \rangle$ belongs to E if and only if S contains an operation $w_j(x)$ where x is in vs_i and x is a replicated data item. From the replication graph definition it follows that only global update transactions can be present among transactions nodes of the graph. A replication graph for a global schedule is not necessarily unique since

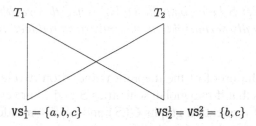

$$\text{VS}_1^1 = \{a, b, c\} \qquad \text{VS}_2^1 = \text{VS}_2^2 = \{b, c\}$$

Figure 12.2. Replication Graph for Example 1

for a given set of transactions there may be many acceptable sets of virtual sites.

A replication graph for the global schedule given in Example 1 is shown in Fig. 12.2. Each of the virtual sites in the graph shown in Fig. 12.2 is at a distinct physical site.

In what follows, we characterize the set of replication graphs for globally serializable schedules. To do so we first define a *reduction process* for a replication graph. We then prove that the reduction process applied to a replication graph results in an empty graph if and only if the global schedule is serializable.

Let S be a global schedule and let RG be a replication graph for S. We define our reduction procedure for RG as follows. We remove from the graph all completed transactions along with all edges incident on it and apply the split rule. If a virtual site node does not have any edges incident on it, we remove that node as well. The graph G' obtained from RG using this reduction procedure, is called the *reduced* graph of schedule S.

For the rest of this section, we consider replication graphs for global schedules in which all transaction are either committed or aborted at all sites. We call such schedules *complete*. Given a schedule S, we construct a reduced replication graph for S by starting with the first operation of S and for each operation we apply the locality, union, and split rules whenever they are applicable. The replication graph RG resulting from this procedure is a reduced one. This follows from the fact that the set of completed transactions is determined uniquely by a given schedule. As a result of the procedure defined above, we remove from the graph all completed transactions. Thus, in the remaining graph no transaction can be removed and the graph is reduced. We denote the reduced graph obtained for S using the above procedure as $G(S)$. The importance of the reduced replication graph stems from the following theorem which was first proven in [6]:

THEOREM 4.1. *Let S be a complete global schedule over the set of transactions T. S is globally serializable if and only if its reduced replication graph is empty.*

The *if* part of the proof of the theorem is based on two lemmas. The first lemma establishes that if two global schedules S and S' are conflict equivalent then their reduced replication graphs $G(S)$ and $G(S')$ are identical. The second lemma states that the reduced replication graph of any serial schedule is empty.

LEMMA 4.2. *Let S and S' be two conflict equivalent global schedules over the set of transactions T. Then their reduced replication graphs $G(S)$ and $G(S')$ are identical.*

The proof of this lemma [6] creates a parallel between the proof that S and S' are conflict equivalent and a proof that $G(S)$ and $G(S')$ are identical. The standard approach to proving conflict equivalence [25] exchanges the order of consecutive steps provided they belong to distinct transactions and do not conflict. For each such exchange, [6] shows that the reduced replication graph is unchanged. First consider a pair of read steps. Then the operations either change an existing virtual site or lead to a virtual site merge regardless of the order of operations. Thus, in either case the same replication graph results. Next consider the case where one of the operations is a write. Then the two steps must reference different data items or there would be a conflict prohibiting the exchange. Therefore, once again, the order of these operations does not affect the replication graph obtained after applying both of these operations.

LEMMA 4.3. *The reduced replication graph for a complete, global serial schedule is empty.*

The proof of this lemma [6] is straightforward. Because the schedule is serial, only one transaction is active at any time. When that one active transaction commits or executes its sp-operation everywhere, it is in the completed state and can be removed from the graph.

Next we consider the *only if* part of the theorem and its proof [6]. If the global serialization graph has a cycle, then none of the global transactions in that cycle could have completed. To see this, note that if, without loss of generality, we consider only those global transactions in the cycle that executed on at least two sites. Each such transaction T_i must write a replicated data item causing it to create a node T_i and edges $\langle vs_i^i, T_i \rangle$ and $\langle vs_i^{i+1}, T_i \rangle$ (if it does not already exist) in the replication graph. No such T_i can complete. To see this, let T_i be the first global transaction in the cycle to attempt to complete. Then at some local site, it would still be preceded by an uncompleted transaction from the serialization cycle. Therefore T_i could commit but could not complete and its edges cannot be removed. As a result, the replication graph must be nonempty.

5. Commit-Oriented Protocol (COP)

In this section, we discuss an optimistic, deadlock-free protocol that requires only two messages per transaction and guarantees global serializability. This is an improvement by a factor of r over the communication overhead required by the protocol in [14]. This protocol, the *commit-ordered protocol*, COP differs from the protocol in [5, 6] in when the replication graph gets updated. Under COP, the replication graph is updated at a **committed** state. We begin by defining a test, **CRGTest**, that is applied by COP when a transaction submits a commit operation at its origination site. The test consists of tentatively applying the locality and union rules to virtual sites in the replication graph and tentatively adding any edges that would be mandated by the definition of the replication graph. If no cycle results, then the test succeeds and tentative changes to the graph are applied. The protocol rules are as follows.

Protocol COP

1. If T_i submits a read or write operation at its origination site $o(T_i)$, the operation is sent for execution. If the executed operation was $w_i(a)$, where a is a replicated data item, assign a timestamp to T_i, if it was not yet assigned. In processing operations, maintain access data set for T_i at each site.

2. If T_i submits a write operation at site $s_r \neq o(T_i)$, check the transaction timestamp. If it is less than the timestamp of the last write operation on the data item, do not perform the write, else send the operation to the local DBMS for execution.

3. If T_i is in the **active** state and submits a commit operation, perform **CRGTest**. If the test succeeds, perform commit. Otherwise, abort T_i.

4. If T_i is in the **committed** state and submits a commit operation, proceed with the execution. If this results in T_i entering the **completed** state, remove it from the replication graph and apply the split rule.

5. If T_i submits the abort operation at its origination site, proceed with the execution. Apply split rule.

COP allows each transaction to proceed at its origination site independently of other transactions that are executing at other sites. The only coordination required is when the transaction submits the commit operation at its origination site. The correctness of protocol COP follows from the following theorem:

THEOREM 5.1. *Protocol COP guarantees global serializability.*

Proof. We prove first that if there is a loop in the global serialization graph of global schedule S, then any replication graph of schedule S also contains a loop. Following that, we observe that protocol COP does not allow loops in the replication graph. Consequently, the assumption that the protocol generates a globally nonserializable schedule would lead to a contradiction. First we prove three lemmas.

LEMMA 5.2. *Let $P = T_1, T_2, \ldots, T_k$ be a path in the global serialization graph for global schedule S contributed by the local schedule at physical site s_1, where T_1 and T_k are global transactions and $T_2, \ldots, T_{k-1}$ are local transactions and $k > 2$ (that is, T_k is the first global transaction after T_1 in P). Then there is a path from T_1 to T_k in any replication graph for S that includes at least virtual site vs_1^1, provided that the split rule was not applied.*

Proof. Let $P = T_1, T_2, \ldots, T_k$ be a path in the global serialization graph for global schedule S contributed by the local schedule at physical site s_1. Every two adjacent transactions in P have a pair of conflicting operations. Suppose that all conflicting pairs are of the ww type. In such a case, T_2 has a write/write conflict with T_1 which is global. Consequently, T_2 must be also global since it writes to a global data item. That is, $k \leq 2$ which contradicts the lemma assumption.

Consequently, suppose that T_1 and T_2 are in a r-conflict. By the union and locality rule, $vs_1^1 = vs_2^1$. Since all $T_3, \ldots, T_{k-1}$ are local, they originate at s_1. The conflict between T_{k-1} and T_k cannot be of the ww type (otherwise T_{k-1} would have to be global too). Consequently, by the union and locality rules, we obtain that $vs_{k-1}^1 = vs_k^1$. Thus, $vs_1^1 = vs_2^1 = \cdots = vs_{k-1}^1 = vs_k^1$. Consequently, the following path satisfies the lemma assertion: T_1, vs_1^1, T_k. □

LEMMA 5.3. *Let $P = T_1, T_2, \ldots, T_k$ be a path in the global serialization graph for global schedule S contributed by the local schedule at physical site s_1, where $T_1, T_2, \ldots, T_k$ are global transactions and each pair of adjacent transactions has a ww conflict on non primary data item. Then, there is a path between vs_1^1 and vs_k^1 that includes transactions T_1 and T_k, provided that the split rule was not applied.*

Proof. Since $T_1, T_2, \ldots, T_k$ are global transactions with every two adjacent transactions in a ww conflict on a secondary data item, by These transactions must therefore have originated at a single physical site s_t and share there the same virtual site vs_1^t. Thus the following path satisfies the lemma assertion: $vs_1^1, T_1, vs_1, T_k, vs_k^1$. □

LEMMA 5.4. *Let $P = T_1, T_2, \ldots, T_k$ be a path in the global serialization graph of global schedule S contributed by the local schedule at physical site s_1, where T_1 and T_k are global transactions. Furthermore, let there be at least one pair of adjacent transactions in P that conflict on a primary data item. Then, any replication graph for S contains a path between T_1 and T_k that includes virtual site vs_1^1, provided that the split rule was not applied.*

Proof. Consider path P. Without loss of generality, we assume that P is built from triples $TR = (P_1 P_2 P_3)$ of segments: segment P_1 of global transactions followed by segment P_2 of local transactions, which, in turn, is followed by segment P_3 of global transactions. The segment of local transactions in the triple may be empty. Two adjacent triples $TR_1 = (P_1 P_2 P_3)$ followed by $TR_2 = (Q_1 Q_2 Q_3)$ satisfy the following condition: $P_3 = Q_1$.

Consider the case that P contains a single triple. If the segment of local transactions in the triple is empty, P consists of only global transactions, and there is at least one conflict on a primary data item. $T_1, T_2, \ldots, T_k$ have originated at the same site s_1 and share the same virtual site there. Thus, the lemma assertion holds.

Suppose now that the segment of local transactions in the triple is not empty. Then, the assertion follows from Lemma 5.3 as follows.

Let $P = T_1, T_2, \ldots, T_i, T_{i+1}, \ldots, T_j, T_{j+1}, \ldots, T_k$, where $T_1, T_2, \ldots, T_i$ is a segment of global transactions, $T_{i+1}, \ldots, T_j$ is a segment of local transactions and $T_{j+1}, \ldots, T_k$ is a segment of global transactions. By Lemma 5.3, transactions $T_1, T_2, \ldots, T_i$ have originated at the same virtual site vs_1 at their common origination site. By Lemma 5.2, there is a path in the replication graph from T_i to T_{j+1} and by Lemma 5.3, there is a path from T_{j+1} to T_k.

Using induction on the number of triples (and consequently, the number of segments of local transactions in P) we obtain the lemma assertion. The Lemma is proven. □

We proceed now with the proof of theorem. Assume to the contrary that the global schedule generated by protocol COP is not globally serializable. Then there is no total order on a set of transactions in the global schedule and the union of local serialization graphs contains a loop shown below.

$$T_1, T_{i1}, \ldots, T_{iq}, T_2$$
$$T_2, T_{j1}, \ldots, T_{jp}, T_3$$
$$\vdots$$
$$T_k, T_{r1}, \ldots, T_{rl}, T_1$$

By Lemma 5.4, either there is a loop in the replication graph, or all global transactions have originated at the same virtual site. In the latter case, the loop shown above could not have occurred since we use the Thomas Write Rule to coordinate execution of ww conflicts. Consider now the former case, where there is a loop in the replication graph. Observe that no transaction from $T_1, \ldots, T_k$ has completed. Thus, none of these transactions could have been removed from the graph as a result of the split rule. Consequently, there is at least one of the transactions whose commit operation creates a loop in the replication graph. It contradicts to the protocol rule that does not allow to proceed commit if a loop occurs in the replication graph. The theorem is proven. $\qquad\square$

In protocol COP, none of the transactions is allowed to wait. Consequently, no distributed deadlocks can occur during the transaction processing. Transactions aborts, on the other hand, could occur. The frequency of transaction aborts is determined by the probability of a transaction generating a cycle in the replication graph.

Let $T_1, \ldots, T_t$ be transactions executed so far by protocol COP such that any adjacent pair of transactions is conflicting. Suppose that an attempt to commit additional transaction T_{t+1} at its origination site creates a loop in the replication graph. This means that the following two conditions hold:

- T_{t+1} has at least two virtual sites in common with transactions $T_1, \ldots, T_t$.

- $T_1, \ldots, T_t$ is a path in the replication graph

To obtain an upper bound on probability of a transaction to be aborted, we assume that if a transaction has at least one data item in common with another transaction, then one of the transactions should be aborted.

Let m be a number of distinct data items at each local site. Without loss of generality we assume that each data item is replicated. Let n be a number of global transactions and let r be a number of different operations in each global transaction. Let $T_1, T_2, \ldots, T_t$ be an arbitrary set of t global transactions do not have any data items in common. There are

$$\prod_{i=0}^{t-1} \binom{m - ir}{r}$$

ways to select t transactions that do not have any data items in common. Let T_{t+1} be a transaction that has at least one data item in common with at least one of the transactions from $T_1, \ldots, T_t$. There are $\binom{(t-1)r}{1} \binom{m-tr}{r-1}$ ways to select a transaction T_{t+1}. Thus, the probability that among $t + 1$ transactions there is at least one transaction that has at least one data item in common with at least one different transaction is:

$$\frac{\binom{n}{t}\binom{(t-1)r}{1}\prod_{i=0}^{t-1}\binom{m-ir}{r}\binom{m-tr}{r-1}}{\binom{m}{r}^{t+1}}$$

Thus, the probability that in a set of two or more transactions at least one is aborted by protocol COP is:

$$\sum_{t=2}^{n}\binom{n}{t}\frac{(t-1)r^2((m-r)!)^{t+1}}{(m-(t+1)r+1)!(m!)^t}$$

We assume that $nr \ll m$. Under this assumption, it is easy to see that the first element of the sum is the largest. Thus, the expression above can be approximated as $(cn^2r^2)/m$, which is an upper bound on a probability of a transaction among given set of n transaction to be aborted by protocol COP.

6. Implementation Issues

In this section, we discuss how our protocol may be implemented so as to minimize communication overhead and tolerate failures.

6.1 Message Overhead

The physical propagation of update values to secondary sites can begin as soon as the write operation has been executed at the primary site. Our protocol restricts only the time at which the updates may be *applied* to secondary copies. This allows increased parallelism in update propagation at the cost of some useless work if a global transaction aborts. In such cases, the messages pertaining to the aborted transaction are purged from the secondary sites' queues. No updates can have been actually applied at these sites as the transaction had not committed at its origination site.

Aside from update propagation, the maintenance of the replication graph represents the main source of message overhead. To compute the message costs of our protocol, we distinguish between long messages that contain graph data and short messages that contain only an acknowledgment, notification of commit or abort, and the like. We ignore transfer of the data itself (update propagation) since that cost applies equally to all protocols.

Our protocol requires graph maintenance only twice per transaction: (1) at the time a transaction attempts to commit at its origination site, and (2) after it completes or aborts. Commits by a transaction at a secondary site must be communicated (once no active transaction precedes it) so that it can be determined when a transaction enters the **committed** state.

To provide an approximate cost estimate for our protocol we make some simplifying uniformity assumptions. Let the system contain n sites, each of which processes t global transactions per second. Assume each transaction updates replicated data at m of the n sites. Let the length (in bytes) of long and short messages be L and l, respectively.

We consider first a central-scheduler scheme, followed by a distributed scheme.

Our protocol requires 1 long message per transaction from its origination site to the scheduler. The scheduler responds with a short message containing permission to proceed or denial thereof. Whenever a transaction commits at a secondary site, that site must inform the scheduler via a short message. Since a transaction cannot commit at a secondary site before it commits at the origination site, we need not include a short message from the origination site to the scheduler. Thus, there are $m - 1$ commit messages. Therefore, we have a total of 1 long and m short messages per transaction, and nt transactions submitted every second somewhere in the system. The communication overhead of our protocol is therefore $nt \cdot (L + ml) = ntL + mntl$ bytes per second.

If we assume $L = 5$ KB and $l = 1$ KB (a packet), and assume 10 sites running 100 transactions per second, each of which updates data on 5 sites, the overhead is 10 MB/sec. Such techniques as grouping several short messages into one can alleviate the overhead by a significant constant factor.

Comparing our protocol to that of [14], which relies on global locking, we find a significant reduction in message overhead. That protocol requires $mnrTl$ bytes per second, where r is the number of data items accessed per transaction, and T is the total number of transactions, including local transactions (thus $T > t$, and most likely by a substantial amount). Thus, we achieve lower overhead by more than a factor of r.

Although this level of overhead may be acceptable, as the desired throughput rate and database size grow, the overhead becomes quite significant. In particular, if the degree to which data is replicated grows linearly in the number of sites then our overhead grows quadratically—a situation that is not acceptable! This blowup in communication cost is inherent in replication [14]. Consider the communication overhead of propagating the updates themselves. If u denotes the number of bytes updates by a transaction, then the update propagation overhead is $mntu$, which grows at the same alarming rate as our communication overhead.

We now consider a scheme for distributed replication graph maintenance. In order to synchronize graph updates, each transaction that is ready to commit is assigned a global timestamp, which is broadcast to all sites. This timestamp specifies the order in which transactions enter the committed state and allows all sites to agree as to the next transaction to attempt to commit. When a transaction attempts to commit, it tests locally for a cycle in the replication graph and then broadcasts its timestamp along with the decision (commit or abort). If the decision is to commit, the changes to the replication graph are included in the decision message.

This scheme depends critically on the availability of a cheap broadcast mechanism as in a local-area network. Under that assumption, there are two broadcasts per transaction, each of which is a long message. The communication overhead for this is $2ntl$. Without broadcast, updates are passed from site to site, with each site incorporating its own changes into the message. In either case, we incur the overhead of sending short messages regarding the completion of transactions at secondary sites.

6.2   Failures and Recovery

In this section, we consider several possible failure modes: data item failure, site failure, and disconnection of a mobile host. Network partitions (other than mobile host disconnection) are not covered as such failures are difficult to handle under our protocol. We also exclude malicious failures in which sites provide incorrect information.

6.2.1   Data Item Failure.   A data-item failure means that a data item is not available for access. If it is the primary copy of the data item that is not available, then any global transactions that have read but not updated the data item before it failed are either aborted or made to wait until the data item becomes operational. Observe that either of these approaches will work, since the other copies of the data item can only be read, and the local DBMS may thus choose either course of action. If the update has already occurred, there is no impediment to the global transaction eventually completing. In any case, recovery from failed data items does not require any additional recovery procedures at the global level.

An alternative approach to primary data item failure is to select a new primary data item among available secondary copies. This is usually done via delegation. That is, each local site has a ordered list of primary copies sites for each data item. These lists are static and thus easily applied at each site when a failure is detected. When the original primary copy is recovered, a message is broadcast to each site and only after each site responds to the message, the original primary copy regains its status by revoking primary copy authority from the backup primary copy. Such an approach guarantees robustness of our protocol in the face of primary copy data item failures.

If a secondary data item copy has failed, then any transactions that originated at the site where the failure occurred and need to access the data item are aborted. Observe that such an abort could not cause a violation of global serializability. If a transaction that is trying to access a failed data item is global, then it did not distribute its updates yet and consequently, its abort cannot cause any aborts elsewhere in the system. If a transaction that is trying to access a failed data item is local, then its abort also cannot cause global serializability violations. Consider now the case when a transaction that needs to access a failed secondary copy did not originate at the site of failure. In such a case, an abort of the replica-propagation subtransaction would not create nonserializability, since the transaction would still be present in the replication graph. After the failed data item becomes available, the aborted subtransaction is restarted.

6.2.2   Site Failure.   If the central-scheduler approach is chosen, the scheduler must be mirrored at another site to ensure fault tolerance. To avoid doubling the communication overhead, the scheduler and its backup should be tightly coupled.

Our protocol is immune to site failures other than failure of the central scheduler. Indeed, if a site fails, then all active transactions at the site failed as well, and thus, these transactions are removed from the replication graph. The only transactions at the failed site that remain in the replication graph are those that have committed but cannot yet be removed from the replication graph. None of these transaction can cause any changes in the replication graph, since any operations that they submit cannot lead to additional edges in the replication graph. Site failure may result in some transactions that have completed their operations at their origination site remaining in the replication graph, pending update of secondary copies at the failed site. The latter may lead to a replication graph that contains transactions waiting for a failed site to be restored; and consequently, it may cause blocking.

We propose a simple solution to resolve these delays. If a transaction has committed at all but a failed site and if it can be removed from the replication graph disregarding the failed site, then we remove the transaction from the replication graph. After the failed site recovers, the replicas are updated in the same serialization order as they would have been if the site had not failed. This is done before the site is re-opened for operations as a part of the recovery procedure.

6.2.3   Disconnection of a Mobile Host.   Disconnection of a single site, as in the case of a mobile computer disconnecting from the network, is the only kind of network partition that our protocol can tolerate easily. If a disconnected site does not contain a primary copy for any data item, then only read transactions can originate at the disconnected site. Since the site is disconnected, none of its data item can be updated. Thus, each read transaction will read a consistent-though-possibly-not-recent copy of the secondary copy. To ensure data availability, the latest committed version of the secondary copies of the data should be copied from the primary sites prior to disconnection. A timestamping scheme can avoid unnecessary copying of data.

Suppose now that the disconnected site does contain some primary copies of data items. Such a case could be treated by transactions originating at other sites similarly to primary data item failure. At the disconnected site, we allow transactions to proceed based on the latest copy of the replication graph available to the site. However, none of the transactions originating at the disconnected site is allowed to commit until the mobile host reconnects. After the connection is restored, the replication graph of the disconnected site is merged with the current replication graph. If no cycles arise, each of the transactions from the disconnected site is committed. Otherwise, transactions that introduce a cycle in the replication graph are aborted and the formerly disconnected site is notified.

7. Conclusions

We have provided an exact characterization of global serializability in the presence of replicated data, using our definitions of virtual site and replication graph. We use this as the basis for our protocol for ensuring global serializability. Our protocol is an optimistic in that it defers testing of the replication graph until a transaction is ready to commit. This achieves a reduction in communication overhead by a factor of r as compared with earlier protocols that guarantee global serializability.

In addition to addressing issues of correctness, we considered message overhead and fault tolerance. Replication presents serious performance challenges if the degree of replication grows as the number of sites grows. The lower overhead and higher concurrency of our protocols as compared with prior work allows broader application of replication. However, achieving full scalability of replication as the degree of replication grows, while guaranteeing global serializability remains an open problem.

References

[1] D. Agrawal, A. ElAbbadi, and R. C. Steinke. Epidemic algorithms in replicated databases. In *Proc. 16th ACM SIGACT-SIGMOD Symposium on Principles of Database Systems*, pages 161–172, Tucson, AZ, 1997.

[2] F. Akal, Y. Breitbart, T. Grabs, H. Schek, C. Turker, and L. Veen. Fine-grained replication, and scheduling with freshness and correctness guarantees. In *Proc. 31st Intl. Conf. VLDB*, pages 565–576, Trondheim, Norway, 2005.

[3] T. Anderson, Y. Breitbart, H. F. Korth, and A. Wool. Replication, consistency, and practicality: Are these mutually exclusive? In *Proc. 1998 ACM SIGMOD Intl. Conf. Management of Data*, pages 484–495, Seattle, WA, 1998.

[4] P. A. Bernstein, V. Hadzilacos, and N. Goodman. *Concurrency Control and Recovery in Database Systems*. Addison–Wesley, Reading, 1987.

[5] Y. Breitbart and H. F. Korth. Replication and consistency: Being lazy helps sometimes. In *Proc. SIGACT-SIGART-SIGMOD Symp. Principles of Database Systems*, pages 173–184, Tucson, AZ, 1997.

[6] Y. Breitbart and H. F. Korth. Replication and consistency in distributed environment. *J. Computer and System Sciences*, 59(1):29–69, 1999.

[7] Y. Breitbart, H. Garcia-Molina, and A. Silberschatz. Overview of multi-database transaction management. *VLDB Journal*, 1(2):181–239, 1992.

[8] Y. Breitbart, R. Kommondoor, R. Rastogi, S. Seshadri, and A. Silberschatz. Update propagation protocols for replicated databases. In *Proc. 1999 ACM SIGMOD Intl. Conf. Management of Data*, pages 97–108, Philadelphia, PA, 1999.

[9] P. Chundi, D. Rosenkrantz, and S. S. Ravi. Deferred updates and data placement in distributed databases. In *Proc. International Conference on Data Engineering*, pages 469–476, New Orleans, LA, Feb.–Mar. 1996.

[10] C. A. Ellis. Consistency and correctness of duplicate database systems. *Operating Systems Review*, 11(5):67–84, 1977.

[11] L. Gao, M. Dahlin, A. Nayate, J. Zheng, and A. Iyengar. Improving availability and performance with application-specific data replication. *IEEE Trans. Knowledge and Data Engineering*, 17(1):106–120, 2005.

[12] E. Gelenbe and K. Sevcik. Analysis of update synchronization for multiple copy data-bases. In *Proc. Third Berkeley Workshop on Distributed Databases and Computer Networks*, pages 69–90, Berkeley, CA, Aug. 1978.

[13] J. Gray and A. Reuter. *Transaction Processing: Concepts and Techniques*. Morgan Kaufmann, San Mateo, 1993.

[14] J. Gray, P. Helland, P. O'Neil, and D. Shasha. The dangers of replication and a solution. In *Proc. 1996 ACM SIGMOD Intl. Conf. Management of Data*, pages 173–182, Montreal, Canada, 1996.

[15] A. A. Helal, A. A. Heddaya, and B. B. Bhargava. *Replication Techniques in Distributed Systems*. Kluwer Academic, Norwell, 1996.

[16] E. Holler. Multiple copy update. In B. Lampson, M. Paul, and H. J. Siegel, editors, *Distributed Systems—Architecture and Implementation: An Advanced Course*. Lecture Notes in Computer Science, volume 105, pages 284–307. Springer, Berlin, 1981.

[17] M. Hsu and A. Silberschatz. Unilateral commit: a new paradigm for reliable distributed transaction management. In *Proc. 7th International Conference on Data Engineering*, pages 286–293, Kobe, Japan, Feb.–Mar. 1991.

[18] H. F. Korth and T. Imielinski. Introduction to mobile computing. In H. F. Korth and T. Imielinski, editors, *Mobile Computing*, pages 1–39. Kluwer Academic, Norwell, 1996.

[19] H. F. Korth, E. Levy, and A. Silberschatz. A formal approach to recovery by compensating transactions. In *Proc. 1990 International Conference on Very Large Databases*, pages 95–106, Brisbane, Australia, Aug. 1990.

[20] E. Levy, H. F. Korth, and A. Silberschatz. A theory of relaxed atomicity. In *Proc. ACM SIGACT-SIGOPS Symposium on Principles of Distributed Computing*, pages 95–110, Montreal, Canada, Aug. 1991.

[21] S. Mehrotra, R. Rastogi, H. F. Korth, and A. Silberschatz. Nonserializable executions in heterogeneous distributed database systems. In *Proc. First International Conference on Parallel and Distributed Information Systems*, pages 245–252, Miami Beach, FL, Dec. 1991.

[22] T. Minoura. A new concurrency control algorithm for distributed database systems. In *Proc. 4th Berkeley Workshop on Distributed Databases and Computer Networks*, pages 221–234, Berkeley, CA, Aug. 1979.

[23] C. Olson and J. Widom. Offering a precision-performance trade-off for aggregation queries over replicated data. In *Proc. International Conference on Very Large Data Bases*, pages 144–155, Cairo, Egypt, Sep. 2000.

[24] C. Olson and J. Widom. Efficient monitoring and querying of distributed dynamic data via approximate replication. *IEEE Data Engineering Bulletin*, 28(1):11–18, 2005.

[25] C. Papadimitriou. *The Theory of Database Concurrency Control*. Computer Science Press, Rockville, 1986.

[26] C. Pu and A. Leff. Replica control in distributed systems: An asynchronous approach. In *Proc. 1996 ACM SIGMOD Intl. Conf. Management of Data*, pages 377–386, Denver, CO, May 1991.

[27] M. Rabinovich, N. Gehani, and A. Kononov. Scalable update propagation in epidemic replicated databases. In *Proc. 1996 Extending Database Technology Conference*, pages 207–222. Springer, Berlin, 1996.

[28] J. Sidell, P. Aoki, S. Barr, A. Sah, C. Staelin, M. Stonebraker, and A. Yu. Data replication in Mariposa. In *Proc. 1996 International Conf. Data Engineering*, pages 485–494, New Orleans, LA, Feb.–Mar. 1996.

[29] R. H. Thomas. A solution to the concurrency control problem for multiple copy databases. In *Proc. CompCon*, pages 56–62, 1978.

Chapter 13

SNAPSHOT ISOLATION: WHY DO SOME PEOPLE CALL IT SERIALIZABLE?

PHILIP LEWIS

*Department of Computer Science, State University of New York at Stony Brook, Stony Brook,
NY 11794, USA. Email:* `pml@cs.sunysb.edu`

Abstract   SNAPSHOT isolation provides a protocol for dealing with concurrent transactions in transaction processing applications. Because applications using SNAP-
SHOT isolation can have very high throughput, many applications are designed
using this protocol.

However, SNAPSHOT isolation can produce non-serializable and incorrect
schedules. One interesting question is: why are there not more complaints from
users that they are getting incorrect results when they use SNAPSHOT isolation?

The most likely answer to that question is that application designers use some
design pattern that produces correct schedules at SNAPSHOT isolation. The
designers are not necessarily selecting a design pattern because it will guarantee
correctness at SNAPSHOT isolation. They are just using design patterns that
seem natural to them, and those patterns happen to produce correct executions
at SNAPSHOT isolation.

This paper reviews some previous work on sufficient conditions for correctness at SNAPSHOT isolation and then presents an example of a design pattern
that is guaranteed to produce correct schedules at SNAPSHOT isolation.

Keywords: database, transaction, SNAPSHOT isolation, infrastructure/state design pattern

1.   Introduction

SNAPSHOT isolation provides a protocol for dealing with the concurrent
execution of transactions in transaction processing applications. Because applications using SNAPSHOT isolation can have very high throughput, many
applications are designed using this protocol. In fact, many of the transac-

S.S. Ravi, S.K. Shukla (eds.), *Fundamental Problems in Computing*,
© Springer Science + Business Media B.V. 2009

tion processing systems we use every day and on which our lives and fortunes depend use SNAPSHOT isolation.

And yet SNAPSHOT isolation does not always produce correct schedules. Many examples can be given of transactions executing at SNAPSHOT isolation that provide incorrect schedules, which result in databases that contain incorrect information.

One intriguing example is provided by Oracle, the largest database company in the world. When an application designer includes a statement in his Oracle SQL program specifying that the application is to be executed at the SERIALIZABLE isolation level, which would guarantee correctness, the Oracle database system does not in fact execute at the SERIALIZABLE isolation level, but instead executes at the SNAPSHOT isolation level, which does not guarantee correctness.

So why are there not a large number of users of such systems (for example Oracle customers) complaining that their applications are not executing correctly, causing their databases to contain incorrect information?

That is the question we address in this chapter. First we review the definitions of correctness and define SNAPSHOT isolation.

2.　　Correctness of Transaction Processing Systems

In the applications we are considering, a database is a collection of data that models some aspects of the state of an enterprise. For example, a bank might maintain a database to model the state of the accounts of its customers. The bank's database is correct if it correctly models the state of its customer's accounts.

One aspect of correctness is that the database must satisfy certain **integrity constraints**. In the bank example, the database might contain a record for each customer containing the balance of that customer's account, and in addition it might contain a record containing the total balance of the accounts of all of its customers. One integrity constraint might be that the total balance must be the sum of the individual balances. If a database satisfies all of its integrity constraints, we say that it is **consistent**.

When an event occurs in the real world that changes the state of the enterprise, a program called a transaction is run to update the database to reflect the change in the state. For example, when a customer of the bank makes a deposit to his account, a transaction is run to update the balance of that customers account and the total balance in the bank.

We say that an update transaction is **correct** if, when it is run all by itself starting with a database that is consistent and that correctly models the current state of the enterprise, when the transaction completes, the database is consistent and the database has been updated to correctly reflect the new state of the enterprise.

If a sequence of correct transactions is run **serially** (each one starting after the previous one has completed), the final database is correct (and consistent). We say that the transactions are **isolated**.

However, serial execution is too slow and does not provide sufficient throughput. Many modern transaction processing systems must execute thousands of transactions per second. To provide this level of throughput, transaction processing systems execute transactions **concurrently**. Many transactions are executing at the same time, and their database access and update operations are interleaved. A particular concern is how to maintain correctness for such concurrent executions.

One sufficient condition for correctness is that the execution be **serializable**. The concurrent execution of a set of transactions is said to be serializable if it has the same effect as if the transactions had executed serially in some order. Each transaction sees the same snapshot of the database it would have seen in the serial order, and the final database is the same as it would have been in the serial order.

Please note that we have defined "serializable" with all lower case letters. Later we will define "SERIALIZABLE" with all upper case letters, which has a related but different definition. Note also that serializable is a sufficient but not necessary condition for correctness. Later we show a non-serializable schedule that is correct.

3. Concurrency Controls, Two-Phase Locking, and Isolation Levels

Most database and transaction processing systems contain **concurrency controls** that can produce concurrent schedules that are serializable. Most such controls are based on **locking**. Before a transaction can access a database item, it must request an appropriate lock from the concurrency control.

A locking protocol is said to be **two-phase** if each transaction obtains all the locks it will ever request before giving up any of its locks (it goes through a locking phase and an unlocking phase). Many systems require that the locking protocol be **strict two-phase**, where all locks are held until the transaction completes.

When a transaction successfully completes, we say that it **commits**. When a transaction does not successfully complete, we say that it **aborts** and any changes it has made to the database are rolled back (undone).

Two-phase locking protocols produce schedules that are serializable. In other words, two-phase locking is a sufficient condition to produce serializable and hence correct schedules.

3.1   Isolation Levels

For many applications, two-phase locking does not provide sufficient throughput. So designers frequently specify that transactions be executed at lower **isolation levels** that do not guarantee serializability and do not guarantee correctness.

The SQL standard defines four isolation levels: SERIALIZABLE, REPEATABLE READ, READ COMMITTED, and READ UNCOMMITTED. All of these isolation levels, except SERIALIZABLE, allow non-serializable and incorrect schedules.

Most database systems allow the programmer to specify the isolation level at which the transactions will execute. Thus a programmer might include in the transaction program the statement

    SET TRANSACTION LEVEL SERIALIZABLE

if he wants the transaction to execute at the SERIALIZABLE isolation level.

We do not go into detail as to the definitions of these isolation levels. The definitions given in the SQL standard specify each level by the types of concurrent behavior it allows and does not allow. However, when these isolation levels are implemented within a concurrency control, each isolation level usually implies a different locking protocol. More specifically the implementation of each isolation level specifies the conditions under which certain locks need not be obtained or can be released earlier than would be allowed by two-phase locking. Fewer locks and early release of locks allows more transaction throughput, but can lead to non-serializable and incorrect schedules.

Thus, the difference between the definitions of "SERIALIZABLE" and "serializable" is that SERIALIZABLE is a locking (or other) protocol that always leads to schedules that are serializable and hence correct. However, some applications executing at isolation levels lower than SERIALIZABLE can also lead to schedules that are serializable and hence correct. (In addition as we have said, some applications that have non-serializable schedules can be correct.)

4.   SNAPSHOT Isolation

SNAPSHOT isolation is an isolation level that was introduced in Berenson, et al. [1] and has been implemented in the Oracle database management system.[1] In fact, Oracle's implementation of "SET TRANSACTION LEVEL SERIALIZABLE" is SNAPSHOT isolation [5]. Thus when the transaction designer specifies that he wants the transaction to execute at the SERIALIZABLE

---

[1] SNAPSHOT isolation has also been implemented in other systems, for example Microsoft's SQL Server 2005.

isolation level, the execution does not in fact execute at the SERIALIZABLE isolation level, but executes at the SNAPSHOT isolation level instead.

SNAPSHOT isolation is attractive because it allows increased concurrency and hence increased throughput. However, as has been pointed out by many authors, starting with Berenson, et al. [1], and as we show below, SNAPSHOT isolation can allow non-serializable and incorrect schedules.

The question then arises: since many programmers of Oracle systems include in their programs the statement "SET TRANSACTION LEVEL SERIALIZABLE" and then expect their transactions to execute serializably, why are there not a large number of dissatisfied Oracle users complaining that their applications are not executing correctly? It seems logical to conclude that a great many real-life transaction applications execute correctly at SNAPSHOT isolation. We return to this discussion later after we define SNAPSHOT isolation.[2]

DEFINITION 4.1. SNAPSHOT Isolation
A schedule produced under SNAPSHOT isolation has the following properties:

- All read operations of each transaction are satisfied using the (committed) snapshot of the database that was current when the transaction made its first read request.

- If two transactions that commit are concurrent (their executions overlap in time), then the set of data items written by one transaction is disjoint from the set of data items written by the other transaction. This is called the **disjoint-write property**. If two concurrent transactions attempt to write the same data item, one of them must be aborted.

Different implementations of SNAPSHOT isolation implement these properties in different ways. We do not discuss these implementations, but we note that in all of these implementations

- Read operations in one transaction do not wait for write operations in another transaction and

- Write operations in one transaction do not wait for read operations in another transaction,

as would occur in a two-phase locking protocol. Thus transaction processing systems that execute at SNAPSHOT isolation can have a higher throughput and execute many more transactions per second than if they had used two-phase locking.

---

[2] This definition is slightly different from, but equivalent to, the one in [1].

$$T_a : r(x)\; r(y) \qquad\qquad\qquad\qquad w(x)\; c$$
$$T_b : \qquad\qquad\quad r(x)\; r(y)\; w(y)\; c$$

(a)

$$T_1 : r(x) \qquad\qquad\qquad w(x)\; c$$
$$T_2 : \qquad r(x)\; r(y) \qquad\qquad\qquad\qquad w(y)\; c$$
$$T_3 : \qquad\qquad\qquad\qquad r(x)\; r(y)\; w(z)\; c$$

(b)

Figure 13.1. Two schedules that are non-serializable and can be produced at SNAPSHOT isolation

4.1 Non-Serializable Execution at SNAPSHOT Isolation

Figure 13.1 shows two examples of non-serializable schedules that can be produced at SNAPSHOT isolation. The schedule in Fig. 13.1(a) exhibits the *write skew* anomaly [1], in which two concurrent transactions read the same set of data items from the same snapshot of the database and each updates some disjoint subset of those items. The schedule in Fig. 13.1(b) does not exhibit any named anomaly. We discuss these schedules again in Sect. 5, where we show that they satisfy a particular property that leads to non-serializable schedules at SNAPSHOT isolation.

Consider the following banking application that might lead to the schedule shown in Fig. 13.1(a). The bank has the requirement that, when a customer has two accounts, the balance in either account can be negative, but the sum of the balances in the two accounts must be positive. Suppose a customer has $100 each in accounts x and y. T_a then reads the balance in each of the accounts, checks that withdrawing $150 from account x would not violate the bank's rule (integrity constraint), and then withdraws $150 from account x, writing $-$50 in x. T_b reads the same snapshot of the database, uses exactly the same reasoning, and withdraws $150 from account b, writing $-$50 in y.

Each transaction, if run serially (or serializably), would have maintained the integrity constraint, but the concurrent execution of the two transactions causes the integrity constraint to be violated and thus is incorrect. Hence for this application, SNAPSHOT isolation can lead to incorrect execution.

4.2 Non-Serializable but Correct Execution

Sometimes non-serializable schedules can be correct. Consider a different application that might also lead to the schedule shown in Fig. 13.1(a): a system that reserves seats for a concert. Assume that the integrity constraint is that the same seat cannot be reserved by more than one person. Suppose there are only two available (not yet reserved) seats, whose availability is stored in the database items x and y. Suppose transaction T_a reads the values of x and y, finds them both available, and reserves x. Concurrently another transaction, T_b, reads the same values of x and y, also finds them both available, and reserves y.

That is a perfectly correct execution. The schedule of those two transactions is identical to the schedule in Fig. 13.1(a) that can be produced at SNAPSHOT isolation. That schedule leads to a correct execution in the seat-reservation application, but led to an incorrect execution in the banking application.

Note that if both reservation transactions had attempted to reserve the same seat, one of them would have been aborted because of the disjoint-write property. A more general formulation of this seat reservation application with more available seats for the concert would also execute correctly at SNAPSHOT isolation.

The reason this particular application works correctly even though its schedules might not be serializable has to do with the *semantics* of the application. A sufficient condition for the semantic correctness of transactions executing under SNAPSHOT isolation is discussed in Bernstein, et al. [2], and we do not discuss it further here.

4.3   Phantoms at SNAPSHOT Isolation

When a transaction, T_1, performs a predicate read,[3] and a concurrent transaction, T_2, inserts a new tuple (row in a database table) that satisfies the predicate (or changes the value of an existing tuple not initially in the predicate so that it satisfies the predicate), the new tuple is called a **phantom**. At all of the SQL isolation levels, except for SERIALIZABLE, if T_2 commits while T_1 is still executing and T_1 were to repeat the same read operation, it would see the new tuple, which can lead to non-serializable and incorrect schedules.

At SNAPSHOT isolation, if T_1 were to repeat the same read operation, it would not see the new tuple, because all reads are satisfied with the snapshot of the database that existed when T_1 made its first read. Because T_1's second read does not see the new tuple, some people would say that the new tuple is not a phantom and that there are no phantoms possible at SNAPSHOT isolation. But as can be seen in the example in the next paragraph, such an inserted tuple can lead to non-serializable and incorrect schedules at SNAPSHOT isolation. And, in fact, if the schedule discussed in the example, had occurred at any of the SQL isolation levels (except SERIALIZABLE), for example, RE-

---

[3] An example of a predicate read that might appear in a banking transaction is "all accounts for which the balance is less then 1000."

PEATABLE READ, everyone would agree that the schedule was an example of a phantom. In the reminder of this paper, we will consider such schedules to contain phantoms.

Consider a task assignment application that assigns tasks to the workers in some enterprise. Suppose the tasks that are assigned to particular workers are stored in a database table with each task stored as a separate tuple. Suppose there is an integrity constraint that a worker can be assigned no more than 10 tasks. Suppose a task assignment transaction reads the predicate corresponding to a particular worker's assignments, counts the number of tuples and finds that he has been assigned 9 tasks, assigns that worker a new task, inserts a new tuple into the table corresponding to that new task, and then commits. A concurrent task assignment transaction assigning tasks to the same worker reads the original value of the predicate, also finds that the worker has been assigned 9 tasks, assigns him a new task, and inserts a new tuple into the table corresponding to that task. The worker has now been assigned 11 tasks, thus violating the integrity constraint.[4] We return to this example in Sect. 7.

4.4 The Read-Only Anomaly

Fekete, et al. [3] points out that even when the transactions that update the database execute serializably at SNAPSHOT isolation, a read-only transaction might see a (consistent) database state that corresponds to a serial order different than the order in which the updating transactions were serialized. Figure 13.2 is an example. T_3 sees the database as if the equivalent serial order were T_1 T_3 T_2, whereas the real equivalent serial order between T_1 and T_2 is T_2 T_1.

We view this anomaly as not too serious because the final database is consistent and correct and the read only transaction sees a consistent view of the database (although perhaps one that never appeared in the serialization of the updating transactions).

5.   A Sufficient Condition for Serializable Execution at SNAPSHOT Isolation

Fekete, et al. [4] addresses a problem similar to that discussed in this paper. They prove a theorem that gives a sufficient condition on the schedules of an application that guarantees that all executions of that application at SNAPSHOT isolation will be serializable.

---

[4] Note that the same phantom situation would result if there were initially a tuple for all possible tasks, with a field for the *Id* of the worker assigned to that task. Initially that field is blank so the tuple would not be returned in the read predicate corresponding to any worker's assignment. If a worker is assigned a task, his *Id* would be put in the appropriate field, and thereafter that tuple would be returned in the read predicate corresponding to that worker's assignment. The exact same phantom situation could then result.

$$T_1: \qquad\qquad\qquad r(y)\ w(y)\ c$$
$$T_2: r(x)\ r(y) \qquad\qquad\qquad\qquad\qquad\qquad w(x)\ c$$
$$T_3: \qquad\qquad\qquad\qquad\qquad r(x)\ r(y)\ c$$

Figure 13.2. A schedule exhibiting the read-only anomaly

We use their theorem in this paper, but our goal is to provide a more intuitive (but less general) condition for correctness and then argue that many applications satisfy that condition.

In their paper, Fekete, et al. [4] use a model of database read and write operations in which, when a transaction performs a write operation based on some predicate, that write operation is replaced by a read operation on the predicate to determine the items to be written, followed by a sequence of individual write operations on each of the items returned by the read. Thus, in this model, there are no predicate writes. We also use this model.

Their paper is based on the idea of conflicts between read and write operations

DEFINITION 5.1. Conflicts

There are three types of conflicts that can occur between two concurrent transactions, T_a and T_b, both of which commit. (Two transactions are concurrent if one transaction starts before the other transaction commits.) The definitions deal with predicate reads, but recall that there no predicate writes.

1. A **read-write** conflict occurs when

   - T_a makes an item or predicate read and T_b later makes an item write of one of the items that was returned by the read, or

   - T_a makes a predicate read and T_b later inserts a new tuple that satisfies that predicate (or changes the value of an existing tuple not initially in the predicate so that it satisfies the predicate).

   The situations described in the second bullet correspond to phantoms.

2. A **write-read** conflict occurs when T_a writes an item and T_b later reads that same item (perhaps as part of a predicate read).

3. A **write-write** conflict occurs when T_a writes an item and T_b later writes that same item.

If any of these conflicts occur, then T_b must be after T_a in any serial (or serializable) ordering of the transactions.

From this definition, it follows that:

LEMMA 5.2 [4]. *When transactions execute at SNAPSHOT isolation, the only possible conflicts between two concurrent transactions that commit are read-write conflicts.*

Proof. Because of the disjoint-write property, there can be no conflicts between two item writes. Recall that there are no predicate writes. Thus there are no write-write conflicts.

Because of the fact that in SNAPSHOT isolation all reads are satisfied with the value of the item (or predicate) in the snapshot of the database that existed when the transaction made its first read, a read cannot read any value written by a concurrent transaction. Thus there can be no write-read conflicts. □

Now we can state the theorem. A formal proof is given in [4].

THEOREM 5.3. *A Sufficient Condition for Serializable Execution at SNAPSHOT Isolation* [4]

All schedules produced by an application executing at SNAPSHOT isolation are serializable if the following situation cannot occur. There are three transactions T_1, T_2, and T_3, such that

- *T_1 executes concurrently with T_2 and T_1 writes or inserts an item that conflicts with a read predicate that T_2 read (in other words the two transactions have a read-write conflict), and*

- *T_2 executes concurrently with T_3 and T_2 writes or inserts an item that conflicts with a read predicate that T_3 read (again the two transactions have a read-write conflict).*

T_1 and T_3 do not have to be concurrent. T_1 and T_3 are allowed to be the same transaction.

Note that this situation occurs in both of the schedules in Fig. 13.1, and hence, by the theorem, both schedules are not serializable. In Fig. 13.1(b), T_1 and T_2 are concurrent with each other and T_2 and T_3 are concurrent with each other, but T_1 and T_3 do not execute concurrently. In Fig. 13.1(a), T_a plays the roles of both T_1 and T_3.

6. The Infrastructure/State Design Pattern

We now return to the question we raised at the beginning of the paper: Why are there not a large number of users of applications executing at SNAPSHOT isolation (or Oracle users who specified the SERIALIZABLE isolation level) complaining that their applications are not executing correctly? We believe that the reason is that almost all applications are designed using some design pattern that guarantees serializability at SNAPSHOT isolation. The designers are not necessarily selecting a design pattern because it will guarantee serializability at SNAPSHOT isolation. They are just using design patterns that seem natural to them, and those patterns happen to produce serializable executions at SNAPSHOT isolation.

We present one such design pattern, the Infrastructure/State (I/S) design pattern. But before we do that, we discuss automatic constraint checking.

6.1 Automatic Constraint Checking

In addition to using some design pattern such as the I/S pattern, we assume that transaction designers use automatic constraint checking. SQL allows designers to specify in their SQL programs that the database system check certain constraints on the database (integrity constraints). Whenever a transaction requests to commit, the database system checks whether allowing that transaction to commit would make one of the specified constraints false, and if so, it does not allow the transaction to commit, but aborts it.

Note that all the examples we have given of incorrect executions at SNAPSHOT isolation involved some integrity constraint becoming false. So if the transaction designer had specified that the database automatically check those constraints, none of those incorrect executions would have taken place. At least one of the transactions in each of these schedules would have been aborted by the system.

However performing automatic constraint checking does not guarantee correct executions. A particular schedule might produce a database that satisfies all the integrity constraints, but is nevertheless incorrect, that is, it does not reflect the desired effects of all the transactions.

As an example, consider again the schedule given in Fig. 13.1(a). Consider the banking application where the only integrity constraint is that when a customer has two accounts the sum of the balances in both accounts must be positive. This time assume that

- T_a is supposed to read the balances in both accounts and deposit an amount in account x such that the total amount in both accounts is twice what it was when T_a started.

- T_b is supposed to read the balances in both accounts and deposit an amount in account y such that the total amount in both accounts is twice what it was when T_b started.

If the transactions had run serially (or serializably), with T_a executing before T_b, the final amount in the first account would be $2x + y$ and the final amount in the second account would be $2x + 3y$. Hence the sum of the amounts in both accounts would be $4x + 4y$, which is four times the sum of the amounts at the beginning of the schedule. This is correct as specified by the intended specifications of the transactions, assuming the transactions had run serially or serializably.

In the SNAPSHOT isolation schedule shown in Fig. 13.1(a), T_a would write $2x + y$ into the first account, and T_b would write $x + 2y$ into the second account. Hence the sum of the amounts in both accounts would be $3x + 3y$, which is three times the sum of the amounts at the beginning of the schedule. This is incorrect (even though the integrity constraint is satisfied).

6.2 The Disjoint-Predicate-Write Property

We define a particular property that is part of the I/S Design Pattern.

DEFINITION 6.1 (The Disjoint-Predicate-Write Property). A schedule satisfies the disjoint-predicate-write property if, whenever a transaction that commits makes a write based on some predicate, no other concurrent transaction that commits inserts a new tuple that satisfies that predicate (or changes the value of an existing tuple not initially in the predicate so that it satisfies the predicate).[5]

Informally, we can say that the disjoint-predicate-write property is an extension of the disjoint-write property to writes based on predicates. Again, informally we can say that schedules that satisfy the disjoint-predicate-write property contain no phantoms that conflict with a write predicate (more precisely no phantoms that conflict with the read predicate that was used as part of the implementation of a write based on a write predicate).

We give some justification as to why we think many applications have this property in Sect. 7.

6.3 Read-Only, Update-Only, and Read-Update Transactions

In discussing the Infrastructure/State design pattern, we consider three disjoint types of transactions:

- **Read-Only Transactions**, which read items, but perform no writes (or inserts or deletes).

- **Update-Only Transactions**, which update all items that they read.

---

[5] Recall that, according to our model, when a transaction makes a write based on some predicate, the write operation is replaced by a read operation on the predicate to determine the items to be written, followed by a sequence of individual write operations on each of the items returned by the read.

- **Read-Update Transactions**, which do not update all the items that they read (there is at least one item that each such transaction reads but does not update).

For the remainder of the paper, we ignore read-only transactions. As we showed in the example of the Read-Only Anomaly, the existence of read-only transactions in SNAPSHOT isolation schedules does not affect the serializability of the transactions that update the database and hence does not affect the correctness of the database. (The database seen by the read-only transaction is the result of some serial order, but not necessarily the order produced by the transactions that update the database, but we do not view that as particularly serious.)

6.4 State and Infrastructure Items and Transactions

In applications that satisfy the I/S design pattern, the database items are either state items or infrastructure items.

DEFINITION 6.2. State and Infrastructure Items

- **State Items.** A state item is an item that contains information about the current state of the business and is updated frequently whenever that state changes.

- **Infrastructure Items.** An infrastructure item is an item that contains relatively long-term information about the infrastructure of a business and is updated infrequently only when the long-term information changes.

For example, in a banking application:

- The infrastructure items might include the depositors' names, addresses, social security numbers, and account numbers, all of which are updated very infrequently.

- The state items might include the account balances, which are updated whenever a depositor deposits or withdraws money from one of his accounts or whenever interest is credited to the accounts.

Similarly, in applications that satisfy the I/S design pattern, the transactions are either state transactions or infrastructure transactions.

DEFINITION 6.3. State and Infrastructure Transactions

- **State Transactions:** A state transaction is an update-only or read-update transaction that can read state and infrastructure items, but must update all the state items it reads and cannot update any infrastructure items. It can do one or more of the following:

- Read one or more infrastructure items
- Write one or more state items
- Read and then update one or more state items
- Insert or delete one or more tuples containing state items.

A key part of the definition is that the only items that a state transaction can read and then not update are infrastructure items and the only items it can read and then update are state items.

Informally, whenever an event occurs in the real world that changes the state of the enterprise, a state transaction is executed, which reads some infrastructure items to determine information that it needs and then updates some state items to reflect the change of state implied by the event.

- **Infrastructure Transactions:** An infrastructure transaction is an update-only transaction that can read and update only infrastructure items. It can do one or more of the following:

  - Read and then update one or more infrastructure items.

  - Insert or delete one or more tuples containing infrastructure items.

A key part of the definition is that an infrastructure transaction can read and update only infrastructure item and must update all items that it reads, that is, it is an update-only transaction.

Informally, infrastructure transactions are run very infrequently whenever infrastructure items need to be updated.

6.5 The Infrastructure/State Design Pattern

Now we can define the I/S design pattern:

DEFINITION 6.4. The Infrastructure/State Design Pattern
An application satisfies the Infrastructure/State design pattern if

- All of its schedules satisfy the disjoint-predicate-write property.

- All the database items are either state items or infrastructure items.

- All the transactions are either state transactions or infrastructure transactions.

Since we want to use Theorem 5.3 to prove when schedules of applications designed using the I/S design pattern and executed at SNAPSHOT isolation are serializable and since a key part of that theorem is read-write conflicts between transactions, we are particularly interested in which transactions can have a read-write conflict.

LEMMA 6.5. *If an application satisfies the I/S design pattern and executes at SNAPSHOT isolation, the only possible read-write conflicts between two concurrent transactions that commit occur when*

- *A state transaction reads some infrastructure item and a concurrent infrastructure transaction writes that item, or*

- *A state transaction reads some predicate consisting of infrastructure items and a concurrent infrastructure transaction inserts a new tuple that satisfies that predicate (or changes the value of an existing tuple not initially in the predicate so that it satisfies the predicate).*

Thus in all read-write conflicts a state transaction does the read and an infrastructure transaction does the write.

Proof. Two infrastructure transactions cannot have a read-write conflict because an infrastructure transaction must write everything it reads, and hence by the disjoint-predicate-write and disjoint-write properties no other infrastructure transaction can do a write that conflicts with that read.

Two state transactions cannot have a read-write conflict due to a read of infrastructure items because another state transaction cannot write an infrastructure item. Two state transactions cannot have a read-write conflict due to a read and then write of state items by one of those state transactions, again because of the disjoint-predicate-write and disjoint-write properties.

A state transaction cannot have a read-write conflict with an infrastructure transaction based on that state transaction's read of state items, because an infrastructure transaction cannot write state items. □

Using this lemma we can prove

THEOREM 6.6. *A Sufficient Condition for Serializable Execution at SNAPSHOT Isolation Based on the I/S Design Pattern*
If an application satisfies the I/S design pattern and executes at SNAPSHOT isolation, all of its schedules are serializable.

Proof. In the statement of Theorem 5.3, in order for a schedule produced at SNAPSHOT isolation to be non-serializable, there must be two transactions, T_1 and T_2, such that T_1 executes concurrently with T_2, and T_1 writes or inserts an item that conflicts with a read predicate that T_2 read. In other words the two transactions have a read-write conflict. Thus, by Lemma 6.5, T_2 must be a state transaction because it does the read.

Also in the statement of Theorem 5.3, T_2 must write or insert an item that conflicts with a read predicate that another transaction, T_3, read. Thus, by Lemma 6.5, T_2 must be an infrastructure transaction because it does the write.

Since T_2 cannot be both a state transaction and an infrastructure transaction, this schedule cannot exist. Since no schedule with the properties specified in Theorem 5.3 can exist, all schedules of applications that satisfy the I/S design pattern and execute at SNAPSHOT isolation are serializable. □

It is interesting to note that if an application satisfies the I/S design pattern and executes at SNAPSHOT isolation, the only type of conflict that can occur between two concurrent transactions that commit is a read-write conflict between a state transaction and an infrastructure transaction. Since infrastructure transactions execute rather infrequently, the number of such conflicts is probably small. (Of course, write-write conflicts can occur between two infrastructure or two state transactions, but in that case one of the transactions will be aborted because of the disjoint-write property.)

7. Justification for the I/S Design Pattern

We briefly give some justification as to why we think the I/S design pattern is natural and hence is used in many applications.

7.1 State and Infrastructure Items and Transactions

The intuition behind the state and infrastructure items and transactions should be clear from their names. As we said, whenever an event occurs in the real world that changes the state of the enterprise, a state transaction is executed, which reads some infrastructure items to determine information that it needs and then updates some state items to reflect the change of state implied by the event. Infrastructure transactions are run very infrequently whenever infrastructure items need to be updated.

The only issue might be: will state transactions read some state items that they do not write? For example, in the ticket reservation application that led to the schedule of Fig. 13.1(a), the reservation transaction reads the items for all the seats (state items) and then writes reservation information into one of those items. Thus that transaction does not write all the state items that it reads and hence does not satisfy the definition of a state transaction. As we have said, that schedule is not serializable, although it is correct.

The question is: would a designer have designed this application in that manner? Probably not. A more natural design would be to have two transactions. The first is a read-only transaction that reads and displays all the available seats for customers to read at their leisure. When a customer wants to reserve a particular seat, another (state) transaction is run to read and then write the item for that seat. Of course, by then someone else might have reserved that seat, in which case the transaction would report that fact. However, that situation might also have happened in the original design, in which case the reservation transaction would be aborted.

If the original design of an application has the property that some "state" transaction reads but does not write some state item (or some "infrastructure" transaction reads but does not write some infrastructure item), the design of that transaction can be tweaked so that it writes back the value it read (or in Oracle the read can be done using SELECT FOR UPDATE) [4].

7.2 The Disjoint-Predicate-Write Property

Before we discuss our justification for the disjoint-predicate-write property, which recall is related to phantoms, we mention that the schedule we gave in an earlier example that led to a phantom cannot occur in the I/S design pattern. In that example, a task assignment transaction read the predicate containing the tuples for all tasks assigned to a particular worker and, based on the number of such tuples, decided whether or not to add a new tuple for another assigned task for that worker. The task assignment transaction should be a state transaction, but a state transaction is not allowed to read any state items that it does not update, and the task assignment transaction reads all the task tuples but does not update them.

A better, more natural design, and one that satisfies the I/S pattern, is to have a separate database item for each worker that contains the number of tasks assigned to that worker. Each task assignment transaction would have to read and update that item. Thus the disjoint-write property, enforced by SNAPSHOT isolation, would not allow two concurrent task assignment transactions for the same worker to both commit. Fekete, et al. [4, 3] call the use of such an item "materializing the conflict" and advocate using such an item to ensure serializability. In this example, we believe that the use of such an item is natural and a better design.

We justify the disjoint-predicate-write property using a number of examples.

- A transaction in a business process updates a set of items based on a predicate at a time when the process is in some stage in which no other item satisfying that predicate *can possibly* be added.

  For example, a state transaction in an order-processing business process might update all the order-items corresponding to a particular order-id (for example, to denote that they have been shipped), at a stage in the process when the entire order has been entered by previous state transactions, and no other order-item with that order-id can be inserted by any concurrent state transaction.

Many business processes go through a stage in which a number of new tuples containing state items appropriate for that process are inserted by one or more transactions, followed by later stages in which those items are read and updated by other transactions in that process.

- A transaction in a business process updates a set of items based on a predicate at a time when it is *very unlikely* that another item satisfying that predicate will be added by any other transaction.

  For example, a state transaction in a bank to credit all accounts with their quarterly interest might be executed at a time when it is very unlikely that a concurrent transaction might be executed to add a tuple for a new account.

  Note that the first transaction is executed at a time selected by the business enterprise, not as a result of some action by a customer. Thus the enterprise can elect to execute the transaction at a time when conflicts are unlikely.

- A transaction in a business process updates a set of items based on a predicate that specifies only a fixed number of items, and the transaction updates all of those items. Thus there is no possible additional tuple which satisfies that predicate that can be introduced by any concurrent transaction in that or any other business process.

  For example, in a banking system, an infrastructure transaction might update the available-credit items in the tuples for the accounts with account-numbers 123, 789, and 347.

8.   Conclusion

We have defined the I/S design pattern and proved that applications designed using that pattern will execute serializably at SNAPSHOT isolation. The pattern is intuitive so that it is easy to verify whether or not a given application satisfies the pattern and, if not, to alter the design slightly so that it does.

We suspect that many existing applications satisfy this or a similar design pattern. The best evidence for the existence of such design patterns is the virtual non-existence of Oracle customers who are complaining that their "SERIALIZABLE" applications do not execute correctly. In all probability, those applications satisfy the I/S design pattern (or perhaps the more general condition in [4]).

9.   Dedication

I would like to dedicate this paper to Dan Rosenkrantz. I first met Dan about 40 years ago when we both worked at the General Electric Research Laboratory. Those were the magic years for Computer Science at G.E., and Dan made important contributions to that magic.

It is particularly appropriate for this dedication to mention that Dan and I worked together on a number of papers related to databases and transaction processing—the subject of the present paper. Two of our joint papers on this topic are reprinted in this volume.

Dan and I are both professional colleagues and personal friends. We have kept up that friendship over the years even after we both left G.E.

Dan has had an exciting and productive career, both at G.E. and at SUNY Albany. He has made important contributions to Computer Science. I wish him a long and happy retirement.

References

[1] H. Berenson, P. Bernstein, J. Gray, J. Melton, E. O'Neil, and P. O'Neil. A critique of ANSI SQL isolation levels. In *Proc. ACM SIGMOD International Conference on Management of Data*, pages 1–10, San Jose, CA, 1995.

[2] A. Bernstein, P. Lewis, and S. Lu. Semantic conditions for correctness at different isolation levels. In *Proc. IEEE Intl. Conference on Data Engineering*, pages 57–66, 2000.

[3] A. Fekete, E. O'Neil, and P. O'Neil. A read-only transaction anomaly under snapshot isolation. *SIGMOD Record*, 33(3):12–14, 2004.

[4] A. Fekete, D. Lierokapis, E. O'Neil, and P. O'Neil. Making snapshot isolation serializable. *ACM Trans. Database Syst.*, 30(2):492–528, 2005.

[5] K. Jacobs. Concurrency control: Transaction isolation in SQL92 and Oracle 7. Oracle White Paper Part No. A33745, 1995. (Additional contributors: R. Bamford, G. Doherty, K. Haas, M. Holt, F. Putzolu and B. Quigley).

Chapter 14

A RICHER UNDERSTANDING
OF THE COMPLEXITY OF ELECTION SYSTEMS[*]

PIOTR FALISZEWSKI[†]
Department of Computer Science, University of Rochester, Rochester, NY 14627, USA

EDITH HEMASPAANDRA[‡]
Department of Computer Science, Rochester Institute of Technology, Rochester, NY 14623, USA

LANE A. HEMASPAANDRA[§]
Department of Computer Science, University of Rochester, Rochester, NY 14627, USA

JÖRG ROTHE[¶]
Institut für Informatik, Heinrich-Heine-Universität Düsseldorf, 40225 Düsseldorf, Germany

Abstract   We provide an overview of some recent progress on the complexity of election systems. The issues studied include the complexity of the winner, manipulation, bribery, and control problems.

Keywords: bribery, computational social choice, control, manipulation, voting

[*] Supported in part by DFG grant RO-1202/9-3, NSF grants CCR-0311021 and CCF-0426761, and the Alexander von Humboldt Foundation's TransCoop program.

[†] URL: home.agh.edu.pl/~faliszew. Current affiliation: AGH University of Science and Technology, Kraków, Poland.

[‡] URL: www.cs.rit.edu/~eh.

[§] URL: www.cs.rochester.edu/u/lane.

[¶] URL: ccc.cs.uni-duesseldorf.de/~rothe. Work done in part while visiting the University of Rochester.

S.S. Ravi, S.K. Shukla (eds.), *Fundamental Problems in Computing*,
© Springer Science + Business Media B.V. 2009

1.   Introduction

Whether it is "more taste" versus "less filling," "peanut butter" versus "chocolate," or "Bush" versus "Kerry" versus "Nader," people have varying preferences. So it is natural that in life preference aggregation, typically via some voting/election scheme, is a central activity. Within the past few months, the authors of this chapter have seen a department's choice for faculty hiring selected by approval voting and a school's faculty senate election held under single transferable vote, and of course countless actions have been taken under plurality rule and under majority rule. Further, in this modern world of processes and agents, it isn't just people whose preferences must be aggregated. The preferences of computational agents must also be aggregated. Indeed, in both the artificial intelligence and the systems communities a surprisingly broad array of issues have been proposed as appropriate to approach via voting systems. These issues range from spam detection to web search engines to planning in multi-agent systems and much more (see, e.g., [14, 15, 32, 12, 16]).

Thus it is clear that elections are important in both the human and the computer worlds. But why should one study the *complexity* of elections? Although the history of looking at the effect of computational power on decision-making goes quite far back [38], the true genesis of the study of the complexity of elections was a spectacular series of papers by Bartholdi, Orlin, Tovey, and Trick that appeared around 1990 [3, 2, 1, 4]. One of the insights that naturally drove Bartholdi, Tovey, and Trick [3] to study complexity issues is that even if an election system has wonderful mathematical properties, if determining who won under the election system is computationally intractable then that system isn't going to be practically useful. Another motivation for studying complexity issues comes from a result known then (the Gibbard–Satterthwaite Theorem), and additional results that have been established since (most notably the Duggan–Schwartz Theorem), showing that every reasonable election system can be manipulated (see [20, 37, 11, 39]). So better design of election systems cannot prevent manipulation. Bartholdi, Tovey, and Trick [2] brilliantly, thrillingly proposed getting around this obstacle by seeking to make manipulation exorbitantly expensive, *computationally*.

The focus areas of those seminal papers from around 1990 were the complexity of the winner problem, the manipulation problem (which regards affecting an election's outcome by changing the votes of voters), and the control problem (which regards affecting an election's outcome by changing the structure of the election—e.g., by adding, deleting, or partitioning voters or candidates). In this chapter, we provide a brief overview of some of the work done on an ongoing project on election complexity that has been pursued over the past decade jointly by the theory groups in Düsseldorf and Rochester. This project has focused on improving the field's understanding of the complexity of winner, manipulation, and control problems, and has also added new directions of inquiry, including the definition and study of election bribery problems. The ultimate goal of the project—which has already been in reasonable part achieved in its manipulation and bribery streams—is to move from simply analyzing individual election systems to finding the source of the complexity of elections. That is, our ultimate goal is to find a simple rule that tells which election systems (perhaps with our focus limited to some broad, important subclass of systems) are computationally simple and which are computationally hard with respect to whichever one of the core questions—winner, manipulation, bribery, or control—is at issue.

By focusing on our own results and interests—though naturally many papers by others are mentioned in the process—we in no way wish to detract from the rest of the enormous body of research being done on related and unrelated topics within the complexity of elections. Indeed, interest in computational social choice theory is at a high level and is still growing, spans fields and countries, and as this is being written the inaugural meeting of a devoted workshop—the (First) International Workshop on Computational Social Choice—is just months away. It is a true, humbling joy to the authors to be part of such a vibrant community with this shared research passion.

Section 2 briefly describes some major election systems. Section 3 studies work showing that the winner problems for Dodgson, Kemeny, and Young elections are complete for parallel access to NP. Section 4 studies work on manipulation and bribery. This work achieves the "simple classification rule" goal mentioned above, and does so on the most important class of election systems—scoring protocols. Section 5 is about electoral control, and studies both the original approach to control and work that extended the control paradigm to the "destructive" case—asking not whether one can make a preferred candidate win, but rather asking whether one can block a despised candidate from winning.

2. Elections and Election Systems: Preliminaries

Throughout this chapter, an election, (C, V), will consist of a finite, though arbitrary in size, candidate set C and a finite, though arbitrary in size, voter set V. It is legal, though a bit bizarre, for an election to have no candidates or no voters.

Our voters will, unless otherwise specified, be input as a list. Each voter will not be associated with a name, but rather will be input simply via his or her preferences over the candidates. The nature of those preferences depends on the election system. For almost all the election systems discussed in this chapter, each voter is specified as a *tie-free linear ordering of the candi-*

dates, e.g., Bush > Kerry > Nader. We will typically refer to that as the voter's *preference list*. For some systems discussed in this chapter—approval voting and k-approval voting—voters are instead specified by *approval vectors*, namely, a vector that for each candidate specifies 1 for approval or 0 for disapproval.

As just mentioned, we generally assume that voters are input as a list. So V might typically be entered as (a natural coding of), for example, the list

$$\text{(Bush} > \text{Kerry} > \text{Nader, Nader} > \text{Kerry} > \text{Bush,}$$
$$\text{Bush} > \text{Kerry} > \text{Nader).}$$

Note in particular that we do not (except when speaking of *succinct* versions of problems—versions where one can list a preference's multiplicity as a binary number) allow one to specify multiplicities of a given preference other than by listing the same preference multiple times. This nonsuccinct approach to input has been the most common one ever since the seminal work of Bartholdi, Orlin, Tovey, and Trick, and reflects nicely the fact that in real life ballots are cast one per person.

In some problems we do allow voters to be *weighted*, but that is quite different than the succinctness issue. For example, a weight-3 voter is an indivisible object that is quite different from three weight-1 voters (since the latter can potentially be bribed/not-bribed/deleted/etc. separately from and differently than each other).

An *election system* (or *election rule*) is a mapping that takes as input an election (C, V) and outputs a *winner set* W satisfying $\emptyset \subseteq W \subseteq C$. So, in contrast with a social choice function, which typically maps from elections to preference-lists-altered-to-allow-ties, election systems focus completely on separating the candidates into winners and nonwinners.

Nonetheless, the literature on the complexity of election systems is a bit schizophrenic. Some areas of this literature—such as most of the work on the complexity of winner problems—focus on the issue of whether a particular candidate is (or can be made to be) a winner. Other areas of the literature on the complexity of election systems—such as most of the work on the complexity of control problems—focus on the issue of whether a particular candidate is (or can be made to be) a *unique winner*, i.e., to be a winner and to be the only winner. In the literature on manipulation one finds multiple examples of focus on winners and of focus on unique winners, but since the seminal manipulation complexity paper [2] focused on winners, we will view that as the "traditional" choice for manipulation.

The abovementioned traditional associations between areas and which of "winner" or "unique winner" to study are largely a matter of taste and often date back to choices made in the seminal papers of Bartholdi, Orlin, Tovey, and Trick. One certainly could choose to diverge from them, and researchers sometimes do. For example, the appendix of [26] reanalyzes the complexity of the winnership problems of Dodgson, Kemeny, and Young elections—whose complexity was previously known for the case of "winner"—for the case of "unique winner," and though it takes some work, shows that in each case the complexity of the unique winner problem is the same as the complexity of the winner problem.

Nonetheless, the traditional choices regarding "winner" versus "unique winner" help unify the literature so that papers within a given research stream— say, the study of electoral control—share the same focus and so can be better compared and contrasted. In this chapter, we respect and follow the traditional choices.

Finally, let us briefly define some of the most important election systems. In *approval voting*, each voter is represented by a 0–1 approval vector. To determine the winner, one component-wise adds the vector from each voter, and all candidates who achieve the largest component-wise sum that appears are winners. For each $k \geq 1$, *k-approval voting* is the same as approval voting, except each voter must have exactly k approvals in his or her vote (and thus we must have $\|C\| \geq k$).

The most important class of election systems is the class of *scoring systems* (or *scoring rules* or *scoring protocols*). A scoring system (for m-candidate elections) is defined by a *scoring vector* $\alpha = (\alpha_1, \alpha_2, \ldots, \alpha_m)$ satisfying $\alpha_1 \geq \alpha_2 \geq \cdots \geq \alpha_m$. Each voter is represented by a preference list, and the ith most preferred candidate on a given voter's preference list gains α_i points due to that voter. Each candidate's point total is the sum of all the points he or she gets. Whoever gets the highest sum is a winner.

Plurality-rule elections are based on the family of scoring systems defined by the scoring vectors $()$, (1), $(1, 0)$, $(1, 0, 0)$, $\ldots$, with the vector appropriate to the number of candidates being the one that is used. *Majority-rule elections* technically are not scoring protocols, but rather are the system using the same scoring vector collection as plurality-rule elections but in which a candidate wins exactly if he or she gets strictly more than $\|V\|/2$ points. Note that approval voting technically isn't a scoring protocol or even a one-scoring-vector-per-election-size family of scoring protocols. However, for each $m \geq k$, m-candidate k-approval voting is a scoring protocol, based on the vector $(\overbrace{1, \ldots, 1}^{k}, \overbrace{0, \ldots, 0}^{m-k})$. Veto elections are based on the family of scoring systems defined by the scoring vectors $()$, (0), $(1, 0)$, $(1, 1, 0)$, $\ldots$.

Condorcet elections are the system in which to be a winner one must have the property that for each candidate d other than oneself it must hold that one is preferred to d by strictly more than half the voters (i.e., one wins all head-on-head majority-rule beauty contests). Such a candidate is called a *Condorcet winner*.

3. Complexity of Winning: Dodgson's 1876 Election System

"I suspect that one of the March Hare, the Hatter, and the Dormouse is guilty," said the Queen, "though I don't know which one is. Thus we—the Duchess, you (Alice), and I—will vote on this matter. Off with the head of any one of the March Hare, the Hatter, and the Dormouse who is preferred to each of the others in pairwise majority-rule contests on whom to execute!"

"You cannot do that," Alice screamed, totally horrified. The Queen replied angrily, "Yes, I *can* do that. This is a rational society where people vote rationally on issues... such as which of those three to behead." And she pointed again to the Hatter, the March Hare, and the Dormouse (who had fallen asleep). "My preference list as to whom to behead is Hatter (I hate him) > March Hare > Dormouse (he is so cute). So shall it be off with the Hatter's head?"

"Not so fast," said the Duchess. "My preference list for whom to behead is March Hare (oh, to rid this world of those creepy long ears!) > Dormouse > Hatter." Suddenly turning to Alice, she asked, "What's your vote?" Alice timidly replied, "If I absolutely must give a list, then my preference list as to whom to behead is Dormouse > Hatter > March Hare."

"Ha!" exclaimed the Queen. "The Hatter is preferred to the March Hare for execution by two to one. Off with the Hatter's head!" "No," replied the Duchess, "the Dormouse is preferred to the Hatter for execution by two to one." "Then off with the Dormouse's head!" cried the Queen. "No," said the Duchess, "the March Hare is preferred to the Dormouse for execution by two to one." "*Then kill the March Hare!*" screamed the Queen, now really quite upset. "Need I remind you," said Alice, "that the Hatter is preferred to the March Hare for execution by two to one? So no one shall be beheaded."

The Queen summarized, "This makes me dizzy. In our rational society, each of the three of us had noncyclic (rational) preferences over these three candidates. And yet when we aggregated our preferences under pairwise majority-rule contests, our societal preference was strictly cyclic: March Hare > Dormouse, Dormouse > Hatter, Hatter > March Hare. Our rational individual preferences aggregated to an irrational societal preference. Since as the Queen I represent the society, perhaps the only fitting penalty is 'Off with *my* head!' "

Lewis Carroll—whose real name was Charles L. Dodgson and who not only was the author of wonderful children's books but also was a mathematician—noticed the same issue the Queen just reached: Rational individual preferences (even with ties not allowed) can aggregate, under pairwise majority-rule contests, to an irrational societal preference. That is, Dodgson rediscovered what is known today as the Condorcet paradox, though he most likely was unaware (see [5, pp. 193–194]) of Condorcet's much earlier work [9]. Note that every election instance having this type of strict cycle over all the candidates in the aggregate behavior is a case where there is no Condorcet winner (though not every election instance having no Condorcet winner is a case of this type of strictly cyclic aggregate behavior). In his 1876 essay "A Method of Taking Votes on More than Two Issues," Dodgson [10] proposed an election system that respects Condorcet winners when they exist, and when they don't exist reflects the philosophy that whoever is "closest" to being a Condorcet winner should be declared a winner. In Dodgson's system, given an election (C, V), each candidate $c \in C$ is assigned a score (denoted by $dscore_{(C,V)}(c)$, and we will write just $dscore(c)$ when the election is clear from context): $dscore(c)$ equals the smallest number of sequential exchanges (called "switches" henceforward) of adjacent candidates in the voters' preference lists that suffices to make c a Condorcet winner. Whoever has the lowest Dodgson score wins in Dodgson's system. When a Condorcet winner exists, he or she is clearly the unique candidate with Dodgson score zero and thus is a (indeed, *the*) Dodgson winner as well.

In the above example, there is no Condorcet winner but switching the Hatter and the Dormouse in Alice's preference list yields Hatter > Dormouse > March Hare. So the Hatter now defeats both the March Hare and the Dormouse by two to one in pairwise majority-rule contests and thus is now a Condorcet winner (in the election for the questionable privilege of being beheaded). So in the above example $dscore(\text{Hatter}) = 1$. Similarly, $dscore(\text{March Hare}) = dscore(\text{Dormouse}) = 1$. If there is no Condorcet winner, Dodgson winners are not necessarily unique, though at least one Dodgson winner always exists in Dodgson elections (except when $\|C\| = 0 \vee (\|V\| = 0 \wedge \|C\| \neq 1)$ holds).

How hard is it to determine whether a distinguished candidate is a Dodgson winner of a given election? Bartholdi, Tovey, and Trick [3] crisply, naturally formalized this problem as follows and also defined two related problems, the scoring and ranking problems for Dodgson elections. A Dodgson triple (C, c, V) consists of an election (C, V) and a distinguished candidate $c \in C$.

Name: Dodgson-winner.

Given: A Dodgson triple (C, c, V).

Question: Is c a Dodgson winner in (C, V), i.e., does $dscore(c) \leq dscore(d)$ hold for each $d \in C$?

Name: Dodgson-score.

Given: A Dodgson triple (C, c, V) and a nonnegative[1] integer k.

Question: Is it the case that $dscore(c) \leq k$?

---

[1] Both [3] and [23] have "positive" here rather than "nonnegative," but it is easy to see that the NP-completeness of this problem is unaffected by that word change (basically because the $k = 0$ case can be tested for in polynomial time).

Name: Dodgson-ranking.

Given: An election (C, V) and two distinguished candidates from C, c and d.

Question: Is it the case that $dscore(c) \leq dscore(d)$?

Bartholdi, Tovey, and Trick [3] proved that Dodgson-score is NP-complete and that Dodgson-ranking and Dodgson-winner are NP-hard. For the latter two problems Bartholdi, Tovey, and Trick left open whether their lower bounds were optimal, i.e., whether their Dodgson-ranking and Dodgson-winner NP-hardness results could be strengthened to NP-completeness or, alternatively, whether their NP-hardness lower bounds could be raised, ideally to some matching upper bound. These open questions were resolved by the following result of Hemaspaandra, Hemaspaandra, and Rothe [23].

THEOREM 3.1 [23]. Dodgson-ranking *and* Dodgson-winner *are* Θ_2^p-*complete*.

Θ_2^p here represents, as is standard, a particular level of the polynomial hierarchy. $P_{\parallel}^{NP}$ is the level of the polynomial hierarchy formed by the class of problems solvable by parallel (i.e., truth-table) access to NP. Quite early, Papadimitriou and Zachos [31] studied $P^{NP[\log]}$, the class of problems solvable by $\mathcal{O}(\log n)$ sequential (i.e., Turing) queries to NP. However, it is now known that $P^{NP[\log]}$ and $P_{\parallel}^{NP}$ are equal [21], and the class they each define is often referred to as the Θ_2^p level of the polynomial hierarchy. There are surprisingly many characterizations of Θ_2^p (see [41])—a tribute to its robustness under definitional variation. From the definitions, Θ_2^p is easily seen to be related to other polynomial hierarchy levels as follows: $NP \cup coNP \subseteq \Theta_2^p \subseteq P^{NP} \subseteq NP^{NP} \cap coNP^{NP}$.

The remainder of this section is mainly devoted to sketching the proof of Theorem 3.1. Our proof sketch proceeds via a series of lemmas. The general proof structure is shown in Fig. 14.1.

The Θ_2^p upper bounds for Dodgson-ranking and Dodgson-winner are easy to see. Dodgson-ranking, for example, is in Θ_2^p via the simple algorithm that, given an instance $((C, V), c, d)$, uses the NP oracle Dodgson-score to

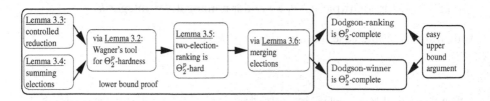

Figure 14.1. Proof structure for Theorem 3.1

compute $dscore(c)$ and $dscore(d)$ by asking in parallel all plausible values of those scores, and by doing so will discover whether $dscore(c) \le dscore(d)$.

Regarding the lower bounds, we show Dodgson-ranking and Dodgson-winner Θ_2^p-*hard* by proving many crucial properties of/operations on Dodgson elections to be *easy*, i.e., we provide polynomial-time algorithms for them. Although this may at first seem counterintuitive, it in fact is natural: Showing that a problem A is $\le_m^p$-hard for a class reflects not just that A has the power to solve all the sets from the class, but also that A is so nicely and simply structured that a polynomial-time many-one reduction from each set in the class can tap into that power. So $\le_m^p$-hardness is itself about simplicity and the power of polynomial-time transformations.

In our setting, some of the easiness results we obtain will be used hand-in-hand with a Θ_2^p-hardness tool of Wagner ([40], see also the surveys [24, 35]), stated as Lemma 3.2 below. Along the lines of the previous paragraph, to link our problems to this tool we must explore the properties of Dodgson elections and in particular how to resculpt them via efficient algorithms.

LEMMA 3.2 [40]. *Let A be an* NP-*complete set, and let B be any set. Then B is Θ_2^p-hard if there is a polynomial-time function f such that, for all $k \ge 1$ and all $x_1, \ldots, x_{2k} \in \Sigma^*$ satisfying $\chi_A(x_1) \ge \chi_A(x_2) \ge \cdots \ge \chi_A(x_{2k})$, it holds that $\|\{i \mid x_i \in A\}\| \equiv 1 \pmod 2 \iff f(x_1, \ldots, x_{2k}) \in B$.*

To exploit Lemma 3.2, we have to do much groundwork. Bartholdi, Tovey, and Trick [3] proved Dodgson-score NP-hard via a reduction from exact-cover-by-three-sets. However, their reduction does not have the properties needed to exploit Lemma 3.2. In contrast, one can achieve these properties by constructing a reduction to Dodgson-score that starts from the well-known NP-complete problem three-dimensional-matching (see Garey and Johnson [19] for specifics on three-dimensional-matching), which we will for brevity henceforth refer to as 3DM. This reduction has the property—which is vastly more restrictive than what is needed merely to achieve a vanilla many-one reduction in this case—that when it reduces to a question about whether a certain candidate has score at most k in a given election, it will always be the case that candidate's true score in that election is either k or $k + 1$.

LEMMA 3.3 [23]. *There is a polynomial-time function f that reduces 3DM to Dodgson-score in such a way that, for each $x \in \Sigma^*$, $f(x) = ((C, c, V), k)$ is an instance of Dodgson-score with an odd number of voters and this instance has the property that: (a) if $x \in$ 3DM then $dscore(c) = k$ and (b) if $x \notin$ 3DM then $dscore(c) = k + 1$.*

Next, Lemma 3.4 shows how to "sum" Dodgson triples in such a way that the Dodgson score of the "sum" equals the sum of the Dodgson scores of the given Dodgson triples.

LEMMA 3.4 [23]. *There is a polynomial-time function dodgsonsum such that, for all ℓ and for all Dodgson triples $(C_1, c_1, V_1), (C_2, c_2, V_2), \ldots, (C_\ell, c_\ell, V_\ell)$ each having an odd number of voters, $dodgsonsum((C_1, c_1, V_1), (C_2, c_2, V_2), \ldots, (C_\ell, c_\ell, V_\ell)) = (C, c, V)$ is a Dodgson triple with an odd number of voters and satisfies $dscore_{(C,V)}(c) = \sum_{1 \le j \le \ell} dscore_{(C_j, V_j)}(c_j)$.*

We now define an ancillary problem that is closely related to Dodgson-ranking and Dodgson-winner.

Name: two-election-ranking (2ER, for short).

Given: Two Dodgson triples, (C, c, V) and (D, d, W), with $c \neq d$ and $\|V\|$ odd and $\|W\|$ odd.

Question: Is it the case that $dscore_{(C,V)}(c) \le dscore_{(D,W)}(d)$?

Lemmas 3.2, 3.3, and 3.4 can be used (together with about two pages of additional argumentation) to obtain Lemma 3.5. Note that 2ER plays the role of the set B in Lemma 3.2, and 3DM plays the role of that lemma's NP-complete set A. Note also that 2ER is in Θ_2^p, so Lemma 3.5 implies that 2ER is Θ_2^p-complete.

LEMMA 3.5 [23]. *2ER is Θ_2^p-hard.*

Finally, Lemma 3.6 shows how to merge two Dodgson elections into a single Dodgson election in a very careful way such that a number of useful properties are achieved. Using this lemma we can transfer 2ER's Θ_2^p-hardness to both Dodgson-ranking and Dodgson-winner. One can think of Lemma 3.6, informally, as akin to a "double-exposure" photograph: Our merged election retains and reflects important information about both its underlying elections.

LEMMA 3.6 [23]. *There are polynomial-time functions merge and merge' such that, for all Dodgson triples (C, c, V) and (D, d, W) for which $c \neq d$ and both $\|V\|$ and $\|W\|$ are odd, there exist $\widehat{C}$ and $\widehat{V}$ such that*

1. *$merge((C, c, V), (D, d, W)) = ((\widehat{C}, \widehat{V}), c, d)$ is an instance of Dodgson-ranking,*

2. *$merge'((C, c, V), (D, d, W)) = (\widehat{C}, c, \widehat{V})$ is an instance of Dodgson-winner,*

3. $dscore_{(\widehat{C},\widehat{V})}(c) = dscore_{(C,V)}(c) + 1,$

4. $dscore_{(\widehat{C},\widehat{V})}(d) = dscore_{(D,W)}(d) + 1,$ *and*

5. *for each* $e \in \widehat{C} - \{c, d\}$, $dscore_{(\widehat{C},\widehat{V})}(c) < dscore_{(\widehat{C},\widehat{V})}(e).$

Space is too tight to cover in detail here the nine pages of proofs for Lemmas 3.3 through 3.6 and Theorem 3.1. But to give the reader at least some flavor of how the proofs work, we illustrate by an example the construction used for proving Lemma 3.6. Let the Dodgson triples (C, c, V) and (D, d, W) be given, where $C = \{a, b, c\}$ and $D = \{d, e, f\}$, V contains three preference lists, $c > b > a$, $a > c > b$, and $b > a > c$, and W contains one preference list, $f > e > d$. Clearly, $dscore_{(C,V)}(c) = 1$ and $dscore_{(D,W)}(d) = 2$. Now construct the election $(\widehat{C}, \widehat{V})$, which is part of the output of the functions *merge* and *merge'*, as follows. The candidate set is $\widehat{C} = C \cup D \cup S \cup T$, where S and T are sets of so-called separating candidates.[2] Voter set $\widehat{V}$ consists of the following preference lists:

1. $c > b > a > \overrightarrow{S} > e > f > \overrightarrow{T} > d,$

2. $a > c > b > \overrightarrow{S} > e > f > \overrightarrow{T} > d,$

3. $b > a > c > \overrightarrow{S} > e > f > \overrightarrow{T} > d,$

4. $f > e > d > a > b > \overrightarrow{T} > c > \overrightarrow{S},$

5. $d > e > f > a > b > \overrightarrow{T} > c > \overrightarrow{S},$

6. $d > c > \overleftarrow{T} > e > f > a > b > \overrightarrow{S},$

7. $d > c > \overleftarrow{T} > e > f > a > b > \overrightarrow{S},$ and

8. $c > d > \overrightarrow{T} > e > f > a > b > \overrightarrow{S},$

where $\overrightarrow{S}$ (respectively, $\overrightarrow{T}$) represents the candidates of S (respectively, T) in some fixed order, and (to avoid interference regarding property 5 of the lemma) $\overleftarrow{T}$ represents the candidates of T in the order that reverses their order in $\overrightarrow{T}$. The first three voters in $\widehat{V}$ simulate V, the fourth voter simulates W, and the remaining voters are so-called normalizing voters. Properties 1 and 2 of Lemma 3.6 are immediate.

For properties 3 and 4 of Lemma 3.6, let us determine the Dodgson scores of candidates c and d in $(\widehat{C}, \widehat{V})$. Note that one switch in, say, the second voter

---

[2] To make the proof of Lemma 3.6 work in general, S and T have to be chosen sufficiently large. In this toy example, however, all properties hold even if $\|S\| = \|T\| = 0$, so all separating candidates could be dropped here.

of $\widehat{V}$ (which is one of the voters simulating V) gives the new preference list $c > a > b > \overleftarrow{S} > e > f > \overrightarrow{T} > d$, and one switch in, say, the sixth voter of $\widehat{V}$ (a normalizing voter) gives $c > d > \overleftarrow{T} > e > f > a > b > \overrightarrow{S}$. By these two switches, c has become a Condorcet winner, so $dscore_{(\widehat{C},\widehat{V})}(c) \leq 2$. But since c needs to gain one vote in $(\widehat{C}, \widehat{V})$ against each of a and d to defeat all candidates by a strict majority, no single switch in the preference lists of $\widehat{V}$ can make c a Condorcet winner, so $dscore_{(\widehat{C},\widehat{V})}(c) \geq 2$. Thus $dscore_{(\widehat{C},\widehat{V})}(c) = 2 = dscore_{(C,V)}(c) + 1$. Similarly, two switches in the fourth voter of $\widehat{V}$ (which simulates W) gives the new preference list $d > f > e > a > b > \overleftarrow{T} > c > \overrightarrow{S}$, and one switch in the eighth voter of $\widehat{V}$ (a normalizing voter) yields $d > c > \overrightarrow{T} > e > f > a > b > \overrightarrow{S}$. By these three switches, d has become a Condorcet winner, so $dscore_{(\widehat{C},\widehat{V})}(d) \leq 3$. Again, since d needs to gain one vote in $(\widehat{C}, \widehat{V})$ against each of c, e, and f to defeat all candidates by a strict majority, no two switches in the preference lists of $\widehat{V}$ can make d a Condorcet winner, so $dscore_{(\widehat{C},\widehat{V})}(d) \geq 3$. Thus $dscore_{(\widehat{C},\widehat{V})}(d) = 3 = dscore_{(D,W)}(d) + 1$. Property 5 uses similar arguments.

As mentioned earlier, Dodgson's system respects the Condorcet winner when a Condorcet winner exists. Since the notion of Condorcet winner is widely considered central and important, election systems with this property have been intensely studied (see Fishburn [18]). Some other examples of election systems respecting the notion of Condorcet winner are those of Young [42] and Kemeny [29, 30]. In Young's system, whoever can be made a Condorcet winner by removing the smallest number of voters wins. Rothe, Spakowski, and Vogel [36] proved that the winner problem for Young elections is Θ_2^p-complete, via a reduction from the problem maximum-set-packing-compare. Kemeny's winners are defined via the notion of a "Kemeny consensus." Each ranking of the candidates (with ties allowed) that is "closest" to the given preference lists of the voters with respect to a certain distance function is a Kemeny consensus. A candidate is a winner in a Kemeny election if there exists some Kemeny consensus in which that candidate is a winner (a highest-ranked candidate, though possibly tied for that position). Hemaspaandra, Spakowski, and Vogel [27] proved that the winner problem for Kemeny elections is Θ_2^p-complete, via a reduction from the problem feedback-arc-set-member.

The three Θ_2^p-completeness results discussed above pinpoint the complexity of the winner problems for Dodgson, Young, and Kemeny elections. Winners in these three systems are not necessarily unique and these three winner problems ask whether a given candidate is *a winner*. However, as mentioned earlier, Hemaspaandra, Hemaspaandra, and Rothe [26] have shown that the unique winner problems for Dodgson, Young, and Kemeny elections are Θ_2^p-complete as well.

Θ_2^p-completeness suggests that the relevant problem is far from being efficiently solvable, and there are many ways in which completeness for this higher level of the polynomial hierarchy speaks more powerfully than would completeness for its kid brother, NP [24]. Since checking whether a given candidate has won should be in polynomial time in any system to be put into actual use, these results show that Dodgson, Young, and Kemeny elections are unlikely to be useful in practice. However, we note that winnership in "homogeneous" Young elections can indeed be tested in polynomial time via integer linear programming [42], that Dwork et al. [12] have proposed an efficient heuristic (called "local Kemenization") regarding the Kemeny winner problem, and that Dodgson winners can be determined efficiently (a) for elections with a bounded number of candidates or voters [3], (b) in Fishburn's [18] homogeneous variant of Dodgson elections [36], and (c) with a guaranteed high frequency of success under a simple greedy heuristic [28].

4. Complexity of Manipulation and Bribery: Scoring Systems and Dichotomy Theorems

The previous section studied the complexity of winner problems for certain election systems. We in this section turn to electoral problems that formalize attempts to influence an election's outcome for the case of a group of manipulative voters (who strategically change their preference lists) and for the case of having someone trying to bribe voters to change their preference lists. The next section studies attempts to influence elections via altering their structure. For a given election system, one would naturally most hope to find that it has an easy winner problem but that it resists electoral manipulation, bribery, and control.

Unfortunately, voters may often be tempted to cast their votes not according to their true preferences but rather insincerely, based on strategic considerations. Consider the following example. Our voting system is the Borda count, a family of scoring protocols that for m candidates uses the scoring vector $\alpha = (m - 1, m - 2, \ldots, 0)$. We have three candidates, a, b, and c, and eleven voters, where five voters have preference list $a > b > c$, five voters have preference list $b > a > c$, and one voter has preference list $c > a > b$. Under the Borda count scoring procedure, candidate a receives 16 points, candidate b receives 15 points, and candidate c receives 2 points. So a is the unique winner. However, from the point of view of voters with (true) preference list $b > a > c$, it might be tempting to report $b > c > a$ instead. This way they might actually make b win. Namely, if all voters whose sincere preference list is $b > a > c$ were to instead cast $b > c > a$ as their votes (and all other votes were to remain unchanged), then b would become the unique winner.

Of course, we would like to have election systems that cannot be manipulated. Unfortunately, a powerful line of work shows that all practically useful systems operating on three or more candidates are open to manipulation. In particular, the Gibbard–Satterthwaite Theorem [20, 37] shows that for each nondictatorial election system that always selects exactly one winner and in which the candidate set is of size at least three and in which for each candidate there is some set of votes that make that candidate a winner, there exists some situation in which a single strategic voter has an incentive to vote insincerely. The Duggan–Schwartz Theorem ([11], see also [39]) obtains an analog of this for the model in which—as in this paper—the winner set is some subset (possibly empty, possibly nonstrict) of the candidate set.

Although manipulation cannot be absolutely precluded in any reasonable election system on three or more candidates, Bartholdi, Orlin, Tovey, and Trick [2, 1] ingeniously proposed to at least make it computationally prohibitive—e.g., NP-hard—for a manipulator (or in later work by others, a coalition of manipulators) to figure out whether (and how) his/her/their vote(s) can be modified so as to make a given candidate win. They found systems *vulnerable to manipulation* (i.e., one can tell in polynomial time whether and how a given candidate can be turned into a winner) and they found systems *resistant to manipulation* (i.e., systems for which the manipulation problem is NP-hard). This line of research has been very actively pursued ever since (see, as just a few of the many examples on or related to this, [6, 7, 13, 22, 17, 34, 33]). As mentioned in the introduction, complexity issues for electoral problems (in particular, manipulation problems) are particularly important in these modern times when preference aggregation is used in multi-agent systems, distributed computing, and Internet applications.

A problem closely related to manipulation is bribery. In (constructive) manipulation, a group of manipulators wants to, by setting their own preference lists, have a given candidate end up a winner. (Destructive manipulation, which analogously seeks to have a given candidate end up a nonwinner, has also been studied [6, 7]. This section deals with the constructive case only.) Bribery is related to manipulation, except that now we look at elections from the point of view of an outside agent who wants to make some candidate win and who has some budget to bribe voters to change their votes. We now formally define these problems for a given election system $\mathcal{E}$.

Name: $\mathcal{E}$-manipulation.

Given: A set C of candidates, a set V of nonmanipulative voters, a set S of manipulative voters with $V \cap S = \emptyset$, and a distinguished candidate $c \in C$.

Question: Is there a way to set the preference lists of the voters in S such that, under election system $\mathcal{E}$, c is a winner of election $(C, V \cup S)$?

Instead of the plain $\mathcal{E}$-manipulation problem presented above, we often are interested in the $\mathcal{E}$-weighted-manipulation problem in which voters, both in V and S, have weights. (In this version of the problem, the set S is usually represented simply as a list of weights of the manipulators.)

The bribery problem for election system $\mathcal{E}$ is defined similarly, except that in bribery the set of voters who can change their preference lists is not part of the input. Intuition might say that bribery thus is more difficult than manipulation, but in fact that is not necessarily the case. We will see (and [17] has a full treatment) that some bribery problems are NP-complete yet their manipulation analogs are in P, some bribery problems are in P yet their manipulation analogs are NP-complete, and sometimes both problems are equally complex.

Name: $\mathcal{E}$-bribery.

Given: A set C of candidates, a set V of voters, a distinguished candidate $c \in C$, and a nonnegative integer k.

Question: Is it possible to change the preference lists of at most k voters such that, under election system $\mathcal{E}$, c is a winner of election (C, V)?

Bribery also has its weighted version, $\mathcal{E}$-weighted-bribery. In addition, bribery can come in a few other natural flavors. In particular, in $\mathcal{E}$-$bribery we associate each voter with a price tag and interpret the integer k as a budget, and we ask whether it is possible to make c a winner by changing the preference lists of voters whose total price does not exceed k. If the voters have both price tags and weights then we call the problem $\mathcal{E}$-weighted-$bribery. Sometimes we also put special restrictions on how to represent weights or prices, and will indicate such restrictions by subscripts.

Throughout this section we will be interested only in manipulation and bribery problems that ask about making the distinguished candidate a winner (as opposed to a unique winner—though we mention in passing that, very often, analogous results hold for both cases, see [17]).

In the remainder of this section we present the flavor of some recently obtained results on manipulation and bribery. We point out that in this section we discuss manipulation and bribery together as if they had been developed at the same time, but this is not really the case. The complexity of manipulation has long been studied, but the study of the complexity of bribery in elections started very recently. Nonetheless, the relationships between these two families of problems are very interesting and natural, and we feel that it is more instructive to present these results together.

One approach to the study of manipulation and bribery would be to study these questions one election system at a time. Let us for a moment do that—by focusing on one of the best-known and most popular election systems, plurality-rule elections—though we will soon seek to wrap many of these results about plurality-rule elections into a broader framework that allows insights into hardness to span many systems. Recall from Sect. 2 that a plurality-rule election with m candidates is described by the scoring vector $(1, \overbrace{0, \ldots, 0}^{m-1})$, so only the top candidate in each preference list matters.[3] First note that, not surprisingly, plurality-rule elections are easy to manipulate.

THEOREM 4.1 [2]. Plurality-manipulation *and* plurality-weighted-manipulation *are in* P.

To prove this theorem, it is enough to observe that if the manipulators want c to become a winner then they should vote for c. ([2] discusses only the unweighted manipulation problem, but clearly weights do not change anything here.)

Now that we know the complexity of manipulating plurality-rule elections, it is natural to ask about the complexity of bribery within such elections. Does the fact that in bribery one has to find some group of voters whose votes are to be changed make the problem more difficult? The answer is no.

THEOREM 4.2 [17]. Plurality-bribery *is in* P.

A greedy algorithm works for plurality-bribery. If we want to make c a winner by bribing at most k voters, we first test whether c is a winner already. If so, we are done. Otherwise, if $k > 0$ then we pick one of the current winners, bribe one of his or her voters to vote for c, decrease k by one (if k becomes negative, this means that we used too many bribes and so c cannot be made a winner), and loop back to testing whether c is a winner already.

This algorithm is very simple and natural. Unfortunately, it does not work for the weighted case or for the case of priced voters. In the weighted case it is not always clear whether one should first bribe the heaviest voter of some current winner or just the globally heaviest voter who does not yet vote for c. In the latter case we get the greatest additional vote weight for c, but in the former

---

[3] There is one issue that one should be aware of when discussing families of scoring protocols such as plurality, veto, or Borda count. Formally, each scoring protocol regards only a fixed, constant number of candidates. When we refer to names such as plurality, veto, and Borda count we typically have in mind the whole family of protocols that involves one incarnation of a particular scoring protocol for each candidate set multiplicity. Thus when we discuss the complexity of plurality-rule elections here, we actually give polynomial-time algorithms that are polynomial both in the number of voters and candidates.

In contrast, when we are discussing scoring protocols in general, we as is standard consider a particular scoring vector and thus a fixed number of candidates. This makes NP-completeness results stronger and polynomial-time membership results weaker. However, we note in passing that Hemaspaandra and Hemaspaandra [22, Sect. 3] provide a formalism and a dichotomy (i.e., complete classification) result for manipulation under uniform *families* of scoring protocols.

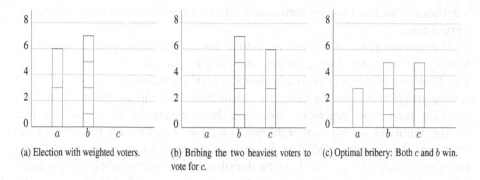

(a) Election with weighted voters.

(b) Bribing the two heaviest voters to vote for c.

(c) Optimal bribery: Both c and b win.

Figure 14.2. Plurality-rule elections where bribing the heaviest voters does not lead to optimal bribery

case we gain some vote weight for c while simultaneously potentially decreasing the total vote weight that c needs to become a winner. (We say "potentially decrease" since if there are multiple winners then the total vote weight c needs to win won't change. But if we keep on bribing the voters of current winners, this decrease will occur eventually.) Let us consider the following example (see Fig. 14.2). We have candidates a, b, and c and six voters with weights 1, 2, 2, 2, 3, and 3. Both voters with weight 3 have a as their top candidate, and all the others have b as their top candidate. Thus a receives a total vote weight of 6, b receives a total vote weight of 7, and c receives no votes. If we bribe the two heaviest voters—the two weight-3 voters preferring a—then c still loses to b. However, if we bribe one weight-3 voter preferring a and one weight-2 voter preferring b then c wins. Examples where bribing the heaviest voters leads to an optimal bribery also exist. This hints that plurality-weighted-bribery may require more than a simple greedy algorithm. Nonetheless, Faliszewski, Hemaspaandra, and Hemaspaandra [17] obtained polynomial-time algorithms for plurality-weighted-bribery and plurality-$bribery.

THEOREM 4.3 [17]. Plurality-weighted-bribery *and* plurality-$bribery *are in* P.

Does this mean that bribery for plurality-rule elections is always in P? Again the answer is no. If voters are weighted and have price tags then the problem is NP-complete.

THEOREM 4.4 [17]. Plurality-weighted-$bribery *is* NP-*complete.*

This theorem follows by a fairly simple reduction from the partition problem, which is the problem that asks, given a multiset of k nonnegative integers, whether the multiset can be partitioned into two multisets that each sum to the same value.

Theorems 4.1, 4.2, 4.3, and 4.4 capture the complexity of manipulation and bribery for plurality-rule elections, showing in particular how the complexity of bribery problems eventually jumps to NP-completeness as we make the setting more and more challenging. However, one can pinpoint the jump's location even more precisely. We have been assuming as our default that all the numbers within our problems (i.e., the weights and the prices) are represented in binary. What if we represent these numbers in unary? Let plurality-weighted$_{unary}$-\$bribery be the plurality-weighted-\$bribery problem with weights represented in unary and let plurality-weighted-\$bribery$_{unary}$ be the plurality-weighted-\$bribery problem with prices encoded in unary. Using a dynamic-programming approach, [17] showed that these problems are in P. What this shows is that the plurality-weighted-\$bribery's NP-completeness hangs by the slenderest of threads: Informally put, if either the weights or prices are represented by fairly small numbers, the problem slips into P.

THEOREM 4.5 [17]. *Plurality-weighted-\$bribery$_{unary}$ and plurality-weighted$_{unary}$-\$bribery are in P.*

The above results on manipulation and bribery for plurality-rule elections capture the complexity of these problems in many important settings. However, as mentioned in the introduction, a far more satisfying goal is to find some simple rule that determines for which election systems bribery and manipulation problems are easy and for which election systems they are hard. Such general results, which we are going to present now as Theorems 4.7 and 4.10 and Corollary 4.9, are known as dichotomy results.

Conitzer and Sandholm [6] observed that, for an election system $\mathcal{E}$ for which the winner problem is in P, if the voters are unweighted and there are a fixed number of candidates then $\mathcal{E}$-manipulation is in P. This result holds because a manipulator can easily evaluate all possible manipulations. The result yields the following corollary (which, though not explicitly stated in [6], should naturally be attributed to that paper). For a scoring vector α, let α-manipulation (respectively, α-weighted-manipulation) denote the (weighted) manipulation problem and let α-bribery (respectively, α-weighted-bribery and α-weighted-\$bribery) denote the (weighted and weighted-plus-priced) bribery problem with respect to the scoring protocol that uses α.

COROLLARY 4.6 [6]. *For each scoring vector α, α-manipulation is in P.*

Can we obtain a sharp, easy-to-use classification result with respect to manipulation for scoring protocols with weighted voters? Conitzer, Lang, and Sandholm [6, 7] took some first steps in this direction. In particular, they observed that for each $m \geq 3$, $(\overbrace{1,\ldots,1}^{m-1},0)$-weighted-manipulation (this is m-candidate veto) and $(m-1, m-2, \ldots, 1, 0)$-weighted-manipulation (this is m-candidate Borda count) are NP-complete. (Note that for two candidates both the Borda count and veto are equivalent to plurality-rule elections, since they all have the same scoring vector, $(1,0)$.) Although certainly interesting, these results don't reach the goal of classifying the complexity of weighted manipulation for all scoring protocols. The problem of full classification was recently solved by Hemaspaandra and Hemaspaandra [22], who obtained the following dichotomy theorem for scoring protocols with respect to α-weighted-manipulation. (The 3-candidate case—and some other cases—of the Hemaspaandra–Hemaspaandra manipulation dichotomy work has been independently obtained by Procaccia and Rosenschein [33]. The 3-candidate special case has also been independently obtained in an unpublished manuscript of Conitzer, Sandholm, and Lang [8].)

THEOREM 4.7 [22]. *Let* $\alpha = (\alpha_1, \ldots, \alpha_m)$ *be a scoring vector. If* $\alpha_2 = \cdots = \alpha_m$ *then* α-weighted-manipulation *is in* P. *In all other cases, this problem is* NP-*complete.*

This result clarifies a few things. In particular, it shows that plurality-rule elections are in fact quite special among scoring protocols, and it shows why scoring protocols tend to jump to NP-completeness at 3 candidates (in particular, the results on veto and Borda count mentioned in the previous paragraph are special cases of Theorem 4.7). Due to space limitations, we omit the proof of Theorem 4.7, which proceeds by a reduction from the partition problem.

Theorem 4.7 is a crisp, natural example of how one can obtain complete characterization results (admittedly, with respect to scoring protocols) regarding the computational complexity of manipulation. It would be great to be able to translate this result from the context of manipulation to that of bribery, in the hope of getting a complete characterization result for bribery. A natural first step would be an attempt to prove, for example, that all bribery problems for each given election system are at least as hard as the respective manipulation problems. Unfortunately, if we want to capture all possible election systems then such a result is impossible. For example, for approval voting the manipulation problem is in P (all manipulators simply approve of just the candidate they are seeking to make win, and no one else), but bribery for approval voting is NP-complete [17]. On the other hand, [17] also constructs an (artificial) election system in which the opposite happens: The bribery problem is in P and the manipulation problem is NP-complete. However, if we stay in the realm of scoring protocols then some extremely useful translations from manipulation to bribery are possible.

394

First, one can observe that if voters have price tags then bribery is just a generalized manipulation. (As an easy exercise, the reader is encouraged to show that this holds.) The following theorem is a slightly weakened version of a result from [17].

THEOREM 4.8 [17]. *For each scoring vector α, α-weighted-manipulation is $\leq_m^p$-reducible to α-weighted-\$bribery.*

Taking Theorems 4.7 and 4.8 together and by inspecting the reduction that underlies the proof of Theorem 4.4, we can obtain the following corollary.

COROLLARY 4.9 [17]. *Let $\alpha = (\alpha_1, \ldots, \alpha_m)$ be a scoring vector. If $\alpha_1 = \cdots = \alpha_m$ then α-weighted-\$bribery is in P. In all other cases, this problem is NP-complete.*

Theorem 4.8 is not entirely satisfactory. Although it translates results on manipulation problems to results on bribery problems, this translation comes at the cost of introducing price tags for voters. In fact, a much stronger translation can be obtained. In particular, using the proof of Theorem 4.7, with much work and problem-reduction trickery, the following dichotomy theorem for weighted bribery with respect to scoring protocols can be shown.

THEOREM 4.10 [17]. *Let $\alpha = (\alpha_1, \ldots, \alpha_m)$ be a scoring vector. If $\alpha_2 = \cdots = \alpha_m$ then α-weighted-bribery is in P. In all other cases, this problem is NP-complete.*

Note that this theorem essentially replaces the word "manipulation" in Theorem 4.7 with the word "bribery." However, achieving this replacement is far from trivial. The proof follows by first observing that the reduction used in [22] can be tweaked to, instead of mapping from the partition problem, map from a restricted version of the partition problem that in effect causes the reduction to produce instances of manipulation problems with certain very special properties. These properties ensure that instances of these manipulation problems can, almost verbatim, be interpreted as instances of the analogous bribery problems.

The above discussion presents results that interrelate bribery and manipulation, and we have seen that doing so helps us obtain broad dichotomy results for bribery. We conclude by mentioning some open problems regarding bribery and manipulation.

One open direction is to seek dichotomy results whose range of applicability is broader than the class of scoring protocols. As mentioned earlier, [22, Sect. 3] already handles uniform *families* of scoring protocols. However, one may hope for even more broadly applicable results. A second open direction is to consider approximation algorithms. This makes sense, for example in the case of bribing priced voters. We would certainly like to know what the cheapest way is of making our preferred candidate a winner by bribery, but we would also be quite satisfied with a cost that—though not the best—is close to optimal. Are there approximation algorithms for plurality-weighted-$bribery or α-weighted-$bribery, where α is some scoring vector? If there are such approximation algorithms for these problems then perhaps there even are polynomial-time approximation schemes. Ideally, we would like to obtain a dichotomy result that crisply classifies each scoring protocol as having or not having a polynomial-time approximation scheme. We hope this section will serve as an invitation to the reader to tackle these open problems.

5. Complexity of Control: Making Someone Win or Keeping Someone From Winning

The previous section covered manipulation and bribery. Although manipulation and bribery are somewhat different issues, they both have the property that only the voted preferences are changed. The structural properties of the election are not changed.

In real life, however, many attempts to influence elections work by seeking to change the structural properties of elections. By structural changes, we refer to such actions as adding candidates, deleting candidates, adding voters, deleting voters, partitioning candidates, and partitioning voters. The term *control* is used to describe issues related to influencing an election's outcome by changing its structure.

We mention in passing that many real-world attempts to influence elections are attempts to simultaneously influence the structure of an election and influence the way voters vote. For example, when an advertisement for candidate c appears on television, it may be simultaneously trying to get voters who most favor d to switch to c, and to get people who already most prefer c but weren't planning on voting to make the effort to go and vote. However, research papers on complexity typically study manipulation and control issues separately. The study of bribery is somewhat of an exception, as bribery, though akin to manipulation, is an atypically flexible form of manipulation, due to the manipulated voters not being fixed as part of the problem input. For this reason, to many people (including the authors) bribery feels somewhat control-like in addition to being very manipulation-like.

For reasons of space, this section will cover control, but with very little stress on formality or even on stating results individually, and instead will simply present an informal discussion about control. We will particularly try to point out what the real-life inspirations are for each type of control. We should warn the reader that in doing so we are taking liberties. For example, we will use as examples some recent American presidential elections. However, in reality, American presidential elections operate under a subtle and obscure system (deeply related, in fact, to partitioning of voters) known as the Electoral College, rather than by direct election by plurality rule. In our informal examples, we will often willfully ignore this and speak as if a presidential election were simply a big plurality-rule election.

We will often discuss both the constructive case—seeking to make a preferred candidate (uniquely) win—and the destructive case—keeping a despised candidate from being a (unique) winner. The complexity of constructive control was first studied in a seminal paper of Bartholdi, Tovey, and Trick [4]. The study of destructive control was initiated much more recently, namely, in work of Hemaspaandra, Hemaspaandra, and Rothe [25]. We mentioned in the introduction that in some subareas of electoral research the focus is on winning and in some the focus is on being the unique winner. For the study of control—in both the constructive and destructive cases—the focus has always been on the case of making a candidate be, or not be, a *unique* winner. Thus, throughout this section, when speaking of our problems or referring to results, when we say (and for brevity and grace we will always just say) winner/wins/winning/etc., we *always* implicitly mean unique winner/uniquely wins/uniquely winning/etc. (the only exception regards the paragraph below on tie-handling rules for subelections, since that directly addresses what happens in subelections when there are tied winners). It is very important to keep this shorthand in mind, since in this section when we say things such as "you can tell whether a despised candidate can be precluded from winning," we always mean "you can tell whether a despised candidate can be precluded from being the unique winner (namely, by either not being a winner at all or by being part of a group of two or more winners)."

Let us start with the issue of *control by adding candidates*. Formally viewed as a set (as all these problems are when seeking rigorous results), this becomes, with respect to some election system $\mathcal{E}$, the sets $\mathcal{E}$-constructive-control-by-adding-candidates and $\mathcal{E}$-destructive-control-by-adding-candidates. The former is defined as follows.

Name: $\mathcal{E}$-constructive-control-by-adding-candidates.

Given: A set C of original candidates, a pool D of potential additional candidates, a distinguished candidate $c \in C$, and a set V of voters with preferences over $C \cup D$.

Question: Is there a set $D' \subseteq D$ such that, under election system $\mathcal{E}$, $c \in C$ is a winner of the election having candidates $C \cup D'$ with the voters being V with the preferences of V restricted to $C \cup D'$?

That is, can we add some of the additional candidates and by doing so make c a winner? As a real-life motivating example, regarding the 2000 American presidential election, if one wanted George W. Bush to win (and Ralph Nader was not at that time running) one might have chosen to add the candidate Ralph Nader if one believed that would split voters away from Al Gore and achieve one's desired outcome. $\mathcal{E}$-destructive-control-by-adding-candidates is defined with the identical "Given" field, but its question regards, naturally, not trying to make a preferred candidate win but rather making a despised candidate not win:

Name: $\mathcal{E}$-destructive-control-by-adding-candidates.

Given: A set C of original candidates, a pool D of potential additional candidates, a distinguished candidate $c \in C$, and a set V of voters with preferences over $C \cup D$.

Question: Is there a set $D' \subseteq D$ such that, under election system $\mathcal{E}$, $c \in C$ is not a winner of the election having candidates $C \cup D'$ with the voters being V with the preferences of V restricted to $C \cup D'$?

The same real-life motivating example works here, except shifted to the case of focusing on an organization who despised Gore and wanted simply to see him not win.

From here on, we often won't formally describe the problems as sets, but will leave the descriptions very informal (even though in our results table we will refer to the formal sets). Interested readers can find the detailed, formal descriptions in [4, 25]. We will also, until the results table, stop mentioning $\mathcal{E}$ explicitly.

Just as one can study control by adding candidates, one can similarly study *control by deleting candidates*. The input is C, V, $c \in C$, and a natural number k, and in the constructive case one wants to know whether by deleting at most k candidates one can make c a winner, and in the destructive case one wants to know whether by deleting at most k candidates (with the deletion of c forbidden) one can ensure that c is not a winner. The same motivating example as above works here. For example, for the constructive case, in both the 2000 and 2004 American presidential elections, some people who wanted Al Gore or John Kerry to win sought to convince/urge/pressure Ralph Nader to withdraw from the race. (Regarding the destructive case, many people whose view was "Anyone but Bush" also naturally wanted Ralph Nader to withdraw.)

Turning to the problems of control by adding voters and control by deleting voters (typically treated as separate, though in the real world these issues interact), in *control by adding voters* (respectively, *control by deleting voters*), one asks whether by adding at most k from a pool of additional voters (respectively, by removing at most k of the initial voters) a given election will make *c* a winner (constructive case) or not a winner (destructive case). A real-world motivation here for considering the case of adding voters is so-called get-out-the-vote efforts. A political party, on the day of an election, might send vans to bring to the polls voters who the party believes favor its candidate but who might without the vans not make the effort to show up and vote. Or a political party might air ads designed to energize some part of its base and get them to decide to show up and vote (e.g., by putting an ad in CACM saying "That other party's candidate, Marty Meanie, if elected will put a tax on every line of code, with a surtax on comment lines. Only by voting can you help prevent that terrible future!"). One real-world motivation for having the case of deleting voters is less openly admitted by parties and groups today, but is widely viewed as occurring: vote suppression efforts. A party might run ads designed to sap the will to get-out-to-vote of the base of its key opponent. Or if one were a media outlet favoring Gore in 2000 and one went on the air and called Florida for Gore while voting was still going on in the more conservative Panhandle part of Florida, that might lead voters in that part of the state not to show up and cast their (more conservative) votes, since they would believe that the state was already a lost cause (here, we are taking into account the Electoral College structure of that election).

Control by voter addition/deletion is also, in a wider view of affairs, related to disenfranchisement—that is, it is related to the issue of which broad groups are, under law, allowed/not-allowed to vote and what hurdles (sometimes via requirements and sometimes via intimidation) are used to in effect prevent broad groups from voting. Using American history for examples, some cases—ranging in modern-day acceptance from the overwhelmingly accepted to the overwhelmingly deplored—of direct exclusions under law include the facts that (today and in the past) children are not allowed to vote, that (today and in the past) resident aliens are not allowed to vote in most elections, that (today and in the past) felons lose their federal vote for life, that (until 1961) citizens living in the US seat of government weren't represented in the Electoral College (and so didn't influence presidential elections), and that (in the past) women and slaves—and in many Southern states all African-Americans—were not allowed to vote. Some American historical cases of exclusion-in-effect via requirements include poll taxes and literacy tests.

For reasons of space, we won't go into detail in defining the various partition schemes, but we mention that partition attempts regarding both voters and candidates occur often in real life. In these schemes, we have more than one voting round, having to do with partitions of the candidates or the voters. We give only examples of the latter, as those are particularly natural. As a first such example, every time an American state legislature does a Congressional redistricting, it may be a type of prepackaged attempt to partition by voters: In a typical redistricting, the dominant party tries to make sure that in as many districts as possible it has enough supporters to hold the seat but not so many supporters as to waste their votes by winning that seat with too much support. (The side that doesn't control the legislature usually refers to such redistricting via the pejorative term "gerrymandering.") As another example of partition by voters, in some American states in elections for various state-wide officials— say, for their US senator—candidates are chosen by separate party primaries in which only members of each given party vote. Then only the winners of those primaries participate in the final election, in which all the registered voters can vote (to make this example work, let us assume that in this state there are no independent voters).

When dealing with partition schemes, one must have some rule as to what happens when there is a tie *in a subelection.* In the results table later, following [25] which first studied these tie-handling models in this context, we use TP ("ties promote") to indicate the rule that all people who tie as winners move forward from subelections, and we use TE ("ties eliminate") to indicate the rule that only unique winners of subelections move forward. Note that the tie-handling rules affect just the subelections, not the final election round of a given partition system (which as is conventional in the study of electoral control always focuses on unique winnership).

This concludes our presentation of the standard types of electoral control. With each existing for both the constructive case and the destructive case, the standard types of control are adding candidates, deleting candidates, adding voters, deleting voters, and, though we did not discuss them in any detail here, three types of partition schemes with each of those three occurring in both the TP and the TE models. So, in brief, there are ten standard types of constructive control, and each of those ten also has a destructive control analog. Each of these twenty control problems is (for each fixed election rule) simply a set. And that set is either computationally easy (meaning it is easy given an instance to decide whether the desired outcome can be achieved using that type of control) or that set is computationally hard (meaning it is hard—say, NP-hard—given an instance to decide whether the desired outcome can be achieved using that type of control).

Indeed, the study of the complexity of electoral control looks at these issues in almost exactly those terms, but with one twist. That twist regards the easy problems. In particular, there are two very different ways a problem might be easy. Consider an election system and a particular type of control for which the type of control at issue can *never* change someone from not being a winner to being a winner within that election system. In that case, the formal control problem (assuming the winner problem—recall that by that we in this section implicitly mean the unique winner problem—for that election system is in P) of course is in P, but for a very uninteresting reason. In that case, we say the problem is *immune* to constructive control: The given type of control can never

Control by	Plurality Construct.	Plurality Destruct.	Condorcet Construct.	Condorcet Destruct.	Approval Construct.	Approval Destruct.
Adding-candidates	*R*	**R**	*I*	**V**	**I**	**V**
Deleting-candidates	*R*	**R**	*V*	**I**	**V**	**I**
Partition-	*TE: R*	**TE: R**	*V*	**I**	**TE: V**	**TE: I**
of-candidates	*TP: R*	**TP: R**			**TP: I**	**TP: I**
Run-off-partition-	*TE: R*	**TE: R**	*V*	**I**	**TE: V**	**TE: I**
of-candidates	*TP: R*	**TP: R**			**TP: I**	**TP: I**
Adding-voters	*V*	**V**	*R*	**V**	**R**	**V**
Deleting-voters	*V*	**V**	*R*	**V**	**R**	**V**
Partition-	**TE: V**	**TE: V**	*R*	**V**	**TE: R**	**TE: V**
of-voters	**TP: R**	**TP: R**			**TP: R**	**TP: V**

Table 14.1. Results on constructive and destructive control. The problem's name is implicitly described by the table, e.g., the top right "V" refers to the case approval-destructive-control-by-adding-candidates. Results due to Bartholdi, Tovey, and Trick [4] are italicized. Results due to Hemaspaandra, Hemaspaandra, and Rothe [25] are in boldface. Key: I = immune, R = resistant, V = vulnerable, TE = ties-eliminate, TP = ties-promote

shift one's preferred candidate from not winning to winning. Immunity to destructive control is defined analogously: The given type of control can never shift one's despised candidate from winning to not winning. If a problem is not immune and is in P, then we say it is *vulnerable*. So when vulnerability holds for a type of control, then that type of control (since immunity does not hold) sometimes actually makes a profound difference, and in polynomial time we can tell whether a given instance is one where the desired constructive or destructive electoral outcome can be achieved. Although knowing that there exists *some way* to achieve the desired outcome is different from knowing some such way, it turns out that for every vulnerability result stated in our results table, Table 14.1, there is an algorithm that not just determines when control can be exerted, but that also gives the exact control actions to take in order to exert the desired control. Finally, if a control problem is not immune and is NP-hard, then we say it is *resistant* to control. Although immunity is the most desirable case (at least if one is not seeking to exert control, but rather is an election-system designer seeking to frustrate those wishing to influence outcomes via control), resistance is also a very desirable case—it means that the general problem of determining whether a given election instance can be controlled is computationally intractable (NP-hard). Although not all NP-hard problems are NP-complete, for every resistance result in our results table an NP upper bound is obvious, so each resistance result of the table in fact represents an NP-completeness claim. (We mention in passing that in the literature election systems that are not immune to a given type of control—that are either vulnerable or resistant to it—are said to be *susceptible* to that type of control.)

We said earlier that we would not stress results, but it certainly makes sense to see what is known. Table 14.1, which is taken from [25], summarizes results on constructive and destructive control. These results are due to Bartholdi, Tovey, and Trick [4] and Hemaspaandra, Hemaspaandra, and Rothe [25], and are about just the collection of election systems that those papers studied. Regarding open directions, we urge the reader to study the control problems of other election systems and to seek to find in a broader way what it is that makes some control problems computationally easy and some computationally hard.

From Table 14.1, some interesting observations are clear. There are settings immune to constructive control that are vulnerable to destructive control. Condorcet elections with respect to control by adding candidates is one such example. Perhaps somewhat more surprisingly, there also are settings immune to destructive control that are vulnerable to constructive control. Approval elections with respect to control by deleting candidates are one such example. Quite interestingly, there are settings vulnerable to destructive control yet resistant to constructive control. In these, you may not be able to efficiently tell whether your favorite candidate can be made to win, but you can efficiently tell whether a despised candidate can be precluded from winning. Condorcet elections with respect to control by adding voters is one such example. Also very interesting is that tie-handling rules can make a tremendous difference. For example, for plurality-rule elections with respect to control by partition of voters, vulnerability holds in the "ties eliminate" model but resistance holds in the "ties promote" model.

Finally, the most glaring observation is that for not one of the systems is it the case that resistance-or-immunity to control holds under all the twenty studied control attacks (ten constructive and ten destructive). Each system studied has good properties (immunity or resistance) under some attacks, but has bad properties (is vulnerable) under other attacks. In fact, at the time the table's work on control was completed (early 2005), no system was proven to be immune-or-resistant to all twenty types of control (or even to the ten constructive types, or to the ten destructive types). However, recently, work of Hemaspaandra, Hemaspaandra, and Rothe [26] has shown how to "hybridize" collections of elections in a way such that the hybrid election has a polynomial-time winner problem if all its constituent systems have polynomial-time winner problems, yet the hybrid system *is resistant to every one of the twenty types of control to which one or more of its constituent systems is resistant.* Simply put, the hybridization scheme combines strengths without adding weaknesses. From that work it now is known that there is an election system (admittedly, an artificial one, since it is built by hybridizing enough systems—some of which had to be constructed just for that purpose—to have, between them, all the right underlying resistances) that is resistant to all twenty standard types of electoral control yet has a polynomial-time winner problem.

6. Conclusions

This chapter has surveyed some recent progress in the complexity of elections, focusing primarily on providing an overview of some of the results obtained to date in an ongoing collaborative research project between Düsseldorf and Rochester. The authors firmly believe that the study of elections is a showcase area where interests come together spanning such CS specialties as theory, systems, and AI and such other fields as economics, business, operations research, and political science. And within the study of elections, the central importance of complexity/algorithmic issues has emerged more clearly with each passing year. Complexity offers a nonclassical yet powerful tool to frustrate those who seek to manipulate or control electoral outcomes. Nonetheless, much remains to be learned. In this chapter's sections, we have tried to point out in passing some of the questions that seem to us the most interesting and urgent. We commend these questions, and this entire area of study, to all readers and most especially to those younger readers seeking a research area that is fresh, promising, enjoyable, theoretically well-grounded, and well-connected to societal applications.

Acknowledgments

We thank S. S. Ravi and Sandeep Shukla for inviting us to contribute to this Festschrift, and we thank Dan Rosenkrantz for his tremendous contributions to the field and his sterling example to all.

Note Added in Proof

The final, accepted version of this chapter was sent in in the summer of 2006. Since then the intense research activity on the complexity of elections—activity that is in part described in this chapter—has continued, and the computational social choice community has if anything become even more vibrant and active. The 2006 COMSOC workshop mentioned in the future tense in this article has by now occurred, as has the 2008 COMSOC workshop, and both were great successes. This present, brief note (added while proofreading the page proofs) is not the right place to attempt to add new references or cover the most recent activity, but we do take this opportunity to mention briefly those cases we know of in which more recent, combined, or successor versions followed papers in the current references. In particular: from [6–8], a paper in *Journal of the ACM*, V. 54, 2007; from [22], a paper in *Journal of Computer and System Sciences*, V. 73, 2007; from [25], a paper in *Artificial Intelligence*, V. 171, 2007; from [28], a paper in *Journal of Heuristics* (to appear); from [33], a paper in *Journal of Artificial Intelligence Research*, V. 28, 2007; and from [34], a paper in *Journal of Artificial Intelligence Research*, V. 33, 2008.

References

[1] J. Bartholdi III and J. Orlin. Single transferable vote resists strategic voting. *Social Choice and Welfare*, 8(4):341–354, 1991.

[2] J. Bartholdi III, C. Tovey, and M. Trick. The computational difficulty of manipulating an election. *Social Choice and Welfare*, 6(3):227–241, 1989.

[3] J. Bartholdi III, C. Tovey, and M. Trick. Voting schemes for which it can be difficult to tell who won the election. *Social Choice and Welfare*, 6(2):157–165, 1989.

[4] J. Bartholdi III, C. Tovey, and M. Trick. How hard is it to control an election? *Mathematical and Computer Modeling*, 16(8/9):27–40, 1992.

[5] D. Black. *Theory of Committees and Elections*. Cambridge University Press, Cambridge, 1958.

[6] V. Conitzer and T. Sandholm. Complexity of manipulating elections with few candidates. In *Proceedings of the 18th National Conference on Artificial Intelligence*, pages 314–319. AAAI Press, Menlo Park, 2002.

[7] V. Conitzer, J. Lang, and T. Sandholm. How many candidates are needed to make elections hard to manipulate? In *Proceedings of the 9th Conference on Theoretical Aspects of Rationality and Knowledge*, pages 201–214. ACM Press, New York, 2003.

[8] V. Conitzer, T. Sandholm, and J. Lang. When are elections with few candidates hard to manipulate? Unpublished manuscript, January 2005.

[9] J.-A.-N. de Caritat, Marquis de Condorcet. Essai sur l'application de l'analyse à la probabilité des décisions rendues à la pluralité des voix, 1785. Facsimile reprint of original published in Paris, 1972, by the Imprimerie Royale.

[10] C. Dodgson. A method of taking votes on more than two issues, 1876. Pamphlet printed by the Clarendon Press, Oxford, and headed "not yet published".

[11] J. Duggan and T. Schwartz. Strategic manipulability without resoluteness or shared beliefs: Gibbard–Satterthwaite generalized. *Social Choice and Welfare*, 17(1):85–93, 2000.

[12] C. Dwork, S. Kumar, M. Naor, and D. Sivakumar. Rank aggregation methods for the web. In *Proceedings of the 10th International World Wide Web Conference*, pages 613–622. ACM Press, New York, 2001.

[13] E. Elkind and H. Lipmaa. Small coalitions cannot manipulate voting. In *Proceedings of the 9th International Conference on Financial Cryptography and Data Security*. Lecture Notes in Computer Science, volume 3570, pages 285–297. Springer, Berlin, 2005.

[14] E. Ephrati and J. Rosenschein. The Clarke tax as a consensus mechanism among automated agents. In *Proceedings of the 9th National Con-*

ference on Artificial Intelligence, pages 173–178. AAAI Press, Menlo Park, 1991.

[15] E. Ephrati and J. Rosenschein. Multi-agent planning as a dynamic search for social consensus. In *Proceedings of the 13th International Joint Conference on Artificial Intelligence*, pages 423–429. Morgan Kaufmann, San Mateo, 1993.

[16] R. Fagin, R. Kumar, and D. Sivakumar. Efficient similarity search and classification via rank aggregation. In *Proceedings of the 2003 ACM SIGMOD International Conference on Management of Data*, pages 301–312. ACM Press, New York, 2003.

[17] P. Faliszewski, E. Hemaspaandra, and L. Hemaspaandra. The complexity of bribery in elections. In *Proceedings of the 21st National Conference on Artificial Intelligence*, pages 641–646. AAAI Press, Menlo Park, 2006.

[18] P. Fishburn. Condorcet social choice functions. *SIAM Journal on Applied Mathematics*, 33(3):469–489, 1977.

[19] M. Garey and D. Johnson. *Computers and Intractability: A Guide to the Theory of NP-Completeness*. Freeman, New York, 1979.

[20] A. Gibbard. Manipulation of voting schemes. *Econometrica*, 41(4):587–601, 1973.

[21] L. Hemachandra. The strong exponential hierarchy collapses. *Journal of Computer and System Sciences*, 39(3):299–322, 1989.

[22] E. Hemaspaandra and L. Hemaspaandra. Dichotomy for voting systems. Technical Report TR-861, Department of Computer Science, University of Rochester, Rochester, NY, April 2005. Journal version to appear in *Journal of Computer and System Sciences*.

[23] E. Hemaspaandra, L. Hemaspaandra, and J. Rothe. Exact analysis of Dodgson elections: Lewis Carroll's 1876 voting system is complete for parallel access to NP. *Journal of the ACM*, 44(6):806–825, 1997.

[24] E. Hemaspaandra, L. Hemaspaandra, and J. Rothe. Raising NP lower bounds to parallel NP lower bounds. *SIGACT News*, 28(2):2–13, 1997.

[25] E. Hemaspaandra, L. Hemaspaandra, and J. Rothe. Anyone but him: The complexity of precluding an alternative. In *Proceedings of the 20th National Conference on Artificial Intelligence*, pages 95–101. AAAI Press, Menlo Park, 2005.

[26] E. Hemaspaandra, L. Hemaspaandra, and J. Rothe. Hybrid elections broaden complexity-theoretic resistance to control. Technical Report TR-900, Department of Computer Science, University of Rochester, Rochester, NY, June 2006. Revised, August 2006. Conference version to appear in *Proceedings of the 20th International Joint Conference on Artificial Intelligence (IJCAI 2007)*.

[27] E. Hemaspaandra, H. Spakowski, and J. Vogel. The complexity of Kemeny elections. *Theoretical Computer Science*, 349(3):382–391, 2005.

[28] C. Homan and L. Hemaspaandra. Guarantees for the success frequency of an algorithm for finding Dodgson-election winners. In *Proceedings of the 31st International Symposium on Mathematical Foundations of Computer Science*. Lecture Notes in Computer Science, volume 4162, pages 528–539. Springer, Berlin, 2006.

[29] J. Kemeny. Mathematics without numbers. *Dædalus*, 88:571–591, 1959.

[30] J. Kemeny and L. Snell. *Mathematical Models in the Social Sciences*. Ginn, Needham Heights, 1960.

[31] C. Papadimitriou and S. Zachos. Two remarks on the power of counting. In *Proceedings 6th GI Conference on Theoretical Computer Science*. Lecture Notes in Computer Science, volume 145, pages 269–276. Springer, Berlin, 1983.

[32] D. Pennock, E. Horvitz, and C. Giles. Social choice theory and recommender systems: Analysis of the axiomatic foundations of collaborative filtering. In *Proceedings of the 17th National Conference on Artificial Intelligence*, pages 729–734. AAAI Press, Menlo Park, 2000.

[33] A. Procaccia and J. Rosenschein. Junta distributions and the average-case complexity of manipulating elections. In *Proceedings of the 5th International Joint Conference on Autonomous Agents and Multiagent Systems*, pages 497–504. ACM Press, New York, 2006.

[34] A. Procaccia, J. Rosenschein, and A. Zohar. Multi-winner elections: Complexity of manipulation, control, and winner-determination. In *Preproceedings of the Eighth Trading Agent Design and Analysis & Agent Mediated Electronic Commerce Joint International Workshop (TADA/AMEC 2006)*, pages 15–28, 2006.

[35] T. Riege and J. Rothe. Completeness in the boolean hierarchy: Exact-four-colorability, minimal graph uncolorability, and exact domatic number problems—a survey. *Journal of Universal Computer Science*, 12(5):551–578, 2006.

[36] J. Rothe, H. Spakowski, and J. Vogel. Exact complexity of the winner problem for Young elections. *Theory of Computing Systems*, 36(4):375–386, 2003.

[37] M. Satterthwaite. Strategy-proofness and Arrow's conditions: Existence and correspondence theorems for voting procedures and social welfare functions. *Journal of Economic Theory*, 10(2):187–217, 1975.

[38] H. Simon. *The Sciences of the Artificial*. MIT Press, Cambridge, 1969. 3rd edition, 1996.

[39] A. Taylor. *Social Choice and the Mathematics of Manipulation*. Cambridge University Press, Cambridge, 2005.

406

[40] K. Wagner. More complicated questions about maxima and minima, and some closures of NP. *Theoretical Computer Science*, 51(1–2):53–80, 1987.

[41] K. Wagner. Bounded query classes. *SIAM Journal on Computing*, 19(5):833–846, 1990.

[42] H. Young. Extending Condorcet's rule. *Journal of Economic Theory*, 16(2):335–353, 1977.

Chapter 15

FULLY DYNAMIC BIN PACKING

ZORAN IVKOVIĆ
Department of Finance, Michigan State University, East Lansing, MI, 48824, USA.
Email: ivkovich@bus.msu.edu

ERROL L. LLOYD
Department of Computer and Information Sciences, University of Delaware, Newark,
DE 19716, USA. Email: elloyd@udel.edu

Abstract   Classic **bin packing** seeks to pack a given set of **items** of possibly varying sizes
into a minimum number of identical sized bins. A number of approximation
algorithms have been proposed for this **NP**-hard problem for both the on-line
and off-line cases. In this chapter we discuss **fully dynamic bin packing**, where
items may arrive (*Insert*) and depart (*Delete*) dynamically. In accordance with
standard practice for fully dynamic algorithms, it is assumed that the packing
may be arbitrarily rearranged to accommodate arriving and departing items. The
goal is to maintain an approximately optimal solution of provably high quality in a total amount of time comparable to that used by an off-line algorithm
delivering a solution of the same quality.

This chapter focuses on three results relative to fully dynamic bin packing.
The first shows that imposing a fixed constant upper bound on the number of
items that can be moved between bins per *Insert/Delete* operation forces the
competitive ratio to be at least $4/3$, regardless of the running time allowed per
Insert/Delete. The second is a **fully dynamic** approximation algorithm for bin
packing that is $\frac{5}{4}$-competitive and that requires $\Theta(\log n)$ time per *Insert/Delete*
of an item. This competitive ratio of $\frac{5}{4}$ is nearly as good as that of the best
practical off-line algorithms. A critical component of this algorithm is that very
small items will be *bundled* together and moved as a single unit. Finally, we
show for *partially dynamic bin packing* (*Inserts* only) and any $\epsilon > 0$, there is an
algorithm with competitive ratio $1 + \epsilon$ that runs amortized polylogarithmic time.

Keywords: bin packing, fully dynamic, approximation algorithm

S.S. Ravi, S.K. Shukla (eds.), *Fundamental Problems in Computing*,
© Springer Science + Business Media B.V. 2009

1. Introduction

In (off-line) bin packing, a list $L = (a_1, a_2, \ldots, a_n)$ of items of size $size(a_i)$ in the interval $(0, 1]$ is given. The goal is to find the minimum k such that all of the items a_i can be packed into k unit-size bins.

Bin packing was shown to be *NP*-complete in [20]. Since that time, bin packing has been a very active area of research in the algorithms and operations research communities (see [4]). Despite its advanced age, bin packing has retained its appeal (more than two decades ago, bin packing was labeled "The Problem That Wouldn't Go Away" [4]) by being a fertile ground for the study of *approximation algorithms*. In the context of bin packing, such algorithms aim to produce a packing that is provably close to the optimal in terms of the number of bins that are utilized.

In this chapter, we study a variation of bin packing known as **fully dynamic** bin packing where:

- items may arrive to, and depart from, the packing dynamically. These are specified using the operations *Insert* and *Delete*.

- items may be moved from bin to bin as the packing is adjusted to accommodate arriving and departing items.

In general, *fully dynamic* algorithms are aimed at situations in which the problem instance is changing over time, and incorporate these incremental changes without any knowledge of the existence and nature of future changes. Related works on *on-line* and *dynamic* bin packing differ from fully dynamic bin packing in that either they do not allow an item to be moved from a bin (of course, this has a predictably bad effect on the achievable quality of the packing), or they restrict themselves to dynamic arrivals (i.e., *Inserts*) of items—there are no departures (i.e., *Deletes*).

This chapter is devoted to fully dynamic approximation algorithms for bin packing with the goal of being "competitive" with existing off-line algorithms. That is, the quality of the approximation produced by the fully dynamic approximation algorithm should be as good as that produced by the off-line algorithms. Further, the running time of the fully dynamic algorithm per *Insert/Delete* operation should be small.

1.1 Background—Off-Line and On-Line Bin Packing

In this section we provide a brief overview of relevant results for approximation algorithms for off-line and on-line bin packing. As noted earlier, the goal of an approximation algorithm is to produce a solution that is "close" to an optimal solution. Approximation algorithms are compared using bounds on the quality of a solution produced by the algorithm. Specifically, the quality of a solution produced by a bin packing algorithm A is its **competitive ratio** $R(A)$ defined as:

$$R(A) = \lim_{n \to \infty} \sup_{OPT(L)=n} \frac{A(L)}{OPT(L)},$$

where $A(L)$ and $OPT(L)$ denote, respectively, the number of bins used by A to pack list L, and some optimal packing of L. Here, we say that A is $R(A)$-**competitive**.

In the domain of off-line algorithms, the value of R has been successively improved [4, 25, 8, 17]. Indeed, it has been shown that there is a *polynomial time approximation scheme* (*PTAS* [10]). Specifically, for any value of $R > 1$, there is an $\mathcal{O}(n \log n)$ time algorithm with a competitive ratio of R [19]. Unfortunately, the running times for these algorithms involve exceedingly large constants (actually, these "constants" depend on how close R is to 1). Among algorithms of practical importance, the best result is an $\mathcal{O}(n \log n)$ algorithm for which R is $\frac{71}{60}$ [17].

With respect to *on-line bin packing*, the problem has been defined strictly in terms of arrivals (*Inserts*)—items never depart from the packing (i.e., there are no *Deletes*). Further, most on-line algorithms have operated under the restriction that each item must be packed into some bin, and it should remain in that bin permanently. In this context, it is known that for every on-line linear time algorithm A, $R(A) \geq 1.536\ldots$ [4]. Further, the upper bound has been improved over the years to roughly 1.6 [15, 16, 18, 21, 23].

The work in [9] focused on a variant of on-line bin packing, again supporting *Inserts* only, in which each item may be moved only a constant number of times from one bin to another. Two algorithms were provided: One with a linear running time (linear in n, the number of *Inserts*, which is also the number of items) and a competitive ratio of 1.5, and one with an $\mathcal{O}(n \log n)$ running time and a competitive ratio of $\frac{4}{3}$.

A related version of on-line bin packing is found in [6] where items may be moved to accommodate an arriving item, but with the limitation that the total size of the items that are moved in response to this arrival cannot exceed a specified constant (the *migration factor*) times the size of the arriving item. A robust APTAS (asymptotic polynomial time approximation scheme [7, 19]) for this problem is given in [6]. The use of a bounded migration factor was introduced by [24] in the context of machine scheduling.

Another notion that is related to, but distinct from, fully dynamic bin packing is *dynamic bin packing* of [3], where each item is associated not only with its size, but also with an arrival time and a departure time (interpreted in the natural way). Here items cannot be moved once they are assigned to some bin other than their permanent removal at their departure time. It was shown in

[3] that for any such algorithm A, $R(A) \geq 2.5$, and that for their Dynamic *FF* (First Fit), $2.770 \leq R(FF) \leq 2.898$.

1.2 The Performance of Fully Dynamic Approximation Algorithms

In this section we discuss the notions of competitiveness and running time in the context of developing fully dynamic approximation algorithms.

We begin by noting that with respect to the definition of *competitive ratio*, there is no need to make a distinction between fully dynamic and off-line algorithms. In each case, these measures reflect the size of the packings produced by the algorithm relative to the size of optimal packings.

With respect to running times, we say that a fully dynamic approximation algorithm B for bin packing has running time $O(f(n))$ if the time taken by B to process an *Insert/Delete* to an instance of n items is $O(f(n))$. If $O(f(n))$ is a *worst case* bound on the running time required by B to process an *Insert/Delete*, then B is $f(n)$-**uniform**. If $O(f(n))$ is an *amortized* bound on the running time required by B to process each *Insert/Delete*, while the worst case bound required by B is $\omega(f(n))$,[1] then B is $f(n)$-**amortized**. Throughout this chapter, we will abbreviate the above and instead refer to *uniform* and *amortized* algorithms, respectively.

The general goal in developing fully dynamic approximation algorithms for bin packing is to design algorithms with competitive ratios close to those of the best off-line algorithms such that the *Insert/Delete* operations are processed quickly. Of particular interest are algorithms that are, in a sense, the best possible relative to the existing off-line methods. For bin packing the best known off-line algorithms require time $\Theta(n \log n)$. Thus, a fully dynamic algorithm that runs in time $\Theta(\log n)$ per *Insert/Delete* is, in that sense, the best possible. Indeed, the fully dynamic algorithm *MMP* that we describe in section 3 runs in precisely this time per *Insert/Delete*.

In the process of handling a sequence of *Insert/Delete* operations, fully dynamic bin packing algorithms are not allowed to "postpone" handling the changes in the packing affected by those operations. Rather, those changes must be made immediately. Thus, fully dynamic bin packing algorithms are required to handle "lookup" queries in addition to the *Insert/Delete* operations. These lookup queries may be arbitrarily interspersed in the *Insert/Delete* sequence and may be either of the following:

- *size*—returns in $\mathcal{O}(1)$ time the number of bins in the current packing;

---

[1] ω-notation is defined as follows: $f(n) \in \omega(g(n))$ if and only if $g(n) \in o(f(n))$ [5].

- *packing*—returns a description of the packing in the form of a list of pairs $(x, \text{Bin}(x))$, where $\text{Bin}(x)$ denotes the bin into which an item x is packed. The running time is required to be linear in the number of items in the current instance.

1.3 The Main Results

In this chapter we describe the three most significant results on fully dynamic bin packing:

- A proof showing that if A is a fully dynamic algorithm for bin packing that moves no more than a fixed constant number of items (worst-case or amortized) per *Insert/Delete* operation, then the competitive ratio of A is at least $4/3$.

- A fully dynamic algorithm *MMP* that is $\frac{5}{4}$-competitive and requires $\Theta(\log n)$ time per *Insert/Delete* operation. This algorithm uses a notion of "bundling" in which a set of very small items can be moved in a single operation so as to avoid the lower bound of $4/3$ from the first result. Relative to the best off-line algorithms, *MMP* has a running time that is the best possible, and has a competitive ratio that is nearly the equal of the best practical off-line algorithms. This is a surprising result even in terms of off-line bin packing, because it is the first practical bin packing algorithm having a competitive ratio of less than $\frac{4}{3}$ that does not rely on packing the items in sorted order. That the algorithm is fully dynamic is all the more remarkable.

- A polynomial time approximation scheme (PTAS) for partially dynamic bin packing where each *Insert* is processed in amortized polylogarithmic time. Partially dynamic bin packing is identical to fully dynamic bin packing except that there are no *Deletes*.

The remainder of the chapter is organized as follows. In Sect. 2 we prove the results relating to moving no more than a constant number of items and the $4/3$ lower bound on the competitive ratio. In Sect. 3 we outline the main ideas behind the *MMP* algorithm. In Sect. 4 we describe the PTAS for partially dynamic bin packing. Finally, in Sect. 5 there are some concluding remarks.

2. Moving a Constant Number of Items Per Operation

A natural approach to developing a fully dynamic bin packing algorithm that runs in a small amount of time per *Insert/Delete* operation is to limit the number of items that are moved from one bin to another in the processing of a single such operation. Particularly appealing is to move at most a constant number of items per *Insert/Delete*. However, in this section we show that imposing such a strong restriction limits the achievable competitive ratio. Specifically we prove the following from [12]:

THEOREM 2.1. *For any positive integer c, if A is a fully dynamic algorithm for bin packing that moves no more than c items (worst-case or amortized) per Insert/Delete operation, then the competitive ratio of A is at least* $4/3$.

Proof. Consider a constant c and an algorithm A meeting the conditions of the theorem. We establish that there are arbitrarily large lists L, and suitably chosen sequences of *Inserts* and *Deletes* of elements of L, for which A produces packings that utilize at least $4/3$ of the optimal number of bins.

We begin by defining *B-items* as items with size greater than $1/2$ and *B-bins* as bins containing a B-item.

Informally, a list that "defeats" A (that is, a list on which A will produce a packing of at least $4/3$ the optimal number of bins) is constructed as follows:

1. Pick an arbitrary (large) integer M,

2. Take M B-items of size $1/2 + \epsilon$ and construct M collections of additional items, where each collection contains a huge number (this number is a function of M, ϵ, and, of course, c) of exceedingly small items of size a, whose cumulative size is precisely $1/2 - \epsilon$,

3. Let L be a list containing all of the items mentioned in step (2) and assume that A packs L,

4. Observe the packing produced by A and suppose that A uses fewer than $4/3$ of the optimal number. Then, we delete all of the B-items from L and, consequently, from the packing. However, because prior to these deletions the B-bins contain a huge number of the items of size a and because A only moves at most a constant number of bins per *Insert/Delete*, it will be impossible for A to consolidate these items in fewer than $4/3$ the optimal number of bins for the resulting set of items.

A formal specification of the construction is given below. Note that the construction of L is aimed at defeating any algorithm A on the basis of A's inability to move more than c items across bins. Intuitively, A will fail not because it is too slow but because it is restricted in its movements, e.g., there is a fixed constant bound on the number of items that can be moved across bins within each *Insert/Delete* operation.

In the remainder of this section we provide a formal proof of the theorem. We begin by selecting an arbitrarily large positive integer M divisible by 6, and then select an arbitrarily small positive number ϵ such that $\epsilon < 1/M$. Finally, we let a be a (small) positive number subject to the following three restrictions:

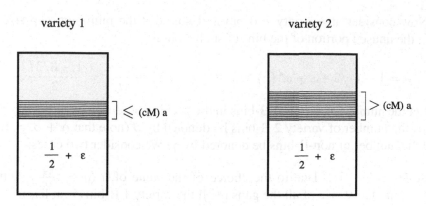

Figure 15.1. Two varieties of B-bins in the packing of L produced by A

1. $\frac{1/2-\epsilon}{a}$ is an integer

2. $a < \frac{\frac{3}{2M}-\epsilon}{cM}$

3. $a < \frac{\epsilon}{cM}$

Now consider the list

$$L = (\underbrace{1/2 + \epsilon, \ldots, 1/2 + \epsilon}_{M}, \underbrace{a, \ldots, a}_{M\frac{1/2-\epsilon}{a}}).$$

Clearly, because $\frac{1/2-\epsilon}{a}$ is an integer, an optimal packing of L requires precisely M bins, where each bin contains a B-item of size $1/2 + \epsilon$ and $\frac{1/2-\epsilon}{a}$ items of size a. Note that all of the M bins in an optimal packing contain items totaling precisely 1.

Now consider the packing produced by A applied to a sequence of *Insert* operations—one for each item in L. In that packing we distinguish between two varieties of B-bins: (1) bins that, in addition to a B-item, contain at most cM items of size a; and (2) bins that, in addition to a B-item, contain more than cM items of size a. We refer to these as variety 1 B-bins and variety 2 B-bins, respectively (Fig. 15.1).

Note that the value of M was chosen so that any sequence of M changes to the packing via *Inserts/Deletes* of items will not result in the removal of all of the items of size a from any of the bins of variety 2, both in the case that the accounting of the number of items that A moves per operation is uniform and in the amortized case.

Now consider any variety 1 B-bin and note that the minimum gap size g (i.e., the unused portion of the bin) of such a bin is:

$$g = 1 - (1/2 + \epsilon + cMa) > 1/2 - \epsilon - cM\frac{\frac{3}{2M} - \epsilon}{cM} = \frac{1 - 3/M}{2}.$$

Let the number of variety 1 B-bins in the packing produced by A be denoted by α, the number of variety 2 B-bins be denoted by β (note that $\alpha + \beta = M$), and the number of non-B-bins be denoted by γ. We consider two cases.

Case 1: $\alpha \geq \frac{2}{3}M$. Due to the choice of the value of a ($a < \frac{\frac{3}{2M} - \epsilon}{cM}$), the cumulative size of all the gaps in all the variety 1 B-bins is at least:

$$\alpha g > \frac{2}{3}M\frac{1 - 3/M}{2} = M/3 - 1.$$

Thus, even under the assumption that all of the variety 2 B-bins in the packing are full, there are still at least $M/3$ non-B-bins in the packing, i.e., $\gamma \geq M/3$.

Case 2: $\alpha < \frac{2}{3}M$. We know that $\beta > M/3$. Note that the cumulative size of all the non-B-items packed into a bin of variety 2 is at most $1/2 - \epsilon$.

Beginning with the packing produced by A when applied to the sequence of *Insert* operations corresponding to the items in L, the algorithm A now processes a sequence of M *Delete* operations that delete all of the B-items from the packing.

In considering the packing that results from this sequence of M *Delete* operations, recall that none of the bins that were variety 2 B-bins before the deletions can be deleted from the packing because each such bin contained more than cM items of size a. In addition, by our choice of a ($a < \frac{\epsilon}{cM}$), all of these bins must have a level strictly less than $1/2$ at the conclusion of the deletion of all of the B-items.

Note also that after the M *Delete* operations, the cumulative size of all of the remaining items is now $M/2 - M\epsilon$ and the size of the optimal packing is now precisely $M/2$ (the latter is guaranteed by the fact that $\epsilon < 1/M$, i.e., $\epsilon M < 1$). Furthermore, the cumulative size of all the items in the β bins that were variety 2 B-bins (before the deletions) does not exceed $\beta/2$. Thus, A requires a certain number δ of additional bins to pack the entire set of items that remain after the deletions:

$$\delta \geq M/2 - M\epsilon - \beta/2 > M/2 - 1/2 \cdot M/3 - M\epsilon > M/3 - 1.$$

Thus, A requires at least $\frac{2}{3}M$ bins to pack the set of items that remain after the deletions, since $\beta + \delta > \frac{2}{3}M - 1$. Because an optimal packing of the items that remain after the deletions requires precisely $M/2$ bins, A must utilize at least $4/3$ of the number of bins utilized by an optimal packing. □

In light of Theorem 2.1, we address the need to move items between bins in response to *Inserts* and *Deletes*. The difficulties related to this issue are twofold. First, such moves need to be carried out in a manner that guarantees small competitive ratios. Second, all of these moves have to be carried out within low running times (i.e., $o(n)$ per *Insert* or *Delete*, because off-line algorithms that achieve any competitive ratio greater than 1 in $\mathcal{O}(n)$ running time are known [7]).

Intuitively, difficulties may arise while handling very small items: the attempt to move a large number of very small items from a bin, item by item, could result in a prohibitively large running time.

An important question is whether there are fully dynamic algorithms for bin packing that are allowed to move $\omega(1)$ items per *Insert/Delete* operation with a competitive ratio of less than $4/3$. That is, would removing the restriction on the number of items that may be moved per operation help? The algorithm *MMP* described in the next several sections answers this question in the affirmative. In *MMP*, the efficient manipulation of very small items is accomplished via **bundling**. The purpose of bundles is to allow the efficient movement of large numbers of very small items at one time: rather than moving these very small items from one bin to another individually, the algorithm moves an entire bundle of very small items.[2] Moving an entire bundle can be accomplished within the same running time as moving a single larger item. Thus, allowing/disallowing the moving of $\omega(1)$ items between bins per *Insert/Delete* operation has a crucial impact on the competitive ratio of fully dynamic approximation algorithms for bin packing.

3. A 5/4-Competitive Algorithm for Fully Dynamic Bin Packing

A natural approach to the development of fully dynamic bin packing algorithms is to adapt existing bin packing algorithms to work in the fully dynamic situation. Unfortunately, this is easier said than done. The difficulty is that most of the off-line algorithms perform bin packing in two distinct stages. First, there is a **preprocessing stage** in which the items are organized in some fashion (this reorganization should have a positive effect on the resulting packing). This is followed by a **packing stage** where the actual packing is accomplished. In the off-line situation this two stage approach is quite natural since the entire list of items is available at the outset. However, in a dynamic

---

[2] Note that this idea was used, albeit in different contexts, in [1] and [9].

environment a two stage process becomes awkward. Consider, for example, the algorithm First Fit Decreasing *(FFD)*, which is $\frac{11}{9}$-competitive. This algorithm first sorts the items and then packs them in order of decreasing size, using the First Fit packing rule.[3] What about a fully dynamic version of *FFD*? Of course, there is no difficulty in maintaining a sorted list of the elements. *But*, there is a great difficulty in maintaining the packing based on that sorted list, because the insertion or deletion of a single item can result in a large number of changes to that packing. It would seem that the packing induced by the sorted list of items is "too specific" to be maintained dynamically, and that perhaps a less specific rule might be of use. Indeed, in this section we utilize the weaker notion of *grouping* [15, 16] as a building block for a fully dynamic bin packing algorithm called *Mostly Myopic Packing (MMP)*. This algorithm will be $\frac{5}{4}$-competitive and will run in uniform time $O(\log n)$ per *Insert/Delete*.

The remainder of this section is organized as follows. The next subsection provides some basic definitions. Section 3.2 discusses the notions of *LLS-maximality* and *M-thoroughness* that play a critical role in *MMP*. In Sect. 3.3 we give a sketch of *MMP* including how the *Insert* and *Delete* operations are handled, along with some critical implementation details. The full description of *MMP* can be found in [14]. Short discussions regarding the competitive ratio and the running time of *MMP* are given in Sects. 3.4 and 3.5, respectively.

3.1 Some Definitions

In this subsection we provide a number of definitions related to items, bins and the contents of bins, that we will use in describing *MMP*. In that context, at any given point in the running of *MMP* we let L be the list of items currently in the packing, with the items ordered in the list from left to right in the order in which they were inserted.

We begin with some simple definitions related to a bin. In particular, for a bin B: $level(B)$ is the sum of the sizes of the items packed in B, $gap(B)$ is $1 - level(B)$ (i.e., the amount of empty space in B), and $content(B)$ is the set of items packed in B. We can assume that the bins are numbered in such a way that every bin has a unique number with the property that, for any two bins, the bin with the lower number is placed "to the left" of the bin with the higher number. In other words, the bins are numbered in increasing order from left to right.

Following Johnson's *grouping* [15, 16], we classify items according to their respective sizes. In particular, an item a is: a B-item (big) if $size(a) \in (\frac{1}{2}, 1]$, a L-item (large) if $size(a) \in (\frac{1}{3}, \frac{1}{2}]$, a S-item (small) if $size(a) \in (\frac{1}{4}, \frac{1}{3}]$, a

---

[3] Informally, bins are ordered from left to right and an item is packed into the leftmost bin into which it will fit.

T-item (tiny) if $size(a) \in (\frac{1}{5}, \frac{1}{4}]$, or a M-item (miniscule) if $size(a) \in (0, \frac{1}{5}]$. Let $\mathcal{B}$, $\mathcal{L}$, $\mathcal{S}$, $\mathcal{T}$, and $\mathcal{M}$ denote the number of B-items, L-items, S-items, T-items, and M-items in L respectively. When the meaning is otherwise clear, the fact that a is a B-item (L-item, S-item, T-item, M-item) will be abbreviated as $a \in$ B (L, S, T, M).

A bin is a B-bin (L-bin, S-bin, T-bin, M-bin) if its largest item is a B-item (L-item, S-item, T-item, M-item). There are several types of B-bins: bins containing one B-item and one L-item, and no other B-items, L-items, S-items, or T-items will be called bins of type BL; bins of type BST, BS, BTT, BT and B are defined analogously. Likewise, there are several types of L-bins, several types of S-bins, and several types of T-bins. The possible types of B-bins, L-bins, S-bins, and T-bins are illustrated in Fig. 15.2. Note that we did not take into consideration the M-items: while it is certainly the case that bins may contain M-items, accounting for them will have no substantive effect on the competitive ratio of *MMP*.

We next introduce a binary relation of **superiority** over types of bins. First, all of the types of B-bins, L-bins, S-bins, and T-bins are superior to M-bins. Second, we consider non-M-bins. Here the following ordering of relevant types of items is assumed: B $\prec$ L $\prec$ S $\prec$ T $\prec$ Z, where Z denotes a fictitious item of size 0. We imagine that each bin contains, on top of its B-items, L-items, S-items, and T-items (M-items may be present, but are being ignored), a fictitious item of type Z (zero), of size 0. Zero items are introduced solely for technical convenience, as their presence will enable us to impose the desired ordering on the types of bins. Thus, in view of the introduction of Z-items, the types of bins are BLZ, BSTZ, BSZ, ..., TTZ, and TZ. For these types of bins, the relation of superiority is defined as the lexicographical ordering over the types of bins. For example, a bin of type BLZ is superior to a bin of type BSTZ. In the remainder of this paper, we omit Z from the notation describing the types of bins.[4] Finally, we will sometimes find it convenient to refer to these types of bins according to their canonical index in this lexicographical ordering, as depicted in Fig. 15.2: a bin of type 1 is a bin of type BL, a bin of type 2 is a bin of type BST, ..., a bin of type 30 is a bin of type T. We assert naturally that if B_j is superior to B_i, then B_i is *inferior* to B_j.

The *allowed* types of bins in the packings produced by *MMP* are BL, BST, BS, BTT, BT, B, LLS, LLT, LL, SSST, SSS, and TTTT, and, of course, M-bins. This restriction may result in at most six unpacked items: one L-item, two S-items, and three T-items. Clearly, these items could be packed into at most two additional bins (a bin of type LTT, and a bin of type SST). *MMP* will utilize the *regular packing*, consisting at all times only of bins of the allowed types, and

---

[4] Although Z is omitted, it is needed to ensure that, e.g., BLZ is superior to BZ.

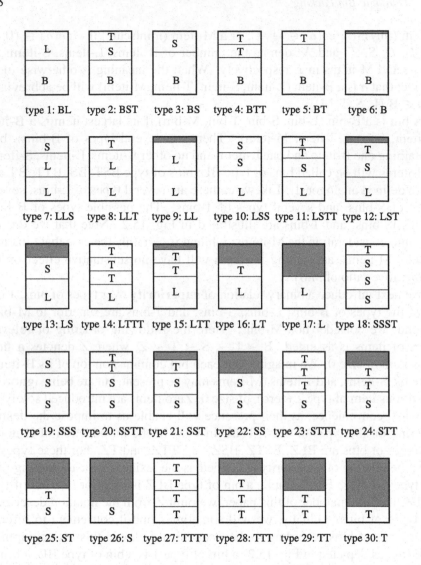

Figure 15.2. Possible types of bins in *MMP*

the *auxiliary storage*, containing the items that are not currently packed into a bin from the regular packing.

3.2   LLS-Maximality and M-Thoroughness

We next define three properties of packings that play a key role for the competitive ratio of *MMP*. We first define the *thoroughness property*. Then we define the *LLS-maximality property*, a property that is similar to, and (much) stronger than, the thoroughness property. Finally, we define the *M-thoroughness property*, aimed at the M-items and their role in the packing. Intuitively, maintaining the LLS-maximality property leads to the competitive ratio of $\frac{5}{4}$ for packings of lists of non-M-items; maintaining LLS-maximality *and* the M-thoroughness property leads to the competitive ratio of $\frac{5}{4}$ for packings of arbitrary lists.

3.2.1 Thoroughness.   We begin with two definitions:

DEFINITION 3.1. Let $\mathcal{P}_{\mathrm{B,L,S,T}}$ be a set of packings of B-items, L-items, S-items and T-items such that each packing $P \in \mathcal{P}_{\mathrm{B,L,S,T}}$ consists only of the allowed types of bins (BL, BST, BS, BTT, BT, B, LLS, LLT, LL, SSST, SSS, and TTTT), where all of the bins of type BL are to the left of all the non-BL-bins, all of the bins of type BST are to the left of all the non-BL-bins and non-BST-bins, etc.

DEFINITION 3.2. Let a packing $P \in \mathcal{P}_{\mathrm{B,L,S,T}}$. Then:

1. Bins of type BL are thorough in P iff there does not exist a B-item b and an L-item l such that $size(b) + size(l) \leq 1$, and the items b and l are either in bins of type inferior to BL in the packing P or in the auxiliary storage.

   The thoroughness of bins of types BS and BT are defined analogously.

2. Bins of type BST are thorough in P iff there does not exist a bin B of type BS in P, where b and s are the B-item and the S-item packed into B, and a T-item t such that $size(b) + size(s) + size(t) \leq 1$, and the item t is in a bin of type inferior to BST in the packing P or the auxiliary storage,

   The thoroughness of bins of types BTT, LLT and SSST are defined analogously.

3. Bins of type LLS are thorough in P iff there does not exist a bin B of type LLT or LL in P, where l_1 and l_2 are the L-items packed into B, and an S-item s such that $size(l_1) + size(l_2) + size(s) \leq 1$, and the item s is either in a bin of type inferior to LLS in the packing P or in the auxiliary storage,

Finally, a packing $P \in \mathcal{P}_{\mathrm{B,L,S,T}}$ is thorough iff all of the above types of bins are thorough in P.

3.2.2 LLS-Maximality.   *MMP* will take some pains to be guaranteed of packing a certain portion of certain L-items and S-items into bins of type LLS (we will call this endeavor "seeking *LLS-coalitions*"). Leading toward this guarantee, we define *LLS-maximality*. LLS-maximality strengthens thoroughness: maintenance of thoroughness does not require LLS-coalitions, and

the absence of coalitions leads to a competitive ratio of at least $\frac{4}{3}$ (see the lower bound example for *FFG* in [15]).

DEFINITION 3.3. Let a packing $P \in \mathcal{P}_{\text{B,L,S,T}}$. Then P is LLS-maximal iff P is thorough, and bins of type LLS are LLS-maximal in P. That is, there does not exist an L-item l_1, another L-item l_2, and an S-item s such that $size(l_1) + size(l_2) + size(s) \leq 1$, and the item l_1 is either in a bin of type inferior to LLS in the packing P or in the auxiliary storage, and the item l_2 is in a bin of type inferior to LLS in the packing P or in the auxiliary storage, and s is in a bin of type inferior to LLS in the packing P or in the auxiliary storage.

The key factor that distinguishes between thoroughness and LLS-maximality is that, unlike thoroughness, when considering whether or not it is possible to pack two L-items and an S-item from bins of type inferior to LLS or the auxiliary storage into a bin, LLS-maximality does *not* insist that the two L-items must come from the same bin. We note that it can be shown that the maintenance of thoroughness, but not LLS-maximality, leads to a simpler algorithm that also runs in uniform logarithmic time per *Insert/Delete* operation, and is $\frac{4}{3}$-competitive (see [11]). An example of a packing that is thorough, but does not have the LLS-maximality property is given in [14].

3.2.3 M-Thoroughness. M-thoroughness is the other key property required for *MMP*. It pertains to the role of M-items in the *MMP* packings. Ideally, we would like to be able to develop a method that would enable *MMP* to pack as many M-items into non-M-bins as possible. However, this is not necessary, as it turns out that maintaining M-thoroughness (a much weaker goal), coupled with LLS-maximality, is quite sufficient to guarantee a competitive ratio of $\frac{5}{4}$.

DEFINITION 3.4. A packing P is M-thorough iff precisely one of the following two conditions is satisfied:

1. There are no M-bins in P, or

2. There is at least one M-bin in P, and all of the non-M-bins have a level exceeding $\frac{4}{5}$ (i.e., a gap less than $\frac{1}{5}$), and all of the M-bins, except for possibly the rightmost bin in the packing, also have a level exceeding $\frac{4}{5}$.

3.3 *MMP Insert* and *Delete* operations—The Key Concepts

In this section we provide a sketch of *MMP* by outlining the *Insert* and *Delete* operations. We do not provide all of the details here and instead refer the reader to [14] for a full description of the algorithm.

In the following two subsections we consider how *MMP* will *Insert/Delete* an item. This is done using three major ideas: *myopic packing*, *bundles*, and *LLS-coalitions*. The latter two of these concepts have already been introduced, whereas the first will be explained in the paragraphs that follow. We begin by discussing how *MMP* packs non-M-items, and then follow with a description of how to pack M-items.

3.3.1 *Insert* and *Delete* of Non-M-Items.

We first consider how *MMP* *Inserts* an item $a \in B \cup L \cup S \cup T$. The key idea is the use of *myopic packing* to maintain thoroughness. This idea, based on Johnson's grouping [15, 16], is that when an item a is being packed, a should be insensitive to previously packed items of "smaller" types than the type of a. Informally, if we think of item a as packing itself into the existing packing, what would a "see" in the bins? Only the items of its own type or of "larger" type. In this sense, a K-item (K is B, L, S, or T) is *myopic* in that it can "see" relatively large items (K-items or larger), and cannot "see" relatively small ones (smaller than K-items).

Based on that view of the packing, a is packed in a First Fit fashion (in a's "K or larger" world). Suppose that B is the bin into which a is packed. Because the item a was packed into B without regard for how full B might already have been due to items of smaller type than a, it may be that B now contains items totaling more than 1. To avoid this situation, *MMP* does this following: When item a is packed into B, there is a forceful eviction from B of all items of smaller type than a. The evicted items will be temporarily "set aside" in the auxiliary storage, and will eventually be reinserted. Before that however, an attempt is made to restore the thoroughness of the packing by trying to pack additional items into B, starting from the available items of the largest type that is smaller than K. That is, the items of the largest type that is smaller than K from the auxiliary storage and from the bins that are inferior to the type of bin the algorithm is trying to reconstruct for B. This effort continues until there are no more available items of that type that can fit with the current bin content. Next, *MMP* continues with the available items (auxiliary storage or inferior bins) of the next largest type until there are no more available items of that type that would fit into the bin, and so on. Here, if an item is taken from some bin, that bin is deleted from the packing, and its contents, except for the item that was taken, are temporarily moved into the auxiliary storage. Upon completion of the filling of B, and the appropriate placement of B into the packing, *MMP* reinserts the items from the auxiliary storage into the packing. Their reinsertion, of course, may disturb some other bins, and move their contents to the auxiliary storage, for later reinsertion. Eventually, all of the items from the auxiliary storage (except perhaps at most one L-item, two S-items, and/or three T-items) are reinserted into the packing, and that packing is thorough.

In addition to thoroughness, *MMP* maintains LLS-maximality. This is done by using LLS-coalitions. To avoid the situation of a list that is thorough, but far from LLS-maximal, an amendment is made to the myopic discipline outlined above. Namely, the insertion of an L-item a is carried out as follows: first, packing a into a B-bin is attempted in a standard myopic fashion. If this attempt fails, then an attempt is made to form an *LLS-coalition* consisting of a, another L-item and an S-item. The latter two can each be sought in any, and not necessarily the same, bin the type of which is inferior to LLS or in the auxiliary storage. If such a coalition is found, then a and the two items are packed into a bin of type LLS, and that bin is inserted into the regular packing. The bins that yielded some or all of these two items need to be deleted, and their remaining content will eventually be reinserted. If the coalition is not possible, the packing of a is completed by resuming the standard myopic steps. Similarly, insertion of an S-item a would involve first packing a into a B-bin in a standard myopic fashion. If this fails, a will seek two L-items coming from any, and not necessarily the same, bins whose type is inferior to LLS or from the auxiliary storage. If two such items are found, an LLS-coalition is formed, and the bin of type LLS is inserted into the regular packing. If not, the packing of a is completed by resuming the standard myopic steps. A careful implementation can guarantee that the added complexity of this *mostly myopic* discipline does not asymptotically add to the running time.

Deletes are implemented as follows: the bin in which a (the item that needs to be deleted) resides is emptied, and deleted. Upon discarding a, the remaining contents of the deleted bin are temporarily moved to the auxiliary storage, from which they are reinserted into the packing as a part of this *Delete* operation.

It turns out that *Inserts* and *Deletes* can be carried out in $\Theta(\log n)$ uniform running time because the number of bins inserted and deleted by an *Insert/Delete* operation is bounded by a fixed constant. Intuitively, the discipline of "touching" only the inferior types of bins provides for the desired running time.

3.3.2   Handling M-Items.   We now consider how *MMP* packs the lists that contain M-items. The goal is to utilize *bundles* to manipulate many M-items at once, within logarithmic uniform running time. At the same time, a proper manipulation of M-items will be important for the M-thoroughness property.

In general, the simplest approach would be to pack the M-items independently of the B-items, L-items, S-items, and T-items by packing them into totally separate bins. This would, however, lead to a competitive ratio greater than $\frac{5}{4}$. Rather, the M-items need to be packed, whenever possible, into non-M-bins. Thus, *MMP* inserts an M-item just like any other item, according to its myopic view of the packing (of course, in this case they actually "see" the entire packing). However, the presence of M-items in the packing gives rise to several important considerations:

First, upon insertion of an M-item a into a bin no items will be evicted— M-items are the smallest items! This makes the insertion of an M-item very efficient.

Second, the insertion of B-items, L-items, S-items, and T-items in situations in which the input lists contain M-items needs to be examined very carefully. In particular, if the algorithm were to follow only the standard approach of myopic packing, its striving to maintain a thorough packing might require relocation of as many as $\mathcal{O}(n)$ M-items, leading to $\mathcal{O}(n \log n)$ time per *Insert/Delete* operation. This would happen both during insertions and during deletions that require relocation of items from the bins of type inferior to that of the bin that is currently being filled. Furthermore, the number of bins that could be inserted and deleted per operation might be huge: it would be possible, for example, to delete as many as $\mathcal{O}(n)$ bins of type BST for the sake of taking a few M-items from each of them and packing those M-items into a single bin of type BL. The disaster does not stop here: each of the items from those many bins of type BST needs to be reinserted, and each reinsertion may again cause an avalanche of deleted bins.

Third, the deletion of an M-item would cause, in case the simple myopic discipline is followed, the temporary relocation of B-items, L-items, S-items, T-items, and potentially many M-items into the auxiliary storage. Packing all of these items back into the bins might be very costly: following the same argument as above, $\mathcal{O}(n \log n)$ time might be required to reinsert a single non-M-item, with many inserted and deleted bins.

Thus, handling M-items in the same manner as the other items will not do. This apparent difficulty is solved by introducing the technique of *bundling*. The idea is that the M-items in each bin (as well as in the auxiliary storage) are collected into *bundles* g_i. All of the bundles in a bin (as well as in the auxiliary storage) have the cumulative size of $\frac{1}{10} < size(g_i) \leq \frac{1}{5}$, except for at most one bundle with cumulative size $\leq \frac{1}{10}$. The former kind of bundle is *closed*, while the latter kind is *open*.

The purpose of bundles is to allow efficient manipulation of large numbers of M-items at one time: in response to the need to move M-items from a bin to the auxiliary storage, or from the auxiliary storage to a bin, the algorithm will only move entire bundles. During this process, when a bundle is inserted into a bin (or temporarily stored into auxiliary storage), the algorithm first checks whether it could be merged with the open bundle, if any, from that bin (or from the auxiliary storage), and, if so, the merging is carried out. This step does not asymptotically increase the running time required for the insertion of an M-item, but it drastically decreases the running time of other operations involving

M-bundles and makes *MMP* fast ($\Theta(\log n)$ running time per *Insert/Delete* operation).

The *MMP* algorithm will treat bundles of M-items like any other item (except for the occasional merging of bundles to maintain the property that each bin (as well as auxiliary storage) has at most one open bundle). Note that a bin can contain at most 10 bundles, hence, loosely speaking, no bin can contain more than 10 items. Bundling is one of the tools used to accomplish *M-thoroughness*. It is natural to ask whether or not the technique of bundling is essential for *MMP*; the answer is in the affirmative, based on the result shown in section 3 establishing that moving only a constant number of items per *Insert/Delete* operation disallows competitive ratios below $\frac{4}{3}$ regardless of the running time.

3.4   Showing that *MMP* Is $\frac{5}{4}$-Competitive

It is shown in [14] that *MMP*'s competitive ratio is $\frac{5}{4}$. That proof is lengthy and complex and is beyond the scope of this chapter. We note only that the proof that $\frac{5}{4}$ is an upper bound on the competitive ratio of *MMP* consists of several major parts. First, it is shown that *MMP* maintains regular packings that are LLS-maximal. Second, it is proven that *MMP* maintains M-thoroughness. Once these two important facts about *MMP* are established, it is shown that, if no M-items are inserted, the competitive ratio of *MMP* is $\frac{5}{4}$. This is the most difficult part of the entire proof. Having proven that fact, an easy application of M-thoroughness shows that *MMP* is $\frac{5}{4}$-competitive for arbitrary lists.

3.5   The Running Time of *MMP* Is $\Theta(\log n)$

As noted in the prior section, *MMP* stores items in two structures: most of the items are maintained in bins in the regular packing, while a few (unpacked) items are in the auxiliary storage. That auxiliary storage is maintained as five min-heaps, one for each type of item. The regular packing will be implemented by storing each bin of that packing at a leaf of a 2–3 tree of the bins, with the bins of type BL placed in the leftmost leaves of the 2–3 tree of bins, the bins of type BST placed in the leftmost remaining leaves (those not holding bins of type BL) of the 2–3 tree of bins, and so on for all of the other allowed types of bins, and, finally, with the M-bins placed in the rightmost leaves of the 2-3 tree of bins. Using these data structures the following theorem is stated and proven in [14].

THEOREM 3.5. *MMP can be implemented to run in* $\Theta(\log n)$ *uniform running time per* Insert/Delete *operation.*

Concluding our discussion of the algorithm *MMP*, we note that, compared to the best practical off-line algorithms, *MMP* is the best possible with respect to its running time and is nearly approximation-competitive with those algorithms (losing but a factor of $\frac{1}{15}$ to the best of those [17]).

4. Partially dynamic bin packing

In this section we study *partially dynamic bin packing* where:

- items may arrive to the packing dynamically (*Insert*), and

- items may be moved from bin to bin as the packing is adjusted to accommodate arriving items.

We consider algorithms for both the uniform and the amortized running time cases. Of particular interest is the amortized case, where we show the existence of a polynomial time approximation scheme (PTAS [10]) for partially dynamic bin packing. All of the algorithms that we describe handle (or can easily be modified to handle) the two "lookup" queries *size* and *packing* in addition to the *Insert* operation.

4.1 Uniform Algorithms for Partially Dynamic Bin Packing

We begin by considering *uniform* algorithms for partially dynamic bin packing. That is, algorithms that handle sequences consisting only of *Insert* operations. Note that all on-line algorithms, the algorithms reported in [9, 14], and all algorithms for fully dynamic bin packing can be directly applied in this situation, even if not designed specifically for such sequences. However, recall that on-line algorithms do not move items from bin to bin as new items arrive, and that fully dynamic algorithms must be designed to accommodate *Delete* operations, as well as the *Insert* operations that occur here.

Nonetheless, since these algorithms are applicable, it is worth noting that all of the results on on-line bin packing reviewed in Section 2 carry over directly. Further, with the exception of one algorithm presented in [9], all of those algorithms are uniform. The best of those algorithms for this context is the algorithm A_2 from [9], which runs in time $\Theta(\log n)$ per operation, and is $\frac{4}{3}$-competitive. The other algorithm presented in [9], algorithm A_1, runs in linear time. That is, amortized constant time per operation, and is $\frac{3}{2}$-competitive. Note that A_1 can easily be made uniform by using some of the techniques developed for A_2 in the same paper and modifying the algorithm slightly. In regard to competitive ratio, the best uniform algorithm for *Inserts* is the algorithm *MMP* from the prior section. Recall that it has a uniform running time of $\Theta(\log n)$ per *Insert* (as well as *Delete*) operation and is $\frac{5}{4}$-competitive.

4.2   Amortized Algorithms for Partially Dynamic Bin Packing

In this section we consider amortized algorithms for partially dynamic bin packing. The main result, more encompassing than the algorithm itself, establishes the existence of a polynomial time approximation scheme (PTAS) for partially dynamic bin packing in which each *Insert* is processed in amortized polylogarithmic time. In particular, we show the following from [13]:

THEOREM 4.1. *Let A be any (off-line) R_A-competitive ($R_A < 2$) algorithm for bin packing. Let $T_A(n)$ be the running time of A, and let $\epsilon > 0$. Then there exists an algorithm A_ϵ for partially dynamic bin packing that is ($R_A + \epsilon$)-competitive, and requires $O(\frac{T_A(n)}{n} \log n)$ amortized time per Insert operation.*

Proof. The algorithm A_ϵ will utilize both the algorithm A and the well-known algorithm for standard bin packing, Next Fit (*NF*).

The algorithm *NF* operates as follows. At the outset, the packing consists of 0 bins. When *NF* receives the first item a_1, it opens a bin B_1, and packs a_1 into B_1. *NF* then packs items $a_2, a_3, \ldots$ into B_1 for as long as each item will fit into B_1. As soon as the first item a_i that does not fit into B_1 appears, B_1 is "closed down" (i.e., no items will be inserted into B_1 in the future, regardless of whether or not they could fit), a new bin B_2 is opened, and a_i is packed into B_2. The subsequent items $a_{i+1}, a_{i+2}, \ldots$ will be packed into B_2 for as long as each item will fit, after which B_2 will be "closed down," a new bin B_3 will be opened, and so on. The performance of *NF* is bounded for every list L as follows: $NF(L) \leq 2\, OPT(L)$, and $R(NF) = 2$ [4, 16, 18]. Note that the running time of *NF* is linear.

The idea behind the algorithm A_ϵ is as follows: *NF* is used for almost every *Insert* operation, and a certain level of supervision is utilized so that when the desired competitive ratio $R(A_\epsilon) = R(A) + \epsilon$ is about to be exceeded, A is used to repack the entire instance inserted so far. Intuitively, this should (temporarily) improve the packing because $R(A) < 2 = R(NF)$. After that repacking, *NF* is utilized until another repacking is required, and so on.

More formally, we begin by considering a sequence of n *Inserts*. Note that, as the *Inserts* take place, the size of an optimal packing grows monotonically from 1 to $OPT(L)$, where $L = (a_1, a_2, \ldots, a_n)$ denotes the list of inserted items. Let $a_{i_1}, a_{i_2}, \ldots, a_{i_k}$ denote the *distinguished* items from L with the following property:

$$a_{i_1} = a_1; \quad \forall j, 2 \leq j \leq k, \quad i_j = min_l : [2\, OPT(a_1, a_2, \ldots, a_{i_{j-1}})$$
$$= OPT(a_1, a_2, \ldots, a_l)].$$

Simply put, the a_{i_j}'s are the sequence of least indices such that $OPT(a_1, a_2, \ldots, a_{i_j})$ is twice as large as $OPT(a_1, a_2, \ldots, a_{i_{j-1}})$, $2 \leq j \leq k$.

Based on these distinguished items, we define the concept of a *stage*: The first stage consists only of the insertion of the first item $a_{i_1} = a_1$. Stage j, $1 < j \leq k$, consists of the sequence of *Inserts* between $a_{i_{j-1}}$ and a_{i_j}, also including a_{i_j} itself. Stage $k + 1$ consists of the sequence of *Inserts* between a_{i_k}, the last distinguished item, and a_n, the last item inserted so far. Because the size of an optimal packing cannot double more than $\lceil \log OPT(L) \rceil$ times, which is $O(\log OPT(L)) = O(\log n)$, the number of stages is bounded by $k + 1 = O(\log n)$.

Now, suppose that A is an algorithm with the performance $(\forall L)[A(L) \leq R(A)OPT(L) + K_A(L)]$ (where $K_A(L) = o(OPT(L))$), To complete the proof it suffices to produce an algorithm A_ϵ from A such that the following three conditions are met:

1. $R(A_\epsilon) = R(A) + \epsilon$

2. For every L, $A_\epsilon(L) \leq R(A_\epsilon)OPT(L) + K_{A_\epsilon}(L)$, $K_{A_\epsilon}(L) = o(OPT(L))$

3. A_ϵ requires only a constant number, say C, of repackings via A in each stage.

Note that the third condition insures that the overall running time of A_ϵ on a list of n items is $T_{A_\epsilon}(n) = T_A(n) \log n$. This is because each item is packed only once via *NF* (when the item is being inserted) and is repacked up to $C(k+1) = O(\log n)$ times via A. Because the running time required to pack each item via *NF* is $O(1)$, the total running time spent on packing via *NF* is $\Theta(n)$. Furthermore, because each repacking requires $O(T_A(n))$ running time and there is a logarithmic number of repackings, all of the repackings require a total of $O(T_A(n) \log n)$ running time. Finally, because $T_A(n) = \Omega(n)$, the overall time required to pack n items via A_ϵ is $O(T_A(n) \log n)$. Note that it also follows that $O(\frac{T_A(n)}{n} \log n)$ is the amortized running time per *Insert* operation.

We next establish a sufficient condition to guarantee that A_ϵ requires only a constant number of repackings via A in each stage.

LEMMA 4.2. *Let OPT_i be the size of the optimal packing immediately after the i-th repacking $(i \geq 0)$ via A. If there exists a constant $\beta > 0$ such that $OPT_{i+1} \geq OPT_i + \lceil \beta OPT_i \rceil$, then the number of repackings via A in every stage is bounded by a constant.*

Proof. The number of repackings in the first stage is 1, thus trivially bounded by a constant.

$A_\epsilon(x)$:
    $L' = append(L, x)$;
    pack x using NF;
    if $A_\epsilon(L') >$ bound then
        repack L using A;
        $\alpha = \left\lfloor \frac{A(L) - K_A(L)}{R(A)} \right\rfloor$;
        bound $= \lfloor (R(A) + \epsilon)\alpha \rfloor + K_{A_\epsilon}(L)$;
        pack x using NF;[a]
    endif;
    $L = L'$;

---

[a] Here only the $A(L)$-th bin of the packing most recently produced by A on L is considered to be open, while the other bins are closed for insertions via NF.

Figure 15.3. Algorithm A_ϵ

It follows from the hypotheses of the lemma that, for every $i \geq 0$, $OPT_{i+1} \geq OPT_i(1 + \beta)$. Now suppose that for some i_0-th repacking a stage other than the first stage has just begun. How many repackings will there be by the end of that stage? Let C denote the number of repackings in that stage. By the definition of stages and the hypotheses of the lemma,

$$2 OPT_{i_0} \geq OPT_{i_0+C} \geq OPT_{i_0}(1+\beta)^C \quad \Rightarrow \quad C \leq \frac{1}{\log(1 + \beta)} = O(1).$$

$\square$

Algorithm A_ϵ is given in Fig. 15.3. The variables L (the list of items) and bound should be initialized prior to the first execution of A_ϵ: $L = ()$, and bound $= 2\gamma$ (the value of γ will be specified later). The description of the algorithm outlines only the essential features. Details regarding the maintenance of information necessary for answering the queries are omitted as their implementation can be easily done within the allowed time bounds.

Note that in A_ϵ the variable α offers, after each repacking via A, a lower bound on $OPT(L)$. It is used to provide a conservative estimate of $R(A_\epsilon)OPT(L) + K_{A_\epsilon}(L)$, the value that should not be exceeded in order to comply with the competitive ratio of $R(A_\epsilon)$.

The algorithm is not yet completely specified because the values of γ and $K_{A_\epsilon}(L)$ are not yet determined. Recall that the goal in the design of A_ϵ is not only to achieve the desired competitive ratio, but also to insure that there are but a constant number of repackings via A at each stage. It is precisely this requirement that requires a careful selection of γ and $K_{A_\epsilon}(L)$.

To insure the growth of the optimal packing between the i-th and $i + 1$-st repacking by at least $\lceil \beta OPT_i \rceil$ (see Lemma 4.2) it is sufficient to require *NF* to pack at least twice as many bins. That is, $\geq 2 \lceil \beta OPT_i \rceil$ bins between the two repackings. Because the competitive ratio of *NF* is 2, this will add at least the required number of bins (i.e., $\lceil \beta OPT_i \rceil$ bins) to the optimal packing. Unfortunately, we are not able to implement this directly in A_ϵ because we do not know the value of OPT_i. Rather, this is accomplished by the use of γ and $K_{A_\epsilon}(L)$ in the following way.

Let the required number of bins packed by *NF* between two repackings be denoted as Δ_i. We desire that:

$$\Delta_i \geq 2 \lceil \beta OPT_i \rceil.$$

We will now refine this condition and demand a stronger inequality. The value of Δ_i will be underestimated by $\lfloor R(A_\epsilon)\alpha + K_{A_\epsilon}(L) \rfloor - \lceil R(A)\alpha + K_A(L) \rceil$ while the value of OPT_i will be overestimated by $\lceil R(A)\alpha + K_A(L) \rceil$, where α denotes the variable from the description of A_ϵ. It is then desired that the following must hold:

$$\lfloor R(A_\epsilon)\alpha + K_{A_\epsilon}(L) \rfloor - \lceil R(A)\alpha + K_A(L) \rceil \geq 2 \lceil \beta \lceil R(A)\alpha + K_A(L) \rceil \rceil.$$

Clearly, then $\Delta_i \geq 2 \lceil \beta OPT_i \rceil$ will follow. The above inequality can be satisfied if we insist that:

$$(R(A) + \epsilon)\alpha + K_{A_\epsilon}(L) - 1 - (R(A)\alpha + K_A(L) + 1)$$
$$\geq 2(\beta(R(A)\alpha + K_A(L) + 1)) + 2,$$

which, after some elementary steps, yields:

$$(\epsilon - 2\beta R(A))\alpha + (K_{A_\epsilon}(L) - K_A(L)) - 2 \geq 2\beta K_A(L) + 2\beta + 2.$$

If the condition $K_{A_\epsilon}(L) > K_A(L)$ is met, then a yet more refined inequality holds:

$$(\epsilon - 2\beta R(A))\alpha \geq 2(\beta(K_A(L) + 1) + 2).$$

The above inequality suggests that there is considerable flexibility with respect to the choice of β. In particular, the value of β can be fixed to any value conforming to the inequality $\epsilon > 2\beta R(A)$. That is

$$\beta < \frac{\epsilon}{2R(A)}.$$

Further, the above inequality also suggests that the required growth of the value of the optimal packing between any two repackings can be achieved if:

$$\alpha \geq \left\lceil \frac{2(\beta(K_A(L) + 1) + 2)}{\epsilon - 2\beta R(A)} \right\rceil.$$

This requirement will be met if the initial packing via *NF* requires at least 2γ bins, where γ can be found as follows:

$$\left\lfloor \frac{\gamma - K_A(L)}{R(A)} \right\rfloor \geq \left\lceil \frac{2(\beta(K_A(L) + 1) + 2)}{\epsilon - 2\beta R(A)} \right\rceil.$$

This condition reflects the scenario in which *NF* would achieve its worst possible packing on the initial items, whereas *A* would produce an optimal packing. Some elementary steps yield the following bound on the value of integer γ:

$$\frac{\gamma - K_A(L)}{R(A)} - 1 \geq 2\frac{\beta(K_A(L) + 1) + 2)}{\epsilon - 2\beta R(A)} + 1.$$

Further simplification yields:

$$\gamma \geq 2R(A)\left(\frac{\beta(K_A(L) + 1) + 2}{\epsilon - 2\beta R(A)} + 1\right) + K_A(L).$$

By the discussion about the worst possible scenario above, it will suffice to set γ and $K_{A_\epsilon}(L)$ to:

$$\gamma = K_{A_\epsilon}(L) \geq \left\lceil 2R(A)\left(\frac{\beta(K_A(L) + 1) + 2}{\epsilon - 2\beta R(A)} + 1\right) + K_A(L)\right\rceil.$$

Note that this condition guarantees $K_{A_\epsilon}(L) > K_A(L)$, as well as all of the other requirements. □

COROLLARY 4.3.

1. *For every $\epsilon > 0$ there is a $(1 + \epsilon)$-competitive approximation scheme A_ϵ for partially dynamic bin packing that requires $O(\log n)$ amortized time per Insert operation.*

2. *For every $\epsilon > 0$ there is a $(1 + \epsilon)$-competitive fully polylogarithmic approximation scheme A_ϵ for partially dynamic bin packing that requires $O(\log^2 n)$ amortized time per Insert operation.*

Proof.

1. Immediate from Theorem 4.1 and the results from [7].

2. Immediate from Theorem 4.1 and the results from [19]. □

5.   Conclusion

There are a number of open questions associated with the fully and partially dynamic bin packing discussed in this chapter. In this section we outline a few of these questions as they correspond to the three main results that we have described.

5.1 Moving a Constant Number of Items Per Operation

There are two major open questions relating to the theorem that restricting the number of items moved per operation to be a constant results in a competitive ratio of at least $4/3$. First, is there any algorithm for this restricted version of fully dynamic bin packing (where the number of items that can be moved between bins per *Insert/Delete* operation is bounded by a constant) with a constant competitive ratio? If there is such an algorithm, is its competitive ratio close to $4/3$? Second, is there a better lower bound than $4/3$? In the case of on-line bin packing, dealing only with *Inserts*, somewhat stronger lower bounds are known: Yao proved a $3/2$ bound [25], and Brown [2] and Liang [22] improved that to $1.536\ldots$. Similar results may be possible for the fully dynamic case.

5.2 Fully Dynamic Bin Packing and MMP

The major unresolved issue here is whether there exist fully dynamic bin packing algorithms (accommodating both *Inserts* and *Deletes*) that attain better competitive ratios. That is, are there algorithms that are α-competitive for some $\alpha < \frac{5}{4}$, and require $o(n)$ time per operation. Here, both uniform and amortized algorithms are of interest.

Other unresolved issues are: (1) what is the nature of the trade-off between running times and competitive ratios of fully dynamic bin packing algorithms for bin packing (both uniform and amortized), and (2) is there a competitive ratio for which there are no fully dynamic approximation algorithms for bin packing featuring sublinear running times (uniform or amortized)?

5.3 Partially Dynamic Bin Packing

The open questions related to partially dynamic bin packing concern the competitive ratio achievable with uniform running time, and the practicality of the algorithms A_ϵ in the case of amortized running time.

Recall that in the uniform case the best known competitive ratio for partially dynamic bin packing is $\frac{5}{4}$ [14]. However, that algorithm was not designed specifically for partially dynamic packing. It is possible that the development of partially dynamic algorithms for bin packing could benefit from the fact that *Deletes* would not be required.

In the case of the amortized running time, we note that the efficiency of the algorithms A_ϵ is primarily determined by the efficiency of their respective "building blocks" A. In particular, if the design goal is to develop a partially dynamic bin packing algorithm (with a good amortized running time) with a small competitive ratio, developing an entirely new algorithm which would not rely on very good but very slow building blocks (e.g., [7, 19]) might be a preferable approach.

References

[1] R. J. Anderson, E. W. Mayr, and M. K. Warmuth. Parallel approximation algorithms for bin packing. *Information and Computation*, 82(3):262–277, 1989.

[2] D. J. Brown. A lower bound for on-line one-dimensional bin packing algorithms. Technical Report R-864, Coordinated Science Laboratory, University of Illinois, Urbana, IL, 1979.

[3] E. G. Coffman, M. R. Garey, and D. S. Johnson. Dynamic bin packing. *SIAM J. Comput.*, 12:227–258, 1983.

[4] E. G. Coffman, M. R. Garey, and D. S. Johnson. Approximation algorithms for bin packing: An updated survey. In G. Ausiello, M. Lucertini and P. Serafini, editors, *Algorithm Design for Computer System Design*, pages 49–106. Springer, New York, 1984.

[5] T. H. Cormen, C. E. Leiserson, R. L. Rivest, and C. Stein. *Introduction to algorithms*. McGraw–Hill/MIT Press, Cambridge, 2nd edition, 2001.

[6] L. Epstein and A. Levin. A robust APTAS for the classical bin packing problem. In *Proc. 33rd International Colloquium on Automata, Languages and Programming (ICALP)*, volume 1, pages 214–225. 2006.

[7] W. Fernandez de la Vega and G. S. Lueker. Bin packing can be solved within $1 + \epsilon$ in linear time. *Combinatorica*, 1(4):349–355, 1981.

[8] D. K. Friesen and M. A. Langston. Analysis of a compound bin packing algorithm. *SIAM J. Discr. Math.*, 4(1):61–79, 1994.

[9] G. Gambosi, A. Postiglione, and M. Talamo. New algorithms for on-line bin packing. In G. Aussiello, D. P. Bovet and R. Petreschi, editors, *Algorithms and Complexity, Proceedings of the First Italian Conference*, pages 44–59. World Scientific, Singapore, 1990.

[10] M. R. Garey and D. S. Johnson. *Computers and Intractability: A Guide to the Theory of NP-Completeness*. Freeman, San Francisco, 1979.

[11] Z. Ivković. Fully dynamic approximation algorithms. PhD Thesis, University of Delaware, 1995.

[12] Z. Ivković and E. L. Lloyd. A fundamental restriction on fully dynamic maintenance of bin packing. *Inf. Proc. Lett.*, 59:229–232, 1996.

[13] Z. Ivković and E. L. Lloyd. Partially dynamic bin packing can be solved within $1 + \epsilon$ in (amortized) polylogarithmic time. *Inf. Proc. Lett.*, 63:45–50, 1997.

[14] Z. Ivković and E. L. Lloyd. Fully dynamic algorithms for bin packing: Being mostly myopic helps. *SIAM J. Comput.*, 28(2):574–611, 1998.

[15] D. S. Johnson. Near-optimal bin packing algorithms. PhD Thesis, MIT, 1973.

[16] D. S. Johnson. Fast algorithms for bin packing. *Journal of Computer and System Sciences*, 8:272–314, 1974.

[17] D. S. Johnson and M. R. Garey. A $71/60$ Theorem for bin packing. *J. Complexity*, 1:65–106, 1985.

[18] D. S. Johnson, A. Demers, J. D. Ullman, M. R. Garey, and R. L. Graham. Worst-case performance bounds for simple one-dimensional packing algorithms. *SIAM J. Comput.*, 3(4):299–325, 1974.

[19] N. Karmarkar and R. M. Karp. An efficient approximation scheme for the one-dimensional bin-packing problem. In *Proc. 23rd IEEE Symposium on Foundations of Computer Science*, pages 312–320, 1982.

[20] R. M. Karp. Reducibility among combinatorial problems. In R. E. Miller and J. W. Thatcher, editors, *Complexity of Computer Computations*, pages 85–103. Plenum, New York, 1972.

[21] C. C. Lee and D. T. Lee. A simple on-line bin-packing algorithm. *J. ACM*, 32:562–572, 1985.

[22] F. M. Liang. A lower bound for on-line bin-packing. *Inf. Proc. Lett.*, 10:76–79, 1980.

[23] P. Ramanan, D. J. Brown, C. C. Lee, and D. T. Lee. On-line bin-packing in linear time. *J. Algorithms*, 3:305–326, 1989.

[24] P. Sanders, N. Sivadasan, and M. Skutella. Online scheduling with bounded migration. In *Proc. 31st International Colloquium on Automata, Languages and Programming (ICALP)*, pages 1111–1122, 2004.

[25] A. C.-C. Yao. New algorithms for bin packing. *J. ACM*, 27(2):207–227, 1980.

Chapter 16

ONLINE JOB ADMISSION

SVEN O. KRUMKE

Department of Mathematics, University of Kaiserslautern, Paul-Ehrlich-Str. 14, 67653 Kaiserslautern, Germany. Email: krumke@mathematik.uni-kl.de

ROB VAN STEE[*]

Department of Computer Science, University of Karlsruhe, 76128 Karlsruhe, Germany. Email: vanstee@ira.uka.de

STEPHAN WESTPHAL

Department of Mathematics, University of Kaiserslautern, Paul-Ehrlich-Str. 14, 67653 Kaiserslautern, Germany. Email: westphal@mathematik.uni-kl.de

Abstract   We consider the problem of scheduling a maximum profit selection of jobs on m identical machines. Jobs arrive online one by one and each job is specified by its start and end time. The goal is to determine a non-preemptive schedule which maximizes the profit of the scheduled jobs, where the profit of a job is equal to its length. Upon arrival of a new job, an online algorithm must decide whether to accept the job ("admit the job") or not. If the job is accepted, the online algorithm must be able to reorganize its already existing schedule such that the new job can be processed together with all previously admitted jobs, however, the algorithm need not specify on which machine the job will eventually be run.

Competitive analysis has become a standard way of measuring the quality of online algorithms. For a maximization problem, an online algorithm is called c-competitive, if on every input instance it achieves at least a $1/c$-fraction of the optimal ("offline") profit. We provide competitive algorithms and lower bounds on the competitive ratio for deterministic and randomized algorithms against an oblivious adversary. Our lower bound results essentially match (up to small constants factors) the competitive ratios achieved by our algorithms.

---

[*] Research supported by the Alexander von Humboldt Foundation.

S.S. Ravi, S.K. Shukla (eds.), *Fundamental Problems in Computing*,
© Springer Science + Business Media B.V. 2009

1.   Introduction

A situation which many of us know: You try to book a cottage in your favorite holiday location for the weekend but the overly friendly person on the phone tells you that they simply can not satisfy your request. If you had called just five minutes earlier, everything would have been fine, but now there is allegedly nothing available. You doubt that this is true. Are they just rejecting your booking request because you just wanted to stay three days and not four? How do they work at all? Better: How *should* they organize their bookings? This must be some easy piece of mathematics!

You sit down and put yourself in the position of the owner of two identical cottages. The holiday season (which we assume without loss of generality to be the time interval $[0, T]$ where $T \gg 1$) is still in the future and you are awaiting for people to make reservations (Fig. 16.1). Naturally, we can assume that the profit you make for a request of length l is l units of money.

A few moments later, the first customer r_1 calls and requests a cottage for the time interval $[0, 1]$. Clearly, we can promise her cottage 1 which gives us a profit of $1 - 0 = 1$. The next customer r_2 requests a cottage in the interval $[1, 2]$. Both cottages are available then, so we accept the booking request and schedule cottage 2 for her (Fig. 16.2). This increases our profit again by one unit. Then, the next customer calls and wishes to get a cottage from 0 to 2. Yikes, we do not have a cottage available during that whole period!

But, let us think one moment. Both cottages are essentially identical and we have not promised r_2 a specific cottage, but only *a* cottage. So, we can simply move his booking from cottage 2 to cottage 1 and we can accommodate the

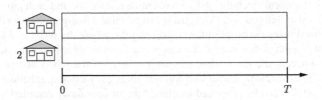

Figure 16.1.   Empty booking table for the cottage-rental problem with two (identical) cottages

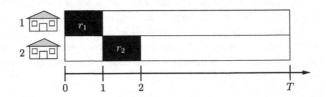

Figure 16.2.   The first two customers have been booked into the plan

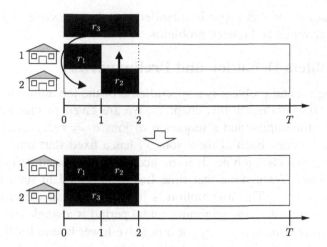

Figure 16.3. By moving customer r_2 from cottage 2 to cottage 1 the new customer r_3 can still be scheduled

request from r_3 (Fig. 16.3). That was not too difficult, after all, was it? And our total profit has risen to $1 + 1 + 2 = 4$.

While we sit back relaxed and content, two more customers call each of which wants to book a cottage for the whole holiday season $[0, T]$. These could be called "ideal customers" in the sense that each of them allows us to fully rent out a cottage at maximum profit. But what is this? No matter how we reorganize our schedule, we can not accept any of them. If we only had known earlier that they would call, we could have rejected the requests of r_1, r_2 and r_3 and made a profit of $2T$ by accepting the "ideal customers" which book the whole season instead of a lousy 4 units. On the other hand, if we reject r_1, r_2 and r_3 and the two "ideal customers" do not call then we have an empty schedule and no profit which is worse than the profit of 4 that we wince at right now. Maybe the cottage rental problem is not so easy?

We have just discovered the *online aspect* of the cottage rental problem. We are facing incomplete information, and even if every time a new request becomes known we compute a new "optimal" schedule this does not necessarily lead to an overall optimal solution.

In general, traditional optimization techniques assume complete knowledge of all data of a problem instance. However, in reality it is unlikely that all information necessary to define a problem instance is available beforehand. Decisions may have to be made before complete information is available. This observation has motivated the research on *online optimization*. An algorithm is called *online* if it makes a decision (computes a partial solution) whenever a new piece of data requests an action.

The remainder of this paper is intended to schedule some light onto the online cottage rental and related problems.

2. Problem Definition and Preliminaries

The cottage rental problem is a special case of the job admission problem, denoted by OJA, studied in this chapter. We are given m machines, a time horizon of T time units, and a sequence of jobs $\sigma = r_1, \ldots, r_n$, which are released one by one. Each of these jobs r_j has a fixed start time a_j and end time $b_j > a_j$, and each job needs to be accepted or rejected before we move to the next one. We assume that time has been scaled in such a way that $\min_j(b_j - a_j) = 1$. This assumption is justified for instance in the cottage rental application where the minimum rental period is a single day (our algorithms still work if $\min_j(b_j - a_j)$ or a positive lower bound for this quantity is known in advance). The goal is to select jobs to be processed such that the sum of the lengths of the accepted jobs is maximized and there exists a feasible non-preemptive assignment of jobs to machines, i.e., such that at any moment in time each machine processes at most one job.

An *online algorithm* for OJA must base its decision for request r_j without knowledge of requests r_i with $i > j$. A standard tool to measure the quality of an online algorithm ALG is *competitive analysis* [22, 6], where one compares for each input sequence σ the profit ALG(σ) obtained by ALG to the optimal profit achievable on that sequence, denoted by OPT(σ).

A deterministic online algorithm ALG for OJA is *c-competitive*, if for any request sequence σ the inequality ALG(σ) $\geq \frac{1}{c} \cdot$ OPT(σ) holds. For randomized algorithms against an oblivious adversary (see [6] for details), one uses the expected benefit $\mathbb{E}[\text{ALG}(\sigma)]$ instead. The *competitive ratio* of an algorithm is defined to be the infimum over all c such that the algorithm is c-competitive.

2.1 Our Results

In Sect. 4 we develop a general lower bound for the competitive ratio of randomized algorithms for the *job admission problem* (OJA). Specifically, we give a lower bound of $\frac{1}{2}(\log T + 2)$ on the competitive ratio of any randomized algorithm against an oblivious adversary, where T is the time horizon.

In Sect. 5.1 we present a first simple greedy-type deterministic $2\Delta_\sigma + 1$-competitive algorithm GREEDY, where $\Delta_\sigma = \max_{r_i, r_j \in \sigma} \frac{b_i - a_i}{b_j - a_j} = \max_{r_i \in \sigma}(b_i - a_i)$ is the maximum ratio of the profit of two jobs.[1] This simple algorithm forms the basis of the improved algorithm C-GREEDY which we present in the following Sect. 5.3. The main competitiveness result is given

---

[1] Recall that time has been scaled in such a way that $\min_j(b_j - a_j) = 1$.

in Sect. 5.3, where we give a deterministic algorithm C-GREEDY that matches our lower bound from Sect. 4 up to constant factors for the case $m \geq \lceil \log T \rceil$. Moreover, we show that for $m \leq \lceil \log T \rceil$ our algorithm C-GREEDY provides a competitive ratio of $2m(\sqrt[m]{T} + 1) \leq 2 \log T(\sqrt[m]{T} + 1)$, which is also optimal up to a constant factor.

2.2 Previous Work

Several variations on the online job admission problem studied in this paper have been considered in the literature. OJA is related to the problem of scheduling equal-length jobs on parallel machines, where the jobs have release times and deadlines and the goal is to maximize the number of jobs completed. Baruah et al. [5] showed that a greedy-type algorithm is 2-competitive for this problem (where jobs arrive over time), a lower bound of $4/3$ for the competitive ratio of randomized algorithms was given by Goldman et al. [15]. Chrobak et al. [11] provided a barely random algorithm with competitive ratio $5/3$. The corresponding offline problem can be solved in polynomial time [4] (see also notes in [11]).

Van Stee and La Poutré [23] considered the problem of partial servicing of online jobs. Here, jobs arrive over time to be rejected or accepted, after which they must start immediately. The algorithm can choose to serve some jobs only partially, and the goal is as here to maximize the profit. The problem is different from ours in its notion of time (new requests cannot appear in the past) and because of the option of serving jobs partially. However, it turns out that several ideas from [23] can be used also to give good algorithms for the current problem.

The problem OJA in this paper can also be seen as a generalized version of online interval scheduling [19], where only one machine is available. However, in the paper [19], jobs arrive over time instead of one by one. Also, there is no pre-specified time horizon. As mentioned at the beginning, another similar problem which has been studied is seat reservations on trains [8, 9]. Here passengers arrive online, specifying their desired connection, and need to be assigned a seat immediately. Differences to that paper are that in making seat reservations, it is assumed that an algorithm is not allowed to reject any passenger for whom there is still room in the train, and they furthermore assume that the seat (in our case: machine) has to be assigned immediately upon request. (The paper [9] considers a slightly relaxed case where each passenger may change seats a fixed number of times during the trip.)

Finally, OJA can also be seen as a call admission problem in an optical network [3, 14, 18]. In our case the network is simply a line. The main difference to optical call-admission on the line is the profit model. For call-admission one

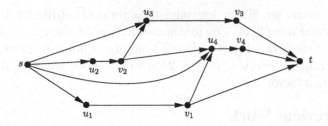

Figure 16.4. A graph G corresponding to a set of jobs $J = \{r_1, \ldots, r_4\}$ with $a_1 < a_2 < b_2 < a_3 < b_1 < a_4 < b_3 < b_4$.

assumes that each job has a uniform value,[2] independent of its length. It seems that this changes the flavor of the problem substantially, since rejecting a large job does not lose you more than rejecting a short job, and generally short jobs are easier to schedule.

3. The Offline Problem

In this section we show briefly how the offline problem corresponding to OJA can be solved efficiently. Given a set of jobs J consider a directed graph $G = (V, A)$ with the following nodes: a source s, a sink t and for every job $r_j = [a_j, b_j] \in J$ two nodes u_j, v_j. Thus, $V := \bigcup_{r_j \in J}\{u_j, v_j\} \cup \{s, t\}$.

For all $r_j \in J$ we have an arc (u_j, v_j) with cost $-p_j$, and the arcs (s, u_j) and (v_j, t) with cost 0. The arc (u_j, v_j) corresponds to the situation where job r_j is accepted. For all $r_i, r_j \in J$ with $b_i \leq a_j$ we introduce an additional arc (v_i, u_j) with cost 0 representing the possibility that r_j can be scheduled directly after r_i on the same machine. All arcs have unit capacity. An example for such a network is shown in Fig. 16.4.

Let f be an integral minimum cost flow of value m in G from s to t. Such a flow can be computed efficiently by standard techniques, see e.g. [1]. We claim that an optimal solution of the job admission problem is given by accepting job r_j if and only if the flow value $f(u_j, v_j)$ on arc (u_j, v_j) is nonzero (that is, it is one by our choice of the capacities).

In fact, every feasible schedule of jobs on m machines gives rise to m edge-disjoint paths in G from s to t, one for each machine (cf. Fig. 16.5). The profit obtained on the machine equals the negative of the cost of the corresponding path.

Conversely, by flow decomposition [1] we can decompose every s-t-flow of value m in G into m disjoint s-t-paths (since the graph G is acyclic, there can

---

[2] The value may depend on the bandwidth of the call but not on its length, which is the path used to route the call.

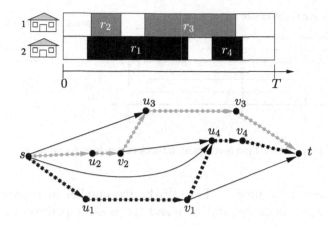

Figure 16.5. Each set of jobs assigned to a single machine in a feasible solution corresponds to an s-t-path in the network G

not be cycles in the flow decomposition). Since every s-t-path corresponds to a set of jobs which can be scheduled on a single machine, these paths specify an assignment of the jobs to the specific machines.

4. Lower Bounds

Let us first consider the question how well a deterministic algorithm can perform in terms of competitiveness. We first start with deterministic algorithms. To this end, let us consider the situation we had in the introduction once more: we scheduled three small jobs but then could not accommodate the two long jobs (which span the whole interval $[0, T]$) any more.

We are given m machines and the time interval $[0, T]$ for scheduling jobs. The basic idea of our lower bound construction is the following. Let ALG be some arbitrary deterministic online algorithm. We first present m small jobs of length 1 each for the interval $[0, 1]$. If the online algorithm accepts all of the jobs, it gets a profit of $m \cdot 1 = m$ and we will then present m large jobs of length T each for the interval $[0, T]$. Thus, the optimal profit is mT and we can force a ratio of T between the optimal and the online profit. What makes the argument slightly more complicated is the fact that ALG need not accept *all* of the jobs of length 1, so it might have some empty space on the machines which can be used to accommodate the long jobs.

THEOREM 4.1. *No deterministic algorithm can achieve a competitive ratio smaller than* $\frac{1}{2}(\log T + 2)$ *for the* OJA.

Proof. Assume that ALG is a c-competitive algorithm for the OJA. The first part σ_0 of the adversarial sequence consists of m jobs of unit size starting at

442

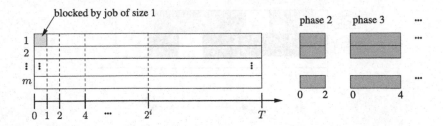

Figure 16.6. Once a job is accepted, it blocks a machine for all future requests

time 0 and ending at time 1. Let $q(0)$ be the number of requests from σ_0 accepted by ALG. Since $\text{OPT}(\sigma_0) = m$ and ALG is c-competitive, we must have that $q(0) \geq m/c$.

We will now continue to present blocks of m requests each of length 2^i for $i = 1, \ldots, 2^{\log T}$. Each request starts at time 0. Let σ_i denote the subsequence formed by the requests of length 2^i. Our total input sequence σ is thus $\sigma = \sigma_0 \sigma_1 \cdots \sigma_{2^{\log T}}$. Observe that each accepted request blocks a machine for future requests (cf. Fig. 16.6).

As we have seen before after σ_0 the online algorithm must have accepted $q(0) \geq m/c$ jobs and thus blocked $q(0)$ machines for future requests. Once the requests in σ_1 have been presented, the optimal solution is to reject all request in σ_0 and accept all the jobs from σ_1 of size 2. Thus, we have $\text{OPT}(\sigma_0 \sigma_1) = 2m$. In order to achieve a competitive ratio of c the profit obtained by ALG must satisfy:

$$q(0) \cdot 1 + q(1) \cdot 2 \geq \frac{\text{OPT}(\sigma_0 \sigma_1)}{c} = \frac{2m}{c}, \qquad (4.1)$$

where $q(1)$ denotes the number of requests accepted by ALG from the subsequence σ_1. We have seen above that $q(0) \geq m/c$. Since all requests from σ_i for $i \geq 1$ give more profit than the unit size jobs from σ_0 we can assume that ALG accepts *exactly* m/c jobs from σ_0. Using $q(0) = m/c$ in (4.1) results in

$$q(1) \geq \frac{1}{2}\left(\frac{2m}{c} - \frac{m}{c}\right) = \frac{m}{2c}.$$

By the same argument as above we can assume that $q(1) = \frac{m}{2c}$, since this leaves ALG with more space for future jobs which are more profitable than the small ones already seen. We will now show by induction on i that in fact the number $q(i)$ of jobs accepted by ALG from σ_i satisfies $q(i) = \frac{m}{2c}$ for $i \geq 1$. The claim has already been established for $i = 1$. Let us assume that we know that $q(0) = m/c$ and $q(1) = \cdots = q(i-1) = m/2c$. We have $\text{OPT}(\sigma_0 \cdots \sigma_i) = m2^i$. By the fact that ALG is assumed to be c-competitive we have:

$$\frac{\text{OPT}(\sigma_0 \cdots \sigma_i)}{c} = \frac{2^i m}{c} \leq \left(\sum_{j=0}^{i-1} 2^j \cdot q(j) \right) + 2^i \cdot q(i)$$

$$= \frac{m}{c} + \left(\sum_{j=1}^{i-1} 2^j \cdot \frac{m}{2c} \right) + 2^i \cdot q(i)$$

$$= \frac{m}{c}(1 + 2^{i-1} - 1) + 2^i \cdot q(i) = \frac{2^{i-1} m}{c} + 2^i \cdot q(i).$$

Solving for $q(i)$ yields $q(i) \geq \frac{m}{2c}$ and by the now familiar argument from above we get that $q(i) = \frac{m}{2c}$. This completes the inductive step.

We are now in the position to establish the lower bound on the competitiveness c of ALG. Observe that the total number of machines blocked by ALG after phase i is $\sum_{j=0}^{i} p(i)$. Since the total number of machines is m we get

$$m \geq \sum_{j=0}^{\log T} p(j) = p(0) + \sum_{j=1}^{\log T} p(j) = \frac{m}{c} + \frac{m}{2c} \log T = \frac{1}{c} m \left(1 + \frac{1}{2} \log T \right).$$

This gives us $c \geq 1 + \frac{1}{2} \log T = \frac{1}{2}(\log T + 2)$ as claimed. □

We now extend our lower bound result to randomized algorithms against an oblivious adversary. The difficulty lies in the fact that it is not clear how a *generic randomized algorithm* RALG looks like. Using the same line of arguments as in Theorem 4.1 we see that RALG only needs to accept m/c unit size jobs *on expectation* and not with probability one. Thus, in order to establish our bound, we make use of Yao's principle [6, 24].

DEFINITION 4.2. A *request-answer game* $(R, \mathcal{A}, \mathcal{C})$ consists of a request set R, a sequence of finite nonempty answer sets $\mathcal{A} = A_1, A_2, \ldots$ and a sequence of cost functions $\mathcal{C} = \text{profit}_1, \text{profit}_2, \ldots$ where $\text{profit}_j \colon R^j \times A_1 \times \cdots \times A_j \to \mathbb{R}_+ \cup \{+\infty\}$. A *deterministic online algorithm* ALG for the request-answer game $(R, \mathcal{A}, \mathcal{C})$ is a sequence of functions $f_j \colon R^j \to A_j, j \in \mathbb{N}$. The *output* of ALG on the input request sequence σ is

$$\text{ALG}[\sigma] := (a_1, \ldots, a_m) \in A_1 \times \cdots \times A_m, \quad \text{where } a_j := f_j(r_1, \ldots, r_j).$$

The *profit* obtained by ALG on σ, denoted by $\text{ALG}(\sigma)$ is defined as

$$\text{ALG}(\sigma) := \text{profit}_m(\sigma, \text{ALG}[\sigma].)$$

A *randomized online algorithm* RALG is a probability distribution over deterministic online algorithms ALG_x (x may be thought of as the coin tosses of the algorithm RALG). The answer sequence RALG[σ] and the cost RALG(σ) on a given input σ are random variables.

THEOREM 4.3 (Yao's Principle). *Let G be any finite request-answer game. Let* ALG *be any online randomized algorithm for G and let $\bar{\mathcal{R}}_{OBL}$(ALG) be the competitive ratio of* ALG *against an oblivious adversary. Let $p(i)$ be any probability distribution over request sequences. Then*

$$\bar{\mathcal{R}}_{OBL}(\text{ALG}) \geq \max \left\{ \min_j \frac{\mathbb{E}_{p(i)}\left[\text{OPT}(\sigma_i)\right]}{\mathbb{E}_{p(i)}\left[\text{ALG}_j(\sigma_i)\right]}, \min_j \frac{1}{\mathbb{E}_{p(i)}\left[\frac{\text{ALG}_j(\sigma_i)}{\text{OPT}(\sigma_i)}\right]} \right\}. \quad (4.2)$$

Proof. See [6, 7]. □

THEOREM 4.4. *Any randomized algorithm for* OJA *has a competitive ratio no smaller than $\frac{1}{2}(\log T + 2)$ against an oblivious adversary.*

Proof. For $i = 0, \ldots, \log T$, consider the sequence σ_i which for each $0 \leq j \leq i$ contains m jobs of length 2^j (thus, σ_i specifies a total of $(i+1)m$ jobs). The jobs in σ_i will be given in increasing order of length, and all requests have a start time of 0. Clearly, for each machine at most one of these jobs can be contained in any schedule and we have OPT(σ_i) $= m2^i$.

We make use of the second bound in (4.2) to derive the lower bound on the competitive ratio of randomized algorithms against an oblivious adversary. Specifically, we give a distribution $p(i)$ over the request sequences σ_i such that for any deterministic algorithm ALG we have

$$\mathbb{E}_{p(i)}\left[\frac{\text{ALG}(\sigma_i)}{\text{OPT}(\sigma_i)}\right] \leq \frac{2}{\log T + 2}.$$

Using Yao's principle from Theorem 4.3 above then yields the desired lower bound of $1/(\frac{2}{\log T+2}) = \frac{1}{2}(\log T + 2)$.

Let $q(j)$ be the number of jobs of length 2^j accepted by a given deterministic algorithm ALG, when given any sequence σ_i where $i \geq j$. Since until the point in time when the requests of length 2^j are given these σ_i are identical, ALG has to make the same decision, how many of these jobs to accept and therefore $q(j)$ has to be identical for all those σ_i.

Thus, when processing σ_i the ratio of the profits by ALG and OPT is

$$\frac{\text{ALG}(\sigma_i)}{\text{OPT}(\sigma_i)} = \frac{\sum_{j=0}^{i} q(j) \cdot 2^j}{m \cdot 2^i}. \quad (4.3)$$

We now derive a probability distribution p over the sequences σ_i such that for each deterministic algorithm ALG we have

$$\mathbb{E}_{p(j)}\left[\frac{\sum_{j=0}^{i} q(j) \cdot 2^j}{m \cdot 2^i}\right] \leq \frac{2}{\log T + 2}.$$

As afore mentioned by using Yao's principle the bound then follows.

Let $p(i)$ to be the probability that σ_i occurs. Then, the expected value of the profit ratio can be computed by:

$$\mathbb{E}_{p(i)}\left[\frac{\text{ALG}(\sigma_i)}{\text{OPT}(\sigma_i)}\right] = \sum_{i=0}^{\log(T)} p(i) \cdot \frac{\text{ALG}(\sigma_i)}{\text{OPT}(\sigma_i)} = \sum_{i=0}^{\log T} p(i) \cdot \frac{\sum_{j=0}^{i} q(j) \cdot 2^j}{m \cdot 2^i}$$

$$= \sum_{i=0}^{\log T} p(i) \sum_{j=0}^{i} \frac{2^{j-i}}{m} \cdot q(j) = \sum_{j=0}^{\log T} \sum_{i=j}^{\log T} \frac{2^{j-i} p(i)}{m} \cdot q(j)$$

Observe that, given a distribution $p(i)$ on the instances σ_i, all deterministic algorithms only differ in the number of jobs they accept of each of the given length classes of jobs. Thus, we can find the deterministic algorithm with the largest expected profit ratio by solving the following integer linear program:

$$(\text{IP1}) \quad \max \quad \sum_{j=0}^{\log T} \sum_{i=j}^{\log T} \frac{2^{j-i} p(i)}{m} \; q(j)$$

$$\text{s.t.} \quad \sum_{j=0}^{\log T} q(j) \leq m$$

$$q(j) \geq 0, q(j) \in \mathbb{Z} \quad \text{for all } j = 0, \ldots, \log T$$

To obtain an upper bound for the optimal solution of this problem it suffices to find a feasible solution of the dual of its linear relaxation, which is given by:

$$(\text{LP1}) \quad \min \quad m \cdot y$$

$$\text{s.t.} \quad y \geq \sum_{i=j}^{\log T} \frac{2^{j-i} p(i)}{m} \quad \text{for all } j = 0, \ldots, \log T$$

$$y \geq 0$$

Observe that the dual (LP1) has only a single variable. Thus, we can easily compute its optimal solution:

$$\min\left\{ my : y \geq \sum_{i=j}^{\log T} \frac{2^{j-i} p(i)}{m}, j = 0, \ldots, \log T \right\}$$

$$= \max_{j=0,\ldots,\log T} \left\{ m \cdot \sum_{i=j}^{\log T} \frac{2^{j-i} p(i)}{m} \right\} = \max_{j=0,\ldots,\log T} \left\{ \sum_{i=j}^{\log T} 2^{j-i} p(i) \right\}.$$

The quality of the bound obtained this way depends on the applied distribution p. The distribution which yields the best bound can be found by solving another linear program:

(LP2) min y

s.t. $\displaystyle\sum_{i=j}^{\log T} 2^{j-i} p(i) \le y$ for all $j = 0, \ldots, \log T$

$$\sum_{i=0}^{\log T} p(i) = 1$$

$p(i) \ge 0$ for all $i = 0, \ldots, \log T$

$y \ge 0$

The optimum is attained for $p(i) := \frac{1}{\log T + 2}$ for $i = 0, \ldots, \log T - 1$ and $p(\log T) = \frac{2}{\log T + 2}$, which can be easily seen by using the Fundamental Theorem of Linear Programming (see e.g. [12]) and the fact that p as given above is a basic solution. Thus, we have

$$\max_{j=0,\ldots,\log T} \left\{ \sum_{i=j}^{\log T} 2^{j-i} p(i) \right\}$$

$$= \max_{j=0,\ldots,\log T} \left\{ \left(\sum_{i=j}^{\log T} \frac{2^{j-i}}{\log T + 2} \right) + \frac{2^{j-\log T}}{\log T + 2} \right\}$$

$$= \max_{j=0,\ldots,\log T} \left\{ \frac{1}{\log T + 2} \left(\frac{2^j}{T} + \sum_{i=j}^{\log T} 2^{j-i} \right) \right\}$$

$$= \max_{j=0,\ldots,\log T} \left\{ \frac{1}{\log T + 2} \left(\frac{2^j}{T} + 2^j \sum_{i=j}^{\log T} \frac{1}{2^i} \right) \right\}$$

$$= \max_{j=0,\ldots,\log T} \left\{ \frac{1}{\log T + 2} \left(\frac{2^j}{T} + 2^j \cdot 2 \cdot \left(\frac{1}{2^j} - \frac{1}{2^{\log T + 1}} \right) \right) \right\}$$

$$= \max_{j=0,\ldots,\log T} \left\{ \frac{1}{\log T + 2} \left(\frac{2^j}{T} + 2 - \frac{2^j}{T} \right) \right\} = \frac{2}{\log T + 2}.$$

This completes the proof. □

5. Competitive Algorithms

In this section we present competitive algorithms for the OJA. The basis of our algorithms is provided by a simple greedy-type algorithm GREEDY which we analyze in Sect. 5.1. This algorithm works acceptably well if all jobs have approximately the same length. In Sect. 5.2 we show how to use randomization in order to turn GREEDY into a competitive algorithm CRS-GREEDY for jobs of substantially different sizes. In Sect. 5.3 we essentially derandomize CRS-GREEDY and obtain the same competitiveness bounds by means of deterministic algorithms.

5.1 A Greedy-Type Deterministic Algorithm

Let GREEDY be the algorithm, which accepts a new job r_j as long as there exists a schedule which contains all previously accepted jobs and r_j. For a given input sequence σ, define its *length ratio* as $\Delta_\sigma := \max_{r_i, r_j \in \sigma} \frac{b_i - a_i}{b_j - a_j} = \max_{r_i \in \sigma}(b_i - a_i)$, i.e., the maximum ratio of two job durations in σ. The algorithm GREEDY does not require that $\min_j(b_j - a_j) = 1$. Our first goal is to establish that GREEDY is $2\Delta_\sigma + 1$-competitive. In the remainder of this section, we will consider a fixed input sequence σ and simply write Δ for Δ_σ.

Let σ_G be the set of jobs, which are accepted by GREEDY and σ_{OPT} be the set of jobs, which are accepted by an optimal offline algorithm. We denote by $X := \sigma_G \cap \sigma_{\mathsf{OPT}}$ be the set of jobs which are accepted by both of these algorithms, $Y := \sigma_G \setminus \sigma_{\mathsf{OPT}}$ be the set of all the jobs accepted only by GREEDY and $Z := \sigma_{\mathsf{OPT}} \setminus \sigma_G$ the set of jobs only accepted by the optimal offline-algorithm.

Consider the schedule that GREEDY outputs. Consider the machines one by one, and on each machine, consider the jobs on it from left to right. Denote the jobs on machine j by $1, \ldots, i_j$, their start times by a_i and finish times by b_i ($i = 1, \ldots, i_j$). Whenever $a_{i+1} - b_i > 2\Delta$, we say that the interval $[b_i + \Delta, a_{i+1} - \Delta]$ is a *gap*. If this happens on machine j, we say that the gap is of type j.

LEMMA 5.1. *Every job in Z has an empty intersection with every gap.*

Proof. Suppose there is a job in Z that has nonzero intersection with some gap of type j. This job could be placed entirely on the machine j, without overlapping the existing jobs on that machine, by the definition of a gap (since its length is at most Δ). So GREEDY would have accepted this job, a contradiction. □

THEOREM 5.2. *For an input sequence σ with length ratio Δ, GREEDY achieves a competitive ratio of $2\Delta + 1$.*

Proof. Take a machine j. Consider an interval between two gaps of type j (or an interval until the first gap/after the last gap/the entire interval $[0, T]$, if there are no gaps on machine j). Call such an interval a non-gap-interval. On machine j, there can be at most Δ idle time at the start and at the end of a non-gap-interval. If this is not true, the gap would have been defined differently. Thus on machine j, some job starts within time Δ of any gap, and after that job finishes, each time within time 2Δ a new job starts, until the next gap appears (at most Δ after the last job completes) or the end of the schedule is reached. Since each job has length at least 1, this means that on machine j, within each non-gap-interval, at least $1/(1 + 2\Delta)$ of the time some job is running in the schedule of GREEDY. This reasoning holds for any machine $j = 1, \ldots, m$. For future calculations, we now say simply that GREEDY is running a job of density ("height") $1/(1 + 2\Delta)$ *at all times* within each non-gap-interval. This does not increase the overall profit of GREEDY and simplifies the comparison to OPT.

On the other hand, in an optimal solution, by Lemma 5.1 no jobs in Z can be running at any time during gaps. Now consider the intervals between two gaps of *any* type in order of increasing starting time. Call these intervals "allowed intervals". We find that all jobs in Z are run only during allowed intervals. However, on each machine, an allowed interval I is a subinterval of a non-gap-interval, so on each machine GREEDY earns (running this job of density $1/(1 + 2\Delta)$) at least $1/(1 + 2\Delta)$ of the length of I. So in total, during I it earns at least $m/(1 + 2\Delta)$ times the length of I, and of course OPT earns at most m times the length of I during I.

Finally, consider a gap G. The only jobs that OPT has accepted and that overlap (partially) with G are the jobs in X that GREEDY is also running, by Lemma 5.1. However, we have modified the GREEDY-schedule by spreading each job out over a non-gap-interval. Thus for a job that runs for t units of time during a gap G, we have that GREEDY earns at least $t/(1 + 2\Delta)$ during G, and OPT clearly earns at most t during G.

This concludes the proof. An illustration is given in Fig. 16.7. □

5.2 An Algorithm Based on Classify and Randomly Select

In this section we show that the GREEDY algorithm from above can be used to obtain a randomized algorithm CRS-GREEDY with competitive ratio $5\lceil \log(T) \rceil$ by applying the classify and randomly select-paradigm [2].

Assume again that the minimum length of an interval is $\min_{r_j \in \sigma}(b_j - a_j) = 1$. We divide the possible input requests into $N := \lceil \log T \rceil$ disjoint classes $C_1, \ldots, C_N$, with $j \in C_i$ if and only if $2^{i-1} \le b_j - a_j < 2^i$. The algorithm CRS-GREEDY chooses class C_i with probability $\frac{1}{N}$. Then, when processing a sequence σ the algorithm ignores all requests not in class C_i and uses GREEDY to process the requests in class C_i.

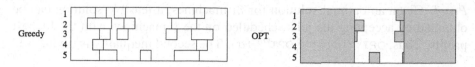

Figure 16.7. An example schedule of GREEDY for an input where $\Delta = 3$. There are five machines, time is on the horizontal axis. All the jobs served by OPT that GREEDY does not serve must be within the shaded areas. Since there is a gap on machine 4, the jobs between the large shaded areas are either both served by GREEDY and OPT, or only by GREEDY

For $i = 1, \dots, N$ let $\sigma_i := \sigma \cap C_i$ and OPT$_i$ denote the total profit of jobs from class C_i accepted by OPT. If GREEDY processes σ_i for some i, it achieves a competitive ratio of 5, since $\Delta_{\sigma_i} \leq \frac{2^i}{2^{i-1}} = 2$. Since there is a probability of $\frac{1}{N}$ that the algorithm picks the class which contributes the biggest part to the optimal solution we can estimate the expected value of the machine time obtained by CRS-GREEDY as follows:

$$
\begin{aligned}
\mathbb{E}\left[\text{CRS-GREEDY}(\sigma)\right] &= \sum_{i=1}^{N} \frac{1}{N} \cdot \text{GREEDY}(\sigma_i) \\
&\geq \frac{1}{N} \sum_{i=1}^{N} \frac{1}{2\Delta_{\sigma_i} + 1} \text{OPT}(\sigma_i) \\
&\geq \frac{1}{5N} \sum_{i=1}^{N} \text{OPT}(\sigma_i) \geq \frac{1}{5N} \sum_{i=1}^{N} \text{OPT}_i = \frac{1}{5N} \text{OPT}(\sigma).
\end{aligned}
$$

Thus, CRS-GREEDY achieves a competitive ratio of $5N = 5\lceil \log T \rceil$.

We remark here that the above algorithm can be modified easily for the case that $\min_j(b_j - a_j) = \varepsilon \neq 1$ is known in advance and then provides a competitive ratio of $5\lceil \log T/\varepsilon \rceil$.

5.3 An Improved Deterministic Algorithm

We will now use GREEDY and ideas from the classify-and-select paradigm to obtain a deterministic algorithm which achieves an improved competitiveness. As in the previous section we first assume that $\min_j(b_j - a_j) = 1$.

LEMMA 5.3. *Suppose that we are given a sequence of jobs σ. For $1 \leq k \leq m$ let* OPT$^{(k)}(\sigma)$ *denote the optimal offline profit achievable using k machines (so that* OPT$(\sigma) = $ OPT$^{(m)}(\sigma)$*). Then,*

$$
\frac{k}{m} \cdot \text{OPT}^{(m)}(\sigma) \leq \text{OPT}^{(k)}(\sigma) \leq \text{OPT}^{(m)}(\sigma).
$$

Proof. Given an optimal solution for m machines, a feasible solution can be obtained by accepting the jobs scheduled on the k machines with the highest profits. Thus, $\text{OPT}^{(k)}(\sigma) \geq \frac{k}{m}\text{OPT}^{(m)}(\sigma)$. The second inequality is trivial. $\square$

Similar to the randomized algorithm CRS-GREEDY, the improved deterministic algorithm C-GREEDY divides the jobs into classes. How this is done, depends on the specific relation between the number m of machines and the time horizon T.

5.3.1 Instances with $m \geq \lceil \log T \rceil$.
In order to simplify the presentation, we first assume that the time horizon $T = 2^k$ is a power of two. In this case, C-GREEDY reserves exactly $\lfloor m/\log T \rfloor$ machines for each of the classes C_i. For each of the $k = \log T$ classes it uses an instantiation of GREEDY to process the jobs.

LEMMA 5.4. *If $T = 2^k$ and $m = k \cdot t$ for some $k, t \in \mathbb{Z}^+$, then C-GREEDY is $5 \log T$ competitive.*

Proof. Similar as in Lemma 5.3 let $\text{OPT}^{(t)}$ and $\text{GREEDY}^{(t)}$ be the respective algorithms which schedule jobs on $t = m/\log T$ machines instead of on m machines. Let OPT_i be the profit of OPT obtained by jobs in class C_i. Then

$$
\begin{aligned}
\text{OPT}(\sigma) \quad &= \quad \sum_{i=1}^{\log T} \text{OPT}_i \leq \sum_{i=1}^{\log T} \text{OPT}^{(m)}(\sigma_i) \\
&\overset{\text{Lemma 5.3}}{\leq} \quad \sum_{i=1}^{\log T} \log T \cdot \text{OPT}^{(t)}(\sigma_i) \\
&\overset{\text{Theorem 5.2}}{\leq} \quad \log T \sum_{i=1}^{\log T} (2\Delta_{J_i} + 1)\text{GREEDY}^{(t)}(\sigma_i) \\
&\overset{\Delta_{C_i} \leq 2}{\leq} \quad 5 \log T \sum_{i=1}^{\log T} \text{GREEDY}^{(t)}(\sigma_i) = 5 \log T \cdot \text{C-GREEDY}(\sigma).
\end{aligned}
$$

$$(5.1)$$

$\square$

LEMMA 5.5. *If $T = 2^k$ and $m \geq \log T$ for some $k \in \mathbb{Z}^+$, then C-GREEDY is $10 \log T$ competitive.*

Proof. For $m \geq \log T$ we have $2\lfloor \frac{m}{\log T} \rfloor \geq \frac{m}{\log T}$. Thus, we get

$$
\text{OPT}(\sigma_i) \leq \frac{m}{\lfloor \frac{m}{\log T} \rfloor}\text{OPT}^{(t)}(\sigma_i) \leq 2\log T \cdot \text{OPT}^{(t)}(\sigma_i). \tag{5.2}
$$

Using the computation from Lemma 5.4, but applying (5.2) instead of Lemma 5.3 in (5.0) gives the desired bound on the competitive ratio. $\square$

We finally extend our result to the general case where T is not a power of two and m is not an integer multiple of $\log T$.

If T is not a power of two, then C-GREEDY simply rounds up T to the next power $2^k \geq T$ of two, so that $2^{k-1} \leq T < 2^k$. Since every instance with given T can be seen as an instance with time horizon 2^k we obtain the following result by applying Lemma 5.5:

THEOREM 5.6. *For $m \geq \lceil \log T \rceil$, the algorithm* C-GREEDY *is* $10(\lceil \log T \rceil) \leq 10(\log T + 1)$-*competitive.*

5.3.2 **Instances with $m < \lceil \log T \rceil$.** If $m < \lceil \log T \rceil$, then C-GREEDY uses a different partition of the machines by using a different classification of the jobs. For $j = 1, \ldots, m$ machine j is only allowed to accept jobs with length between $T^{\frac{i-1}{m}}$ and $T^{\frac{i}{m}}$. This way we obtain m classes where for each class i the ratio of the longest and the smallest possible jobs is $\Delta_i = \sqrt[m]{T}$.

THEOREM 5.7. *For $m \leq \lceil \log T \rceil$,* C-GREEDY *has a competitive ratio of* $2m(\sqrt[m]{T} + 1)$.

Proof. Analogously to the two preceding proofs, we can upper bound the optimal offline profit as:

$$
\begin{aligned}
\text{OPT}(\sigma) \quad &\leq \quad \sum_{i=1}^{m} \text{OPT}^{(m)}(\sigma_i) \\
\overset{\text{Lemma 5.3}}{\leq} \quad &m \sum_{i=1}^{m} \text{OPT}^{(1)}(\sigma_i) \\
\overset{\text{Theorem 5.2}}{\leq} \quad &m \sum_{i=1}^{m} 2(\Delta_i + 1)\text{GREEDY}^{(1)}(\sigma_i) \\
\overset{\Delta_i \leq \sqrt[m]{T}}{\leq} \quad &m \cdot 2(\sqrt[m]{T} + 1) \sum_{i=1}^{m} \text{GREEDY}^{(1)}(\sigma_i) \\
= \quad &m \cdot 2(\sqrt[m]{T} + 1) \cdot \text{C-GREEDY}(\sigma). \qquad \square
\end{aligned}
$$

The input sequence from Lemma 4 of [23] can be adapted for the current problem by letting all jobs have the same starting time (since jobs no longer arrive over time but in a list). This gives a lower bound of $m(\sqrt[m]{T} - 1)$ for any online algorithm. This means that the algorithm C-GREEDY is optimal up to a factor of slightly more than 2.

We note that the deterministic algorithm C-GREEDY can be modified to handle that case that $\min_{r_j \in \sigma}(b_j - a_j) \neq 1$ but this quantity (or a lower bound $\varepsilon > 0$ for it) is known in advance. In this case in all competitiveness bounds T is replaced by T/ε in the expressions.

6. Conclusions

Going back to our initial story, we have discovered organizing the bookings for cottages is not a trivial task, at least not, if booking requests arrive online. The competitive algorithms presented in this chapter all work by classifying customers according to the length of the desired booking interval and then treating each "customer class" separately. In fact, the lower bounds tell us that such a classification makes sense.

So, if your holiday location works in a competitive way, the initial suspicion that our request was rejected just because we asked for three days instead of four may be justified. On the other hand the theoretical lower bounds are somewhat discouraging. Even randomization does not help. On the other hand this can also be viewed as good news, or would you prefer the owner of the cottages to flip coins in order to decide about your bookings?

References

[1] R. K. Ahuja, T. L. Magnanti, and J. B. Orlin. *Networks Flows*. Prentice Hall, Englewood Cliffs, 1993.

[2] B. Awerbuch, Y. Bartal, A. Fiat, and A. Rosén. Competitive non-preemptive call control. In *Proceedings of the 5th Annual ACM-SIAM Symposium on Discrete Algorithms*, pages 312–320, 1994.

[3] B. Awerbuch, Y. Azar, A. Fiat, S. Leonardi, and A. Rosén. On-line competitive algorithms for call admission in optical networks. *Algorithmica*, 31:29–43, 2001.

[4] P. Baptiste. Polynomial time algorithms for minimizing the weighted number of late jobs on a single machine with equal processing times. *Journal of Scheduling*, 2:245–252, 1999.

[5] S. K. Baruah, J. Haritsa, and N. Sharma. On-line scheduling to maximize task completions. *Journal of Combinatorial Mathematics and Combinatorial Computing*, 39:65–78, 2001.

[6] A. Borodin and R. El-Yaniv. *Online Computation and Competitive Analysis*. Cambridge University Press, Cambridge, 1998.

[7] A. Borodin and R. El-Yaniv. On randomization in on-line computation. *Information and Computation*, 150(2):244–267, 1999.

[8] J. Boyar and K. S. Larsen. The seat reservation problem. *Algorithmica*, 25:403–417, 1999.

[9] J. Boyar, S. Krarup, and M. N. Nielsen. Seat reservation allowing seat changes. *Journal of Algorithms*, 52:169–192, 2004.

[10] B. Chen, A. P. A. Vestjens, and G. J. Woeginger. On-line scheduling of two-machine open shops where jobs arrive over time. *Journal of Combinatorial Optimization*, 1:355–365, 1997.

[11] M. Chrobak, W. Jawor, J. Sgall, and T. Tichy. Online scheduling of equal-length jobs: Randomization and restarts help. In *Proceedings of the 31st International Colloquium on Automata, Languages and Programming*. Lecture Notes in Computer Science, volume 3142, pages 358–370. Springer, Berlin, 2004.

[12] V. Chvátal. *Linear Programming*. Freeman, New York, 1983.

[13] A. Fiat and G. J. Woeginger, editors. *Online Algorithms: The State of the Art*. Lecture Notes in Computer Science, volume 1442. Springer, Berlin, 1998.

[14] E. Gassner and S. O. Krumke. Deterministic online optical call admission revisited. In *Proceedings of the 3rd Workshop on Approximation and Online Algorithms*. Lecture Notes in Computer Science, volume 3879, pages 190–202. Springer, Berlin, 2005.

[15] S. A. Goldman, J. Parwatikar, and S. Suri. Online scheduling with hard deadlines. *Journal of Algorithms*, 34:370–389, 2000.

[16] M. Grötschel, S. O. Krumke, and J. Rambau, editors. *Online Optimization of Large Scale Systems*. Springer, Berlin, 2001.

[17] J. A. Hoogeveen and A. P. A. Vestjens. Optimal on-line algorithms for single-machine scheduling. In *Proceedings of the 5th Mathematical Programming Society Conference on Integer Programming and Combinatorial Optimization*. Lecture Notes in Computer Science, pages 404–414. Springer, Berlin, 1996.

[18] S. O. Krumke and D. Poensgen. Online call admission in optical networks with larger wavelength demands. In *Proceedings of the 28th International Workshop on Graph-Theoretic Concepts in Computer Science*, Lecture Notes in Computer Science, volume 2573, pages 333–344. Springer, Berlin, 2002.

[19] R. J. Lipton and A. Tomkins. Online interval scheduling. In *Proceedings of the 5th Annual ACM-SIAM Symposium on Discrete Algorithms*, pages 302–311, 1994.

[20] C. Phillips, C. Stein, E. Torng, and J. Wein. Optimal time-critical scheduling via resource augmentation. In *Proceedings of the 29th Annual ACM Symposium on the Theory of Computing*, pages 140–149, 1997.

[21] D. B. Shmoys, J. Wein, and D. P. Williamson. Scheduling parallel machines on-line. *SIAM Journal on Computing*, 24(6):1313–1331, 1995.

[22] D. D. Sleator and R. E. Tarjan. Amortized efficiency of list update and paging rules. *Communications of the ACM*, 28(2):202–208, 1985.

[23] R. van Stee and J. A. L. Poutré. Partial servicing of on-line jobs. *Journal of Scheduling*, 4(6):379–396, 2001.

[24] A. C. C. Yao. Probabilistic computations: Towards a unified measure of complexity. In *Proceedings of the 18th Annual IEEE Symposium on the Foundations of Computer Science*, pages 222–227, 1977.

Chapter 17

A SURVEY OF GRAPH ALGORITHMS
UNDER EXTENDED STREAMING MODELS
OF COMPUTATION

THOMAS C. O'CONNELL

*Department of Mathematics and Computer Science, Skidmore College, Saratoga Springs,
NY 12866, USA. Email:* `oconnellT@acm.org`

Abstract   There has been a great deal of recent interest in the streaming model of computation where algorithms are restricted to a single pass over the data and have
significantly less internal memory available than would be required to store the
entire stream of data. Because of the inherent difficulty of solving graph problems in the streaming model, a number of extensions to the streaming model
have been considered, namely the Semi-Streaming model, the W-Stream model,
and the Stream-Sort model. In this chapter, we survey the algorithms developed
for graph problems in each of these models. The survey is intended to be tutorial
in nature although familiarity with graph algorithms is assumed.

Keywords: streaming, stream-sort, graph algorithms, communication complexity

1.   Introduction

   With our ever increasing ability to generate enormous amounts of information, comes a need to process that information more efficiently. In particular,
we need to be able to process data that cannot fit into internal memory (i.e.
RAM) and to do so in such a way that our access to external storage is efficient. Recently, there has been interest in a model of computation called the
streaming model which has its origins in [14] and also in [17]. In the streaming model, the data is presented sequentially in a single pass while the internal
memory available is sufficient only to store a small portion of the data. The
motivation for the streaming model is that sequential access to disk can be

S.S. Ravi, S.K. Shukla (eds.), *Fundamental Problems in Computing*,
© Springer Science + Business Media B.V. 2009

implemented very efficiently yet making multiple passes over large data sets may be prohibitively expensive or, in some cases, impossible because of the transient nature of the data.

A number of papers consider computing various statistics in one pass over a stream [2, 18]. However, determining the types of graph problems that can be solved efficiently when the graph is presented as a stream of edges is also an important research question. For many graph properties, it is impossible to determine whether a given graph has the property in a single pass using $o(n)$ space where n is the number of vertices in the graph [11]. (One notable exception is the problem of computing the number of triangles in a graph for which a 1-pass streaming algorithm appears in [4].) Because of the inherent difficulty in solving graph problems in the 1-pass streaming model, extensions to the streaming model have been proposed. The most obvious extension is to allow multiple passes over the stream with the hope that the number of passes will be quite small in relation to the size of the stream. In [14], it is suggested that studying the tradeoff between the number of passes and the amount of space required by streaming algorithms is an important research topic.

Beyond allowing multiple passes there are three main extensions currently discussed in the literature:

1. The *Semi-Streaming model* [12] in which the algorithm is given $\Theta(n \log^k n)$ space where n is the number of vertices in the graph and k is any constant. In this case, the algorithm has enough internal memory to store the vertices but not necessarily the edges in the graph.

2. The *W-Stream model* [20] in which the algorithm is allowed to write an intermediate stream as it reads the input stream. This intermediate stream, which can be at most a constant factor larger than the original stream, is used as the input stream for the next pass.

3. The *Stream-Sort model* [20, 1] in which the algorithm is not only allowed to create intermediate streams but also to sort these streams in a single pass.

In this chapter, we survey the algorithms that have been developed for these extended models. For a more general survey of streaming algorithms, see [18] and [3].

While the emphasis of this chapter is on the actual algorithms developed, we begin with a discussion of lower bounds on the space required to solve graph problems in the streaming model to motivate the discussion of the other models.

2.   Lower Bounds

When receiving an input graph $G(V, E)$ as a stream, we assume, unless otherwise stated, the graph is given as a stream of edges $(u, v) \in E$ in no particular order. If the graph is weighted, an additional weight component is added to each edge, giving us data items of the form $(u, v, w(u, v))$. Some lower bounds on the space required for streaming algorithms can be proven using counting techniques. For example, in [6], lower bounds are provided for deterministic and randomized algorithms for $O(1)$-pass streaming algorithms for finding common neighborhoods of vertices. Another approach to proving lower bounds is to use results from communication complexity [16]. We provide a brief description of the main ideas behind the communication complexity approach below.

2.1   Communication Complexity

The **two-party communication complexity** model originally defined in [24] consists of two players A and B. The players' combined goal is to compute a function $f : X \times Y \rightarrow Z$. When computing $f(x, y)$, Player A is given x but does not know y while player B is given y but does not know x. To compute the result, the players must communicate their private information to each other. The **communication complexity of** f is the number of bits of information that must be exchanged for f to be computed. In other words, if we define the cost of a communication protocol for the two players to be the number of bits that must be exchanged to compute $f(x, y)$ in the worst case, the communication complexity of f is the cost of the communication protocol with the least cost. The **one-way communication complexity** of a function f is the communication complexity of f when Player A is allowed to transmit information to Player B but Player B cannot transmit information to Player A. For example, consider the following problem referred to as **Bit Vector Probing** in [14]:

DEFINITION 2.1. In the **Bit Vector Probing (BVP)** problem, Player A is given a bit string x of length n, while Player B is given an index $i, 1 \leq i \leq n$. The objective of the two players is to output the i-th bit. In other words, $f(x, i) = x_i$.

The (two-way) communication complexity of this problem is $\log n$ since B can simply send A the index i and A can output x_i. The one-way communication complexity where B is prohibited from sending any information to A is n. (See [16] for details on this and other results in communication complexity.)

In [14], results from communication complexity are used to study several graph problems related to database queries as well as other problems relating to databases. In each of the graph problems, a directed multigraph is given as input. The vertices of the graph can be partitioned into k sets, $V_1, V_2, \ldots, V_k$, such that each edge is directed from a node in V_i to a node in V_{i+1} for some $i, 1 \leq i < k$. Four different types of queries are considered:

- Max: Let u_1 be the node of largest degree in V_1. Let $u_i \in V_i$ be a node of largest degree among those incident to u_{i-1} for $2 \leq i \leq k$. Find u_k.

- MaxNeighbor: Let u_1^* be the node with the largest outdegree in V_1. Let u_i^* be the node of largest degree incident on u_{i-1}^* for $2 \leq i \leq k$. Find u_k^*.

- MaxTotal: Find a node $u_1 \in V_1$ such that u_1 is connected to the largest number of nodes of V_k.

- MaxPath: Find nodes $u_1 \in V_1, u_k \in V_k$ such that they are connected by the largest possible number of paths.

In [14], Henzinger et al. prove that a 1-pass streaming algorithm requires $\Omega(kn^2)$ space to solve any one of these problems where $n = \max_{1 \leq i \leq k} |V_i|$. They also prove that a p-pass algorithm for MAX requires $\Omega(kn^2/p)$ space and provide a p-pass, $O(kn^2 \log n/p)$-space algorithm for MAX. For the remaining three problems, 1-pass, $O(kn^2 \log n)$-space algorithms are provided.

Rather than restate the proofs from [14], we provide a lower bound proof for a more familiar graph problem, namely determining whether a graph is bipartite, to provide the flavor of the communication complexity arguments for space lower bounds on streaming algorithms. We can reduce BVP to Bipartiteness as follows:

Given a bit string x of length n, Player A adds an edge (u, u') to the stream, and, for each $j, 1 \leq j \leq n$, such that $x_j = 1$, Player A adds an edge (u, v_j). Player A then runs the hypothetical streaming algorithm for Bipartiteness on the stream, pausing when all edges have been read. Player A then passes the contents of the streaming algorithm's memory to Player B. Player B then takes the query i, initializes the streaming algorithm with the memory contents provided by Player A, and runs the streaming algorithm on the stream consisting of a single edge (v_i, u') effectively restarting the streaming algorithm from where Player A left off. Player B outputs 0 if the streaming algorithm indicates that the graph is bipartite, and outputs 1 otherwise.

To see that Player B outputs the correct result notice the graph described by the entire stream consists of vertices $V = \{u, u', v_1, v_2, \ldots, v_n\}$ and edges $E = \{(u, u'), (u', v_i)\} \cup \{(u, v_j) : x_j = 1, 1 \leq j \leq n\}$. (See Fig. 17.1.) If $x_i = 1$, then (u, u'), (u', v_i), and (u, v_i) are all edges in the graph which implies that the graph is not bipartite. If $x_i = 0$, then none of the v_j's are adjacent to u'. In this case, the graph is bipartite with u on one side of the partition and all the other vertices on the other side. Therefore, the graph constructed is

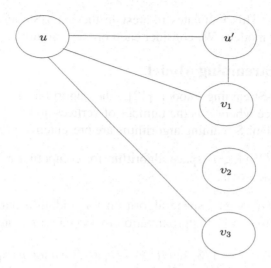

Figure 17.1. The graph constructed by the reduction of BVP to Bipartiteness when $x = 101$ and $i = 1$. Note that the graph is not bipartite because of the triangle $(u, u'), (u', v_1), (v_1, u)$

bipartite if and only if $x_i = 0$. Since the one-way communication complexity of BVP is n, Player A must have passed n bits of information to Player B in the worst case. Therefore, any streaming algorithm for bipartiteness must use n space in the worst case where n is the number of vertices in the graph.

Many natural graph problems share a characteristic with bipartiteness that leads to similar reductions from BVP and consequently the same lower bound [11].

DEFINITION 2.2 [11]. A graph property P is **balanced** if there exists a constant $c > 0$ such that, for all sufficiently large n, there exists a graph $G(V, E)$ with $|V| = n$ and a vertex $u \in V$ such that:

$$\min \left\{ |V_{P,u}|, \left|\overline{V_{P,u}}\right| \right\} \geq cn$$

where $V_{P,u} = \{v \in V : G'(V, E \cup \{(u, v)\})$ has property $P\}$ and $\overline{V_{P,u}} = V - V_{P,u}$.

THEOREM 2.3 [11]. *In the 1-pass streaming model, testing a graph for any balanced graph property requires $\Omega(n)$ space where n is the number of vertices in the graph.*

In [11], Feigenbaum et al. point out that many graph properties such as including a vertex of a given degree, bipartiteness, and including a path between a given pair of vertices are balanced. They conclude that the 1-pass streaming model with an $o(n)$ space limitation does not provide enough power for graph problems. This motivates interest in the Semi-Streaming, W-Stream, and Stream-Sort models. We consider each of these in turn.

3.   Semi-Streaming Model

In the Semi-Streaming model [12], the algorithm is allowed to use $O(n \log^k n)$ space where n is the number of vertices and $k \geq 1$ is a constant. The following Semi-Streaming algorithms are presented in [12]:

- a 1-pass, $O(n \log n)$ space algorithm for computing a bipartition for a graph if one exists,

- a 1-pass $O(n \log n)$ space algorithm for finding a maximal matching and, therefore, a $1/2$-approximation to a maximum matching,

- for any $\epsilon, 0 < \epsilon < 1/3$, an $O(\frac{\log 1/\epsilon}{\epsilon})$-pass, $O(n \log n)$-space, $(2/3 - \epsilon)$-approximation algorithm for finding a maximum matching in a bipartite graph,

- a 1-pass, $O(n \log n)$-space, $(1/6)$-approximation algorithm for finding a weighted matching.

Additionally, it is mentioned that an algorithm from [22] can be adapted to give an $O(\log_{1+\epsilon/3} n)$-pass, $O(n \log n)$-space, $1/(2 + \epsilon)$-approximation algorithm for weighted matching.

One of the key computational benefits of the Semi-Streaming model is that there is enough space to store the connected components of a graph using a disjoint-set data structure [7]. Furthermore, the connected components can be computed in a single pass. In [12], the connected components of the graph are used in a 1-pass algorithm to determine whether a graph is bipartite. The disjoint set data structure is augmented to include a color for each vertex, either Red or Blue. The algorithm proceeds as follows:

1. Initially, color each vertex Red.

2. For each edge (u, v) in the stream,

    (a) if u and v are in the same connected component and u and v have the same color, return failure. (The graph cannot be bipartite in this case since the color of any vertex in a connected component uniquely determines the color of every other vertex in that connected component. In this particular case, if u and v have previously been assigned the same color, the graph is not 2-colorable, i.e., bipartite.)

    (b) if u and v are in different connected components then

       i if u and v have the same color, flip the color of all the vertices in v's component

      ii merge the two connected components.

3. Return the coloring as the bipartition of the graph.

The algorithm runs in a single pass and uses $\alpha(m, n)$ time per edge where α is the inverse Ackermann function (see [7]).

Maintaining the connected components can also be used in an algorithm for computing the minimum spanning tree for a graph [12]. The algorithm is a streaming version of an algorithm which appears as a remark in [21]. As we read the edges from the stream, we keep track of the connected components in memory. For each connected component, we also maintain a minimum spanning tree (MST), which can be stored in $O(n \log n)$ space since the total number of edges in all the spanning trees is $O(n)$. The complete algorithm is as follows:

1. For each edge (u, v) in the stream

    (a) if u and v are in different components then union the two components and create a minimum spanning tree for this new larger component by merging the two components' minimum spanning trees and adding edge (u, v),

    (b) else add (u, v) to the MST for the component (creating a cycle) and remove the heaviest edge on the cycle created.

2. Assuming the graph is connected, only one component remains. Return the corresponding spanning tree as the result.

3.1   Spanners

Just as the connected components are a useful representation of a graph that maintain connectivity information, a spanner is a representation of a graph that maintains approximate distance information. Formally, we have the following definition:

DEFINITION 3.1. An (α, β)-**spanner** for a graph $G(V, E)$ is a subgraph $H(V, E')$ such that $E' \subseteq E$ and for any vertices $x, y \in V$, $d_G(x, y) \leq d_H(x, y) \leq \alpha d_G(x, y) + \beta$ where $d_G(x, y)$ and $d_H(x, y)$ are the distances from x to y in graphs G and H respectively. When the additive constant β is 0, we simply refer to the spanner as an α-spanner.

A Semi-Streaming algorithm to find a $(\log n)/(\log \log n)$-spanner is mentioned in [12]. An algorithm for constructing a $(1 + \epsilon, \beta)$-spanner of size $O(n^{1+\delta})$ in a constant number of passes and using $O(n^{1+\delta} \log n)$ space appears in [9].

A randomized Semi-Streaming algorithm that constructs a $(2t+1)$-spanner for an unweighted graph in one pass appears in [11]. With probability $1 - \frac{1}{n^{\Omega(1)}}$ the algorithm uses $O(tn^{(1+1/t)} \log^2 n)$ bits of space. The per edge processing time is $O(t^2 n^{(1/t)} \log n)$. Using this algorithm, the all-pairs distances in a graph can be $(2t+1)$-approximated. An extension to the spanner algorithm that provides a $((1+\epsilon)(2t+1))$-spanner for weighted undirected graphs is also presented in [12]. The idea behind the algorithm is to make sure that for every edge $(u,v) \in E$ that is not included in the spanner, the distance between u and v is at most $2t+1$. This ensures that the spanner is a $(2t+1)$-spanner since, every edge in a shortest path in the original graph can be replaced by a path of length $(2t+1)$ in the spanner. The idea is to maintain trees of height $\leq \lfloor t/2 \rfloor$ that represent dense parts of the graph, connections between trees of height $= \lfloor t/2 \rfloor$, and miscellaneous edges to represent sparse parts of the graph. Since the height of each tree is $\lfloor t/2 \rfloor$, the distance between any two vertices within the same tree is $\leq t$. The key to the algorithm is to ensure that for any edge (u,v) in the graph, u and v are either in the same tree, in two trees that are connected by a single edge, or connected by a path including miscellaneous edges that is not too long. The complete algorithm has a randomized labeling procedure to achieve the desired results. The reader is referred to [11] for details.

3.2   Sparsification

In [11], Feigenbaum et al. suggest a general approach for designing algorithms for the Semi-Streaming model and improving the running time per edge using the idea of sparsification from [10]. Sparsification is a technique for designing dynamic algorithms to test graph properties. It relies on the property having a strong certificate. A *strong certificate* for a property P and graph G is a graph G' on the same set of vertices such that for any graph H, $G \cup H$ has property P if and only if $G' \cup H$ has property P. A strong certificate G' for property P and graph G is said to be *sparse* if G' has at most cn edges for some constant $c > 0$ where n is the number of vertices. Since the Semi-Streaming model provides enough space to store a sparse certificate and $O(n)$ edges, we can read $O(n)$ edges at a time while maintaining a sparse certificate for the property in question. This gives us the following theorem:

THEOREM 3.2 [11]. *Let P be a property for which a sparse certificate can be found in $f(n,m)$ time where n is the number of vertices and m is the number of edges in the graph. There is a 1-pass Semi-Streaming algorithm that maintains a sparse certificate for P using $f(n, O(n))/n$ time per edge.*

This result and the work by Eppstein et al. [10] leads to Semi-Streaming algorithms for bipartiteness, connected components, and minimum spanning tree with better time per edge than previous algorithms. It also results in new Semi-Streaming algorithms for 2, 3, and 4-vertex connectivity, 2, 3, and 4-edge connectivity, and for constant edge connected components.

4.   W-Stream

While the Semi-Streaming model extends the streaming model by allowing more space, in the W-Stream model [20], algorithms are allowed to write as well as read streams. In each pass, the last stream written (or, in the case of the first pass, the input stream) is read and a new stream is written. This certainly seems like a reasonable extension to the streaming model as long as we do not allow the streams to grow too large. Therefore, the size of the streams written will be restricted to be within a constant factor of the size of the original input stream. While adding the ability to write intermediate streams would appear to provide more power to the streaming model, a p-pass W-Stream algorithm using s space can be simulated by a p-pass streaming algorithm using $p \times s$ bits of space [20]. Thus, when the number of passes is relatively small, the ability to write intermediate streams does not provide significantly more computational power. For example, a $(\log n)$-pass, $(\log n)$-space, W-Stream algorithm can be simulated by a $(\log n)$-pass, $(\log^2 n)$-space, streaming algorithm. In [8], however, Demetrescu et al. prove that when the space is $O(1)$, there are problems that can be solved using intermediate streams that cannot be solved without intermediate streams no matter how many passes are allowed. They also suggest that the total number of items processed is a better measure of the computational complexity of algorithms in the W-Stream model than the number of passes. They prove that the following problem, called FORK, can be solved with an $O(\log n)$-space W-Stream algorithm while processing $O(n)$ items. An $O(\log n)$-space streaming algorithm, on the other hand, would require $\Omega(\log n)$ passes and, therefore, processes $\Omega(n \log n)$ items [8].

DEFINITION 4.1 [8].   In the **FORK** problem, we are given two vectors x and y of n numbers each such that $x_1 = y_1$ but $x_n \neq y_n$. Our objective is to find an index i, called a fork, such that $x_i = y_i$ but $x_{i+1} \neq y_{i+1}$.

While reading and writing a single stream as in the W-Stream model certainly seems like a reasonable extension to the streaming model it also seems to be a bit too restrictive. Why not allow multiple streams to be read and written simultaneously? For example, the FORK problem which requires $p \times s = \Omega(\log^2 n)$ passes in W-Stream [8], can be solved in $O(\log n)$ space and two passes if we are allowed to read and write two streams. In the first pass, simply write A to one stream and B to another. In the second pass, move through A and B in lock step looking for the first index i at which $A[i] \neq B[i]$. In [20], Ruhl points out that these types of algorithms have been studied previously as tape-based algorithms [15]. Ruhl proposes an alternative model called *Streaming Networks* which is equivalent in power to the tape model and proves several results relating the power of Streaming Networks to the models discussed in this chapter. A complete discussion of the Streaming Network model is beyond the scope of this chapter.

In addition to the separation results above, two algorithms are presented in [8] along with a detailed analysis of the tradeoff between the number of passes versus the amount of space required by the algorithms. The problems considered are finding the connected components of an undirected graph and directed single-source shortest path. For both problems, any W-Stream algorithm using s bits of memory requires $\Omega(n/s)$ passes [8]. (Throughout the remainder of this section, we take n to be the number of vertices and m to be the number of edges in the graph.)

4.1 Connected Components in W-Stream

A deterministic W-Stream algorithm for finding the connected components of an undirected graph that uses s space and $O((n \log n)/s)$ passes is presented in [8]. The idea behind the algorithm is to repeatedly find the connected components of subgraphs of G where these subgraphs are small enough to fit into memory. Once such a connected component is found, it can be compressed into a single vertex for the next iteration. As groups of vertices get compressed, a representation of the original vertices within each connected component must be maintained. Therefore, there will be two parts to the intermediate streams. Part A will hold the edges from the compressed graph. Part B will contain a representation of the connected components found so far. This representation will consist of an edge from each original vertex v to the representative vertex for the component containing v.

The algorithm repeats the following until there are no more edges in the graph:

1. Read edges from Part A of the stream, storing each new vertex encountered in memory. As edges are read, maintain the connected components seen so far by maintaining a spanning forest. Continue reading edges until the internal memory is exhausted or until all the edges from Part A have been read. Let H be the subgraph induced by the edges that have been read and stored in memory.

2. Read all remaining edges from Part A of the stream if any. As each such edge (u, v) is read, determine whether u and v are part of the same connected component in H. Let

$$c(x) = \text{the vertex representing the component in } H \text{ containing } x$$
$$\text{if } x \in H$$
$$= x \text{ otherwise.}$$

If $c(u) \neq c(v)$, write $(c(u), c(v))$ as an edge in the new stream for the compressed graph. In this step, all the connected components are compressed down to their representatives. Any vertex in G that is adjacent to a vertex in a connected component from H will now be adjacent to the representative of the component.

3. At this point the connected components of H have been found and the compressed graph has been written to the new stream. It is possible that some vertices that were previously representatives of connected components in G are no longer representatives since their components could have been merged into a larger component. If this is the case, we need to update Part B of the stream so that every vertex in such a connected component points to the representative of the new larger component. To do this, read the edges from Part B of the stream. As each edge (u, v) is read, write $(u, c(v))$ to Part B of the new stream and, if $u \in H$, mark u in memory as having been written to Part B of the new stream.

4. The entire stream has been read and most of the connected component information has been written to the new stream. However, there may be vertices in H whose connected component information have not been written to the new stream—vertices in H that were not included in the connected component information for G after the previous iteration. To remedy this, find each vertex $u \in H$ that was not marked as having been written to Part B of the new stream in Step 3 and write $(u, c(u))$ to Part B of the new stream.

Using the reduction of connected components to bipartiteness from [20], this algorithm can be extended to provide an $O((n \log n)/s)$-pass, s-space, W-Stream algorithm for bipartiteness. It is an open question whether this W-Stream algorithm for connected components can be extended to find a minimum spanning tree as was done with the Semi-Streaming algorithm for connected components.

4.2   Single-Source Shortest Paths

A randomized W-Stream algorithm for the directed single source shortest path problem restricted to instances in which the edge weights are positive integers bounded by some number C appears in [8]. With s space, the algorithm makes $p = O(Cn \log^{3/2} n/\sqrt{s})$ passes. The distances returned are correct with high probability and the size of each intermediate stream is $O(m + n\sqrt{s/\log n})$. The idea behind the algorithm is that, given any constant l, a shortest path between any two vertices can be viewed as a sequence of shortest paths between intermediate pairs of vertices where each of the intermediate shortest paths has length $\leq l$. If we can find shortest paths of length up to l for all pairs of vertices, we can splice these shortest paths together to get shortest paths of length $> l$. There is no known algorithm for finding shortest paths between all pairs of vertices even for limited path lengths in the W-Stream model, so instead a random subset of vertices is chosen to serve as the intermediate sources. A streaming version of Dijkstra's algorithm can be run on each of these intermediate sources. We will explain this streaming version of Dijkstra's algorithm since the ideas used may be applicable to other problems.

4.2.1   Finding Distances Up To l from a Single Source Using Dijkstra's Algorithm.   Recall that in each iteration of the main loop in Dijkstra's algorithm, the vertex u with minimum estimated distance from the source is extracted from the priority queue. Each edge (u, v) out of u is then "relaxed", i.e., the estimated distance to v is reduced to the distance of the shortest path to v over the edge (u, v) if this distance is smaller than the previous estimated distance from the source to v. (See [7] for a complete description of Dijkstra's algorithm). The difficulty in implementing Dijkstra's algorithm when the space is restricted to $o(n)$ is that the priority queue cannot be stored in memory. Instead the priority queue must be stored on the intermediate streams created during each pass through the data. To simplify the exposition of the algorithm, let's first consider the case where we want to find all shortest paths of length $\leq l$ from a single source, a. If we have the priority queue stored in the stream, extracting the vertex with minimum priority can be done in one pass. However, relaxing all the edges coming out of that vertex would be problematic if the priority queue were simply appended to the stream of edges. (Since relaxing a single edge would require a pass through the entire stream, the entire algorithm would require at least m passes through the stream in the worst case.) An alternative idea, would be to store a copy of the priority queue after each edge as a linear array containing the priority of each vertex. In addition, we would have to store a boolean value with each priority to indicate whether or not the vertex has previously been removed from the queue. In other words, the stream would look like:

$$e_1 [(p_1, f_1), \ldots, (p_n, f_n)] \, e_2 [(p_1, f_1), \ldots, (p_n, f_n)]$$
$$\cdots e_m [(p_1, f_1), \ldots, (p_n, f_n)]$$

where e_i is the i-th edge, p_j is the priority of $v_j \in V$, and f_j indicates whether v_j has been removed from the queue.

If we relax edge $e_1 = (u, v)$, we can update the priority for v in the copy of the priority queue that comes immediately after e_1. Now suppose $e_4 = (u, w)$ is the next edge in the stream coming out of u. This edge needs to be relaxed.

As with edge e_1, we can relax e_4 by updating the priority of w in the copy of the priority queue coming immediately after e_4. Note that the various copies of the priority queues are now out of sync. However, each priority queue maintains the necessary invariant that the priority of any vertex is greater than the actual length of the shortest path to that vertex. The extract-min operation can still find the vertex with the minimum priority in one pass because the vertex on the queue with the minimum priority can be found regardless of whether it also appears with a larger priority elsewhere in the stream.

The algorithm as described would require intermediate streams of size mn. Notice, however, that the only priority that can be updated in the copy of the priority queue immediately following edge (u, v) is v. Therefore, we only need to keep a single priority after each edge in the stream. This reduces the size of the intermediate stream to $O(m)$.

We can optimize the algorithm further in terms of the number of passes by allowing the extract-min operation to find multiple vertices in the case there are ties for the minimum priority. In other words, the extract-min operation will create a pool of vertices in memory that consists of up to k vertices that have minimum priority where k is such that the space constraint is obeyed. In this way, the number of extract-min passes is bounded by $n/k + l$ since there can be at most n/k times in which the priority does not change from one pool to the next, and at most l times when the priority does change from one pool to the next (assuming the weights are positive integers). Since there is one relaxation pass for each extract-min pass, the total number of passes is $O(n/k + l)$.

4.2.2 Finding Distances Up To l from Multiple Sources Using Dijkstra's Algorithm.
To be useful in solving the single source shortest path problem by spicing together paths of length $\leq l$, the algorithm above must be extended to handle a set of sources A. This can be accomplished easily enough by maintaining $|A|$ priority queues in the same manner as was done with one source. In other words, in the intermediate stream, after each edge we would write a priority for each source. If the number of vertices k allowed in each pool for the extract-min operation is $s/(|A| \log n)$, the total number of passes is $O(n/k + l) = O(n|A| \log n/s + l)$. The size of the intermediate streams is $O(m|A|)$. The size of the intermediate streams can be optimized to $O(m + n|A|)$ by preprocessing the stream to create many groups of contiguous edges in the stream where the endpoints of the edges in each group are the same. The priority queue information for a vertex is then maintained only after each group rather than after each edge. For complete details, see [8].

4.2.3 The Complete Single Source Shortest Path Algorithm.
Using the algorithm above as a subroutine, the general single source problem can be

solved when edge weights are positive integers $\leq C$ for some number C as follows:

1. Randomly choose a set A of $\sqrt{s/\log n}$ vertices including the true source a_0 to serve as the intermediate sources.

2. Use the algorithm above to compute distances up to $l = (\alpha C n \log^{3/2} n)/\sqrt{s}$ from each of the vertices in A to every other vertex in the graph where α is any constant > 1. Let $d(a_i, v)$ be the distance from source $a_i \in A$ to vertex $v \in V$. This distance information is stored in memory.

3. Build a new graph G^* on the vertices in A such that there is an edge between a_i and a_j if and only if Step 2 found $d(a_i, a_j) \leq l$. Set the weight of this edge to $d(a_i, a_j)$. G^* can be created in one pass and stored in memory as an adjacency matrix using $|A|^2 \log n = s$ space. This graph gives us a concise representation of the shortest paths computed in Step 2 between the sources in A. These are the paths that we will splice together to create paths of length $> l$ in the original graph.

4. Compute the shortest paths from source a_0 in G^* using any single source shortest path algorithm. Let $d^*(a_0, a_i)$ be the distance from a_0 to a_i in G^* for each i.

5. For any vertex v for which we did not compute a shortest path $\leq l$ in step 2, we set its distance to $\min_{a \in A}\{d^*(a_0, a) + d(a, v)\}$.

All distances $\leq l$ are computed correctly in step 2 since a_0 is one of the vertices in A. Distances of length $> l$ could be computed incorrectly. For example, if a poor choice of random vertices for A resulted in a vertex $v \in V$ being a distance of more than l away from each $a \in A$, the distance computed for v would be ∞. Demetrescu et al. prove, however, that with probability at least $1 - 1/n^{\alpha-1}$, each distance $> l$ is computed correctly in Step 5. The number of passes required is $O(\alpha C n \log^{3/2} n/\sqrt{s})$.

5.   The Stream-Sort Model

It is argued in [20] and [1] that the crucial limitation of the streaming model is not in its inability to write intermediate streams but in its inability to write sorted intermediate streams. They prove that a p-pass, s-bit, W-Stream algorithm can be simulated by a p-pass, $(p \times s)$-bit, streaming algorithm and that sorting a stream can be accomplished by a p-pass, s-space, W-Stream algorithm only if $p \times s \geq$ the size of the stream [20]. The latter result is a consequence of a result from [5]. Since sorting large data sets can be done efficiently with today's hardware [23], adding a sorting primitive to the W-stream model seems appropriate. This leads to the Stream-Sort model. In each pass through the data, we can either produce an intermediate stream as in the W-Stream model or sort the stream according to some partial order on the items in the stream. The partial order must be computable on a Turing machine M with an s-bit memory, i.e., M is given two items and returns the order of the items. M does not maintain an internal state between comparisons. On the other hand, we explicitly allow the local memory to be maintained between streaming passes.

In [20] and [1], it is suggested that an algorithm in the Stream-Sort model be considered efficient if the number of streaming and sorting passes is $O(\log^k n)$ for some constant k. Efficient Stream-Sort graph algorithms for undirected s-t-connectivity, directed s-t-connectivity, bipartiteness, minimum spanning tree, maximal independent set, tree contraction, detecting cycles in an undirected graph, and minimum cut appear in [20] and [1]. Each of the algorithms is randomized. As with the models discussed in the previous sections, we present a Stream-Sort algorithm for connected components, which is from [20] and [1].

5.1   Connected Components in Stream-Sort

Although the algorithm presented in [20] and [1] is for s-t-connectivity, we amend it slightly to output the complete connected components of a graph. The final stream created by this algorithm will have the connected components listed as pairs of vertices and component labels similar to the format used in [8] and discussed in Sect. 4.

The algorithm repeats the following until there are no more edges in the graph.

1. Assign a random $3 \log n$ bit integer to each vertex in the graph.

2. Label each vertex with the minimum number among those assigned to itself and its neighbors.

3. Merge all vertices that receive the same label.

4. If a representative of a connected component is merged then update the representative for all vertices in the corresponding component.

The idea is that by assigning random labels to each vertex and merging vertices based on neighboring labels, the number of vertices in the graph decreases by a constant factor in expectation during each iteration [1]. This implies the expected number of iterations is $O(\log n)$. As we will see below, each iteration requires a constant number of passes through the stream.

Assume the input stream is given as a list of vertices followed by a list of edges and that each edge (u, v) appears as both (u, v) and (v, u) since the edges are undirected. The edges are assumed to be in no particular order. The computational benefit of sorting is that it gives us the ability to group together information that may be distributed in a variety of places in the stream. For example, when looking for the minimum label among a vertex v's neighbors, we need to find all the edges incident on v and the labels of those vertices, yet the edges incident on v do not necessarily appear near each other in the stream.

The implementation of this algorithm in the Stream-Sort model is described below. For concreteness, we provide an example for the first iteration on a graph consisting of a straight line through four vertices in Table 17.1.

Repeat the following until there are no more edges in the graph:

1. In one pass over the stream, replace each vertex v_i by a vertex-label pair (v_i, l_i) where l_i is the random number assigned to v_i. If this is the first iteration, append the initial connected component information with each vertex serving as its own representative.

2. For each vertex, we need to find the lowest label assigned to itself or its neighbors. To do this efficiently, we would like to group the labels for all of a vertex's neighbors together in the stream. We proceed as follows:

   (a) Sort the stream so that the list of edges emanating from v_i appear right after the vertex label (v_i, l_i) for each vertex v_i. In addition, move the connected component information to the end of the stream.

   (b) In one pass over this new stream, add an "edge label" (l_i, u) following each edge (v_i, u). This edge label indicates that u is adjacent to a vertex labeled l_i.

   (c) Sort again to group these edge labels with the vertex label for the endpoints of the original edges. In other words, vertex label (v_j, l_j) will be followed by the list of edge labels (l_i, v_j) for edges coming into v_j. Put the actual edges at the end of the stream to get them out of the way.

   (d) Now in one linear pass over the stream determine the smallest number assigned to v_i or its neighbors for each i. This can be done in one pass since each vertex label (v_i, l_i) is followed by a list consisting of an edge label (l_j, v_i) for each vertex v_j adjacent to v_i. In other words, v's label and the labels of all its neighbors are now grouped together in the stream. This number becomes the new label for v_i. Update each vertex-label pair in the stream to reflect the new labeling.

3. Update the connected component information as follows:

   (a) Sort the stream so that the list of component pairs (v_i, v_r) appears immediately after the vertex label (v_r, l_r) for the representative vertex v_r.

Table 17.1. A trace of the first iteration of the connected components algorithm for the graph consisting of a straight line through four vertices, v_1, v_2, v_3, v_4. Since ordered pairs are being used to describe edges, labelings, and component information, we will differentiate between each of these types of pairs. We use $e(v_1, v_2)$ to represent the edge (v_1, v_2), $C(v_1, v_r)$ to represent that v_1 is in the connected component represented by v_r, and $L_V(v_1, l_1)$ and $L_E(l_1, v_1)$ to represent the vertex-label and edge-label pairs used in the algorithm. To save space, let $[E]$ be the complete list of edges unchanged from the previous step and $[C]$ be the complete list of connected component pairs unchanged from the previous step

Step	Stream
Initial	(v_1) (v_2) (v_3) (v_4) $e(v_1, v_2)$ $e(v_2, v_1)$ $e(v_2, v_3)$ $e(v_3, v_2)$ $e(v_3, v_4)$ $e(v_4, v_3)$
1	$L_V(v_1, 20)$ $C(v_1, v_1)$ $L_V(v_2, 10)$ $C(v_2, v_2)$ $L_V(v_3, 30)$ $C(v_3, v_3)$ $L_V(v_4, 40)$ $C(v_4, v_4)$ $[E]$
2a	$L_V(v_1, 20)$ $e(v_1, v_2)$ $L_V(v_2, 10)$ $e(v_2, v_1)$ $e(v_2, v_3)$ $L_V(v_3, 30)$ $e(v_3, v_2)$ $e(v_3, v_4)$ $L_V(v_4, 40)$ $e(v_4, v_3)$ $[C]$
2b	$L_V(v_1, 20)$ $e(v_1, v_2)$ $L_E(20, v_2)$ $L_V(v_2, 10)$ $e(v_2, v_1)$ $L_E(10, v_1)$ $e(v_2, v_3)$ $L_E(10, v_3)$ $L_V(v_3, 30)$ $e(v_3, v_2)$ $L_E(30, v_2)$ $e(v_3, v_4)$ $L_E(30, v_4)$ $L_V(v_4, 40)$ $e(v_4, v_3)$ $L_E(40, v_3)$ $[C]$
2c	$L_V(v_1, 20)$ $L_E(10, v_1)$ $L_V(v_2, 10)$ $L_E(20, v_2)$ $L_E(30, v_2)$ $L_V(v_3, 30)$ $L_E(10, v_3)$ $L_E(40, v_3)$ $L_V(v_4, 40)$ $L_E(30, v_4)$ $[C]$ $[E]$
2d	$L_V(v_1, 10)$ $L_V(v_2, 10)$ $L_V(v_3, 10)$ $L_V(v_4, 30)$ $[C]$ $[E]$
3a	$L_V(v_1, 10)$ $C(v_1, v_1)$ $L_V(v_2, 10)$ $C(v_2, v_2)$ $L_V(v_3, 10)$ $C(v_3, v_3)$ $L_V(v_4, 30)$ $C(v_4, v_4)$ $[E]$
3b	$L_V(v_1, 10)$ $C(v_1, 10)$ $L_V(v_2, 10)$ $C(v_2, 10)$ $L_V(v_3, 10)$ $C(v_3, 10)$ $L_V(v_4, 30)$ $C(v_4, 30)$ $[E]$
4a	$L_V(v_1, 10)$ $e(v_1, v_2)$ $L_V(v_2, 10)$ $e(v_2, v_1)$ $e(v_2, v_3)$ $L_V(v_3, 10)$ $e(v_3, v_2)$ $e(v_3, v_4)$ $L_V(v_4, 30)$ $e(v_4, v_3)$ $[C]$
4b	$L_V(v_1, 10)$ $e(10, v_2)$ $L_V(v_2, 10)$ $e(10, v_1)$ $e(10, v_3)$ $L_V(v_3, 10)$ $e(10, v_2)$ $e(10, v_4)$ $L_V(v_4, 30)$ $e(30, v_3)$ $[C]$
4c	$L_V(v_1, 10)$ $e(10, v_2)$ $L_V(v_2, 10)$ $e(10, v_1)$ $e(10, v_2)$ $L_V(v_3, 10)$ $e(10, v_3)$ $e(10, v_3)$ $L_V(v_4, 30)$ $e(30, v_3)$ $e(10, v_4)$ $[C]$
4d	(10) (30) $e(30, 10)$ $e(10, 30)$ $C(v_1, 10)$ $C(v_2, 10)$ $C(v_3, 10)$ $C(v_4, 30)$

(b) Update the representative in each component pair to be the new label for that representative. In other words, the component pair (v_i, v_r) becomes (v_i, l_r). Note that the labels become the vertices in the next iteration.

4. We need to update the edges so that edge (v_i, v_j) is replaced by edge (l_i, l_j) in the compressed graph. This can be done as follows:

   (a) Sort the stream so that edges emanating from v_i appear right after vertex label (v_i, l_i) and the connected component information appears at the end of the stream.

   (b) In one pass over this stream, produce a new stream of edges where each edge (v_i, u) is replaced by (l_i, u). This updates the first component of each edge in the compressed graph for the next iteration.

   (c) Now sort this stream so that each vertex label (v_j, l_j) is followed by the list of edges (l_i, v_j) coming into v_j.

   (d) In one pass over this stream, produce a new stream of edges where each edge (l_i, v_j) is replaced by (l_i, l_j). This updates the second component of each edge in the compressed graph for the next iteration. Also remove self-loops of the form (l_i, l_i) and replace each vertex label by the label alone—the labels becoming the vertices for the next iteration. In a second pass, remove duplicate vertices.

In the end, the remaining labels in the stream represent the connected components and each pair (v_i, l_i) in the connected components portion of the stream indicates the connected component in which v_i is a member. In the example from Table 17.1, notice that after the first iteration, we have determined that v_1, v_2, and v_3 are in the same connected component which is represented by the new vertex 10. In the next iteration, we will find that v_4 is also in this same connected component (although the representative could be 30 depending on how the random numbers are assigned).

Since the expected number of iterations is $O(\log n)$ and each iteration requires a constant number of passes, the expected number of passes is $O(\log n)$. Since the only information required to be stored in memory at any one time is a small number of labels and vertices, the total amount of space used is also $O(\log n)$. Recall that in W-Stream this problem requires $\Omega(n/s)$ passes using s space. Having the ability to sort, therefore, provides a significant computational advantage for this problem. This algorithm is used in [20] and [1] as a subroutine in Stream-Sort algorithms for bipartiteness, directed s-t-connectivity, and minimum spanning tree.

6. Summary and Conclusions

We have discussed a number of graph algorithms for the three main extensions to the streaming model—Semi-Streaming, W-Stream, and Stream-Sort. In each model there is a need to maintain some compressed representation of the information contained in the graph. For example, maintaining connectivity information has proven extremely useful in all three models. In [20], a number of open problems for the Stream-Sort model are listed including developing algorithms for breadth-first-search, depth first search, topological sort, and directed connectivity. The W-Stream algorithm from [8] for single source shortest path discussed above can be used for breadth-first search and can achieve a sub-linear number of passes using sublinear space. (By taking $s = \sqrt{n} \log^3 n$ for example, the number of passes required would be $n^{3/4}$.) It would be interesting to see whether sorting can be used effectively to bring this down to polylog passes and space.

Interest in the streaming model of computation is not likely to subside anytime soon especially in the data mining community. The algorithm for finding coherent threads in search results from [13] for example, is mentioned to be efficiently implementable in the Stream-Sort model. In addition, Ruhl points out in [20], that the implementation of the PageRank algorithm discussed in [19] can be done efficiently in the Stream-Sort model. As more people investigate the streaming model, consideration of graph algorithms in streaming model variants will become increasingly common.

7. Thank You Dan

Dan Rosenkrantz was Chair of the Computer Science department at the University at Albany—State University of New York, while I was a graduate student. It is one of my great regrets that I never got to work with Dan on any problems since his problem solving skills are legendary. I felt Dan's presence in the department in other ways however. Every presentation I made to the department I made with Dan in mind since Dan would surely find the slightest hole in any argument. I remember at least one occasion where my wife wondered aloud whether I really needed to go over my presentation yet again and I responded, "I have to. Dan Rosenkrantz is going to be there." I consider it a great honor to contribute this chapter to a book celebrating Dan's career although I do so with a bit of trepidation. I hope he doesn't find any holes.

Acknowledgment

I would like to thank Mike Eckmann for many helpful comments and suggestions.

References

[1] G. Aggarwal, M. Datar, S. Rajagopalan, and M. Ruhl. On the streaming model augmented with a sorting primitive. In *Proc. 45th Annual IEEE Symp. Foundations of Computer Science (FOCS'04)*, pages 540–549, Rome, Italy, 2004.

[2] N. Alon, Y. Matias, and M. Szegedy. The space complexity of approximating the frequency moments. *J. Computer and System Sciences*, 58(1):137–147, 1999.

[3] B. Babcock, S. Babu, M. Datar, R. Motwani, and J. Widom. Models and issues in data stream systems. In *Proc. 21st ACM SIGMOD-SIGACT-SIGART Symp. Principles of Database Systems*, pages 1–16, Madison, WI, 2002.

[4] Z. Bar-Yossef, R. Kumar, and D. Sivakumar. Reductions in streaming algorithms, with an application to counting triangles in graphs. In *Proc. 13th Annual ACM-SIAM Symp. Discrete Algorithms*, pages 623–632, San Francisco, CA, 2002.

[5] Z. Bar-Yossef, T. Jayram, R. Kumar, and D. Sivakumar. An information statistics approach to data stream and communication complexity. *J. Computer and System Sciences*, 68(4):702–732, 2004.

[6] A. L. Buchsbaum, R. Giancarlo, and J. R. Westbrook. On finding common neighborhoods in massive graphs. *Theoretical Computer Science*, 299(1-3):707–718, 2003.

[7] T. H. Cormen, C. E. Leiserson, R. L. Rivest, and C. Stein. *Introduction to algorithms*. McGraw–Hill/MIT Press, Cambridge, 2001.

[8] C. Demetrescu, I. Finocchi, and A. Ribichini. Trading off space for passes in graph streaming problems. In *Proc. 17th Annual ACM-SIAM Symp. Discrete Algorithms*, pages 714–723, Miami, FL, 2006.

[9] M. Elkin and J. Zhang. Efficient algorithms for constructing $(1 + \epsilon, \beta)$-spanners in the distributed and streaming models. In *Proc. 23rd Annual ACM Symp. Principles of Distributed Computing*, pages 160–168, St. John's, Canada, 2004.

[10] D. Eppstein, Z. Galil, G. F. Italiano, and A. Nissenzweig. Sparsification: a technique for speeding up dynamic graph algorithms. *J. ACM*, 44(5):669–696, 1997.

[11] J. Feigenbaum, S. Kannan, A. McGregor, S. Suri, and J. Zhang. Graph distances in the streaming model: the value of space. In *Proc. 16th Annual ACM-SIAM Symp. Discrete Algorithms*, pages 745–754, Vancouver, Canada, 2005.

[12] J. Feigenbaum, S. Kannan, A. McGregor, S. Suri, and J. Zhang. On graph problems in a semi-streaming model. *Theoretical Computer Science*, 348(2-3):207–216, 2005.

476

[13] R. Guha, R. Kumar, D. Sivakumar, and R. Sundaram. Unweaving a web of documents. In *Proc. 11th ACM SIGKDD Intl. Conf. Knowledge Discovery in Data Mining*, pages 574–579, Chicago, IL, 2005.

[14] M. Henzinger, P. Raghavan, and S. Rajagopalan. Computing on data streams. In *External Memory Algorithms*. DIMACS Series in Discrete Mathematics and Theoretical Computer Science, volume 50, pages 107–118. American Mathematical Society, Providence, 2000.

[15] D. E. Knuth. *Sorting and Searching*. The Art of Computer Programming, volume 3. Addison–Wesley–Longman, Redwood City, 2nd edition, 1998.

[16] E. Kushilevitz and N. Nisan. *Communication Complexity*. Cambridge University Press, New York, 1996.

[17] J. I. Munro and M. S. Paterson. Selection and sorting with limited storage. *Theoretical Computer Science*, 12(3):315–323, 1980.

[18] S. Muthukrishnan. Data streams: algorithms and applications. In *Proc. 14th Annual ACM-SIAM Symp. Discrete Algorithms*, page 413, Baltimore, MD, 2003.

[19] L. Page, S. Brin, R. Motwani, and T. Winograd. The pagerank citation ranking: Bringing order to the web. Technical Report 1999-66, Stanford Digital Libraries, Nov. 1999.

[20] M. Ruhl. Efficient algorithms for new computational models. PhD Thesis, Department of Computer Science, MIT, Cambridge, MA, 2003.

[21] R. E. Tarjan. *Data Structures and Network Algorithms*. SIAM, Philadelphia, 1983.

[22] R. Uehara and Z. Chen. Parallel approximation algorithms for maximum weighted matching in general graphs. *Information Processing Letters*, 76(1-2):13–17, 2000.

[23] J. S. Vitter. External memory algorithms and data structures: Dealing with massive data. *ACM Computing Surveys*, 33(2):209–271, 2001.

[24] A. C. Yao. Some complexity questions related to distributive computing (preliminary report). In *Proc. 11th Annual ACM Symp. Theory of Computing*, pages 209–213, Atlanta, GA, Apr.–May 1979.

Chapter 18

INTERACTIONS AMONG HUMAN BEHAVIOR, SOCIAL NETWORKS, AND SOCIETAL INFRASTRUCTURES: A CASE STUDY IN COMPUTATIONAL EPIDEMIOLOGY

CHRISTOPHER L. BARRETT

Department of Computer Science and Network Dynamics and Simulation Science Laboratory, Virginia Bioinformatics Institute, Virginia Polytechnic Institute and State University, 1880 Pratt Drive, Blacksburg, VA 24061, USA. Email: cbarrett@vbi.vt.edu

KEITH BISSET AND JIANGZHUO CHEN

Network Dynamics and Simulation Science Laboratory, Virginia Bioinformatics Institute, Virginia Polytechnic Institute and State University, 1880 Pratt Drive, Blacksburg, VA 24061, USA. Emails: kbisset@vbi.vt.edu, chenj@vbi.vt.edu

STEPHEN EUBANK

Department of Physics, Network Dynamics and Simulation Science Laboratory, Virginia Bioinformatics Institute, Virginia Polytechnic Institute and State University, 1880 Pratt Drive, Blacksburg, VA 24061, USA. Email: seubank@vbi.vt.edu

BRYAN LEWIS

Network Dynamics and Simulation Science Laboratory, Virginia Bioinformatics Institute, Virginia Polytechnic Institute and State University, 1880 Pratt Drive, Blacksburg, VA 24061, USA. Email: blewis@vbi.vt.edu

V. S. ANIL KUMAR AND MADHAV V. MARATHE

Department of Computer Science and Network Dynamics and Simulation Science Laboratory, Virginia Bioinformatics Institute, Virginia Polytechnic Institute and State University, 1880 Pratt Drive, Blacksburg, VA 24061, USA. Emails: akumar@vbi.vt.edu, mmarathe@vbi.vt.edu

S.S. Ravi, S.K. Shukla (eds.), *Fundamental Problems in Computing*,
© Springer Science + Business Media B.V. 2009

478

HENNING S. MORTVEIT

Department of Mathematics and Network Dynamics and Simulation Science Laboratory, Virginia Bioinformatics Institute, Virginia Polytechnic Institute and State University, 1880 Pratt Drive, Blacksburg, VA 24061, USA. Email: `hmortvei@vbi.vt.edu`

Abstract   Human behavior, social networks, and the civil infrastructures are closely intertwined. Understanding their co-evolution is critical for designing public policies and decision support for disaster planning. For example, human behaviors and day to day activities of individuals create dense social interactions that are characteristic of modern urban societies. These dense social networks provide a perfect fabric for fast, uncontrolled disease propagation. Conversely, people's behavior in response to public policies and their perception of how the crisis is unfolding as a result of disease outbreak can dramatically alter the normally stable social interactions. Effective planning and response strategies must take these complicated interactions into account. In this chapter, we describe a computer simulation based approach to study these issues using public health and computational epidemiology as an illustrative example. We also formulate game-theoretic and stochastic optimization problems that capture many of the problems that we study empirically.

Keywords: interaction-based computing, theory of simulations, agent-based models, biological, socio-technical and information systems, urban infrastructures, discrete dynamical systems, computational complexity, combinatorial algorithms

1.   Introduction

Social networks represent relationships among individual agents. Social networks are not generally static; they evolve over time. Certain aspects of this change arise from structural adaptations such as reciprocity, transitivity, etc. However, changes in social networks also occur as a result of the behavior of individual agents comprising the network. Conversely, individual characteristics and behaviors can depend on the social network to which the agent belongs. For example, it is well known that in many social situations, the behavior of individual agents mimics those of other agents with whom they interact. In other words, individual behaviors and social networks co-evolve. Examples include fashion trends in schools, market practices of firms based on strategies used by successful firms, etc. Social scientists often refer to the change in network structure as *selection* [22–24], and change in individual characteristics as *influence* [17, 23, 24]. See [1, 7, 2, 9, 8, 10, 11, 33, 18] for work done at the interface of game theory, network formation and individual behavior. We also refer the reader to the work of [12, 29, 30] for theoretical as well as empirical research on the subject of treating selection and influence processes in a network simultaneously.

In this chapter we further motivate and study the joint evolution of selection and influence in social networks in an important application context—spread of infectious diseases. Furthermore, we also consider another component that affects this dynamic—public policy. In classical models used in computational epidemiology, individuals do not adapt their contact behavior during epidemics. For example, they do not endogenously engage in social distancing (protective sequestration) based on disease prevalence. Rather, they simply continue mixing (often uniformly) as if no epidemic were under way. Although potentially a reasonable assumption for non-lethal infections such as the common cold, it is known to fail for lethal diseases such as AIDS. People may be expected to adapt their contact patterns when they perceive a potential threat due to the onset of avian influenza. This will likely result in substantial changes in the social networks that in turn will alter epidemic dynamics. In other words, individual behaviors and the social contact networks that they generate interact and co-evolve. *For brevity we will call the problem of co-evolution of Public policy, Individual behavior and interaction Network as the* **PIN** *problem for the rest of the chapter.*

We begin by describing a computer simulation based approach to study such questions. These simulations use a detailed representation of social contact networks; such a representation is crucial for studying the questions related to co-evolution. We then describe a set of experimental results using our simulations that seeks to analyze these questions in the context of developing public policies for pandemic influenza planning. In the last section of this chapter, we formulate these questions as questions in stochastic optimization and game theory. We hope that these mathematical formulations will serve as starting points for researchers interested in algorithms, operations research and game theory in making further progress in this new and exciting research area.

2. The PIN Problem in Computational Epidemiology

Urban infrastructures have been designed for efficient functioning during normal operations. During crises, however, people's behavior can change so drastically as to render the infrastructure practically useless. Recent blackouts in the Northeast US (2003) and hurricanes such as Rita and Katrnia (2005) demonstrate this amply. In the event of an influenza pandemic, changes in the structure of the social contact network due to behavioral changes are the most important yet difficult to predict factors in determining the spread. The question of how to respond to crises most effectively is very complicated, involving public health systems, regional and urban population dynamics, economic effects, critical infrastructure availability and public policy.

It is well understood that planners must take individual behavior into account when preparing for crises. However, it is not as well appreciated that social responses to public policy can significantly impact the efficacy of public policy and disaster response. Human response, public policies and specific crisis situations are intricately intertwined with one another, making it impossible to obtain a clean simple formal model and solution. Furthermore, policy interventions can have unanticipated consequences due to complex feedback between changing conditions, individual expectations, and social connectivity.

Policy planning has been a central focus of epidemiological research over the years. In addition to empirical observations, practitioners have relied on mathematical models for understanding and comparing different public health policies and making recommendations. These models involve stochastic disease processes on social contact networks. Due to computational considerations, most work in epidemiological modeling has focused on *static* social networks. However, social networks change quite a bit during an epidemic. For instance, policies put in place by public health authorities such as school closures, quarantine, and face masks cause significant changes to the social network. Equally important though is the role of individual behavior in transforming the social network. The recent SARS epidemic (2003) served as an excellent example of how both these factors changed the social network. Thus, mathematical methods for analyzing epidemics based on models of static social contact networks are unlikely to give practical insights into the spread of diseases. We illustrate the issues by two examples.

EXAMPLE 1. First, a simple yet important decision faced by millions of people throughout the country every day during cold and flu season: should I go to work today, even though I have symptoms of a cold or flu? The immediate economic impact of absenteeism due to colds and influenza in the United States in 1980 is estimated to have been $6.5 Billion [31]. While some fraction of these infections arise from exposure outside the workplace, many and perhaps the majority occur because a co-worker decided the consequences of possibly transmitting the disease were less important than the certain consequences of staying home. Indeed, the term *presenteeism* has been coined to describe the problem.

Let us examine the factors involved in this decision more closely. Society pressures us in many ways to go to work even when we may be sick: lack of paid sick leave, need to complete tasks, fear of being seen as a malingerer, desire to be perceived as critical to an organization's success, etc. Personal interactions with co-workers can influence the decision either way. The influence co-workers exert may be tied to whether they have themselves been sick. Furthermore, when a person chooses to stay home, it affects the social network at work in at least two different ways: one is simply the removal of the sick person as an active influence in decision-making (note that this biases the influence of the remaining people by removing precisely those who would argue for staying home); the other, more subtle, effect is a change in the probability that co-workers will be infected, and thus a possible change in their influence on the decision.

EXAMPLE 2. A second example is the individual decision whether and when to flee in the face of a crisis. As recent mass evacuations have clearly shown, we do not know the best way to clear people out of a city. Much of the uncertainty stems from poor understanding of the effects of individual decisions on the process. How is a person's decision to leave related to official evacuation orders and to decisions made by social contacts? How does it relate to the perceived congestion in the transportation system? How will a household prepare to evacuate and how long will preparations take? What additional demands will be placed on the transportation system as geographically dispersed households gather? How can we take advantage of existing mass transportation resources? How do all these choices depend on timing of an official announcement?

The factors affecting decision making discussed in the above examples, namely, uncertain consequences and conflicting motivations between micro and macro levels for individuals—are at the heart of issues such as non-compliance with public policy and, more generally, breakdown of the rule of law in society. The examples, though complex, are amenable to analysis. By adding features such as public policy decisions and a co-evolving "epidemic" of panic, we can create even more realistic, though inherently more complicated, representations of decision-making with immediate applicability to crisis response and longer-term broader applicability to modeling civil order.

3. Network Based Computational Epidemiology

Computational Epidemiology is the development and use of computer models for the spatio-temporal diffusion of disease through populations. The basic goal of epidemiological modeling is to understand the dynamics of disease spread well enough to control it. Potential interventions for controlling infectious diseases include pharmaceuticals for treatment or prophylaxis, social interventions designed to change transmission rates between individuals, physical barriers to transmission, and eradication of vectors. Efficient use of these interventions requires targeting sub-populations that are on the critical path of disease spread. Computational models can be used to identify those critical sub-populations and to assess the feasibility and effectiveness of proposed interventions.

The spread of infectious diseases depends both on properties of the pathogen and the host. An important factor that greatly influences an outbreak of an infectious disease is the structure of the interaction network across which it spreads. Descriptive models are useful for estimating properties of the disease, but the structure of the interaction network changes with time and is often affected by the presence of disease and public health interventions. Thus generative models are most often used to study the effects of public health policies on the spread and control of disease.

Aggregate or collective computational epidemiology models often assume that a population is partitioned into a few sub-populations (e.g. by age) with a regular interaction structure within and between sub-populations. The resulting model can typically be expressed as a set of coupled ordinary differential equations. Such models focus on estimating the number of infected individuals as a function of time, and have been useful in understanding population-wide interventions. For example, they can be used to determine the level of immunization required to create herd immunity.

In contrast, disaggregated or individual-based models represent each interaction between individuals, and can thus be used to study critical pathways. Disaggregated models require neither partitions of the population nor assumptions about large scale regularity of interactions; instead, they require detailed estimates of transmissibility between individuals. The resulting model is typically a stochastic finite discrete dynamical system. For more than a few individuals, the state space of possible configurations of the dynamical system is so large that they are best studied using computer simulation.

See [1, 7, 9] for work on use of game theory to study problems in epidemiology. See Kermer [21] for one of the early work on integrating behavioral and epidemiological models; the work however used traditional differential equation based mean field modeling. Recent work by Epstein et al. [13] has used individual based models to study this interaction. Excepting the work of [13], we are not aware of any other work that uses individual agent based models to study the PIN problem in epidemiology.

3.1   SimDemics

SimDemics is a tool for simulating the spread of disease on a social contact network. A brief overview of **SimDemics** is provided here. Further details can be found in [3, 14, 16, 5]. It details the demographic and geographic distributions of disease and provides decision makers with information about (1) the consequences of a biological attack or natural outbreak, (2) the resulting demand for health services, and (3) the feasibility and effectiveness of response options. See [3, 14, 15] for further details. The overall approach followed by disaggregated models consists of the following four steps.

Step 1 creates a synthetic urban population by integrating a variety of databases from commercial and public sources. It yields a set of synthetic individuals and households located geographically, each associated with demographic variables. Synthetic populations preserve privacy and confidentiality of individuals and yet produces realistic attributes and demographics for the synthetic individuals in the following sense: a census of our synthetic population yields results that are statistically indistinguishable from the original census data, if they are both aggregated to the block group level.

Step 2 creates a synthetic social contact network. This is done by first assigning synthetic individuals a set of activity templates based on several thousand responses to an activity or time-use survey. These activity templates include the sort of activities each household member performs and the time of day they are performed. various machine learning and data mining techniques are used for this task. By integrating, this data over all individuals, we get a minute-by-minute schedule of each person's activities and the locations where these activities take place. This information can now be used to synthesize a *time varying social contact network* represented by a (vertex and edge) labeled bipartite graph G_{PL}, where P is the set of people and L is the set of locations. If a person $p \in P$ visits a location $\ell \in L$, there is an edge $(p, \ell, label) \in E(G_{PL})$ between them, where *label* is a record of the type of activity of the visit and its start and end points. Synthetic generative methods such as the ones used here are necessary to develop a realistic representation of large urban scale social contact network; such a network cannot be constructed by simply collecting field data.

Step 3 consists of detailed simulation of the epidemic process. The computational model used is called a *graphical probabilistic timed transition system*. The within hosts disease evolution is represented as a probabilistic timed transition system (PTTS). There is one transition system per individual. The state transition of a given PTTS corresponding to an individual depends on its own state, the time, a set of random bits and the state of its neighbors in the dynamic interaction network created in Step 2.

Step 4 consists of representing and analyzing various public policies and interventions using a combination of partially observable Markov decision process (POMDP) and n-way games; these formalisms allow us to capture sequential decision making processes related to interventions and individual behavioral changes in response to disease dynamics. The POMDP is specified succinctly using a co-evolving dynamical system described in the next section. It is thus exponentially larger than the problem specification and is intractable to solve optimally in general. As a result, we use efficient simulations and heuristics to solve the PIN problems. A key concept is that of *implementable policies*—policies or interventions that are implementable in the real world.

SimDemics maintains a parameterized model for the state of health of each person, and updates this continuously based on interaction with other people, and transmission of a disease through these contacts. This enables us to estimate both the geographic and demographic distribution of the disease as a function of time. It also allows us to evaluate the impact of different intervention policies, such as vaccination and quarantine.

This is an important feature of **SimDemics**. Indeed, the success of most policies and plans depends on their ability to anticipate and adapt to all possible outcomes. However, many of the tools used to describe the range of outcomes and to quantify their relative magnitudes are based on static estimates, whereas in a crisis situation, the responses authorities make depend greatly on real-time situational awareness. **SimDemics** allows the synthetic people to change their behaviors and interactions based on their individual situation as well as characteristics of the entire population.

4. A Mathematical Model to Capture Co-Evolution

We will use a discrete dynamical system framework to capture our co-evolution between disease dynamics and individual behavior. The basic framework consists of the following components: (i) a collection of entities with state values and local rules for state transitions, (ii) an interaction graph capturing the local dependency of an entity on its neighboring entities and (iii) an update sequence or schedule such that the causality in the system is represented by the composition of local mappings.

We formalize this as follows. A **Co-evolving Graphical Discrete Dynamical System** (CGDDS) S over a given domain $\mathbb{D}$ of state values is a triple $(G, \mathcal{F}, W)$, whose components are as follows:

1. Let $V = \{v_i\}_{i=1}^{n}$ be a set of vertices, and let $(g_i)_i$ be a vertex indexed family of graph modification functions $g_i: \{0,1\}^n \longrightarrow \{0,1\}^n$. The functions $(g_i)_i$, through their applications, defines an indexed sequence of graphs $G = (G_r = G_r(V_r = V, E_r))_r$ with labeled edges and vertices. The graph G_r is the **underlying contact graph** of S after r applications of functions g_i. It is assumed that the edge $\{v_i, v_i\} \in E_r$ for all r and for all i. We set $m_r = |E_r|$.

2. For each vertex v_i there is a set of local transition functions $\{f_{v_i,d}\}_d$ where $f_{v_i,d}: \mathbb{D}^d \longrightarrow \mathbb{D}$. Let $N(i,t)$ denote the set of vertices consisting of v_i and the neighbors of v_i at time t, and let $d_t = |N(i,t)|$. The function used to map the state of vertex v_i at time t to its state at time $t+1$ is f_{v_i,d_t}, and the input to this function is the state sub-configuration induced by $N(i,t)$.

3. The final component is a string W over the alphabet $\{v_1(s), v_2(s), \ldots, v_n(s), v_1(g), \ldots, v_n(g)\}$. The string W is a schedule. It represents an order in which the state of a vertex or the possible edges incident on the vertex will be updated. Here $v_i(s)$ intuitively specifies that the state of

the vertex v_i is to be updated; $v_i(g)$ specifies that one or more incident edges will be updated.

From a modeling perspective each vertex represents an agent. Here we will assume that the states of the agent come from a finite domain $\mathbb{D}$. The maps $f_{v_i,j}$ are generally stochastic.

Computationally, each step of a CGDDS (i.e., the transition from one configuration to another), involves updating either a state associated with a vertex or modifying the set of incident edges on it. The following pseudo-code shows the computations involved in one transition.

Initialize $t = 0$
Repeat Until W is empty
  (i) Let r be the first symbol in W.
  (iii) **If** $r = v_i(s)$, update the state of the vertex v_i as follows:
    (a) Let degree of node v_i in G_t be d_t. Node v_i evaluates f_{v_i,d_t}. (This computation uses the *current* values of the state of v_i and those of the neighbors of v_i in G_t.) Let x denote the value computed.
    (b) Node v_i sets its state s_{v_i} to x.
  (iii) **If** $r = v_i(g)$, update the edges incident on v_i as follows:
    (a) Use current graph G_t to compute g_{v_i}.
    (b) Let G_{temp} denote the new graph.
  (ii) Set $t = t + 1$, $G_{t+1} = G_{temp}$ and delete r from string W.
End Repeat

Let F_S denote the **global transition function** associated with S. This function can be viewed either as a function that maps $\mathbb{D}^n$ into $\mathbb{D}^n$ or as a function that maps $\mathbb{D}^V$ into $\mathbb{D}^V$. F_S represents the transitions between configurations, and can therefore be considered as defining the dynamic behavior of an CGDDS S.

We make several observations regarding the formal model described above.

1. We will assume that the local transition functions and local graph modification functions are both computable efficiently in polynomial time. In agent based models used in social sciences these are usually very simple functions. Furthermore, the functions g_{v_i} need to be specified using a succinct representation, rather than a complete table which will be exponentially larger.

2. The edge modification function as defined can modify in one step a subset of edges simultaneously. An alternate model could have been where a vertex is allowed to change exactly one edge at a time. We have chosen the former due to the specific application in mind. In all our applications,

when an agent decided to not go to a location (either due to location closure as demanded by public policy or due to the fear of contracting the disease) its edges to all other individuals in that location are simultaneously removed while adding edges to all the individuals who might be at home.

3. The model is *Markovian* in that the updates are based only on the current state of the system; it is possible to extend the model wherein updates are based on earlier state of the system.

4. We have assumed that there is exactly one function for each arity for each node. This can be relaxed easily, similarly these functions will, in general be stochastic.

4.1   Specifying PIN Problems in CE Using Co-Evolving Discrete Dynamical Systems

We briefly outline how PIN problems in Computational Epidemiology can be specified using CGDDS. In all the situations considered in this paper, we can make certain simplifying assumptions due to the specific dynamics that we consider. In **SimDemics**, we have a notion of a **day**. A day is typically 24 hours but can be smaller depending on the specific disease. We *assume* that the social contact network does not change in the course of a day. This is a realistic assumption due to the time scale of disease evolution (time it takes for a person to be infectious or symptomatic after being infected). As a result, the schedule can be specified as a sequence of days wherein we only consider disease dynamics over the entire population followed by a step in which there is a change in the social contact network.

We can make this a bit more precise as follows: We denote the functional modules for mobility, disease propagation and activity generation by M, D and A, respectively; these are described in Appendix. Each individual is assigned a set of initial activities based on their preferences, demographics, and infrastructure constraints in the activity assignment module A. The module M assigns locations to all entities based on the current set of activities which in turn induces the current contact graph, or social network. Using the contact graph, the module D computes the next stage which is disease dynamics. This corresponds to updating the disease state of every individual in the network over one day. The activity generator A uses the current disease state to update the current activities. Models of individual behavior or policy that affects individual behavior constitutes this module.

In general, the dynamics is time dependent and is generated by iteration of the composed map F given by

$$F = D \circ M \circ A.$$

This is illustrated on the right in Fig. 18.1. Notice that this is already a substantial simplification over all possible choices for the string W.

Interventions and behavioral changes can be broadly categorized based when they occur:

1. *Non-Adaptive*: Non-adaptive interventions and behavioral changes occur before the start of the simulations. The non-adaptive interventions unrealistically assume the population does not change during the course of the epidemic and is limited to studying treatments that have a permanent effect, like vaccination.

   Letting the initial state of the system be x_0, the final state of the system can be written as $x(t) = F^t(x(0))$ as $(D^t \circ (M \circ A))(x(0))$, illustrated on the left in Fig. 18.1.

2. *Adaptive*: The adaptive strategies on the other hand, incorporate changes in the movement of the people, treatments that have only temporary effects (antiviral medications are only effective when being taken), and wholesale changes to the interactions within the population (like school closure). This is represented most generally as $x(t) = F^t(x(0))$ as $(D \circ M \circ A)^t(x(0))$. We can now differentiate various strategies by how frequently M and A are applied as compared to D. In other words, we view the dynamics as the following composition: $(D^{t/r} \circ M \circ A)^r(x(0))$, where the exponents reflect the different time scales. This can be viewed as degree of adaptation. Policy based change in the social network is usually caused by changing the behavior of a set of individuals in some uniform way. Furthermore, it is natural to expect that these changes do not occur often. Individual behavior based changes on the other hand can occur every day—individuals can change their behavior and thus their probability of contracting a disease on a daily basis. A simulation is computationally most efficient when t is small, since it amounts to fewer updates to the social network and individual behavior. On the other hand, making t small makes the simulation less realistic since the

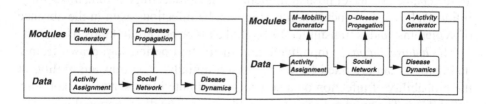

Figure 18.1. The left diagram shows the data flow for disease dynamics without feedback, that is, where e.g. interventions do not alter activities. The diagram on the right shows data flow with feedback from the disease dynamics to the activities

interaction between individual behavior and disease dynamics is not well represented.

5. Computational Experiments

This section illustrates how complicated PIN problems can be specified and studied using computational models such as **SimDemics**. See [6] for additional details. We will compare the effectiveness of both adaptive and non-adaptive interventions on the same population with the same contact network, using disease models of the same disease (pandemic strain of influenza). Non-adaptive interventions are done before the epidemic starts—in this setting, we (unrealistically) assume that the activities of all people are unchanged during the experiment. Adaptive interventions, on the other hand, are done based on the information available about the epidemic, and can change as the epidemic proceeds. The interventions we will consider include medical (such as administration of vaccines and anti-virals), governmental (such as school closures), and societal (such as social distancing)—some of these interventions are external, and some are endogenous, i.e., people themselves implement them.

These computational experiments show the following:

- They illustrate the qualitative differences between adaptive and non-adaptive strategies and highlight the need for more realistic dynamic modeling.

- They illustrate the power of **SimDemics** modeling system in terms of (i) its ability to handle various kinds of adaptive and non-adaptive interventions, (ii) handle large instances.

5.1 Basic Experimental Setup

The contact network we study models a population of about 8.86 million people in Chicago. The network is constructed by synthesizing information from a number of different sources [4]. We model pandemic influenza with all the characteristics of normal influenza, with a much higher transmissibility. Influenza has a short incubation period, can be infectious even in the absence of symptoms, and is transmitted through the air or by certain kinds of contact.

The *heterogeneous* symptomatic and incubation periods are drawn from a distribution, and are fixed for every person initially. The transmissibility, or the probability of infection on a contact, per minute is chosen to be 0.000048 and 0.0003. The number of initial infections is 4. The disease model in Experiment 2 differs from the one in Experiment 1 in by incorporation of additional states needed to capture the effects of the antiviral treatment, but the gross features are still the same.

Parameter	Values
Social network	Chicago, 8.86M individuals
Transmissibility (τ)	0.000048 and 0.0003
Age groups	0–5 (group 1), 6–15 (2), 16–20 (3), 21–60 (4), >60 (5)
Number of people intervened	50K, 100K, 150K, 200K, 250K, 300K, 400K, 500K
Number of initial infections	4
Number of iterations	50, 2 initial infection sets, 25 iterations per set
Policies	random, high degree, high vulnerability, household with specific activity types, specific age groups

Table 18.1. Summary of parameters used in experimental studies

We describe below the specific experiments we perform and the various experimental parameters.

- We choose two values for the transmissibility parameter τ, namely $\tau = 0.000048$ and $\tau = 0.0003$.

- We choose 25 different sets of initial infections and run 2 random iterations for each of them, for a total of 50 iterations. We then compute an *average run*, where the number of new infections on each day is the average of the new infection number on this day in the 50 iterations, and report the measures based on the average runs.

- For each vaccination policy, we consider the following sizes (where K means thousand): 50K, 100K, 150K, 200K, 250K, 300K, 400K, 500K.

- For random people, we choose a subset of given size from the population uniformly at random. This trivial vaccination scheme can be viewed as a benchmark for evaluating effectiveness of other vaccination schemes.

- An individual is *active* if his/her activities belong to many types, or s/he lives in the same household with an active individual. The list of active people is determined from the given contact network and has about 500K people.

- We have five age groups: 0–5 years in age group 1; 6–15 years in age group 2; 16–20 years in age group 3; 21–60 years in age group 4; older than 60 years in age group 5. We are especially interested in age groups 2 and 5, i.e., school kids and seniors.

5.2 Experiment 1

Non-Adaptive Interventions: Study the effect of pre-vaccination of specific sub-populations assuming no changes in behavior throughout the course of the epidemic. Here we will compare vaccination policies targeting the following sub-populations:

- randomly chosen people

- people of high degree

- people of high vulnerability

- active people

- people of a specific age groups

While many other policies and groups can be explored, even in this static case, these groups are chosen to illustrate a sample of the types of policies that can be represented in this modeling environment. We measure the effectiveness of these policies in terms of the percentage decrease in the epidemic size as compared to the unmitigated case as well as the unit efficiency. We will need some notation in order to define these measures formally. For subset $A \subseteq V$ of people, we let $\mathcal{I}_A(G)$ denote the set of infected people, when the people in A are immunized, subject to some specific starting conditions, and disease model in the contact network $G(V, E)$. Mathematically, vaccinating a person is equivalent to either removing a node from the network, or reducing its incident infection probabilities. Note that $A = \emptyset$ means no vaccination, i.e., *base case*. The two measures we use to compare different policies are:

- the *percentage decrease in epidemic size*, defined as:

$$\text{DES} = \frac{|\mathcal{I}_\emptyset| - |\mathcal{I}_A|}{|\mathcal{I}_\emptyset|}$$

- the *unit efficiency of vaccination*, defined as:

$$\text{UE} = \frac{|\mathcal{I}_\emptyset| - |\mathcal{I}_A|}{|A|}$$

Results and Analysis: The most basic question is which policy is the most effective for a given disease. We are also interested in finding a policy that is easy to implement from a public health point of view. These policies would be compared empirically in the sections that follow.

The two measures (DES and UE) are plotted against vaccination size in Figs. 18.2 and 18.4 for the case $\tau = 0.000048$ and in Figs. 18.3 and 18.5 for the case $\tau = 0.0003$.

The effectiveness of vaccination is highly dependent on who is selected for vaccination and what the transmissibility of the disease is. When the disease has high transmissibility ($\tau = 0.0003$) vaccination policies have little effect

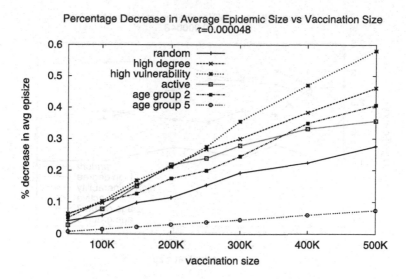

Figure 18.2. Percentage of decrease in average epidemic size ($\tau = 0.000048$)

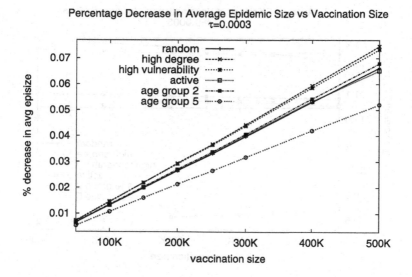

Figure 18.3. Percentage of decrease in average epidemic size ($\tau = 0.0003$)

(Fig. 18.3): even if half a million vaccinations are given (5.6% of the population) there is only a 7% decrease in epidemic size (6.3% of the population). If these vaccines were not randomly assigned, but specifically given to people older than 60 then they are even less effective, only decreasing the epidemic size by 5.1% which is even lower than the vaccination percentage

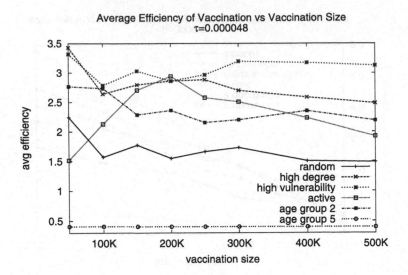

Figure 18.4. Average unit efficiency of vaccination ($\tau = 0.000048$)

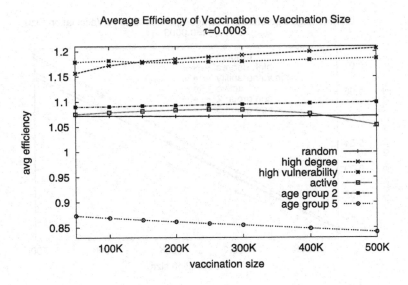

Figure 18.5. Average unit efficiency of vaccination ($\tau = 0.0003$)

(5.6%). The effect is only slightly greater for less transmissible diseases: with $\tau = 0.000048$ the epidemic is decreased by 8%. The limited effect of vaccinating those over 60 is a result of the low connectivity of this population. They are more susceptible to severe effects of the disease, however, so vaccination ensures lower mortality, which was not considered in these simulations.

To further illustrate the impact of who is vaccinated, note that schemes where "high degree" individuals are vaccinated result in significant decrease of epidemic size. For instance, in Fig. 18.2 ($\tau = 0.000048$) when half a million "high degree" individuals are vaccinated the epidemic size is decreased by more than 45%. Furthermore, if the "high vulnerability" individuals are vaccinated the epidemic decreases by almost 60%. Identifying these individuals requires complete knowledge of the contact network and in the case of vulnerability, requires previous simulations and analysis. It is more realistic to identify people that are in high risk age groups or have behaviors that might put them at higher risk. Figure 18.4, shows that vaccinating school children aged 6–15 is much more efficient than simply vaccinating random individuals. Additionally, *active* individuals, who engage in many types of activities (i.e. school, work, and/or college) or live with an individual with these activities, may be relatively easy to identify. Vaccinating these individuals is also shown to be more efficient than random vaccination.

The effectiveness of vaccinating "high degree" and "high vulnerability" people stands to reason given the significant reduction of overall degree that their removal would produce. However, these strategies require perfect knowledge of the contact network. Additionally, note that the effectiveness of the strategies is based on the assumption that the social network does not change. Individuals that are high degree before the arrival of an epidemic disease, may not have high degree under epidemic conditions. The evolution of the contact network under these conditions can also cause individuals that might not be obviously high degree to become more highly connected (for instance health care workers).

Nevertheless, even assuming a fixed contact graph, significant insights into the effectiveness of various vaccination schemes can still be made. For instance, the effectiveness of vaccinating high degree individuals suggests that it might be useful to identify individuals in a specific age groups or individuals carrying out specific trade (e.g. emergency care workers) as potential targets.

5.3 Experiment 2

Adaptive Interventions: Study the effects of dynamic changes to the social network, treatments with antivirals, and changes in individual behaviors throughout the course of an influenza epidemic. An effective vaccine for pandemic influenza is not likely to be available until the pandemic is well established. Currently available antiviral medicines used for treatment of influenza have limited efficacy in preventing infection and are likely to be in short supply. Without these tools, control of an influenza pandemic must be attempted through more general infection control measures. This experiment studies the effectiveness of a collection of interventions both together and in isolation as

494

well as the sensitivity of when they are implemented. The interventions are dynamically triggered at different points in the epidemic and the timing of these triggers is also studied. The interventions are designed to reduce the opportunities for infections by removing infectious people from circulation, reducing their infectivity through treatment, and keeping potentially infectious people from transmitting disease before they develop symptoms. These interventions drastically alter the daily activities of many of the people in the simulation, and these dynamic changes can effectively control the epidemic.

Experimental Setup: As mentioned earlier, the same population with the same contact network are exposed to the same disease modeled on a highly infectious influenza, as was done in Experiment 1. However, the interventions modeled are very different. They are derived from interventions recommended in federal pandemic planning documents[1] and require that they be dynamically applied under conditions specific to the individual. The modeling environment is designed to accommodate these kinds of interventions, and thus allow the simulation to closely represent what might actually occur in reality.

The specific interventions we will consider are:

1. Case isolation: once an individual experiences symptoms of the disease, they remain home through the duration of their illness.

2. Case treatment and household quarantine: if a case is diagnosed, they are administered anti-viral medications (reduces their infectivity and duration of illness) and all household members are given prophylactic anti-viral medications (reduces their chance of infection) and are quarantined at home until no one in the household is sick.

3. School closure: all schools are closed, some children remain at home while the remaining substitute other activities during normal school hours. An adult in the household of a young child (less than 15) must stay home to supervise them.

4. General social distancing: 50% of people eliminate all non-essential activities (shopping, visiting, recreation).

5. Workplace social distancing: to reduce workplace exposure, workers in large offices interact with 50% co-workers.

These interventions were studied across different levels of adherence to the interventions (30%, 60%, and 90%) and were implemented at different points in the progress of the epidemic (from 0.0001% of the population to 10% of the

---

[1] See http://www.whitehouse.gov/homeland/pandemic-influenza.html.

Prevalence trigger	Cumulative proportion ill
Never	44.7%
10%	20.3%
1%	3.9%
0.10%	2.0%
0.01%	1.7%
0.001%	1.7%
0.0001%	1.7%

Table 18.2. Epidemic size decreases when the interventions are implemented at lower prevalence thresholds

Compliance	Early threshold (0.01%)	Later threshold (0.1%)
30%	1.7%	2.0%
60%	0.1%	1.3%
90%	0.1%	1.2%

Table 18.3. Epidemic size decreases when societal compliance with interventions increases

population infected, or 9 cases to 886,000 cases). All permutations were not studied due to limits on computational resources.

Results and Analysis: The modeled disease epidemic can be completely controlled by the adaptive interventions. The overall magnitude is significantly curtailed when the interventions are triggered at a lower level of disease prevalence. Similarly, when societal compliance increases the size of the epidemic decreases.

The size of the epidemic is very sensitive to when the interventions are instituted (Table 18.2). An uncontrolled epidemic, i.e., when the interventions are never implemented, leads to nearly half the population becoming ill. Even if the interventions are not applied until after the epidemic has made 10% of the population ill, the interventions are able to prevent half of these infections. Interestingly, there is a limit to how effective the interventions can be, even if implemented at levels of infection in the population that would be impossible to detect (0.01% to 0.0001%) they cannot completely prevent the epidemic. While the overall attack rate may be the same, note the difference in the timing and shape of the epidemic (see tables below). The epidemic that follows the interventions triggered at 0.01% peaks nearly three weeks earlier but has the same area under the curve, which could translate into other changes in the population were there further adaptive measures in place.

The levels of compliance with the interventions also have an effect on the size of the epidemic, though less so than the timing of the intervention (Table 18.3, Fig. 18.6). Similarly, at the extremes of the control (both 60% and 90%) the overall attack rates are limited to the same level, but shape of the

496

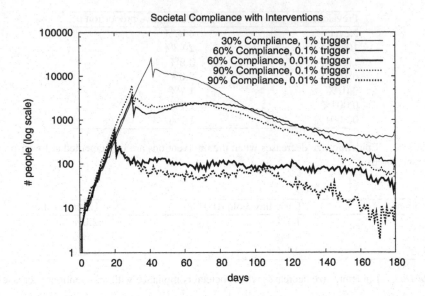

Figure 18.6. Epidemic curves by levels of compliance and time of intervention: Scenario 2—30% compliance and trigger at 1% prevalence; Scenario 3—60% compliance and trigger at 0.1% prevalence; Scenario 4—60% compliance and trigger at 0.01% prevalence; Scenario 5—90% compliance and trigger at 0.1% prevalence; Scenario 6—90% compliance and trigger at 0.01% prevalence

epidemic curves are different, which in turn could have an effect on additional adaptive measures.

5.4   Comparing Adaptive and Non-Adaptive Strategies

The two case studies above tell different stories to Public Health policy makers, with varying levels of refinement. The non-adaptive strategies studied on the static network can be useful for informing permanent modifications to the potential disease transmission network, such as vaccination. These approaches could determine which groups are best suited for vaccination when supply is limited, or could be used for planning how many vaccines are needed to control an epidemic. However, they can not answer questions about behavior modifications based on an individual's state. The adaptive strategies studied using the **SimDemics** modeling environment are designed to handle these exact types of dynamic changes to the social network. This more flexible architecture allows the exploration of a wider range of public health policy options, and can reproduce behaviors in the system that may not be obvious. The transparency in the representation of the framework also allows for a more direct interpretation of the results, which allows for greater understanding across a wider audience of policy makers. The framework still requires some coarse adjustments based more on time and average behavior of the model, and full situational awareness. Further refinement of these adaptive strategies is needed so that the implementation of all these strategies is more fluid and evolving.

6. A Mathematical Formulation

We have seen how one can use computer simulations to study the effects of various adaptive and non-adaptive interventions to control the spread of avian flu through a social network. In this section, we will try to formulate many of these questions as combinatorial questions in stochastic optimization, game theory, dynamical systems and algorithms. This serves to expose the reader to various mathematical formalisms, each capturing a different facet of the underlying problem. Nevertheless, our primary goal is algorithmic here—we concentrate on the algorithmic issues arising in these formalisms. Often the questions are based on a simplified mathematical abstraction of the realistic situation; nevertheless, we believe that this allows us to formulate questions that might be tractable in the sense of obtaining rigorous mathematical proofs. Progress on these questions will help us understand and guide simulation based experimental results.

6.1 Preliminaries: A Simplified Model

Let V denote a population. We refer to individuals in V as nodes. Let $G(V, E)$ denote a contact graph on this population—each edge $e = (u, v) \in E$ denotes that the individuals u and v come into contact and can infect each other. The spread of infection is assumed to be a stochastic process. For each edge $e = (u, v) \in E$ let $r(e)$ (also, sometimes denoted by $r(u, v)$) denote the probability of the infection spreading from u to v per unit time—this is sometimes referred to as the infection rate. Let $\tau(u)$ denote the time that node u remains infected. Note that the infection rates need not be symmetric, i.e., $r(u, v)$ and $r(v, u)$ need not be the same. We will assume that $r(u, v)$ does not vary with time, though this happens in reality. Most disease models have additional states. For instance, there is an *incubation period*, which is the period right after the infection, in which the individual is infected, but not yet contagious. Let $I(u)$ denote the incubation period for node u. We let $\bar{r}$, $\bar{\tau}$ and $\bar{I}$ denote the vectors specifying the above quantities for all nodes and edges. We will use $\bar{x}$ to denote the initial conditions: $x(v)$ denotes the probability that v is infected initially.

We will be considering discrete time models for epidemics, where the probability that node v does not get infected by node u in t time steps after u got infected is given by:

$$\Pr[\text{node } v \text{ not infected}] = (1 - r(u, v))^t \qquad (6.1)$$

In an epidemic model such as SIR, each node u recovers and becomes immune $\tau(u)$ time steps after becoming infected. In endemic models such as SIS, node u returns to the susceptible state after this time. A crucial assumption made in almost all epidemic models is that of *independence*: we assume that the spread of infection from a node u to node v is completely independent of the infection from a node u' to node v. Similarly, an infected node u spreads the infection to each neighbor v, independent of the other neighbors of u. This is a central assumption in almost all the epidemic models and the analytical results based on percolation. However, there exist other epidemic models, such as the *Descending Cascade Model* [20], in which this independence assumption does not hold.

6.2   Policy Planning Problems

We begin by formulating one of the policy planning problems studied earlier empirically—determining whom to vaccinate—as a stochastic optimization problems. The optimization issue arises because of limited resources, e.g., of vaccines—this raises the question of whom to vaccinate so that the "public good" is maximized. However, public good can be defined in a number of ways, and therefore, there is no unique solution. In this section, we will take an easy route by just attempting to determine a policy that minimizes the epidemic size. This gives us the following problem, which we call the Vaccination Problem, following our earlier results in [16], which we denote by $\mathsf{VP}(G, \bar{r}, \bar{\tau}, \bar{I}, \bar{x}, k)$:

- **Given:** Contact graph $G(V, E)$, which is directed, an SIR disease model, as described in Sect. 6.1, which is specified by the vectors $\bar{r}$, $\bar{\tau}$, $\bar{I}$, and a parameter k, and a vector $\bar{x} \in [0, 1]^n$, which describes the initial conditions—$x(v)$ denotes the probability that node v is infected initially. The most common starting conditions are: (i) there is a single node v such that $x(v) = 1$ and $x(w) = 0$ for all $w \neq v$, or (ii) $x(v) = 1/n$ for each v.

- **Objective:** Choose $S \subseteq V$, $|S| \leq k$ so that the number of nodes infected when the disease is run on $G[V \setminus S]$ is minimized. In the initial conditions where some specific nodes are infected, none of them should be in the set S.

The SIR model leads to several simplifications in the formulation of the above problem, and relates it to percolation. First, the incubation period $I(u)$ of node u plays no role in the expected epidemic size. Also, the above formulation does not care for the temporal aspects, and so it suffices to simply consider the effective infection probability on edge $e = (u, v)$ as $r'(e) = 1 - (1 - r(e))^{\tau(u)}$. Let $G(r')$ denote a random subgraph of G in which each edge e is retained with probability $r'(e)$. Also, consider a simple initial condition $\bar{x}$ in which there is a single node s with $x(s) = 1$ and $x(v) = 0$ for all $v \neq s$. Thus, the $VP(G, \bar{r}, \bar{\tau}, \bar{I}, \bar{x}, k)$ problem can be restated as:

- Choose a subset $S \subseteq V$ with $|S| \leq k$ such that:

- The expected number of nodes reachable from s in the (random) subgraph $G(r')$ is minimized—the expectation here is over the random subgraphs $G(r')$. If the initial condition $\bar{x}$ is different, the expectation above would also be over different choices of initial sets, by sampling from $\bar{x}$.

The above formulation is the simplest possible one, but is already nontrivial. It remains non-trivial even if we consider the simplest possible disease model in which $r(e) = 1$ for each edge (modeling a "highly infectious disease"), as the following result from [16] shows:

THEOREM 18.1 [16]. $VP(G, \bar{r}, \bar{\tau}, \bar{I}, \bar{x}, k)$ *is NP complete if $r(e) = 1$ for each e, and there is a node s such that $x(s) = 1$ and $x(v) = 0$ for all $v \neq s$. For any $\epsilon > 0$, there is a polynomial time bi-criteria approximation algorithm that deletes a set S of $O((1+\epsilon)k)$ nodes, so that the number of nodes reachable from s in $G[V \setminus S]$ is $O((1 + 1/\epsilon)OPT)$, where OPT denotes the optimum solution to this problem.*

The complexity of the $VP(G, \bar{r}, \bar{\tau}, \bar{I}, \bar{x}, k)$ for more realistic disease models (i.e., when $r(e) < 1$) is likely to be #P-hard, and determining this remains an open problem.

Adaptive Policies: The VP problem described above corresponds to a *non-adaptive* vaccination policy. Using the stochastic optimization framework developed by [28, 32, 19], we can formulate an *adaptive* version of this problem, which we call Adaptive Vaccination Problem (AVP). In this formulation, the nodes to be vaccinated, or deleted do not have to be chosen in one shot. Instead, a feasible solution corresponds to choosing set S_i at the start of the ith time step. As in [28], we assume that there is an inflation factor σ_i in step i, so that the cost of choosing set S_i in step i is $\Pi_{j \leq i} \sigma_j |S_i|$; following [28], we also assume that $\sigma_i \geq 1$. The $AVP(G, \bar{r}, \bar{\tau}, \bar{I}, \bar{x}, k, \bar{\sigma})$ problem is defined in the following manner:

- The quantities G, $\bar{r}$, $\bar{\tau}$, $\bar{I}$ and $\bar{x}$ are defined as before. The parameter k denotes the total cost that feasible solution must have, and $\bar{\sigma}$ specifies the inflation factor.

- **Feasible Solution:** This is a sequence of disjoint sets $S_1, S_2, \ldots, S_\ell$. The set S_i denotes the set of nodes to be vaccinated on the ith timestep.

The set S_i can be chosen after observing the state of the epidemic in the ith step.

- **Objective:** Choose a feasible solution $S_1, \ldots, S_\ell$ such that the inequality $\sum_i (\Pi_{j \leq i} \sigma_j)|S_i| \leq k$ holds and the expected number of infected nodes is minimized.

In reality, only *partial* information is known about the epidemic reliably at each step, and the AVP problem above can be easily modified to incorporate this aspect.

The 2-person Vaccination Policy Game: We now consider a variant of the AVP problem as a 2-person game. One player is the policy maker who has to choose the vaccination policy, and the second player is "nature", which decides on the spread of the epidemic, following the framework of *Games against Nature (GAN)* [27].

We denote this game as $\mathsf{VPG}(G, \bar{r}, \bar{\tau}, \bar{I}, \bar{x}, k, \ell, M)$. Let P denote the single player, and let N denote nature. The game runs in rounds with P and N playing alternately. N plays first, and infects nodes according to the starting condition $\bar{x}$, i.e., each node v is infected with probability $x(v)$, independently of other nodes. Then, P plays, and it can decide to vaccinate (or delete) up to ℓ nodes. In the next round, N plays, and spreads the infection to the unvaccinated neighbors of the infected nodes, according to the disease model specified by $\bar{r}$, $\bar{\tau}$ and $\bar{I}$. Let S_i denote the set of nodes chosen to be vaccinated by P; we must have $\sum_i |S_i| \leq k$. The goal is to decide whether there is a vaccination strategy for P, specified by the sequence of sets $S_1, S_2, \ldots$, such that $\sum_i |S_i| \leq k$ and the total number of infected nodes is at most M. Is this problem PSPACE complete, as some of the other GAN problems are?

6.3 Individual Behavior Problems: A Game Theoretic/ Dynamical Systems Viewpoint

A common problem with implementation of policies is compliance. This is especially true in the case of vaccinations, which may have side effects and involve additional costs, and in the case of directives to "stay home", might simply be infeasible. Incentives are needed to make people comply. An interesting way to give an incentive could be to enter all the people who get vaccinated into a lottery—such schemes have also been studied in other settings, such as voting. This scenario immediately leads to interesting game theoretic questions, since each individual now has a set of conflicting costs and rewards, and has to make a choice that would optimize his or her perceived utility. There are several papers that study game theoretic questions [1, 7, 9] related to epidemics on networks. However, these results either assume that the graph is very simple, or that the disease model is very simple. The approaches in [7, 9] use differential equations and mean field approximations to formulate realistic disease models on complete mixing networks (cliques). The paper by Aspnes, Chang and Yampolskiy [1] is much closer to our models, in the sense that the network is general, but the disease model is simple and assumes a "highly contagious disease". Extensions of this game have been studied in [26, 25]. There are, admittedly, several difficulties with these non-cooperative formulations, e.g., it is hard for nodes to compute their utility functions, and there is no persuasive reason for equilibria to exist. However, the structure of these games may give useful insights into their dynamics. We also give equivalent dynamical system formulations of these games.

The Vaccination Game (VG) This game is denoted by $VG(G, \bar{r}, \bar{\tau}, \bar{I}, \bar{x})$, and is defined in the following manner. Each node corresponds to a player, and a strategy for player v is denoted by a quantity $a_v \in [0, 1]$, which is the probability that node v decides to get vaccinated; vaccinating a node is equivalent to lowering the infection probabilities on all edges incident on v. The disease model is specified by $\bar{I}$, $\bar{r}$ and $\bar{\tau}$, and $\bar{x}$ gives the initial conditions, as discussed earlier. We formulate the utility function U_v for node v as

$$U_v = a_v C + \Pr[v \text{ gets infected}]L,$$

where C denotes the cost (or reward) of getting vaccinated, and L denotes the cost of getting infected. The probability that node v gets infected is defined over the initial condition $\bar{x}$ and the strategy $\bar{a}$.

One of the main problems of interest is to study the structure of equilibria, if they exist, and compare their cost to that of a social optimum. Aspnes et al. [1] consider a simple disease model, in which a node gets infected if there is a path to it from an infected node, and the disease can start initially at any node, i.e., $x(v) = 1/n$ for each v. For illustration, consider a pure strategy $\bar{a}$. Suppose $a_v = 0$ for some node v. Then $\Pr[v \text{ gets infected}]$ is proportional to the size of the component containing v, after all the nodes w with $a_w = 1$ are deleted. This is illustrated in Fig. 18.7. For this model, Aspnes et al. [1] show that pure Nash equilibria always exist, and can be completely characterized in terms of the quantity $t = Cn/L$—a strategy profile $\bar{a}$ is a Nash equilibrium provided:

1. every component in $G_{\bar{a}}$ has size at most t, and

2. flipping the strategy of a node v from 1 to 0 gives a component of size strictly greater than t.

They also show that computing Nash equilibria that have minimum total cost is NP-complete, but a simple switching strategy always converges to an equilibrium. Finally, the cost of the worst Nash equilibrium can be $\Theta(n)$ times

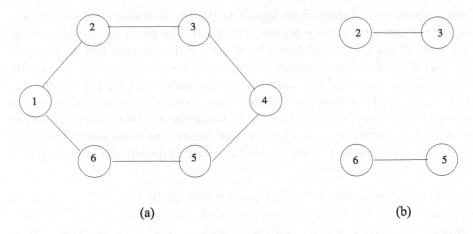

Figure 18.7. (a) A sample contact graph. (b) The components resulting from the strategy $\bar{a}$ with $a_1 = a_4 = 1$ and the rest being 0. The probability that any of the nodes $2, 3, 5, 6$ gets infected is $1/2$

the social optimum. Extending these results to more general disease models remains open questions.

The Multi Stage Policy Game (MSPG): While the above questions are mathematically interesting, an inherent difficulty with the above model is that it is hard for individuals to estimate their costs. In light of this, we will consider the following multi-stage version of this problem. We call this the Multi Stage Policy Game (MSPG), and it is denoted by $\mathrm{MSPG}(G, \bar{r}, \bar{\tau}, \bar{I}, \bar{x})$. In this game, the strategy a_v of player v is actually a vector, and $a_v(i)$ denotes the probability that v stays home—people find it much easier to decide whether to stay home or not, when an outbreak has started, than deciding the utility of getting vaccinated. Node v can choose $a_v(i)$ depending on how many nodes in its neighborhood are infected. The main objective would be to study this as a dynamical system and explore its limit distribution, and the parameters that influence these distributions.

Preliminary empirical results related to this problem can be found in [13]. A simpler variation of the above based on differential equations was formulated and studied in [21]. The model proposed here is more general and network based which makes the problem substantially harder. The MSPG and VPG games are instances of anti-coordination games [8]—it is in the interest of a player to get vaccinated or stay home if a lot of people around her are not doing so. The realism in the contact network and disease model make this a very rich problem area. In addition to the limiting distributions of these games, the computational complexity of these problems is an interesting problem.

6.4   Discussion of the Different Formulations

The different theoretical problems formulated above deal with specific aspects of epidemic processes and policy planning—the different variants highlight the richness of this area, and the limitation of any single theoretical model to capture all of its complexity. The computational complexity of these problems is in general an open question.

As an example, we consider the VP and AVP problems and their computational variants. The complexity of computing the expected number of infected nodes, N_{inf}, for initial conditions $\bar{x}$, when set S_i of nodes is vaccinated at step i, is not exactly known. As mentioned in [20], it is not known how to compute this quantity, even when all the nodes to be vaccinated are chosen in step 1 itself, though it is a reasonable conjecture that this problem is #P-hard. An (ϵ, δ) approximation to N_{inf} can be computed by a simple sampling scheme:

---

1. **For** $i = 1$ to t **do**

    (a) Generate a random instance of the bond percolation process, by retaining each edge with probability $r'(e)$, as defined earlier in the discussion of the AVP problem.

    (b) Let Z_i denote the number of nodes reachable from the initial infected nodes, specified by $\bar{x}$.

2. **Output** $Z = \frac{Z_1 + \cdots + Z_t}{t}$

LEMMA 18.2. *For $t \geq n^2/\epsilon^2\delta$ we get an (ϵ, δ) approximation to $E[N_{\text{inf}}]$, i.e.,*

$$\Pr[|Z - E[N_{\text{inf}}]| > \epsilon E[N_{\text{inf}}]] \leq \delta$$

Proof. Clearly, $E[Z] = E[Z_i] = E[N_{\text{inf}}]$ for each $i = 1, \ldots, t$. Therefore, by Chebyshev's inequality, we have

$$\Pr[|Z - E[Z]| \geq \epsilon E[Z]] \leq \frac{var(Z)}{\epsilon^2 E[Z]^2} \leq \frac{var(Z_1)}{t\epsilon^2 E[Z_1]^2}$$

$$\leq \frac{E[Z_1^2]}{t\epsilon^2 E[Z_1]^2} \leq \frac{n^2}{t\epsilon^2} \leq \delta$$

for $t \geq n^2/(\epsilon^2\delta)$. $\qquad\square$

The above sampling works only because N_{inf} takes integral values in the range $\{1, \ldots, n\}$. It would not immediately work for other problems, such as determining the probability that a node v gets infected.

An interesting question is whether the AVP and VPG problems are PSPACE complete. In light of the above discussion of an (ϵ, δ) sampling for N_{inf}, is it possible that reasonable polynomial time approximation algorithms exist for these problems?

7. Concluding Remarks

We have described an agent based modeling approach to study the interaction between public policy, individual behavior and spread of infectious disease in an urban region. Our experimental results demonstrated how realistic modeling considerations can impact the disease dynamics; the modeling framework is general enough and yet efficient to undertake such studies. Further development of the modeling framework is necessary for modelers to study this interaction. We also described formal mathematical questions that arise when studying these complicated interactions. Most of the computational complexity as well as the algorithmic questions arising in this context are open problems and represent interesting directions for future research.

8. Thank You Dan

The group members of Network Dynamics and Simulation Science Laboratory want to wish Professor Daniel Rosenkrantz a happy retirement from active academics. He has been a collaborator for over eight years now; the computational theory of discrete dynamical systems to understand computer simulations of socio-technical systems was developed jointly with him. Dan's contributions and insights to the development of this theory have been invaluable, and his continued collaboration with us is a source of new ideas and inspiration. Madhav Marathe would like to express a special note of thanks and gratitude to Dan for being his teacher, mentor, colleague and a friend over the last 19 years.

Acknowledgments

We thank the members of Network Dynamics and Simulation Science Laboratory; the work presented here is based on work done by the entire group over the last 10 years. This work has been partially supported NSF Grants Nets CNS-062694, HSD SES-0729441, and NECO CNS 0831633, CDC Center of Excellence in Public Health Informatics Grant 2506055-01, NIH-NIGMS MIDAS project5 U01 GM070694-05, and DTRA CNIMS Grant HDTRA1-07-C-0113. Computational support for the work was provided in part by the National Science Foundation through TeraGrid resources provided by NCSA, TACC and PSC.

References

[1] J. Aspnes, S. Chang, and Yampolskiy. Inoculation strategies for victims of viruses and the sum-of-squares partition problem. *J. Comput. Syst. Sci.*, 72(6):1077–1093, 2006.

[2] V. Bala and S. Goyal. A non-cooperative model of network formation. *Econometrica*, 68 (5):1181–1231, 2000.

[3] C. Barrett, J. Smith, and S. Eubank. Modern epidemiology modeling. *Scientific American*, 292(3):54–61, 2005.

[4] C. L. Barrett, R. J. Beckman, K. P. Berkbigler, K. R. Bisset, B. W. Bush, K. Campbell, S. Eubank, K. M. Henson, J. M. Hurford, D. A. Kubicek, M. V. Marathe, P. R. Romero, J. P. Smith, L. L. Smith, P. L. Speckman, P. E. Stretz, G. L. Thayer, E. V. Eeckhout, and M. D. Williams. Transims: Transportation analysis simulation system. Technical Report LA-UR-00-1725, Los Alamos National Laboratory Unclassified Report, 2001.

[5] C. L. Barrett, K. Bisset, S. Eubank, V. S. A. Kumar, M. V. Marathe, and H. S. Mortveit. Modeling and simulation of large biological and information and socio-technical systems: An interaction-based approach. In *Proc. Short Course on Modeling and Simulation of Biological Networks, AMS Lecture Notes, Series: PSAPM*, 2007.

[6] C. Barrett, K. Bisset, J. Chen, B. Lewis, S. Eubank, V. S. A. Kumar, M. Marathe, and H. Mortveit. Effect of public policies and individual behavior on the co-evolution of social networks and infectious disease dynamics. In *Proc. DIMACS DyDAn Workshop on Computational Methods for Dynamic Interaction Networks*, 2007.

[7] C. Bauch and D. Earn. Vaccination and the theory of games. *Proc. Natl. Acad. Sci.*, 101(36):13391–13394, 2004.

[8] Y. Bramoulle, D. Lopez-Pintad, S. Goyal, and F. Vega-Redondo. Social interaction in anti-coordination games. *International Journal of Game Theory*, 33(1):1–19, 2004.

[9] R. Breban, R. Vardavas, and S. Blower. Inductive reasoning games as influenza vaccination models: Mean field analysis. In arXriv: q-bio.PE/0608016, 2006.

[10] N. Durlauf and P. Young. *Social Dynamics*. MIT Press, Cambridge, 2001.

[11] G. Ellison. Learning, local interaction, and coordination. *Econometrica*, 61:1047–1071, 1993.

[12] M. Emirbayer and J. Goodwin. Network analysis, culture and the problem of agency. *American Journal of Sociology*, 99:1411–1454, 1994.

[13] J. Epstein, J. Parker, and D. Cummings. Coupled contagion dynamics of fear and disease: A behavioral basis for the 1918 epidemic waves: Mathematical and computational explorations. Technical Report, Brookings Institute, 2006. Presentation made at the MIDAS meeting.

506

[14] S. Eubank, H. Guclu, V. S. A. Kumar, M. Marathe, A. Srinivasan, Z. Toroczkai, and N. Wang. Modeling disease outbreaks in realistic urban social networks. *Nature*, 429:180–184, 2004.

[15] S. Eubank, V. S. A. Kumar, M. Marathe, A. Srinivasan, and N. Wang. Structural and algorithmic aspects of large social networks. In *Proc. 15th ACM-SIAM Symposium on Discrete Algorithms (SODA)*, pages 711–720, 2004.

[16] S. Eubank, V. S. A. Kumar, M. Marathe, A. Srinivasan, and N. Wang. Structure of social contact networks and their impact on epidemics. In *AMS-DIMACS Special Volume on Epidemiology*, 2005.

[17] N. Fredkin. *A Structural Theory of Social Influence*. Cambridge University Press, Cambridge, 1998.

[18] S. Goyal and F. Vega-Redondo. Learning, network formation, and coordination. *Games and Economic Behavior*, 50(2):178–207, 2005.

[19] N. Immorlica, D. Karger, M. Minkoff, and V. S. Mirrokni. On the costs and benefits of procrastination: Approximation algorithms for stochastic combinatorial optimization problems. In *Proceedings of the Fifteenth Annual ACM-SIAM Symposium on Discrete Algorithms (SODA)*, pages 684–693, 2004.

[20] D. Kempe, J. Kleinberg, and E. Tardos. Influential nodes in a diffusion model for social networks. In *Proc. International Colloquium on Automata Programming and Languages (ICALP)*, pages 1127–1138, 2005.

[21] M. Kermer. Integrating behavioral choice into epidemiological models of the aids epidemic. *The Quarterly Journal Of Economics*, CXI:549–573, 1996.

[22] P. Lazarsfeld and R. Merton. Friendship as social process. In T. Abel and C. Page, editors, *Freedom and Control in Modern Society*, Van Nostrand, New York, 1957.

[23] R. Leenders. Models for network dynamics. *J. Mathematical Sociology*, 20:1–21, 1995.

[24] R. Leenders. Structure and influence, statistical models for the dynamics of actor attributes, network structure and their independence. PhD Thesis, Amsterdam, 1995.

[25] M. Mavronicolas, V. Papadopoulou, A. Philippou, and P. Spirakis. A network game with attacker and protector entities. In *Proceedings of the 16th Annual International Symposium on Algorithms and Computation (ISAAC 2005)*, volume 3827, pages 288–297, 2005.

[26] T. Moscibroda and R. Wattenhofer. When selfish meets evil: Byzantine players in a virus inoculation game. In *25th Annual Symposium on Principles of Distributed Computing (PODC)*, pages 35–44, 2006.

[27] C. Papadimitriou. Games against nature. *Journal of Computer and System Sciences*, 31:288–301, 1985.

[28] R. Ravi and A. Sinha. Hedging uncertainty: Approximation algorithms for stochastic optimization problems. *Math. Program.*, 108(1):97–114, 2006.

[29] T. Snijders, C. Steglich, and M. Schweinberger. Modeling the co-evolution of networks and behavior. In K. van Montfort, H. Oud and A. Satorra, editors, *Longitudinal Models in the Behavioral and Related Sciences*. Routledge/Taylor & Francis, New York, 2006.

[30] C. Steglich, T. Snijders, and M. Pearson. Dynamic networks and behavior: Separating selection from influence. Technical Report, University of Groningen, The Netherlands, 2007. Available at http://stat.gamma.rug.nl/snijders/.

[31] W. Stewart, J. Ricci, E. Chee, and D. Morganstein. Lost productive work time costs from health conditions in the United States: Results from the American productivity audit. *Journal of Occupational & Environmental Medicine*, 45(12):1234–1246, 2003.

[32] C. Swamy and D. Shmoys. Approximation algorithms for 2-stage stochastic optimization problems. *ACM SIGACT News*, 37(1):33–46, 2006.

[33] P. Young. *Individual Strategy and Social Structure: An Evolutionary Theory of Institutions*. Princeton University Press, Princeton, 1998.

Author Index

S.S. Ravi, S.K. Shukla (eds.), *Fundamental Problems in Computing*,
© Springer Science + Business Media B.V. 2009

Subject Index

S.S. Ravi, S.K. Shukla (eds.), *Fundamental Problems in Computing*,
© Springer Science + Business Media B.V. 2009

512